MUSIC IN A WORD

Volume 1

Learning to Write 1972–1997

Ira A. Robbins

Trouser Press Books

Cover design by Kristina Juzaitis / February First Design

Uncredited photographs were taken by the author.

ISBN: 978-0-9842539-7-5

LS261

First printing January 2022

www.trouserpressbooks.com
https://hopp.bio/tpbooks
books@trouserpress.com

Table of Contents

Preface

One of my enduring childhood memories, from the age of six or seven, was wanting an assignment. My sister Sara, who was in junior high, always had homework to do and, oddly, I envied her for that. My undeveloped brain had already developed a desire for direction, responsibility and deadlines.

As a student, I was only a recent graduate from nap time, but there was already something about the idea of being given a chore with a deadline that scratched some psychic itch: in a family of high achievers, I must have sensed a need to prove myself, to meet a challenge, to perform reliably and with competence. Of course, I had no way of knowing that would lead me to a lifetime of journalism and publishing, but that's just what it did.

Why do I write about music? I've given that question a lot of thought, and I have discerned subliminal motives of mine that are less than flattering. On one hand, it's the desire to share what moves me, to offer the benefit of serious consideration and historical knowledge to the young and curious. On a deeper level, however, it springs from a desire to be accepted and appreciated, to establish standing in the world that I hungered for as a child. In a mild, bloodless way, there's a competitive aspect to it, an internal quest for acknowledgment and approval from one's peers and public.

Expressing ideas and having an audience willing to consider and perhaps endorse them is, as we have learned in the era of social media, a powerful and addictive attractor. (Social media has had other profound forms of impact on what I do as well: easy virtual contact with artists that was never before possible, feedback from readers that once relied on the post office is now a few easy clicks away and ideas expressed in public must now be defensible and virtually bulletproof.) The ability to articulate original views in public, then, becomes a competitive sport, a way to prove one's mental mettle on the battlefield of words. Lacking demonstrable physical prowess, writing is a flex, a chance to show off a skill in public. And the egotism involved is both external and internal. Writing is a self-administered test of creative intelligence, like a crossword puzzle or a brain-teaser puzzle, with a risk of failure. I may surprise myself with a clever observation or phrase I didn't know was in me — or I may not. I imagine songwriting is like that for those who can do it well.

If you've never thought about ideas that way, it may sound overblown and absurd, but there are elements of all that in my journalism. And (forgive a mixed metaphor) I have worried at times that playing David to a perceived rock music Goliath can come awfully close to directing stored anger at a straw tiger.

In going through this stuff, I see clearly how the radical politics of my youth provided a blueprint for my us-against-them understanding of the music business, seeing the independent and indomitable spirit of left-wing activists reborn in the scrappy self-belief of indie rock bands and the malevolent cynicism of a capitalist government alive in the stifling commercialism of the big record companies. Time and again, I wrote about the malign role of major labels and the righteous efforts of underdogs to survive with or without them. Perhaps it was a bit one-note simplistic, but I don't have any regrets about sticking to those guns all these years.

I imagined it would be fun delving back through my long career in music journalism, rereading long-forgotten old pieces, remembering fascinating encounters with rock and roll's colorful characters, seeing where my critical judgment was spot on and where I got it all wrong, remembering fun times and wild adventures, wan memories confirmed and augmented by a bit of new research.

I was, to an extent, wrong. Although I can find great pleasure in being reminded of things I have experienced, especially those I had forgotten, it turns out (as rendered in a sort-of-Yiddish version on a small wooden plaque that hung for many years over my grandparents' fireplace) "Ve git too soon oldt und too late Schmart."

It has been sobering, embarrassing and rewarding to read the cocksure arrogance of my youth: the harshness, the ignorance, the disappointment in artists I once adored as they fell short of whatever it was I wished them to be...

or *not* to be. I have always attributed those failings to a combination of enormous passion and extremely high standards, a personal form of elitism that ruled out all but a few. Maybe that's too generous an analysis, I don't know. True, age has softened me. I no longer (well, rarely) feel the personal affront, the rank offense, that mediocrity or worse in culture music once prompted. It's become harder to understand how or why I could once have felt so profoundly aghast at a record. Did that make me a discerning hardass or an intolerant jerk? Do exceedingly high standards that lead a critic to disdain so much make one commendably demanding or just reflexively difficult? Maybe there were other forces in play, things that colored my views and triggered rancor when levelheaded consideration would have been more appropriate. I've come across a lot of regrettably negative (often amplified by a misplaced sense of disappointment — but at what?) hasty impressions of albums I now treasure. I really wish I'd spent more time thinking before writing in the '70s.

Taste, of course, is highly mutable. While doing an inventory of my record collection (a year-long pandemic project), I've pulled out albums that I haven't played in decades and found my experience of them often at odds with my recollection of them. The wailing blues solos I once so admired are now trite riffs I've heard a thousand times. Voices whose sandpaper grit once conveyed sincerity and passion now strike me as shrill. Endless studio jams that were the hallmark of bands free to be can't end soon enough. World music in languages that I once found off-putting now warms me. And while the adrenaline rush of loud-fast rock that speeds the heart rate of a teenager can be physically distressing to an older person, I still love listening to punk records (just not as loud as I once did). I haven't joined others of my generation in gravitating toward Americana, jazz or classical, but I do understand the appeal more cerebral music has for older, more sophisticated, perhaps jaded, listeners as their instinctive core moves up the body.

Over time, I have become more mindful of how much work goes into the creation of a record. While that's not really germane to thoughtful critical consideration, I might have given that human element a little more consideration. There are no participation awards in my world, but a little regard for the effort that artists put in might have tempered the intensity of my responses. I definitely could have cut down on the adverbs.

Still, I have to admit that it bugs the shit out of me when people rave about art that seems ordinary or derivative, lazy, pat, arbitrary, unearned, vulgar, dumb, witless. These days (especially at the time of this writing, during the 2020–'21 lockdown), that art is more likely to be movies, books and television than records, but the sense I have of standing alone against a tidal wave is the same, and it's one I can recall having as far back as 1968, when I came out of a theater, unaided by the psychedelics so many found essential to appreciation, wondering just what the fuck *2001: A Space Odyssey* was supposed to be about. While that willingness to inhabit a tiny minority space on the fringes has made me open and sympathetic to all sorts of culture that lives below the popular radar, it conversely makes widespread critical favor a potential poison pill for me.

For reasons I can't completely explain, my taste remains doggedly narrow, "quirky," if you must. I've become one of those people who, metaphorically if not quite literally, only likes foreign films with subtitles. And so popular taste can feel oppressive in its indiscriminate appreciation of unqualified efforts. Easy though it may be for an indie rock fan to disdain mainstream music for all the obvious reasons (at least until the rise of poptimism, which made the embrace of crass vacuity a hip badge of omnivorous cultural enlightenment), it amazes (OK, infuriates) me when "friends" — that large peer group of a sort, whose enthusiasms and opinions social media ably collates and shares — bang on about a record or a movie or a TV show utterly lacking in wit, originality or charm. What do people see that I don't? I get that sometimes the problem is a specific prejudice or a matter of taste: I'm not big on costume dramas, fantasy or slapstick. For those, I generally refrain from exposure and comment. Same goes for jazz and classical music — I know better than to pretend my opinion about an art form for which I have never developed an adequate appreciation has any public value. I recognize the difference between not understanding a piece of art and not liking it. There are actors I can't stand watching; whatever the opposite of the ineffable quality of charisma is, they've got that for me in spades. And everyone has their dealbreakers: I couldn't watch *Breaking Bad* because the constant brutality obscured any of the show's possible qualities; the constant anachronistic cursing in *Deadwood* turned me off (and I'm a *big* fan of swearing).

I have a book of R. Crumb's letters titled *Your Vigor for Life Appalls Me*; quite a pungent title, that. In my world, I am baffled (and occasionally appalled) by people who gladly embrace and praise so much of what comes their way. I'm sure they're sincere, but I can't imagine how anyone can feel that way. As I understand the psychology, a positive pleasure response is either connected to a previously unknown desire that has been unexpectedly filled or an established inclination prodded with familiarity. So, a record you've never heard before can be thrilling... *and* a record you know well can be intensely enjoyable when you know every word and note before they're sung or played. I expect those are very different mental processes, but both feel to me like narrow passageways with numerous filters through which only a very few candidates can flow.

Are there people so devoid of discernment that nearly everything they encounter can be pleasurable? I know I'm at least mildly anhedonic, which is either a root cause of my demanding standards or a symptom of the same impulse. Still, I'd like to believe that developing and applying a reasonably consistent critical sensibility has equipped me to judge quality without relying solely on an atavistic sense of pleasure. I can identify quality entertainment even if it doesn't entertain me; conversely, I can enjoy garbage that I would never truly defend.

Still, how can anyone love so wantonly? I suspect that people who say they enjoy all kinds of music generally haven't given enough serious thought to it; the attenuated response that reads to them as highly favorable is perhaps stimulated by the merest of touches. But those of us who obsess over culture, who slice, dice, weigh and savor it, swish and spit, analyze, debate, self-criticize and doubt it, have erected higher walls around our pleasure centers. Our receptors are small and particular, awaiting just the right unexpected stimuli to tingle. Like a proofreader who spots no errors, a critic who likes nearly everything simply isn't doing the job. Shock of the new is not an open invitation, it's a landing strip that demands just the right approach. Bell curves don't just apply to the economy, they distribute the likelihood of excellence, average and awful as well. I know my quality threshold setting is unreasonably high, but I like it that way.

It's impossible for me to go back and reassess the state of mind that informed the callow judgments I typed out on the seafoam green Hermes manual in my father's office in our Manhattan apartment. I wish I'd had more maturity and context, more knowledge, more curiosity. Our blank slates at birth incorporate what we learn of the world as we go, interpreting it with all the information and awareness we have gathered. But that fluid process is never-ending. All of this work is frozen in the time it was written, a snapshot captured by a person less skilled, less aware, less conscientious than I would become. And having built myself a credible platform from which to pontificate without barriers, boundaries or guidance, I could write with unchallenged self-assurance; there are idiotic assertions of insufferable smugness here that are almost unbearable for me to read now.

Subject to prevailing values, there are assertions and opinions strewn through this book that fall far short of what I would now consider fair and just. I'd wager that nearly every male rock critic active in the early '80s wrote a "Girls With Guitars" article. What seemed like well-meaning support of our musical sisters then is now ineluctably lame.

It's embarrassing — decades later — to see the limits of what I knew, declarations of youthful naïveté that now leap off the page as arrogant stupidity. In cases of governmental malfeasance, the question is often what did X know and when did X know it? For me, it's more like what didn't I know and when did I finally learn it?

Naturally, I'd like to go back and fix some of my humbling shortsightedness here, but that would be dishonest. Other than excising a few inexcusable shames and fixing some confounding typos, I'm willing to take my retrospective lumps by sharing this stuff either as written or as published. On the other hand, it is entirely possible to look at a bylined article that clearly establishes its provenance, find the ideas and writing clever, erudite, illuminating even and yet have no recollection of writing it — or even a reasonable belief that such a thing was possible. It's like finding a forgotten box in the back of your closet — it clearly belongs to you, but you don't know how it came to be there. So, yes, some of my work collected here both surprises and impresses me. After enduring the dross of my early flailings, I hope others feel the same.

I take full credit *and* blame for what I've written. I've endeavored to gather both the good and the bad, but that doesn't mean I'm equally proud of all of it. Certainly not.

At this stage of life, whatever value I may possess as a cultural elder is in what I recall, what I can share about events I witnessed, what analytic wisdom I can summon about times I lived through. Unfortunately, those memories are fixed and fading; I'm not about to remember anything new about a show I haven't thought about in 40 years. I am at once incredibly glad that my work led me to record so much of that in words at the time and sorry that I can't reexamine those experiences with the deeper understanding of things age has granted me.

So, why, after all of *that*, have I undertaken *this*? Retirement after 22 years from a mid-level management job in syndicated radio left me with both time and a yen for some retrospective stock-taking. I began several archival projects: organizing and digitizing my interview tapes, scanning the run of *Trouser Press Collectors' Magazine*, relaunching the *Trouser Press* website, going through my files, augmenting the concert lists I've kept since the '80s and doing an inventory of my record collection. (If you're curious: a total of 35,000 LPs, CDs and 45s.)

Then I got a query from a one-time *Trouser Press* contributor (forgive me, but I can't recall who) asking for permission to include that work in a collection he was preparing (of course!). A light bulb went off. A lot of music writers have published anthologies of their work; I've never thought that held much appeal beyond a tiny audience and so would be futile to pitch. (I do, however, own a shelf of other writers' collected works.) For much the same reason, I've always resisted the idea of a proper *Trouser Press* anthology, although I do value the ones I have for other publications (*Bomp, Punk, Creem, Crawdaddy, Touch and Go, No Depression, Mad*).

But having self-published two novels as E-books, I realized I could just do it myself. As I thought about it, I decided to make it a combined anthology and memoir, sharing oft-told (as well as previously untold) tales that people have always seemed to enjoy the telling of.

I've kept a lot of documentation: binders of clippings, converted computer discs, file cabinets of drafts, press bumpf, reviews and research. So, I went to work, sifting through all the writing I've done and deciding how to present it. I spent a year tinkering with it and now have it organized into three volumes, a total of nearly a million words. (Hence the fused arthritic joint in my right index finger. Awaiting the start of a conference call a few years back, a colleague correctly identified my presence by the audible violence of my hunt-and-peck typing.)

Assembling all of this material in one place opens me up to examination that might uncover cases of critical inconsistency, of turnabouts and rethinks, of self-plagiarism and contradiction. Errors of fact, hapless predictions and once-faddish views that now seem quite absurd. I'm sure there are plenty of those collected in these three volumes, and I don't relish the prospect of having them brought to my attention. But it would be absurd to assume that the human mind can steer a straight and true course, without a few wrong turns along the way, for nearly half a century. And most people don't commit so many thoughts, observations and opinions to print for posterity.

Maybe, in these late innings, I don't really care. I know that I've given it all my best, most honest shot, so if I have inadvertently screwed up a few times along the way, I don't feel that bad about it.

I am very proud of my small contribution to the world of rock music. Over the years, countless friends and strangers have graciously thanked me for turning them on to specific artists or genres and praised *Trouser Press* for providing a knowing lifeline to lonely music fans in need of a sympathetic voice. A few artists have expressed their appreciation to me as well. That's both meaningful and gratifying, since I became a music critic out of an innate desire to proselytize, to share my discoveries and enthusiasms with others, to preach the gospel of music that mattered to me. Yes, despite my hard-earned reputation as a curmudgeonly grouch, my impetus for doing this was always positive.

As best I can recall, I have been published in *Addicted to Noise, The Big Takeover, The Broadway Local, The Chicago Tribune, Circus, Circus Raves, CMJ New Music Monthly, the CODA Collection, Crawdaddy (Feature), Creem, eMusic, The Encyclopedia Britannica, Entertainment Weekly, The Forward, Good Times, Guitar World, Hartford Courant, Los Angeles Times, Mojo, Music & Sound Output, The Music Gig, Musician, New Musical Express, New Route, New York Daily News, New York Newsday, Newsday, New York Post, New York Times, Parade, React, Record, Request, Rolling Stone, Salon, San Francisco, Chronicle, Savory NY, Spin, Star Hits, Tower Pulse!, Tracks, Trouser Press, Trouser Press Collectors' Magazine, TV Guide, Video, Video Insider, Video Review, Village Voice, VSDA Reports* and *Zoo World*.

I apologize in advance that some of my specific experiences are mentioned more than once. When you write for a living, it's inevitable that memories come up in various contexts and get recycled from time to time.

No one need point out that I have allowed myself the license to include pieces that fall outside the 25-year period (1972–1997) specified in the subtitle of this book. But anyone who can take reliable issue with a fact as I've depicted it, please let me know and I will make a correction. Ditto for typos, etc. Thank you for reading.

New York City
January 2022

Acknowledgments

Like most people of my generation, the primary influence on my musical taste was radio (in order: WMCA-AM, WNEW-FM, WKCR-FM, WLIR-FM, WDRE-FM) and the music press, especially *Creem* and the *New Musical Express*.

Also, albums borrowed from the New York Public Library, all the music magazines I've read, all the opening acts I've seen, all the promo records I've received, reviews I've edited and countless stray encounters along the way.

I would be remiss if I did not gratefully note these invaluable individual contributions to my musical awareness:

- Andy and David Yale for Bob Dylan
- Scott Marden for the Who
- Pete Townshend and Lenny Kaye for Eddie Cochran
- Dave Schulps for the Bonzo Dog Band, Roxy Music, Sparks and many more
- Robert Schainbaum for David Bowie
- Linda Danna for the Fast and Suicide
- Regina Joskow for Soul Asylum and Marvin Gaye (at least)
- Monica Dee and Art Black for Green
- Paul Rambali for Joy Division
- Alan Fielding for Frank Sidebottom
- Anthony DeCurtis for the Vulgar Boatmen
- David Sheridan for the Jesus and Mary Chain
- Bobbie Gale for Fountains of Wayne
- Tim Sommer for Neu!
- Michael Azerrad for the Pulsars
- Jackson Griffith for the Queers
- Doug Brod for the Fags (I know how this sounds...)
- Freda Love Smith for Robbie Fulks

I also need to thank whoever at Google built the handy online tool that converts printed material into text files in Google Drive. Anonymous software engineers: I couldn't have done this without you.

And my deepest gratitude to everyone who ever played a part in *Trouser Press*.

In lieu of a dedication, I'd like to acknowledge some of my important, imperfect heroes for their instruction and inspiration. My profound thanks for the laughs *and* the tears.

Pete Townshend, Bob Dylan, Robert Downey Senior, Vivian Stanshall, Bobby Seale, Jimmy Carter, Pete Seeger, Mona Simpson, Muddy Waters, René Descartes, George Studdy, Dusty Springfield, Mickey Mantle, The Rev. Martin Luther King Jr., Paul Williams, Chuck Berry, John Lennon, David Bowie, Miriam Linna, Joe Meek, Sam Cooke, Ray Davies, Malcolm X, Twiggy, John Otway, René Magritte, Joe Strummer, Karl Rodman, Lenny Kaye, R. Crumb, Sister Rosetta Tharpe, Brian Wilson, Tom Lehrer, Aretha Franklin, Gary Stewart, Keith Richards, Lillian Roxon, Vladimir Ilyich Ulyanov, Tommy Smothers, Blossom Dearie, Charles M. Schulz, Kingsley Amis, Wendy Carlos, Chuck D, Elvis Costello, Peter Sellers, Raquel Welch, Bryan Ferry, Al Feldstein, Hugh Hefner, Chris Sievey, Shirley Chisholm, Soupy Sales, Phil Spector, Sandrine Bonnaire, Eddie Cochran, Nik Cohn, Muhammad Ali, Alan Betrock, Greg Shaw, Samuel Shem, Red Skelton, Nick Kent, Dr. Seuss, W.C. Fields...

...and whoever came up with the line "I've suffered for my art, now it's your turn."

A Few Memories

Things that I swear happened (but which now seem totally implausible, even to me)

◆ The Lemon Pipers' "Green Tambourine" was a number-one hit in 1968. I have a blurry recollection of seeing them play a short promotional set around that time in the hip clothes section of a New York department store (A&S? Gimbels? Korvettes? Macy's?) The detail that stuck with me is that one of the musicians pulled out a hatchet and chopped up a guitar at the finale. In 2020, I was able to reach the band's singer, Ivan Browne, and he more or less confirmed it. "I have a vague memory of doing that. Don't remember the store." And while he doesn't believe any instruments were sacrificed that day, he did say, "Bill Bartlett, the guitar player, did that! Chopped the edge of his Mosrite double neck with an axe. Not at a store. That was very early '68. Had to be a big performance somewhere."

◆ When I was nine or ten, in the first public know-it-all display of my childhood, my two-years-older next-door neighbor (and still a friend) Kay Schoenwetter and I gave a "lecture" on dinosaurs (along with the Yankees, they were my first childhood obsession), complete with a mimeographed handout (drawings possibly mine), at the beloved Brooklyn Children's Museum, a few blocks from our apartment building.

DINOSAURS

by Kay Schoenwetter and Ira Robbins

DINOSAURS lived a long time ago. There are no dinosaurs living today. The most you could probably find is a fossil. A FOSSIL is the bone of an animal buried in the ground for thousands of years.

The name "fossil" comes from a Latin word <u>fossilis</u>, which means "dug up".

FOSSILS

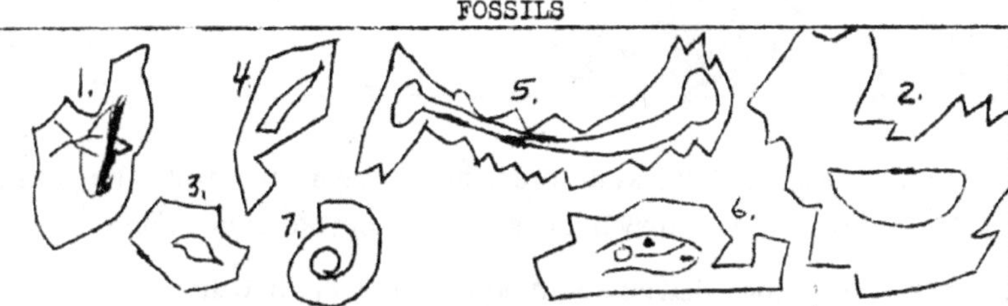

1. Insect imbedded in rock after millions of years. 2. Foot bone of a brontosaurus. 3. Back toe of a tyrannosaurus rex. 4. Claw of an allosaurus. 5. Cracked leg bone of a brontosaurus. 6. Head of diplodocus. 7. Fossil snail.

Some were flying dinosaurs; for example Rhamphorhynchus and Pteranodon. Some dinosaurs lived in the water; Diplodocus was one of these. Some were land dinosaurs.

DIMETRODON was a land dinosaur. He fed on small animals along the shores of lakes. He had two sets of sharp teeth, and a "sail". He was 7 feet long.

This is TYRANNOSAURUS REX. He was "king of tyrants". He had 4 inch dagger-like teeth to tear the meat that was his diet. Here he is chasing a Brontosaurus who will be lucky if he can get into a nearby lake before he is caught and eaten. He was 50 feet long from nose to tail.

◆ Thanksgiving 1969: Seeing the Rolling Stones at Madison Square Garden as a teenager, I was rushing down from my cheap seat in the nosebleeds toward the stage when I ran smack-dab into Janis Joplin. (According to Holly George-Warren's 2019 bio, Joplin did in fact attend that concert!)

◆ Thanksgiving 1973: Dave Schulps and I are browsing in the original Village Oldies when the only other customer in the shop, a small man in a watch cap and pea coat, mistakes Dave for a store employee and asks him something about Lee Hazlewood records. The curious consumer? Bob Dylan.

◆ While waiting to interview Alex Harvey at SIR studios in Manhattan in 1976, a door opened to one of the rehearsal rooms and inside I could see Bob Dylan, Joan Baez and a handful of other stars, maybe Roger McGuinn. It was only weeks later that I learned of the Rolling Thunder Revue, which is what was gestating there. (Another memory of the experience — being shooed away from the loo by a bodyguard so Dylan could do his business without company.)

◆ In 1972, attending a concert at Philharmonic Hall (which became Avery Fisher Hall the following year and is now Geffen something or other) called *Folk Variations* that starred Phil Ochs, Doc Watson and David Bromberg, I wound up in a backstage dressing room with a lot of people, including Ochs. I have no idea how or why I got there.

◆ In 1997, knowing that Steve Albini's band Big Black had released a 45 of "He's a Whore" and that Sub Pop co-founder Jonathan Poneman played in a Seattle Cheap Trick tribute band called Sick Man of Europe, I suggested to Cheap Trick that they could earn some well-deserved indie cred by getting the former to produce a single that the latter could release. I made the CT – JP introduction (I didn't know Albini other than reading his column in *Matter* and once having to nag him about an overdue $50 bill for an ad in *Trouser Press* for his indie label, Ruthless Records), and this was the result. That was their only Sub Pop engagement, but Albini also recorded their widely bootlegged raw remake of *In Color*.

◆ When Dave and I interviewed Ron Wood in 1979, Keith Richards came in from an adjacent hotel room, on all fours, carrying his son Marlon, a toddler at the time, on his back. He stopped in to chat with us about some of his favorite reggae artists and shared their plans for a side band called the Barbarians. I sheepishly mentioned that the name was already in use (a fact gleaned from Lenny Kaye's *Nuggets* set, which contains their maudlin garage rock classic "Moulty"). I don't know what happened after that, but when the tour was announced, their band was billed as the New Barbarians.

◆ I once saved Ahmet Ertegun's life. At CBGB one night in the '90s, seeing Ghost of an American Airman, a now-forgotten Irish band Atlantic had just signed, I was standing to the right of the sound board, behind a tall metal filing cabinet. Ertegun, the chairman of the company and already a bit frail in his early 70s, watched the show briefly from the raised section of the club and then made his way down the three or four stairs behind me. As he did, he tripped and pitched forward, his bald pate's potentially fatal trajectory toward the cabinet's sharp metal corner blocked only by my back. He landed against me, regained his balance and went on his way without saying a word. So far as I could tell, he never saw me or realized what had happened. (Coincidentally, his death a dozen years later was the result of a fall he took at a Rolling Stones concert.)

◆ In the 1990s, I played guitar and sang in the new wave mash-up punk cover trio Utensil (named after a fictional outfit mentioned in the Jim Jarmusch film *Night on Earth*) with my multi-talented friends Michael Azerrad (drums) and Jim Merlis (bass, on loan from his main band, Honus Wagner). We did a workshop gig that was serendipitously attended by Jody Stephens of Big Star during a CMJ convention and then a "secret" warm-up gig at which we billed ourselves as Spork. We made our proper debut at CBGB (thanks, Louise!) on a Friday night, 11 September 1992, a show that was previewed in the *Village Voice* (thanks, Bob!) and then unexpectedly reviewed in *Rolling Stone* (!). David Fricke's incredibly generous piece remains one of my proudest moments.

> *Rolling Stone*, 29 October 1992
> The eyeglasses were a dead giveaway. Everybody in the band wore 'em. And the set list had "concept" scrawled all over it: Nineties-style grunge-rock make-overs of late-Seventies and early-Eighties New Wave hits, running the high-camp gamut from "Turning Japanese," by the Vapors and the Dickies' "Manny, Moe and Jack" to an ingenious medley of Nena's "99 Red Balloons" and "In the City" by the Jam.
>
> Only a bunch of rock writers would dream up something so delightfully screwy, and Utensil, a New York band that made its world debut at CBGB a few weeks ago, features two of the best. Singer-guitarist Ira Robbins is the co-founder of the late, great *Trouser Press* magazine and the editor of the acclaimed *Trouser Press Record Guide*. Drummer Michael Azerrad is a frequent contributor to this magazine. Bassist Jim Merlis is a ringer — a publicist at Columbia Records — but he looks the part (specs, exploding hippie-ish hair), and he can play...

The piece went on to recommend that we record, and we did: "Ça Plane Pour Heroin" along with three other tracks ("Our Lips Are Sealed," the Buggles' "Clean Clean" and Devo's "Uncontrollable Urge," with a detour into Led Zeppelin's "Misty Mountain Hop") at Coyote Studios in Brooklyn, produced by Andy Shernoff of the Dictators, and — through our industry connections — obtained vague promises from Sub Pop and Creation to release two each as singles, which would have been amazing if they had actually happened. I did, however, send our rendition of her song to Jane Wiedlin, who replied with a friendly note that now hangs on my record room wall.

Three months later, we returned to the CBs stage to open for Flaming Lips. At a later gig, we got Ira Kaplan of Yo La Tengo (who had at one time written reviews for *Trouser Press*) to take my place for the first song because everyone kept mixing us Iras up and we thought it would be funny to confuse things further.

◆ In 1976, Linda Danna and I were hoping to hold our wedding reception at Max's Kansas City, but after the ugly dustup between Handsome Dick Manitoba and Wayne County, who was Max's resident DJ at the time, we were told that we couldn't have the Dictators play the party, so we booked a space at the Essex House on Central Park South and didn't have any live music after all.

◆ In 1999, when Kristina Juzaitis and I had our belated wedding reception, Yo La Tengo played a lengthy set of perfectly selected covers which I wish had been recorded, since the night's drinking blotted it all from my memory. I do know that their set included songs by the Who, Bonzos and Kinks as well as a bunch of new wave classics.

◆ Sometime in the '90s, I ran into Bob Geldof outside a hotel ballroom during a music convention. We had met once or twice in 1977 or 1978 (I may have been present when Dave interviewed him for *Trouser Press*) and he greeted me by name. Either he has total recall or I simply imagined it.

◆ In April 2010 I had the enormous privilege of "opening" a show for the great Neil Innes (R.I.P.) at the Record Collector in Bordentown, New Jersey: he sang, I read an excerpt from my first novel. He was kind and friendly. We'd met before — I interviewed him in the '80s — but my debt to him and the Bonzos is incalculable, and this was a singular honor for me.

◆ I sort of auditioned for the Dictators one time. They needed a bass player, but for some reason I ended up playing Ross the Boss's white Les Paul Custom with the band for a minute. Although I was friends with two members of the band, I was never any sort of a contender, but I do relish the memory.

◆ To my utter delight, I appear in a Pete Frame family tree ("Smouldering in the Bowery...One") thanks to organist Jimmy Destri's brief membership in my first band, Knickers. (He soon got a better offer and joined Blondie.) We played loud punk-pop before there really was such a thing, rehearsed for a year and did one gig opening for the Fast at Mothers in 1975 before breaking up. We released a posthumous single ("Drums of Love" b/w "Denunciations") produced by the late Ian (real name: Ira) North of Milk 'n' Cookies. You can find those tracks on Bandcamp.

Knickers began when my bass-playing *Trouser Press* colleague Jim Green met singer-songwriter Stephen Gallo working in a record shop; Jim got me in to play guitar and write songs with Steve. Then we pushed Jim out. (I am not proud of that, but I've been forgiven and we are still close friends.) In came Kathleen Turner's future ex-husband, Jay Weiss, on bass. Drummers included Harry D'Antonio (later a mainstay of my good pal Russell Wolinksy's band, the Sic F*cks; he died of COVID in 2022) and fine-art painter and memoirist Duncan Hannah (also RIP). My first wife, photographer Linda Danna, sang backup.

Knickers, 1975: Jay Weiss, Stephen Gallo, Ira Robbins; Harry D'Antonio at rear. Photo by Linda D. Robbins

◆ British national treasure Pete Frame was kind enough to allow *TP* to publish some of his amazing scholarship for grossly inadequate remuneration. And I have never forgotten his fortuitous proffer of Stiff Records T-shirts when he was the label's press officer in London in 1978 — they came in handy when Ian North, with whom I was staying (his flatmate was a German call girl who was never there), fucked off for the weekend without warning and left keyless me out in the street. I felt extremely conspicuous idling unhappily for hours on a residential street in Fulham. I finally gave up, got a taxi to the one cheap hotel I knew, in Russell Square, and enjoyed the comfort of clean "If it ain't Stiff it ain't worth a fuck" shirts, telephoning at regular intervals until Ian returned, with a bland apology, on Monday.

◆ Notable rock artists I've seen on the New York City streets or subway more than once: Gibby Haynes of the Butthole Surfers, Richie Stotts of the Plasmatics and Jim "Foetus" Thirlwell.

◆ Bands I've played guitar and/or sung in: Gorilla (aka Hank Frank and the Hot Dogs), Knickers, Utensil, Pippi Eats Cherries, Ira and the Ashtray, Heather Has Two Mommies, Who, The (that's one band) and the Editors NYC.

◆ I have been onstage with Cheap Trick, Velvet Crush, Lisa Loeb, Elliot Easton, Mark Eitzel, Amy Rigby, Kelley Deal, Heavenly, the World Famous Blue Jays, the Mary Janes, Scott Kempner, Dennis Diken, Sal Maida, the Baskervilles and Binky Philips. I've also taken part in one-off tribute bands for the music of Lester Bangs, the Who, Cheap Trick and the Bureau of Alcohol, Tobacco and Firearms.

Starting Out (1954 – 1974)

You *could* call it ironic...

Graduating high school in the fall of 1971, ambivalent as I was about the value of higher education at a time of great political turmoil in America, I enrolled in a two-year technical school primarily so I could avoid two things: reading and writing.

Radical politics and loud rock music (and girls) were my only real interests in life. Literature — both the consumption of and the creation of — felt extraneous. I was certain that college, at least the liberal arts version my friends were headed to, would be a waste of time. They were looking forward to sex and drugs; I was reading underground newspapers and grappling with my father's extensive Lenin library. (There is no need to add the obvious Lenin / Lennon quip here.)

I had already attended five different public schools and lived through nearly as many repetitions of the course in basic English grammar, a Groundhog Day experience that left me overdosed on parts of speech, tenses, agreement and dangling modifiers — but also inscribed the rules firmly enough to last a lifetime.

I was 17 years old, living with my folks on Manhattan's Upper West Side. Whether I liked it or not, I had to do something to address my future. Mr. Wernicke, an awful teacher I'd had in eleventh grade, had queered my childhood ambition of becoming a chemist and left me with one remaining ambition: to pass the difficult test for a first-class FCC radiotelephone license and qualify for an off-mic engineering career in radio. That was going to take some study. City College, which was free at the time, was an option (and a family tradition), but I also applied to RCA Institutes, a bare-bones Manhattan job factory on West 31st Street, right near Penn Station, that offered associate degrees in electrical engineering. Bolstered by the surprising offer of a full scholarship from the school, I viewed two years of academic servitude as a damn sight better than four, so I enrolled. I would continue to study math and science in the service of potential employment and happily leave words to others.

My father, a voracious reader in his youth, consumed several serious magazines, some left-wing political weeklies and the *New York Times* (which he always brought home folded to the editorial page, which at the time faced the obituaries and led me to wonder why he was so morbid) without fail. He owned a huge library, but I never once saw him crack open a book that was not about philately. (He also didn't care for sports, go to the movies or partake of modern culture. He only watched the business reports and news on PBS.) Once I'd finished the Hardy Boys and a bunch of baseball biographies, I wasn't much interested in books, either. No, I'm not proud of that.

The following spring, a brief bout of mononucleosis blocked my academic progress for a few weeks; it was decided that I would need to retake the quadramester — a year later. So, I transferred to another local institution, biting the bullet for a full four-year Bachelor of Science in Electrical Engineering.

Two years later, a bored B+ junior at Polytechnic Institute of New York, I co-founded the magazine that would launch my lifetime in musical journalism. Conveniently, that project discouraged the recruiters I met with from thinking me sufficiently devoted to engineering to be a viable employment prospect. Asked about my hobbies and outside interests (for engineering students, that's almost a trick question), I thought it would show initiative and imagination to mention that I published a rock magazine in my spare time. How wrong I was: none of them offered me a job. If my burgeoning interest in writing intuitively disqualified me from the career path I'd been studying for, all I could do was go with that.

I realized as an adult that, while school failed to inspire a taste for reading or writing, both were always in my blood, no matter how clueless I may have been at the time about it. In fact, as a young boy, I had already done a fair bit of writing. My mother, whose education was in biology but whose career took her from an executive role in a hospital workers' union to X-ray technician for a Brooklyn doctor and then, late in life, to join my father in the philatelic world, had an unbridled creative streak that manifested in countless ways, from photography to sewing dresses for my sister to making marionettes for a show I wanted to stage and cloth figures of some favorite cartoon characters (Snoopy, Quick Draw McGraw) as presents for me. She was an ambitious and resourceful cook and baker. We went camping and canoeing on the Schuylkill River in Pennsylvania; she even showed an active interest in pop art. In addition to allowing me to paint two murals on my bedroom wall — a *Peanuts* panel in full color, which I produced using a pantograph (I have *zero* talent for drawing), and a Yellow Submarine — she made a remarkable art piece fashioned from soaked-off Campbells soup can labels. Now framed, her '60s homage to Andy Warhol hangs just outside our kitchen and invariably receives admiring comments from visitors.

My father, who got his degree at City College in political economy, earned his living from philately (rare stamps). But he had extensive experience in both printing and political activism. For those reasons, odd though it may have been for a family of lower-middle city dwellers, we always had a mimeograph machine at home. (Kids: think of it as prehistoric Xerox machine or a rudimentary printing press.) It was, in its day, the essential tool for producing fliers, signs, manifestos and other rabble-rousing propaganda. And, as it happened, for running off a rock fanzine.

When I was a wee lad, my mother helped me "write" a brief story, which she bound into booklet form. We also collaborated on a one-act (well, one-scene) play. In January 1963, when I was eight, we published the solitary issue of *The Marks Weekly*, a two-sided rexographed "newsletter" about the Brooklyn street (St. Marks Avenue in Crown Heights) on which we lived. The handwriting is hers. I have no idea what I contributed to my first brush with the world of journalism, but that is in fact how I got my start. And I don't recall the project seeming at all out of the ordinary.

The Yales and Starks were neighbors, friends and classmates. Later that year, Andy Yale and his older brother David introduced me to the music of Bob Dylan. I had heard "Blowin' in the Wind" by Peter Paul & Mary, so when they played *Freewheelin'* for me, I couldn't understand why some guy with such an awful nasal voice was trying so hard to sing it.

⇒ My first rejection letter!
I was nine and had sent in some rubbish poem for consideration to *School Bank News*, a publication for kids that was owned by the bank at which I had a tiny savings account. The paper cost two cents (free for schoolchildren). While my submission didn't pass editorial muster, the consolation prize ("pencils... sent herewith") was an encouraging reward.

School Bank News

GRACE BRADBURN
EDITOR

PUBLISHED BY
THE EAST NEW YORK SAVINGS BANK
BROOKLYN, N. Y.

February 7th, 1964

Dear Ira:

~~We received~~ and ~~were glad to~~ have your recent contribution to School Bank News. All that are received cannot possibly be published because we do not have space for them. Therefore, we have to take those which at the time seem to us to be the best.

Perhaps you have read the quotations: "If at first you don't succeed, try, try again" -- "Practice makes perfect".

To those who send contributions for publication which indicate real effort, we usually send a pair of pencils, and these are sent herewith.

Cordially yours,

Grace Bradburn
Grace Bradburn
Editor

Enclosure

THE LIBRARY AT 725 ST. MARKS

KNOWLEDGE IS POWER

A "MARKS WEEKLY" NEWS CORRESPONDENT INTERVIEWED HARDY FRANKLIN, COORDINATOR OF DISTRICT LIBRARIES. HERE ARE QUESTIONS AND ANSWERS:

Q: What could you do about children who are NOT INTERESTED IN reading?

A: "I would get a book on a subject the child liked. It would be heavily illustrated and encourage the child to read."

Through this brief interview, the "Marks Weekly" has established confidence in Mr. Franklin.

IF YOUR OUTGO EXCEEDS YOUR INCOME, YOUR UPKEEP CAN BE YOUR DOWNFALL.

Poetic Masthead

There was a paper called "The ST. MARKS"
Run by the Robbins, the Yales and the Starks.

So, how did I come to believe myself to be a person who should analyze and critique anything? My first academic brushes with literature put me at serious odds with that very notion. Beginning in junior high, English teachers would bang on about the themes of the books we were told to read. I had a hard time with that idea. As I understood it, themes were what authors had in mind but didn't bother to say; I was never good at hidden meanings, so those notions often eluded me. (Maybe that's why engineering suited me — I like empiricism better than guesswork. Semiotics? Get to fuck!)

So, while I may have had some grasp of satire, parody and parable — I got that *Animal Farm* and *Rhinocéros* were about totalitarianism, *The Jungle* was about the evils of industry and *Tom Sawyer* was about tricking yokels into painting fences — those elusive "themes" were always beyond my ken. When I was told that the theme of *Lord of the Flies*, that grisly chronicle of youthful descent into savagery, was man's inhumanity to man, that settled it for me. I fixed on that as the one-size-fits-all theme. From then on, whether the evidence was there or not (this was during the Viet Nam war, so there was a lot of man's inhumanity to man on the nightly news), whenever any question about theme was posed, I could confidently shoot my hand in the air: it could only be that one thing, the all-purpose, all-encompassing purpose of serious literature: *man's inhumanity to man*.

I found ways to express my resentment at being told to discern meaning behind archaic words in old books I had no interest in reading. An English teacher seeking to bridge the generation gap once trotted out Simon & Garfunkel's "The Boxer" and asked us to analyze it. (I'm pretty sure I volunteered "man's inhumanity to man," at least under my breath.) It was thought at the time that we cynical young counter-culturalists could be drawn into an appreciation for classic literature if pop lyrics were portrayed as poetry, an attempt to use what we knew to trick us into caring about a culture that we found impossibly remote. We never went for it. We were the new generation, and we had no taste for *Ethan Frome* (Edith Wharton, 1911) or *Silas Marner* (George Eliot, 1861) — two books still in the public school curriculum in the late 1960s — no matter how many "Eleanor Rigby" references a teacher could summon up.

The teacher offered some ideas about the boxer as a symbol of I forget what and then moved the class discussion to some couplet of Simon's, trying to instill particular significance into the word choice. The leading question was what was meant by the words he chose. I shot up my hand and said he was just sticking in a word that rhymed, that it meant nothing more than that and any attempt to aggrandize it with significance was bullshit. In what might be thought of as my instinctive first gesture toward music criticism, I also complained about the awkward melodrama of the reverb-soaked snare used to accent the refrain. (Perhaps if I had known that was Hal Blaine's contribution, I might have appreciated it more.)

An unrelated school memory: when a teacher in fourth or fifth grade taught us that candles burn by incinerating the wick as the melting wax slows its progress, I knew she was wrong. I already had my doubts about her because she pronounced the word "reverberation" as "rev-ERR-burr-AY-shun," and this was more than I could bear. At home that night, I prepared an experiment, using a fully burnt wooden match in a small tray of paraffin to demonstrate that it was the rising petroleum fumes from the wax which burned *around* the wick and could do so even if the wick was already incinerated, that I brought in for show and tell the next day. I don't recall any repercussions from that, but the teacher must have *hated* me. Hell, *I* would have hated me. (In junior high, well into the cold war, I got sent to the principal's office after telling a social studies teacher that I didn't mind the thought of living in Russia. My dad came to school the next day and read them the free speech riot act.)

And an aside: it took exactly two attempts at acting to convince me I had no talent in that department: a day camp swipe at *The Man Who Came to Dinner* and a junior high production of *Candide* in which I was supposed to slap someone in the cast, a thespian obligation I could not carry out due to my adolescent crush on the young actress.

In high school, I wrote what I thought of as a book, although it only amounted to a ring binder of hand-written (in semi-legible script) pages that I titled *Funkomania: A Bookette of Our Times*. Inside, as I explained, "This book is written exactly how I talk. It may not appear very cool in print, but books should be truly expressive of the author's manner. My manner is rather four-lettered. Sorry, but this book is realistic, and reality is not always as nice & polished as carefully prepared manuscripts. This is not meant to be pretentious." (Actually, it was overheated and lame.)

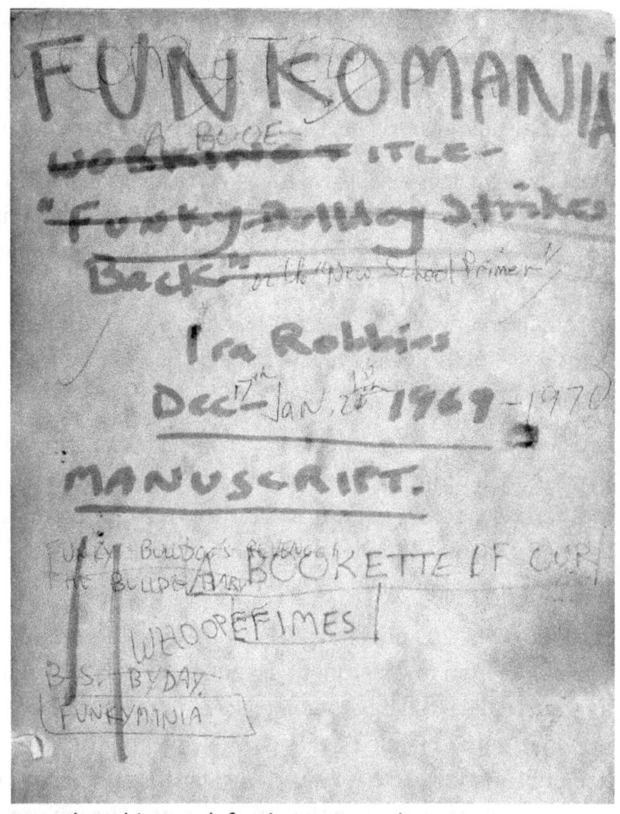

I'll stop there other than to note that — preceding Karl Ove Knausgård by 35 years in trying to produce "art" from an account of an ordinary life — chapters bear such scintillating titles as "The Yard," "Home Room," "Social Studies" and "The Tale of the 3 AM Hairy Coffee Machine" (credit my years of listening to Jean Shepherd for that one.)

Around that same time, I joined a group of grassroots political activists in my new neighborhood, the Upper West Side of Manhattan, and helped commandeer an abandoned corner building that we turned into HQ for, among other things, a left-wing community newspaper cleverly named *The Broadway Local* for a subway line that served the neighborhood. I worked on that, mainly as a typesetter, which was done on an IBM system that essentially slaved a Selectric typewriter to a tape cartridge memory unit the size of a file cabinet. We had some sort of arrangement with OBU (One Big Union, a reference to the International Workers of the World, aka the Wobblies), a radical women's group with a loft in Sheridan Square, and it was their equipment we used late at night. I was a shitty two-finger typist (still am), so I handled the output work, printing out columns of type on rolls of blindingly white clay-coated paper. We had some sort of labor trade worked out for the use of their gear, so I got asked to help out on a project they had gotten — I think it was Abbie Hoffman's *Steal This Book*. I don't think I bothered to read what I was outputting, but I did take home some of the discarded galleys. Haven't seen a trace of them in decades. (I was an opponent of the Yippies and always found Hoffman's farcical approach to radical politics reprehensible. So there.)

I was a red diaper baby (i.e., my father had been in the Communist Party of the USA). We lived on East 13th Street (the block on which *Taxi Driver* later placed "Sport" Harvey Keitel and his brothel) in a neighborhood then considered part of the Lower East Side but later absorbed into the East Village. Around the turn of the century, my mother's father lived deeper in the heart of the Lower East Side, on Hester Street. He told me stories about relocating down the fire escape at the end of the month because his parents couldn't pay the rent.

When I was two, we moved to a seven-and-a-half room apartment in a large building with a grand courtyard in Crown Heights, a no-longer-prosperous section of Brooklyn, which is why my lower-middle-class family of four could afford to live there. My bedroom, which was situated at the end of a long hallway that I used to fantasize about filling with water and swimming down, was 15' x 20', larger than many studio apartments! My sister Sara lived in what were once maids' quarters — two small rooms behind the kitchen; she had her own bathroom. I learned to read at a very young age thanks to Dr. Seuss books and Hardy Boys mysteries and was introduced to rock and roll the year I turned nine. My first conscious exposure was Del Shannon's "Hats Off to Larry," heard during a 1963 visit to our next-door neighbors' summer house in the Catskills. Then, in January of 1964, I was in my sister's room when her table radio blared out "I Want to Hold Your Hand" and I was off to the rock and roll races.

The following year, we began going to Washington D.C. to march against the war in Viet Nam, another link in the chain of left-wing political activity. I spent that July at Camp Thoreau, a small progressive sleepaway in Wallkill, New York, where I took guitar lessons from Mike Meeropol, the elder son of Julius and Ethel Rosenberg. (His brother Robbie was our sports counselor and taught us to play soccer. I was serving as goalie when a brisk kick of his hit my bare shin and ricocheted back at least 30 feet. Bright red for a week.) Two grandchildren of the legendary singer and actor Paul Robeson were fellow campers. It was that kind of place and I absolutely loved it, returning for the entire summer of 1965 and a month in 1966.

One early trace of the impulse to become a music critic: as a child, after returning from a Saturday matinee at the theater on Bedford Avenue and Eastern Parkway with my friends, I would insist on recounting the film's plot to my mother. I was terrible at it — lots of "Oh, wait, I forgot to tell you about..." digressions and backfills — but she listened patiently. It must have been tedious for her, but she was, as in all things, a patient good sport who always had time for her family.

I attended P.S. 289 until the fifth grade, when overcrowding in our newly built school building (poor planning, that) two blocks from my apartment led our entire class to be sent elsewhere for sixth grade, either to a middle school in an even tougher neighborhood adjacent to mine or to one miles away just north of Kings Highway in Flatbush, which was then upper-middle-class and largely Jewish. (None of this was my decision. I was not even aware that a decision had to be made, just that I was changing schools.) So, at the age of 11, my best friend Gregory Trent and I, along with a bunch of our Crown Heights classmates, began commuting to PS 238 (I never knew it was Ruth Bader's alma mater!) via a two-bus-one-subway route that involved a walk past the housing project built on the site of Ebbets Field. I have joked that I was sent to help integrate a white school, but the class and culture shock for me was nothing compared to what my Black classmates must have experienced. I don't recall outright antagonism, but there was a lot of awkwardness and an abiding sense of being in someone else's world where none of us quite belonged.

Those kids had grown up together in a sheltered, nearly suburban idyll of private houses, cars, comfort and financial security, while our parents lived paycheck to paycheck in a crowded slum where men played conga drums late into the night in Brower Park and only a few of my neighbors didn't live in apartments: they owned brownstone row houses. Our Flatbush classmates never came to visit us, but we did socialize; I attended a number of parties at their houses; some were seven-minutes-in-heaven/spin-the-bottle makeout parties that later struck me as awfully precocious behavior for a 12-year-old.

For grades seven and eight, we went to Cunningham JHS on East 17th Street in the same neighborhood. I celebrated my thirteenth birthday with a "kitchen sink," a huge ice cream concoction for ten glucose fiends, at Jahn's Ice Cream parlor on Nostrand Avenue and Avenue Z. It was only years later — after countless glasses of milk, fondues, cream-cheese-and-olive sandwiches (a personal favorite) and milkshakes that I learned what lactose intolerance was — and why my stomach had been a mess all those years. (I think it was my first girlfriend's mother, Mrs. Wolf, who alerted me; I'd never heard of the affliction, but it did explain the mild stomach distress I'd endured all through my milk-drinking years.) When I started high school and the combination of stress and early hours played havoc with my digestive system, a gastroenterologist fed me a bucket of barium, X-rayed my innards and prescribed Milpath, a mild sedative and muscle relaxant related to Miltown, the very idea which of which put me in the conceptual company of bored suburban housewives, like the ones summoned to mind by "Mother's Little Helper." I recoiled at the connotation and was switched to Valium, taken at lunch, which made me nod off during drafting class at 1:30 every day. The teacher must have thought I was on drugs (which, in fact, I was).

Rocked by the Radio

TrouserPress.com, 14 June 2020

I owe a lot to the Good Guys: Joe O'Brien, Jack Spector, Harry Harrison, Dandy Dan Daniel, B. Mitchell Reed, Dean Anthony and Gary Stevens.

Beginning around 10 years of age, just as the British Invasion began, my introduction — nay, initiation — to music came through the tiny speaker or the knotted, white-wired earplug of a trusty Viscount transistor radio, my battery-powered connection to WMCA-AM, one of the few New York radio stations that played rock and roll in the mid-'60s.

"Radio 57 — first on your dial." That made it easy to tune in, even though the signal was audibly weaker than nemesis WABC, perched 20 clicks higher at 77. (The bandwidth for AM frequencies is in the hundreds of kilohertz, so the station was actually tuned in at 570 kHz. Whatever — it's not like I had a problem with the non-mathematical way batting average percentages were expressed. And 57 was what it said on my radio's tiny tuning window.)

Other than the folk songs I learned at Camp Thoreau, my early taste in music was entirely formed by what I heard on WMCA. (As a kid, I bought and owned very few records. My big sister gave me some singles, but my small allowance led me to rely on LPs borrowed from the library; when I became a writer and got on mailing lists, my tiny teenaged collection began its inexorable growth.) I was a slave to the sound, obsessed with every song, contest, countdown, joke and news report the station pumped out. I picked up and devoured *Go* magazine, the national giveaway music paper (edited by Robin Leach!) sponsored by local radio stations, weekly from the counter of some store on Kings Highway on my way home from seventh and eighth grade. And the station's weekly chart for home study. Naturally, it contained precisely 57 hits of the week, some designated as the week's "Sure Shot" and others noted, no doubt with pride, as "Former Sure Shots" that had borne out program director Ruth Ann Meyer's early taste-spotting confidence. (Now that I think about it, what data was used to rank singles? I guess when you're a kid receiving the gospel, you don't question who came up with it.)

To distinguish itself from the more showbizzy WABC and the less showbizzy WINS (which went all-news in mid-1965), MCA called its deejays the Good Guys, had them sing funny songs in unison and emblazoned the slogan (in singular form) under a smiley face squiggle on the bright orange sweatshirts you could win by sending in a postcard and then waiting to hear your name announced on the air. I tried and tried and tried but finally was able to snag one for $3.00 during a rare retail sell-off by the station; although it fit me when I was a stocky 12-year-old, it's now roughly the size of a chunky baby. How does that happen?

I recorded broadcasts by placing a rectangular microphone directly face-to-face on the radio speaker and running it into the reel-to-reel tape recorded I got for my 12th birthday. (I could either have that or a shotgun, my father said at the time. I definitely made the right choice.)

Half a lifetime later, I was myself gainfully employed by a radio company (in a completely off-mic capacity) and had a colleague, Mike McCann, who'd been an oldies (now called "classic hits") jock in several markets. One day, I accompanied him to an event at which he introduced me to Dan Daniel, who had the afternoon shift on MCA and played the countdown my friend Gregory Trent and I listened to religiously after school. I've met a lot of famous people, but I admit I was overwhelmed. I told the toweringly tall Texan how much I owed him for my musical education and thanked him for setting me on the path of my life. He couldn't have been nicer. (Daniel died in 2016.)

The reason I bring all of this up is because of an MP3 I was sent, a three-hour 1968 WMCA aircheck. Beyond the simple nostalgia of hearing my 14-year-old world captured in amber, it's an amazing document of rock radio's youth, before the audience was fragmented into a dozen narrowly focused isolation tanks. It's a window into a time when pop music was a thousand things all at once, when youth culture welcomed the myriad results of its awakening with open arms and embraced whatever flowed forth. I listened to the file once and was transported; but I was also provoked into thinking about what it all meant, then and now. So, I played it again, this time with a Word file open.

19563
DEAN ANTHONY'S "OFF-KEY" SINGING CLUB
Official Member
THIS CARD ENTITLES MEMBER TO SING "OFF-KEY" WITH ANY AND ALL RECORDS PLAYED ON WMCA WITHOUT FEAR OF EMBARRASSMENT OR CRITICISM.
SING MORE NOW . . . EVEN THOUGH YOUR FRIENDS ENJOY IT LESS!
SING ALONG WITH DINO ON YOUR RADIO

It's Thursday, September 12th. Joe O'Brien (known on the air as J.O.B.), whose square-jawed Irish *punim* now puts me in mind of the swabbies on *McHale's Navy*, has the day off, and Ed Baer — "The Big Bad Baer" — is holding down his 6:00-to-10:00 morning drive slot. (The file only includes the first three hours of the shift.) It sounds like a lovely fall day, 62 degrees going up to the 70s, on what would have been the fourth day of the first week of public school — had the city's teachers not gone on strike. (Actually, the 12th was the only day in two months that they were not on strike; they'd begun the walkout on Monday the 9th but ordered back to work, futilely, three days later. By Friday, they were gone till November. (Not to get too far off topic, some parents and kids crossed the picket lines and held "liberation schools" to provide us with some form of education in their absence. That was my introduction to high school.) Despite the likelihood that most of the station's audience is home with nothing to do that morning, Baer makes no mention of the strike, although early on, after reading a commercial script for a furniture store in Yonkers that mentions "the kids are back in school," he ad libs, "we hope." (The every-half-hour news breaks, which must have addressed the city's top story, are edited out, so there's no evidence of how the strike was covered.)

Ed Baer

The show begins with a jingle singing "hello" in a variety of languages. With enough reverb to suggest an empty bank vault, Baer dives right in with Jeannie C. Reilly's "Harper Valley PTA," a clever blast of small-town turnaround loaded with sexy snark, sly innuendo (having a rhyme set up a likely line ending in "full of shit" but then using "hypocrites" instead), Dobro and y'all-type drawl. How amazing was it that this straight-up country song was a hit on a rock radio station in New York City, of all places? Despite the city's sizable African-American population with Southern roots, a good portion of the station's listeners probably knew little about that culture beyond what they'd seen on *The Beverly Hillbillies* (about to begin its seventh season as the tenth most popular show on TV), *Green Acres* (heading into its fourth) and *The Andy Griffith Show*, which had just wound up an eight- season run as the top-rated show on the air. The song is sarcastic, sure, but its judgment remains fixed inside its local milieu, not of it.

Baer back-announces the song (radio jargon: ID the title and artist of a record after playing it) then tells a mild joke about the smallness of Harper Valley, with a blast of canned laughter (probably on a tape cartridge, pulled off a rack and stuck in a player by the show's engineer). Then a (yikes!) cigarette commercial.

The Beach Boys' pulsing "Do It Again," currently number-16 on the station's survey, is up next, followed by a commercial and O.C. Smith's glacially paced, lushly arranged R&B-flavored "Little Green Apples," already a much bigger hit than it was for the white Texan who cut it as more of a country song six months earlier. Baer enthuses about it in his introduction: "Glad to hear O.C. Smith's version of the great Roger Miller song." (A little credit please for the song's writer, Bobby Russell.) It's a sweet sentiment, sure, but who believes that small, sour fruit are one of God's most notable creations, worthy of elevating in song?

Baer reels off last night's baseball scores then plays a lengthy jingle selling malt liquor (yikes again) and reads an ad for Barney's, the clothing store on 7th Avenue and 17th Street on its way to becoming a national brand, that includes a chance to win a pair of tickets to the Electric Circus. The fabled downtown discothèque had been the site of happenings by the Velvet Underground and the Fugs; by '68, Cat Mother and the All-Nite Newsboys, a good-time outfit a lot less outré, was the house band. But it was still a crazy place. (Larry Packer of Cat Mother: "There was a room there called the foam rubber room, a dark room. I remember my aid being enlisted to carry an ODed dead body out of the foam rubber room. A young lady.") So, let's imagine some random kid from Queens shopping for his bar mitzvah suit and winding up loose in one of the city's hippest night spots as a result. Yay for commerce crossing the culture gap.

Speaking of gaps...Baer spins "Over You," a song I barely remember by Gary Puckett and the Union Gap. "Lady Willpower" and "Woman, Woman," sure. Ditto "Young Girl." But this surging ballad doesn't ring any bells. (Not that it has any role in my knowledge fail, it's a really bad song, full of melodramatic swells, Bonanza-like strings, ridiculous lyrics and an abrupt melodic turn.) He notes that it was the previous week's Sure Shot, probably an easy call after three consecutive Top 5 hits for the Civil War-garbed quintet.

An awful diet desert spot for the no-sugar gelatin Shimmer ("rhymes with slimmer") precedes a surprising airplay selection: Status Quo's psychedelic classic, "Pictures of Matchstick Men." (Baer actually says the name correctly — STAY-tuss, not STAH-tuss.) The uncharacteristic song, which relegated one of the world's most popular straight-up rock and roll bands from the '70s on to be a one-hit wonder in America, is a marvel of trippy lyrics, studio flanging and wah-wah guitar wash. Oddly, the second time I saw the band play in New York, at Irving Plaza in 1997, the audience was primarily Mexican; Quo was a big deal south of the border, capable of filling soccer stadiums and bullfighting rings there.

You might hear the Quo song as a museum piece, but it sounds a lot more relevant half a century later than the next number, Ray Stevens' "Mr. Businessman." (Are they programming alphabetically here?). The lyrics of this dated topical relic are something to behold, as they mention "bigger cars, bugger houses" and "term insurance for your wife" as well as "your harlot" and "your charlatan analyst."

Billboard called Stevens "the #1 novelty recording artist of the past 30 years"; this one sits in his chart discography between "Harry the Hairy Ape" and "Gitarzan," so it's hard to tell if Stevens was truly despairing of the lifestyle damage done by capitalist business conformity, pointing a figure at a particular executive who wronged him, or just stirring the soup, making it up for provocative fun.

After a newsbreak with Herb Norman on the half-hour, Baer returns with groovy number-six on the weekly survey: "Girl Watcher" by the O'Kaysions. Based on sound, especially the singer's honeyed melisma (if not the name's resemblance to the O'Jays), I always imagined a Black soul group, but this sheet music makes the North Carolina outfit look like a square suburban wedding band. A later photo, however, has them in straight-up fake-hippie duds. Their lighthearted pop breeze, like a lot of the music on the station this day, has the peppy innocence of an arrangement for the Fifth Dimension, but that doesn't hide the fact that it's a leering ode to the harassment of women.

The basement makeout parties of my youth were redolent — at least in my memory — of Wind Song perfume from Prince Matchabelli (for the ladies) and Hai Karate aftershave or cologne (for the men). The produced spot Baer introduces for the latter is a real wheeze: "A SPECIAL RADIO COURSE IN HOW TO MAKE SCARY-SOUNDING NOISES IN CASE YOUR GIRL LOSES HER HEAD OVER YOUR HAI KARATE." (The insulting pseudo-Japanese gimmick, probably inspired by the martial arts on display in spy films starting with *Goldfinger*, promoted in shamelessly oversexed TV commercials, was that the aroma makes women lose control, wanton lust that must be fought off martial arts.) Baer riffs on the spot afterwards, weakly joking that karate lessons have made his hands such lethal weapons that he is afraid to applaud.

"1, 2, 3 Red Light" was the second of three million-sellers by New Jersey's 1910 Fruitgum Company. While other successes of the genre were studio confections whipped up by Kasenetz and Katz or one of the era's other Svengalis, these guys were — contrary to common belief — an actual band originally known as Jeckell and the Hydes and wrote some of their own material (if not their hits). Other than the scant, flimsy lyrics, it's no worse than a lot of what was on the charts in 1968: well-produced, the mix emphasizing handclaps over than multi-voice lead singing and backing vocals. The key change comes out of nowhere and the whole thing is done in less than two minutes.

The hour's second cigarette commercial (it would be another few years before tobacco products were banned from the airwaves) promotes one of Madison Avenue's dumber slogans: "It's not how long you make it, it's how you make it long." Baer gives the baseball scores again and then dives into a lengthy commercial break: Castro Convertible (I always wondered how the furniture manufacturer avoided being negatively impacted by sharing the name of the Cuban leader, an arch-villain to many Americans), orange juice, a dry-as-dirt PSA about environmental training for building superintendents, a weather check and a poorly produced spot for *The Young Runaways*, a lurid appeal to parents' worst nightmares (or a likely guidebook for disaffected teens.) Perhaps the Ramones had this tagline — "There's no stopping The Young Runaways" — in mind when they wrote "Cretin Hop" a few years later.

Then it's back to the music with "Hey Jude," the week's number-one song (and one Beatles song I would be happy to never hear again). Baer plays six of its seven-plus minutes and enthuses "I love that" before throwing to a news break, again omitted from the MP3. (Another cigarette spot, this one read by newsman Steve Powers, is included.)

Baer's traffic report leads into "Born to Be Wild," the second single in a row to be a favorite on both AM and FM radio of the '60s. That MCA's playlist could embrace country and bubblegum on one end all the way to what is now thought of as proto-metal on the other makes it a hallmark to the diversity that, at the time, didn't seem like a concern to programmers. And it certainly didn't matter to listeners. Motown? Great! The Rolling Stones? You bet! The Mamas and the Papas? Love it! Frank Sinatra? Sure, why not. That situation would change very soon, but we certainly enjoyed it while it lasted.

The next spot Ed reads, for Blue Cross/Blue Shield medical insurance (not nearly as much a part of our lives then as it is now), is so rich with respect and praise for doctors that it could have been played during the 2020 pandemic. But what follows is one for the time capsule. From the "Community Bulletin Board" comes "a strange happening at the Architectural League's gallery [on East 65th Street] this evening — people who go will be asked to step on to a scarlet acetate strip stretched around the block. The strip will then be cut into pieces, leaving people in various combinations. What happens will be a lesson in communication, behavior and participation. Sounds like fun." And the next plug is for the showing of a Greta Garbo film in a church. Generation landslide!

Before getting back to the music, Baer plays a jolly jingle for a money lender (you try singing "the full amount you have in mind"), reads those baseball scores again, plays another cigarette spot (it's terrifying how big a portion of the station's advertising comes from the tobacco industry) and only then introduces "Down in the Boondocks," Joe South's proto-Marxist evocation of the impediments to inter-class romance recorded by Billy Joe Royal in 1965, as "a Good Guy goldie." (Wikipedia notes that the song's hook — a choppy, upcurled guitar figure — was copied from a 1963 Gene Pitney recording of the Bacharach-David composition "24 Hours From Tulsa." Coincidentally, the O'Kaysions included a version on their *Girl Watcher* album.)

Coming up on the half-hour, Baer plays Jose Feliciano's cover of "Light My Fire." Blind, Puerto Rican, a virtuoso player of nylon-string guitar and a soulful, big-voiced singer, Feliciano occupied a strange position in pop — emerging from the Greenwich Village basket scene, his youth (22 at the time), uniqueness and winning sincerity made him a popular entertainer but where other folkies (Richie Havens, for one) were warmly embraced by the incipient *Woodstock* nation, Feliciano tacked too hard to the mainstream to be considered hip. Yet, here he was, doing the nearly unthinkable by spinning the Doors' year-old chart-topping signature song — a lusty roar of organ and near-psychedelia that, alongside "Born to Be Wild," was as much a generational anthem as any — into a gently acoustic bossa nova, freestyling the lusty words into cheerful romance, erasing the image of a leather-trousered Adonis in the thrall of Bacchus and who knows what else. Defanging Morrison's horny creation, Feliciano made it appealing to a much wider audience and had nearly as big a hit with it. But his success was not without controversy.

A month after this spin on WMCA, Feliciano — again displaying his guts and artistic conviction — sang a reworked (what would now be called, cloyingly, "reimagined") version of "The Star-Spangled Banner" at Tiger Stadium before Game 5 of the World Series and triggered (another modern coinage) racist blowback from "patriots" who objected to the funky, folky desecration of their beloved theme. "It was a disgrace, an insult," baseball fan Arlene Raicevich of Detroit told the Associated Press. "I'm going to write my senator about it." Bernie Gray, also from Detroit, said, "It sounded like a hippie was singing it." Slugger Roger Maris of the St. Louis Cardinals told *The Boston Globe*, "I don't think it was the proper place for that kind of treatment. Maybe I'm a conservative." Pitcher Dick Hughes offered, "Thumbs down all the way. That's a conformist's song and should be sung the way it was written."

Coming out of the AWOL news break, with no introduction or identification, the next voice you hear is Richard Nixon's, accepting the Republican nomination for president a month earlier, calling for a reduction in U.S. foreign aid. Turns out it's a campaign ad, one that sounds frighteningly like it could be airing today except that the words are actually coherent.

Nixon would not have appreciated the song that follows: "People Got to Be Free," a wonderfully idealistic '60s sentiment that still sounds great. Pigeonholed as a singles band thanks to, duh, a run of really great singles, the Rascals never really got the respect they deserved, although they worked hard to make strong albums. When they were still the *Young* Rascals, I saw them at a 1966 Murray the K Easter show at the Brooklyn Fox (also on the bill: Joe Tex, Mitch Ryder & the Detroit Wheels, Jay & the Americans, Little Anthony & the Imperials, Deon Jackson, the Shangri-Las, Patti LaBelle & the Bluebells, the Gentrys and the Royalettes. AM radio's stylistic diversity in the flesh.)

A pain reliever ad, then a station medallion give-away (Lisa Bellaran of Old Bridge, NJ: "You have 10 minutes to call PLaza-2 9944"). A Google search turned up the fact that she didn't just send in post-cards to radio stations, a few years later she was one of the kids who added their voices to Alice Cooper's "School's Out." And she appeared on Broadway. Disappointingly, the aircheck does not reveal whether she called in or not.

A jingle oversells the benefits of chewing gum, then another cigarette ad. On to the week's Sure Shot, the Fifth Dimension's "Sweet Blindness," which oversells the benefits of drinking. Laura Nyro was fighting to establish herself as a performer at the time, but her songs had no trouble rocketing up the charts for other artists. In fact, this is a somewhat slipshod rendition, with a giddy arrangement suitable for *Love American Style* and vocals that miss a few intended notes. (To be fair, Nyro's own rushed, offhand rendition *Eli and the Thirteenth Confession* doesn't do the song justice, either.)

An Eastern Airlines ad unwisely bases its sales pitch on the variety of food served on flights ("Something Else"), and an Amoco spot promotes the relatively novel idea of credit, urging customers to see America, "charge it all and take up to a year to pay." (Which reminds me of *The Man From the Diners' Club*, a wildly dated 1963 comedy starring Danny Kaye as a company clerk who inadvertently issues a credit card to a mobster — played by Telly Savalas, no less — and has to retrieve it.)

Which is *still* not as dated as the next song to hit the station turntable: "Shake Rattle and Roll," the born-to-be-mild version by Bill Haley and His Comets. This surprising (for 1968) echo from the far end of the station's oldies spectrum (1954) connects it to the dawn of rock and roll during an explosively progressive era that had already canonized sounds and styles unthinkable a decade earlier. Still, even while jettisoning a lot of the Eisenhower era and replacing it with protest marches hair, Afros and love beads, the youth of 1968 retained a measure of respect for certain blasts from the past: Chuck Berry was on a Fillmore East bill with the Who in June 1969, recognized as a father to the sons, and Sha Na Na, that slightly arch tribute band to music of the '50s, played *Woodstock*. Still, it's amazing to me that no one who wasn't meant to grasped what a "one-eyed cat peepin' in a seafood store" signified.

A confusing ad for shoes sets up "Hush," Deep Purple's surging cover of the show's second (!) Billy Joe Royal number written by Joe South. What are the chances of a heavy British rock band landing on a recent and relatively obscure American song (Royal's version didn't reach the Top 40 upon its release in 1967), putting it on their first album (where it joined renditions of "Help!" and "Hey Joe" and five originals) — and breaking big in America in the process? A similar tactic, which worked for Vanilla Fudge ("You Keep Me Hanging On") that same summer, had been road tested a few years earlier by Otis Redding ("Satisfaction"). It's hard to guess whether such cross-pollination fed into radio's diversity at the time or was a way to game the system, getting a song back on the air in a new style. This wasn't Pat Boone deracinating R&B for an isolated audience, this was musicians bringing what they liked to an otherwise unfamiliar audience, much as Cream was able to popularize the work of Robert Johnson.

fabulous 57

Joe O'Brien Harry Harrison Jack Spector Dan Daniel Gary Stevens Dean Anthony

wmca good guys

WMCA Radio 57 - Countdown Survey for the Week of March 10, 1966

1. BALLAD OF GREEN BERETS - SGT. BARRY SADLER
2. *#19TH NERVOUS BREAKDOWN - Rolling Stones
3. CALIFORNIA DREAMIN' - Mamas & Papas
4. BOOTS ARE MADE FOR WALKIN' - Nancy Sinatra
5. *#NOWHERE MAN - Beatles
6. ELUSIVE BUTTERFLY - Bob Lind
7. DAYDREAM - Lovin' Spoonful
8. SHAKE ME, WAKE ME - Four Tops
9. *SOUL & INSPIRATION - Righteous Brothers
10. THIS OLD HEART OF MINE - Isley Brothers
11. 634-5789 - Wilson Pickett
12. #HOMEWARD BOUND - Simon & Garfunkel
13. BABY, SCRATCH MY BACK - Slim Harpo
14. #LISTEN PEOPLE - Herman's Hermits
15. LOVE MAKES WORLD GO ROUND - Deon Jackson
16. HUSBANDS & WIVES - Roger Miller
17. LIGHTNIN' STRIKES - Lou Christie
18. STOP! - Moody Blues
19. I FOUGHT THE LAW - Bobby Fuller IV
20. *#SURE GONNA MISS HER - Gary Lewis
21. RAGS TO RICHES - Lenny Welch
22. I'M SO LONESOME I COULD CRY - B.J. Thomas
23. MY BABY LOVES ME - Martha & Vandellas
24. SPANISH FLEA - Herb Alpert
25. ONE MORE HEARTACHE - Marvin Gaye
26. #La La La - Gerry & The Pacemakers
27. Uptight - Stevie Wonder
28. Don't Mess With Bill - Marvelettes
29. #My World Is Empty - Supremes
30. It's Too Late - Bobby Goldsboro
31. My Prayer - Johnny Thunder
32. *Inside — Looking Out - Animals
33. Ain't That A Groove (Part I) - James Brown
34. Get Ready - The Temptations
35. Time Won't Let Me - The Outsiders
36. Good Lovin' - The Young Rascals
37. Magic Town - The Vogues
38. Stop Her On Sight - Edwin Starr
39. *Kicks - Paul Revere & The Raiders
40. *One Track Mind - Knickerbockers
41. Juanita Banana - The Peels
42. *Nessuno Mi Puo Giudcare - Gene Pitney
43. The Rains Came - Sir Douglas Quintet
44. The Love You Save - Joe Tex
45. Somewhere - Len Barry
46. Walkin' My Cat Named Dog - Norma Tanega
47. Time - The Pozo-Seco Singers
48. Little Latin Lupe Lu - Mitch Ryder
49. Memories Are Made of This - The Drifters
50. The Phoenix Love Theme - The Brass Ring
51. I Can't Grow Peaches - Just Us
52. You're Gonna Lose Your Clown - Ray Charles
53. *A Sign Of The Times - Petula Clark
54. *Rhapsody In The Rain - Lou Christie
55. *Till The End Of The Day - Kinks
56. Satisfaction - Otis Redding
57. I'll Take Good Care Of You - Garnet Mimms

COUNTDOWN TOP 25 DAILY WITH DAN DANIEL 4-7 PM

#Former Sure Shot

*Heard First in New York on WMCA

SURE SHOT ! *LEANING ON THE LAMPPOST - Herman's Hermits

2 Great Talents—2 Great LP's

TOM JONES **NOEL HARRISON**

The final hour of the show repeats the 6:00 am sign-on, includes a more detailed traffic report and then, perhaps staying on that topic, gives "1, 2, 3 Red Light" another spin. I remember once being home from school, sick in bed, and being shocked and disappointed during a long day's listening at how often the week's hits were repeated. But I don't remember ever hearing a creepy Excedrin commercial that (a) claims to contain an anti-depressant (what, caffeine?) and (b) advises women suffering from menstrual cramps to wash their hair or try on lipstick to feel better.

Another thing I don't remember is the crossover success of Sergio Mendes' easy-listening take on "Fool on the Hill," sung by Lani Hall (Herb Alpert's missus), which reached number-six in *Billboard* that summer. Beatles covers were common as muck in the '60s — everyone wanted to ride their coattails with sure-fire songs — and tried them in every possible style, frequently glossing over the subject matter as if it didn't matter. (Like this one.) The Beatles included the song on *Magical Mystery Tour*; it was never a single for them, still the royalties rolled in.

Baer follows a somber commercial — Nikoban lozenges "for real help in breaking the cigarette habit" — with a flip (and probably inadvisable) joke, gives the ball scores one more time, whips off a dumb one-liner about sports and then digs out another golden oldie, this one from 1958: Bobby Darin's "Splish Splash," good clean (ahem) fun just short of being a novelty record. In time's telescope, the difference of a decade after a half-century feels far less pronounced, but I imagine the generational gulf between some of the songs played on this show must have felt huge. I was a young teenager at the time, so that song was a hit years before I started listening to the radio and — unless it got regular airplay — was probably unfamiliar to a lot of us. "Mack the Knife" was ubiquitous, so I expect I knew Darin's name, although I was not aware I was beginning my high school education at his alma mater.

Continuing the crass promotion of unhealthy products, a Tastykakes spot targeting kids stakes a dubious claim to "nutritional value." But then on to something of real value: the Equals' "Baby Come Back." The tremendously exciting bi-racial English/Caribbean band, whose lead singer would score a much bigger solo hit 15 years later with "Electric Avenue" (yep, Eddy Grant), was also the originator of "Police on My Back," which the Clash covered to fine effect on *Sandinista!*, and loads of other great stompers like "Michael and the Slipper Tree," "Green Light," "Black Skinned Blue Eyed Boys," "Softly Softly" and "Rub a Dub Dub," a sexier version of "Splish Splash." I can definitely recommend the *Viva Equals!* compilation.

Baer sounds like he's suppressing a chuckle during his pitch for Gerber baby food, but that's forgotten when he plays the number-ten song, Marvin Gaye and Tammi Terrell doing "You're All I Need to Get By." My favorite Ashford & Simpson production and composition, it's simple, short (2:38, although here it's faded out under Baer's praise around 2:18) and sung with bountiful heart and soul, rising from an intimate declaration to a glorious testimony, and then repeating the ride again. It's still so spine-tingly fine all these years later and heartbreaking to think that she died, 24 years young, less than two years later. Few singers ever delivered a better performance than she does here.

Another awful cigarette spot, a news break and then — before another shoe commercial — a passionate Bill Medley single, "Brown Eyed Woman" (written by Barry Mann and Cynthia Weil; no patch on Van Morrison's "Brown Eyed Girl" from the previous year). He had recently broken up the Righteous Brothers and was struggling to rekindle the duo's success on his own. He never really did and reunited with Bobby Hatfield in the mid-'70s.

Wrapping up hour three, coming up to 9 am, Baer reads a spot for the start of horse racing season at Belmont Park and then gives the week's top song, "Hey Jude," its second spin of the morning. And that's where the MP3 ends.

MCA changed to talk radio in 1970; for a lot of us, you could say the 1960s ended there and then. Truth be told, I'd already switched over to FM, mainly the far more expansive WNEW-FM, and looked down my nose at the hype and tight playlists of my former sanctuary. ◆

Where It All Began

My attendance at the Bronx High School of Science began in the fall of 1968 during the New York City teachers strike, an ugly, angry and racially charged battle for community control of public schools between a powerful (and largely white) labor union and Black activists in the Ocean Hill and Brownsville sections of Brooklyn. Unwilling to sacrifice our education to politics, some of our parents and a few mutinous progressive teachers broke into the building and held what were called "liberation classes" for any students willing to cross a picket line for their education while adults battled over its future. The strike went on for two months and made the start of school a lot more dramatic than it otherwise would have been.

Near the end of that first year, Fred Wasser — my bosom buddy of 50-plus years, who I met on the first day of regular classes at Bronx Science when a biology teacher sent us to fetch a stack of textbooks for the class — introduced me to my future partner-in-crime Dave Schulps, whose knowledge and enthusiasm for rock'n'roll outstripped mine. (He says no one called him Dave until I did; in my head, I can still hear his mother call him David in her Polish accent.) He did far more to set me on my life's course than anything, or anyone, else in high school.

I don't recall the process which melded our musical, historical, cinematic and journalistic instincts into what would become the rich soil that grew *Trouser Press*. In short order, we were obsessing over the Who, *Putney Swope* and the Bonzo Dog Band. The only points where our enthusiasms diverged was politics, a subject in which he professed no interest ("super-apolitical" was the phrase he used at the time) and, a bit later, pot. (He indulged, I didn't.)

Without doubt, our brotherhood — which has endured all these years — profoundly impacted our lives. The enthusiasm we shared about music became a source of strength and confidence to both of us and led us to our futures.

Our first ambitious project together was Dave's idea to assemble a genealogy of British rock musicians. In that pursuit, we spent hundreds of hours in the Lincoln Center library, poring through microfilm of *Melody Maker*, jotting down every name, date and band membership we came across. Dave developed a nomenclature to abbreviate instruments, which came in handy when I was covering concerts.

Cycling through the horizontal rush of images could be nauseating, but we delighted in each discovery we could add to the data bank. To this day, the mere mention of some obscure band we uncovered during that time can elicit a shared chuckle. So, hello to Mogul Thrash, Grunt Futtock, Piblokto, Hapshash and the Coloured Coat, Gnidrolog, Balls, Bronco, the Rockin' Berries, Warm Dust, Bob Kerr's Whoopee Band and Hackensack!

A few years on, the book *Rock Record* and Pete Frame's family trees made it clear we weren't the only ones of such a mind, and that that there were rock and roll scholars out there who knew *way* more about this stuff than we ever would. That point was underscored for me decades later when Frame authored *The Restless Generation*, a monumental account of the prehistoric days of British rock and an astonishing trove of pre-Beatle facts, characters and connections.

Closer to home, Greg Shaw's *Bomp!* and Alan Betrock's *Rock Marketplace* ushered us into the rabbit hole of rarities, B-sides and foreign releases, sparking a mild record collecting hobby my father's nominal efforts to pull me into his professional obsession, philately (rare stamps), was never able to accomplish. Other things I collected as a kid: baseball cards, matchbooks, coins and sugar packets printed with the names of restaurants we'd eaten at (*that* didn't end well).

When we began interviewing some of those artists we'd read about and notated, being able to mention a bit of their history proved to be enormously helpful. More than one British rocker, upon being asked a moderately informed question by a couple of brash young Americans, jokingly marveled, "You know more about me than I do!"

M 2

* Van Morrison VG -	Them / Van Morrison
Ken McDowell V -	Them /
* Dave Mason G B V -	Deep Feeling / Traffic / Mason, Wood, Capaldi & Frogg / Traffic / Dave Mason
Dave Munden D -	Tremeloes
Chris Mercer S -	John Mayall / Juicy Lucy / Keef Hartley Band /
John Moorshead G V -	Aynsley Dunbar Retaliation /
Mick Moody G	Tramline / Juicy Lucy / 73- Snafu
John McCoy	Tramline /
Leo Mannings D	Savoy Brown /
Mitch Mitchell D	Riot Squad / Jimi Hendrix Experience / Ramatam /
Jamie Muir PN	Heavy African Gudgel Boris / King Crimson /
Andrew McCulloch D	Shy Limbs Manfred Mann / King Crimson / Arthur Brown / Fields / Greenslade
Brian Miller P	Isotope / Gary Boyle Band Isotope
Nigel Morris D	Isotope / Gary Boyle Band Isotope
Tris Margetts	Spontaneus Combustion
Gary Margetts	Spontaneus Combustion
John McGuinness PO	Stone the Crows /
John Mealling	If
Ray Martinez G-M	-70- Spring / Gypsy
Trevor Mee GFV -	63-67 Pink Bears / 67- The Late Unicorn
Patrick Martin BV	63-67 Pink Bears / The Late / Unicorn
William Murray D	Kevin Ayers / Mellow Candle

Good Times and Bad Takes

My first paid writing gig ("paid" being more accurate than "professional," which would egregiously overstate my level of achievement) was a record review published in *Good Times*, a weekly giveaway paper based in and focused on the NYC suburb of Long Island, New York. (To its credit, "America's oldest regional entertainment newspaper" has loads of recognizable names on its alumni list, including Kurt Loder, Dave Fricke, Eric Van Lustbader, the late Stan Mieses, the late John Swenson, Leonard Maltin, photographer Richard Aaron, label exec Dennis Fine and journalist/artist manager Barry Taylor.)

For the paper's going rate of two dollars, Andy assigned me to "review" *Rough Edges*, a collection of Sir Douglas Quintet leftovers issued by Mercury Records after Doug Sahm had left the label. With shamefully brazen youthful hubris, I decried the concept of "cashing in" as if I'd uncovered a Star Chamber conspiracy, smugly displayed my ignorance of pioneering rock writer-cum-Mercury A&R man Paul Nelson, who compiled the album, overlooked John Swenson's liner notes, sideswiped Johnny Winter, stupidly twitted the album title and otherwise offered little but condescension and unearned indignation.

Regarding the abundance of noted typos and grammatical mistakes, younger readers are reminded that in the days before one could E-mail text files, pieces had to be keyed in to the typesetting system from typewritten pages. So, lots of potential for transcription mistakes, although some of the errors were probably mine.

On the strength of this, I would gladly support a law restricting permission to review records to writers who've learned the basics of critical thinking, spelling and adequate cultural regard.

Doug Sahm
Rough Edges
Good Times, 3 May 1973

There is a ploy in the record trade which is know [*sic*] as "cashing-in." When someone becomes popular (i.e. valuable), any dreck that they may have left in their wake is assumed to be important (i.e. profitable). Remember the rash of "earliest" Johnny Winter albums which were released at the height of his fame? They were an embarrassment to evryone [*sic*] involved, and mainly proved that somewhere in the dark past of each brilliant musician, there lies a fumbling klutz.

Around 1971, Doug Sahm and the rest of the Sir Douglas Quintet ended a three year association with Mercury Reocrds [*sic*]. Sir Doug had had an erratic, almost manic-depressive kind of on-again, off-again career with some hugely successful songs ("Mendecino [*sic*]," "She's About a Mover" but also plenty of nothings. With no backup band, Doug Sahm looked liked [*sic*] a has-been until the fateful sessions in late 1972 while he was recording *Doug Sahm and Band* for his current label, Atlantic. You know who dropped by and gave the album the golden touch, putting fame (and I suppose some fortune) back into all [*sic*] Doug's life.

Anyway, the folks on E. Wacker Drive found out that their has-been is now a somebody, but on a different record company. This must have caused great consternatin [*sic*] and some rolling heads out in Mercury-ville, so they sent someone named Paul Nelson to dig up old tapes from Mercury's basement to see if they could piece together, as if by wizardy [*sic*], just one more album by the defunct, but now saleable Sir Douglas Quintet. Well he did, and they did, and, oh boy, what a mistake it was! This still-born illegitimacy is called *Rough Edges*, credited mostly to Doug Sahm (y'see he's the one they're cashing-in on) even thouh [*sic*] it is admitted on the jacket that the entire Quintet is responsible for the sounds on this disc.

Rough Edges is well titled, since it mostly contains off-the-cuff, informal and unfinished recordings made around 1969, unmixed until a fellow described on the cover as an A&R man was given the job of assembling a piece of music from essentially a disorganized series of notes. The raw material shines through in spots, and some of it might be

DOUG SAHM
ROUGH EDGES

There is a ploy in the record trade which is know as "cashing-in." When someone becomes popular (i.e. valuable), any dreck that they may have left in their wake is assumed to be important (i.e. profitable). Remember the rash of "earliest" Johnny Winter albums which were released at the height of his fame? They were an embarrassment to evryone involved, and mainly proved that somewhere in the dark past of each brilliant musician, there lies a fumbling klutz.

Around 1971, Doug Sahm and the rest of the Sir Douglas Quintet ended a three year association with Mercury Reocrds. Sir Doug had had an erratic, almost manic-depressive kind of on-again, off-again career with some hugely successful songs ("Mendecino," "She's About A Mover") but also plenty of nothings. With no backup band, Doug Sahm looked liked a has-been until the fateful sessions in late 1972 while he was recording **Doug Sahm and Band** for his current label, Atlantic. You know who dropped by and gave the album the golden touch, putting fame (and I suppose some fortune) back into all Doug's life.

Anyway, the folks on E. Wacker Drive found out that their has-been is now a somebody, but on a different record company. This must have caused great consternatin and some rolling heads out in Mercury-ville, so they sent someone named Paul Nelson to dig up old tapes from Mercury's basement to see if they could piece together, as if by wizardry (sic(, just one more album by the defunct, but now saleable Sir Douglas Quintet. Well he did, and they did, and, oh boy, what a mistake it was! This still-born illegitimacy is called **Rough Edges**, credited mostly to Doug Sahm (y'see he's the one they're cashing-in on) even thouh it is admitted on the jacket that the entire Quintet is responsible for the sounds on this disc.

Rough Edges is well titled, since it mostly contains off-the-cuff, informal and unfinished recordings made around 1969, unmixed until a fellow described on the cover as an A&R man was given the job of assembling a piece of music from essentially a disorganized series of notes. The raw material shines through in spots, and some of it might be godd if this album had been completed with the participation and/or supervision of the musicians involved. It wasn't, and that's why this record is a disaster. There is an entire page of 7-point liner notes which try desperately to justify and dignify the trashy way that this slop was thrown together; produced with such bland efficiency as befits some 'teeny top fifty band.' Every song is faded out identically, possibly to cover up the fact that there are no endings on any of these grade-B tapes.

If Doug Sahm were the new messiah, then it would expected perhaps even desirable, for old tapes to be dusted off, and not-quite-great albums released for the music-starved public to lap up. **Rough Edges** is not in that class, though, it is simply Mercury's pitiful attempt at skimming something off Doug Sahm's new success! I hope that this album will find it's way only into collections of S. D. Quintet freaks, not gullible record buyers who were impressed by Dylan showing up or **Doug Sahm & Band**. Don't get fooled again!

—**Ira Robbins**

godd [*sic*] if this album had been completed with the participation and/or supervision of the musicians involved. It wasn't, and that's why this record is a disaster. There is an entire page of 7-point liner notes which try desperately to justify and dignify the trashy way that this slop was thrown together; produced with such bland efficiency as befits some 'teeny top fifty band.' Every song is faded out identically, possibly to cover up the fact that there are no endings on any of these grade-B tapes.

If Doug Sahm were the new messiah, then it would [be] expected[,] perhaps even desirable, for old tapes to be dusted off, and not-quite-great albums released for the music-starved public to lap up. *Rough Edges* is not in that class, though. It is simply Mercury's pitiful attempt at skimming something off Doug Sahm's new success! I hope that this album will find it's [*sic*] way only into collections of S. D. Quintet freaks, not gullible record buyers who were impressed by Dylan showing up or [*sic*] Doug Sahm & Band. Don't get fooled again! ◆

Lucky for me, the standards for music journalism back then were spotty; willingness, enthusiasm and conviction often supplanted a lack of knowledge or skill. While a more demanding editor might have read this shameful display of arrogance and quashed my journalistic hopes and dreams right then and there, I was, as my dad used to say, off to the races.

Out of curiosity, I played the LP for the first time in 45 years and, honestly, I still find it to be a minor release from a generally credible figure. Starting with a silly autobiographical number, "Sir Doug's Recording Trip," the first side is weak, the selections of an overly generous aficionado. Side 2, however, is delightful enough to warrant the release and illustrates Sahm's eclectic musical range. This is exactly the sort of vault excavation that would become commonplace — and valued — in the reissue era.

I was a sophomore at Brooklyn Poly when I began writing for the student newspaper in November 1972, but the weekly *Polytechnic Reporter*'s circulation and editorial ambitions were no more impressive than its name. I'd put up my hand as a music fan and was given a shot, not a difficult feat in a student body of veterans on the G.I. Bill, immigrants and pocket-protector nerds. Over the next few years, my contributions included a dig at Don McLean, an enthusiastic review of the New Lost City Ramblers, something about Led Zeppelin and a lukewarm take on Joni Mitchell's *For the Roses* which ended with the unforgivably trite line "...this is another collection of her songs to be listened to and reckoned with." Likewise, I must disavow these unwarranted attacks on some great Quo numbers.

Status Quo

Hello

Polytechnic Reporter, October 1973

It's not well known here, but Status Quo is one of the oldest bands still operating in England. With a history that stretches back more than a decade and a lineup which contains, presently, all the founding members, they're a virtual rock and roll redwood. They almost qualify as challengers to the Who for longevity without personnel changes, but they lost a member a while back and although he was never replaced, so that disqualifies them. The Nashville Teens and Rolling Stones have been around longer than anybody, but not without major changes in the musicians, so the Who get to keep the trophy.

Status Quo is kind of a misfit, musically. In 1968, as Chuck Berry's contemporaries were trying to psychedelicize their way into the hearts and ears of a new, mid-sixties generation, six-year-old Status Quo donned Kinks suits and hit the bigtime with a pop single called "Pictures of Matchstick Men" which quickly landed them in a pile of matches à la Grand Funk for the cover of an album called *Pictures of the Status Quo*. They were IN, just like a thousand fly-by-night mod bands that era. This only lasted a few more successful singles, and after the absurdity of clowny [????] wore in, they changed the suits for jeans and began playing straight-ahead rock and roll.

Back in 1969, the organist left and then there were four. As a result, the Quo got even more raw and basic. A couple of albums later, just over a year ago, they released Piledriver, which contained one great song, actually a hit single "Paper Plane," and not much else. In retrospect, it now sounds every bit as dull and simpleminded as it did then, when I made a fool of myself by calling Status Quo a "young behemoth band" in an unpublished review. They were playing together when I was in third grade!

Hello, released in England months ago, is simply more of the same stuff that was on *Piledriver*. The lyrics are improved and more intelligent, and a few of the songs are out of the standard Quo character, but they still do a good deal of old Canned Heat rhythms and 12-bar rock pieces. Nothing about this record is bad, but it just isn't something you could sit down and listen to.

The keynote of Status Quo's sound (as Canned Heat's standard riff was the one from "On the Road Again") are what are called "sixths." Chuck Berry always uses 'em (it's when the pinky of the left hand keeps bouncing on and off the A or D string, two frets above the chord, in three-quarters time) and so does Lennon, prominently in the opening few bars of "Revolution," not to mention a trillion other guitar players, myself included. Every song on *Hello* is built around sixths and there's no need for such overkill. Because of the sixth overpopulation they've been given the title of "England's number one Boogie Band" which only means that their stuff is so rhythmically simple that you can dance to it. Anybody can play sixths and do the same thing.

There isn't enough variation on *Hello* to keep it interesting front to back, but there are a couple of good songs which rise above the boredom, notably "Caroline" and "Roll Over Lay Down." A few of the others are debatably interesting, but it doesn't seem to be worth the investigation.

"Yes, Watson, I have considered the question. Damn nuisance, isn't it?"
"Well, for God's sake, Holmes, what do you suggest?"
"Save your money Watson. There'll be other records."
"That Holmes is brilliant, isn't he? Harrumph!" ◆

The Start of Something Big

In November 1973, Dave Schulps, home from college in Washington DC, and I — Who freaks and budding record geeks, haunters of cut-out bins in record shops all over New York — attended a small afternoon get-together in Yonkers, just north of Riverdale, where Dave's folks lived. We were invited by Frank Reda — obsessive Kinks and Yardbirds fan, prescient selfie master and serious record collector — who we had run into on a couple of occasions.

We were never really friends. As much as I appreciated his inadvertently fateful role I'm getting around to, he was too manic to spend much time with. He visited me once when I was still living with my parents. Late in the evening, he asked if he could stay over. I demurred and showed him the door. The next morning, I saw him coming out of the stairwell by the elevators where he had evidently spent the night. He died in 2019, but there's a swell Facebook group dedicated to his memory.

At Frank's house, along with uber-collector (just one of his many significant roles in the rise of New York rock) Alan Betrock, John Overall and Frank's brother Mike, we met Karen Rose, a Jeff Beck and Peter Frampton fan who had been the editor of the Brooklyn College student newspaper. She was a few years older than us and already had a real grown-up job as an editor at the company that published *True Romance, True Experiences* and other such magazines. We three hit it off, perhaps because we were dilettantes compared to the others, or maybe owing to simple volubility. On the Number 1 train headed back to Manhattan, Karen and I decided to start a fanzine. Roughly put, we would model our publication after Greg Shaw's *Who Put the Bomp!*, with added inspiration from *Creem*, Betrock's *Rock Marketplace*, Jon Tiven's *New Haven Rock Press*, *Melody Maker* (to which Dave and I shared a sea-mail subscription) and *Zigzag*, the history-minded London monthly.

We three talked it over and finally settled on a name for our imagined venture: *Trans-Oceanic Trouser Press*. I don't recall anything about how it progressed from there, but we kicked around a bunch of ideas and eventually started writing articles and reviews for the first (and perhaps only) issue.

Over winter break at the end of 1973, high school chum Jeffrey Gross and I set out to hitchhike from New York City to Montreal. It wasn't the smartest idea. Our plan was to pinball through three upstate universities (SUNY Binghamton, Cornell and Syracuse), where we could stay with fellow Bronx Science graduates, en route to McGill, where the kid brother of another was now a freshman. The New York portion of the program went well; I spent a couple of happy afternoons in the Syracuse University library drafting an article about the Pink Fairies for the inaugural issue of *TOTP*.

But the border-crossing leg, weather-wise, was a nightmare. We got caught in a blizzard and found ourselves knee deep in snow trying to catch a ride as the sun set. We nearly had to crawl across a frozen bridge. After surviving all of that and somehow managing to get within range of Montreal, were able to flag down a pair of French-Canadian brothers in a beater that lacked working windshield wipers to brush away the sleet. When the driver took his hands off the wheel to roll a cigarette (or more likely a joint), his brother in the passenger seat reached over to steer with his left hand. Cowering behind them, Jeffrey and I silently mouthed our goodbyes to life. But we survived.

Here's the kicker, the coda that always puts me in mind of the farcical misadventures of "Alice's Restaurant": we got to the McGill dorm and knocked on the door of our intended host only to be told that he'd gone home to New York for the week. Luckily, Jeff had an aunt in Montreal, and she kindly took us in. The next morning, defeated and no longer keen to spend a few days in the city, my parents arranged plane tickets for us and we flew home.

I didn't exactly devote myself to *The Reporter*, but I did grasp that my minor contributions made it easy to wangle free records and concert tickets. With a letter of introduction proffered by the paper's editor, I snuck a chukka-booted foot inside the door of the rock critic establishment. As Dave was also writing about music for his college paper, when he came home for holidays, we would meet up and make our label (and PR firm) rounds to see what free records we could snag. New York was still the center of the American music business, and we did those outings like rock and roll Halloween. A lot of the companies had designated college reps — Barb Pepe of Atlantic was especially kind to us — but we were not above waltzing in, announcing ourselves to the receptionist and asking if there was anyone we could talk to. Sometimes we would get in to see a press person who wasn't too busy, or we would get a name and pay a return visit at a later date. We met loads of wonderful folks that way — Susan Blond at United Artists, Ida Langsam at Ren Grevatt, Bob Merlis at Warner Bros. and Janis Schact at Sire. We also had a couple of Who-specific stops on our route — Decca/MCA Records and Premier Talent, Frank Barsalona's booking agency, where Nancy Lewis worked and was generous with press photos and posters. On one visit to MCA, we had the name of Gary Buttice, a promo guy we hoped to get in to see; we found juvenile humor in mispronouncing it and laughed about it in the elevator going up. Of course, when we got off, he'd been in the car with us... I don't think we got any records from him.

In early 1974, as we were preparing the first issue of *Trouser Press*, I got a record review assignment from Arthur Levy, an editor at *Zoo World*, a *Rolling Stone* wanna-be out of Florida. I am forever grateful to Arthur for the kindness he showed me and the opportunity he offered (probably no one else wanted it); our epistolary relationship turned into friendship when he moved to New York and became a staff writer for Atlantic Records. What a mensch!

Jan Akkerman was the guitarist in the Dutch group Focus (known for the execrable "Hocus Pocus"), but as a solo artist he had classical ambitions. I did my best to understand his music, which was well outside my ken; this time, given my ignorance, I tried to be generous and respectful rather than patronizing and harsh. (I still needed to work on the finer points of punctuation.) So, this was my first appearance in a national publication.

TABERNAKEL
Jan Akkerman
ATCO SD 7032

Ever since the inception of classical-rock (the Nice? the Electric Prunes? Kim Fowley?), it has been evident that the most serious proponents would someday forsake the excitement of rock for the intellectually virtuous career of a classical musician. From time to time, this has happened, more often than not on a solo album (Rick Wakeman, Thijs Van Lerr, Jack Nitzsche). However, on the rock-hand side of the classical-modern boundary, classically oriented rock bands have experimented with various mixtures of the two forms, from simply using classical instruments or stealing Baroque riffs (early Procol Harum, Yes, Electric Light Orchestra) to deeper involvement, with orchestral accompaniment (Nice, Moody Blues) or by playing jazzed-up versions of long-haired compositions (ELP, N.Y. Rock and Roll Ensemble, Nice).

For his second solo album, *Tabernakel*, Dutch guitarist Jan Akkerman of Focus has combined songs displaying both types of classical-rock with one long finale which summarizes the record and shows off his many instrumental abilities. Specifically, there are four distinct styles covered on *Tabernakel*. For five cuts on side one, Akkerman plays alone, on lute and/or acoustic guitar. Although the lute, an ancient forerunner of the guitar, generally sounds rich and pleasant, the one employed here has annoying resonances which (unless it's just dreadful production) tend aurally to push the listener down a well. The music itself is accompaniment to a pair of dances popular in Europe five hundred years ago, Pavin and Galliard.

Side one also includes a pair of orchestral ventures in which Akkerman again plays lute and guitar, but the character of the music is very different. The modern influence (or perhaps too many Late Shows) is clear on "(Meditations) Javeh" a dreadfully trite shred of movie soundtrack. The other, "Britannia" shows what can be done creatively with the collaboration of an orchestra.

In contrast to the heavy classical drift, there is "House Of The King," a product of the 'intermix' school. With sitar, electric guitar, the support of the two rhythmic thirds of Beck, Bogert and Appice and the symphonic orchestra, Akkerman has succeeded in creating a bouncy Dutch equivalent to "Classical Gas." Incidentally, the lead melody, carried by the sitar, prevents *Tabernakel* from being declared totally unhummable. "House Of The King" would even make a good single, it's the right length and it's got everything.

Profile, Jan Akkerman's previous solo, reserved a whole side for a twenty minute suite of McLaughlin-King Crimsonesque diddling. For this record he has put together a shorter, more interesting epic called "Lamm" which proves his instrumental versatility plus a command of several different musical styles. Like a reprise ending a musical, all the preceding participants are recalled: sitar, lute, electric and acoustic guitar, the orchestra (including a church organ and a chorus) and the Bogert-Appice add-on rock band. Not without a series of awkward transitions, "Lamm" swings through Gregorian chants, a pop raga, a drum solo, some flashy guitar riffs, a Moody Blues session, and a lute-flute duet before resolving majestically with a beautiful medieval chorus. Unfortunately, this closing minute doesn't justify the confused collage which precedes it. The same thing is generally true of the entire album. Even though each individual piece of music is, by itself, successful, *Tabernakel* has no continuity or coherence. In these days of wholly conceived productions, it comes off, by comparison, as a Jan Akkerman sampler. Given such high quality material, if some attention had been paid to structure and flow, a much better album could have been created. As it stands, it's well worth listening to...one cut at a time.—IRA ROBBINS

Jan Akkerman

Tabernakel

Zoo World, 28 February 1974

Ever since the inception of classical-rock (the Nice? the Electric Prunes? Kim Fowley?), it has been evident that the most serious proponents would someday forsake the excitement of rock for the intellectually virtuous career of a classical musician. From time to time, this has happened, more often than not on a solo album (Rick Wakeman, Thijs Van Leer, Jack Nitzsche). However, on the rock-hand side of the classical-modern boundary, classically oriented rock bands have experimented with various mixtures of the two forms, from simply using classical instruments or stealing Baroque riffs (early Procol Harum, Yes, Electric Light Orchestra) to deeper involvement, with orchestral accompaniment (Nice, Moody Blues) or by playing jazzed-up versions of long-haired compositions (ELP, Nice, New York Rock and Roll Ensemble).

For his second solo album, *Tabernakel*, Dutch guitarist Jan Akkerman of Focus has combined songs displaying both types of classical-rock with one long finale which summarizes the record and shows off his many instrumental abilities. Specifically, there are four distinct styles covered on *Tabernakel.* For five cuts on Side One, Akkerman plays alone, on lute and/or acoustic guitar. Although the lute, an ancient forerunner of the guitar, generally sounds rich and pleasant, the one employed here has annoying resonances which (unless it's just dreadful production) tend aurally to push the listener down a well. The music itself is accompaniment to a pair of dances popular in Europe five hundred years ago, Pavin [*it's pavane, actually*] and Galliard.

Side One includes a pair of orchestral ventures in which Akkerman again plays lute and guitar, but the character of the music is very different. The modern influence (or perhaps too many *Late Shows*) is clear on "(Meditations) Javeh" a dreadfully trite shred of movie soundtrack. The other, "Britannia," shows what can be done creatively with the collaboration of an orchestra.

In contrast to the heavy classical drift, there is "House of the King," a product of the 'intermix' school. With sitar, electric guitar, the support of the two rhythmic thirds of Beck, Bogert and Appice and the symphonic orchestra, Akkerman has succeeded in creating a bouncy Dutch equivalent to "Classical Gas." Incidentally, the lead melody, carried by the sitar, prevents *Tabernakel* from being declared totally unhummable. "House of the King" would even make a good single, it's the right length and it's got everything.

Profile, Jan Akkerman's previous solo, reserved a whole side for a twenty-minute suite of McLaughlin-King Crimson-esque diddling. For this record he has put together a shorter, more interesting epic called "Lamm" which proves his instrumental versatility plus a command of several different musical styles. Like a reprise ending a musical, all the preceding participants are recalled: sitar, lute, electric and acoustic guitar, the orchestra (including a church organ and a chorus) and the Bogert-Appice add-on rock band. Not without a series of awkward transitions, "Lamm" swings through Gregorian chants, a pop raga, a drum solo, some flashy guitar riffs, a Moody Blues session and a lute-flute duet before resolving majestically with a beautiful medieval chorus. Unfortunately, this closing minute doesn't justify the confused collage which precedes it. The same thing is generally true of the entire album. Even though each individual piece of music is, by itself, successful, *Tabernakel* has no continuity or coherence. In these days of wholly conceived productions, it comes off, by comparison, as a Jan Akkerman sampler. Given such high-quality material, if some attention had been paid to structure and flow, a much better album could have been created. As it stands, it's well worth listening to...one cut at a time. ◆

I sharpened my writing (and my critical scalpel) on other albums I reviewed for *Zoo World* in 1974: *Heavy Metal Kids* ("mediocre"), Hawkwind's *Hall of the Mountain Grill* ("an album that can truly be enjoyed"), *Bad Company* ("thrillingly informal"), Cockney Rebel's *Psychomodo* ("thoroughly strange"), a pair of Finnish prog albums and *June 1, 1974* by Ayers-Cale-Nico-Eno (favorable). I also reviewed a concert by the progressive Italian band PFM.

At the same time as I was doing that and working on *TOTP*, with its devout focus on British rock, much of it from the past, I was going to a lot of shows by young bands on the burgeoning New York underground scene. Max's Kansas City was still a Bottom Line sort of label showcase venue — I didn't see the legendary Bob Marley/Bruce Springsteen double bill, but in May 1973 I *did* witness a completely unknown Andy Kaufman — either as a plant in the audience or randomly freestyling his own performance art without invitation — interrupt Kinky Friedman and the Texas Jewboys onstage several times to tell intentionally inept variations on the chicken-crossing-the-road joke in his silly foreign-man voice ("Mr. Kinkyman! Mr. Kinkyman!"). There was also a Martin Mull "living room" show I remember mainly for the fact that he was wearing khaki trousers and visibly wet himself during the set.

I'd gotten my first exposure to the idea of bands doing it for themselves, well outside the control or indulgence of record companies and standard venues, on 30 March 1973, when the Planets — an Eddie Cochran-loving quartet of longhairs in colorful crushed velvet trousers led by my Camp Thoreau pal and fellow Who freak Binky Philips — booked themselves a gig at the Brooklyn Academy of Music. (For contrast, other shows I saw in the early months of that year included Canned Heat, Genesis, Slade and Bill Monroe — I was, and remain, a bluegrass fan.) It is no overstatement to say that the very idea of seeing someone I knew, just a year my senior, who didn't have a record out, play a full-bore loud-as-fuck rock and roll concert in a genuine theater was a total mind-blower. In my decade of rock fandom, I had never imagined such a thing possible.

I saw the Planets loads after that, in all sorts of Manhattan dives, including CBGB, Kenny's Castaways, Max's and Mothers, as well as Coventry in Queens. Then came the Ramones, Television, Blondie et al. Meeting ballet-dancer-turned-rock-photographer Linda Danna in April '74 (we got married two years later) led me to the Fast, Patti Smith, Wayne County, the New York Dolls, Suicide, Milk 'n' Cookies, Tuff Darts, the Marbles, Mumps, Miamis, Talking Heads, Heartbreakers, Dead Boys...

CBGB was hopping in those days, and we were regulars, bouncing between the club and the rhymingly named Phebe's, a café just up the Bowery, for nicer toilets, a piece of pie and a respite from bands we didn't like.

The other local band early on my radar was the Dictators, who I knew because guitarist Top Ten was in reality my high school pal and Gorilla bandmate Scott Kempner, another Who freak. Bassist-singer-songwriter Andy Shernoff (as Adny Shernoff) was a *Creem* writer and editor of a cool fanzine (*Teenage Wasteland Gazette*). The Dics were signed to Epic Records, had a rock critic booster in R. Meltzer and bigtime production-management in Blue Öyster Cult masterminds Sandy Pearlman and Murray Krugman. They didn't gig a lot in those days, but I did see them on a two-stage bill with the Dolls at Coventry in Sunnyside, Queens in January 1975. (Two years later, they headlined a legendary New York show at the Palladium, supported by the Michael Stanley Band and, ahem, AC/DC. Admission was $3.50.)

In the summer of 1975, I pitched *Rolling Stone* on a piece about the underground New York scene. (I was not a regular reader — it felt like the establishment to me and so the object of both disdain *and* envy.) Said scene was then an insular collection of a few dozen bands and a few hundred fans, none of whom envisioned its potential much beyond the skelly neighborhoods that housed the clubs. There was no reason in the early '70s to suspect any of these bands would get signed, go on tour, be on MTV, sell millions of records or get elected to the Rock and Roll Hall of Fame.

Well after my entreaty, I got a rejection note from *Rolling Stone* Senior Editor Ben Fong-Torres. The article he refers to ("N.Y. Club's Talent Search: Anybody Listening?") was a one-page reported recap by Ed McCormack of a month-long CBGB unsigned bands festival that ran in October. At the time, I assumed my idea had been stolen and the rejection of it held up until a replacement could be produced, but I'm sure that wasn't the case. I know that Ben, an important and influential pioneer in rock journalism, is a good man.

Sept. 30

Dear Ira,

Thanks but no thanks on your proposal for a summer job (the New York rock consumer's guide). We have neither the interest nor the space for such a piece. In fact, in the Patty Hearst issue, we did a page on the "festival" of the "Top 40 Unrecorded Bands" of NY, and that seems to me to be about the right way and size.

Any other story ideas, however, are welcome, and should be sent to Chet Flippo in our New York office.

Best,

Ben Fong-Torres

Ben Fong-Torres

Creem and Before

Creem, which was the best rock magazine in America of the early '70s (and knew it!), regularly ran this little house ad, a clarion cry to self-expression that probably did more to encourage rock critic wannabes into print than any J-school. (Mascot drawn by R. Crumb.)

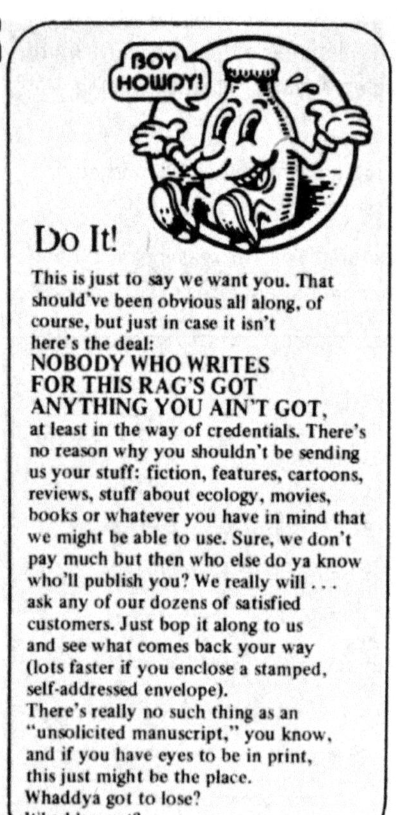

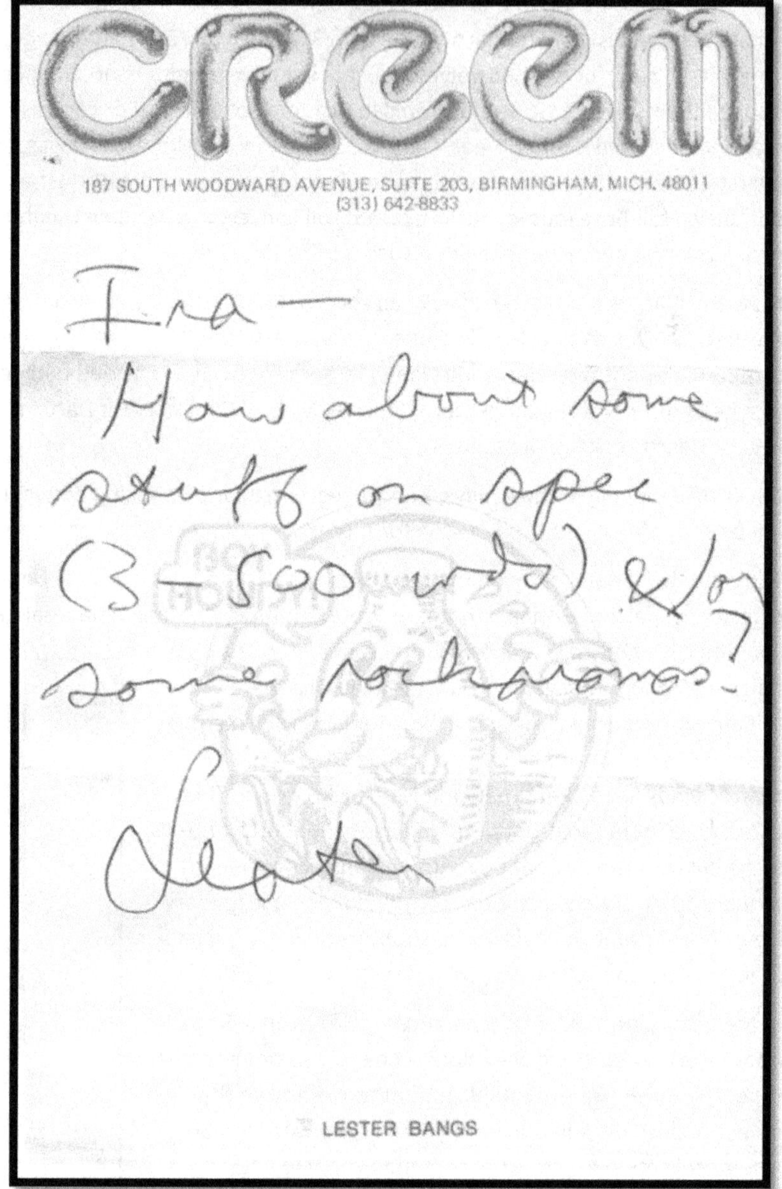

CREEM

187 SOUTH WOODWARD AVENUE, SUITE 203, BIRMINGHAM, MICH. 48011
(313) 642-8833

Ira—
How about some stuff on spec (3-500 wds) &/or some rockaramas?

Lester

LESTER BANGS

My high school classmate Hank Frank had managed to get a Sparks LP review published in *Creem*; in the hopes of following suit, I submitted a couple of unassigned record reviews. I guess I didn't keep any copies of what I sent off, but the note from Lester Bangs provided motivation for me to keep trying. In October 1977, with *Trouser Press* on my CV, I finally got into *Creem* (thanks to ace editor Susan Whitall) with my weird and poor excuse for a feature titled "Pink Floyd's Heart of Darkness: A Crash Course in Pig Latin" which ended on this particularly odd note: "...I've always loved miserable rock, and these days, the Floyd are about as miserable as any band I've ever heard."

Billy Bragg

A decade later, I was a more regular contributor to *Creem*; record reviews mostly, but also a Cheap Trick feature that is included in Volume 2 of *Music in a Word* and this short Billy Bragg profile.

I've restored one paragraph that was deleted from this story, which I like a lot. I attended a reading Billy did in New York a few years ago and was able to grab him for a brief chat afterwards. He's still an absolutely fantastic fellow and a crusader for many good causes.

Bragging With Billy

Creem, April 1987

For a homely socialist who literally couldn't get arrested in New York a few years ago, self-described spokesperson-for-a-generation Billy Bragg has done alright for himself. "My mum'll be getting the third gold record by Christmas, I should imagine." An artless but effective singer/string-banger with an extraordinary songwriting gift, Bragg is proof that politics has a viable, valuable place in pop music and vice versa.

"Just because I dress like / this doesn't mean I'm a communist." With few exceptions — only Phil Ochs, Bob Dylan and Bob Marley readily come to mind — protest singers have generally proven incapable of simultaneous commitment to both social conscience and social lives. To his credit, the cheerful 28-year-old is as articulate and serious praising organized labor as he is chronicling failed romance. "Life is not all politics. If pop music were only political it'd be incredibly dull and humorless. Likewise, life isn't all shagging girls, driving cars fast and getting pissed. It's a mixture of all those things, and my job" — as he refers to music — "is to reflect them."

"A nation with their freezers full are dancing in their seats while outside another nation is sleeping in the streets." Bragg's personal introduction to America came in 1984, when he turned up at the New Music Seminar, guitar in hand, amp strapped to his back. For busking loudly in the convention's hallways, he "got ejected from the [New York] 'ilton. Then we did it in the streets and a copper came up and said, 'Move along'." Recalling Elvis Costello's 1977 arrest for playing in front of a CBS Records' confab in London, Bragg demanded to be busted, but to no avail. "I remember saying through me speakers, 'For chrissakes, what does someone have to do to get arrested in New York City?'"

"When the world falls apart, some things stay in place." What of Elvis Costello — does this year's angry young man scorn the 10-year veteran of the emotional wars? "As far as I'm concerned, he's the best writer in the

English language. We singer-songwriters in Great Britain owe him a lot." Indeed, Bragg shares Costello's zeal for country and soul music. "American audiences find it strange to see English artists singing what they think is redneck music." But, he says, naming the cultural crossover connection between urban Blacks and rural whites that may be invisible to this nation's class-unconscious masses, "It's all working-class music."

Onstage at Manhattan's Ritz in November, he introduces a brilliant cover of the Jackson 5's "I'll Be There" and his own bone-chilling "Levi Stubbs' Tears" with a windy but amusing lecture on the miraculous healing power of Motown records. After inserting "I Fall to Pieces" into "Honey I'm a Big Boy Now" he chides the audience for its ignorance of Patsy Cline. Later, he expands on the topic. "Patsy was fucked over by the industry and fucked over by her manager. She was undoubtedly the greatest female country singer that ever lived." Mention of Wanda Jackson yields more excitement. "She's brilliant! What a voice!" And one more: "If Phil Ochs had seen the Clash when he was 19 years old, he'd have made records like I make now." You don't hear that kind of talk much anymore, except in Nick Tosches's books.

Bragg brings that same conviction and enthusiasm to socialism (not Marxism, in case your folks want to pick a fight about it). He's very much involved in the Red Wedge, an activist cooperative of well-known musicians which supports Britain's Labour Party against Mrs. Thatcher. Besides countless benefit concerts and political rallies, he's performed in Eastern Europe and the Soviet Union. "I was in Kiev for three days. We did one song on a TV show, a gig for the morning shift of an electronics factory and another at Kiev University." His three albums contain songs of worker solidarity ("There Is Power in a Union," "Which Side Are You On"), attacks on the press ("It Says Here") and the government ("Ideology," which pointed paraphrases "Chimes of Freedom" in both melody and lyric) and comments on foreign affairs ("Help Save the Youth of America"), among other socio-political concerns.

"A letter came one morning that she would not let me see..." Pointed, deceptively slight phrases chopped up with jagged blurts of distorto guitar strumming give Bragg's records a depth of intelligence and political/emotional significance their spartan presentation may not immediately suggest. The records' punkily unpolished sound may leave some oblivious to the songs' melodic beauty. (*Life's a Riot With Spy Vs Spy* was cut solo as demos; *Brewing Up* also has scant embellishment. The relatively busy new LP, *Talking With the Taxman About Poetry*, benefits from selective but significant assists by Smith Johnny Marr and others.)

Bragg is heartily open to interpretation. "When I've finished a song, that's what I see for it. If anyone else wants to come along and improve on that original idea, I'm only too pleased to hear that." The most notable Bragg cover to date is Kirsty MacColl's rendition of "A New England," a wonderful smothered-in-production job which its author "likes very much."

Bragg describes his job as "a responsibility to talk about certain subjects," adding that he's "willing to talk about 'em until I'm blue in the face." But — and this is a welcome break in the long-winded tradition of wordy folksingers and angry young men in general — he says, crediting Berry Gordy; "I'm a great believer in the maxim that if you can't say it in three minutes it ain't worth saying." Oh, go ahead. We'll keep on listening. ◆

My *Circus* Act

One national magazine more willing to take a chance on young me was *Circus*. Unlike most of the '70s rock press, *Circus* was published by an experienced adult (Gerry Rothberg, a former *Esquire* editor who created *Hullabaloo* magazine and moved it toward an older demographic as *Circus*, was nearly 40). They had a swank office in a glass tower at 747 Third Avenue in Manhattan. Kathi Stein and future soap opera writer Stephen Demorest were the managing editors; Paul Nelson looked after the review section; Frank Rose (later at *New York*) was Senior Editor; Lance Loud was on the masthead as Assistant Editor. Kathi let me have her *Metal Machine Music* advance, which I found in a slush pile leaned against her office wall; I still have it.

How did I come to write for *Circus*? Other than contributing editor Andy McKaie, who I'd written for at *Good Times*, I wasn't in with any of those folks. Jon Tiven, who I knew a little, was also a contributing editor; perhaps he provided an introduction. Jon, who broke the rock writer mold by being a stylish dresser and went on to become a successful songwriter, producer and musician, started publishing his fanzine, *The New Haven Rock Press*, in 1967, so full marks to him for that. At the end of 1971, I happened to be carrying an issue of it while waiting at the Carnegie Hall stage door for Keith Moon to emerge after hosting a show by Sha Na Na. He'd worn a glittering ball gown and high heels on stage but was in civilian clothes when he appeared on the street. Plucking up my courage, I thrust the *NHRP* at Moon and asked him to sign the cover. I happened to recount my experience to Jon later at some press event and he was a bit put out about it. I'm sorry, but I didn't have a *Trouser Press* with me at the time.) If Jon had anything to do with my writing for *Circus*, then I guess he got over it. So, thanks for that.

In any case, I started off doing short, front of the book pieces — on Be-Bop Deluxe, Crack the Sky, Phil Manzanera, Jeff Beck — for *Circus*'s editorially indistinguishable sister publication, *Circus Raves*, in 1975. By the end of that year, they had erased the titular distinction between the two magazines and *Circus* had become a bi-weekly.

In December, I got my first full feature assignment: 750 words on the problems Jethro Tull faced in touring America. I was told to call Terry Ellis, the head of Chrysalis Records as well as the band's manager, for a phone interview. But when I posed the angle I'd been given to him as my opener, he flatly denied that was the case. The rest of the conversation was a desperate effort on my part to get something, anything, I could use. The line on the Milton Glaser-designed cover was more or less the opposite of the assignment: "TULL: Why They Don't Play Hard-to-Get."

In an issue also containing pieces on Dylan, Springsteen, KISS (who became a *Circus* mainstay), the Kinks, the Faces, Neil Sedaka and the Abominable Snowman (!), my poorly written story goes off in several directions at once, haphazardly combining history with box office reports and Ellis's appraisal of the band's itinerary. I didn't miss too many lame observations or band talking points.

Jethro Tull — The Band That Might Gig Anywhere

Circus, 20 January 1976

"Jethro Retire Hurt!" blared the headline in a major British magazine just over two years ago, when a spokesman for the group announced an "indefinite" end to Jethro Tull's live appearances, blaming the move on the extreme negative reaction which their then-current album, *A Passion Play*, received from the British critics. To the audiences who had already seen the intricate concept album presented live, the move came as quite a shock. However, before calling it a day, Tull agreed to play a scheduled American tour in order to fulfill contractual commitments. That tour and the one which they did a year later (after unretiring) proved one fact beyond the shadow of a doubt: regardless of the critics, Jethro Tull is one of the most popular super-groups in the world.

Their power to draw people to concerts has surpassed, in quite a few major cities, that of such concert titans as the Who, Led Zeppelin and even the Stones. However, playing only the biggest cities, although extremely profitable, is not Ian Anderson's idea of the best way to reach his audience. That's why on their 1975 tour of America they included quite a few dates at colleges and in smaller cities, covering ground that most top groups usually ignore.

This fall, for example, in addition to larger towns like Wichita, Toledo and Milwaukee, they hit places like Norman, Oklahoma (University of Oklahoma), Normal, Illinois (Illinois State) and Easton, Pennsylvania (Lafayette College). They even played a high school auditorium in Joliet, Illinois. "At the beginning of the year they decided to play a hundred dates," explains long-time Tull associate Terry Ellis. "We worked out three tours to take care of the cities we wanted to hit and found that it only added up to 85. Since they hadn't played colleges for a while, they thought it would be fun. They've always played a lot. They have always done, say, three tours a year in the States. They've always reached out and played towns other than the main cities."

OBLIGATIONS CAN BE FUN: Why? Well, as Ian Anderson told *Circus* a few months ago, "If you're a musician and going to play to people at all, you've got an obligation to go wherever people are and not just wherever the money is right." Terry Ellis has another explanation. "They enjoy it," he says. "They don't go on the road just to promote albums or make money to pay their roadies' wages, they actually do enjoy playing concerts. Ian's not happy unless he has a full schedule of touring or recording or doing interviews. He enjoys working. He doesn't have that many other leisure activities."

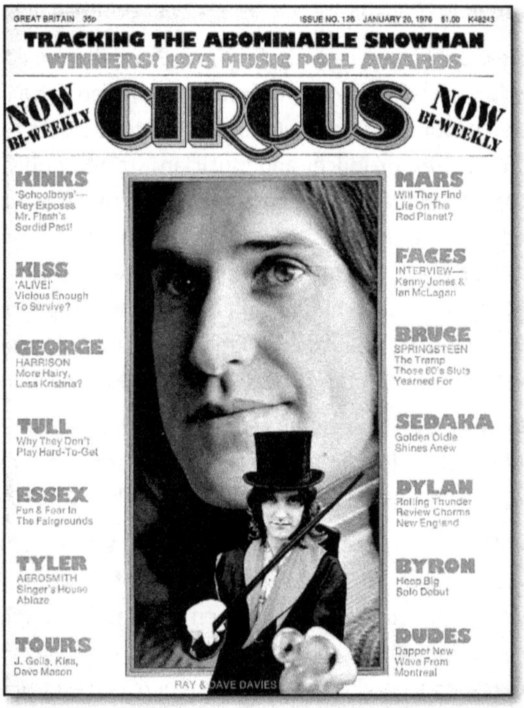

Like any other group with a lot of touring under their belts, Tull has done some interesting roadwork. They rank high in the U.S. sweepstakes for most visits. (Also in the running is Humble Pie, but they're out of business ....) In their 18 American tours, one finds quite a bit more history than in the case of your usual one-tour-a-year British superheavy.

Since their first appearance in the States, so many personnel changes have swept through the band that Ian is the only original member left. It was on the strength of Mick Abrahams' brilliant work on the instrumental blues "Cat Squirrel" (from the debut disc, *This Was*) that the band came over to tour early in 1969. The airplay which the song received created quite a stir among guitar freaks who thought Jethro was the performer's name; the three-month tour which that excitement prompted lost $20,000. They were more successful when they returned soon after, second-billed to Led Zeppelin. But before Tull recorded their second album, *Stand Up*, Abrahams left and was replaced by Martin Barre (who is still in the band). By the time Glenn Cornick left two tours later, Tull was headlining at important halls like the Fillmore East and making enough money to pay off debts.

At this point public reaction to their live appearances was still more impressive than their record sales, but the release of *Aqualung* early in 1971 changed all that. Hailed near and far as a classic album of heavy riff-rock, combined with the unmistakable trademark of Ian Anderson's wild flute playing, it featured two new members: Jeffrey Hammond-Hammond, the bassist who replaced Glenn Cornick, and John Evan, whose keyboard work has made a profound impression on Ian's music. But even though its phenomenal success made them a major concert attraction, Tull kept up their brutal touring pace. They returned to the States twice during the summer of 1971; between visits, Barriemore Barlow exchanged seats with the band's original drummer, Clive Bunker, giving them their current line-up.

JETHROMANIA: In the summer of 1973, Tull staged their biggest and most successful tour yet. Set up in three five-week sections, it included three nights in the immense Los Angeles Forum in the middle of the second leg. No one was prepared for the incredible number of Jethro Tull fans who turned out when tickets went on sale in June.

One-and-a-half hours after the box office opened, the three-night gig — 54,000 seats in all — was completely sold out. A fourth show was added and sold out just as quickly. The shows got great notices from just about every paying fan who went. But only two months later, the group announced its retirement.

While the reviewers in Britain heaped criticism (Anderson termed it "abuse") on *Passion Play*, both live and on record, Tull began the final part of their gigantic U.S. tour. In late August they hit New York, just barely satisfying the demand with four sold-out shows. Soon afterwards, Ian Anderson secluded himself and began writing Tull's next album, *War Child*, which eventually turned out to be an answer to the critics' putdown of the band's work. Although they resumed live work in England after a year's rest and recording, it wasn't until January 1975 that they returned to the United States. Determined to grind their detractors into the ground, the tour was set up bigger and longer than the previous one. When they appeared at the Forum this time, they established a new record — five nights, 85,000 tickets sold! No other band had ever drawn so many people there in one week. And the concerts were a resounding success with the fans, clearly demonstrating that even in retirement, Tull could outdraw any band going.

"Their drawing power is just a fact of life," says Ellis. "They've been playing long enough to have a strong reputation as a live act. When they play, people come to see them, either because they've seen Tull before, or they've heard that they should be seen."

Quite a few writers have attempted to explain Tull's live popularity in more detail, but none have really succeeded. The most obvious factor, however, is the incredible amount of showmanship and visual effects that make up the non-musical aspect of their concerts. Anderson is a firm believer in the "vaudevillian" side of rock and roll, so everything from films to actors to comedy routines between the musicians are to be expected onstage during a set. "What Ian does onstage is very much self-expression of the music, which also happens to be entertaining and exciting to watch," Ellis explains.

At one time, the only attention grabber was Ian Anderson's manic posturing onstage as he went running about and flailing his flute in the air. Now, no Tull show is complete without a quartet of classical violinists to open the proceedings, a female valet to serve Mr. Anderson's onstage needs, dancers in Walt Disney drag, a giant rabbit, smoke, flares, sirens and searchlights. All these theatrics only increase the audience's enjoyment of the music because of the complex interplay between the two. As with a three-ring circus, there's something exciting to see or hear every minute when Tull comes to town. ◆

I liked Tull. They were an exciting live act (I saw them in July 1969 on a Central Park bill with the Paul Butterfield Blues Band) and one of the few to successfully undergo a major musical course correction after one album: the debut was largely stone-cold British blues (including a ferocious version of "Cat Squirrel"), led by guitarist Mick Abrahams (whose subsequent outfit, Blodwyn Pig, was one of the handful of bands I saw at the Fillmore East, opening for Chicago and Johnny Winter in November 1969). I lost interest as time went on, but that turned to disgust at a 1995 Anderson solo show. From my *Newsday* review: "Anderson explained the harp-accented 'In the Moneylender's Temple' as being about a thieving accountant the band once had; later he asked if there were any Jews in the audience and dedicated the middle-Eastern 'At Their Father's Knee' to them."

I subsequently wrote a feature on Uriah Heep and supplied a detailed Who discography to accompany an article someone else wrote. And that was the end of my trip to the *Circus*.

One lasting benefit I got from the *Circus* experience was a lesson in giving and getting editorial direction. It helped an amateur like me to learn that magazines had their own stylistic requirements which could be articulated in documents like the following first page of the one *Circus* editor Kathi Stein handed me. I have since written a number of writers guides for contributors to various publications and have always kept this one in mind.

CIRCUS Magazine Features Writing Guide

Following are some of the points that should be covered in a normal Circus album story, and the accepted method of structural organization. Within this framework, writers are encouraged to exhibit as much personal flair and insight as they desire in their style of presentation.

Opening paragraph-- A lead which hooks the reader, catapulting him into the story. Usually a quintessential anecdote or quote, it should epitomize or reflect somehow on the main angle of the story which is all spelled out in paragraph 2.

Angle paragraph---- What the point of the story is. (What kind of creature is X, what makes him a touchstone for the people he attracts, what's he trying to prove, and how well does he succeed, etc.) This news angle paragraph announcing the new album gives the reasons why we're writing about this character--that is, something just happened (in this case the release of an LP, or a tour) and if you read on you'll find out all about it.

summarize import of the new LP in 1 or 2 lines

History flashback-- Review X's career for a couple of pages, showing how he's evolved as an artist or personality or whatever up to the present. (If this were a Genesis tour story, you might review the masks Peter G. has worn in the past and then point out why he dropped them in favor of Rael's leather jacket--how well past tours

Trouser It to Me! (1974 – 1984)

Trouser Press, which I later called "a whim whose time had come," stumbled into existence casually but ended up dominating my life for more than a decade — and remains a significant part of my world and identity.

For a complete archive of issues, visit www.trouserpress.com.

Trans-Oceanic Trouser Press made its first public appearance as a homemade fanzine outside of the Academy of Music on East 14th Street on March 9, 1974. I wrote about the magazine's whirlwind debut week for my college paper, incorporating a bit of concert reviewing to give it some heft. I drafted the manuscript in longhand, with the penmanship that earned me several suggestions as a kid that I had a likely future as a doctor.

The Lost Week

Polytechnic Reporter, March 1974

Preface: Having published (on March 9th) issue #1 of the *Trans-Oceanic Trouser Press*, an Anglophiliac rock magazine which I co-edit, I proceeded to spend a manic week selling them at the most likely spots, namely several concerts around the city. Luckily, but not at all accidentally, there were four between Saturday the 9th and Saturday the 16th, all of which featured English bands. Of these, I had tickets for the two Saturday shows. After two concerts and two pre-concert selling sprees, I was ready to pack it in.

Saturday the 9th: Collated 24 pages for 400 copies, packed them into knapsacks and shopping bags, put them in subway lockers and split home to eat and to suit up for the evening's work. Met some co-workers and headed downtown to the Academy (of Music) on East 14th Street where 10cc, Brian Auger's Oblivion Express and Rory Gallagher were scheduled to start at 8:00. Standing outside in the on-off drizzle, screaming at the top of my lungs, I sold some copies, but no landslide. By 8:00, the street was streaming with wet youth types, looking to buy or grub tickets and/or dope. I went in after a while, sold a few more, then dashed for my seat as 10cc came on stage and began tuning up. Enjoyed their tight, melodic set immensely. I wish they did "The Dean and I," but everything they did do was brilliant, so the loss was minimal. Sold a lot during the first intermission, then sat down (stomping on many toes since my seat was in the middle of a long, occupied row) to watch the legendary rock/jazz piano/ organist make a dull fool of himself with a back-up group that clung tightly to one note for hours on end. Panicking with boredom, I climbed out into the aisle, ducked back to the lobby and sold a pile of copies very quickly. Lots of famous types floating around — 10cc's New York debut had been heavily promoted by UK/London Records.

Rory Gallagher ran on stage, so I skedaddled for my seat. I love Rory's records, but now I know that he's great on stage as well. For two hours, backed by a genius drummer, a rockin' bassist and a top electric pianist, he knocked out original tunes as well as some traditional blues pieces which Rory played on acoustic instruments. One AM or so, I limped home, wasted but happy.

Monday, March 11th: New York's best hometown band, the Planets were playing at Kenny's Castaways on the East Side, and I hadn't seen them for over a year, so I plopped down a buck and went in. In a smoky audience of 100 or so, the spectators included top rock-writers, most of the New York Dolls and other assorted glitter types. Almost sold a copy of *TOTP* to one of the Dolls, but friend's advice and lack of nerve prevented me. Next time...

The Planets were only good (the stage was tiny and looked awfully crowded) but guitarist Binky Philips knocked out everyone, including record scouts and reviewers in the audience.

Wednesday the 13th: Met my partner in a record store (natch), picked up *Trouser Presses* and headed down to the Garden for to hawk at the Deep Purple gig. It was freezing cold, windy and everything, and the Purple People didn't make life any easier. I got into arguments with cynical old snots, couldn't sell to young (13-14) suburban types (none of them were interested in music, or so they said — you figure it), got nasty glares and giggles from the druggies — a wonderful collection of 18,000 lovelies. In two hours of this nonsense, the two of us sold 40 *TOTP*'s. What a drag.

Friday the 15th: Van Morrison at the Felt Forum. The weather was nice, but the people weren't. The Garden was running one of those '50s [oldies] circuses and old Teddy Boys were crawling all over the place, confusing the already poor situation. Around on 8th Avenue, where the Forum opens its doors, teenys [*sic*] wiggled around trying to buy tix for this long since sold out concert. There were hundreds of buyers, but only a few sellers and they were all pro scalpers, asking 15 – 20 bucks. The upshot of the affair was that no one was interested in buying a magazine until they could find a ticket and nobody was finding tickets. I split home empty-handed. (I did, however, carry a briefcase full of *Trouser Presses*.)

Saturday the 16th: I'm about done for. The word "no" followed by silence, a sneer, or occasionally "Thanks" has begun to infiltrate my nightmares. Cracking up is near at hand, but in hand, as usual, are a couple of hundred neatly stapled *Trouser Presses*. This is it — the last real chance to sell. We've got to move 150 copies and the scene is 14th Street again. Foghat, Peter Frampton and Maggie Bell — two shows: 8 and 11:30 or thereabouts. I'm down in the threatening rain around 7:00 and so are the ticket grubbers. The fifteen-year-olds are drunk out of their heads, puking in doorways and it's not even dark yet. I don't know if the holiday had anything to do with it, but I doubt that it did these dregs crawl out every Saturday night. The hordes begin to arrive, the roster of pinprick pupils and cracked teeth completing a rather Daliesque scene of youthful decadence. I really couldn't take the scene, bummer, like y'know man but duty called and I dived into the crowd, mouth blaring, and I sold pretty well. Inside, I skipped Maggie Bell and went on with my work around the rip-off candy counter, the only part of the Academy with visible lighting. I sat down to watch Frampton — what an incredible guitarist; every bit as good as I'd been told. Skipped Foghat — they're okay. but this was the fourth time, and they don't vary their show all that much. Sold another couple of hours in the lobby and then out in the pouring rain to chance it with the late show line. Not too receptive, and I was rather miserable getting soaked, so I hustled over to the BMT and split for home to watch TV flicks.

Altogether, we (well, mostly me) sold 300 copies, made lots of friends and got very little praise from those nice enough to stop and chat. Next issue — May 1st. That gives me just six weeks to get psyched up for this insanity again? Oh my God! ◆

All we had at the time was a PO box and plans for a second issue (on the back of *TOTP 1*, I wrote "...if you like this debut and want issue #2, we suggest...you adhere 25¢ to the blank and send it to us, along with a 10¢ stamp. Then you will be sure not to miss #2, whenever it comes out, which should not be too long 'cause we've become addicted to stencil correction fluid. ...How many more issues do you suppose we'll get out? How much do you trust us?")

But the bug bit and we blithely shouldered the responsibility of a more or less bi-monthly publishing schedule. From there, things evolved slowly. Our first official acts were to file a dba certificate with the county clerk and (belatedly) acquire a peddler's license and a resale number that allowed us to flog the magazine to passersby. As time went on, we acquired (not in this order) volunteers, staff, writers, printers, pages, color, typesetting, advertising, distribution, office space, postal permits, incorporation, loans, interns, payroll, promotion, tax returns, equipment leases and many other elements of a proper business. Which, after a fashion, is what we became.

I've told the story many times. Here's one rendition:

Interview by Steven Ward

RockCritics.com, 2001

Trouser Press was a rock fanzine you started with Dave Schulps in 1974. The fanzine quickly turned into a professionally done and well-respected rock magazine that was forced to close almost 10 years later in 1984 because of financial pressure. Do you miss putting out a monthly music magazine and do you think you would ever get involved in something like that again?

Actually, finance was only one of the factors that contributed to my decision to end *Trouser Press* in 1984. The music world had changed, music media had changed, the lives of the staff had changed, our audience had changed — all of which conspired to make the original thrill of having a credible forum to do with as we saw fit feel more like a Sisyphean duty to fill up a bunch of damnably empty pages every month. The emotional rewards, for me at least, had dissipated in the face of MTV's ability to make new wave bands come alive, with audio and video, in a way we couldn't match on paper. Part of why we existed was because commercial American radio completely ignored the bands we cared about and college radio was only beginning to matter in the new world.

MTV, in its early-'80s infancy, lunged for the colorful (read: new wave) and the video-savvy (that meant English, since the UK use of video to promote bands on TV was already established, albeit not in such a concentrated way) acts — Adam Ant, Duran Duran, Stray Cats (Americans who started their career in London), Culture Club, the Cure, Depeche Mode, et al. That wasn't all we did, but they stepped on our toes a lot.

I was frustrated at our fiscal insecurity and, turning 30 after 10 years of doing *Trouser Press* and nothing else, I discovered that real life, adult life, couldn't be postponed indefinitely. Plus there was only so much rejection of the mainstream possible if staying in business was a goal. We unintentionally had a new audience — teenyboppers excited by our coverage of their faves but too young to share our sensibilities and our skepticism: one cover story on Duran Duran that attacked the band's flaws caused howling letters of disillusionment and anger from kids who just wanted the good news on how cute they were. How could we put them on the cover and not worship them? It made sense to us — a big story is a big story, and a band is a mix of good and bad. Little did we know that no one else thought that way. These days, what serious publication dares think that way?

Which brings me to the question you actually asked — do I miss it? Sure. It was fun to publish completely independent music reportage and criticism. *Trouser Press* stood for things. Our readers thought of us as a friend with strong opinions. We clearly favored cool bands over old-hat stooges, but we had a real respect for veterans and their complex careers. We (I) loved Cheap Trick, the Who, Roy Wood, Sparks, Todd Rundgren and the Clash. We (I) hated Bruce Springsteen and all the manly Americans who bellowed rather than sang. We thought Patti Smith might be over-rated and we couldn't cope with LA's hardcore punk (a generational failure, no doubt). But we had a huge soft spot for the enigmatic charmers in the Residents.

It was all seat-of-the-pants, idiosyncratic, irreverent self-indulgence, but it was wonderful fun. It sucked getting dicked around by record companies, advertisers, distributors and all the rest. I took it all personally — I can vividly recall arriving full of enthusiasm and optimism to our 13th floor office on Fifth Avenue on many occasions only to discover that the morning's mail contained a few bucks in checks on days when the rent, or payroll, or a $20,000 printing bill was due. It wasn't just the money, really, it was the feeling of powerlessness, that the enterprise we put so much of our lives into could so easily be derailed by another company's incompetence or bankruptcy, or the record industry suspicion that print advertising wasn't of any real use to them. It was a tough and lonely battle, externally and internally. We didn't learn until it was over how many people we were important to.

Having started out so small and informal, we never grew into a well-run organization — although we got our work done and seemed on top of things, how we did it was always pretty slapdash. When I look back at the old issues, they look and read better to me than I remember them from the creative side. It was that kind of experience — hard to watch the food being prepared but tasty once it got on the table.

So, yeah, there are parts of it I miss. But after it was over, I was able to regain friendships that were seriously challenged by working together, and that means a lot to me to this day. I look back and see how well *Spin* did after we quit — not that the two are in any way connected, but if we'd had some of their money and a bit of encouragement, maybe we could have become a much bigger deal than we ever were. When I decided I'd had enough, I looked around for a buyer. I had an accounting firm groom us for a sale but there were no serious takers, although we did have discussions with a sheet music publisher that ended up nowhere.

I'm glad to have done *Trouser Press* and glad not to be doing it anymore. Sometimes you have to know when to leave what you've done frozen in time and let others carry on. Fortunately, the *Trouser Press* books — which we started doing in 1983, while the magazine was still up and running — provided 15 added years of continuity for me, the magazine's name and its ethos.

Would I do it again? I've always said if someone wanted to put up a million bucks, providing the business acumen and leave me alone to be the editor, I'd love to run another music magazine. Our slow but steady approach to business was fine in some ways, but a lack of initial capital was ultimately fatal, dooming us to be a small-time operation even when we might have done a lot more. I was never a businessman, and we were never able to get past print-it-they-will-read idealism. Successful magazine publishing, I discovered, involves a lot more than a good editorial "product" — it needs a marketing push, professional salespeople, distribution expertise, muscle, resources and management discipline — none of which we ever had [enough of]. Oh well.

Trouser Press was started because you wanted to cover bands that mainstream rock mags were ignoring. That turned out to be a lot of British rock and progressive rock bands in the mid-'70s. As time went on, non-mainstream acts turned into the punk/new wave/alternative wing. During the magazine's last few years, did you consider yourself or the magazine a champion of "alternative" bands or just scribes chronicling the bands that were non-mainstream?

It's nice of you to use the verb "champion," since that is exactly the reason why we put out the magazine. At the outset, our view of what mainstream rock magazines were overlooking included history as well as obscurity, so we latched onto the past (namely British Invasion bands) as well as pub rock, prog-rock and assorted marginal artists few publications cared about. But we were hardly doctrinaire about it. (As you may recall, both Genesis and King Crimson were considered prog bands at the time.) In the first two years (12 issues) of what was initially known as *Trans-Oceanic Trouser Press*, we covered the Who, Mott the Hoople, Todd Rundgren, Peter Frampton, Steve Harley, Marc Bolan, Brian Eno, the Rolling Stones, Status Quo and Roxy Music — among others.

Confession: As the mid-'70s wore on, we found ourselves covering bands we knew we were supposed to care about but actually didn't (privately, we referred to them, using a bit of borrowed British slang, as "wallys"). I was opposed to making too much of the New York underground scene we all loved and took part in, because we didn't want to be seen as locally obsessed. It wasn't as if bands like Blondie or Television or Talking Heads would ever escape the Bowery (as I foolishly believed) and be able to be heard by anyone outside the metropolitan New York area. (Bear in mind that most CBGB/Max's groups never released any independent records, and major labels were very slow to come calling. Then came the deluge, and in retrospect we quickly found out how naïve that view had been.)

Flash forward to the early '80s. New wave had become new romantic; the class of '77 was either dead or digging itself into a rut of decreasing quality and originality. The pop stars we could stomach — Adam Ant, the Go-Go's, Culture Club, Cyndi Lauper, Madness, Squeeze, Stray Cats — were just that, pop stars, which made them less emotionally rewarding to champion. U2, R.E.M., Blondie and others were numerically significant and good, but there weren't enough of them for a monthly. So, yes, in a sense we were phoning it some of the time, and that hypocrisy really made us lose enthusiasm for the whole enterprise. Meanwhile, we were somewhat removed from the indie rock stuff that was exciting. The Dead Kennedys, Neighborhoods, X and Pere Ubu were cool by us, but Black Flag was really not appealing to me musically in 1982. They sounded like the era we'd just come out of, minus the insight and credibility. (OK, so I was wrong about that.)

When I think of a rock critic who specializes in new wave or alternative music, I automatically think of Ira Robbins. Do you think you have been unfairly tagged with that title or do you think the connection is an apt one?

Unfair but hardly unwarranted. My musical interests, taste and areas of expertise, I'm happy to say, extend further than A Flock of Seagulls to the Butthole Surfers, but I suppose we all have to be typecast for something, so I can't really complain. And I *did* title the first *Trouser Press* book a "guide to new wave records," so who am I to quibble?

Long before there were skinny-tie bands, I was devoted as a fan and journalist to the Who. (When I handed Pete Townshend a copy of *Trans-Oceanic Trouser Press* #3, the second issue of ours to feature his band on the cover, in 1974, he took it to be a Who fanzine rather than a generalist rock magazine.) I've cared about Bob Dylan, blues, soul, folk music and British rock of the '60s my whole sentient life — one of my best recent CD purchases was an old Canned Heat live album I had worn out on vinyl. Glam / glitter is also a favorite era of mine (Roxy Music / Slade / T. Rex). I also love old-school hip-hop, Blossom Dearie, bluegrass, smart singer-songwriters and Humble Pie.

I would hate for people to assume, based on my writing and editing work, that I woke up in the mid-'70s, decided the Vapors were the bomb and never gave it another thought. By the time Elvis, the Pistols, Clash, Stranglers, Vibrators, Damned, Buzzcocks, Pere Ubu, Devo, etc. crossed my radar, I'd been a professional music journalist for five years and a devoted rock and roll fanatic for 15. And I've kept involved, active and enthusiastic to this day. I've co-produced a J. Geils compilation, written liner notes for Yardbirds reissues and the Electric Light Orchestra box set, reviewed the *Broadside* collection and done a lot of other things regarding music — all because I wanted to.

Tell me about your favorite rock magazines in the early '70s. What were you reading before you started Trouser Press and what rock critics were your favorites? Which ones influenced you?

I have trouble recollecting exactly what I was reading in those days, but I can tell you with some surety that future Dictator Scott Kempner turned me on to *Creem* in high school, and I found that very inspiring. I was desperate to write for it and sent them a couple of pitch letters/spec submissions which elicited an encouraging scrawled note from Lester Bangs. But my classmate Hank Frank was the first to get a record review — of a Sparks LP, I think it was — published. I was green with envy! By 1971, I was buying *Melody Maker* and subscribing to the *New Musical Express* (which came months late, via sea mail, rolled into a baton-like tube). In 12th grade at Bronx Science, future *TP* co-founder Dave Schulps and I would read it furtively behind the large fume-gathering hoods on our desks in an elective chemistry course. I had read *Hit Parader* and *16 Magazine* occasionally as a kid. *Creem* was a revelation. *Rolling Stone* meant nothing to me (unless the Who was on the cover) and continued not to for years — I only got interested when my ambitions as a writer grew to see it as a magazine I'd like to write for. (Which I had.)

Magazines that strongly influenced our thinking about *Trouser Press* were *ZigZag* (genealogy and history, crossed with incomprehensible devotion to the wrong kinds of American rock), *Crawdaddy* (general excellence), *Bomp!* (record collecting and discographies), *Phonograph Record* (serious, entertaining scribing), *The Rock Marketplace* (the mail auction ad business of which we took over when Alan Betrock folded it to launch *New York Rocker* — this was before *Goldmine* became the *ne plus ultra* of that realm), *Let It Rock* and the British weeklies.

Dave Schulps and I discovered that the New York Public Library owned a collection of *Melody Maker*, going back for decades, on microfilm. Dave had this idea of researching British rock using them, so we spent untold hours at the Lincoln Center library, going cross-eyed and seasick as the scratchy old images raced by, writing down every British musician we could find reference to, which bands they had been in and when. Dave came up with a coding system for instrumentation which I use in note-taking to this day: G/V/K/Y/B/D — guitar, vocals, keyboards, synthesizer, bass, drums — etc. We would write this stuff on sheets of notebook paper, listed vaguely alphabetically, by musician's name, and attempt to put their careers in chronological order. Then we would go to the stores that sold cutouts and look up the names on records' back covers to see what we could add to our knowledge base and our record collections.

Dave — who turned me on to the Bonzo Dog Band, Roxy Music, Sparks and a whole of other profoundly formative music — was a fiend for this stuff and we both learned a lot of bizarre details we would later trot out at interviews and frequently shock subjects with the extent of our knowledge of their careers. (The same idea later became a series of books called *Rock Record*. But we did it first.)

If guys like Robert Christgau and Greil Marcus were considered academics and Lester Bangs and Richard Meltzer were considered gonzo writers, would it be fair to say that the stuff you and your writers were doing at Trouser Press was more historical? Maybe like what Lenny Kaye and Greg Shaw were doing at the time?

Only at the beginning. As *TP* went along, especially when the underground scene and new wave started making contemporary music good and exciting again, our emphasis on history faded out. When we started, in 1974, glam was mostly done and there really was a lull in innovation and novelty. So, history made us feel like we were doing something valuable — anyway, it was how we learned about music. We were thirsty for info on what had gone before (in the '60s, at least. There wasn't much a whole lot of acknowledged pre-Beatles enthusiasm in our house.) But once things in the music world got good, history started feeling musty and ass-backwards as a journalistic ideal, so we downplayed it. But we never cut it out completely.

At the outset, we were fans who recognized that there was a lot we didn't know. We weren't serious record collectors (a joke around our place was to say "The more you pay, the better it sounds" as recognition of how out-of-touch serious collectors could get about music as artifact, not art), but we were devotees of rock history who also loved contemporary music. Lenny Kaye was a hero of mine — his liner notes are responsible for my ever-since obsession with Eddie Cochran — as was Paul Williams, although I wasn't as fully aware of his work. Most of the music writers I admired were English — Nik Cohn, Roy Hollingworth (who I buttonholed in a champagne-induced stupor, mine if not his, at a legendary Hawkwind after-show party in NYC in '73), Chris Charlesworth, Charlie Murray, Nick Kent, Pete Frame (who became a contributor to TP), Mick Farren (ditto).

We were completely clueless when we started. There were three people involved — me, Dave and the late Karen Rose, who Dave and I met at a guy's house in Yonkers. We were into the Who. She was into Jeff Beck. We all knew a couple of people and inveigled them into writing for the magazine. The two cornerstone pieces we got under our belts in the first year were a huge multi-part Yardbirds history by a great guy Karen knew or met called Ben Richardson and a fine Animals retrospective by David Fricke, who was still living in Philadelphia and was writing for a local weekly. My dad knew *his* dad through the stamp business.

We did what came naturally, which was to write as exhaustively as we could about the bands and music we loved. Pete Townshend wrote back in reply to the first issue. Lenny Kaye contacted us to say he dug the mag. Dave Marsh looked us up and bought us lunch a year or two in. Kathy Miller, who was a pal of Lester's and a regular contributor to *Creem*, as well as a former partner in crime of my first wife, the rock photographer (and NY Dolls fan club co-founder) Linda Danna, wrote some great glam-rock profiles for us.

ANDY FRASER & PAUL RODGERS

Dave and I had met Richard Meltzer and Nick Tosches at publicity director Susan Blond's office at United Artists Records when we were both writing for our respective college papers before we started the magazine. We were faintly connected to Meltzer through our high school Who pal Scott Kempner (R. wrote an article for *Fusion* magazine that was supposed to be about the high school band me, Dave, Scott and Hank Frank had that got so far as "rehearsing" in my parents' living room a couple of times, perfecting a version of "Do You Believe in Magic" that no one else ever heard us play.) At UA, where he and Tosches were blagging sealed, unpunched promos they could sell (and rejecting any that didn't qualify), R. gave us a crucial bit of advice: to always put something in your writing that's just for your own amusement, like ending one word with "s-h" and then starting the next with "i-t." I'm sure that beats anything I might have learned in journalism school, had I ever attended one.

We didn't have any money (the founding capital for *TOTP* was $60 to buy 10 reams of mimeograph paper, a box of stencils and a couple of tubes of black ink). We didn't know any of the name brand writers personally and were too shy to meet them. (Dave did get chummy with Gordon Fletcher, a *Rolling Stone* contributor in DC.) We certainly didn't imagine they'd be interested in our dinky little enterprise, so we got people we knew, or met, or who found us and volunteered to do writing for the magazine. We kind of knew what we liked, so we knew when we were on to good things. Dave and I both did lots of writing — he emerged as one the magazine's main feature writers once he finished college and came back to New York in 1975 — but we were up for almost anything if it seemed credible and worth reading. Within a year of our starting, Jim Green and Scott Isler had joined the staff; Jim as a singles columnist and feature writer (not to mention distribution manager) and Scott as the art director (and editor in training). Both became major contributors to the magazine over the rest of its life.

Tell me about your staff at Trouser Press. *Did any go on to do bigger things at more mainstream rock mags. I know Scott Isler went on to do some great stuff at* Musician.

I've always been very proud of our alumni and how they spread into various roles in the industry. Jim Green has written for a lot of publications and done liner notes for Rhino as well as build an incipient acting career. Dave, who now lives in LA, and I work for the same radio company; he's done plenty of writing over the years for a lot of different publications in the US and UK. Tim Sommer, who came to work for us a teenaged intern and stayed to become an indie-rock columnist, has already had several brilliant careers, writing for *Sounds*, newscasting for VH1, rocking in Hugo Largo, signing Hootie and the Blowfish to Atlantic and so on. John Leland, who was also an indie-rock columnist for *TP*, was on staff at *Newsday* and *Newsweek*, [became] the editor of *Details* and is now a reporter at the *New York Times*. Jon Young, who was a contributor for many years, has kept up the good work for numerous publications while working in a real job. Steven Grant is a big wheel in the comics world. Joel Webber, our first ad director, co-founded the New Music Seminar [*not quite: he became one of its three directors a year or two in*], put out some very cool records and became an A&R man at Island Records but died in his early 30s of a congenital heart defect. Steve Korté, our second and final ad director, moved on to an editor's job at *Star Hits* magazine and has continued to prosper in other publishing realms.

You never had guys like Marcus or Christgau write for any of your record guides. The writers are always younger, less-known writers. Was that by design because those writers were more in touch with newer, outside the fringe music or did you want to give those younger writers a chance?

Yes. I don't like Marcus's writing at all, and Christgau has his own record guides to do (for which I have, on one or two occasions, loaned him records), so there's no chance of either of them being involved in a *TP* book. On the other hand, Neil Strauss, David Fricke, Karen Schoemer, Gary Graff, Greg Kot, Michael Azerrad, Tom Moon, Jim DeRogatis and many other highly regarded, well-established not-entirely-young writers have all contributed.

Basically, I've always lived and worked outside the rock critic establishment. I've never been friends with any of the big shots (except for Lenny Kaye and Paul Williams, whom I met in the early '90s) and I've never written for them. Nor most of them for me. I started in rock journalism on the outside and have, for better and worse, remained there for most of my career. I've never been in the "in" crowd.

Did you ever have bigtime rock writers in Trouser Press*?*

Over the life of the magazine, we did publish some big names (Lester Bangs, Pete Frame, Mick Farren, Roy Carr, Gloria Stavers, Chris Salewicz, Dave Marsh), but none of them other than Farren were regular contributors or in any way more than momentarily identified with the magazine. We had some future stars (David Fricke, Kurt Loder, Paul Rambali, Pete Silverton) and some really cool interns (like Fall album cover painter Klaus Castenskiold), but by and large we just picked people whose work we liked. We grew our own.

By the way, although the perception is that women writers were shut out of rock journalism until the post-punk '80s, we used a lot of women writers, not as a political statement but because they knew their shit and wanted to write for us. We didn't exclude anybody who could help. (Plus the magazine was co-founded by a woman.) Toby Goldstein, Marianne Meyer, Karen Schlosberg, MT (Marilyn) Laverty, Kris DeLorenzo, Kathy Miller and Galen Brandt all come immediately to mind, and I'm sure there were others. ◆

In April 1979, *Trouser Press* ran an article about Jim Morrison written by Gloria Stavers, whose byline I knew from reading *16 Magazine*, where she was the editor and sometimes referred to herself as GeeGee. I recall being impressed at seeing names like John Coltrane and Al Jackson Junior in her pages, along with ads for some instrument company featuring Frank Zappa. She managed to make a teenybopper magazine subversive. I don't recall the reprint arrangement that led to this note (she died the following year at 55), but she was a great, important figure in music and it was a thrill just to have a small professional interaction with someone I'd looked up to as a kid.

GLORIA STAVERS
405 EAST 63rd STREET
NEW YORK CITY 10021

8-23-82

Mr. Ira Robbins
Trouser Press

Dear Ira

This is to confirm my conversation with your office last week, following up with the appropriate reminder. Please co-sign one copy and return to me. The others are for you and/or TP files if needed.

If you have a copy of the April '79 issue I would love to have one; also, a couple of recent issues so I can see what you guys are up to.

Sincerely,

Gloria

Gloria Stavers

encl: reprint agreement
copies of material from
April '79 (Jim Morrison story) issue

Gloria Stavers, creator
and owner of said material

copies: GS, IR & TP mag.

encl: photo-copies of material

We had plenty of other adventures:

◆ The call I got in the office one day from a woman I knew who said she was in a hotel room somewhere, had just fucked Iggy Pop and was delighted to confirm the rumors about the size of his cock.

◆ Dave Schulps' encounter with Jimmy Page that resulted in the most informative and expansive historical interview the guitarist has ever granted. A sitdown set for the Plaza Hotel in New York during Led Zeppelin's Madison Square Garden stand in 1977 kept getting pushed back until the band decamped for Los Angeles, with Dave in hot pursuit. Once there, he was kept waiting by the pool for the better part of a week until Page finally deigned to talk. The classic story we got out of it was well worth the effort, but it led to insane deadline anxiety at the time.

◆ The time Wendy O. Williams — towering on platform boots and probably barely clad — strutted into our shabby Times Square office to drop off a Plasmatics ad.

◆ Scott Isler's attempt to honor Devo's bizarre request to be interviewed by Linda Lovelace for the cover story of issue 70, which ended when her boyfriend-cum-manager Chuck Traynor threatened Scott's life over the phone just for calling. Her seemingly safer replacement was William S. Burroughs, but the resulting meeting of the minds at Burroughs' New York City residence, the Bunker, proved a lot less edifying than we'd hoped: they spent a lot of their time together discussing the purchasing and consumption of recreational drugs. Just to amplify the disappointment, Burroughs amanuensis James Grauerholz later included our interview in a book without seeking permission or giving credit. Years later, that led to it appearing, again *sans* credit or permission, in Italian *Rolling Stone*.

◆ A disagreement over whether or not we could run yellow ink in a half-page Jonathan Richman ad that led gangly ad salesman Joel Webber (R.I.P.) and I to wrestle each other over a desk.

◆ When our two-room office was in the heart of Times Square (147 West 42 Street), we used to see Joe Franklin, who I think had an office there as well, in the lobby. There were also occasional sightings of Andy Warhol, whose wigmaker had offices in the building.

◆ The Joey Ramone cover shoot David Godlis did for our final issue, during which the candles on the cake set fire to the "10th Anniversary" sign we had typeset for the occasion. The resourceful photographer cobbled a replacement together on the spot. Years later, some enterprising greeting card company got hold of the image and revised it for wider and more durable appeal. (I hope Godlis got paid.)

◆ The one time we asked Lester Bangs (R.I.P.) to write for us, he sold the Ramones article we assigned him to the *NME* without crediting *TP*, so it looked like we reprinted it, rather than the other way around. We were angry and he was unrepentant, but given our paltry pay scale, we had a lot of nerve. The article appeared in issue 33 (November 1978) and is available online.

◆ Dave's phoner with Elvis Costello — the artist's first contact with an American journalist — ended abruptly when Elvis's estranged wife called on the other line.

That wasn't El's only hasty exit. After his awful racist remark about Ray Charles, Costello held an abashed press conference in a conference room at Black Rock (CBS) in New York, sweating through questions from African-American journalists unimpressed by whatever it was he was supposed to be famous for. During one of his futile attempts to explain it away as drunken stupidity, I happened to glance at the back of the room and saw his manager, Stiff Records co-founder Jake Riviera, silently draw a finger across his throat. He'd decided that was enough, or that it was not helping. Elvis clammed up and walked out of the room. (On the next page is the first letter I got from Jake, accompanying Stiff's initial 45s.)

Hello

Thought that you might dig our shit. This is the bumpf so far. We'll keep ya upto date, Hows about a sub to your rag?

Best Wishes

Jake

P.S. Records coming under seperate cover.

Karen Rose

Although we were good friends in the magazine's early days, *Trouser Press* co-founder Karen Rose and I had a falling out that I never fully understood. What began as routine editorial disagreements over artists, coverage, contributors and direction evolved into ugly acrimony. Sides were taken and factions formed. The rows turned ugly, especially when it came to the selection of photographs taken by a friend of hers or those taken by my photographer girlfriend.

Karen withdrew from an active role in the magazine but remained a shareholder in the corporation we had formed. Distrust, tension and resentment escalated. A lot of it was personal, some of it was petty: we literally argued over whether her masthead credit should be Publisher *Emeritus* or Publisher *Emerita*. There was some silliness over the band Starry Eyed and Laughing. The annual stockholder meetings we were required by law to convene were charged and testy. Other than that, the only reason we had any contact after that was because she placed ads in *Trouser Press* for Rock Read, the visionary mail-order music book business she founded.

Beyond the hurt and confusion, I was truly sorry about the end of our friendship. Karen was an exceptional character, the kind of person who gets things done. She was a small woman with a big laugh and a mane of red hair. She was smart, charismatic, organized, funny, determined, unique and enthusiastic. (And a keen copyeditor, as this note reveals.) I both liked and admired her.

Well after the magazine — and my contact with her — had ended, I learned, nearly three years after the fact, that she (a non-smoker) had died of lung cancer in 1989. As she chose to keep her illness completely private, the sad news came as a total shock. I don't know her exact dates, but she couldn't have been more than 38 years old.

Karen was an extraordinary person. I gratefully and proudly acknowledge her primary role in the creation and ascendance of *Trouser Press*. We never would have done it without her. ◆

OFFICE MEMORANDUM

DATE: may 8, 1974

DEPT: Accounting FLOOR:

TO: Ira Robbins

FROM: Karen Rose

RE: TOTP finances

Money collected from #1 by the time we started #2	67.25
Subs for #2, added payemnt for #1, and Ira's donation	81.95
	149.20
Total cost for #2	142.20
	7.00 left
Money collected since sale date of 4/30 for #2 up till night of 5/7/74	106.62
Total now going into #3 → though there are more sale dates, and money should be coming in from D.C., Houston, and East Side Books and Discount	113.62

Trouser Press Turns 40

On March 23, 2014, we threw a 40th *Trouser Press* anniversary and reunion party at Bowery Electric in New York. Bands played, friends who hadn't seen each other in decades got to catch up and we all had a wonderful night of memories and music. I gave a speech to express my gratitude. Rereading it now, there isn't a word I would change.

The story of *Trouser Press* resembles the story of a band. We met in high school, got things going in college, had fun for a while, involved a lot of great people, made no money, broke up and then got famous.

What began as a whim on a southbound #1 train ended up consuming my life for 11 years. And, ultimately, brought us all here tonight.

Thanksgiving 1973. Dave Schulps and I — besides encountering Bob Dylan in the original Village Oldies — hauled ass up to Yonkers for a record collectors hang with a bunch of strangers who, like us, were into British Invasion bands. We weren't full-on collectors, more like amateur trainspotters, but that got us in. We ended up riding downtown with one of the people we met there, a redhead named Karen Rose, who worshipped Jeff Beck and had edited the Brooklyn College newspaper. By the time we got off the train, the three of us had decided to publish a fanzine. I was 19 years old and it just didn't seem like that big a deal.

In creating *Trouser Press*, we billed ourselves as outsiders — "an alternative to the alternate alternatives" is how we put it in a pre-publication mailer. "We have nothing to alienate anybody — no famous writers, no big names, no money, or anything that might make us elitist (or successful)." Truer words...

Using my father's mimeograph, a rented Selectric typewriter and a T-square wielded by High School of Art and Design student Barbara Wolf, we pulled together a first issue, with articles to match the March 1974 concert schedule in New York. Our idea was to hawk the mag in front of venues with articles about the bands playing there. So, come March 9, 1974, we planted ourselves in front of the Academy of Music on East 14th Street, at a show featuring 10cc, Brian Auger and Rory Gallagher.

The opportunity to rave about music we loved was pretty seductive. And the odd perks — a personal letter from Pete Townshend in response to the first issue, free records, a paid subscription from Gene Simmons — made a future seem possible. In short order, our all-volunteer army grew to include Jim Green, Scott Isler and Sue Weiner.

We didn't invent anything, but we knew who to emulate. *Crawdaddy, Rock Marketplace, Bomp, Zigzag, Creem*, the *NME* — that was where words about music changed things for me. Paul Williams, Lenny Kaye, Greg Shaw, Nik Cohn, Nick Kent, Nick Tosches, Alan Betrock, Billy Altman, Ellen Willis, Richard Meltzer, Joe Fleury, Lillian Roxon — they were as much my heroes as the bands they wrote about.

We never had a clear sense of what the magazine meant to anyone. Until we stopped. Since 1984 I have been amazed by how durable a concept, a memory, an ideal *Trouser Press* turned out to be. Whatever that is, *Trouser Press* is more of it now than it was 30 years ago, when our obituary ran in *Rolling Stone*. "Voice of pop-rock underground folds after 10 fan-filled years."

And fans we were. Musicians told us we knew more about them than they did. We came prepared, and despite our deep-seated snark, we always gave artists a fair shake. If it was Moogy Klingman patiently enduring the questions of three rank amateurs, Steve Harley challenging me over stuff I'd read in the British weeklies, Hugh Cornwell of the Stranglers being a complete prick to staff photographer Linda Danna, Lou Reed playing his asshole character to the hilt with Scott or Jimmy Page giving Dave the most detailed accounting of his career by the pool at the Beverly Hilton, it all became *Trouser Press*.

None of us set out to be in charge, we just fell into roles, roles for which we were wholly unsuited. I was certainly not cut out to be a businessman, and I take full responsibility for the failure of *Trouser Press* to become a sprawling media empire, the *Pitchfork* of its time. But the people involved all had talent, spirit and imagination: art director Judy Steccone, Kathy Frank, Steve Korté, photographer Ron Gott, Mark Fleischmann, Louise Greif, Wayne King, Kenn Lowy, John Gallagher, Dan Zedek, David Fenichell, Craig Campbell.

What ultimately made Trouser Press worth its ink was the incredible world of creative talent we stumbled onto. The list of greats who placed themselves in the pages of *Trouser Press* still shocks me. David Fricke, Pete Silverton, Ebet Roberts, Mick Farren, John Leland, Jon Young, Gloria Stavers, Laura Levine, , Jim Sullivan, Tim Sommer, Wayne King, Bill Flanagan, Marianne Meyer, Steven Grant, Dave Godlis, Pete Frame, Jim Sullivan, Paul Rambali, Mitch Kearney, Laura Fissinger, Kurt Loder, John Walker, Marilyn Laverty, Cary Baker, Amy Horowitz, Savage Pencil, Barbara Kagan, Roman Szolkowski....

And they did it for peanuts. I am embarrassed at how little we were able to pay such valuable people. I have no defense for that except that we didn't have any money. Simple as that. We operated as a collective of sorts, and everyone's contribution was part of a group effort to accomplish something worthwhile. I am gratified and relieved that many of them went on to far more lucrative success.

We even had world-class interns: Tim Sommer, Fran DeFeo, Pearl Lieberman, Linda Walker, Eric Hoffert, Adam Auslander, Jay Paquette, Miriam Kuznets and others, many of whom built distinguished careers in the music world and beyond.

Speaking of beyond: Karen bowed out of an active role in the magazine after a few years and went on to found Rock Read, a company of her own that sold music books by mail order. An Amazon of the '80s, you might say. Like many of the people who knew and admired her, I was shocked by her death in 1989 from cancer.

Jim Green brought his gangly Berkeley pal Joel Webber into the Sam Goody's record store where we both worked in early 1976 and I hired him on the spot to be our ad director. With his energy, his bravado and height, Joel was a boon to our fledgling operation, although we did once end up throwing each other over desks in our tiny Times Square office. I watched in awe as he went on to a career as a director of the New Music Seminar and an A&R man at Island Records. Joel's 1988 funeral was a heartbreaker.

Mick Farren, who died last summer, was a true rock legend. I never imagined we deserved to have him write for us, certainly not for what we were able to pay him, but I was proud as hell every month when he came in with his *Surface Noise* column. Mick was a great writer, but he was much more than that. A crucial '60s figure in British politics, bands, culture and publishing.

Back to the living, and then I promise I'll stop. Dave Schulps and I have stayed friends for 45 years, and I can assure you that I would not be here tonight if not for him. He shaped my musical taste and redirected my life. Without realizing it at the time, we took a leap together that changed us both. We share a lot, we do — just ask us to recite the dialogue from *Putney Swope* in synch if you want proof — but we're very different people, and a couple of years spent putting out a magazine made some of those ways abundantly clear. I had the perseverance — or lack of imagination, call it what you will — to stick it out for 10 years, dealing with the nuts and bolts of running a small business, while Dave went off to manage a band before settling into the career he still excels at: reporter, interviewer and writer.

Since the magazine ended, I've gotten a lot more credit for *Trouser Press* than I deserve. Dave is not the only other person who gave the magazine its truth and soul, but he certainly leads that list. Simply put, *Trouser Press* would not have existed — or mattered — if not for him. ◆

The Speedies

To expand on something I mentioned in that speech, *TP* interns proved to be a successful lot: Tim Sommer became a well-known writer, a VH1 star, leader of an adventurous band (Hugo Largo) and the A&R man who signed Hootie and the Blowfish. Fran DeFeo become a VP of Publicity at Columbia Records and now has her own company. Claus Castenskiold is an artist who designed the cover of at least one Fall album. Linda Walker got into artist management. Miriam Kuznets is a psychiatrist. Pearl Lieberman has worked in TV and on documentary films. A few more names have since come back to mind: Eric Blumberg and Jane Lupo. And I seemed to have neglected to mention Rod Granger, David Fenichell, Danny Cornyetz, Louise Greif, Linda Francischelli, John Gallagher and Kenn Lowy, all of whom worked for us for a time.

Eric Hoffert was, at the time he and his pals were dropping by our office, a student at my old high school, Bronx Science, where they had formed a colorful and glamorous power-pop band called the Speedies, who ended up being managed by one *Trouser Press* staffer and had their first single produced by another. They were, for a time, very popular on the local scene and developed a following of fans who, in the fine tradition of the Beatles being pelted by jelly babies (beans), threw cereal at them onstage. They got opening slots for some top touring bands, including the Jam. In 1980, I wrote a bio for the band, was later used as liner notes of a retrospective CD.

Someone might once have observed that if a rock band could be designed to have the irresistible appeal of junk food, nothing could stand in the way of success on the order of Corn Flakes. The Speedies, a new prototype, are filling that role perfectly. In fact, they see themselves as the breakfast cereal rock organization — a sweet to be craved insatiably by American youth.

Now in their second year of product evaluation, the Speedies are looking more and more like a successful test. With regional experimentation yielding stunning results in the Northeast, the next stage of the planned introduction is a national roll-out, wherein the Speedies will soon be as well known in Pasadena as they are in their own homes.

Meet the creative team behind the Speedies conceptualization:

GREG: The clean-cut, fresh-faced rhythm guitarist also handles back-up vocals and humility chores for the group. An A- student, recently graduated from one of the Apple's better public high schools, Greg plans to live out his days in Brooklyn. (Until the subway fare goes down.)

ERIC: The studious longhair, Eric plays psychedelic lead guitar and sets the Speedies on a steady course to stardom by being responsible for medium-range strategy. Another good student also recently graduated from the public school system of New York. Also a Brooklynite and Yankee fan.

JOHN CARL: The suave, handsome one plays bass, sings back-up and draws fans (especially female variety under the age of 20) to gigs like ants to a picnic. Shops at Fiorucci, lives in Queens, plans to die happy.

JOHN MARINO: The band's resident poseur and singer. The trendy, outrageous Speedie who adds class and theatrics to an otherwise intensely serious organization. Lives in Manhattan, has forgotten everything he ever learned in school and is looking forward to more and better closets for his outfits.

ALLEN: Every band needs an adorable, crazy drummer like Mickey Dolenz. Allen not only looks better but has the chops and the zaniness to win both fans and rhythm awards. Another Brooklyn boy.

The report to date: The Speedies rose from the failed ashes of the Middle Class in early 1979. Played first six months sans bassist, managing gigs all over the city, nonetheless. (There are open-minded club owners who don't mind underaged bands with unconventional line-ups.) Gigs have been limited to weekends (because of the educational careers of some of those involved), but some stellar appearances including repeated total sell-outs of such luminous niteries as Hurrah, Max's, Trax and Irving Plaza, as well as a highly successful date opening for the Jam in front of several thousand screamers at the Palladium.

The Speedies recorded and released their first single on Golden Disc Records, selling hundreds of copies in the first few days. Airplay and label interest has been mounting steadily, and constant invitations to appear are weighed carefully at strategy sessions by the group's planning caucus. At this instant, possible TV and classy club appearances are on the docket, and interest from overseas has been registered.

The Speedies are poised, ready to spread their joyous pop noise across the width and breadth of the United States. Will the youth of America find that they fill a discernable need? Will they acquire some of that disposable income that powers this nation's entertainment industries? Will the record business give them a fair shake or a royal screwing? Will General Foods ask them to record cereal jingles?

For the answers to these and other pressing questions, stay tuned to the Pop Culture Station in your area and keep an ear perked for the unique snap, crackle and pop of Speedies brand rock'n'roll. Nag your parents for money to buy Speedies. Hold your breath 'til your face turns blue! The Speedies want to be your breakfast cereal!! ◆

The Speedies released two 45s, the second of which was produced by Clem Burke of Blondie and then came to a natural stop. Lead guitarist "Eric Pop" (Hoffert) became a software engineer and helped create Apple's QuickTime. "Greg Zap" grew up to be Gregory Crewdson, a world-famous art photographer and Yale professor. (Prophetically, the band's first single was "Let Me Take Your Foto"). And drummer Allen Hurkin-Torres ("Allen Zane") became a New York State Supreme Court judge. Yes, it's true.

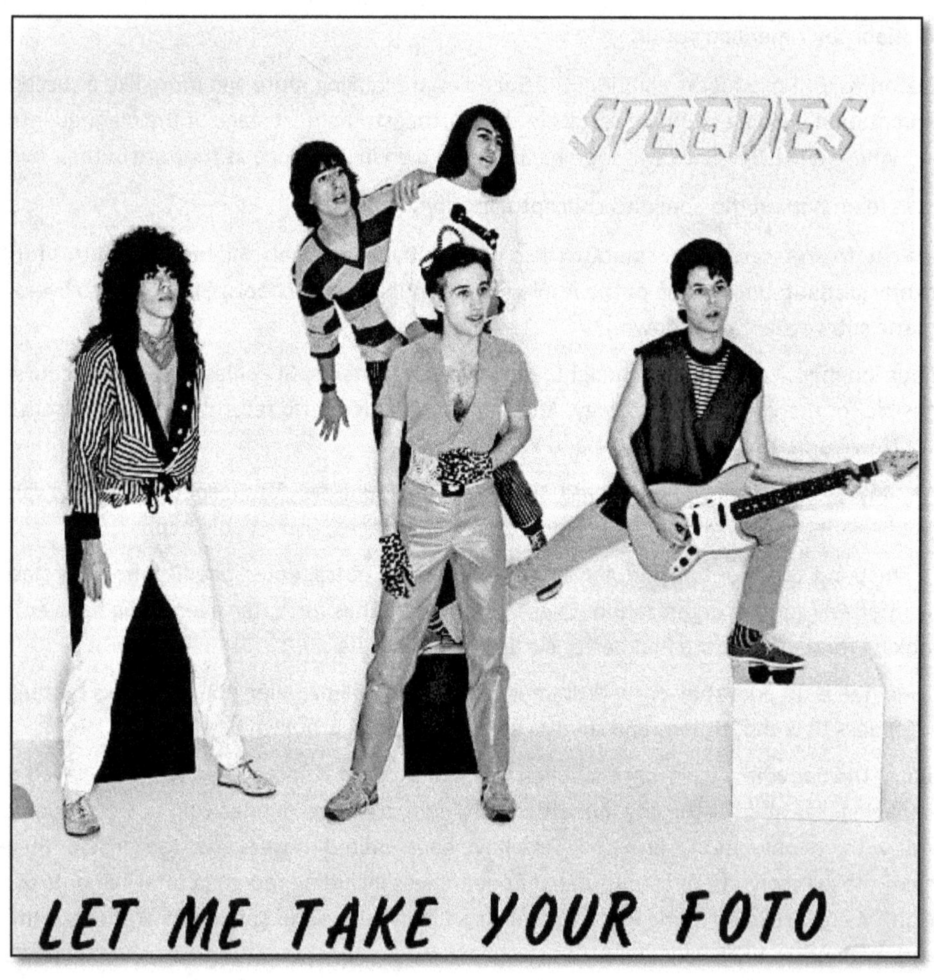

Early Interviews

The first musician I ever interviewed was Mark "Moogy" Klingman (R.I.P.), who in 1974 was a studio owner, solo artist and keyboard player in Todd Rundgren's band, which I think was the main reason for our interest in him.

Utterly ignorant as to how such things were done, Dave, Karen and I went to Moogy's Chelsea loft (aka Secret Sound) to speak with him in June 1974. He couldn't have been nicer to three rank amateurs. (The KID acronym was a collective byline we never used again.) Our rambly Q&A ran in two parts (issues 5 and 6) later that year.

26

Moogy Klingman Meets the KID

By the KID

No one accuses the Trouser Press of not knowing a sucker when it sees one. And when we found out that Moogy Klingman -- ace Todd sideman and a most worthy talent in his own right, with musical, compositional, and production credits you can read about below -- flipped out over the review of his 1972 solo endeavour (definitely a bargain bin classic) in TOTP #1, we immediately asked him for an interview. Moogy was quick to oblige, so one eve in mid-Who week (6/12/74), the inimitable KID (that's the TOTP editorial staff, Karen, Ira, and Dave, en masse) invaded The Secret Sound studio and then Moogy's adjoining apartment. We gawked at the equipment, spoke briefly of Todd's upcoming productions (The Hello People, Felix Cavaliere, and, of course, Utopia), shook hands on Moogy's and Karen's mutual idol, Fred Astaire, and said the following:

K: Where did the name Moogy come from?
M: That comes from when I was two, my brother was three, my sister was six and my sister used to call me Marky that was short for . . . that was long, a nickname for Mark, and my brother tried to call me Marky but not being able to speak so well it came out Moogy. I used the name pretty steadily till I was about 12 or 13 and then I decided that I was an adult so I shouldn't use it anymore so I stopped using it, still my close friends called me Moogy, but it's still a hassle to tell people that's my name -- I always have to tell them three times and I usually have to tell the story how I got the name. . . .
KID: (chuckle chuckle)
M: I don't mind telling it though . . . but I started using it again professionally because it seemed to have more of a snap to it than Mark. I started to really dislike the name Mark, it seemed to be bland, a really bland name.
I: You used it as sort of your middle name also.
M: Yeah, sometimes I do that. It's really Mark William, but that's like trying to

let people know, anyone that knows me, that Mark Klingman and Moogy Klingman are the same person, so I started to say Mark was called Mark Moogy Klingman, but up to that point I was only known as Mark Klingman, but now I've dropped the Mark, so it'll just be Moogy from now on, I think.
D: Now everyone has the idea that you play synthesizer.
M: Yeah, but it was before. My name came before the synthesizer . . . and now I do play it. Life is strange, isn't it?

THE LONG ISLAND SOUND

D: Tell us about Glitterhouse.
M: Yeah, that was my first group. I'll try to give you a short musical history. The Glitterhouse: When I was in Great Neck [Note: That's on Long Island, N.Y.], when I was 16, there was a group called The Justice League, which was really The Glitterhouse, which was the biggest group in Great Neck and the coolest, and I started trying to play piano again.
D: How long ago was this?
M: This was -- I was 16, about eight and a half years ago and I started playing piano again. I started when I was about 12 and took lessons for about two years and played in Dixieland bands. In fact I had a Dixieland band that appeared on Wonderama with Sonny Fox and I was the leader and I got interviewed by Sonny when I was 12.
I: Did you get games and prizes and stuff?
M: I don't know. You know how stardom is. You don't remember too much when you're on Wonderama, you're just blinded

The Stranglers

I have been asked many times — as, I expect, anyone who does this sort of work has — about the people I've interviewed: the biggest names, the best talkers, the biggest surprises. And the inevitable "Who's the worst interview subject you've ever had?" Dave once had a hard time with Andrew Eldritch of Sisters of Mercy, who insisted that questions put to him be answered by a new member of the band who hadn't played on the latest LP. We've all faced the gaping silence of monosyllabic answers and artificially impaired conversationalists, but one that stands out for me is Hugh Cornwell of the Stranglers, who spent a 1977 conference room chat at A&M Records in New York expectorating into a paper cup and asking the photographer who accompanied me to the session, who happened to be my wife, about her cunt (his word, not mine). I admired his band, but his misplaced display of punk rudeness was well out of order. Of course, that was the band's early ethos (see "London Lady" for evidence), so I shouldn't have been surprised.

This photo, taken by Linda Danna Robbins during that unpleasant encounter, appeared in *TP* 22, but the article it illustrated was by Pete Silverton. (I must have decided to not do anything with the interview.) Two months later, I wrote this review.

Stranglers

No More Heroes

Trouser Press, December 1977

It's so hard to decode the Stranglers. After you've gone through the easy observations about Dave Greenfield's keyboard sound and its relationship to Ray Manzarek, all the obvious stuff one gets from an album cover that features a rat, and the simple revulsion that can be gleaned from songs about sewers and other horrible environs, it's extremely difficult to understand two things about the Stranglers. First, why did their debut album sell almost 200,000 copies in England, and second, what are they really about?

Meeting Hugh Cornwell was an interesting brush with self-consciousness to the nth degree (his, not mine). The man tries so hard to be repulsive and iconoclastic that he comes off as a bit of a fake. Somehow, I don't find myself believing that he eats little children for dinner. But I could be wrong.

What isn't questionable is the fact that the Stranglers know what they want and how to get it. Their sound is instantly identifiable, a jaunty combo with lots of funky bass and trollopy synthesizer/organ. Their songs are chock full of interesting lyrics about all sorts of things — a friend that jumped off a bridge, seducing young girls, a Trotsky eulogy, the hypocrisy of school — but the one consistent factor is the bitterness, the total lack of positive emotions. "Bring on the Nubiles" is as crass a song about sex as ever is likely to be written ("Lemme lemme fuck ya fuck ya" etc.).

The Stranglers are without a doubt the gloomiest, nastiest band ever. Whether or not it's real makes little difference at this stage. Either you accept the Stranglers and revel in their mire or reject this sort of thing out of hand and transfer directly to the Carpenters school of sweetness and light. I suppose I find myself somewhere in the middle: I can appreciate the darkness and sinisterness as well as the music, but I don't think I'd let my sister marry a strangler. Something better change. ◆

John Lydon Lunches

I had a similar experience years later when I met John Lydon in a New York hotel room on a promotional tour for his first (of, so far, three) memoir. Although it was a fruitful interview, he ate sushi while we spoke and displayed an overt display of scorn (for an American? A journalist? A fan?) that could have been better saved for someone with a lot less admiration and respect for him and his music. Whatever shred of civility he allowed to slip through that got me to generously refer to him as "charmingly insufferable" I can't recall.

Rotten Is as Rotten Does

Newsday, 1 May 1994

John Lydon, the erstwhile Johnny Rotten, is not a nice man. And he's the first to admit it. As the keening lead singer of England's notorious Sex Pistols in the late '70s, he spewed venomous lines like "I am an anti-Christ ... I wanna destroy the passer-by!" from a point unnervingly between irony and conviction. Three pages into his recently published autobiography, *Rotten: No Irish No Blacks No Dogs*, Lydon calls himself "a spiteful bastard ... if I can make trouble, then that's perfect for me." And holding forth in a pricey suite at Manhattan's Parker Meridien hotel, the charmingly insufferable Lydon waxes theatrically splenetic for the amusement of a wary journalist.

"Hopefully [the book] will annoy a lot of people, because people do need to be annoyed from time to time," says Lydon, looking up from a unilateral lunch of sushi. "It's the only way you can wake them out of their slumber.

"For 17 years, people have fiddled about with my history and rewrote my life story for me. I decided enough is enough: Here's the truth. I wanted to smack you in the face with it. I'm fed up with people fantasizing: The reality is far more interesting."

The reality Lydon has put together (with the help of Keith and Kent Zimmerman, who did all the interviews, other than with Lydon, that make up this oral history) is at once irritating and entertaining, a do-it-yourself indulgence full of historical amplifications and bizarre assertions ("I thought it would have been silly to go play New York. It was pointless. They had already decided that they hated us..."). Who knew the future Johnny Rotten was once a day-care teacher? Or that Lydon saw a role model in Laurence Olivier's film portrayal of Richard III? "I thought it was the most splendidly vile thing I'd ever seen. I couldn't present myself as a nice little pop star, because I knew I was pig-dog ugly and I had to find a way around that." But Lydon splits hairs on the significance of his efforts. The book mentions seeing the film "a long time before I conceived Rotten." In person, he counters a question on that remark with, "I didn't conceive of Rotten as a character, that's just the way I decided to present myself."

Lydon, whose gift for condescension and haughty crankiness belies his poor, working-class London roots, just might be Oscar Wilde reincarnated as Gore Vidal. Quick, acerbic intelligence adds a razor edge to his contempt, which caroms between principled opposition to "ignorance and prejudice, class systems, lousy attitudes and establishment figures" and vendettas against old punk-rock nemeses like the Clash. "I know from an insider's view what that band are all about," says Lydon. "They're [bullshit] and they're out for money."

Actually, the whole notion of punk rankles the man most music fans would be quick to identify as the genre's figurehead. "I would never have used the name punk," he scowls. "It's dis-*gus*-ting."

For all their shattering impact on the rock world, the Sex Pistols had a brief, chaotic existence, from late 1975, when the quartet was unveiled, to November 1976, when its first single was released, to January 1978, when Lydon uttered his famous valediction ("Ever get the feeling you've been cheated?") from San Francisco's Winterland — the final stage in the Pistols' inexorable implosion.

"We ended when we had to. From there on in it really would have been repetition. We had no hope in God's hell of making album number two. It just wouldn't work." As Lydon notes in his book, "Anti-fashion became a fashion unto itself. Then it was time to move on." In terms of the future, "I don't like reunions. I will never ever repeat my past. I will not go on the stage and perform those songs with the Pistols ever again." [*Which is, of course, exactly what he did for six months two summers later, guiltily calling it* The Filthy Lucre Tour.]

During their brief lifetime, the Sex Pistols made a handful of phenomenal singles ("Anarchy in the UK," "God Save the Queen," "Holidays in the Sun"), one album (*Never Mind the Bollocks, Here's the Sex Pistols*), a U.S. tour documentary (Lech Kowalski's *D.O.A.*) and no small measure of history; in its wake came an eight-year court case between Lydon and manager Malcolm McLaren, a film (*The Great Rock 'n' Roll Swindle*), a bunch of inferior post-Rotten recordings, an endless parade of imitators, the overdose death of bassist Sid Vicious and a plethora of albums, including a compilation snidely titled *Flogging a Dead Horse*.

The Pistols staked out a position of unflinching antagonism ("blatant attacks on anything and everything that got in my way," is how Lydon characterizes his lyrics), playing hard-edged, charged-up rock of enveloping intensity, topped off by the acid sneer of Rotten's sideways melodicism. "You can't be dealing with conventionalism," he says of his inimitable singing style. "You just gotta do what you do and [fuck] everybody else, [fuck] the rules and regulations.

"I was left literally penniless when the Pistols expunged me. I managed to pull through. I don't think money, or lack of it, is where problems are. If you have ideas, you'll find the cash." And, he adds, "I've never been short on ideas."

The idea Lydon had after the Pistols was Public Image Ltd., a group whose determined rejection of pop music convention has resulted in some of the most challenging sounds ever issued by a major record company. In recent years, shifting lineups of musicians have helped Lydon produce some truly wonderful records that absorb relatively normal melodicism and give it back wrapped in barbed wire. Right now, Public Image is on a year's hiatus while Lydon makes a solo album, promotes his book and assembles a Pistols documentary from 600-plus hours of previously unscreened live and interview footage. "If you want to know what the Pistols were like, then watch that. But don't ask us now, approaching our 40-mid-crisis years, to go back on the stage and pretend we're 18 again, 'cause we're not." ◆

Here's the full transcript. I have to say, reading this for the first time in 27 years, it's a perfectly good — and seriously entertaining — interview. I don't know why he pissed me off so much at the time. I suspect — and here comes a dirty little secret of my profession — I would have liked him to respect me for my knowledge and enthusiasm, to admit me to an outer ring of the inner circle of people who were around and aware in 1977. I was disappointed when he treated me like some ignorant jackal come to poke the bear and hear it growl. (But it's entirely on me that I was possessed to begin the interview on the weird note that I did.)

John Lydon, 12 April 1994

The death of [Dr. Feelgood singer] Lee Brilleaux?

Is he dead? I obviously don't think very much at all. they seem to be snuffing it like flies. it's just another funeral I won't be attending.

The McLaren bio and Glen Matlock's book

I don't know about the Malcolm bio at all. I just put my little piece together because, for 17 years, people have fiddled about with my history and rewrote my life story for me. I decided enough is enough: here's the truth. I wanted to smack you in the face with it. it's myth-breaking, that's all. I'm fed up with people fantasizing: the reality is far more interesting.

For 17 years, no matter what I do, people refer to other people's points of view on my life. and I've had enough. I just want to clear it all out once and for all. this is the final full stop, I would hope. I know there'll be more lesser pieces of work coming out, but they really won't matter anymore.

Will Paul Cook write a book?
I don't think he's capable.

Conceiving of Rotten as Richard III
I didn't conceive of Rotten as a character, that's just the way I decided to present myself. I loved Olivier's Richard III, I thought it was the most splendidly vile thing I'd ever seen. I couldn't present myself as a nice little pop star because I knew I was pig-dog ugly and I had to find a way around that. that was my conclusion. I might have got it wrong, but it somehow worked. it's no big deal, it's just what people do.

Your book suggests you contrived this presence to affect...
It's not a contrivance, it's just the way things are. That's why influenced me the most; lo and behold, the end results did its bit.

How did you keep a lid on the intellectualism and musical awareness the book now acknowledges?
You can't really be wasting your time with other people's idiocies and pontifications because you'll never achieve anything if you indulge in that, at least not at that specific time. you can read it later when it doesn't matter, and it's lost its bite. you've just got to move forward all the time.

Would it have been shocking if the NME *had reported you as a former daycare instructor?*
Not to me! But that's the kind of stuff they would not bother to print. this is the mythologizing and the nonsenses that go on. I've always been absolutely, specifically honest. I had major rows with McLaren at the time about things... Capital Radio is a classic example. I was asked to go on and play some records. Malcolm thought that would all be Iggy Pop and the Stooges or the New York Dolls, which I had very little interest in. I have very varied tastes. Big, big row. Breaking the myth. But I think the truth is far more interesting and you will achieve a lot more by being honest.

Punk acknowledged reggae as a serious influence...
Did punk? That all came after me, that followed. And then reggae suddenly became a fashion accessory and that was the end of that.

People saw punk groups as tough, rootless and angry at the world...
I'm still fighting the same battles as I was then: ignorance and prejudice, class systems, lousy attitudes, establishment figures...

Has adult success taken any of that ground away from you?
I don't know if I've had any success. You're here. I'm not living in a squat — is that a sign of success? That's something you do when you're young, but you move on.

Not everyone gets to. Look around the streets of New York.
Yes, well not everyone's got a brain and knows how to use it.

I'm not denying your entitlement.
Many people do.

How does one maintain an anti-establishment stance when has one has ....
This isn't a stance, that's the point. I don't like being told what I can and cannot do. As long as I don't hurt anyone, I cannot see where the problem is. I won't make mediocre music. I'm not interested in going with the flow or even being remotely competitive with anyone. I'm not interested at all. as fine as that is left out of my life then everything's all right. but of course record companies will try to dictate. Even your own audience will try to dictate. and it's just too bad.

How shocked was Virgin when you delivered the first PiL record?
They were very unhappy.

You must have been delighted...
Yes, I was...No, I wasn't now I look back on it because they withheld its release date and it was available in bootleg form three months before it was officially released, which did not make me very happy. I've been plagued by bootlegging and the likes. it just shows you can't really trust your own record companies, 'cause that's the only place the tapes could have come from.

PiL's accomplishments: a new beachhead of objectionability. You could have just gone on and done some form of the Pistols indefinitely.
There wouldn't be any sense of achievement or purpose to that. you can't just paradiddle on the same note forever and a day; there's no joy. nothing to be achieved. Fuck the money, fuck art. Just do what you believe in.

How did PiL come about? You and [Jah] Wobble?
No, it was my band. It wasn't Wobble's. I put it together and invited them in one by one. lo and behold we just lumbered our way through rehearsals and somehow or other songs came out of that. Public Image works because it's different people, completely different attitudes and backgrounds, clashing vigorously. there's no one brainstorm going on. there's no dictatorship in anything I do, it always has to be a sharing thing.

But you get your way
I formed it. I'm the axle.

Producer Stephen Hague / commercialism
I've got problems with the Hague productions. I like the lunacy and the ridiculousness of being so structured, but it's just a little wimpy. still jolly good, and I like the lyrics I was putting together around that period, too. One thing I can't share, I can't have people writing songs for me. I have to be the mouthpiece, and I have to thoroughly believe in what I'm doing to do that properly.

The song "Seattle"
Hysterical, hunh? we were stuck in Seattle for a week and a half with nothing to do in midtour 'cause gigs were cancelled — or whatever the reason, I can't remember now, it seems so long ago — so we just worked. we rented a room in the hotel and rehearsed, and that song came out and lo and behold the Seattle scene followed it. I hope the two are not connected.

The song "Public Image" and the sound of U2.
I've said this for years: how bass, from Wobble's end, suddenly became a dominant force in rock music, which it certainly wasn't beforehand. It was just this boomy noise in the background, just another person to balance the stage.

What did the Zimmermans do?
They helped me with the editing and they did some of the interviews for me, because, quite frankly, there's no way I could on God's Earth interview my own father. He would wind me up, 'cause as much as I'm a wind-up merchant, believe me, I've learned everything from him. he does it ever so much better. it could never, ever have happened. I was there. I watched this go on, but I took a back seat.

Which interviews did you do yourself?
None. just myself, I do me, myself. I talked to other people and was in and out all the time. It's taped interviews.

Did you write out or tape your contributions?
Tape. this book's about 3 years in the making for me. initially I sat down and tried to write it all out, but I was pontificating too much and falling in love with the way sentences are formed rather than the content. it's a terrible thing. I'm not practiced enough in that way. I can write songs, but I can't expand with facts.

Transcription: there's nothing worse than listening to yourself babble.
It's agony. I don't like my own voice. Isn't that funny?

Comparisons of his singing to Bryan Ferry's
You can't be dealing with conventionalism. you just gotta do what you do and fuck everybody else, fuck the rules and regulations. besides, I'm much more into drama and dynamics anyway. I like the way things are said as much as you're saying.

You entered the Pistols to be as irritating as possible to as many people.
Not specifically originally, no. But I learned at certain gigs that that would be the best way to handle the audience. when the response is absolutely ignoring you or merely thinking you're nice, well then you do something about that. because it's all about action and reaction. as long as an audience leave with some sense of they either hate you or love you then it's fine. when you're just mediocre that's the kiss and you're in the wrong industry from there on in. I'm not naturally antagonistic. it comes from reacting to situations.

You developed a facility for it.
I've always been sharp, and I don't miss opportunities.

Self-defeating careerism. The Pistols repeatedly shot themselves in the foot.
Yes, but not deliberately so. that's just what occurs quite naturally to us. all my friends to this day are that way, all the people I work with in Public Image are that way inclined. we don't do what is considered the correct route because the correct route is wrong. I'm not Debbie Gibson and I don't want to work with anyone that thinks like that.

There comes a time when not taking the correct route leaves you with no path to follow...
I don't think so. I've never been short on ideas.

Steve Albini is an endlessly critical character.
That's just negative for the sheer hell of it. I'm sorry but I'll argue this point about anarchy, too. it's no good just being an anarchist if you don't have something to replace what you're destroying with. otherwise it's just futile farting-in-the-wind stuff. I'm sorry, but I'm always two stages ahead of that. it's not just chaos for no particular reason.

Was that the dividing line between you and Malcolm?
I'm not sure. Malcolm's a smart boy. we just have differences of opinion on very many things.

But he saw chaos as an end in itself.
Possibly so, but I think a lot of that was personal jealousy that he was not in the driving seat so he would have to constantly reinvent his position and the only way he could really do that was by destroying things for no particular reason, creating animosities and instigating arguments that really led us nowhere, led us in circles. we ended when we had to. we done what we done and that's it. from there on in it really would have been repetition. we had no hope in god's hell of making album number two. it just wouldn't work. they couldn't cope with the songs I was writing at that point and I couldn't deal in any shape or form with what they were doing.

The post-Rotten Pistols material — was that circulating before you left?
No, it all came after. you have to look at it honestly: Sid doing Eddie Cochran versions, there's nothing new or rebellious about that.

They were good versions...
So what? The original's better. Steve and Paul's stuff ("Oh You Silly Thing," etc.) was exactly what it said, a silly thing.

[The band] had lost its unity. They were squabbling over royalties and things like that. As you must know about me, I won't have any of that. If you work with me everyone gets an equal share, regardless of who's doing the most work or the least. When you stop that kind of squabbling, you keep things together. If egos get in the way it's impossible.

Was any of the litigation with Glitterbest over songs?
No, they couldn't argue that. they tried to gain access to the publishing, but it doesn't work that way. [*Hotel employee comes to door. Rotten dispatches him politely, closes the door and mutters "Dimwit."*] Now, what was I waffling? That was one area when Glitterbest's lawyers were inefficient, much to our benefit.

Endless Pistols albums
It's all the same stuff regurgitated. the "Kiss This" product which came out last year, I put that together. but that's because Virgin had already committed themselves to re-releasing and rather than it being a lousy package I thought I'd move in and make it a once-for-all everything that was on the shelf and they've got nothing left to tamper with. That's it. I had to remix a lot of that stuff, the tapes were so buggered up. they were stored in the worst possible ways possible. serious deterioration.

The pre-LP bootleg Spunk?
Don't know. no one sent me a check so don't ask me to explain or justify it. I can't stop it. the amount of people that bootleg off the Pistols, I'd be in the courts for years trying to stop it. I don't care that much anyway. if people are stupid enough to buy bootlegs and know they're being ripped off for inferior product, then they're welcome to it.

Who controls the Sex Pistols recordings at this point?
I'm chairman of the board. Steve and Paul and I are equal shareholders. we make all decisions. Malcolm has nothing to do with it. he's out. it cost me money and 8 years of my life debating the point. I was left literally penniless when the pistols expunged me. to form public image was a living nightmare. I had no cash, no nothing. I managed to pull through. I don't think money or lack of it is where problems are. If you have ideas, you'll find the cash.

Talk about the Swindle *film*
The first 30 seconds were a masterpiece and then... All that *Swindle* stuff, that's nothing to do with me. that came after, when I was gone.

The abortive contracts with EMI and A&M
You don't deliberately organize these things. nobody wants to lose their workload, their distributor. in hindsight, of course, Malcolm would say he planned it that way but that isn't the truth. I don't see any joy in fantasy. well, not that kind. we all have our fantasies of girls doing things to each other...[*cackles*]....

It's just all pop. By its very nature I am a pop star, regardless of what I might smugly think of myself, that's what it comes down to. [*uproarious mirth*]

What about today's 17-year-olds...
Don't use the name punk, in the same way I wouldn't have used the term rock and roll or Teddy Boy when I started. I would never have used the name punk, either. it's disgusting.

Alternative music
I don't find very much content in so-called alternative music. They do love their doom and gloom and self-pity. That's not fun for me.

They have a sense that things are not right that it's worth fighting against even if they don't have a clue.
If they don't have a clue, then what the fuck are you talking about then? Leave the mind games to the intelligent and plod on relentlessly. I see an awful lot of self-pity in the alternative scene and I find that a bit hard to stomach.

The Pistols' lyrics: more ironic than self-pitying?
Hardly self-pitying. blatant attacks on anything and everything that got in my way.

"Pretty Vacant"?
That's a piss-take. That's not a deliberate statement. That is from a moron's point of view. This doesn't mean I'm a moron for saying it. I'm an actor! I was acting!

People miss the point...
What can you do? You can't work everything to your lowest common denominator.

You can defend yourself from being misunderstood.
We didn't really get the opportunity. By the time the poison had set in, I found it was best to just ignore it and move on and get on with PiL.

Your solo album
We decided to take a year off with PiL, and so rather than getting bored I decided to just do everything myself for one album for Atlantic. I built a little studio to do exactly that in. I'll have no one to blame except myself if it all goes wrong, and I really enjoy that pressure. It's not PiL. It's just me on my own. I'm not working with anybody.

A one-man project?
Yes. I've only just got through learning how to use most of the equipment. Modern technology moves along at an alarming pace. But it's good fun. I've had to make myself computer friendly. It's much easier than it used to be in analog, in the old days. It's just a challenge. I've only just begun.

When did PiL last tour?
I forget. Last year sometime. I've been so damn busy with everything else. Sorry, I'm not in a reflective mood right now.

Frequency of PiL records...
I don't have anything to prove and I don't make records until I'm good and bloody ready. I'm not going to chuck out fodder just because some record company wants to make some money. It's of no interest to me.

Who's in the group?
The same people that were when I left it. Temporarily. On vacation.

Are they all making solo records as well?
Yeah. And I'm not here to brag about their little pieces. I don't need the competition.

Have you totally lost touch with Levene?
I don't like him anymore. His drug indulgences really piss me off. He became very useless and lazy. I went through all that with Sid, and I wasn't going to repeat it. Not with anyone. it's not worth it.

Steve Jones?
Stopped it. I think he's now getting religion, which is worse. He goes on those weird trips where they all bond together in the nude in a tent...Retreats. Jesus, how insane!

Where do you live?
I pay my tax in London. And wherever work takes me is where my big beautiful bottom is plonked.

What brought you to Atlantic Records?
They're the only ones that would pay me. Tim Sommer got me the deal. I like him. He tries hard. But the poor sod is going to have to try a hell of a lot harder. I don't think he knows what he's taken on. Or maybe he does. Then more power to him.

The book
It's no revival attempt. It's a reaction to bullshit, that's all it is. Special in its honesty. If anyone young out there ever dreams of joining this industry, please read and learn. There are many pratfalls, and I'm warning you about more than enough of them. I've opened my mouth here and I think it's worth listening to. That's my point of view on it. Hopefully it will instigate very many points of view. Hopefully it will annoy a lot of people, because people do need to be annoyed from time to time. It's the only way you can seem to wake them up out of their slumber and this mass acceptance of blandness.

Attack on the Clash
I know from an insider's view what that band are all about. They're bullshit and they're out for money. Hence the reformation.

Other punk bands
We've nothing to do with any of them. never have been. don't want anything to do with anything they're getting up to. They all existed because we existed. and gave not one word of thanks to that fact. and set themselves up directly to compete. This is the nonsense and crud I had to face weekly from the likes of Joe Strummer. "We'll be bigger than the Pistols!" The nonsenses coming from the man. sounds like grumpy old Matthau character, fighting old battles. the notion of competition — pop music obligates such arrogance, but certainly credit was given. What kind of attitude's that? It's got nothing to do with 'I love the music,' full stop. They came out of jealousy; we came out of originality. There's the fine line between us.

Response from Glen Matlock or anyone else slagged off in the book?
I don't slag him off. I just tell it like it is. He's probably a perfectly nice person but I don't like him, and I can't help that. And there's no reason for me not to like him, as I say. I just don't. He's had his say, hasn't he? His book came out and it was just non-stop rubbish, yapping on about my sisters and things. I don't have sisters. What on earth is the man talking about?

The Raincoats reunion?
I heard about it. I don't like reunions. I will never ever repeat my past. I will not go on the stage and perform those songs with the Pistols ever [cough] again. It can't possibly work.

Involvement in Julien Temple film documentary
All the unreleased live footage that's never been seen, interviews and the like. It was just festering away, rotting on some horrible warehouse shelf. I'll release it as a documentary, probably about an hour-and-a-half long. I wouldn't want it to be any longer. Jesus, our career was basically an hour-and-a-half. and just let it run chronologically and not add any talking heads from today. everything will be as it happened then and leave well enough alone. if you want to know what the pistols were like, then watch that. but don't ask us now, approaching our 40 mid crisis years, to go back on the stage and pretend we're 18 again, 'cause we're not. of course, he was closer to 21 at the time....

Were a lot of shows filmed?
Yeah. a hell of a lot. we're talking huge amounts. like 678 hours of unseen footage. the entire American stuff. here on bootleg was only seen the Winterland gig and from a very lousy angle, which is very depressing angle.

*Jon Savage's book [*England's Dreaming*]? Did you take exception to it?*
I took exception to most of it. I think it was all him yapping on about his very good friend Malcolm. I found it disgraceful that he completely seems to have ignored women's role in all of this. Again that would have to have something to do with his pink triangle attitude, wouldn't it?

Whatever the reasons, ignore he did. It's the results that matter. And I think that was unforgivable. There's a few lines here and there, tersely dealt with. Shocking. The whole punk thing was total equality. Across the board. No matter class war. No nothing of that shite. No sexism. And he just missed it. It's the most important element of it and he completely missed it.

The kids who populated the punk movement didn't get it either.
Very many didn't. That's right. But Sid's death put a big knocker on everything anyway. From there on in it was pointless to try and make sense out of it. Once heroin and drug addiction and suicide had been entered into the scheme of things, it's just well to forget it. Start again someplace else.

That was your response to Sid's death?
Absolutely. I had no pity for him. I'd given that up several years before. ◆

Welcome to the Working Week

With *Trouser Press* still more or less an unpaid hobby for me that could be worked on at night and on weekends, I had two jobs after finishing school in the summer of 1975. The first — thanks to my *Trouser Press* colleague and chum Jim Green — was at the Rockefeller Plaza branch of the Sam Goody record chain, where he had landed after returning to New York from college in Berkeley, California. (Record store jobs were a virtually mandatory rite of passage for music journalists in those days.) I was assigned to the cassette department, which was kind of a drag — I've never felt the same affection for tapes that I do for vinyl — but the job had amusing aspects, like the occasional appearance of Lauren Bacall, who shopped there, and a recently resigned *National Lampoon* co-founder, who needed a catch-up (on cassette) of the music he'd missed while he was working twenty-hour days entertaining American college students. Otherwise, most of my customers were tourists asking for tapes of whatever was in the charts at the time.

Aside from Bernie Bornstein, the comical figure who managed the store, and a visit now and again by Mr. Goody himself (yes, there was a Sam Goody!), I have two vivid memories of that experience: the day Jim brought in his gangly Rather Ripped Records pal Joel Webber to meet me so I could hire him to sell advertising for *Trouser Press* and the day in October 1975 that whatever radio station was playing over the store PA premiered *Who by Numbers* by airing it in its entirety. Listening to lyrics that felt extremely personal to a devoted Who fan, I was moved to tears: a powerful experience in a most inopportune setting.

After I'd had enough of retail, I lucked into a handoff from my Brooklyn Poly classmate Michael Abram: a part-time gig in the two-person service department of Gotham Audio on Washington Street in the West Village. Run by an imperious but charming Austrian named Stephen Temmer (referred to by us as "the GLC," for God-Like Creature), the company was the exclusive importer of Neumann microphones, the *ne plus ultra* German brand standard in recording studios, and my job was to clean and repair them. I worked for Joe Leung, a tough little guy with an opaque sense of humor. Every day, a couple of U87s or maybe an old U47 turret mic would arrive in the mail (they now sell for $3,000 – $5,000) for us to service. Some came from Stevie Wonder's home studio, others from places like the Record Plant, the Hit Factory or Wally Heider. My degree in electrical engineering was of limited value: the work involved blowing off dust, swapping out ruined connectors, replacing power supplies and very delicately cleaning the gold-plated membranes on which the whole thing relied. The part cost a few hundred dollars; working on it was a tricky task that involved soldering tiny leads without spattering anything onto the membrane.

It wasn't a bad job, a bit stressful at times, but fair enough. I got to listen to WNEW-FM while I worked, which is how I heard Scott Muni and Elton John get absolutely shit-faced on the air one afternoon and make juvenile remarks about Kiki Dee, her swollen "tits" and "that time of the month." The inadvertent worst moment of my employment at Gotham was the time I had an old mic plugged in with the outer case removed; someone in the room said something that caused me to turn around and my hand brushed a live contact that carried 240 volts of DC power from a transformer. I was knocked off my stool and onto the floor, my limp arm quivering like a plucked bow. No permanent damage, but a lesson learned. I never did that again.

Temmer, who later put up the money to launch *Christopher Street* magazine, knew of and respected my other professional pursuit, and once expressed a shared sense of our (albeit widely disparate) roles as leaders: it was our job to look out for problems and fix them before they become disasters. Coming from someone so accomplished and affluent, I took that as a great compliment. When he died of AIDS in 1992, his obituary in the *New York Times* contained a number of remarkable facts: he advised Watergate prosecutors on the gap in the White House tapes, was involved in the renovation of Avery Fisher Hall and once served as the general manager of WBAI-FM.

The Undertones

It was an absolute delight meeting the Undertones on their second trip to the States, in 1980. (Their first, the previous year, had them opening for the Clash — a great bill that I saw on 20 September 1979 at the Palladium, with Sam & Dave as well).

They were still wide-eyed kids from Derry, high-spirited and pinch-me amazed to be back in America. We met up in a Manhattan diner (I still don't know why we writers tolerated such rubbish environments for interviews). Here's a bit of my account from *TP* 54, September 1980:

Sire Records, their worldwide label, is buying lunch, and the race is on to see who among three of the band — singer Feargal Sharkey, guitarist Damian O'Neill, and bassist Mickey Bradley — can take best advantage of the freebie (apparently, to judge from their gusto, a novel experience). After commenting on (and avoiding) an item listed on the menu as "English fish and chips," they all order spreads, but Feargal runs into a bit of a language barrier when he attempts to order a Coke float. The waitress, patient yet uncomprehending, hears what amounts to "caoulk flaoute," and that's not in her repertoire. Without the slightest evident annoyance, Feargal lets one of the Americans at the table translate for him, and the lunch gets under way.

A few hours later, appetites whetted by nothing more than a five-block walk back to the hotel followed by an equally short stroll to the evening's venue, the entire band gathers around a makeshift buffet to chow down yet again — this time in a large (and functioning) bathroom set aside as the band's "dressing room" and hospitality suite. They're waiting for the roadies to finish setting up the stage downstairs so that they can run a soundcheck. We start talking about touring, and I wonder aloud whether or not the group is, as published in numerous articles, reluctant to leave their Irish roost for roadwork. "I've never felt like that. I've always wanted to get away," laughs guitarist John O'Neill. Brother Damian agrees: "This tour's better than the last one [in the UK]. I'm enjoying it more. Every time we tour England, we're a little bit bigger, and that makes it a lot easier. The halls are better; we stay in better hotels; we get meals after soundchecks." Maybe these guys are genuinely grateful to be sitting in a bathroom in New York, eating cold cuts and drinking American beer. They've undoubtedly seen worse times along the way. ◆

Michael Bradley photographed by John Leland

They were blindingly good live, great tunes precision-played at lightning speed. Their records stayed wonderful even as they moved in calmer stylistic directions. I loved getting mailings from the Rocking Humdingers fan club under the direction of their manager, who I got on with quite well. After Feargal left to launch a solo career, Damian and John formed That Petrol Emotion, another solid rock outfit with a more pronounced Gaelic (and political) orientation.

I've seen the Undertones a couple of times since they reformed with a new singer — a little different, but not so much as to be any less enjoyable. And their songs will never lose their charm.

I heartily recommend Mickey Bradley's highly entertaining memoir, *Teenage Kicks: My Life as an Undertone*. He and I got to spend some time together in New York the last time the 'tones (all the originals except for Feargal, and no less of a super-fun band!) came through. Now the host of a weekly music show on Irish radio and a solid family man, he's still the same gobby cutup onstage that he was as a giddy teenager.

Objection Lessons

A lot of rock critics have used contrariness to establish themselves — bucking consensus, championing rubbish or attacking sacred cows in order to get noticed as someone with a unique perspective. Chuck Eddy did it, Chuck Klosterman did it; I suppose the late Chuck Young did a bit of it as well. (Three Chucks? Weird!) The most recent online wielder of that particular axe is onetime *TP* columnist (and dear friend) Tim Sommer, who really gets a kick out of winding people up with indefensible positions he enthusiastically defends.

I always wonder how sincere those broadsides are; a critic can and should argue any firmly held belief, no matter how unique, but I would hate to think of critical grenades being lobbed as a careerist ploy. As a card-carrying curmudgeon, I've argued plenty of unpopular positions, so maybe I'm the wrong person to point that particular finger. But, in my defense, at least I've largely refrained from voicing my objections to Bruce Springsteen and the Grateful Dead in print.

No such self-restraint impeded me in the fall of 1977 when I felt a strong sense of disappointment and naïve disillusion that new wave (which, at the time, meant *all* of it, not just skinny ties and synthesizers, but punk and incipient indie in all of its myriad forms) was going down the same commercial path rock had always done; it's hard to remember if I could even conceive of an alternative. In the throes of d.i.y. magazine publishing, however, I felt self-righteous about the purity of not selling out and proud of the alternate music industry sprouting all around my little world. (This was probably in some ways an echo of my experience with radical politics in the previous decade. Movements and rock music make uneasy bedfellows.) The tipping point for me might well have been the "punk fashion" display I spotted in the window of Macy's. Burning with righteous indignation, I wrote a screed that served as the magazine's October cover story.

The Sex Pistols released *Never Mind the Bollocks* that month; the first Clash album had been out in the UK for half a year but had yet to receive an American release. There were two Ramones LPs in the shops; two by the Stranglers, one by Blondie, one by the Damned, one by Elvis Costello and one by Talking Heads. Generation X, Wire, X-Ray Spex and the Adverts had all released great singles but nothing more. The Damned had been the first to traverse the ocean and play at CBGB; none of their British peers had yet made the trip.

So, what was I doing decrying a movement in an issue that also contained enthusiastic features on two of its heroes: the Pistols and Stranglers? (No answer needed, that's rhetorical.)

I loved the cover image, a beautiful Robert Burger spray-painting of Johnny Rotten copied from a photo in which he affected a crucifixion pose. I got Rob to add a black armband and a T-shirt that read "NEW WAVE R.I.P."

This was certainly the most precarious limb I've ever climbed out on, editorially speaking. It rambles, goes on too long, has stretches of incoherence and rides a very high horse. I'm not sure how much sense it made or makes, but I'm glad it got written. (I've deleted a few words and one extraneous sentence I don't understand.)

After zipping up the body bag, of course, we continued to write about those bands for another five years — but maybe my point was never to bury the king, just to bitch about the fancy clothes he was wearing while claiming to be naked. Judge for yourself.

As a preface to the article that follows it, I am reproducing a letter from Chiswick Records founder Ted Carroll because it supports a pet contention of mine: that "new wave" was what the British media initially (this is mid-1977!) called the musical movement now thought of as "punk," and that the American use of "new wave" to mean skinny ties and bands with colorful MTV videos was a belated perversion of the term — which never would have applied to Chiswick acts like the Radiators From Space, Motörhead or the evil Skrewdriver, a ramalama band that morphed into avowed neo-Nazi propagandists.

3 Kentish Town Road London NWI

267·2474

Ira Robbins,
Editor,
Trouser Press,
147 West 42nd Street,
New York,
NY 10036.

13th July 1977

Dear Ira,

Thanks for your letter dated May 25th. As you can imagine from the delay in replying, things are muchos busy here. I am enclosing one copy each of our most recent singles from (S.9.) RADIO STARS up to the current release (S.15.) "No-One" by the legendary JOHNNY MOPED. I am also enclosing under separate cover additional copies of these records including 12" copies of the MOTORHEAD single and also a couple of extra COUNT BISHOPS albums. Also enclosed are a few biogs and we are enclosing other biogs and promotional material with the other records under separate cover.

Also will write you a more lengthy letter on the London New Wave scene as soon as I get a spare moment. We are as excited as I am sure you are by what is happening here at the moment. Lots of energy and new groups cropping up every day.

Are Jim or Dave or any of your other writers coming to London this year? I would love for you to do something on RADIO STARS who I think are going to be ginormous. We have an EP coming out in three weeks time from them and also an album at the end of September. Also in the pipeline are albums from SKREWDRIVER, RADIATORS FROM SPACE and MOTORHEAD. We are very excited about the RADIATORS and SKREWDRIVER albums which we feel will establish both these groups as strong contenders in the new wave immortality stakes.

Will write some more soon. Thanks for your letter.

Yours sincerely,

Ted Carroll

The New Wave Washes Out

Trouser Press 22, October 1977

It may come as a bit of a shock, especially if you were just getting used to the idea, but Britain's new wave movement is over. Fini. Kaput. Although it has unalterably changed the course of rock music, the movement that was created in the British rock press has died partly through the sensationalist coverage given it in the regular journals of our day. Because of a variety of internal contradictions and external oppositions, this unique and wondrous era has ended.

Lest anyone jump to the incorrect conclusion that 287 bands have simultaneously bit the dust, it is not the music that has stopped but merely the driving creative force that brought bands such as the Pistols, Clash, Damned, Jam, Vibrators, Eater et al. into a position of national note: something they might never have achieved on their disconnected own. New wave will continue to be used as a banner, both to label diverging musics and to reject, exploit and defuse some; but articles now appearing purporting to be about the new wave are merely reporting the vestiges of a dinosaur that has not had the good sense to freeze. By the time the U.S. press and radio picks up on the British bands, there will be so little left to say about the movement that they will wonder why they are giving it coverage. There ain't nothing there anymore.

From here on in the bands are on their own. No amount of brave talk or camaraderie will coalesce the same emotions that brought these groups into existence. Along with the independent record labels and the new wave fanzines, they will have to make their way on the basis of individual talent and/or creativity. It won't do any longer to write songs about boredom and anarchy; if you've got nothing unique to present, you're just an artifact, a relic who didn't hear that the bandwagon has run out of gas. Crapshit bands, ones who "made it" solely through the sufferance of the times (anonymity in the crowd), will fade and die as quickly as they appeared, leaving naught but a few disposable records to prove their moment of glory. So long; don't call us...

On the other hand, the truly meaningful talents that have shot into stardom courtesy of the press-fed new wave publicity have a few months to beat the clock and prove themselves to have some lasting merit-more than just their initial inspiration — to carry themselves for a few years. Like the Merseybeat movement, it wasn't until six months after the initial explosion that you could tell the bands who had it from those who just sounded like everybody else and couldn't progress off their lily pad.

As in the Merseybeat boom, there are several historical eras against which the new wave can be weighed. Twenty years ago, the entire birth of rock'n'roll from the embers of R&B, country and blues was the biggest and baddest of the lot, changing the entire world of music overnight. Pioneers who opened the doors to a load of rockers who had been denied a chance put it on the line; the smart ones survived, the turkeys didn't. Since the '50s, there have been several revolutionary periods in rock: San Francisco in 1966-67, London and Liverpool in 1963-64, glitter-rock in

1972, and the accompanying art-school movement beginning that same year. While each of these major shifts have had long-lasting and far-reaching effects, the 1976-77 new wave has been the first instance where the social and cultural conditions have changed the music. In all the other cases, the music has been affected by forces within itself, new talents emerging and leading a new path. In the new wave the change was based on the objective social conditions facing British kids: out of work, full of teenage frustration and fed up with the stiff-lipped British acceptance of their fate. When your culture abandons you, create a new one. And that's just what they did.

The result of this grass roots movement has been the complete revitalization of the entire British music scene, and a major impact in other countries. A year ago, the British music papers were desperate for things to write about, so uneventful was the general atmosphere. Now, if a new Stones album comes out it may be a few issues before they can find space to mention it, so full of new wave news are they. Obviously, this is largely uncalled-for gossip about bands that have captured media/public (it doesn't matter which) attention and have become sensationalist fodder that sells papers. When someone pointed out recently that nothing was happening in the UK except for the new wave it was necessary to mention that the papers don't cover anything else, which doesn't rule out the chance that other, less eye-catching events are taking place. They merely aren't being covered.

Signs of this revitalization more trustworthy than press linage are the surge of new bands (some first-rate) and the popularity they have attained. Some of the records that have been created are classic, and they might never have emerged had there not been the vacuum waiting to be filled. New bands are breaking rules that were in effect for the entire history of rock, bringing minimalism to music in a way that has been hinted at for years but was never successfully achieved. The influx of energy and inquiry makes the new wave the most-needed change in rock music this decade. Though many people have rejected it out of hand, they will not avoid its influence in later work done by more mainstream bands.

So, what's wrong? When the reports began to suggest early this year that the new wave was growing into something much more important than just an ersatz New York type scene (i.e., lots of bands not making it), some basic problems became apparent. The development of a cohesive movement put a time limit on bands who had become too successful to continue to claim the political integrity of being just like their audience — kids on the dole with no future. While the ordinary rock fan was no better off than he had been (unless the identity of a new culture is a good substitute for a paying job), the bands had gained a job, a life and a future. Unlike the culty American bands of radical persuasion (the MC5 make a good f'rinstance), the British bands could not stay unsuccessful enough to remain honest to their fans. With all the press and public interest in the Pistols and their kind, groups were meeting with more sales and fame than many established first-tier bands (the week the Stranglers' album was number-four, Pink Floyd was number-five). Unassuming young punks were becoming media superstars, whether they cared to be or not. In the eyes of their original fans, no amount of fancy backtalk could prove that they weren't becoming just like the alienated groups against whom they were supposed to be rebelling.

In some cases, fame and fortune were the unconsidered result of an honestly pure artistic desire to state their feelings musically. Maybe. However, few bands have made a serious attempt to stem the tide. Even the Pistols, with their knack for getting thrown off labels, have earned as much in a year of near inactivity as a successful band does in a prosperous year. There's certainly no reason for them not to make money, but it's not a very revolutionary thing to do. After all, where do EMI's pounds come from? If you aren't totally blind to the fact that rock'n'roll is and always has been primarily a business that just happens to proffer a culture we all hold near and dear, then there is nothing at all wrong with new wave bands making money in the normal sell-records-sell-tickets fashion. As long as punters are willing to plunk down their money, the unavoidable chain of grey suits with their contracts and open palms will be there to collect their share. Them's the breaks. It doesn't change the music. Usually.

The real hypocrisy arises when bands refuse to admit they are charter subscribers to the great R&R dream — the Big Time. Maybe they see it a bit differently than those who preceded them, but there aren't any new wave bands who have convincingly showed their opposition to the notion of fame and fortune — their distaste for the trappings, perhaps, but not the idea. Whether they say it or not, every punk band in England and America is just as fascinated by the Eric Carmen theory of Hit Record-dom as Peter Frampton is. I'm not knocking rock'n'roll success, but musical careers built on nihilism and anti-superstardom seem a bit wobbly when the groups begin to accept the star's life. Why walk when you can ride? Just because Joe Strummer of the Clash was arrested for spray-painting a slogan on a wall doesn't change the fact that he got off with a fine. A kid off the street probably wouldn't have. It's just one of those incontrovertible facts of life; when you become famous, your life changes.

There have been some telling remarks in the press recently. Johnny Rotten on the subject of unprovoked attacks on his person by reactionary thugs: "I don't want the star trip. All those silly twats trying to kick me off the street — they don't realize what they're doing. They're just turning me into another superstar." If it were only that simple.

Let's talk about co-option. Every movement has to be co-opted to be destroyed; I think Lenny Kaye said that. In the past few months, the new wave has been the subject of almost every possible form of exploitation: films, best-of albums, foreign tours, press junkets — the works. There's nothing left to be taken. For the bands there's no turning back. Once you've done the major halls there are no club gigs for you, no future if you can't meet expenses. The new wave bands aren't gonna give their money away to charity; nihilism is not an altruistic affair.

If the two basic principles of the new wave are (a) total opposition to everything dull, boring and stagnant and (b) a refusal to take anything seriously, a few troubles arise. Bands like the Damned have put a lot of effort into remaining ridiculous, but there's just so far it can go. When interviewed for the absurdist NBC-TV report on the new wave, Rat Scabies of the Damned proudly declared he'd like nothing better than to make a million dollars. If he intends to pursue that goal, the Damned will find themselves becoming serious before long. (In passing, while we're on the subject of silliness, a song titled "I'm Bored" appears on the first Bonzo Dog Band album, recorded in 1967. Viv Stanshall as proto-punk?)

Along with the induction of new wave bands into the rock hierarchy comes the inevitable onset of dry rot; no band can stay fresh forever. The idea of permanent change (essentially a political theory, but then many features of the new wave are Maoist) leads each new band that comes along to reject everything preceding. Now that the Pistols are stars, they get lumped in (from the newcomer's point of view) with all the star bands, such as the Stones. The difference between 30,000 and three million pounds a year seems inconsequential compared to 30 a week. (As long as the Stones have come up, remember that they were the original rebellious bad boys of rock, peeing on gas stations and such. It certainly didn't kill them to trade street-fighting for jet setting, but they were also able to change their public outlook.)

Like Keith with his drug problems, the Pistols and other new wave bands have no chance of being inducted into the good guy hall of fame. They are working hard at being rude and obnoxious, gaining legions by their outrage. That's nothing new, but the foolish English authorities are so paranoid that they are terrified of these paper punks and have taken unreal steps to ban live performances and hound the groups legally wherever they venture. This is the confusing factor: the new wave exists only as long as its enemies believe that it exists. A very shaky foundation.

For all its fatality, the new wave has served a few long-range functions. (I still can't believe the new wave fashion show in Macy's window.) Providing the opportunity for a veritable monsoon of young bands (some talented) to make their way from the clubs to the jukeboxes in a matter of months, not years, is the sort of situation that should always exist. Instead of farty old record execs signing three new bands a year, always choosing the ones that sound like whatever's currently popular (that of course being the reason for the worldwide magnanimity toward punk bands), both adventurous establishment record people and newly founded labels (designed to meet the needs of an industry expanding creatively much faster than normal outlets were prepared to comprehend) have made the break and taken some very long shots, some of which have turned into gold mines. Elvis Costello and Joe Strummer would've remained frustrated hackers, playing cheap gigs to 10 people had open-mindedness not suddenly entered a business not known for its interest in talent. Where would the Stranglers be without the publicity of Hugh Cornwell wearing a (ooh-isn't-it-'orrible) T-shirt with one four-letter word printed on it to a concert one night. That sort of nonsense was gobbled up furiously by the sensationalist British press, making national villains out of a rock band. It's happened before, it'll happen again.

The other wonderful thing the new wave accomplished was the return of marketing techniques that actually add something. In this, the decade of the salesman, where a hit record is a scientific process only scarcely involved with music, the idea of putting a record out in blue plastic, or with a nice picture sleeve — just the idea of making singles an important item, not a trailer of coming attractions for an LP — is worth celebrating. Granted, singles are harder to store, but a lovingly produced single by a talented three-minute artist is worth lots more than a drecky album by a tasteless schnook whom the research department deems of star quality. Thank you Stiff, Chiswick and Island for leading the way and for CBS Polydor and Virgin for following. Special mention to EMI for never quite catching on.

Getting back to my original point, new wave has ended. From here on in everything that arises will be an imitation. There can be only one set of leaders per movement and this one's have already risen to the surface. Sorry, all the good jobs have been taken; come back and file an application when the next movement begins. Or begin it yourself. The style has been set, and now it's the duty of those who pioneered it to give it up. If they have the creativity and the good sense they will refuse to become the stagnant heads of a dying movement. It's all been done; the new wave has run its course. From stinky little clubs where unknown bands all sounded alike, to the scramble for the free ride provided courtesy of the media over-blitz, the new wave has been transformed from a fresh revolution to a stale mockery. Before it all. gets totally sour — Johnny Rotten posters, etc. — the top groups should make the suicidal move and jack it in (wake up, you're only dreaming). Even the camaraderie that tied the young bands together has broken down to bitter disputes over bookings, contracts and egos.

As the groups have begun to feel their own power, they are learning how to wield it — at promoters, at record companies, at the press. It's just a matter of time before they begin staving off enthusiastic fans with burly gorillas in concert aisles. But then that's the way it's always been, hasn't it? ◆

The Dean Speaks

In January 1979, Robert Christgau's annual *Pazz & Jop* essay in the *Village Voice* was titled *New Wave Hegemony and the Bebop Question*. I rather liked being a member of an Anglophiliac cabal, but it did sound a bit like eye of newt might be involved, when all we were doing was marveling at boxloads of brilliant music. (The line about Edmunds that is obscured by the crease is "as Brit-purist as r&r gets." I'm not sure how Devo got into that sentence.) In any case, this gentle dig was received with a lot more good humor than his inflammatory 1983 reference to *Trouser Press* as "a journal white supremacist enough to make *Rolling Stone* look like a hotbed of affirmative action."

so happens that there are a lot of orthodox new wavers toward the end of the alphabet, including three of *Trouser Press*'s Anglophiliac cabal, and suddenly artists like Dave Edmunds (as Brit-purist as r&r gets), Devo (whose marginal early showing had encouraged us to hope they wouldn't place at all), and Generation X (accomplished but by no means original—or principled—power-pop punks) were vaulting upwards. This was turning into new wave hegemony, and I don't like hegemony of any sort. Not even the sudden success of my own favorite record of the year, Wire's *Pink Flag*, warmed my heart.

Five Years

This stock-taking interview was done in recognition of our fifth anniversary by the estimable David McGee, then on the staff of the number-two music business trade magazine, *Record World*, and subsequently the founding editor of *The Record*.

Record World, February 1979

Since issue number one in March 1974, *Trouser Press* has been a constant source of lively, prescient and historically accurate rock journalism. Unlike many fanzines, which it nominally is, *Trouser Press* is distinguished by solid writing as well as by iconoclastic viewpoints; at the same time, its evolution from a two-color publication on newsprint (circulation: 250) to four-colors on slick paper (circulation: 40,000) has made it as visually appealing as any of the renowned establishment music magazines. Such professionalism accounts in part for *TP*'s longevity; for while the number of fanzines to have sprung up over the years is great, the number to have survived long enough to celebrate a fifth anniversary is infinitely small.

In the following *Dialogue*, Ira Robbins, who along with Dave Schulps and Karen Rose founded *TP*, discusses the publication's growth, its prospects for the future and its special place in rock journalism.

What's unique about Trouser Press? How has it survived for five years?
It's survived for five years out of sheer inexhaustibility. It's outlasted everything that could stop it: lack of money, lack of time, lack of people. What's unique about it has changed over the years. When it began, we felt sort of a professional attitude about musical fandom. We wanted to be literate, and we wanted to be informative, but we also wanted to be very emotionally involved. We felt that the commercial magazines that existed at the time were sometimes factual, rarely historical and rarely emotional. So they weren't of any use to us. The fanzines that existed were emotional but badly done; they suffered from a lack of literacy. Historical facts very badly presented and badly laid out. We tried from the beginning to be as visually effective as possible and to be as professional as we could. We tried to come out on time, we tried to be businesslike about what we did.

During the magazine's first year, we sat down one day and decided that all the news we were writing about was pretty much English and that there wasn't anything coming out of America that was interesting. Back in '74, if you were a rock or pop fan, there really wasn't anything in America. All the bands that are superstar bands now were just starting out in England in '74: 10cc was doing its first tour, ELO had just spun off the remains of the Move, Rod Stewart and the Faces were a large band but not cosmically superstars. We felt that the only good music was coming out of England, so we aimed ourselves specifically at English rock music and maintained exclusivity up until about our 20-something issue. Exclusivity to the point where a band had to be English to be in the magazine or had to be relevant to English music — the Raspberries for example, or Todd Rundgren. And we developed from there. That's the bulk of the magazine's history up until a year and a half ago: strictly English and very adamant about it. Our slogan was "America's Only British Rock Magazine." [*That was a borrowing from* Creem, *of course*.] Nobody understood but everyone got the meaning.

How is the magazine considered in the music industry itself? Has its longevity increased its credibility?
It's added to our credibility, and in some ways detracted from our ability. A lot of people in the business take us for granted. We're in that funny nether world: we're not big enough to push record companies around, nor are we small enough to sort of sneak in the back door. We can no longer go up to people backstage at gigs and say, 'Can I ask you ten questions?' which we might have done a few years ago. Now it's important for us to play the full-scale game. We have to go along with this kind of thing because that's the way it's done, and if we're going to do a feature that's credible and isn't going to look like everybody else's feature, we've either got to do it a month before everyone else does it or six months after or something like that.

In the industry, we're treated differently by different people. I think we're largely respected, probably much more than our circulation warrants. I have a feeling [that] publicists come after us sometimes harder than they might go after another magazine with comparable circulation. We are still discriminated against because of our size. We've been told "*Time, Newsweek, Rolling Stone* and the trades are doing this interview and you're not." And it might be someone we've really put up a lot of time and effort to do. Surely not everyone in this business understands the magazine. There are maybe half a dozen people who have really been with us from the very beginning, who from the minute they figured out what we were about supported us, and that means getting advertising, getting interviews, answering the phone when we called. There are still people in the industry who think we're no more important than the *Waukegan Express*.

How important do you think Trouser Press is in the whole scheme of things?
There's no empirical data to judge whether or not we make bands happen. There's circumstantial evidence to indicate that we help bands along. That doesn't prove anything. We've done reader surveys and found that our readers buy a lot of records. We've also asked our readers if they would buy a record because they read a review of it in *Trouser Press*. We got a very high response to that question. Something like 30 or 40 percent of our readers said they had bought records more than once because of a review in our magazine. So, if you're talking about 40,000 people who buy six albums a month, 20 or 30% of whom listen to *Trouser Press* before they go buy records, then maybe a couple of hundred thousand record sales a year are in some way influenced by *Trouser Press*.

Who reads Trouser Press? From your surveys have you gathered a typical reader profile?
We've found that our readers are generally older than most other rock magazine readers, 22, 23, the others being 18 to 20 from what I've read of other magazines' surveys. Fairly literate: most of our readers are college-educated. Our median age is 22, but we have readers up to the late 30s. I think they find this magazine more to their taste than the more youth-oriented magazines. We don't bend over backwards to make ourselves attractive to 12-year-olds. We would love it if 12-year-olds read the magazine, because I think we have as much to say to them as anybody. I don't doubt the intelligence of 12-year-olds to be able to read and understand this magazine. I speak of 12 as a figurative age. I mean people in high school, up to high school age. There's certainly nothing in *Trouser Press* that they can't understand if they want to read it. The rock business tends to look down on kids, tends to package things so simply that they can't be missed. And certainly, the most successful bands of the past few years have been bands that have appealed to very young audiences. They don't sell Eno dolls, you know. But our readers are basically very intelligent, and we try to be there for them without alienating people who might not be as literate.

Obviously Trouser Press in its fifth year is qualitatively different from TP number one. What specific changes have been made over the years to make the publication more attractive to readers and to advertisers?
We approach problems one at a time. For instance, if Time-Life puts up five or six million dollars to start a new magazine, everything is basically sorted out beforehand. We've gone through six-month periods of deciding that the magazine doesn't look good enough and working very hard to improve its appearance. Then we might go through a period where we feel distribution needs work. We have a small staff; we don't have department heads that can take care of everything. The full-time staff of the magazine is currently five; at times it has been three.

The first three years of the magazine there were no paid employees; it was a hobby, after-hours, meet at my apartment on Saturday and edit the magazine. Which is about the hardest way of doing anything. At one point we decided it was important for us to stop being a bi-monthly and become a monthly. We finally went monthly in September of '77, and I can distinctly remember planning that move at a meeting in '77. The problem we faced then was in trying to support ourselves, being out of college and all that. As a bi-monthly the magazine didn't turn over enough money to afford salaries or rent or anything else. As a monthly we could double the amount of income, we could amortize wages and so forth. We spent some six months planning to go monthly, which meant redesigning the magazine, because we wanted to make a big splash. We redesigned the logo; we changed the kind of paper we were using; we started running four-color covers. That was a major jump for us. That was the move we feel put us on the map. Before that we had two-color covers on sort of cheesy paper, and as much as we might like the magazine, we realized there was a quantum difference between us and the other rock magazines. Now I think we've built ourselves to the point where, without being particularly obnoxious about it, the difference between us and the other rock magazines is not that huge. It's a bridgeable chasm where before it wasn't.

We've also gone through periods where we decided the editorial content of the magazine wasn't up to snuff. At one point we realized we were running ourselves into the ground by covering bands that had no commercial potential. Potential isn't the right word. No commercial perception. People weren't buying enough of their records to make them want to buy a lot of magazines. We decided we didn't want to be a cult magazine anymore; it was important for us to branch out and be more adaptable and more generally interesting, without sacrificing what makes the magazine special.

Over the past year and a half we phased out the British exclusivity. We didn't sit down and say we didn't want to be British anymore; we just realized that the number of bands we could write about that could also sell records had become fairly small. The bands that we started writing about when we began had become so successful that we had dropped them. The nature of the magazine has always been anti-superstar. We figure magazines like *Circus* and *Creem* can write about superstars. They don't need us. And when you're talking about people like Rod Stewart, Elton John, Mick Jagger or someone like that there's really not that much you can say about them that hasn't already been said. We've always felt a strong sensitivity toward not repeating what everyone else has said.

We don't feel we exist to churn out commercial product. We exist because we have something left to say about music, we have some sort of critical evaluation that's worth putting over. What we did decide is that the bands that weren't superstars or weren't on the up and coming didn't exist; there's no middle ground anymore. And we found that there were more bands in America that we wanted to write about than there ever were before. Bands like Cheap Trick, Cars, even Boston, which we haven't written about, but which shows, if not progress commercially, a return to the kind of music we've been writing about all along. If we could drop our superficial decision about what we were going to write about and then evaluate the type of music that's being made, we could find a lot more in America worth writing about. And we did.

While you've made all these changes, you've also maintained a recognizable fanzine editorial approach. That is, one can still find in TP lengthy, investigative accounts of artists' careers. As you've sought to expand your appeal, have you ever questioned the validity of this type of reporting, particularly in a period when the trend seems to be toward the quick read?

Certainly there are articles we did in the first year or two of the magazine that we haven't done since, real detailed, note-by-note, album-by-album histories. We think we've outgrown that; we think our readers have outgrown that too. There's a point in fanzine type of writing where you're basically turning out biographies of groups. I don't remember exactly when, but we decided we couldn't keep doing that and keep the magazine interesting. We didn't want to be a dry, technical journal for rock intellectuals. We tried to juice up the quality of the magazine, so we introduced short features.

The front of the book is made up of one-page articles on bands that we don't feel for one reason or another at this point deserve a whole feature. Might be a group we've just done a feature on six months ago, or it might be an event, or something like that. But we will do fairly huge articles, like the recent John Lennon cover story. We gave up [on] getting an interview with Lennon. The guy just doesn't do interviews, he can't be found, no one works for him, he doesn't have a record company. But we felt it was important to write an article on John Lennon at this stage just because no one else has.

That's a large part of our credo: doing things other people haven't done or won't do. The thing we have going for us now is — well, the English word for it is "suss," you know, being able to figure out what needs doing. We try not to be simply responsive to record companies calling us up and saying, 'We've got so-and-so in town for an interview.' We don't like to do that.

Are your editorial decisions ever based on who's hot on the charts or what's in vogue at the moment?
No. We're sensitive to it, and I'd be lying if I said we decided to not do an article on someone because they were hot at the moment. The difference between us and the other magazines in that regard is that we tend to sense who's going to be hot because they're good. Or who's going to be interesting because they're good. And we'll go out on a limb on the basis of very little information. For instance, we did a cover story on Elvis Costello that came out exactly the same week as American CBS put out the first Elvis Costello album. There's no magic there: Elvis had been very successful in England, and the buzz on Elvis in the British papers had been building to a fever pitch by the time the album was finally released here, which was almost six months after the album came out in England. So, there was no mystery. We didn't expect Elvis to be very successful here. We would like to have believed he would be, but there was no reason to think he'd be any more successful than a hundred other really talented British bands that had had albums released here and had quietly disappeared.

We don't take credit for making anyone a star, but I think we've established ourselves as a trend indicator. People look to us to see what we have to say about things because we've earned the right by having been correct a bunch of times and by also knowing who's interesting. People may disagree with us in terms of what we think is going to succeed, but they rarely disagree with us critically. We've managed, amazingly enough, the people who run the magazine, to stay fans. We still get excited about bands. It may have a lot to do with why the magazine maintained its quality, its personality. We haven't given up. There are people who put out magazines who couldn't possibly care less about what goes on in rock and roll, and one band to the next it's no different: it's just all music or all commercial product. We're still very opinionated: there are bands we love and bands we hate. This magazine still hates bands; there are bands we don't write about because we just don't like them. There are bands we've avoided up to now doing articles on and can't perceive in the near future doing articles on, solely on musical content.

We have our standards. We've loosened our reins in the last two years; we've let bands go through that we previously would have never touched. But we decided we had to broaden our base in terms of the kinds of bands we were writing about. We found ways to write about bands that we previously didn't expect to write about. But we had to get over our own prejudices to a degree and try out things that we wouldn't normally have done. ◆

Marc Bolan

Like I said in the *Record World* interview, *Trouser Press* often ran articles without artist interviews. With our early historical bent, pieces could be based on research, not contact. When we got more interested in the present, we did grab opportunities to speak with artists whose work we admired, but we never considered their participation a prerequisite for decisions about coverage. We wouldn't have anyone dictating to us what we could write about or when. Other publications may have felt (and still feel) it essential to offer quotes as evidence of access or insightful value, but that was never our view. We also became wary of letting Q&A transcripts substitute for actual writing. There's no great achievement in hiding behind quotation marks, letting them serve as a signifier of artist contact and relieving the writer of having to provide thoughtful commentary or useful information. Sometimes, sure.

Writers have jumped through flaming rings of shit trying to bring home the transcribable bacon editors demand, but it's not always worth the bother. A lot of stars have nothing to say. That shouldn't stop you from writing about them. I nearly wept at the scene in *Almost Famous* where the Cameron Crowe character knocks miserably on his subject's hotel room door for the umpteenth time, pleading for the sitdown on which he imagines his career hinges; something like that has happened to all of us. *Rolling Stone*'s 1995 Weezer profile included a depiction of writer Mim Udovitch's futile effort to interview Rivers Cuomo; lack of access couldn't stop her from producing a great article.

At 5,750 words, this may have been the longest piece I ever wrote for the magazine; with all the second-hand sources, borrowed quotes and tick-tock structure, it reads like liner notes. In 1991, I got to apply some of the same enthusiasm to annotate an American T. Rex collection. I began that essay like this:

> Marc Bolan — the showman ego of Little Richard reborn as a working-class Cockney Jew — had already been a psychedelic rocker in John's Children and was a mystical elf singing wispy acoustic poesy to English hippies when he decided, in 1970, to steer Tyrannosaurus Rex into the all-electric present. As Britain's most rabidly worshipped pop band since the Beatles, T. Rex ushered in the maniacal era of glam-rock, making a profound contribution to the 1970s' musical sensibility.
>
> Bolan was a pop star through and through. This charismatic charmer given to outrageous boasts was an ingenious songwriter with an unmistakable voice and sonic signature. The creator of a nonsense universe that meant the world to millions, he could build endlessly memorable songs on the simplest of ideas, giving familiar styles a unique personal twist. But he wasn't above releasing inferior records and staging atrocious live performances, or self-abusing himself into overweight oblivion. The utter embodiment of rock'n'roll's flash and trash, Bolan was both a cardboard cutout and an important innovator, an intuitive innocent and a glitzy cynic.

A Wizard, a True Star: Marc Bolan's brief blaze of glory

Trouser Press, May 1980

If anyone in the annals of rock'n'roll has ever fully deserved to be called a "pop star," Marc Bolan certainly tops the list of candidates. A fully self-propelled invention, Bolan was neither a great musician nor a visionary rock prophet, yet he achieved a level of almost inconceivable fame and reopened the door for many of the more extreme rock idols of the '70s. He created a style that was widely imitated and must be given a lot of credit for the resurgence of singles bands in England and around the world.

Unlike some of the other superstars of his prime era — Bowie, Elton John, Gary Glitter, Suzi Quatro — Bolan blended a strong and single-minded sense of direction with an uncanny ability to sound dignified while delivering mostly insipid and simplistic lyrics. (The MB Award for same goes, a few years later, to Jonathan Richman, the manchild of Massachusetts.) Someone once observed that Marc wrote lyrics on the back of used matchbooks in the elevator riding up to a recording session, and another listen to some of those dusty 45s does little to contradict that notion. Yet Bolan (and millions of his fans) found something significant and comprehensible in T. Rex songs, and many lives were touched by them. One thing is clear from a reexamination of the T. Rex catalogue: Bolan may have written seemingly simple songs, but he was no dunce.

Marc Bolan's career can be divided roughly into three phases — the ultra-mod youth who found no difference between modeling clothes and playing music; the adorable pixie poet/hippie musician; and the boogie boy chart king who ruled a nation. The final stage — Bolan's decline into middle age before his recovery and fatal car crash at the age of 29 — is represented poorly by recordings from those years and seems, in retrospect, superfluous to the accomplishments of his heyday.

Before he died in 1977, Bolan, whose stature had been sorely diminished for a few years, was attempting to return from has-beendom with a revised self-appraisal of both his music and his importance. With the knowledge that he could scarcely expect to be appreciated for rehashing old riffs, he made a record, his last, that stood on its own and allowed his death to be — although tragic — a dignified finish to his legend. It is fitting that he should be remembered for his achievements, not for the sad patches in between.

It is almost impossible to describe just how big the band was throughout the non-American world between 1971 and 1974: comparisons to Beatlemania were common in the British press (rock and otherwise), and the idolized Bolan lived in forced isolation because of the legions of fans that followed his every move. At one point, as a result of a lawsuit in which he was involved, a national British newspaper published Bolan's address (an apartment in London's Little Venice), forcing him to abandon his flat and relocate permanently within hours of the paper hitting the streets. The mob scene that surrounded his home made it impossible to even throw out the trash, and someone had to carry it downstairs for his nibs, where it was investigated thoroughly by the faithful.

At the time of T. Rex's supreme reign, there were a trio of British chart factions controlling the leftovers: glitter bands (largely inspired by Bolan's sense of campy glamour) such as Slade, Chicory Tip and Gary Glitter; the younger and less rock-oriented teenybop (and weenybop!) outfits like the Osmonds, Dawn, Gilbert O'Sullivan and David Cassidy; and the slumming high-talents who could establish themselves through 45s and go on to make adult LPs (Roxy Music, David Bowie, and, to an extent, Roy Wood). Not too much of this phenomenon arrived intact on American shores, although the homegrown non-rockers found it easiest to export themselves onto the charts here. Few of the more outrageous acts made any real headway here (some not until a few years later, if at all), but no one took as frustrating a fall as Marc Bolan, who fully expected to recreate his preeminence in the record world on this side of the Atlantic. While the group had some legitimate hit records here, Bolan was never able to capture enough hearts and minds of American youth to build a base from which to dominate.

Young British record buyers have historically had more tolerance for (and interest in) new trends and fads in music, and they embraced Marc Bolan without hesitation, with all his odd visual styles and self-absorbed literary pretensions, as both a heavyweight rocker and as a delicate acoustic nymph, spinning tales of arcane fantasy. In America, on the other hand, the confusion was too... confusing. While the kiddie fan magazines ran pieces under headlines such as "Marc Bolan Sings for You and Answers 40 Funky Questions" (f'rinstance, "What three tips would you give a girl who wanted you to like her?"), the more "serious" rock press treated us to quite the opposite: "I'm too raunchy — they (the fan mags) can't use me in that way. I'm not going to sit down and do those pictures." Not only was the audience confused — did they expect twee folk diddling or heavy metal guitar boogie? — so was Bolan. In various interviews done on several tours, the Metal Guru struck out in a number of different directions, showing an overall plan to conquer America that changed by the minute. Each ploy that failed was replaced by a more desperate one — on his last tour here he took to whipping his guitar on stage. ("I don't think anyone's ever whipped a guitar on stage before," he told Lillian Roxon in 1973.) Does that sound like a musician confident of his own abilities?

T. Rex's records sat right in the middle of the British glam scene — a little too heavy for children (not that it stopped millions from buying and loving them) and a bit on the silly side for serious aesthetes. After establishing themselves through hit singles, other bands either disappeared or tilted off in more satisfying (and credible) directions; T. Rex was the only major band to stick to its guns and stay in the charts. For a while, the Top 10 in the UK was populated by the worst novelty junk and MOR mush, so Bolan's ongoing success through the slush years only further proved the popularity and endurance of his music. The magic was certainly there.

In the beginning, there was 13-year-old Mark Feld, spotted by a photographer on assignment for *About Town* magazine looking for sharp mods to use in a fashion layout. A fop of the top caliber, Feld became a famous face, and his photogenic puss was well on its way to immortality via every printing press in Great Britain. A youngster confident of his future fame, Feld spent his teenage years doing interesting things like living in Paris with a wizard, playing in a duo with Cat Stevens and procuring a recording contract at the ripe age of 18. Decca, home of the Stones in England, released his first disc, "The Wizard" b/w "Beyond the Rising Sun," under the name of Marc Bowland, which was subsequently adjusted to Bolan. He recorded a number of other tracks for Decca, but only one other single was released during the term of his contract with the company. (Years later, when T. Rex was an established act, another company bought and issued those tracks, without Bolan's consent, as an LP entitled *The Beginning of Doves*.)

Marc's producer for these early sessions was Simon Napier-Bell, whose work with the Yardbirds had made him widely known; the project occupying him in 1966 was a weird pop band called John's Children. With such future luminaries as Andy Ellison and John Hewlett (best known for his behind-the-scenes work with Sparks, Dickies and Milk 'n' Cookies), John's Children had a few hits on their own, but when they fired their guitarist in early 1967, Napier-Bell put Bolan in his place. The group had just signed to the newly-formed Track Records, and according to Bolan, "wanted a Pete Townshend type figure, a writer/guitarist/creator, and they thought I'd fit the bill." His first assignment was to create another hit for the group, which he did, a little rocker called "Desdemona," which was banned from the BBC airwaves for imagined indecency. The single sold well in Europe, and so the group was shuttled off to do a German support tour with labelmates the Who. Bolan described the song: "It took me 25 seconds to write. The story's rather complicated and difficult to explain." The shapes of things....

Before long (a few months, actually), Bolan and John's Children set off in different paths, a result of some excessive studio tampering with Marc's songs; in his words, "I could feel that I wasn't going to get the freedom I wanted personally." Leaving the safe nest under less-than-ideal circumstances, Bolan attempted to assemble a five-piece group to play psychedelia like the band Tomorrow, but some question about the ownership of the instruments arose, and the record company took away all their toys, down to the very last electric guitar.

And so, out of necessity, the acoustic duo, Marc Bolan and Steve Peregrine Took, dubbed Tyrannosaurus Rex, was born. They plied their audible wares in all of the obvious haunts in London — in subways, streets and underground clubs — rarely for money, but then this was the Summer of Love, so why worry?

In an extensive interview [published] in the book *Voxpop*, Bolan recalled the era. "I went to Joe Boyd, who was doing the Incredible String Band. I wanted him to produce us, and we did some tracks — with Danny Thompson on cello — but they weren't quite right. Apple Records was trying to cop us because we'd been playing at Middle Earth [one of London's two major underground rock clubs at that time]. We used to play there for nothing, without any amplification — just me and Steve. The word got about that something was going down, and we had about five record company offers, including Apple."

The next figure who requires introduction at this point is Tony Visconti, 20 years old at the time, earning his growing reputation as an arranger and studio wiz for the Move. (His partner, Denny Cordell, was the producer of the Move's early records, and he often used Visconti to add brass, strings and woodwinds. His work is most obvious on the first Move LP. In later years, Visconti took his musical and technical talents to work with David Bowie, Procol Harum and numerous others, including Thin Lizzy and Sparks. One might guess that his influence on Roy Wood and co. ultimately led to the classical bent that sired ELO ... but that's another article entirely.)

With Bolan and Took, Visconti got his first steady job as a producer, although there couldn't have been very much for him to do on the early sessions. In later years, his influence and skill would help guide Bolan from hit to hit — it seems clear that the mix of heavy rock with squeaky voices and smooth strings was as much his doing as Marc's. As mentor, friend and producer through 1974, Visconti deserves a lot of credit in the T. Rex saga.

The two young moguls, Visconti and Cordell, caught the two hippies in a club one night and offered them a chance to make a single. Bolan had been down that route with John's Children as well as on his own, and wasn't interested — for him, it would have to be an album or nothing at all. Visconti was sufficiently interested to arrange a deal with an EMI subsidiary, and within weeks Marc and Steve were in Advision studios recording their album, which was released in early '68. According to Marc, the record cost about $1,000 to make (take that, Knack!), but there couldn't have been many problems involved in putting acoustic guitar, bongos and vocals on tape.

Towards the end of the brief session, they recorded "Debora" for release as a single. An appealing little bit of nursery nonsense, it mainly consists of Bolan repeating the name semi-scat fashion. It had all the ingredients of Bolan's early approach, as well as clues to his later manifestation: wobbly vibrato vocals mixed with an occasional gutsy howl, spirited guitar strumming, galloping bongos and an indefinable shimmering quality. With the help of ace deejay John Peel, it made the Top 30 in Britain, and Tyrannosaurus Rex were on their way.

The album, released soon after the single, was named *My People Were Fair and Had Sky in Their Hair...But Now They're Content to Wear Stars in Their Brows*. It set the tone for a semi-mystical lyrical fixation that Bolan never abandoned. Dedicated to "Aslan and the Old Narnians" (a C.S. Lewis reference) and containing a spoken Bolan fairy tale read by Peel, the record debuts the car fixation that later pulsed through countless T. Rex numbers in ordinary acoustic tunes named "Hot Rod Mama" and "Mustang Ford." Not a very peace/love subject to write songs about, but that's the Bolan enigma in a nutshell. From mod to popstar to metal folkie without missing a beat.

What stands out most on the record is Marc's singing. One of the few truly distinctive voices in recorded music, Bolan had the control of a top-notch jazz singer and the pipes of a reedy Donovan. Starting out each line with breezy smoothness, an aggressive wobble would take hold by the end of each phrase, turning the sense from soft to tough, edging towards downright nastiness in spots. Over the years, Bolan's voice became lower, less capable of the vibrato and less flexible, replacing the fragility with a measure of surliness.

Bolan's songs at this stage suffer from a lack of definition — pop classics they weren't. In retrospect, the importance of the first two LPs (the other is *Prophets, Seers & Sages*) was in allowing Bolan to develop both his singing technique and his fantasy world pastiche of Tolkien, science fiction, mythology and nonsense. With those two weapons firmly ensconced in his bag of tricks, Bolan was fully prepared to deal out his future.

Until the partnership with Steve Took evaporated in late 1968 as a result of the latter's desire to exert a stronger musical influence, the duo had established themselves as a leading underground force around England, attracting the sort of following that musicians who sit cross-legged on stages attract. After their third album together, *Unicorn*, was released in America they came over to tour (on a bill with the Turtles, hence the later Flo & Eddie connection), but spent most of the trip falling apart and returned home separately. The first Tyrannosaurus Rex was extinct.

Where *Prophets* had stuck closely to the style and sound of the first LP, *Unicorn* showed an attempt to develop beyond the skeletal base. Steve Took had branched into instruments beyond measly bongos and actually played a drum kit in spots. Bolan, who was becoming a much better guitarist, was also growing as a singer, and came through louder and clearer than before. The songs, a bit more involved melodically, showed lyrical promise as well, with Bolan weaving languid metaphysical tales about "Chariots of Silk," "Warlord of the Royal Crocodiles," "Iscariot" and the "Sea Beast." The production, which utilized such clever studio gimmickry as backwards recording and off-speed distortion, adds to the songs; the most successful coupling being "Catblack (The Wizard's Hat)," almost a rock recording in timbre. The album also includes the second John Peel dramatic reading, dedicated to "The Three Friends of Hiawatha." (I still prefer the Bonzos' *Gorilla*, which is dedicated to "Kong, who must have been a great bloke.")

After the departure of Steve Took, Bolan, legend tells, discovered his replacement, Micky Finn, in a macrobiotic restaurant in Notting Hill. Finn, who had been in an outfit named Hapshash and the Coloured Coat, evidently impressed the auto-enthusiast elf with his monster motorcycle. Bolan hired him on the spot. Finn fit into Took's shoes perfectly, playing bongos, tabla and all the other diddly instruments so integral to the manufacture of twinky faerie music. But it didn't lead down quite the same path. Finn had been a rocker. Bolan had been a rocker. Visconti had worked with rockers. The pair's first LP together showed what Boley had been saving his shillings for: an electric guitar to replace the one so unceremoniously repossessed by Track.

The new decade brought many changes to Marc Bolan's life and career. In February, he married June Child, who also served as secretary, driver, personal manager and confidante. Around the same time, he and Micky recorded *Beard of Stars*, using electric guitars, bass and keyboards, making it a significant transitional step between acoustic and rock. The vocals — a mixture of high and low harmonies — add a distinctive touch that pervades later work. The production is smoother and more sophisticated (by this stage Visconti was earning his pay thanks to the increasing complexity of the work) and employs less tricks and more substance. The team was getting closer to the future, but they weren't there just yet.

As 1970 wore on, Bolan faced a major predicament. The band was fairly successful, but not in the way he'd always envisioned. His literary aspirations were increasing — a book of poetry published in '69 (*Warlock of Love*) sold 40,000 copies — and he arrived at a point where he contemplated chucking music in favor of writing prose. (What a mistake that would have been. Bolan's popularity as a poet had little to do with his talent in that field: without the record sales his future as an author would have been slim indeed.) "I had offers for screenplays — I was going to get into novels and science fiction — but it meant giving up six months, which I wasn't prepared to do." He decided to do one last record before making a final decision. "Ride a White Swan," recorded at Trident Studios with young engineer Roy T. Baker, solved Bolan's dilemma once and for all. Released on the newly created Fly label (a Denny Cordell undertaking) around October 1970, it was all that Marc Bolan — with a newly shortened band moniker, T. Rex — needed to insure a future as a teen idol.

"Ride a White Swan" b/w "Summertime Blues" and "Is It Love" shows no drastic change in direction, but the three cuts rank with Bolan's best, and sound as fresh and pleasurable today as they did ten years ago. With roughly the same instrumentation — electric guitar, bongos, handclaps and that voice — the attitude is the crucial difference. For a semi-terrestrial folknik, the choice to record an Eddie Cochran / Genuine Rock and Roll Classic verged on sacrilege as far as parochial fans were concerned, and Bolan knew it. The way they do the song, however, makes criticism foolish — it might as well be a Chopin étude for all the lack of rock'n'roll energy or volume. A little acoustic guitar, a lot of bongo, an amazing vocal — nothing to challenge the Who's supercharged live version of about the same time, yet the message is clear: wood nymph or not, Bolan was ready to rock out. "Is It Love" opens with a raunchy Bolan countdown and builds into a beautiful tune punctuated by some fierce lead guitar which Bolan must have pulled out of a hat. On *Beard of Stars*, Bolan had poked at his electric like a palsy victim, with no feel or energy, but in the intervening months someone must have shown him which end was up (he spent a lot of time with Eric Clapton, if that's any help), and he rocks here in the finest fuzzbox-processed tradition.

The centerpiece of this magnificent single is a simple toe-tapping 2:20 piece of pop perfection. As a two-man rock overdub job, it's rudimentary enough to make the cheesiest garage hackers blush, yet the accomplishment is enormous. In the same vein as Buddy Holly's simple trio, Marc and Micky used a non-drum percussion field (handclaps mostly) to set the tempo, and a persistent guitar figure from the Book of Berry to attract the ear. On top of it all, Bolan's smooth, clear voice drives the melody home, with just the right insouciance to carry it off. The lyrics — simple but endearing — tie the whole package up neatly. "Swan" made number-two in the British charts and spent nearly four months in the running. Whereas Tyrannosaurus Rex had sold substantial albums, it was clear from the very start that T. Rex was going to be a singles band.

For a long-playing debut, *T. Rex* (March 1971) has an incomplete relationship with the hard-rock-group format. With Marc and Micky playing all the instruments (plus vocals on one track by the soon-to-be indispensable Flo / Eddie larynx squad and strings arranged by Visconti), there isn't a whole lot of flat-out boogie. Instead, the hoppy bopping of "Swan" is expanded into longer and more intricate escapades on one hand — and shorter, simpler pop ditties on the other. Bolan's vocals are enchanting throughout, delving into deep skat turf, sailing clearly through charming melodies and curling in that amazing vibrato. The use of strings to follow the hook riff adds to the uniqueness of the LP's sound, and the cover (Marc with Les Paul and Micky) ties up the whole package into a classic T. Rex album.

From that point on — when the newly energized sound received a warm welcome in the record marketplace — the future was clear for T. Rex, and only the formality of actually hiring sidemen to reproduce the record on stage remained. (Interestingly, this meant that every song recorded in the future would pretty much have to use the full rock complement, erasing the flexibility afforded to a two-man multi-track outfit. If T. Rex made Bolan a tentative rocker, the addition of two more musicians finished the job.)

The first to be hired, Steve Currie, was a bassist whose limited portfolio included stints with the Rumble and the Meteors. Drummer Bill Legend was actually drafted a bit later when Bolan realized that Finn couldn't be a regular drummer and play congas as well. Convinced that T. Rex wouldn't be the same without congas, he insisted on adding Legend (real name Fifield — the name came from his group with Mickey Jupp).

SO, T. Rex became a conventionally arranged rock'n'roll band, and Marc Bolan became a certified popstar, with all the accompanying accoutrements — trainloads of adoring fan mail, crowds hanging around the front door, press lined up to get the latest scoop on the still-young "overnight sensation." For Bolan, the responsibility of runaway celebrity quickly became a burden, and although he would never admit it (being the egocentric he appeared to be), the effects of being the center of attention in England were not all salutary. He quickly became smug and cocky, and the string of chart-topping singles that led to the Beatle comparisons (not to mention the crowd hysteria dubbed "T. Rextasy" in the media) aided in detaching Marc from the constraints of real life. For the first year (after all, the group didn't go through the roof instantly — it took a few months), he seemed intact and in control, but by early '72, the press began highlighting a few of the cracks in his armor, and an acrimonious (and largely press-provoked) public joust with old friend David Bowie, whose career was heating up in the wake of Bolan's, did little to help paint Bolan as a well-adjusted artist. The image of a spoiled-brat-rock-god jealous of the competition and unable to conceive of the problems of the real world became the prevalent one, and Marc seemed to have neither the inclination nor the ability to dispel it. In New York, on the full group's first tour, he and June threw dollar bills from a hotel terrace to the plebs below. In the same city, two years later, on another tour, he told writer Lillian Roxon, "I'm too big a star to worry about promoting myself. I am, after all, a living legend."

T. Rex chalked up two 1971 number-ones ("Hot Love" and "Get It On") as well as a number-two ("Jeepster") released against Bolan's wishes by Fly after the end of their contract. The singles showed great strides in both conception and execution, and a new world of heavy boogie had been created: Bolan's bizarre lyrics painting a private dream powered by relentlessly catchy metallic hooks. The LP released in the summer of '72 (containing two of the singles and a number of similar tracks in addition to some oddities), *Electric Warrior*, shows the completely realized electric Rex, although it contains a few tunes that hark back to an earlier era. With the full lineup, the clever use of hand-claps and percussive guitar is replaced by straightforward drumming, and the increased employment of Flo & Eddie drives the T. Rex sound into a powerful, identifiable groove that eventually would devolve into a repetitive rut.

A few of the cuts on *Electric Warrior* are quite different from the others. The shrill "Rip Off" contains the instant oblivion couplet "rocking in the nude/feeling such a dude," while "Lean Woman Blues" amounts to a typical (but not for Bolan) 12-bar blues workout. "Cosmic Dancer" is basically an acoustic song overlaid with heavy drums and lots of strings. In retrospect, it's hard to think of *Electric Warrior* as anything more rock'n'rolly than a folk LP with drums and fuzzbox. It's a really good record, but not as weird as it seemed at the time.

Americans found the burgeoning Bolan phenomenon mildly amusing, picking "Get It On" (retitled "Bang a Gong" here) over the other T. Rex singles that were issued, and making it a Top 5 hit, while the LP it was on barely made the top half of the heavy hundred. A few attempts to put the band over live on American shores failed to ignite anything comparable to the wild scenes common in England, and the big hype push mounted by Reprise only served to embitter critics and record buyers who expected the apocalypse and got a mediocre hour of clichéd boogie. Frustrated and confused, T. Rex — a band that sold the equivalent of 14 million singles in England in one year — headed home to a progressively crazier scene.

Pop-rock enjoyed phenomenal success in England between 1972 and '73, with a wide variety of idols to woo the teenyboppers. Bowie began having hit singles; Slade put four in the upper echelons in less than 12 months; Gary Glitter shook his paunch before millions; Sweet, Elton John, Chicory Tip and David Cassidy (for the kids in England, the clear difference between Keith Partridge and Mr. T. Rex was not so evident) regularly populated the charts, stages, airwaves and front covers of England. Marc Bolan was the uncrowned king, the only one to stay at the top for a long time. His fashions (outrageous and campy) were followed, his pronouncements accepted as gospel and his ability to sell records — the final measure of pop stardom — seemed eternal. His post-Fly company, EMI, created a special label/license for him, and everything released bore his picture and the name "T. Rex" in lieu of EMI. The prefixes further displayed his majesty's preeminence — MARC for singles, BLN for albums.

In an attempt to immortalize his fame, Bolan arranged with his friend Ringo Starr to make a documentary/concert film in early '72. (*Born to Boogie*, with its trademark [image] of Marc sitting on a tiger's back, opened in England at the end of the year, and did land office business for a while before disappearing. It was never shown widely in the States.) Bolan went off to Paris and Copenhagen and recorded a new album, *The Slider*; Fly repackaged some of his older material and released a set called *Bolan Boogie*.

The demi-god began to show some signs of wear. In a confusing interview with Michael Watts of the *Melody Maker* on the eve of *The Slider*'s release in the UK, Bolan rambled on at length about a variety of topics that show some of his problems. "I'd cut all the tracks for *Slider,* and I just said, 'Screw it.' I did a Brian Wilson. I said 'F— the album! I don't wanna put it out. I just don't ever want to record again.' And I went away for a week, came back and played the tapes and thought they were great. So, there you go... Obviously we're very much bigger because we're two years ahead of him (Bowie) and it's not the same riff either. I welcome David, 'cause I know he's a wise cat... There's always a Beatles and a Stones, and at the moment they are trying to get someone to run alongside T. Rex, which I think is admirable. David is into a whole different school from us... The song 'Main Man' is about me: 'As a child I laughed a lot / Now it seems I cry a lot' — I've never cried so much in my whole life as this last year."

The Slider is without a doubt the definitive T. Rex album — it contains the full gamut, the entire artillery and very few weak spots. (It may not be as enjoyable as the *T. Rex* set, but this is the one to refer to for a quick course.) There are a lot of great numbers — from the ominous title track to the hits "Telegram Sam" and "Metal Guru," both bolstered by strings and Kaylan / Volman. In between, there are two should-have-been A-sides, "Rock On" and "Baby Strange," and the haunting "Main Man." Nothing particularly profound here — Bolan had certainly perfected the art of the minimal lyric, and much of it borders on juvenile nonsense, but that's T. Rex for you. *Slider* is the last album on which Bolan has any connection at all to the delicacy and tenderness that permeated his earlier work, both vocally and creatively. The signs of encroaching middle age were clear, and the bloat that was setting in physically and esthetically signaled the end of innocence for the child star.

By the time of his next album, *Tanx* (March 1973), that lost naïveté had been replaced by a somewhat surly, aggressive voice and overtly violent imagery. His career, though intact, was no longer on the rise, and the sale of LPs, starting with *Tanx*, began to slow. As this particular outing contained no singles (one B-side, actually), it was a mistake for T. Rex, and it was quickly passed over in favor of the ongoing string of 7-inch delights that were being dished out. Bolan, unfortunately, had bought his own press, and believed that he could do no wrong. This baker's dozen of half-assed boogie retreads showed not a whit of charm and taste, and contained only one real good tune, "Born to Boogie," amid the dross. Bolanites disappointed by *Tanx* were at least able to enjoy the trio of singles that had preceded it: "Children of the Revolution," "Solid Gold Easy Action" and "20th Century Boy" — all ace T. Rex hits.

After 1973, Bolan's mistakes began to compound themselves, and they were intensified by various outside forces: a frustrating failure to prevent Track from issuing an album's worth of pre-Tyrannosaurus Rex demos and singles, a split with his wife, an end to his professional relationship with Tony Visconti, some confused attempts to break America, and a variety of uninspiring sidemen. The most notable influence on Bolan — starting with the 1974 *Zinc Alloy and the Hidden Riders of Tomorrow* album is Gloria Jones, whose pervasive vocals dictate the soul/disco direction that the music takes. A real Claudia Lennear/Merry Clayton-type gospel wailer, The Gloria Jones (as she is billed on the record sleeve) became the most important character in the rest of Bolan's life. She changed his music, bore him a son (Rolan), and was driving the car in the crash that killed him. For the fans of T. Rex's bubblegummy singles, the new-sound band (by this time billed as Marc Bolan and T. Rex) was not to their taste. The larger lineup also damaged the group's live popularity: with seven or eight people on stage, the sound wasn't tight or interesting, and Bolan's incessant soloing showed the failure rather than the success of his music. On the last US tour, in Fall '74, an overweight and tired Boley seemed a self-indulgent caricature of his former lithe self. The writing was definitely on the wall: his failure was no longer limited to this side of the Atlantic.

After a couple more LPs and an endless stream of occasionally excellent singles (about three a year), Bolan sank from sight. He moved to America to avoid tax problems, stopped touring and doing interviews, hung around with other has-beens, and seemed out for the count. He became an alcoholic and acquired a drug "problem." End of story?

Not quite. In 1976, Bolan — cleaned up and out, thinner and better groomed than ever, looking roughly like someone who might be 29 — made a stab at a return to the record business. With no remorse or high expectations, he put together a band (consisting, ironically, of Bowie stalwarts), made an album and, in March '77, went on the road, hiring the Damned (whose first LP had just appeared) as his opening act. *Dandy in the Underworld*, while not a masterpiece, is a coherent, respectable piece of music, and it proved that Bolan still had the spark of genius that had powered him from the outset. He became the host of a weekly TV rock show (*Marc*) and seemed to be functioning well as an au courant rock elder. He had filmed a number of episodes, including a painfully ironic one with Bowie as guest (featuring a duet by the two old rivals), when a car crash took his life, one week short of his thirtieth birthday.

Although Bolan never regained the prominence he'd attained in T. Rex's heyday, his reemergence in the last year of his life served to have his ghost be remembered for his triumphs, not his failures. For a gentle soul who brought pleasure to millions, it's fitting that he should stand as a figure of excellence, for there are enough wonderful songs in his large discography to last anyone a lifetime. ◆

Oddly, I gave Bolan a quick backhand in this ponderous, narrow-minded and not entirely defensible account of one decade's music, belched out in order to herald the beginning of another. I have included this piece mainly for its semi-valid historical snapshot and because it does contain a few keen observations.

Remember Those Fabulous '70s? A musical stroll from *Woodstock* to punk

Trouser Press, January 1980

The best characterization of rock'n'roll's third decade is that of 10 years spent revising, refining and recalling the music of the '60s. While '50s bands established the framework, it was during the '60s that the pioneering of relevance to the '70s was accomplished. In the last ten years rock has walked a fine line between nostalgia for early bands and the need to make the record business as sophisticated, crass and mass-oriented as possible. As a result of this paradox, the decade's style has lurched from minimalism to runaway complexity, from homogenized mainstream to the unbelievably arcane. This has been a fascinating period for the development of rock music, but one which has relied on the assumption that nothing really original is possible — only novelty in packaging or synthesizing of existing forms.

Since the English invasion of 1963, rock can be empirically defined as the employment of primarily electric (amplified) instruments in a small band format, the songwriting largely (if not exclusively) done within the band. Unlike their forebears in the '50s, modern groups have had much greater control over their careers, from writing and choosing songs to production to tour planning to album cover artwork. The change has indelibly altered the shape and direction of the music as well as the business. Early groups, often with no marketable writing ability, lacked the clout to stand up to record companies, which were by and large viewed as benevolent giants who could not be gainsaid. Starting with the Beatles, Stones and Bob Dylan, power began shifting to creative artists. Popularity was translated into self-determination by artists able to threaten labels with non-cooperation and not worry about their careers suffering. Throughout the '60s bands went further: producing and/or managing themselves, working with others in various capacities, and ultimately forming their own record labels to handle their affairs and those of musicians they cared to aid and abet. For a while it appeared that every major band would end up on its own label, leaving regular companies to act merely as manufacturers / distributors. However, the financial pressures of running a business forced a number of these labels to fold.

Throughout the '40s and '50s, record companies treated their artists as little more than hired help; as a result, they were ill-prepared for the onslaught of well-managed, self-reliant bands they faced (and signed) in the mid-'60s. By the end of that decade the music industry itself had been infiltrated by newcomers whose sympathies lay more with the bands than their employers' corporate structures. Labels signed whatever looked hot, then waited to see if their investment would deliver goods they could market successfully. Record companies could pick the entrants but not tell them how to run.

The '70s returned some degree of power to the labels. After realizing that established bands could not be steered or forced to deliver, companies looked for stooges instead. If one style or image proved commercial, why not clone copies who wouldn't complain when told what to do? Labels discovered they need not sit on their hands waiting for long shots to attract a mass audience; whatever is proven popular (either recently or not) can be duplicated and sold in huge quantities to susceptible rock consumers. Hence, we have been saddled with mainstream rock that goes nowhere (except as self-parody) until an external force breaks the circle — at least temporarily. Late-'60s and early-'70s rock became more a commodity and less a culture. It was not long before *Woodstock* fans' sense of identity began to be lost in a morass of mass-produced T-shirts. Unlike the '60s, rock fans in the '70s were forced to endure talentless nobodies with little interest in music beyond fame, fortune and drugs.

Since at any given moment rock consists of overlapping styles and trends, the '70s can only be divided into several hazy periods — from December 1969, when the Woodstock Nation snapped out of its drug-induced torpor at Altamont Raceway, to February 1979 and Sid Vicious's death from terminal stupidity. Along the way we survived glam/glitter, heavy metal, fossils that wouldn't quit, power pop, all the ghosts of rock'n'roll past, punk, electronics, reggae, disco, colored vinyl and enough hype to fill the Grand Canyon. What have we got to show for it as we meander into another decade?

Actually, quite a bit. In the past 10 years there has been a near-steady stream of listenable rock among the waves of garbage. Given the basic modes created in the '60s — pop, heavy metal, guitar/blues, folk-rock, progressive, good-timey and punk — all that remained for '70s groups to do (at least until they used technology to create novel instrumentation) was recombine them into synthetic styles and make them seem fresh through marketing and promotion techniques. Even though much '70s music sounds original, there haven't been any conceptual breakthroughs this decade. Rock has been refined, improved, disguised, adapted — but not born again.

We entered the calendar '70s a scant four months after the giants of the first great rock age appeared together for the first and last time at Woodstock. The cast of that event provides a good reference point to refresh fading memories. The Who was between *Tommy* and *Who's Next*. Creedence Clearwater Revival was all over AM radio. Jimi Hendrix was a few months shy of recording a live set at the Fillmore East with the Band of Gypsys. Johnny Winter's second album hadn't yet been recorded. Crosby, Stills, Nash and Young, Canned Heat, Janis Joplin, Mountain and the Band were all major stars of the day.

At the end of 1969, Mick Taylor had been a Stone for only six months. The Beatles had broken up and released several solo projects before *Let It Be* appeared. Bowie's "Space Oddity" was big in the British charts. Dylan had appeared at the Isle of Wight Festival before a quarter million fans and was between *Nashville Skyline* and *Self-Portrait*. The Doors were still going strong; Blind Faith had come and gone in the wake of Cream. Elton John was just about to become a huge star in America. LPs listed for $4.98. New faces of the day included Alice Cooper, Led Zeppelin, Hot Tuna, Emerson, Lake and Palmer, James Taylor, Iggy and the Stooges and the MC5. Lou Reed, Rod Stewart, Peter Green and Todd Rundgren had all recently launched solo careers.

The artists who topped the 1970 record charts continued to dominate the first few years of the decade: McCartney, Led Zeppelin, Simon and Garfunkel and CSN&Y, among others. Bands that were about to alter the course of music were around but hadn't gained popularity to affect any changes. Meantime, among all the deaths and breakups, rock in 1970 was populated with rehashed mediocrity: Grand Funk Railroad, J. Geils, Cat Stevens, the Carpenters, David Cassidy and Chicago are hardly the stuff of which great leaps forward are made. The popularity of wimpy acoustic/soft rock (later to become the LA sound of the Eagles, Linda Ronstadt and Jackson Browne) forced rock fans to settle for pathetic geeks trading on the void left by the demise or inactivity of late-'60s power bands.

An important break in the monotony came in 1972, when some creative British bands visited the States and met a homegrown scene of increasing significance. The David Bowie/Alice Cooper axis made for a cataclysmic shift in rock's face and sound. *Killer* went gold, proving that morbidity, sex and nihilism were no longer taboo; Bowie influenced fans and bands in everything from fashion to sexuality to music and lyrics. Even though neither made music too far from the norm, each affected the media powerfully through on- and off-stage theatrics — a new concept for rock. Makeup, totally fake imagery and costumes attracted and amazed; many bands of questionable ability achieved greater fame among bored and gullible audiences than might have been possible had they appeared strictly as themselves.

By early 1973, theatricality was a dominant force. A New York four-piece playing basic rock'n'roll painted their faces and wore stupendous costumes in an attempt to allow no aspect of their lives to enter into their rock fantasy. KISS merchandised not only the music but pure image: toys, dolls and paraphernalia bearing their faces and costumes. They quickly became one of the biggest moneymakers of all time.

The New York Dolls were also the offspring of Alice and Bowie to a degree. They tried to combine stage and real life, attempting to be as outrageous in their daily existence as they were in front of a crowd. Few presumed Alice Cooper wore his makeup in the daylight, but Dolls fans would hardly be surprised at anything their heroes might do. Like Iggy Pop and Lou Reed, the Dolls bore the air of serious decadents — no international jet set parties for this crew. They earned the cachet of ultimate abandon when their original drummer died in London, where the band had been invited to open a major concert for the Faces. And this was before they had signed a record contract!

Bowie's legacy was a huge collection of bands wearing feminine clothes and too much makeup, singing spacy songs with a touch of Jacques Brel. There was, however, one other character causing much imitation (even by Bowie himself): Marc Bolan. A former pop star and folkie, Bolan had shortened the name of his acoustic duo Tyrannosaurus Rex to T. Rex, gone electric and melded together rhythms, boogie, Spectorish production and inanely simple lyrics. It wasn't good for much except fun, but it sold like crazy. Although he predated Bowie's arrival on the charts by a full year, Bolan never commanded equal power or respect. While Bowie became an overnight media mogul by taking charge of the careers of those around him, Bolan kept toiling away, hit after hit, at intellectual fodder like "Metal Guru," "Telegram Sam" and "Bang a Gong."

Among the bands to emerge or change as a partial result of Bowie were the awesomely well-conceived and executed Roxy Music, Mott the Hoople (whom Bowie singlehandedly revitalized), bubble gum escapees Sweet, a femmed-up Rod Stewart, Slade, Suzi Quatro and Gary Glitter. Some of those glamsters were successful in America, where the competition included teenybop stars the Osmonds, David Cassidy, the Jackson 5 and Rick Springfield. The appeal to both ten-year-olds and older audiences was significant when the alternative was Seals and Crofts, Loggins and Messina, America and other gutless wonders. For a year or so non-stop foolish fun was the order of the day; catchy melodies, dumb lyrics and big guitar chords were all over airwaves and turntables.

Popular as glitter may have been for a short time, most of the bands who profited from it couldn't grow beyond the narrow limitations and faded away after the fad died down. There must be a lot of satin stretch pants hanging in the backs of once-luxurious closets these days.

By 1974 rock was definitely not well. As a disposable commodity, the music has always required regular change and development to stay active and healthy; but aside from a few bands trying relatively new things (e.g., Genesis and the Strawbs) there was little excitement. Most of the great '60s bands had settled into a comfortable pattern of infrequent tours and record releases, satisfied to live their ritzy lives away from the rabble that would fill any hall (no matter how mammoth or remote) where they might choose to appear. As a result, superstars produced little music of any quality; disaffected fans lost interest in the idols of their youth and removed some of the comfy security the musicians thought they could always expect.

They were also challenged by the rising popularity of bands with ingenuity and originality: Genesis, Electric Light Orchestra, Sparks, Cockney Rebel, Be-Bop Deluxe and Queen made rock shoot off in a different direction by the end of the year. Unfortunately, the tendency towards intricacy, delicacy and heavy studio orientation was a short-lived blessing; within a few short years these bands had become overblown, self-possessed and disinterested in any ongoing creativity. The bright hopes of 1973 and '74 had become old nuisances by 1976.

New York in the wake of the Dolls underwent a brief dip, then reorganized itself into a very active, vital testing ground for a new crop of bands. In late 1974 Patti Smith, Television, the Ramones, Blondie and others were appearing regularly on the sleaze circuit; label interest, unlike media attention, was slow in developing.

In England, glitter was followed by pub rock. An unpopular name for a popular music, pub bands played around London with one foot rooted in various American styles (country, R&B, '50s) and another in sweaty British rock'n'roll energy. Unable to enter the mainstream at first, they found places they could play without being big stars. Pub owners were glad to have a cheap way to increase business, and the bands were grateful for a place to play and make a little money. London's club scene was similar to New York's only in that the groups themselves created the venues. The music being played in the two cities was as different as day and night.

Their directions were very different as well. By mid-'75, the leading pub bands had developed into nationally known stars. Dr. Feelgood particularly made their tight R&B very popular in England and Europe. New York bands, long considered too weird for national exposure by the powers that be, continued "underground" until early '76, when acclaim for Patti Smith's first LP snowballed into contracts for the Ramones, Television, Blondie, Talking Heads and others.

In London energetic rockers were making it while more laid-back bands weren't. Age and enthusiasm counted a lot in the public eye, and before long a younger, "punkier" outfit than the Feelgoods — Eddie and the Hot Rods — had the country in an uproar. In retrospect it's now easy to see that the pub bands were leading directly to the new wave bands that supplanted them in 1976.

Interestingly enough, some of the pub rockers were able to challenge punk outfits by proving to have a good deal more mainstream appeal (especially in America) than the aggressive pogo bands. While the Pistols were washouts with the American public and press, pub-grown entries — Elvis Costello, Graham Parker, Nick Lowe, Ian Dury, the Motors, the Records, Ian Gomm — all met with reasonably favorable receptions. As far as most American rockers are now concerned, these older and wiser pub vets are the only good part of the new wave.

It is also fascinating to note how easily these old-timers could jump from stagnant musical styles to positions of leadership with the most competitively hip trendies on two continents. But then, considering how strongly rooted their current styles are in the past, perhaps this is merely a case of opportune recycling.

While New York (and other US hot spots) bands were waiting for record moguls to come down and sign them up, clever folks in disparate locations were taking matters into their own hands. Independent labels had been around for a while (Beserkley in California, Skydog in France, Chiswick in London), but two small-time band managers brought enough world focus on their Stiff Records to make small labels viable and significant. Stiff provided a way for talented newcomers to reach potential fans without submitting to the existing industry's preset rules and whims. By making the label (est. summer 1976) at least as interesting as the bands whose records it released, Stiff created a strong identity to attract attention in record shops.

By the end of 1976, other small labels in a number of British and American cities were operating on a regular basis. The number of new bands who got their only possible shot (including some who became very successful) through small labels has been a source of constant amazement among established companies, who had themselves convinced nothing salable had escaped them. When independents began suffering from the same ingrown sense of protective stupidity that had led them to exist in the first place, newer outfits emerged to fill the fringe void; the situation, at least in England, has been one of continual growth and replacement, channeling a steady flow of new bands into the rock arena.

Thanks in large part to the early indies, the reigning superstars of the late '70s found their comfortable existences threatened by young upstarts who quickly nudged them aside — first in the music press, then in the record stores. (That is, in England; it took Americans a while longer to catch on. As of this writing, it's not 100 percent clear they have caught on.) Unfettered by the arduous long wait between forming a band and having a record released, the new crop burst onto the scene in full bloom; there was none of the discouragement or bitterness that usually afflicts 30-year-old "overnight sensations" who have been slogging away in seedy dives for five or ten years. Some new bands hardly deserved the chances they got, but enough freshness and quality was uncovered to warrant tolerance of a few bad apples.

For rock fans with open minds, new wave bands provided welcome relief from the alienation of stadium concerts by bands that could only bother to show up in any given area once every few years. Why bother waiting to drop $15 for the Stones, Who or Fleetwood Mac when $5 was enough to see the Ramones, Talking Heads or Blondie in a small club any weekend? These new bands were accessible and bore none of the mythical untouchability of the stadium giants. They put out records often, toured a lot, and made themselves available to their fans. Kids once again had bands they could identify with and root for. For those of us who remember the '60s vividly, the first year or two of the new wave — until it got crass and sour all over again — felt very similar in spirit and in that indefinable sense of an overall movement.

While the new wave was setting everything to right in England (1976-78), the American record industry was caught up in a near-fatal merry-go-round of seemingly limitless platinumania. Some very familiar bands began selling LPs in unprecedented quantities, surprising all except perhaps record companies who were quick to claim credit for effective marketing strategies. Fleetwood Mac, Peter Frampton, Steve Miller, Bob Seger and a few others had been struggling for a decade or more each, with little hope of success. Suddenly, each shifted direction towards the middle of the road and began collecting royalty checks fit for royalty. At the same time, record companies' newly refined sales forces and techniques turned some (relatively) new names — Meatloaf, Boston, Heart, Eddie Money — and the revived Bee Gees into tremendously successful commodities.

The failure of many of these guaranteed profit-makers to repeat their sales performances the next time out caused a panic in the industry that wiped the smug grin off the faces of many top execs. This somehow allowed the infiltration (onto radio and into the charts) of a slew of new wave-affiliated bands. Without any desperate need to sell records in the multi-million quantities, groups with some sense of pride in their accomplishments (and a definite commitment to the new wave — either in theory or reality) brought America its first real dose of change in the second half of the '70s. The Cars, Cheap Trick, Blondie, Police, Shoes, Joe Jackson, Elvis C., the Heads and, yes, even the Knack stuck a foot in the door and swung a sagging industry back into a period of optimism and creativity.

And that's where we are as we enter the '80s. Some old names are still in the charts, although their music can hardly stand up to earlier achievements. (Witness Dylan, the Who and Elton John.) Although they may still please new fans, new bands will have to work to stay popular among rock consumers. Quite a few promising bands are just entering the arena, and independent labels haven't totally lost their original purpose, stray as they might.

In a very real sense, we're back where we started, but the 10-year route around the circle has produced quite a few bands and records of long-lasting greatness. Rock's early naïveté is undoubtedly gone forever, but the spirit that drives young people to make energetic noise shows no sign of abating. If anything, the '70s proved that rock can be as sophisticated as any techno-culture or as minimal as fingerpainting. That's a major revelation for many.

There were some fairly dead spots in the '70s, but only boredom could have laid the foundation for the momentous changes that have taken place. The '70s were a period of middle age for '60s bands and the pop record industry; however, a continuing stream of new rock fans with open eyes and ears provided a perpetual appetite for novelty. Some of us old fogies may wistfully recall the old days, but we have to face the fact that rock thrives on mass appeal; great bands can't stay small and survive. The continuous replacement of obsolete dinosaurs with rebellious newcomers has kept rock thrilling for me for almost 20 years now. I, for one, am certainly looking forward to another great 20 years. Let's rock in the year 2000! ◆

The End of the Line

I may have rocked, as it were, into the new millennium, but the magazine didn't make it through Orwell's prophetic year. The end of *Trouser Press* was traumatic — and a ton of work — for me. It took a lot of pondering to decide to shut it down and then to work out when and how to do that. Turns out ending a monthly magazine is rather like stopping a boulder that is rolling downhill: there's a lot of momentum to contend with.

I've often been asked why the magazine stopped; there was no single reason. We were out of money, short on enthusiasm and hope, marginalized by the rise of MTV, bored with the colorful editorial corner we'd painted ourselves into (the Adam Ant cover was our best-selling newsstand issue). Encroaching adult cynicism flourished in captions and editorial asides, making us — for the first time — feel hypocritical about prominently featuring artists we didn't especially like or even respect. (Big difference from criticizing artists whose value we recognized and appreciated.) I was tired of being poor, sick of baling the sinking vessel and depressed about all of it (which hastened the end of my first marriage). I felt responsible for my colleagues, guilty about those to whom we owed money, frightened for my personal future but, ultimately, unable to go on with what increasingly felt like a weighty yoke.

Failure is a huge emotional burden when it's your own doing and you can't think your way out of it. I tried to find a buyer for the magazine, to no avail. Huge, unexpected returns from our European newsstand distributor put us deep in debt; our sales in America were disappointing as well. The thought of escaping the pressure became too appealing to ignore. Once my mind was made up, setting a timetable was easy — we were about to reach ten years of publication. I was about to turn 30 and thinking about ending my first marriage. Those round numbers appealed to my mathematical instincts. I had hoped we could get to 100 issues, but the timing didn't work.

Stopping a magazine turned out to be a lot more complicated than starting one. I told the staff and announced my plan to go out with a bang. So, without telling anyone outside the office that we were about to pull the plug (our printer would never have printed the final issue, our distributor would not have shipped issues to newsstands, and it would have obliterated advertising sales), we produced a retrospective issue (number 96) and planned a 10th anniversary party at Irving Plaza. Kathy Frank, a friend from high school who was our typesetter when she wasn't managing a local band called the Panic Squad or staging Rock Against Racism events with the Yippies, arranged things with the club. We hit up some record labels for unpaid talent and somehow got Jason and the Scorchers to headline, along with the Planets, my friend Binky Philips' band, a longtime personal (and *Trouser Press*) fave, and the gone-tomorrow Here Today. A fine time was had by all that night (although the bar tab presented to me at the end of the night was hundreds of dollars more than I expected it to be; as we were broke, that put a bit of a damper on things for me.) Rumors of our plan started going around the club, which led to a lot of hemming, hawing and outright fibbery. Regardless, we had a blast.

The next day, once I was able to drag my hungover corpse into the office (at 212 Fifth Avenue, now the New York address of the world's richest man...), we started telling people the truth. With everyone else gone (the staff had been six full-time and a couple of part-timers, maybe an intern or two, at the end), I settled in to try and collect moneys owed, pay bills, arrange a replacement magazine for our subscribers (which turned out to be *The Record*, *Rolling Stone*'s monthly music publication; my friend Wayne King was an editor there and I was able to make a deal with Wenner's fearsome business manager, Kent Brownridge), return photos to photographers and sell a filing cabinet of press photos to *Goldmine*, fulfill back issue orders and otherwise attend to the matter of winding things up. It took months, but I was able to hire a longtime *TP* correspondent, David Sheridan, who was working in a shoe store at the time (and is now a chief financial aid officer at a top university), to give me a hand with the work.

I prepared a letter ahead of time to explain what was happening — and why — to those who needed to hear it from me. I don't think anything here is untrue or unrealistic, but it definitely has the best face I could put on it.

This past week, *Trouser Press* celebrated our tenth anniversary. It's hard to believe that it's been a decade since we mimeographed and stapled our primitive first issue, but it has. We've received many kind words of congratulation recently, and many friends have offered good wishes for the magazine's next ten years. Unfortunately, in the words of an ancient Anglo-Saxon poet, "There is no future." After much sober (and not so sober) consideration, we've decided that the 10th Anniversary issue (*TP* 96 / April 1984) will be the final one.

Although money problems have plagued *Trouser Press* since the beginning, that is not the basis for this decision. Truthfully. it would have been easier to opt for continuing were there no financial pressures, but surviving ten years of near-insolvency makes virtually any challenge of the checkbook endurable. Why *Trouser Press* is stopping has more to do with why it began in the first place and how the role and nature of the rock press has diminished and changed over the years. It comes down to the realization that we've basically accomplished what we set out to do, and that our feelings about music and writing and the record business have less and less in common with our readers. We've become reasonably skilled at this rock magazine game, but the ability to publish a credible issue every month isn't the same as knowing why we should. Rather than muddling on with reduced enthusiasm simply out of inertia or lunging for the commercial jugular and selling out to the latest big thing, we want *Trouser Press* to end with grace and dignity.

Good sense and realistic modesty prevent overestimating or overstating the impact *Trouser Press* has had, but it would be highly gratifying if we could claim some credit for abetting and possibly aiding such commendable developments as the mushrooming of do-it-yourself records, the proliferation of imports, the acceptance of new wave and fringe musics, and the spread of mail-order record sales. Hopefully, *Trouser Press* has exposed readers to some worthwhile bands and records, maybe given some artists the boosts they needed, inspired a few fanzines into existence. Knowing that *TP* has contributed something to the rock culture more than justifies the extraordinary work many fine people put into creating ninety-six issues, not to mention all those trees that gave up their lives.

Finally, I want to offer my deepest gratitude to everyone who has supported *Trouser Press*, and to anyone who agrees with us that rock'n'roll should be played for love, not money. I also want to offer my encouragement for independent musicmakers everywhere. And last but absolutely not least, thanks to our readers, who are the smartest rock fans in the country. ◆

Trouser Press, R.I.P.

Parke Puterbaugh, a charming and erudite North Carolinian who had reviewed a few records for us and was on staff at *Rolling Stone* (and, coincidentally, lived a half-block from the apartment where I grew up), did a wonderful thing in 1984 by pitching and writing a full-fledged obituary for *Trouser Press* that ran in *RS* 422. I am ever grateful for that honor. A framed copy of the page (see overleaf) hangs in my house, proof that there can, in fact, be life after death.

Regarding the end of *TP*, Parke quoted me saying, "It's like building a statue in sand and then watching the tide come up." The photo caption summed up my feelings nicely: "I hope we made some sort of difference."

A freelancer named Larry Williams came to our soon-to-be-vacant office at 212 Fifth Avenue in the Flatiron District (the building was subsequently converted to condos and is now, of all things, Jeff Bezos's New York address!) to photograph me for the piece; we spent an hour or two moving desks and boxes around to produce an arty background for my dejected doorway pose. When he told me how much he was getting paid for the assignment I ruefully joked that we could have stayed in business another week or two for that amount.

A few issues later, *Stone* ran this colorful, metaphor-mixing letter from Tony Dela Cruz of Honolulu. I happened upon it recently and was tickled:

> There are going to be some people who, never having read *Trouser Press*, will consider Ira Robbins the Jim Jones of rock journalism, an off-center cult leader who brought his temple down when his religious context no longer seemed to make sense. Then there are those of us who saw *TP* as the Dr. Pepper of the mag racks. *TP* stood for the little guy. It gave more than a few writers their first national bylines and reviewed records radio stations wouldn't even have looked at. I feel like a friend just committed suicide. I've also got a good-sized New Wave record collection that will never sound the same.

I put so much time, energy, creativity and thought into *Trouser Press* for the entirety of my twenties that — while I regret none of it and have reaped many benefits from it since — I came to see that it had exacted a significant personal cost. (A marriage, for one thing.) I wasn't cut out to be a businessman, and we had all suffered for my inexperience and fecklessness. I certainly didn't reap any financial rewards for my efforts. The year after the magazine ended, during which I did freelance writing and delivered a new edition of *The Trouser Press Record Guide*, my income doubled. Endings ... beginnings ... all that.

Being so closely identified with a single publication and a particular style of music, perhaps being thought of as either a publisher *or* an editor *or* a writer, I was never welcomed into any of the city's journalism cliques and so lost out on professional opportunities I saw many of those in those in-crowds enjoy. The rock critic establishment favored its own, so I missed out on employment opportunities that went to peers. No doubt I could have put myself forward more, but even when I did manage to overcome those professional insecurities, my efforts came to naught. I *was* hired for a prestigious position at *Newsday* almost through no fault of my own, but serious campaigns that I mounted to procure editorial positions at *Rolling Stone*, *Entertainment Weekly*, the *Village Voice*, *The New Yorker*, *Newsweek*, *Blender* and *Playboy* got me absolutely nowhere. Book pitches got shrugged off. Sandlot stuff, to be sure (*pick me!!!*), but it was emotionally trying back then. And, yes, I have clung to a measure of resentment about that all these years.

OBITUARY

'Trouser Press' magazine, March 1974—April 1984

Voice of pop-rock underground folds after ten fan-filled years

BY PARKE PUTERBAUGH

Like all obsessive fans and collectors, the rock & roll inveterates who published *Trouser Press* magazine enjoyed chancing upon the undiscovered and creating something as undeniably romantic as a pop-rock underground. Working out of a cramped, stereo-less office in midtown Manhattan, they wrote for 60,000 readers who felt the same way about music that they did. These were people who believed, says *TP*'s founder and publisher, Ira Robbins, "that rock is an art form that deserves to be discussed and appraised for its creative aspects, not just for its financial aspects."

Trouser Press lent an ear to all kinds of music when few others would listen. In its early days, the magazine championed some of the more interestingly offbeat progressive bands coming out of the U.K. and off the continent. In the late Seventies, *TP* made a dogged stand on behalf of punk and New Wave, otherwise received with hostility by the American media. To struggling overseas bands of all stripes, "we were like the USO," says Robbins. "We were reaching out to them and giving them coverage in America, which they wanted." And needed, in order to establish a foothold in the U.S.

Some of the obscure acts touted early on by *TP* were Genesis and Queen, ELO and King Crimson. As for the New Wave phenomenon, *Trouser Press* would have the final word by compiling a well-received encyclopedia – *The Trouser Press Guide to New Wave Records* (Scribners, 1983). The commercial ascendance of New Wave in the Eighties meant sweet vindication for *TP*, but also created an editorial dilemma: how to juggle a fickle young audience stuck on pinup stars like Boy George and Adam Ant with an older, more serious readership that preferred discographies and erudite dialogue from its heroes. Ultimately, that dilemma contributed to Robbins' decision to fold the magazine. *TP*'s April issue was its last.

The shutdown came exactly ten years after Robbins and several of his friends created *Trouser Press* "as the last resort of a rejected rock critic." There were plenty of fanzines being published in the do-it-yourself spirit, but *TP* managed to combine basic fanzine enthusiasm with solid journalistic skill. It took off right away. "I characterized it as a whim whose time had come," Robbins says. "It was too easy not to do it."

The start-up cost was a mere sixty dollars; the first five issues were run off on Robbins' parents' mimeograph machine, hand-stapled and peddled for a quarter outside rock shows at Manhattan's Academy of Music (now the Palladium). Back then, Robbins was publishing his pet project on a bimonthly basis and calling it *Trans-Oceanic Trouser Press*. The title was a play on the initials of *Top of the Pops*, Britain's TV music show. The "Trouser Press" was borrowed from the Bonzo Dog Band song of the same name. Soon, *TP* was billing itself as "America's Only British Rock Magazine," an identity that set it apart from the pack.

Ira Robbins closes the door on a decade: 'I hope we made some sort of difference.'

Issue number one featured the Who on the cover and included stories about Rory Gallagher, King Crimson and bootleg Beatles albums. For the most part, *Trouser Press* had the market to itself. "The coverage of British bands in most American magazines was uninformed at best and disinclined at worst," Robbins recalls. The situation would change over time, but so would the magazine. By 1977, *Trouser Press* had transcended the "fanzine" tag; that year, Robbins and company ran their first color cover, of Peter Gabriel, and *TP* began appearing on the stands every month. In July 1978, they even put an American, Todd Rundgren, on the cover.

By then, *Trouser Press* was also giving its full-force endorsement to punk and New Wave, and the staff found itself way out on a limb. "The response from the American record companies was, 'New Wave is stupid; we don't want it. You can cover it all you want, but you're not going to convince us to release these records over here,' " Robbins remembers. "And the media picked up solely on the nihilistic sputterings and self-mutilation of the more outrageous costumers. Yet all it took was to hear 'Anarchy in the U.K.' or 'God Save the Queen' " – the Sex Pistols' first singles – "and it was rock & roll love at first sight."

But after championing New Wave in its infancy, *TP* castigated it at the first signs of corporate co-optation. Such were the perquisites of independence that Robbins could put a likeness of Johnny Rotten, wearing a T-shirt that said NEW WAVE R.I.P., on the cover of a 1977 issue and write inside that "this unique and wondrous era has ended." Robbins' bold declaration was, of course, highly debatable and, he allows, premature. It did vex him, however, to see New Wave threatening to become part of the commercial mainstream – which was inevitable.

Still, Robbins claims to have been happiest "around '78, '79, when the records were great and we pretty much had a free hand to do anything we wanted. I look back on those issues and am amazed at the stuff we accomplished simply because we didn't know any better." In those days, *Trouser Press* was reviewing, in one form or another, as many as 150 records in a single issue.

In 1981, the magazine signed a national distribution deal. But while *Trouser Press* was reaching more people than ever, Robbins and his charges were having trouble mustering as much excitement over, say, Culture Club as the Clash. Then, too, "the music, the record industry and the people involved have changed," says Robbins. "Even the writers have become more industry-oriented, because they're working in a milieu that is not particularly conducive to independent thought."

There were financial pressures, as well. In the end, Robbins chose not to "lunge for the commercial jugular" by placing the popular video bands of the day on cover after cover and writing, with diminished enthusiasm, for an audience he no longer recognized. Not that the decision was an easy one. "It's like building a statue in sand," Robbins says wistfully, "and then watching the tide come up."

What has been lost with *Trouser Press'* demise, Robbins feels, is "a national forum for whatever might happen next. We've always been flexible enough that if we felt something was really great, we'd change the whole magazine around for it. There was no one to tell us not to."

Trouser Press, R.I.P. ●

PHOTOGRAPH BY LARRY WILLIAMS

VIDEO Magazine (1985 – 1989)

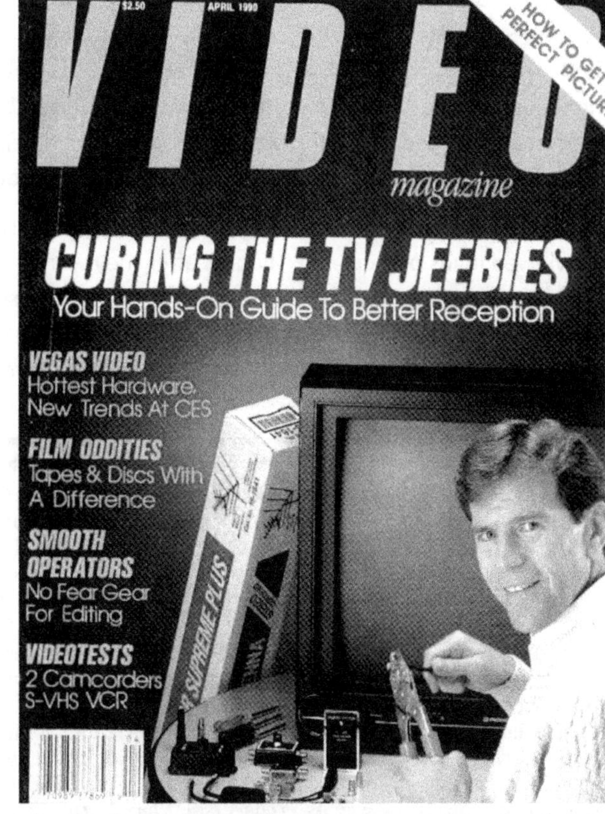

After winding down (or, I suppose, winding up) the business end of *Trouser Press* at the end of 1984, I turned to freelance work to pay the bills (a feasible option in those days), and found it far more lucrative than employing myself had been. That was fine for a couple of years, but after I got divorced and started living alone for the first time in my life, the charm of co-habiting in solitary with a cat (even the incredible feline one-off that was Bobo) wore off. As the pandemic has reminded so many, working at home can become a lonely, isolating drag.

Mark Fleischmann, a Columbia University grad who had been a *Trouser Press* contributor and editor of *Trouser Press Collectors' Magazine*, had joined the mainstream magazine ranks with a job at *Video*, the smaller of the two main consumer monthlies serving the burgeoning medium, both from the hardware side ("8mm, How Far How Fast?") and the "software" side — movies, TV and made-for-video releases on Beta, VHS and laserdisc.

Mark kindly sent freelance work my way, reviewing music-related releases. Even more helpfully, upon his exit from *Video* in 1987, he recommended me to the editor-in-chief, Doug Garr, who hired me to take over his role. At the age of 33, I had my first regular job: Senior Editor of Programming at *Video* magazine.

The June 1986 issue contained a laughably odd editor's note announcing my arrival. "Robbins is the kind of guy we refer to as a 'software specialist.' He stays up late sifting through much of the prerecorded videotape that finds its way into our offices.... He has seen more rock videos than he cares to remember (some he does care to remember, however)."

Along with a steady and perfectly adequate paycheck, I got an office, endless videotapes (some of which I still have) and the occasional opportunity to attend film junkets. As a bonus, I got back some of the professional self-respect that was lost in the shuttering of *Trouser Press*.

Video was a recent addition to the Reese Communications stable, a father-son publishing operation previously known for what we affectionately referred to as "dick books" — lurid noir pulp magazines *True Detective, Master Detective* and *Inside Detective*, staffed by a collection of *Barney Miller*-type oddballs plus a beautiful young Guyanese-American woman who seemed completely out of place there — and the porn mag *Beaver* (stop me if you've heard this slogan before: "more gash for your cash"). The company had dropped the latter in a bid for legitimacy as the son, Jay Rosenfield, jumped into the home video market in the late '70s.

Reece (Maurice) Rosenfield was a doddering but intimidating geezer who never spoke to us; Jay ran the company and was friendly, calm and generally reasonable about things. The staff included Technical Editor Lancelot Braithwaite, a voluble Trinidadian chap with a disconcerting wandering eye (ocularly, that is; I don't mean to imply any errant behavior) and the generosity to loan colleagues (and often conveniently forget to ask for the return of) video equipment he'd received to review. The business manager was a goon who smoked like a chimney and looked like a demoted mafiosi. I didn't know it at the time, but Art Director Lonnie Heller was a New York graffiti legend.

I inherited a colorful collection of freelancers, including the top-notch Frank Lovece (author of a book on the sitcom *Taxi*), Tom Soter, Steve Daly, Clifford Meth, Tim Onosko, Steven Levy and Michael Musto (before he became a nightlife legend). It was Frank who we turned to at the eleventh hour to replace a future-of-media piece we'd commissioned Isaac Asimov to write when we discovered that he'd previously published it elsewhere. Someone above me still wanted to see the prestigious byline we'd paid a handsome fee for; sight unseen, Asimov agreed to take credit for an article he had not written so long as he could keep the money.

Video was great real-world experience for a self-taught journalist. I had a lot of freedom, got to watch TV for a living and reviewed loads of movies six months after they were in theaters. (Now that I watch movies exclusively on cable, I'm still having delayed reactions to films others have long since stopped talking about. Check me out on FB, weighing in on last year's controversial releases!) The work was not especially taxing, so I had time for freelance projects, including another edition of the *Trouser Press Record Guide*.

Robert Downey's second chance

Many film directors acknowledge the role video has played in giving their work a second life, but Robert Downey (father of Robert Downey, Jr., the hot young actor) has gained an even greater appreciation of the medium's salutary possibilities. Last year, Downey made *Rented Lips*, a film written by and starring Martin Mull. But he was unhappy about the way its producers had edited it. "I had improvised a lot," he explains, "and they used the wrong takes." Granted a week in which to finish the cut, Downey was unable to undo the creative damage.

Enter IVE, the company which acquired theatrical and video rights to the picture prior to its release. Downey knew an executive there who offered him the chance to recut the film to his own taste. "It was a miracle," the director says. "I got back in the editing room with an assistant and in four weeks we cut and mixed it again. We showed it to IVE and they couldn't believe it was the same movie." That second version of a tale about two serious documentarians (played by Mull and the late Dick Shawn) who wind up directing an absurdist porno film is the one which played briefly in theaters and is now in video stores.

Downey first made his mark two decades ago as the brilliantly black-humored underground auteur of such pioneering social satires as *Chafed Elbows* (1966), *Putney Swope* (1969) and *Greaser's Palace* (1972). (All of those, as well as subsequent efforts like the 1980 teen comedy *Up the Academy*, have been issued on video but are nearly impossible to find.) In those days, he used a regular circle of actors, some of whom (including Allen Garfield, Antonio Fargas and Allan Arbus) have become well-known above-ground film and television stars.

Another actor in that rep company was Downey's son, who appeared at various stages of childhood in *Greaser's Palace*, *Pound*, *Jive* and other films. In *Rented Lips*, he plays porn star Wolf Dangler, a role originally written for a 50-year-old. Fortunately, his dad "think[s] that's the way to cast—against type. He was terrific, and fun to work with," says the proud poppa. "All I have to do is give him absurd intellectual tips and that kicks him into whatever he's doing." **—Ira Robbins**

Movies on S-VHS debut in Japan, Beta fans unite

Ever since Super VHS was introduced last year, the lack of pre-recorded software has been a major obstacle to its widescale acceptance. With under a million S-VHS VCRs presently in American homes, not one domestic company has announced plans to release videocassettes of theatrical films in the format.

But take heart—while the future may

22 VIDEO NOVEMBER 1988

With the freedom to cover pretty much anything that struck my fancy, I took the opportunity to do phone interviews with Crispin Glover (that was weird), prankster Alan Abel and my idol, film director Robert Downey.

We had actually spoken before. When I was 16 or so, I called in to Barry Gray's talk show on WMCA-AM and innocently asked his guest to define "jizm," a word I'd heard for the first time in his film *Putney Swope*. Downey laughed out loud at my question and was equally amused years later — after we'd become friends — when I reminded him of it.

Although I'd seen him recently and was aware of how badly Parkinson's disease had affected him, Bob's death in July 2021 hit me hard. He was an absolute joy to hang out with, an endless fount of wit and knowledge on a wide variety of subjects, that rare culture hero who turned out to be even better in person.

I'm not sure how good I was at reviewing films, but I took the work seriously, ignored conventional wisdom and fashion and gave it my best shot. I certainly did appreciate the opportunity to broaden my cultural scope as a critic.

River's Edge

Video, November 1987

In the 1960s, the parents of America considered radicalized, violence-ready students an unprecedented threat to the status quo. When that group graduated to white-collar conservatism, callous, drug-addicted muggers took over as public crime nightmare number-one. But it turns out there was another, more dangerous social group — bored, middle-class teen losers — waiting in the suburbs. In recent years, quiet communities have been shattered by acts of absurd violence: ceremonial killings by juvenile cults, murders committed over social standing, copycat suicides.

One such event — the 1981 rape and murder in northern California of a 14-year-old girl by her boyfriend — provided the basis for *River's Edge*. Public outrage that classmates knew of the deed — some actually went to view the corpse but didn't feel moved to do anything about it — gave screenwriter Neal Jimenez and director Tim Hunter (who co-wrote *Over the Edge*, another offbeat movie about teen alienation) the inspiration to create this year's most gripping, insightful and extraordinary film. *River's Edge* explores a terrifying world of apathy, irresponsibility and misplaced morality, a depressing realm of unstable, alienated youngsters without one solid clue about life. Their bizarre sense of loyalty, family and reality (mis)guides all their actions: an explorer following a map's reflection in a funhouse mirror would have a better chance at finding the correct path. While it remains as sympathetic as possible, *River's Edge* neither romanticizes nor justifies the kids' views or behavior. Parental incompetence and pop culture's fantasy/reality blur are the only explanations offered.

Although Frederick Elmes' masterfully blunt camerawork loses much of its bleak beauty on video (a problem shared by his previous film, *Blue Velvet*), *River's Edge* remains a blazingly intense work. Besides sharply realistic dialogue and weird, high-strung direction, the film's magic comes from its brilliant cast. As Layne, the braying, self-important ringleader, Crispin Glover is amazing, an uncontrollable jumble of nerves, rage and chaotic ideas. Railing at his homicidal buddy, Layne whines, "You have no sense of pride, no sense of loyalty... why do you think Russia is gearing up to kick our asses?" Dennis Hopper, playing a lunatic one-legged ex-biker, offers a strangely helpful adult moral perspective. Keanu Reeves, as Matt, reluctantly discovers more humanity in himself than in his friends.

As bad as these teens are, the most unsettling aspect of *River's Edge* is its parting suggestion that we ain't seen nothing yet. Matt's 12-year-old brother is far more depraved than he is; the prospect of these zeros reproducing is too horrible to contemplate. *River's Edge* is a must-see that should give pause to even the most cynical social observer. ◆

Full Metal Jacket

Video, August 1988

Every entry in the growing body of films about the American experience in Vietnam has, to some degree, considered how the war's brutality converted innocent teenagers into numb, semi-human weapons with an appetite for death. Half of *Full Metal Jacket*, the genre's most powerful and disturbing work, is devoted to Marine boot camp — the intentional side of that process — and the rest to the aftermath, the painful discovery of the moral issues that accompany bullets. Although not without flaws of ethos and character, the arrival of *Full Metal Jacket* reduces *Platoon* to a mere war movie and reaffirms Stanley Kubrick as one of cinema's true masters.

With a depersonalizing buzzcut, the film introduces a bunch of recruits falling into the clutches of super-Marine drill instructor Hartman (R. Lee Ermey). In a spectacular center-stage performance, he terrorizes them into submission with a barrage of foul-mouthed (but uproariously funny) invective. His relentless berating and bullying is hysterical, a torrent of putdowns that, given its essential reality (Ermey, an ex-Marine who served as technical advisor on the film, knows whereof he bellows), can amuse only those at a safe distance.

As the savage course turns children into disciplined killers, a crack begins to develop. The slow-witted Private Pyle (Vincent d'Onofrio) surges out of the sea of faceless crewcuts, a born loser in a world that doesn't tolerate failure. When the entire company is penalized for his mistakes, smart and sensitive Private Joker (Matthew Modine) turns from friend to foe in a ritual signifying his dwindling moral fortitude. That's the final straw: graduation day brings an end to Pyle's Marine career.

The rest of the film takes place in 'Nam, during the bloody Tet Offensive. Narrator Joker, now a *Stars & Stripes* reporter, has lost his moral balance. He sports both a peace sign and the slogan "Born to Kill," but can't explain why. "It's something about the duality of man," he offers lamely to an absurd colonel who explains the war by claiming that "inside every gook is an American waiting to get out."

At this point, Kubrick throws the thematic ball in the air. Joker's dilemma is obvious — a burning and suicidal desire for action, coupled with uncertainty about the war's righteousness — but the film never delves into it. Kubrick leaves the issue unexplored and unresolved. A sniper later draws a deadly bead on Joker and another Marine has to save him. When challenged to finish the job, Joker must make an ultimate choice. Can he kill the vanquished enemy? Is he still human? We see the decision — Kubrick captures his internal struggle with an unflinching focus on Modine's anguished face — but the questions aren't answered.

That hollowness resonates in the ponderous but ambiguous soliloquy that ends the film. As Marines stroll through a battlefield singing the Mickey Mouse theme, Joker intones, "I am in a world of shit, yes, but I am alive. And I am not afraid." Is that really it?

Kubrick's meticulous filmmaking wraps this bare-bones tale in totally controlled and determined direction, poetic camera work that re-creates Southeast Asia in vivid colors and believable performances that never falter. *Full Metal Jacket* is a deeply sad masterpiece that maddeningly refuses to judge its own characters but nonetheless speaks volumes about the effects of war on humanity. ◆

Beverly Hills Cop II

Video, April 1988

Given the altogether sorry creative history of cinematic sequels, it's both a surprise and a pleasure to report that *Beverly Hills Cop II* neatly breaks that tradition by improving on the original in virtually every way. The second film, set two years later, employs another routine crime plot to divert scam-happy Detroit detective Axel Foley (Eddie Murphy) to Los Angeles, where he merrily runs afoul of the stellar bad guy triumvirate (Jurgen Prochnow, Brigitte Nielsen, Dean Stockwell) as well as an apoplectic police chief. Although Murphy's élan managed to carry the first film, which was otherwise generally laughless and clumsy, to huge box office success, this time he's looser, more self-assured and funnier, in a blockbuster that is better looking, more sharply written and directed, and better acted than its predecessor.

The same gang of Beverly Hills cops is on hand — Detective Rosewood (Judge Reinhold), the world's worst driver, twisted by the sequel's screenwriters into a fringe weirdo living in a house full of plants and guns; Sgt. Taggart (John Ashton), his long-suffering partner with marital problems; and Captain Bogomil (Ronny Cox), Foley's former foe, whose attempted murder draws him to the West Coast. The previous picture was spent dissolving the antagonism between them and Foley; *II* takes their warm friendships as given. That rapport is used to narrow the focus on the absurdly resourceful hero, who breaks up the nefarious crime gang while confounding the ludicrous Chief Lutz (Allen Garfield) and evading the long-distance ire of Inspector Todd (Gil Hill). A silly repeat performance by Paul Reiser, as well as cameos by Hugh Hefner and Gilbert Gottfried (as an accountant with a bizarre approach to bribery), all add to the entertainment.

But as funny as Murphy's incessant wisecracks, put-ons and vulgar asides are, there's a fatigue factor: too much of a good thing. At one point, he pretends to be a delivery man carrying "sound-seeking projectiles" to get onto a shooting range where he wants to interrogate someone. While his terrorization of the officious receptionist is briefly amusing, he could just as easily have asked for an appointment. Likewise, stealing a mansion (that's right) and conning his way into a private nightclub by introducing Sgt. Taggart as Gerald Ford are transparent contrivances to give Murphy more comedic opportunities.

The pacing is otherwise expert, and the score's urgent electronic rhythms complement the high-tech crime scenes. Garfield is hilarious as the outraged bureaucrat dead set on disciplining everyone under his jurisdiction; as his Detroit counterpart, Hill sputters and threatens Axel with more humor and conviction than the first film.

All told, a remarkably solid sequel, and the first one in memory that actually makes the likelihood of further episodes something to anticipate rather than dread. ◆

While I befriended Assistant Editor Lou Kesten (a wry puzzle genius with a taste for horror films, now an editor at the Associated Press) and Adam Phillips (who went on to a long career at Marvel), I also formed lasting bonds with Doug Brod and Glenn Kenny, editors at the rival *Video Review*. But by far the greatest benefit of my time at *Video* came in July 1987 with the arrival of an attractive and intriguing Associate Art Director, Kristina Juzaitis.

Reader, I married her.

Sure, it took a decade or so for that happy ending to a very twisty road — including a brief second marriage for me and a couple of boyfriends for her — but that was more than two decades ago now. The rest of my life truly began at a drafting table on West 34th Street.

In a lucky break for our bit of the media world, film studios all had an interest in promoting the video after-market. And so they began inviting our small coterie of video journalists along to the ludicrously extravagant junkets that were standard for Hollywood film promotion. Some of the junkets were in swanky New York hotels, but a lot of them weren't. So, many months before we had any call to write anything (our participation was rolled into the pre-release film promotion, so we had to wait for the video to come out, six months or more down the road), we got whisked off — all expenses paid — to places like London, Memphis and Palm Springs. (My travels also included twice-yearly trips to Las Vegas and Chicago for the Video Software Dealers Association convention and the Consumer Electronics Show, but we had to do real work and make our own way at those. The junkets were carefully and luxuriously structured, nearly effortless if the film didn't completely suck and generally fun-packed.) We stayed at top hotels, ate in fine restaurants, usually got some local entertainment thrown in and all we had to do was watch a film and then spend a morning doing round-robin interviews with the talent. A hell of a perk for a lowly journalist.

Meeting the then-little-known but disarmingly smart (yes, and gorgeous) Sharon Stone at a 1988 roundtable for *Action Jackson* was a more memorable experience than anything in the silly film itself. Novice actress (and Harvard student) Meredith Salenger (and now married to Patton Oswalt) at the junket for *Dream a Little Dream* was a far more interesting person than her famous co-stars, Corey Feldman and Corey Haim, who were way less cool than they thought they were. I got to speak with Michael Caine, Jerry Lee Lewis and June Allyson, had a wee next to John Doe, toured Sun Studios in Memphis and Elvis's home in Palm Springs and had a drink and a natter with Norman Mailer after he directed the film of his novel, *Tough Guys Don't Dance*.

Great Balls of Fire

This 1989 junket, for which we put up at the fabulous Peabody Hotel (gotta love the fountain ducks!), first introduced me to the marvels of Memphis BBQ. It also got me in a room with Jerry Lee Lewis, who was both hard of hearing and ornery, which led to a tense moment as one of us Northern city boys asked a question that he took the wrong way and got hot about. We were used to high-strung stars with sensitivities that might lead to an abrupt walkout, but this felt more like the escalating prelude to a bar fight. (Nothing happened, but phew!)

On the last night, our corporate host stood us for rounds of an expensive Jack Daniels special reserve that, combined with the subsequent glut of beers and ribs at the Rendezvous, left me so hung over that I could not answer the bell for the morning press conference with Winona Ryder, on whom I had a bit of a fan-boy crush. Disappointed and queasy, I lay in bed and tried not to hurl as the room rotated around me. I had a flight home early that afternoon, but packing my bag would mean standing up and looking down at it, which was far too vertiginous to manage. After a long while, when I was finally able to throw my shit in the case, I slunk out through the lobby to get a taxi.

Dennis Quaid stokes rock's Fire

Video, December 1989

It's strange enough seeing a familiar actor like Dennis Quaid portraying someone as well-known as Jerry Lee Lewis. But when the star of *Great Balls of Fire* turns up in a Memphis hotel to talk about his movie, months after the shooting, with the same blond dye job, period shoes and the remnants of an artificial Southern accent, the line between reality and acting blurs.

Although viewers might not realize it from Quaid's extravagant caricature of one of the 1950s' greatest white rock and rollers, Quaid took the role very seriously. "I had a responsibility to Jerry Lee Lewis, and I needed his blessing. Before we started, I told him if I can get it close to your heart then I'll be able to sleep at night.

"You can't invent a character like Jerry Lee Lewis," Quaid observes. "It's certainly more fun than playing Pat Boone."

This isn't Quaid's first real-life role. "Playing Gordo Cooper in *The Right Stuff* was a gas. He was my favorite astronaut when I was a kid," Quaid recalls. "I prefer playing real people. I try to get to the truth of a person then fictionalize it."

And therein lies one of the problems with *Great Balls of Fire*, which fizzled theatrically this summer. The film, which primarily addresses Lewis's career from 1956 to 1958, is less a musical docudrama than a stylized love story about his marriage to a 13-year-old second cousin, Myra Gale Brown. By purchasing the rights to Myra's 1982 memoir (republished this year as a tie-in), the filmmakers were able to portray some of the people actually involved in Lewis's life, according to producer Adam Fields.

But director Jim McBride was concerned with making an entertaining film, not a documentary. He conceived of it as a fantasy, and several scenes, like a dance number on the steps of Myra's school that resembles the opening of *High School Confidential* (a 1958 movie in which Lewis appeared), bear this out. In any case, the film's fabricated facts and improbable chronology only magnify Quaid's bizarre performance.

Still, if Jerry Lee Lewis "didn't like something, I worked as hard as I could to change it," Quaid recalls. "This is the only movie I've ever done where I'd like to do Part Two. Jerry Lee's life is so rich, the whole thing needs to be done."

In the meantime, Quaid's pursuing his own musical career. He has a band, a contract with Capitol Records, a forthcoming album and the memory of working with the one and only Killer. "The musical education I got from him is invaluable. He had his effect on me." ◆

Al Pacino

We were a jaded lot, we video reporters, so talking to famous actors was no problem. Neither was asking difficult questions amid the friendly softballs endemic to junketeers. I have never been much of an Al Pacino fan, so when we met at a hotel roundtable for *Sea of Love*, a tense 1989 murder mystery with Ellen Barkin and John Goodman, I was unafraid to query him on a detail in the film that bugged me. As the actor was born in the Bronx, I wondered, how could the detective he plays do something *no* New York native, *especially* a cop, would ever do? He was a bit nonplussed by the question but did manage a clever reply. This is the short piece that came out of that exchange.

Sea of Love

Video, May 1990

"One of the things I look for in a script," says Al Pacino, "is the dilemma in a character." After the disastrous reviews and commercial failure of 1985's *Revolution*, a more germane dilemma was how one of America's finest actors could regain his momentum as a movie star. Despite a long and distinguished career in such films as *Scarface, Serpico, The Godfather* and *Dog Day Afternoon*, Pacino had lost his box office power. Following *Revolution* (which he defends only to the point of saying, "I thought there were some interesting scenes"), he returned, as he often has, to his first love — theater. He appeared in an Off-Broadway production of *Julius Caesar* and developed various projects, including an experimental film of a play called *The Local Stigmatic*.

It took the sexy police thriller *Sea of Love* to reintroduce Pacino to the movie-going (and, with its recent arrival on tape, video-renting) masses. The New York native, now 50, brings believable maturity to the role of a rumpled detective who foolishly falls in love with a prime suspect (played by Ellen Barkin) in the murder case he's investigating.

Frank Keller, Pacino explains in a soft, raspy voice, "is a guy with mid-life problems. He has a drinking problem. He's been asked to retire from the job he's done for 20 years. He has no love interest in his life, and Freud says work and love are all there is. He needs love, communication with someone."

The script by noted Bronx novelist Richard Price gives *Sea of Love* a convincing dose of contemporary New York culture. But why would a smart New York cop repeatedly open an apartment door without knowing who's outside? "We shot in Canada, where things are different," Pacino quips. ◆

Please Rewind

The beginning of the end of my professional idyll at *Video* came when editor-in-chief Doug Garr left; his successor, a suburban single mom who'd come from a trade magazine for convention planners, was a culturally ignorant master of the obvious. Her editorial ideas were rubbish and the freelance friends she pushed me to use were inappropriate for our needs. She was grossly unsuited for the job but, as I understood it, came cheap. I did my best to get along with her until the day she sheepishly admitted that she had killed her cat by inadvertently closing it in a folding bed.

Judy Sawyer lasted longer than any of us expected her to, but her replacement was no improvement. Art Levis, a cocky video veteran, took an instant dislike to me. Managing Editor Stan Pinkwas, a likable, cultured and hard-working reformed bohemian with a stint at Shakespeare and Co. in Paris on his résumé, stopped being my ally and became Art's weapon against me. I had my own complaints. Stan was fond of coverlines that included the *Beaver*-like phrase "bang for your buck." We nearly came to blows when I bridled at his suggestion to shorten the caption on a photo of actress Mary Elizabeth Mastrantonio by IDing her as Mary Mastrantonio. When they went behind my back to assign a programming story I had nixed, I called bullshit and quit.

I was still on the masthead as Senior Editor in the November 1989 issue; the following month I was lumped in with a bunch of freelancers as a "contributing editor"; a junior colleague, Ken Korman, now had my former title.

entertainment
WEEKLY
MOVIES
WINTER FILMS:
THE BIG WEEP
PRINT
HIP HUGGERS:
THE STERNS AND
THE SIXTIES
KIDS
NEW ZORRO:
HERO OR ZERO?
VIDEO
STONES SAGA:
NO SATISFACTION
TV
COMPELLING
'KENNEDYS'
$1.95 (CAN. $2.50)
BEYOND THE GRAMMYS
In today's divided,
divisive music scene,
NENEH
CHERRY &
K.D. LANG rise
above
the rest by stirring up
smart new sounds
THE MIX MASTERS
CHERRY (INSET) AND LANG

Entertainment Weekly (1989 – 1999)

In 1989, when *People* magazine TV critic Jeff Jarvis succeeded in convincing the powers that be at Time Inc. to launch *Entertainment Weekly*, a magazine dedicated to covering pop culture in a novel way, I got up my gumption and applied for a job. As Jarvis envisioned it, the magazine would include sections on TV, movies, books, music and video, each its own department staffed by an editor, an associate editor, a reporter, a critic and an assistant. Looking ahead from my gig at *VIDEO* magazine, I could happily envision myself with a new full-time gig reviewing albums — or overseeing the person who did.

I managed to secure a meeting with Jarvis in September, but on the day, I had the second worst prolonged allergy attack of my life. I was well off my game: my ears were clogged, my throat was hoarse, I couldn't stop sneezing, I hadn't slept well and I wasn't thinking clearly. We had a nice conversation, but nothing came of it.

I caught two breaks, however, when Sue Byrom, the veteran English journalist who had been my editor when I freelanced for the *New York Post*, was hired to run the music department. And Jim Meigs, who had been the editor of *Video Review*, got the video section to run and saw me as uniquely situated to review music videos; as I had done at *Video*, I also wrote about movies on tape.

The wonderful David Browne was brought over from the *Daily News* to handle music features, but the staff critic Sue selected was Greg Sandow: a towering figure with a white leonine mane who knew lots about classical music. While he had the swagger of self-confidence in person, his early stabs at writing about rock and rap were riddled with uncertainty borne of unfamiliarity.

A few months after he finally brought the magazine to market in February 1990 (with k.d. lang on the debut issue's cover), Jarvis was pushed out and the clear-cut structural policies he had instated were rethought. The music section opened up to freelancers, and I began contributing record reviews — mostly reissues — as well. I was fast and reliable, so I got lots of work there. In issue 40 (16 November 1990) alone, I wrote about albums by Monie Love, Eno/Cale, Roxy Music and Gang of Four as well as the Roky Erickson tribute set.

EW ran a lot of capsule reviews ("Recordings at a Glance" was the initial section hed), quixotic efforts to shoehorn a thoughtful artistic judgment into 75 words of largely explanatory consumer-guide prose (thank god for parentheses), capped off with a letter grade for those easily swayed consumers who couldn't wade through an entire paragraph. With nuance and balance impossible to finesse, they were essentially dressed-up Ebert thumbs in print. It is actually harder to write that short, but my *Trouser Press Record Guide* work had prepared me, so that's what I did.

The magazine paid its freelancers very well. At one point, they cut back on the length of record reviews — but didn't immediately change the generous per-piece rate. One Saturday morning, I sat down and reviewed three reissues, an easy enough assignment. For a total of maybe 350 words in all, I pocketed a month's rent. That inadvertent beneficence came to a quick end, but then another potential jackpot emerged: a verbal offer for a retainer deal that would have me contribute a handful of record reviews a week — two days of easy work, max — in exchange for enough dosh to obviate the need for any other remunerative labor. There was some period of waiting while approvals were to be acquired, so it dragged on a bit. Just a matter of days before the promised retainer contract was to be on its way to me, the editor who had offered me the deal got shitcanned, and that was the end of that.

Sandow became music editor, David Browne took over as staff critic and Elysa Gardner (who went on to a big writing career after leaving the magazine) the department assistant. Later on, the music staff was wise to hire Tom Sinclair. Ron Givens took on the job of assigning record reviews, and he kept me gainfully busy covering reissues until Greg's editorial tinkering became too much for me to bear. I am, however, eternally grateful for the one valuable piece of writing advice I got from him: never end a sentence or a paragraph with a weak word or thought.

A random sample of the many capsule reviews I did for *EW* and the letter grades I was obliged to assign:

Bob Geldof *The Happy Club* (Polydor) With his monumental Live Aid achievements now receding into history alongside his punk days in the Boomtown Rats, Bob Geldof has found himself a handsome, comfortable-sounding niche somewhere between Van Morrison and Bob Dylan. Geldof's third (and best) solo album, an inventive blend of Irish folk and modern pop, offers politics, religion, tender memories and playful fun — engaging intelligence with loads of heart. **B+**

Ride *Smile* (Sire/Reprise) Noisy guitar distortion is often a mask for artistic ineptitude, but this London [*oops: Oxford*] quartet uses its fuzzboxes, feedback and wah-wah to create gusts of tuneful rock & roll excitement. Smile wraps eight delicate pop songs in a chaotic storm, daring listeners to weather the onslaught and enjoy their charm. **B**

Bettie Serveert *Palomine* (Matador) The captivating Dutch quartet Bettie Serveert pulls you in with its gentle indie-pop demeanor and Carol van Dijk's cool, conversational vocals — then unleashes a storm of jagged guitar noise. *Palomine*'s remarkable feat is that its quiet arrangements never undersell the offbeat songs — and turmoil can't shake the music's sturdy foundations. **A-**

Styx *Edge of the Century* (A&M) Seven years after breaking up, Styx — at best, an overblown bar band with clumsy English art-rock pretensions — is back in business, testing the commercial climate for richly sung schlock. Although Midwestern sincerity and solid creative effort prevent this derivative album, *Edge of the Century*, from sounding entirely crass, the gaping lack of originality (these guys have obviously been listening to a lot of rock radio) guarantees its mediocrity. **C**

Information Society *Hack* (Tommy Boy) That old joke about watching the TV commercials and ignoring the shows applies to this New York synth trio's second album. When Information Society layers sound bites — from TV, radio, records, and the telephone — over hip-hop beats, *Hack* conveys the chaos of urban streets with a palpable sense of reality. Unfortunately, these exciting moments are surrounded by plodding and badly sung techno-dance songs. **D+**

Trashmen *Tube City!: The Best of the Trashmen* (Sundazed) The Trashmen were not only goofy enough to play surf-beat instrumentals while living in Minnesota, they had the demented inspiration to create 1963's greatest junk-rock novelty, "Surfin' Bird." *Tube City!* is a vintage dance party with the deliciously cheesy ambience of an atrocious beach movie. Garbage doesn't get any sweeter than this. **A+**

Texas Instruments *Magnetic Home* (Doctor Dream) These unpretentious ramblers on the indie-rock highway build their alternative rock thing on folk roots of the '60s: Bob Dylan, San Francisco psychedelia, the Buffalo Springfield. Magnetic Home, the Austin quartet's fourth album, has energy, charm and several memorable songs, but its casual, one-take ambience doesn't suit long journeys. **B-**

Bobby Fuller Four *The Best of the Bobby Fuller Four* (Rhino) Like the great Eddie Cochran a decade earlier, Bobby Fuller was a multitalented rock & roll original whose many creative achievements never received adequate commercial recognition and who died tragically in his early 20s. Fuller's engaging music, recorded in 1965 and 1966, has been popularized via numerous cover versions, but the real thing has freshness and sincerity that make it special. Cut from newly recovered master tapes that give *The Best of Bobby Fuller* a real sonic advantage over Rhino's corresponding Golden Archive Series vinyl/cassette compilation, "I Fought the Law," "Another Sad and Lonely Night" and "Let Her Dance" (plus other fine, if lesser-known, tracks) make this an essential retrospective. **B+**

Ice-T *The Classic Collection* (Excello/Rhino) Ya gotta give Ice-T his props: he was kicking serious West Coast rap before anyone. If these old-school tracks from the mid-'80s don't quite sound like the arrival of a courageous and controversial superstar, Ice-T's smart, funny rhymes still make this introduction to his story worth perusing. **B+**

Ben E. King *Anthology* (Atlantic/Rhino) Ben E. King, the magnificent voice and author of 1960's "Stand by Me," poured warmth and sincerity all over the hits he recorded as a Drifter ("There Goes My Baby") and as a young solo soulster. But King ultimately lacked the stylistic authority of a great artist, and the diverse songs from his later career don't all inspire such conviction. **B-**

Dictators *The Dictators Go Girl Crazy* (Epic) Although the Dictators never became "The Next Big Thing" (as they promised on the first track of this 1975 debut), *Go Girl Crazy*'s junk-generation culture and smart-aleck sensibility did provide an essential blueprint for '70s punk. With its TV references and homely vocals, this ground-breaking and long-unavailable album continues to inspire underground groups everywhere. That the "Teengenerate" quintet boasted a brilliant pop songwriter (Andy Shernoff) and a world-class hard-rock guitarist (Ross the Boss) only helps make this unserious album a serious milestone, a tune-and laugh-filled revelation. If you want to know who introduced wrestling and White Castle hamburgers to rock & roll, spread the joy of remaking '60s pop classics ("I Got You Babe," "California Sun") with bratty irreverence, and proved that rock-band rules were made to be broken, the Dictators are your men. **A**

Wanda Jackson *Rockin in the Country* (Rhino) Blessed with the sexiest voice since Elvis Presley, Wanda Jackson defied white female stereotypes of the late '50s with sizzling rockabilly and rock & roll singles considered too hot to be hits. Hitching her country roots to the rhythm & blues wagon, Wanda added a devastating come-hither tone that spoke volumes. *Rockin' in the Country*, a concise retrospective (14 tracks; 18 on CD), contains the best of her bad-girl classics ("Let's Have a Party," "Fujiyama Mama," etc.), but gives equal time to her less rambunctious Nashville country work of the '60s. **B+**

The Scepter Records Story

Although Scepter Records was a hit factory in the '60s, the label never had the cachet of a Motown or Sun. Scepter's commitment to picking top material rather than blazing stylistic trails was probably what kept its public profile low — and makes the three-CD *Scepter Records Story* (Capricorn) such a thrilling surprise. This well-stocked jukebox of great rock and roll singles — the Shirelles' torchy "Soldier Boy," the Isley Brothers' raving "Twist and Shout," the Kingsmen's classic "Louie Louie," and B.J. Thomas' drippy "Raindrops Keep Fallin' on My Head" — must seem mighty eclectic. But when Scepter reigned, rock & roll was mighty eclectic — a confusion of R&B, pop, and country that embraced almost anything with a beat and a hook. More than three dozen Top 40 hits guarantee the box's appeal, but, more importantly, it expertly depicts an era when music was just music. **A-**

> Dear Mr. Robbins,
>
> I was so excited by your eloquent review of the Scepter Records collection. As producer of the box set and as a huge fan of *Trouser Press* and your book, I was really tickled to death. I can't tell you how many times I ran to the news stand to buy the newest *Trouser Press* when I lived in Manhattan.
>
> I sent your review to Florence Greenberg, Scepter's founder, and to producer/songwriter Luther Dixon, both of whom were thrilled and asked me to convey that to you.
>
> I hope to meet you one day and always look forward to seeing what new albums and projects you're writing about! Thank you very much for reviewing the Scepter box set, and for your kind words.
>
> Sincerely,
> Diana
> Diana Haig
>
> Thanks, Ira!
>
> DH/ms

The response I received was *so* gratifying; I wish the review had been long enough to merit such fulsome praise.

Jerry Lee Lewis *The Jerry Lee Lewis Anthology* (Rhino) Filling two discs with the unnatural force of ill-nature that is Jerry Lee Lewis requires scant exertion: the Killer has recorded enough momentous sides of rock & roll fire and country misery to load a collection twice the size. Like few singers in pop, Lewis constructed his vividly recognizable persona almost entirely on other people's songs, making them his own through sheer will. Only a sucker would bother cutting this career-spanning deck: it's stacked with aces. **A**

Dave Bartholomew *Spirit of New Orleans: The Genius of Dave Bartholomew* (Imperial/EMI) Fats Domino was Dave Bartholomew's most successful studio protégé, but by no means his only star. As documented on these two discs of vintage New Orleans R&B, the fabled producer-songwriter-bandleader-performer also wove his infectious, low-key spells with Shirley & Lee, Smiley Lewis, Roy Brown and others. (Some of them featured here on tunes popularized by the Fat Man.) The sound is as murky as the Mississippi, but Bartholomew keeps the grooves flowing like the smoothest bourbon. **B**

Soul Asylum *Grave Dancers Union* (Columbia) A powerhouse with a poetic soul, Soul Asylum should finally get their commercial due with this hard-hitting album. Mixing up chunky '70s riffola, a stirring country ballad and punky vehemence, the Minneapolis quartet slams its best cards on the table, splashing lyrical wit into hundred-proof spirit. **A**

Beat Happening *You Turn Me On* (Sub Pop) Beat Happening give inspired amateurism a good name. On its fifth album, the wily and winsome Northwest trio draws stick-figure pop songs with just voice, electric guitar and skeletal drums: a charming racket dressed in childlike innocence. **A-**

Big Black *The Rich Man's Eight Track Tape* (Touch and Go) Barbed with oblique political venom and the most abrasive sounds ever coaxed out of electric guitars, this reissue of a reissue of mid-'80s issue by Chicago's uncompromising Big Black seethes with scrawny punk antagonism and virulent musical imagination. **B**

Ramones *Mondo Bizarro* (Radioactive) The Ramones became a punk-rock institution through their single-minded devotion to one thing: elementary tunes with stupid lyrics, played hard and simple. Ideally, every great Ramones song sounds like every other; creative ambition has been the band's occasional undoing. The quartet's twelfth studio album is prudently no social climber, but with so much of their own punk junk to recycle, why cover a Doors song and swipe the chorus of "I Won't Let It Happen" from glam-rockers Slade? **B-**

Nazareth *No Jive* (Griffin Music) Ten years after the presumed extinction of this Scottish dinosaur — a bluesy hard-rock quartet known for its brutal version of a Joni Mitchell ballad — Nazareth comes lumbering back to life, good as new. Still running on stubborn chutzpah, this once-mighty '70s beast, stranded in an inhospitable environment, somehow sounds right at home. **B**

Occasionally, an ambitious reissue project was deemed worthy of a lead review.

Hip-Hop History: Street Jams and Electric Funk

Entertainment Weekly, 21 February 1992

Popular music thrives on its myths. According to the lore, Elvis Presley invented rock'n'roll, and the Sex Pistols were the original punk band. But he didn't, and they weren't. If casual observers imagine that rap began with Hammer, the fact is many other MCs had to look for the perfect beat before he could sell it to Pepsi-Cola.

The sounds of an urban youth culture dubbed hip-hop first emanated from schoolyards and clubs across the Bronx and Harlem in the late 1970s. Initially, rap's lively skeleton of booming beats, manic turntable maneuvers and urgent voices — music as hard and real as the city itself — was confined to New York, another subway rider stuck underground.

But rap found a way out and, despite lingering prejudice and reservations, mainstream culture now rocks to its rhythmic rhymes — from pop charts to advertising. Even Rhino Records, the golden-oldies label whose exhaustive reissues are the ultimate tributes to music ranging from soul and British rock to the Monkees, is paying its respects, planting the roots of rap firmly into serious music history. An annotated compilation of vintage singles on four individual albums, Street Jams introduces hip-hop's heritage to the world it helped create.

Street Jams devotes two discs to rap itself and two to mostly instrumental "electric funk," tracks dominated not by rappers but by the producers, keyboard players and turntable masters who also provided the rappers' backing tracks. What emerges is a musical revolution that began modestly but gained creative juice as newcomers rushed to out-innovate each other. *Street Jams*' 1979–1985 timeframe predates rap's vast commercial impact (few of these pioneers were around long enough to enjoy it), so the greatest hits of hip-hop would be a drastically different collection. But no understanding of the music's genesis is possible without the tracks preserved here.

Compared to the brutal roar of some current artists, *Street Jams: Hip-Hop From the Top Part 1* comes in like a lamb. Beneath the boastful party banter of Sugarhill Gang's 1979 "Rapper's Delight" (a fundamental record, but mild-mannered enough to reach the *Billboard* Top 40 with lines like "Guess what, America? We love you!") and Kurtis Blow's wryly polite "The Breaks" (1980), rap's groundbreakers built their musical house on a familiar disco foundation. That wasn't enough change for a restless new generation; structures had to be stripped down to yield a stark, minimalist style younger African-Americans could call their own.

Rap outgrew the innocence of party music when Grandmaster Flash and the Furious Five delivered "The Message," a grim 1982 diary of life in the rotten Apple. Tinged with menace but poetic in its perception, the song contained a memorable refrain ("Don't push me, 'cause I'm close to the edge"). In its realistic portrayal of an urban nightmare shared by many of its listeners, the song first suggested rap's potential to unite and empower a generation. Rap was becoming, as Chuck D. of Public Enemy put it, CNN for Black America.

Hip-Hop Part 1 outlines the music's origins; *Part 2* more or less follows its development, capturing the early growth of rap's diversity, from Kurtis Blow's 1984 celebration of "Basketball" to the rock-hard syncopation of Run-DMC's momentous 1983 debut, "It's Like That." The album also touches on the vinyl fracas begun by UTFO's "Roxanne, Roxanne." The 1984 single of frustrated pick-up lines engendered numerous salty reply records from women, one of which, "The Real Roxanne" by Roxanne with UTFO, follows it here.

Back in the clubs, dancers began moving to music with the same punch as rap but fewer verbal distractions. *Electric Funk Part 1* is a pulse-quickening document of what they heard: the visionary Afrika Bambaataa (whose hugely influential 1982 "Planet Rock" made dynamic street music out of arty German synthesists' robotic disco), keyboardist Herbie Hancock (who dropped in from the fusion-jazz world to sample hip-hop techniques, earning a 1983 Grammy for his wild breakdancing soundtrack, "Rockit") and the turntable wizards who dreamed up new ways to "play" records. *Part 2* is the era's hangover: a tedious hour of wretched disco singing, Darth Vader voices, drum programs and other clichés of the electronic age.

For all the care and enthusiasm that obviously went into compiling, annotating and mastering *Street Jams*, however, the set has its shortcomings. Non-chronological sequencing and the absence of production credits obscure the developmental flow. The songs are jammed together with abrupt transitions, and some tracks seem misplaced: an early rap performance by Ice-T is consigned to *Electric Funk*. In terms of gaps, Blondie's 1980 hip-hop/pop hybrid "Rapture" would have been an enlightening inclusion; the omission of "White Lines," Melle Mel's 1983 cocaine warning, is more serious. Doug E. Fresh is nowhere to be heard. Instead, crucial cuts (especially those on *Hip-Hop Part 1*) are surrounded by instrumentals, novelties and mediocre tracks of dubious significance. And three *Funk* appearances by Newcleus, whose label Rhino evidently owns, is at least one too many.

Still, *Street Jams* fulfills its cultural mission with more than enough early landmarks, invigorating tracks that practically force you to dance. This in-depth retrospective vividly conveys how rap grew from a variation on existing dance music into a distinct force by stripping away the remnants of the past, leaving only the beats and rhymes needed to build a profound musical future. ◆

Movies

Notwithstanding the experience I'd gained at *Video* magazine, I had an amateur's depth and expertise in film, which made me well-suited to review home videos for *Entertainment Weekly*. The magazine had a proper film critic (Owen Gleiberman) for new releases; the video after-market needed something less. I was neither inclined to nor capable of impressing anyone with my grasp of auteur theory, a semiotic analysis of John Wayne's role as an icon of the romantic tradition in the mythology of the American West or the trans-cultural values of Korean film noir.

Not talking down to readers was an *EW* credo; my lack of academic film knowledge ensured that I couldn't even if I'd tried. (I did, however, have to check my elitist scorn for mainstream rubbish.) Jim Meigs, a top-notch editor, was wise enough to recognize that and gave me lots of work. It didn't hurt that two other *Video Review* alumni I knew were also on the magazine's staff: David Hajdu (author of *Positively 4th Street*) and my good friend Doug Brod.

Smack in Your Face

Entertainment Weekly, 14 February 1997

If *Trainspotting* (1996) is, as some have claimed, an irresponsible advertisement for heroin use, the Smack Council had better start looking for a new agency. Despite its raves for the rush — "Take the best orgasm you've ever had, multiply it by a thousand, and you're still nowhere near it," effuses narrator Mark Renton (Ewan McGregor) — *Trainspotting* ultimately depicts the disastrous consequences of addiction with unsparing irony. Disconcertingly free of moral outrage but illustratively down on dope, *Trainspotting* is a potently unglamorous shot in the arm of junk cinema, an ugly little genre that can easily be tracked on video.

Otto Preminger and Frank Sinatra famously broke the taboo more than 40 years ago, entering the abyss of drug addiction via *The Man With the Golden Arm* (1955). Set to Elmer Bernstein's jazzy noir score, the right-minded tale was courageous for its time but now looks overheated and quaint. Reformed junkie and poker dealer Frankie Machine (Sinatra) returns from prison with big dreams of going straight as, of all things, a drummer. But no amount of good intentions can keep him from the devilish temptations of a pusher (Darren McGavin). At this melodrama's lurid peak, Frankie goes cold turkey, politely entreating the valiant Molly (Kim Novak), "If you love me, kill me, please."

By the '70s, heroin had become such a well-known social disease that America was ready for a tougher, more contemporary view. With a script by Joan Didion and John Gregory Dunne, *The Panic in Needle Park* (1971) graphically depicts street-level addiction as a one-way ticket down. Compelling, unflattering performances by its stars rivet this grim romance between a cocky New York grifter (Al Pacino) and the mild-mannered Midwesterner (Kitty Winn) he corrupts. Tagging along on the couple's aimless parade of scores, hits, crimes and arrests, the film occasionally takes on the appearance of cinema vérité, and video amplifies the impression of TV-news reality.

A generation later, *Drugstore Cowboy* (1989) removed the sensationalism and raised the stakes. Discarding *Needle Park*'s oh-my observations, the film treats the lifestyle of "shameless full-time dope fiends" as stable and nearly viable. Going so far as to feature William S. Burroughs as a wizened junkie ex-priest decrying the "demonization" of narcotics, maverick director Gus Van Sant (*To Die For*) cozies up to Bob and Dianne Hughes (Matt Dillon, Kelly Lynch), happy-go-lucky ringleaders who rob pharmacies and get high on the swag. Rich with pharmacological detail, weird drama and such droll insights as "[junkies need] something to relieve the pressures of their everyday life...like having to tie their shoes," this disarming and bittersweet movie doesn't judge its characters but treats the consequences of their actions as a natural payoff of their drug thefts. When Bob cleans up only to meet another fate entirely, he takes it in stride, just like a cowboy.

The faint-hearted may prefer *London Kills Me* (1991), a drug movie that hardly touches the stuff. In a flimsy directorial debut that preceded *Trainspotting*'s heroin haze of Scottish youth culture, screenwriter Hanif Kureishi (*My Beautiful Laundrette*) doesn't trouble his pitiful posse of small-time dealers and squatters with much evidence of their chemical dependency. In fact, lead loser Clint (Justin Chadwick) expends far more effort trying to steal shoes for a job interview than he does feeding his habit. As one addict grumbles: "Druggies are boring, small-minded, stupid. The people are enough to put you off taking the stuff." If Kureishi disagreed, he might have made a more substantial film.

Which is exactly the source of *Trainspotting*'s devastating impact. Adapted from Irvine Welsh's bleakly funny episodic novel, the movie likes its nihilists: Scottish drug buddies Renton, Sick Boy (Jonny Lee Miller) and Spud (Ewen Bremner), plus their vicious alcoholic mate Begbie (Robert Carlyle) and the ill-fated Tommy (Kevin McKidd). Between fixes and capers, they talk up a slang-happy storm, debating James Bond movies, analyzing their habits, chatting up underage girls. A deliriously profane spew of sex, ODs and videotape, *Trainspotting* leavens the stomach-turning scatology and violence with a savvy soundtrack and surreal invention.

Vibrant and colorful, the film abstains from sermonizing to tug at the conundrum of voluntary self-annihilation. In a voice-over during the boisterous opening scene — a foot race with police through Edinburgh streets, set to the thumping urge of Iggy Pop's "Lust for Life" — Renton articulates the paradox. "Choose life," he proposes, in one of the cast's most easily understood accents, the comprehensibility of which improves with rewinding. "Why would I want to do a thing like that?" In their explorations of drugs and the people who love them, these videos all provide clues to that deadly riddle. ◆

Love Gets Real

Hate her concert act all you want, but with The People Vs. Larry Flynt*, Courtney Love launches a movie career more in the tradition of serious thespian Cher than acting wannabe Madonna.*

Entertainment Weekly, 6 June 1997

It's written in the entertainers' bible: If thine image offends thee, try another medium. For music stars straitjacketed by an unwanted reputation, movies offer a handy escape route. With one suitable (and songless) project, acting can (as with Cher) — but doesn't always (as with Madonna) — drastically alter mass perceptions.

When director Milos Forman (*Amadeus, Ragtime*) set about polishing a reprehensible sleazemonger into an endearing free-speech hero in *The People vs. Larry Flynt*, he also afforded another infamous figure the chance to improve a nasty reputation.

To the public mind, Courtney Love of Hole is alternative rock's baddest bad girl. Only Roseanne gets more consistently scabrous and malicious press than this inflammatory loudmouth. But risks are her business, and so, in a career move comparable to stage-diving in a short dress, Love cast her cinematic lot with Althea Leasure — the stripper who married Larry Flynt, ran *Hustler* magazine during his jail time and finally drowned in a tub, an HIV-infected drug addict.

Though the role is more of a stretch than, say, playing a rowdy rock singer, the similarities between Leasure and Love — a onetime stripper, ex-heroin user and the widow of Kurt Cobain — are obvious; Love does slip smoothly into the skin of this assertive, outrageous woman devoted to an equally unconventional mate. She looks great in Althea's salad days — all big bright eyes, plush mouth and trim figure — and goes luminously to hell at the end. While Forman pursues his entertaining but blinkered agenda of painting Flynt (Woody Harrelson) as a victimized reprobate, Love fishes an exhilarating personal victory from the narrow straits separating her and the role. She emerges a disciplined, talented pro able to hold her own (despite a wavering regional accent) in the skilled company of *Oscar*-nominees Harrelson and Edward Norton (as Flynt's long-suffering attorney).

Love got a *Golden Globe* nomination for *Flynt* but as yet has made no plans to act again. Next, she should expand her dramatic scope and submerge herself in a less likely role. That's the hallmark of Cher's distinguished movie career (*Mask, Moonstruck, Mermaids, The Witches of Eastwick*), which long ago eclipsed her singing. On screen, the outlandishly attired pop goddess is a marvel of modesty, favoring down-to-earth characters who wouldn't have a clue how to get into a black leather bustier. **B+**

Control

TrouserPress.com message board, 21 September 2007

From now on, biographies of musicians should only be made by directors with a painter's eye and deep personal knowledge of their subject. Granted, that will seriously cut into the number of such films to be created, but if Anton Corbijn's *Control*, a shatteringly beautiful and haunting look at the brief existence of Joy Division and its doomed lead singer Ian Curtis, is the final entry in the often-execrable bio-pic genre, that's fine. He so surpasses the form's mundane language that his film sets an impossible standard for others to attempt.

Echoing the hollowness and placid despair of the band's music, Corbijn — who began his career as a rock photographer, with Joy Division and U2 among his primary subjects, and expanded his visual palette as a video director — all but ignores the tropes of the form. He foregoes the easy freeze frames of familiar images, the clear-cut hagiography, the overnight stardom. There are two passing "and then I wrote" setups — for "Control" and "Love Will Tear Us Apart" — but Corbijn makes little of them, sparing viewers pat explanation in favor of a more ambiguous suggestion of creativity's crooked path. Instead, the essence of Curtis's words inspires the language of the film.

Time after time, Corbijn pauses to insert riveting artistic statements without slowing the flow of what, at two hours, is a long film. A casual street conversation that suddenly cleaves Curtis's marriage is eloquent in its composition: the lens stays focused on his stationary body while her increasingly blurred torso walks toward it, accompanied by the inevitable repertoire selection. Obvious and simple, yes, but the synchronized impact is devastating. Elsewhere, signal events in the band's story are re-created without fanfare (in the case of their signing to Factory, played for laughs; in the case of a gig that ends in a riot, as blood sport) and set in context of the story, rather than as buoys to cover the gaps in it. The result is an intensely intimate demythification of a band that for many people is nothing but a myth.

Based on a memoir by Curtis's widow Deborah (who co-produced the film), the story is frighteningly predictive of Kurt Cobain's rise and death: each miserable winner, made increasingly disconsolate by the success they only thought they wanted or needed, left behind a wife, a baby and a band bigger than their dreams. Yet it is impossible to think of Courtney Love assenting to — much less sketching out — a portrait as nuanced, sad and blameless as this. Curtis here is a complex figure who travels from generic English glam kid — a little insular and difficult, sure, but optimistic and open to the future — to a despairing epileptic star frightened into hanging himself seven years later. With nothing to go on but illusion and fantasy, I'm not going to quarrel with the characterization of caring intimates with no evident historical axe to grind, and ultimately accuracy isn't an issue. What makes this so compelling is the depiction of amateurs fumbling their way toward fame, guided by one visionary who never lost his sense of being an outside observer even as hordes of admirers surrounded him. The pivotal moment that is never convincingly depicted in movies about rock bands — the transubstantiation of desire into achievement — is simply erased here. The closest Joy Division comes to a eureka moment is when manager Rob Gretton — played to the hysterical hilt by Toby Kebbell — interrupts a rehearsal to inform them of a two-week tour of America, the one Curtis would fatally cancel hours before departure time. Considering that they were coming to play clubs in what would have likely been a money-losing more-or-less replication of their European treks, it's not exactly a number-one record or a command performance for the Queen. (Not that either of those things would have suited Joy Division in the slightest...) In fact, the quartet was beatified but broke.

The film makes nothing of the hard graft of creativity, perhaps accepting the devaluation of rock effort. Play some notes, bang a drum, sing some shit and you've got a hit song. Bands don't get good overnight or receive the secret of success in a fax, they improve by imperceptible bits — a good gig, a bad gig, a song that shocks them into believing in their own talent — and that's the tenor of this story. Joy Division's album artwork and chilly sound set them atop a post-punk glacier, and this film melts it out from underneath them. Bernard Sumner is a nervous little twerp, Peter Hook a careless thug, Stephen Morris the good-looking cipher-drummer. And in the center, Curtis is a ball of confusion, working his civil service job, marrying his first girlfriend, losing his heart to a Belgian beauty and channeling it through a songwriting prism that either tells his story in the clearest possible terms or siphons something else entirely into an aching art of isolation. ◆

Record Reviews: Who Needs 'Em?

Salon, 1 January 2013

Part One

I could be wrong, but — adding together a decade of *Trouser Press* magazine, five *Trouser Press Record Guides* and a whole lot of freelance writing — I may have reviewed as many albums as any American rock critic this side of Bob Christgau. From adroit to inept, I've offered my full faith and credit to a small percentage of them, attacked some (with the fierce indignation generally reserved for orphan-robbers, World Series goats and career criminals) and juggled the rest. I suppose I've shared a few valuable insights, but no doubt just as often I've come up empty, papering over ambivalence with utilitarian description.

How often was I right? Even if we can stipulate that there is a "right," it's hard to say, since the inconstancy of life synchs unreliably with value judgments that have been frozen in time. What was on the money in 1978 may seem horribly naïve in 1988 and condescending by 2008. Plus, a critic continues to hear and learn long after committing an appraisal to print, and that both alters the context and expands culture's possibilities. When it comes to records which no longer live clearly in my memory, even going back for a refresher listen promises only a slim chance of summoning up enough sense of who I was and what I knew at the time to extrapolate what I was feeling when I wrote what I did.

I have never heard "Hats Off to Larry," the single that first introduced me to the existence of popular music 51 years ago, without truly feeling the pain and bitterness of Del Shannon's words. I had not yet loved and lost at the time (well, maybe a guinea pig or two), so the song's sentiments were practically worthless to me, but I was still moved in some way that I can't possibly remember. By the time I began thinking about music seriously, with the instinctive self-awareness that would oblige me to become a critic, I could better understand why it was a heart-wrenchingly great record, and I have never changed that estimation of it.

On the other hand, I was such a fan of the song "Snoopy Vs. the Red Baron" in sixth grade that I drew the dastardly Fokker pilot *Sieg Heiling* on a piece of cardboard with Magic Markers and mailed it off. (I have no idea how I knew where to mail it.) In any case, it came back autographed by Charles M. Schulz. But for all that, I have no need, or desire, to ever hear the Royal Guardsmen again. It was a novelty record, and I was susceptible to its short-lifespan charms. But time has clarified its merits. While I surely would have felt differently in my ignorance circa 1967, I would now leave the song, which, other than the "10 – 20 – 30 – 40 – 50 or more" chorus, has faded from my consciousness, off any list of the rock era's thousand greatest 45s.

But if my critical sensibilities were undiscerning as an adolescent, emotional responses were already driving my musical tastes. Growing up when I did, loving the Beatles was a given (my white skin and brown bangs led a Black classmate to call me Ringo in my last-day-of-fifth-grade autograph book in 1964), but their songs of loss, longing and alienation — "You've Got to Hide Your Love Away," "Nowhere Man," "We Can Work It Out," "You're Gonna Lose That Girl" — were the ones that hit home to me; they provided helpful commentary on my sebaceous spin-the-bottle romantic life at the time. (As much as I would like to claim professional certainty about the particular merits of those songs compared to the more assured and optimistic songs they accompanied on the American editions of *Rubber Soul*, *Help!* and *Yesterday and Today*, I lack the means to identify and quarantine the role a girl who I liked at the time played in my adolescent musical appreciation.)

While my estimation of some music I've lived with for decades has risen or fallen, my aesthetic values haven't changed much, and I am only occasionally taken aback by opinions I once expressed. Blame it on stubbornness or subconscious ass-covering, I honestly can't manage any kinder words now than I did at the time for Sting's early solo work, Jane's Addiction, Barenaked Ladies or any barrel-bound fish I have shot at. Now and again, I stop and reexamine my disdain for Bruce Springsteen. (My friends have all heard the spiel, and I was once included in a newspaper article about rock crit apostasy because of it: my other dissensions from the party line include Gram Parsons, Aimee Mann, Little Feat, Tom Waits, Captain Beefheart, Radiohead, PJ Harvey and Wilco.)

It's hard to keep reactions to individual albums from hardening into overly general views of the artists who make them: like her, hate them. The very nature of rock fandom, amplified by the professional responsibilities of a critic who is asked for consistency, Top 10 lists, all-time favorites, star ratings, two-sentence recaps and all that, leads listeners to divide the vast world of music-creators with whom they come into auditory contact into two camps: rock and rot. (Well, maybe three: rock, rot and *rule*.) And that brings with it the risk of prejudgment. It would take the most disciplined of critics to approach each album she or he considers as a white label mystery before forming a response to it.

On 12/12/12, as the world braced breathlessly for the fantasy league pairing of a living Beatles with three living members of Nirvana at that night's Hurricane Sandy charity concert, I was moved to spit out this Facebook hack at Foo Fighters:

> "...one of the most well-intentioned worthless bands ever to have a career. There is not a single song in their repertoire that could not have been written by a 15-year-old. Grohl's singing begins and ends with a shriek, and no one else in the band seems able to slow him down or build him up. His heart is in the right place, he's a most honorable rock star, and he was a tremendous asset to Nirvana. But I wish he would just go the fuck away."

A resourceful observer quickly posted this paragraph from www.TrouserPress.com and used it to challenge my critical consistency:

> With an immediate return to form in "The Pretender," *Echoes, Silence, Patience & Grace* is the Foos at their hardest-rocking. The album balances loud and soft, from "Long Road to Ruin," "Erase/Replace" and "Let It Die" (with a Smear solo) to "Stranger Things Have Happened," "Come Alive" and "Summer's End." The instrumental "Ballad of the Beaconsfield Miners" showcases Grohl's acoustic guitar chops, while the piano-driven "Home" provides a lovely ending to an excellent album.

Reads like a case of flip-floppery, doesn't it? Not so fast.

I didn't write that paragraph (many of the reviews on the site are the combined work of various critics; Pete Crigler actually penned that bit), but a while back I *did* write this segment of the same entry:

> "I don't owe you anything" screams Dave Grohl over and over in "I'll Stick Around," and it sounds at once like a desperate chant against evil thoughts, a bitter testimonial to history and the needed disposal of some traumatic baggage. "I'm alone and I'm an easy target," he worries two songs later.
>
> The spotlight is hardly an ideal hiding place, but maybe the former Nirvana drummer (whose career began in Washington DC, in Dischord punk band Scream and such lesser luminaries as Dain Bramage) is just facing his fears. Stepping out from behind the relative safety of his monstrously battered kit, Grohl writes, plays guitar and sings in the Foo Fighters, an ambitious return to active duty following Nirvana's sudden death in 1994.

> Recorded before the band's actual formation, *Foo Fighters* is entirely Grohl's doing save for a bit of guitar playing by Afghan Whigs frontman Greg Dulli. (The quartet's final lineup, pictured but not named on the record, includes guitarist Pat Smear, originally of Los Angeles' legendary Germs, a solo artist and, most recently, a touring member of Nirvana, plus the former rhythm section of Seattle's Sunny Day Real Estate: bassist Nate Mendel and drummer William Goldsmith.) On record and in concert, Grohl emerges as a potent frontpunk with a limited vocal range, good songs, ample enthusiasm and too much imagination to simply replicate the signature sound of the band that made him famous.
>
> Roaring with guitar distortion like a fission furnace threatening imminent disaster and underpinned by a seismically massive bottom, *Foo Fighters* clearly takes some of its stylistic cues from Nirvana. The lunging bass, oblong chord progression, abrupt time shift and vocal style of "Alone+Easy Target" are unmistakable; "This Is a Call" and "I'll Stick Around," both written in the wake of Cobain's suicide, manifest his influence on Grohl's music. But other songs — the quiet, harmony-tinged "Big Me," the lightly sung verses of "Good Grief," the distorto-pop reverie of "Floaty," the overload frenzy of "Weenie Beenie," the swinging bop of "For All the Cows," the metallic riff rip of "Wattershed" — push the album beyond Grohl's past, outlining a more diverse approach Foo Fighters have yet to fully realize. The rock-solid delivery of the simple tunes, which have sketchily significant lyrics and catchy hooks, makes them seem like more than they are, and that won't wash twice. Having made a successful lift-off, Foo Fighters still has to find and reach an ultimate target.

So, yes, in 1996, listening to the first Foo Fighters album in the wake of Kurt Cobain's suicide, I found some qualities in it to praise. But I also raised a red flag as to the band's challenging future. And therein lies the rub. An auspicious start looks an awful lot like beginner's luck in the rear-view mirror as the long-range trajectory of a career stretches out. (Out of curiosity, I listened to the album again, and, while it has some strong, ambitious tracks that make it worth hearing, it runs out of gas halfway and succumbs to functional filler. In this case, I can stand by what I wrote.)

Grohl is a great drummer and seems to be a cool guy with good taste in bands and a healthy skepticism about the meaning of rock stardom. But his band's records are more often overwrought and pedestrian than original or engaging: hard rock as a concept, not a creative format. I've seen them live on TV a few times and watched a horrendously bad festival show once, all of which hardened my suspicions into disdain. That said, the 88 words I spouted in an informal setting hardly depicts the band in full and is certainly not what I would submit for publication, but I will, in the future, resist the temptation of citizen screaming.

Regrets, I've had a few. I don't care that I have pissed off fans of numerous bands by not praising their idols; the inevitable "argument" that worship or popularity proves quality (call it the McDonald's defense) remains specious and irrelevant. But I hate to realize that something intangible affected me that wasn't there in the music, and that I succumbed to the temptation of being an asshole rather than a responsible commentator. I was needlessly scornful of Patti Smith's *Horses* in 1976 and still can't explain exactly why. I've never become a fan of hers, but that album is not what I made it out to be. I warmed up to Hole's *Live Through This* a year after the fact and found Television's first two albums far more wonderful in the '90s than I did in the '70s. And I cannot tell a lie: I thought the Ramones were a ridiculous travesty the first two times I saw them.

Maybe some of it owes to lack of engagement: music can be consumed at many levels, from background noise to meaning of life, but I suspect that cultural wisdom can also be compromised by letting a public persona intrude. That's never fair and rarely illuminating. An album is a mysterious product of numerous forces; lots of people you wouldn't want to hang out with have made great albums, and lots of terrible albums have been made by wonderful people. It's an elusive goal for critics to factor characters out of the art they produce.

Part Two

Trouser Press was seven years old when "Video Killed the Radio Star" introduced MTV. Radio and its stars didn't die, but the magazine did. (There were other factors as well, and I certainly don't blame anyone.) In offering America a colorful look at the new romantics and other heirs to new wave's post-punk flowering, Music Television made an end run around commercial radio at a time when college radio had yet to provide a viable alternative. Our franchise was bands that were, by their very nature, never going to get a tumble at Top 40. We introduced them to discerning gourmandisers who wanted to know about what they couldn't tune in to hear. MTV put that music — not all of it, but enough — on free display for anyone with cable television. The most pungent evaluations we could print about the music of Devo, New Order, R.E.M. or Ultravox, say, was no match for the easy and free experience of hearing — and *seeing* — them on TV. MTV came, we went, album reviewing continued.

The form actually grew in stature for a while, as daily papers and general interest magazines reconsidered their longstanding indifference toward pop music. But the undermining of the form was not through. Perhaps you've heard about the Interwebs? With the explosion of digital musical distribution, virtually any music that you become aware of can be heard in a matter of moments. We have moved from do-it-yourself to find-out-yourself. For those who still seek some external guidance, there are if-you-like-then-you'll-like crowdsourced programs to do the necessary hand-holding.

The other, more amorphous, toxin to *Trouser Press*'s ideals arrived the following year from *USA Today*, which traded the values of journalistic leadership for reader-pleasing servility. It made perfect commercial sense, of course — give the people what they want rather than challenge them in any potentially off-putting way, like with stuff they don't know about — but the mainstreaming of that idea converted a proud media industry into slaves of public ignorance rather than a weapon against it. Television, from sitcoms to CNN, has often been guilty of that, and the same mercantile ruthlessness reined in radio, degraded the understanding and employment of language, turned Hollywood into an explosive-rigged pimple factory and ultimately led us down to the schoolyard syllogisms of the 2012 election.

As the estimable British music journalist Charles Shaar Murray put it, reflecting back on his days working at the *New Musical Express* in the 1970s, "I'd rather lose a slow reader than talk down to a bright one." In Pat Long's excellent book, *The History of the NME*, CSM goes on to say, "A lot of the other papers were talking down to their readership...We were always trying to stimulate or intrigue."

I once had an editor at a general interest magazine who saw his role as protecting readers from the terrifying possibility of an unfamiliar word or reference. So, record reviews had to be immediately comprehensible to all, even those with zero interest in the subject. (I won't deny that much of the jargon and genre designations habitually employed by music writers doesn't illuminate anything for anybody. "Jangling," "plangent" and "gutbucket" leap to mind but eliminating crutches is different from removing intelligence.) It was a terrible test, to stop every few words and add a subordinate clause to ensure that no adult would be left behind. "It's not as if I'm asking you to write 'God, the deity...'" he once told me. But that's what it felt like. The writing came out sounding like the condescension of a remedial ed teacher. "Like black leather jackets and motorcycles, the Southern offspring of R&B and country known as rockabilly is inextricably identified with wild youth of the 1950s. The slap bass, flashy guitar runs, canyonlike echo and frantic (or tremulous) singing — punctuated by whoops and hiccups — of great rockabilly records can deliver as many delinquent thrills as a lurid biker movie." I wrote that and would have gladly omitted all of it to be able to say more about the particular rockabilly in question, rather than explaining what it was.

Like they told us in school, look it up! I grew up with a newspaper in one hand and a dictionary in the other, and I owe my vocabulary to finding out what I didn't know and fixing it. I do that to this day. Sure, there are writers too dense to bother with (who wants to stop every sentence to translate English into English?), but I was raised to get that other people knew more than me, and it was my job to try and catch up. To wit, my reading of British music papers as a teenager was a weekly education in bands, in styles, in slang. I loved being schooled and still do.

So, when I came to publish a music magazine, my principled but naïve stewardship proceeded from the same ethos of leading, not following, our imagined audience. (Let me not overblow this: we were never so self-serving as to willfully ignore what our audience cared about, we just declined to be limited by it.) Our founding goal was to share our enthusiasms and interests, and if we found a rotten apple in the basket, we never saw the harm in announcing that. We had moxie. Putting a band on the cover of *Trouser Press* did not ensure favorable coverage inside: if the artist merited a cover due to significance (or, to be candid, the occasional lack of a viable alternative), what our writer had to say about them, pro or con, wasn't [preordained].

As we got closer to the end in the early '80s, I was genuinely shocked to have readers complain that we were doing a "bait and switch" by criticizing an act we enticed them into buying the magazine for. If they expected that front cover placement was an assurance of puffery inside, that was never the contract in my mind. I suppose hatchet jobs have been given featured placement since then, but I don't disagree that it sounds like wildly warped editorial judgment for the post-critical age.

We were too small and bloody-minded to play the collusion games with labels or artists, and certainly not afraid of our readers. In 1998, Marilyn Manson allegedly roughed up *Spin* editor Craig Marks for breaking a deal to put him on the cover. His record sales tanked, and the magazine changed its bet. That's not giving your audience a lot of credit. You only plan by SoundScan if you have no faith in your magazine, your readers or your editor. *Spin* no longer exists as a print publication. (Neither does *TP*, and our worst dust-up was an angry letter from a publicist for a photo spread we did of the KISS action figures she provided in a lewd dollhouse tryst with a bunch of Barbies.)

So, the question that faces us as 2013 arrives is what value do record reviews now serve? In one sense, they have taken on the role of Amazon customer reviews. Music that is exotic, obscure, unfamiliar or unknown can certainly benefit from exposure, even of the most minimal sort. (I've heard that *Pitchfork* wields a lot of clout in that regard.) But that's not the same as serious music criticism, a valiant pursuit which is in such awful decline.

Record reviews are now brief, upbeat and simple: "download these songs, they're good." Beyond that service, writers don't provide much real value. They are unlikely to establish a strong connection with their readers, as no sense of prejudices and predilections can emerge from four sentences (at least one of which is going to be strictly informational). Here is the critical half of a current *Rolling Stone* T.I. review, which I grabbed at random: "Incorporating everything from sex-rap with R. Kelly to power balladry with Pink to raging trap-rap with Meek Mill, his eighth album fuses lordly self-mythologizing with epic self-searching; a version of Leonard Cohen's 'Hallelujah,' puts the T.I. saga in proper perspective." (The extraneous comma is not mine.) Jon Dolan goes on to quote two lines of the song and concludes, "Even in torment, he only rolls VIP." It's hard to accept that drivel as a legitimate descendant of the thought-provoking insights a writer like Ellen Willis or Paul Williams routinely delivered in their work. And you can't even blame space. They are simply kowtowing to the preferences of those readers who care the least.

Part Three

Having thusly thrown in the towel, I'd like to return to the beginning (or something like it) and look (well, listen) at the subject through the other end of the proverbial telescope.

As I've written way more album reviews than any other type of journalism, that means I must lay claim to any number of hasty judgments, wild presumptions, haphazard guesswork, received wisdom and rash opinionating. Sometimes I might have had weeks to absorb and consider a release before committing a review to paper or screen; other times, the whole process, from slitting the shrink wrap to printing out a final draft, might have been shoehorned into a few hours. When I was working against an impossible deadline on the fifth and final *Trouser Press Record Guide*, I could dispatch a relatively generic record in the time it took to play it. I know that sounds horribly cavalier and unfair, but it was sometimes the case.

Back in the day, we had advance (*not* "advanced") cassettes and a record company bio, sometimes even a lyric sheet. For major releases, sometimes we'd have to sit in a label conference room while the album — which we could not take with us — was played once. (Yes, that was as daunting a task as it sounds.) Otherwise, we were on our own, armed only with whatever we had read or seen or heard.

The amount of relevant knowledge one brings to review a record is significant, but in a paradoxical way. We have a responsibility to the reader to provide factual content about the release, but the less you know, the freer of extraneous influence you can be in your evaluation. That's a good thing. The more conscious you are of who an artist is, what they have previously done or said, how people feel about them, how popular they are, who they've been compared to, the harder it can be to form a truly independent sense of what you're hearing. It's no coincidence that many critics say more or less the same thing about a significant release; I suspect there is, for some writers, reassurance in having one's impressions confirmed by colleagues. And don't discount the fear of being seen as uncool. While doing that intentionally has worked wonders for a couple of previously cited contrarians, in general a lot of reviewers lack the guts to call bullshit on a critical darling. (In the early days of rock journalism, when the reviewing population was small and self-important, savage attacks on big albums were common. Unthinkable as such iconoclasm would be today, *Rolling Stone* famously ran John Mendelssohn's attack on Led Zeppelin and Jon Landau's dismissal of *Are You Experienced*, while Nik Cohn deemed most of *Abbey Road* "an unmitigated disaster" in the *New York Times*. And legend has it that Eric Clapton ended Cream after the trio's LPs were brutally trashed in the press.

The theoretical high ground for reviewers is an absolute vacuum, a space in which one forms judgments and perceptions and theories without internal prejudice or outside influence and then acquires adequate knowledge to avoid misapprehensions and misguided analysis. Would that were possible. It's not. The best I can do is take what I know, what I've read, what I've heard and what I imagine and set it aside long enough to really hear the music. It's not a perfect system, but that's the human mind for you.

In the thousands of reviews I've written, there have certainly been some fabulous misfires. I'm pretty disheartened to re-read reviews I did for *Trouser Press* that flop around helplessly, allowing other people's opinions (mainly the idol-thrashing British weeklies at the time) to shape my thinking. I suspect I was in too much of a hurry to think enough to write real criticism; a lot of these seem more like track-by-track narrations than thoughtful appraisals. It is disappointing to see the whiffs, the superficial considerations and the careless dismissals of records by great artists.

The worst of it, of course, is when a record you delivered a judgment on in a vacuum goes on to become a classic or a best-seller. Hindsight is a motherfucker. There is no way, years later, to make the case that "I didn't know how big a deal this was going to be when I wrote about it and if I had I would have..." without sounding pathetic.

The only reason to care about how successful a record is likely to be is to adjust the amount of consideration — time and space — it merits. Reviewing is not A&R work; my job is not to identify potential superstars or platinum sure-things. But a record that will probably move millions (and I mean that in both senses) may warrant more scrutiny than one few will ever care about. Not that I value one over the other. As I wrote in a *Trouser Press* record guide,

> "Some artists are truly worth picking apart; everything they've committed to posterity bears some critical scrutiny. Unlike other record guide editors, I don't presume to boil artists down to their widely known works or forgive them their early missteps. This is an egalitarian exercise: within the stylistic and philosophical framework in effect here, those who declare themselves musicians and produce work for public consumption are treated seriously regardless of success or obscurity. That's why a prolific and intriguing artist who has never sold in the five figures might well be covered in an entry far longer than an obvious platinum act with two albums. It's about the music, not the numbers."

In my view, every album, every single, every concert is of equal potential merit. I don't care if it's a cassette in a hand-drawn case or a CD manufactured by major label, the possibility of great artistic value exists for me. I go with what I hear, not who has endorsed it or how much money it stands to make. ◆

Rolling Stone

Nevermind is the most remarked-upon album review I ever wrote for *Rolling Stone*, but it was just one of many I had in the magazine in the '80s and '90s. Lisa Henriksen, the first reviews editor to give me assignments, was great to work with until she ghosted me. It bothered me like hell for a while, and I've always wondered who I pissed off enough to earn expulsion from the *RS* ranks; I nursed a few buddy-club theories about that. In any case, she eventually left, my black spot was either rescinded or forgotten, and I resumed writing for her successors: David Wild, Anthony DeCurtis and Nathan Brackett, all of whom were generous and supportive.

My first review for the magazine was *Geffery Morgan*, which I called "UB40's first completely engaging album" in February 1985. It got three-and-a-half stars. Those ratings were not in use when this one (my third contribution) appeared five months later but did return a few years later.

Bryan Ferry
Boys and Girls
Rolling Stone, 18 July 1985

When Bryan Ferry first began making solo records in 1973, his apparent goal was to forge a path radically different than what he was writing and performing with Roxy Music. So, while the group produced utterly original, unconventional music, Ferry perversely made albums of songs by other artists, from Dylan to the Beatles to Motown, singing them as if he'd never heard them before.

Ferry eventually dropped the gimmick (though Roxy surprisingly picked it up on occasion) and devoted himself to the band as it became steadily more mainstream. Now that Roxy Music is defunct, Ferry seems determined to keep its sound going on his own. If *Boys and Girls* resembles a semi-funky follow-up to Roxy's 1982 swan song, *Avalon*, credit the cast of musicians, many of whom contributed to both. Conspicuous by their absence, of course, are Phil Manzanera and Andy Mackay, Ferry's former partners. But three ace guitarists — David Gilmour, Mark Knopfler and Neil Hubbard — are prominently featured, and several tunes have sax work that recalls Mackay's characteristically sinuous sound. Considering the subordinate role Mackay and Manzanera had taken in recent years, *Boys and Girls* could have been billed as a Roxy Music album and no one hearing it would have demurred.

Ferry is unquestionably one of the greatest, most influential vocalists of our time. He has also authored numerous brilliant songs. On *Boys and Girls*, his singing is typically above reproach; his writing, however, is quite another matter. The nine songs (all his, including one collaborative effort) are distressingly short on melody: "Slave to Love," the album's first single, is a worthy — and not dissimilar — successor to *Avalon*'s "More Than This," but "Sensation" and "The Chosen One" are merely adorned one-note grooves over which Ferry meanders in search of a discernible melody, "Windswept" and "Don't Stop the Dance" are appealing but skimpy. The rest of the record is smooth, attractive and utterly forgettable.

Boys and Girls is instrumentally exquisite, the top-notch players — Nile Rodgers among them — turning in economical, inventive performances deftly orchestrated by Ferry and his co-producer, Rhett Davies, into mild, state-of-the-art dance tracks. The guitar work is especially good, with restrained soloing providing the record's most exciting highlights. There isn't a moment here that doesn't shine with enormous skill taste, stylishness and artistic integrity, Unfortunately, the flimsy content ultimately makes this record a frustrating exercise. ◆

Red Hot Chili Peppers
Freaky Styley
Rolling Stone, 24 October 1985

After nearly two decades of racial division, popular music is in the midst of an overdue and exciting (if modest) effort to integrate itself. One particularly happy result is the pairing of George Clinton with the Red Hot Chili Peppers. Having dallied with Thomas Dolby on his own new album, the P-Funk overlord furthers his far-reaching stylistic influence by schooling the Los Angeles quartet in the ways of the venerable funkmaster.

A fairly outrageous bunch to begin with, the Chili Peppers raise their butt-shaking dementia to new heights of prurient rhythmic frenzy under their producer's sage if zany guidance. *Freaky Styley*, the Peppers' first full-length album, is wilder, rougher, funnier and funkier than their self-titled EP, which was no semiotics colloquium itself. From the psychedelicized guitar, subliminal background voices and urgent, aggressive dance beat of "Jungle Man" to "Yertle the Turtle," a weird animal kingdom fable, the Peppers bump, vamp, rock, leer and growl their unique musical mutation that borrows songs from Sly Stone ("If You Want Me to Stay") and the Meters along with assorted moves from Clinton, James Brown, Peter Wolf and others. They dabble in egotistical rap ("Nevermind") and nubile punk ("Catholic School Girls Rule") and toss in poetry delivered in a Brooklyn accent, a horny folk chant, a brief political commentary and "Blackeyed Blonde," which can only be described as Aerosmith meets Isaac Hayes. Drummer Cliff Martinez's wicked backbeat and Flea Balzary's popping, percolating bass provide the relentless energy drive for Anthony Kiedis's often smutty vocalizing and Hillel Slovak's guitar work, a mix of crazed solos, nostalgic wah-wah and rhythmic scratching. A sharp horn trio from the Clinton camp adds appropriate punctuation, helping to obscure the songs' tendency toward tunelessness.

The Peppers' quasi-orthodox hard funk might appear to be an imitation of Black music for a white audience, but they're actually irreverent, punky rockers with a jones for rhythm & blues vernacular (lyrical and musical) and a commitment to humor, variety and unbridled stylistic independence. Along with Fishbone, Was (Not Was), the Beastie Boys and others — white and Black — the Chili Peppers are taking advantage of the current crossover free-for-all to universalize funk by expanding its limits and incorporating new ingredients without diluting the basic bump. Fed up with the empty calories of effete high-tech dance records? *Freaky Styley* is stick-to-the-ribs rock that puts meat back in the motion. ◆

I was introduced to the Sundays' music by KCRW-FM in Santa Monica — in person. In February 1989, I was in L.A. promoting the third edition of the *Trouser Press Record Guide*. Dave Schulps (who had moved out west) and I were being interviewed by the late, great Deirdre O'Donoghue. Playing a round of blind date, she asked for our first impressions of some new records live on the air. One of them was a 12-inch import of "Here's Where the Story Ends." We both loved it on the spot. I pitched *Rolling Stone* on a review as soon as I got back home.

Sundays
Reading, Writing and Arithmetic
Rolling Stone, 14 June 1990

To join the ranks of sophisticated pop ensembles with female vocalists — whose membership includes the Cocteau Twins, 10,000 Maniacs and, on occasion, Everything but the Girl — a band must meet certain stylistic criteria. The guitar-based sound must be politely electric, near but outside the boundaries of folk rock, and delicate but not flimsy. Lyrics should be intelligent, even a bit arty. Appealing melodicism is crucial, as is a stylish, genteel reserve.

The Sundays not only qualify for acceptance in this postmodern club, the London quartet deserves an honored place in its hierarchy. *Reading, Writing and Arithmetic* is an alluring slice of lighter-than-air guitar pop, a collection of uncommonly good songs graced by Harriet Wheeler's wondrous singing. While her bandmates play with shimmering economy, Wheeler brings an exceptionally expressive voice to bear on the rich melodies and homely lyrics that offer offbeat thoughts about life, love and the English climate.

The album's finest tracks — "Can't Be Sure," "Here's Where the Story Ends" and "Hideous Towns" — have an uplifting spirit that can render a potentially unpalatable line like "Desire's a terrible thing, but I rely on mine" intriguing. "Skin & Bones," "You're Not the Only One I Know" and the soaring, minor-key "My Finest Hour" ("...was finding a pound on the Underground") are further demonstrations of the Sundays' easy charm.

The sound is as spacious and tastefully appointed as an art gallery. Co-producer Ray Shulman achieves remarkable sonic transparency by capturing only what's essential to shape the songs. On several numbers, guitarist David Gavurin picks our discrete notes, strumming a chord here and there for dramatic effect. Driven by an unvarying rhythm drone in "Can't Be Sure," Gavurin's steady guitar pattern tugs against the expansive, segmented melody, cleverly turning a simple tune into a small gem — one of the many in the masterful lesson *Reading, Writing and Arithmetic* delivers. ◆

Loath as I am to acknowledge it, I've really gone off Richard Thompson. As is virtually mandatory for rock critics of a certain age, I was a full-fledged fan and wrote about him with great relish and regard several times. Now I simply cannot abide the sound of his voice. His playing remains unassailable, but I have not intentionally pulled out a Thompson album (other than *Shoot Out the Lights,* which remains a beloved touchstone of romantic collapse for me) in ages. I stand by this review, but I won't be listening to the album again any time soon.

Richard Thompson
Rumor and Sigh
Rolling Stone, 11 July 1991

An exceptional guitarist whose catalogue of memorable songs has been widely covered by admiring peers, Richard Thompson is — twenty years into the personal odyssey that outlines his solo career — both the embodiment of British folk-rock and its most prominent refugee. Steeped in tradition but no longer defined by it, he remains true to his idiosyncrasies, sharing provocative character studies and frank insights without concern for parochial stylistic sensibilities.

Thompson's records have generally kept to simple arrangements, free of adornments that might distract from his songs' emotional impact. Whether motivated by commercial or creative impulses, he now seems amenable to more ambitious treatments. *Rumor and Sigh*, his third album produced by Los Angeles keyboard player Mitchell Froom, allows a varied menu of thoughtful settings to provide an alternate focal point to the typically fascinating wordplay and striking melodies.

Froom fleshes out songs about love, madness, drunks, sex offenders and old 78s with a variety of non-synthesizer keyboards, a few medieval instruments and a solid dose of Thompson's guitar work, which ranges here from a teasing refrain that underscores the narrator's romantic disappointment in "I Misunderstood" to the country figures in "Keep Your Distance" to the riveting rock solo that closes "Mother Knows Best," an anti-Thatcher diatribe oblique enough to render the resignation of its target irrelevant. The crisply catchy "Read About Love," a witty poke at sexual ignorance, borrows a Cheap Trick riff; "You Dream Too Much" ends in a hail of feedback. If that doesn't send hidebound Fairport Convention fans over the cliff...

Ironically, the album's most affecting number, "1952 Vincent Black Lightning," is an unembellished folk ballad. Fingerpicking an acoustic guitar with enough rhythmic power to dance to, Thompson laments a modern couple and a vintage motorcycle in a completely traditional form, making a resonant connection between his rootsy past and open-minded present. The weirdest track here is "Psycho Street," a spoken set of grotesque vignettes that indulges Thompson's worst tendency towards theatrical delivery.

Thompson's concerns and approaches are probably too offbeat for acceptance in the bland pop world, so the redirection of *Rumor and Sigh* may be an academic exercise, sales-wise. But like the row of Oscars that should belong to Al Pacino or the plaque of Phil Rizzuto that has yet to hang in baseball's Hall of Fame, a hit album would be the long-denied but richly deserved reward for an exemplary career. ◆

Jesus and Mary Chain
Darklands
Rolling Stone, 3 December 1987

In its own way, the Jesus and Mary Chain's second album is just as audacious as the band's controversial debut, *Psychocandy*. On that album, the Chain offered up melodic pop drenched in noise and feedback. *Darklands*, the impressive follow-up, reveals enviable conceptual mettle, as the group sets aside its characteristic Ramones-in-a-blender sound for spacious, echo-laden politesse. Jim and William Reid, the singing and guitar-playing brothers at the Scottish band's core, are still writing virulently downcast songs, but have elected to proffer them with restraint, rather than in a wash of disorienting fuzz.

Featuring the incomparable gems "Happy When It Rains" and "April Skies" — loud, minimalist pop symphonies with irresistible hooks and unsettling lyrics — *Darklands* also reflects the Reids' diverse influences. "Cherry Came Too" gently raids the Beach Boys' "Surfin' Safari" for part of its melody; the slow surge of "On the Wall" invites Velvet Underground comparisons; and "Deep One Perfect Morning" suggests *Blonde on Blonde*-era Dylan.

Judging by the inclusion of one borderline-chaos piece, "Fall," the brain-beating din that made *Psychocandy* so incredible has not been banished forever. But in helping the band control its distortion habit, co-producer Bill Price gives the affecting material precedence over what was heretofore, to some, a distracting presentation. The paradox of simple tunes bathed in cacophony may have originally generated notoriety for the group; the strength of these enticing songs from the dark side is reason enough to stay excited. ◆

Five years later, I got a second turn at the J&M plate, and I'm really proud of this one. "Constipated ennui"... "velvety subterranean torpedo packed with viscera"... "at once redundant and essential"? Ooh, yeah! I seem to have forgotten the stylistic point I made about *Darklands*, but it *was* nearly five years later. This is the version I submitted; what ran had some of the best bits pruned away.

Jesus and Mary Chain
Honey's Dead
Rolling Stone, 14 May 1992

An appetite for self-destruction, any psych major can tell you, is just a cry for attention. So, when Jim Reid of the Jesus and Mary Chain wheezes "I wanna die just like Jesus Christ...I wanna die just like JFK..." — lines that kept "Reverence" (the first single from *Honey's Dead*) off British TV — he's obviously just jerking society's chain. And when he and brother William later run the same lyrics over a stretch of Jonathan Richman's "Roadrunner," the song's death wish dissolves into wry self-mockery.

Seven years after inventing the genre, the pioneers of noise-pop (three chords and a distortion pedal, hold the truth) are still building their castles of fuzz in the same sandbox. Since firing off the landmark *Psychocandy* — a velvety subterranean torpedo packed with viscera — in 1985, the Chain hasn't added many links to its creative development. The Reids seem perfectly content to recycle their elementary songs and limited vocabulary endlessly while others carry their sharp-edged toys off to new stylistic playgrounds.

But one brilliant idea is better than none, and the Reids navigate their small pond with consummate skill and the indefatigable enthusiasm of children. Recovering from the constipated ennui of 1989's *Automatic, Honey's Dead* is looser, livelier fun: chewy bites of irresistible nod-pop demagoguery rhythmatized by a stuttering dance beat, barbecued in woolly guitar static and slathered with echo.

Disciples of both Andy Warhol and Lou Reed, these Velvet Underground acolytes revel in the decadence of their willful, indifferent shallowness. "Teenage Lust" is not only unromantic, it's not even sexy, yet the lyric wraps up tabloid-era vacuity with blunt efficiency. Similarly, the infectious "Far Gone and Out" skewers media blitz with phrases like "television-sick and television-crazy." Elsewhere, *Honey's Dead* pivots on "Reverence," whose deliberate, take-that-U2! music possesses the conviction its lyrics lack, and "Rollercoaster," a 1991 UK single which makes the most of a simple melody hook and a touching plaint "Don't put me down..."

On an unwavering mission to explore every corner of one divine inspiration, the Jesus and Mary Chain is proof that monomaniacal dedication is one of rock & roll's most powerful gimmicks. At once redundant and essential, *Honey's Dead* elevates tackiness to art and reduces music to junk. Now *that's* entertainment. ◆

I got to review some seriously obscure records for *Rolling Stone*, which suited me down to the ground. No one else wanted to them, and my instinct to proselytize made me keen to write about music with limited commercial potential. Plus, I had a lot better chance of booking work if I stuck to lesser-knowns, since the A-list assignments generally went to staffers. (Speaking of which: a friend proofreading at *Stone* once gave me the marked-up galleys of a Jann Wenner review of Dylan's *Slow Train Coming,* and there was barely a sentence that hadn't been challenged, changed or deleted. If you want to know who can really write and who needs to be carried across the finish line, always ask a copy editor. I once heard of a Famous Writer Who Shall Remain Nameless whose much-vaunted debut column in a Very Important Magazine took staffers several days to reshape into publishable form.)

I worship this band. From the first time I saw the Steed + Twiggy cover of *And Don't the Kids Just Love It*, I was drawn to the TVPs' unique blend of pop culture obsession and outsider art, of tender romance and painful insecurity. Odd, amateurish and profoundly English, they set off a lot of my pleasure sensors. I've liked a lot of bands who see the world as their bully, but no one else has made of that what Daniel Treacy has. When I first got their albums, some of them with handmade covers, the TVPs were an opaque mystery; it wasn't until I found a half-page article in the *NME* that I even knew Dan's name or anything else about the group. I saw them play in New York and London in the early '90s, chatted with Daniel once or twice and was honored to take part in a 2004 tribute concert for him when he was ill. In a true mitzvah for great music, my friend Steve Yegelwel, an A&R man with admirable taste for obscure bands from the UK, signed the TVPs (as well as the Pooh Sticks, another favorite of mine) to the Atlantic imprint he worked for, and I got to write about the very happy result.

Television Personalities
Closer to God
Rolling Stone, 24 June 1993

Even in the great tradition of eccentric Englishmen, the Television Personalities are a cult unto themselves. An artless art band, an unpopular pop group, the deliberately guileless trio has sustained a 15-year career with determined amateurism and a wellspring of '60s pop culture memories. Led by singer-guitarist Daniel Treacy, the TVPs proffer vulnerable delights and bewitching neuroticism strewn with jagged bits of psychedelic noise.

Closer to God, the London group's sixth studio album, dispenses with such past proclivities as crackerbox production, sloppy tunings and time-tunnel nostalgia for an unclouded look into Treacy's heart and soul. This intense but orderly 79-minute collection about love, faith, aging and emotional collapse cuts deeply, but with a whimsical, witty touch. Sketched in simple guitar-bass-drums arrangements that suggest a stripped-down Byrds of uncertain vintage, the songs are colored in and textured by violin, saxophone, melodica and the flashback sound of tabla drums.

Treacy drops names like Leonard Cohen, Edvard Munch and Timothy Leary into the wide emotional panorama he addresses here. Candid personality debates fill "Razorblades and Lemonade," an uncertain suicide note ("On a very good day I can be so adorable") set to a jolly waltz perversely complete with children's chorus; "This Heart's Not Made of Stone," a tenderly ambivalent lover's apology; and "Me and My Big Ideas." Meanwhile, romantic bliss ("Coming Home Soon," "Little Works of Art") cohabits with the disarming seriousness of "My Very First Nervous Breakdown."

The author of past songs about David Hockney, Syd Barrett and Salvador Dali returns to topical commentary with "Goodnight Mr. Spaceman," a merry dig at the Ecstasy drug scene and the band Primal Scream: "This record is sponsored by Pepsi / I've taken three e's / But I still can't dance like Bobby Gillespie." The centerpiece is the magnificent eleven-minute title track, a harrowing, feedback-splashed confession of a Catholic upbringing. Like a dotty uncle whose amusing madness can turn maddening on a penny, the TVPs come calling with a kit bag of fascinating dreams and disturbing nightmares. Invite these scruffy charmers in and they may never leave. ◆

This next review, which was my second for the magazine, has not aged well; I regret the myopic and prejudiced use of phrases like "gay rock mantle." But consider the context. At the time, out rock stars (as opposed to out dance-music stars) were relatively rare (Elton John was married to a woman!), and the rare gay artist who didn't downplay the specifics of his or her desire risked being relegated to a niche market. With one explicit declaration in song, Tom Robinson had struck a powerful blow for widespread appeal, but Frankie Goes to Hollywood, who I used as a jumping off point here, were far more demonstrative in their embrace and promotion of gay culture. Sadly, I was still stuck in the mindset that gay performers would predominantly appeal to a gay audience, an archaic assumption that, for commercial reasons, held sway for a long time. (How I let myself use the awful "time will tell" phrase is another matter entirely.)

I once gave the subject some thought in this introduction to my *TrouserPress.com* entry on Melissa Etheridge:

> Since rock'n'roll is essentially sexual, it's inevitable that the private lives and public styles of people who create popular music become a pivotal issue to some of those who consume it. Fans of all but the most distant performers see themselves or their desires reflected in their icons, scattered through a shattered prism of social pressures, lyrical messages, contrived images and personal realities. Before young women began significantly integrating rock's male preserve in the last decade, the rote formulation that prevailed was simple-(minded): boys wanted to be their heroes, while girls wanted to sleep with them. That thesis suffered gamely through several confusing phases (the cross-dressing and camp of glam rockers and the new romantics, a rash of celebrities claiming to be bisexual, the willful asexuality of punk), surviving into the arena-rocking late '80s, thanks to manly men like Jon Bon Jovi, Bruce Springsteen and Sting. Then came uncloseted (and closeted) lesbians and gays, and it was back to the role-model drawing board.
>
> Given the permutations of male/female straight/gay fans and performers (for non-math types, that's 16 possible matchups), the erasure of old presumptions creates a whorl of new cross-currents. Boys want to be them, and girls want to sleep with them? Boys want to sleep with them, and girls want to be them? Straight girls wish they were lesbians so they could be better fans? Gay people don't care if the music's good so long as it specifically addresses or includes them? Straight people think the music's cool but can't deal with (or don't ask and don't want to know about) the performer's orientation? As Ray Davies once observed, it's a mixed-up, muddled-up, shook-up world, and — in a self-obsessed inversion of pop music's onetime role as a generation's defining culture — identity politics have become an aesthetic factor of rock life.

Quickly followed by Pet Shop Boys and many others, Bronski Beat heralded a new era — an unmistakably gay act widely accepted by all. Eclipsed by the ethereal strangeness of Jimmy Somerville's singing, the discussion of his sexuality didn't last much longer than it took people to embrace "Smalltown Boy."

Bronski Beat

The Age of Consent

Rolling Stone, 25 March 1985

Now that Frankie [Goes to Hollywood] has proven to be a remote-controlled sham with less depth (not to mention stage presence) than its sloganeering T-shirts, the gay-rock mantle has fallen onto London's Bronski Beat, an unabashedly glad-to-be-gay synthesizer trio. Their impressive but uneven debut album offers several killer dance tracks powered by Jimmy Somerville's unique, piercing falsetto, but it also contains some painfully trite message lyrics and a campy selection of cover versions that undercuts the band's serious side. Evidently undecided as to their stance, the Bronskis alternate between intense, evocative chronicles about the challenges of being young and gay, and routine love-sex pieces no more enlightened than any macho heterosexual boast. Still, few bands have the courage to embrace a controversial topic, and these guys deserve credit: they neither exploit nor soft-pedal their gayness, they simply reflect it in song.

"Smalltown Boy" is a memorable tour de force, a powerful audio film about escaping provincial intolerance, made charming by an unpolished performance (note the tempo acceleration just before the first verse) and non-electronic-sounding synthesized minimalism. Somerville's winsome tale is convincing, and the ingenuous lyrics — if not quite James Baldwin prose — ring of truth and pain. "Junk" adopts a tense, urban urgency to deliver scowling lyrics about disposable culture; "Heatwave," a jazzy finger-popping number, features a brilliant, scar-laden vocal performance. "Why?," though a great high-energy song with just-right brass work by New York's Uptown Horns, suffers in spots from overly strident singing: one of this LP's problems is that Somerville's voice is best enjoyed in limited doses.

Besides often excellent songwriting, what makes *The Age of Consent* remarkable is the deceptively low-tech sound of the (uncredited and unspecified) electronic instruments. Bronski Beat hardly sounds like a synth band, and this modern dance record doesn't suffer from the pounding clichés of electro-disco. Under producer Mike Thorne, the variety of instrumental voices and arrangements sustains the album while remaining subordinate: clearly preeminent, Somerville's singing is the band's only consistent identifying feature.

Like the protagonist in "Smalltown Boy," Bronski Beat is young, uncertain and facing numerous challenges. Given their outspokenness and the disastrous record of topical bands, they'll have a thorny future, contending with bigotry as well as the immutable expectations of their audience. They are clearly an original talent, but only time will tell if they can remain true to their ideals and survive the confines of their advocacy. ◆

Trouser Press enthusiastically supported the Residents — and vice versa — for a long time. We felt a real kinship to their determinedly outsider art as well as their clever professional and ambitious approach. Perhaps because he had gone to school in Berkeley, Jim Green became our in-house Residents specialist. We regularly reviewed their records; his lengthy feature on Ralph Records ran in issue 54. They were a steady advertiser; we respected the group's wish to remain anonymous and hidden within their eyeballs (oddly, I later gravitated to another orb-encased artist, Frank Sidebottom) and dealt with a fellow named Jay Clem as the public face of the secretive group. In a strange coincidence that I had no inkling of at the time, my future sister-in-law Diane Juzaitis (R.I.P.) was the Cryptic Corporation's lawyer for a while. I was pleased at the opportunity to share them via *Rolling Stone*.

Residents

The King and Eye

Rolling Stone, 8 February 1990

Cloaked in anonymity, the Residents have spent 15 years playfully dancing around music's strangest regions to create a vast, influential and mostly enjoyable body of willfully anti-mainstream work. Bizarre vocals, dizzying concepts and blithe disregard for rules and tradition are the hallmarks of this mysterious San Francisco group — the band's members are unnamed, always masked and have never been publicly identified — which has proven equally adept at audio realizations of Eskimo culture, intricate narrative epics and scabrous parodies of '60s pop.

Puckish reinterpretation of musical icons has always been a Residential hobby; the Beatles and Stones were early targets. Recent albums have paid affectionate, if patently irreverent, tribute to James Brown, Hank Williams and others. With *The King and Eye*, the Residents confront rock's ultimate figure, launching an invasive cultural exploration into Elvis Presley's musical core. More insidiously perceptive than most critics, the Residents dismantle and rebuild 16 of his standards, from "All Shook Up" to "Burning Love," offering radical new ways to hear the commonplace.

Cruelly but kindly pushing the songs to the limits of recognizability, the Residents deliberately strip away everything familiar to reveal previously hidden depths of passion, leering sexuality and gripping drama. Such dusty jewels as "Viva Las Vegas," "Return to Sender" (expanded into an epic of misery and abandonment) and "Teddy Bear" are reborn in twisted melodies, imposed rhythms, radical rearrangements and distended vocal phrasings rendered with an exaggerated Southwestern drawl. Along with the provocative music is additional food for thought: In the five segments of "The Baby King," an adult and two young children discuss Elvis's psyche and symbolism.

The King and Eye is no mere Cat in the Hat mischief. Focusing a giant jaundiced eye on the unassailable achievements of a genuine rock god, the Residents have made a powerful and passionate statement about the man, the myth and the music that is bewitchingly entertaining and brilliantly enlightening. ◆

Vic Chesnutt
About to Choke
Rolling Stone, 12 December 1996

A rusty, banged-up sign with hand-painted words swings slowly over a porch in a soft Georgia breeze, conveying its simple promise without need of neon. Parked beneath it in an old wheelchair, strumming a battered acoustic guitar, sits Vic Chesnutt, singing to his own breeze.

Over the course of five remarkable albums — including one under the name Brute, with backing by Athens homeband Widespread Panic — Chesnutt has emerged as the smartmouth of the South, a cockeyed charmer with a rare gift for acute observation. Volunteering both sweetly offbeat yarns and soul-searing annals of self-defeat, Chesnutt has so far avoided mainstream radar while attracting a sizable cult of fans, some of whom paid tribute on the star-packed *Sweet Relief II: Gravity of the Situation* album.

His profile thus raised by the well-meaning efforts of Smashing Pumpkins, Garbage, Live and the like, Chesnutt joins the major-label fray with the gorgeous *About to Choke*. Perhaps fretting about the integrity police who inspect underground artists taking the upward plunge for evidence of commercial ambition, Chesnutt reverses the sonic progress of his recent releases with skeletal, casual-sounding arrangements that make the elemental radiance of his songs (and his noticeably strengthened singing) more plain.

The gently spiced "Tarragon," the meteorological "Swelters" and the pharmaceutical "Hot Seat" make do with spare acoustic guitar, while piano proves a mellifluous foil for Chesnutt's syncopated elocution on "Myrtle." On the jazzy "Little Vacation" ("Robert's Rules of Order will be observed"), he uses keyboards to form his own small combo, adding a delightful mouth-made trumpet solo.

Elsewhere, others join Chesnutt for small-scale acoustic and electric rocking. A rhythm section bolsters the Soul Asylum-like surge of "Giant Sands" and the shuffling beauty of "New Town," which is as finely drawn a cameo of a growing burgh as any [other] American poet's. Three additional guitarists bolster the emotional vehemence of "See You Around," a compelling letter-song which describes a soured friendship with such finality that the mesmerizingly repeated titular refrain becomes a warning as much as a pledge. But then a distant echo of "Myrtle" closes the album, softening the enigmatic salutation into a tender farewell. ◆

The late Vic Chesnutt was a unique and wonderful character, a miracle of grace under pressure. His story, his tender songs, his despairing but optimistic outlook, his twisted wit, his creaky voice, his wild musical imagination and his incredible personal charm were all testaments to a spirit and a talent that seemed capable of leading him anywhere he could dream to go, even with a nearly useless body. His monumental gifts made the impact of his 2009 suicide even more painful and sad; I encourage anyone who discovers the wonders of his music to read Kristin Hersh's powerfully moving *Don't Suck, Don't Die* memoir of their friendship.

It took me a minute to catch onto Vic from his Texas Hotel releases, which were generally known in indie circles because of Michael Stipe's generous encouragement as producer. But once I boarded his creaky jalopy and heard the profound depths of poetry and atmosphere that issued from this small, twisted body in a wheelchair, I was all in.

This is the introduction to my *TrouserPress.com* entry on his albums:

> Countless artists can produce convincing creative facsimiles of heartbreak and its many guises — alienation, guilt, regret, self-flagellating misery — in song, but none meets the task with more bitter pleasure, honesty or crooked-smile charm than the inimitable Vic Chesnutt. Phrasing his lyrics idiosyncratically in a cracked, unsteady voice, strumming simple acoustic guitar patterns from his wheelchair, the real auteur of Athens, Georgia produces aggressively vulnerable records that turn predictable emotions inside out, using the wrenching pathos of his sublime (but intentionally rough-hewn), self-effacing poetry. For an illuminating introduction to a unique figure, Peter Sillen's half-hour 1993 documentary film *Speed Racer: Welcome to the World of Vic Chesnutt* is available on videocassette.
>
> This colorful and witty storyteller doesn't need to be reminded of his failings — he's more than ready to sing about them, in a synergy of life and art that closes around his slight figure like a noose. In the bleak corrosion of Chesnutt's tender idealism, a highly literate mind in a ruined body becomes a willful primitive with a ferocious and highly developed sense of irony. His skilled songwriting burns with reality's pain while glowing with imagination.

Interviewing him for a 1994 *Newsday* piece about resurgent singer-songwriters (which also included the late Paul K and Jack Logan) was an absolute delight. We spoke inside Irving Plaza, following his soundcheck for a show that inadvisably put him in front of a Live (the band) audience. (Angelfish, Shirley Manson's little-noticed pre-Garbage band, was third on the bill.) I hope he liked talking to me a tenth as much as I enjoyed meeting him.

From that article:

Georgia's Vic Chesnutt, 29, has made three albums in twice as many years (and about as many days of studio time), the result of prodding by his friend and sometime record producer, R.E.M. singer Michael Stipe. On the current *Drunk*, Chesnutt delves deep into his own personal abyss — which includes the wheelchair he's needed since driving a car, under the influence, into a ditch 11 years ago — with a wicked, knifelike sense of irony and moral ineptitude ("my non-sense of preservation," he quips) that redirects recriminatory guilt from self-pity into simple, searing art. Chesnutt makes the most of his rickety Southern charm on such songs as "Kick My Ass" and "Dodge" ("I bent over backwards to misbehave / It's a holy wonder I didn't just flip on over into an early grave").

"I worry that there's nothing universal in my songs," says Chesnutt, who recently presented his ramshackle folk art on a national tour with MTV darlings Live. "But I really don't care. I don't beg people to be listening to me or nothing." Chesnutt gets his satisfaction elsewhere. "I feel the best when I'm writing a tune. It gives me some kind of a charge. I can't think about people listening to it in the future.

"For some people, listening to my music is a lot like watching a movie," he says. "Even if they don't relate to it personally, they might can appreciate my story, or just the circumstance around it. A lot of my songs are rather vague, 'cause I try to hide my specific meaning in metaphors and [stuff] like that. It's what writers do. I write my Bukowski songs, too, where I don't spare no punches. But I like to challenge myself. Language is a heavy deal to me.

"Every day, I get more and more sight in my mind's eye, so I can probably write more and more songs. I haven't written the songs that I need to write yet." ◆

Some unused quotes from the 7 June 1994 interview done for that piece. As affecting as I found him at the time, this is heartbreaking to read knowing of his 2009 suicide:

Born in Florida, lived in Georgia my whole life, except for a brief stint in California and a brief stint in Knoxville. Grew up outside of Zebulon, GA. I was in a new wave band, a new romantic band, I guess you'd call it. The singer wanted to be David Bowie. In the early '80s. I was in an industrial band at the same time. we had analog keyboards, with hundreds of effects. There was only two of us in the band. The band was called Dinosaur. The other guy committed suicide, so then I got in another band, playing strummy wummy music in Athens. I went to school there, like everyone else. but I didn't graduate. I should have, but I was too busy being distracted. I ate a bunch of acid and then went to Latin class, and I had to leave during the middle of the class, and never went back. I was studying English. I was good at math, too.

I've been in the [wheelchair] about 11 years. It was 1983, Easter morning. I was in a car wreck. Drunk. I was the only one in the car. Ran into a ditch. I blew the horn, though. It wasn't my fault — I blew the horn. I don't remember it at all. I was 18, drunk. Idiot. Not that I'm any smarter now.

I started writing songs when I was a little kid. I was really into music. My grandaddy played music. Whenever he'd pull out his guitar, even when I was a toddler, I'd be right there at his feet, listening to him play. He played country music. He hated bluegrass, he was more into the swing...and the pop music from when he was a youngster.

I started out on trumpet. I played it in the band since third grade. Once I got a guitar that was the end of my trumpet playing. I love trumpet. I wish I could play it now. I wrote songs on it.

I knew Michael [Stipe] from Athens, met him in clubs and stuff. I was in a band called the LaDeDas, and he liked them. We always talked in the coffee shops.

I recorded the first album in 1988. Most of the songs were written between 1985 and 1988. After the accident, I couldn't play guitar for a long time, so I was playing keyboards a lot. I love wild keyboard music. None of the keyboard songs survived. When I started playing guitar [again], that's when I started writing more songs. I still have 100s of cassette tapes.

I did have theories for that first album, *Little*. I was really into singing and playing as quiet as you could play and singing really quiet. That was what I was into at the time. That album was thrown together in one day. I just recorded it, I didn't know it was going to be an album or nothing. Michael gave it to [Texas Hotel]. They wanted to release it, and I said no way. I wanted to record all my songs in one big album and put it out. At first they said yes, then they said they wanted to put out this. I had a hundred or so songs. It would have been stupid. I wanted to make a record like *Double Nickels on the Dime*.

I'm bad about self-abuse, and I'm good at putting the blame all inward. It's true that's what a lot of my songs are about. It's a little self-indulgent. I didn't beg people to be listening to me or nothing; I wasn't like Urge Overkill or anything: *pleeeeze love meeeeee*! They made me do it. It's all Michael's fault. He made me do it. ◆

Do It Yourself: Punk Will Never Die

Anarchy in the UK/UK Punk I (1976-77)
The Modern World/UK Punk II (1977-78)
Teenage Kicks/UK Pop I (1976-79)
Starry Eyes/UK Pop II (1978-79)
Come Out and Play/American Power Pop 1 (1975-78)
Shake It Up!/American Power Pop II (1978-80)
The Blank Generation/The New York Scene (1975-78)
We're Desperate/The L.A. Scene (1976-79)
Mass. Ave./The Boston Scene (1975-83)
Rolling Stone, 4 February 1993

Leon Trotsky devised the theory of permanent revolution, but it took Marlon Brando in *The Wild One*, shrugging off the question "What are you rebelling against?" with a cool "Whaddaya got?," to give perpetual change its cultural currency. There was plenty of "whaddaya got" in the mid-'70s. Pop music was a cynical marketplace ruled by aging aristocrats hopelessly alienated from their audience. While arena-goers complacently ate cake off platinum plates, a scared, angry generation found strength in loud, fast punk rock, the metronome for a chaotic world.

Riding a seismic "New Wave" of rebellion, the subculture forded the gap between band and fan to build a do-it-yourself alternative to dinosaur rock. Faster than a one-two-three-four countdown, up sprang bands, labels, magazines, stores and venues — a complete autonomy kit. The lunatics didn't take over the asylum. They simply declared themselves sane and went out to play.

Of course, the punks were full of shit. They claimed to be nihilists but embraced capitalism, gaining fame by feigning apathy. They scorned the past while plundering it; any ideas of their own were immediately xeroxed into clichés. New Wave was born to live fast and die young — but it left a smoldering corpse that keeps flaring up. Besides founding an ongoing independent music industry and a value system that counts music before money, New Wave produced many of the decade's most inspired records — electrifying anthems that lit into youth and society with a cackle and a cattle prod.

Fifteen years later, the future that punks couldn't envision has swung around to celebrate them. *DiY* makes New Wave nostalgia official on nine individual volumes of punk and pop from a five-year period beginning in 1975, when rock insurgents first coalesced into a New York underground. By 1980, younger grassroots groups would emerge to push the revolt into styles from synth pop to ska, but *DiY* doesn't go that far. Neither does it reveal the full extent of the music's diversity — angry young auteurs like Elvis Costello and Graham Parker are AWOL, as are the early exponents of hardcore, industrial and the mod revival — but more volumes are planned. In this large nutshell, *DiY* offers today's alternative rockers a proper introduction to their roots. Nirvana may represent the ultimate validation of everything '70s punk stood for; the irony is that other Lollapaloozers are exactly what it opposed.

Anarchy in the UK and *The Modern World* collectively amount to a spot-on review of first-wave Brit punk's greatest hits — musically speaking, that is: none of these 38 singles ever troubled Casey Kasem. The Clash declined to appear, the two Sex Pistols items are inferior demos and the small roster of second-stringers (999 and the Lurkers, but no Ruts or Members) is hair-splittingly arguable. But quintessential ramalama from bands that really mattered — the Damned, the Jam, Generation X, Buzzcocks, the Boomtown Rats, X-Ray Spex, Wire, the Stranglers, the Vibrators and so on — re-creates the thrill of getting New Wave import singles in those days and being amazed by almost every one. This definitive pogo party is rich with great songs; unlike many of their disciples, the original bands tempered three-chord aggression with melodies and hooks. The two discs (which should have been packaged together) throw up a megadose of catchy adrenaline with a still-tangible sense of urgency.

Britain's pure-pop practitioners — merry seditionaries revitalizing the tired three-minute song form with a new sense of adventure — were connected to the safety-pin brigade largely via similar sensibilities and indie-label affiliations. *Teenage Kicks* has fathers (Nick Lowe, the Motors) emerging from the retro-minded world of pub rock with an eye toward reinvesting melodic guitar music with youthful spunk and sons (the Undertones, Squeeze, Skids, XTC) discovering the pop potential within punk. *Starry Eyes* shines with the wit and charm of the Records, Joe Jackson and Bram Tchaikovsky but squanders slots on the superannuated Searchers and the insignificant Starjets.

The paradox of American power pop is that it sounds commercial but isn't truly meant to be. Ultimately rooted in the Beatles and the Beach Boys, power pop flowed into New Wave via two stylistic channels: the Raspberries, who mined nostalgia for hit records, and Big Star, whose quixotic idealism didn't sell beans. To purists, ambition — not to mention success — is anathema, but *Come Out and Play* and *Shake It Up!* randomly mingle idiosyncratic indie-pop cult legends like Chris Stamey, Shoes and the Nerves with major-label insiders like Cheap Trick, Billy Squier's Piper and Fotomaker. Why not go all the way and get the Knack? Twinky tunefulness runs rampant, but one disc of underground pop would have sufficed. Too much innocuousness — power pop should only seem meaningless and disposable — leaves the records adrift in *DiY*'s sea of significance.

In a dubious democratic gesture, New York, Los Angeles and Boston each rate a *DiY* volume. *Blank Generation*'s Bowery stars — Patti Smith, the Ramones, the Dictators, Television, Richard Hell, Blondie, Suicide, the Heartbreakers (no Talking Heads, though) — were New Wave's pioneers; Britain's punk uprising was the direct result of the bands on this monumental disc. By comparison, *We're Desperate* makes an unconvincing case for Southern California's received rebellion. X's whiny title tune and the psychotic entropy of the Germs' "Forming" are credible punk artifacts; although some of the same musicians made better music later on, the scene's pre-hardcore stars (the Dils, the Zippers, the Plugz, the Dogs, Springsteen wanna-bes the Furys) sound derivative and monochromatic. *Mass. Ave.* camouflages the patchiness of Boston's diverse New Wave scene by extending the time frame.

For all its naïve bravado and denial, New Wave really did have a future. Punk didn't completely burn out before it could fade away, and this fiery requiem pours a welcome stream of gasoline on its embers. ◆

I thought I did a pretty decent job with that review, but at least one reader disagreed.

> Ira Robbins' brash, self-serving review of Rhino's punk and power-pop series felt too much like a crash course on the movement by someone who fancies himself its peerless authority. Just because Robbins published Trouser Press, does that make him the obvious choice for the assignment? It's as if there's some universal consensus that he's the one with the expertise, while in fact your staff reviewers have done a fine job reviewing punk all along. He says that two discs of power-pop is too much, while it actually barely scratches the surface. He misses the point that there has never been a widely-distributed record devoted to such music, much less a CD (or two). And in an all too predictable move, Robbins pans the L.A and Boston collections, while praising the one that chronicles the scene in his home city of New York. Most, if not all, of the music on that one is easy to find on other CD's. And perhaps had Robbins grown up in L.A. or Boston, he would have greater appreciation of those cities' contributions. His review stinks of bias and misses the whole point of the Rhino series: to bring to the fore some very excellent and hard to find music.
>
> Jordan Oakes
> St. Louis, Missouri

Jordan Oakes, in fact, *is* a peerless authority on power pop (editor of the fine *Yellow Pills* fanzine and compiler of a series of unassailable CD collections under the same name), so I didn't resent his rancor: he's a good guy, and I hope I didn't reply. (In 1996, I got a very nice note from him regarding my Cheap Trick box liner notes.)

But none of us could hold a candle to the devotion, knowledge and enthusiasm of Gary Stewart, the mastermind behind Rhino's incredible efforts to collect, codify and exalt so much great music of the past in countless compilations and box sets. I worked for Gary on a number of projects, starting in 1990 with the notes for a Sparks compilation. In 2003, Dave Schulps and I collaborated on the liner notes for Gary's lovingly assembled four-CD set *No Thanks! The '70s Punk Rebellion*, an achievement I had tried and failed to do for Rykodisc.

I first met Gary in late February 1989, when we were both guests on *Li'l Art's Poker Party*, a public access TV talk show hosted by the inimitable Hollywood rock and roller Art Fein. I was in Los Angeles doing promotion — including an amazingly fun in-store at Book Soup, where I met a lot of my West Coast colleagues for the first time — for the third edition of the *Trouser Press Record Guide*. (Grudgeful memory note: I had to set up and pay for the trip myself; my publisher couldn't see its way clear to making any such effort or expenditure on the book's behalf.)

I had corresponded with Gary at Rhino but was happy to finally meet him. And then I was completely bowled over when he mentioned owning the single I had made with my mid-'70s band, Knickers. We had pressed a thousand copies of "Drums of Love" b/w "Denunciations" and sold maybe 200 copies via relentless mail-order ads in *Trouser Press*. I still have a few boxes of them in a closet. Gary not only owned a copy, he remembered the songs a decade later. And said he had sung one of our numbers at a party!

The other thing that impressed me was when Art pulled out a portable cassette player and tested our mettle by playing the first two or three seconds of a record to see who could identify it from that scant evidence. Gary could, and he could it do it without hesitation. Me, I lumbered behind lamely like a thumbless *Jeopardy!* contestant, feeling utterly humbled by the display of such skill at recognizing of records I well knew.

After compiling just about everything there was to compile at Rhino, Gary went on to a second career at Apple Music and a significant sideline in fundraising and charity work. His 2019 suicide was a terrible shock. We had not been in touch for some time, but had a lot of friends in common, and the outpouring of love and respect for him was incredible. A memorial event I attended in New York a few months later shed some light on the dark challenges that undermined his will to live but did nothing to lessen the enormity of the tragic loss to the music world. And seeing Gary on screen in Edgar Wright's 2021 Sparks documentary opened that wound all over again.

Sloan

Smeared

Rolling Stone, 15 April 1993

In Halifax, Nova Scotia, a remarkable young quartet called Sloan listens and learns, reflecting and refracting, working out ways to improve on the cool records they're hearing. Smeared, the diverse debut from this post-alternative chop shop, marries Nirvana's thrash bottom to twinky harmony vocals, puts My Bloody Valentine on a budget with a beat, drops the art ballast from Sonic Youth, uncovers the soft underbelly of Dinosaur Jr. and takes sixteen years off Cheap Trick. While running down a college-radio playlist of ingredients, Smeared transcends mere style scavenging through guileless enthusiasm. In the grooves of this irresistible platter, Sloan's catchy tunes and witty post-adolescent lyrics collate into a distinct and winning personality that sounds anything but calculated.

"Underwhelmed" cleverly explores didactic issues of grammatical propriety for surprising amorous potential. Between noting that the title is not a dictionary word and that an otherwise desirable classmate's spelling is "atrocious," Sloan manages to add Hollies-quality harmonies to Cobain-strength guitar rock and keep it from sounding precious. With guest vocalist Jennifer Pierce and a buzzing breeze of guitar distortion invoking an Anglo dream-pop aura, "I Am the Cancer" handily pulls off a trick chord progression while cutely deconstructing romance down to its "kiss me, kiss me, now you're s'posed to miss me" basics. Likewise, the supremely catchy "Sugartune" compresses years of power pop tradition into a modern spitball of unbridled fun without letting it go all gummy. And while the instrumental track of "500 Up" strongly suggests *Daydream Nation*, the handsomely interwoven harmonies point the song towards chipper jangle-pop.

Like white blues bands of the late '60s, the medium of underground rock — its textures and sources — is threatening to become its essence, as too many groups that have the style don't bother much about content. Armed with all the right moves and material well worth cranking, Sloan may very well be the Cream of the crop. ◆

Robyn Hitchcock

Moss Elixir

Mossy Liquor (Outtakes and Prototypes)

Rolling Stone, 17 October 1996

Have wit, will travel: Robyn Hitchcock's penchant for fanciful wordplay is a calling card that doesn't open every pop-music door. At his best, Hitchcock is an ingenious student of both Edward Lear and the surrealists, revealing odd truths by fantasizing about odder absurdities. While insightful enough to admit in song his desire to be "a pretty girl so I could look at myself in the shower," Hitchcock can also become tiresomely drunk on his own cleverness. But over the course of 15 adventurous solo albums that filtered the '60s sounds of the Beatles, Pink Floyd and the Byrds through a modern looking glass, the English singer and guitarist has demonstrated acute intelligence, uncommon melodic designs and a mariner's skill for finding his way back home from forays into dead seas. This time, he's sailing along with a sure sense of direction.

Although *Moss Elixir* stops short of the solo minimalism of 1990's *Eye*, it untangles the sometimes-strained complexity of 1991's *Perspex Island* and 1993's *Respect* with unfussy arrangements that field a single guitar or a full electric band to the same glowing effect. With cagey horns, wafty background vocals and a brisk beat, "De Chirico Street" is *Moss Elixir*'s most decisive-sounding track, but the song's hallucinatory narrative — in which "numbers turned to fingers and the fingers turned to flies" — is as reality-challenged as a Salvador Dali clock.

The rhythmically aggressive "Devil's Radio" better illustrates the element of forthrightness that has been growing in Hitchcock's work. Dropping jokey references to Stalin and Mao Tse-tung at the outset, Hitchcock proceeds to the more serious issue of broadcasting evil [by taking a swipe at Rush Limbaugh.] Likewise, Hitchcock's generation-gap dig in "Alright, Yeah" bespeaks a more mature mindset than the noir drollery of "Man With a Woman's Shadow."

Those open to a full dose of Hitchcock's latest prescription will need to locate the limited-edition and quietly superior companion, *Mossy Liquor (Outtakes and Prototypes)*. Besides alternate versions (some with strings and piano) of six *Moss Elixir* numbers — including "Alright, Yeah" translated into Swedish and a longer but no less beautiful "Heliotrope" — it doles out six extra songs, most notably "Trilobite," which details eons of paleontology in three comical minutes. ◆

Butthole Surfers

Independent Worm Saloon

Rolling Stone, 10 June 1993

Is nothing sacred? This alternative thing has definitely spun out of control when the Butthole Surfers — America's worst underground rock nightmare, a band that began terrorizing jaded scenesters when Alice was in training Chains and *still* has problems getting its name printed in family newspapers — is allowed to release an album on a reputable major label.

With 46-year-old ex-Zeppelin bassist John Paul Jones adding little more than appropriate incongruity as producer, the Texans abandon the double-cross nihilist irony of 1991's *Piouhgd* — no Garry Shandling tributes or so-bad-they're-bad Donovan covers this time — for a no-holds-barred return to basic twisted aural chainsaw massacre overload. (There is, however, one banjo-driven ballad on which Jones plays bass.) If *Independent Worm Saloon* offers little in the way of songs to hum, few records can beat it for sheer guitar-choking feedback ecstasy.

Track after track, the rhythm section lays down a juggernaut of '70s punk-metal boogie (or, in one case, a waltz) while guitarist Paul Leary and singer Gibby Haynes whack the shit out of whatever strings and whammy bars can survive their mutilating onslaught. Following Surfers tradition, Haynes's absurd acid fantasies, like "Who Was in My

Room Last Night?," are delivered through various electronic distortion devices, reaching a funny-voice pinnacle in "The Annoying Song."

Although the protectors of public decency could probably care less by this point, the Buttholes still work overtime to offend, whether by screaming "I don't give a fuck about the FBI" in "Goofy's Concern," offering a spoken-word vignette about recycled sweets ("Chewin' George Lucas' Chocolate") or beginning "Clean It Up," a number which ultimately devolves into a lengthy impressionist re-enactment of the bombing of Dresden, with a minute of garish audio vérité spew noises.

Ironically, in the face of such current socio-musical affronts as Nine Inch Nails and Billy Ray Cyrus, the Surfers' savage psychedelia sounds timidly unfocused and faintly quaint. The veteran band's raging inferno tears an entertaining enough hole in the ozone, but these wild-eyed slackers hail from a different hell than today's sonic reducers and [actually] seem out of step. Kicks just keep getting harder to find... ◆

Vulgar Boatmen

Anthony DeCurtis, who had deservedly gotten the *Rolling Stone* reviews editor job I coveted, called me one day and asked me to review the second Vulgar Boatmen album. I gathered he had a personal connection to the band (it turned out Robert Ray had been his college professor), but it was only later that I realized Walter Salas-Humara of the Silos was a founder of the band and that Dale Lawrence had been in the Gizmos, an early Indiana punk band I semi-liked. The band name rang a bell, though. This make-believe album by Blobbo Stumpsky and the Peasants (a moniker coined by Tim Sommer) was reviewed in *Trouser Press* 44 in 1979, our attempt to ape the brilliant *Rolling Stone* put-on review of the Masked Marauders. I don't recall who actually wrote the piece, Tim or me.

Blobbo Stumpsky and the Peasants
Vulgar Boatman
Russo AD 1917

It was not common knowledge until very recently that the Soviet Union had an under-ground rock scene, and the very notion of Red Punks comes as a shock to the preconceptions most of us hold about life behind the Iron Curtain. Yet here is absolute proof of a very au courant rock consciousness, alive and kicking. There is very little information provided in the packaging of this mysterious album, which leaves the music as the final resort for judging the quality of Russia's premier new wave band. Comrade Stumpsky apparently threw away a promising Olympic career as the world's fattest acrobat to become the bearded and disgusting leader of this five-man, one bear musical monstrosity.

Formed in late 1978, the Peasants had been appearing at a tiny punk club in Leningrad ("The Borscht Belt") when Stumpsky, drowning his sorrows (expulsion from the Olympic team for an extra X chromosome) staggered in, drunk as a skunk, during the group's soundcheck. He passed out cold in the men's room and didn't awake for several hours, by which time the show was in full swing, and the only exit was across the stage. Passing among the musicians, Blobbo picked a fight with the Peasants' lead singer, one Vermin Festrovsky, and beat him unconscious, forcing the band to end their set early. Terrified of the vodka-soaked behemoth who had caused their predicament, the Peasants took the cowardly route, and invited Stumpsky to be their new vocalist.

It wasn't long before BS & the P's were granted an audition before the state-run record company, CBS (Classic Bolshevik Sounds), and signed to a long-term contract. This is their first album recorded under that agreement, and it certainly is an off-beat piece of work. There are a few potential singles here (although none have been officially sanctioned by the commissar in charge of the label), most notably the garishly overproduced "Nazdrovia" and an obnoxious Clash soundalike, "Red Riot." The other 17 tracks are short snippets, a bit like Wire or the Cure, except that the abundant use of ethnic instruments — balalaika, Kurdish nose flute, kudzu and alto *messerschmidt* — tends to make all the songs a bit samey sounding. All in all, this debut shows more promise for the Russian punk scene's future output than for its current lack of originality. If these comrades ever make it to America's shores, looking for a little of that long green they've read so much about, one has to hope they get stuck on a triple bill with Meatloaf and Black Oak Arkansas. Maybe a little down-home redneck charm will give them a real feel for where America's head is at. Go back to Russia where you belong! —*Nikita Kentski* ◆

I have no idea how this next item came to be, whether some clever reader was joining in the fun or a staffer was stretching out the charade. I doubt it was my doing. In any case, we ran this in the *Hello It's Me* letters column of *Trouser Press* 46 (January 1980).

> To the Editor:
>
> You've blown it again, TP. First by allowing some mush-head asshole bozo-brain by the name of Nikita Kentski to review Blobbo Stumpsky & the Peasants' debut LP (TP 44). Second, by failing to realize the sociological and cultural significance of this record's release.
>
> Kentski's historical and factual errors were downright embarrassing. To begin with, Blobbo (real name: Alexandria Blobbo) was not an acrobat, he was a shotput champion. His band includes three bears — dancing ones at that — not one; didn't comrade Nikita note the grunting female background harmonies on "Rainy Night in Moscow (Cold War Blues)"?? The tale about Blobbo's induction into the band was just a press release/bio fantasy. Blobbo originally joined the Peasants as one of the dancing bears; four weeks into their *Great Ukraine '78 Tour* they realized he was one of them during the bear's choreographed strip act in the Peasants' best tune, "The Sovkhoz Shuffle."
>
> *Vulgar Boatman* is a masterpiece. "Nazdrovia" is not "over-produced" as that twerp Kentski says; the combination of 10 electric lutes and five 13-string mandolins is absolute perfection. Kentski even neglected to mention the Peasants' greatest tunes: their Jan & Dean tribute "(Hammer & Pop) Sickle," the pro-capitalist "Lovers for Levis" and their anthem "Bring Back the Troops (Cuba Calls)." Not to mention their independently released 45 (pre-LP) on their own Ballet Records ("Belorussia Rocks"/ "Defect or Not Defect").
>
> Rather than simply write Nikita Kentski off as a duppy numb-bulb snocone, let me rather assume he merely missed the point of Vulgar Boatman. Fuck you, Nikita Kentski; your review was stupid and unfair. I was under the impression that music mags assigned reviews to writers who knew what they were talking about. You have done one of the few truly great groups that ever existed a serious injustice, so FUCK OFF, YANKEE CRETINS. I doubt you have the guts and moral responsibility to print this.
>
> Jack Hammer
> Kansas City

Back in the real world, I took the assignment and immediately loved *Please Panic.*, so thank you to Anthony for that. I became a huge Boatmen fan, saw them on the second stage of *Lollapalooza* in St. Louis in 1993 and ended up becoming dear friends with Janas Hoyt of the Indiana faction.

I've written other things about the group over the years, including a feature for the *Observer* and notes for a German reissue of the band's third album, *Opposite Sex*.

Vulgar Boatmen

Please Panic.

Rolling Stone, 28 May 1992

Since *Help!* first led unwary adolescents to believe the Beatles all slept in a row of sunken beds, rock groups have been seen as nuclear families: autonomous social organizations facing the world as self-contained units. While that conception has been extended by amorphous clusters of musicians guided by a central creative force — more like a franchise than a family — there is still no structural precedent for the clan of the Vulgar Boatmen.

The group's two pilots — singing guitarists Robert Ray and Dale Lawrence — reside, respectively, in Gainesville, Florida and Indianapolis, Indiana. They rarely perform together, co-write songs by exchanging cassettes and contribute separately to the recording process. Each leads a lodge of local musicians, calling on members for live or studio work according to need and availability. A loose organization with two distant nuclei promises stylistic chaos, but *Please Panic.* delivers exactly the opposite. The album could not be more focused or consistent; in tone and content it seems the result of a single artistic vision. While a few songs rhythmically suggest the chugging languor of the Grateful Dead, the Boatmen's gently intense guitar pop most often sounds like a country cousin to the hermetically close-knit Feelies.

More precise and polished than the Boatmen's highly praised debut (1989's *You and Your Sister*), *Please Panic.* is a patient, translucent collection of eloquent beauty and delicate vigor. Spartan arrangements give it subtle allure. A few chords, near-subliminal bass and an austere backbeat — plus occasional viola or organ accents — paint the unprepossessing melodies in muted watercolor hues with strong, straight pen lines. Behind the clear, artless vocals, each carefully chosen note is absolutely essential. *Please Panic.* weaves its considerable power into studied simplicity: songs tick like clockwork but pulse with strength.

The emotional depths suggested in elusively vague lyrics of unresolved relationships — "We Can Figure This Out," "Fool Me," "You Don't Love Me Yet," "I'm Not Stuck on You," "Allison Says" — are illuminated with flickers of melancholy and quiet obsession, but numbers expressing a more positive view ("You're the One," "There's a Family") don't erase the uncertainty from the music. In these adult songs, life's complexities can only be alluded to. *Please Panic.* is a rich, rewarding record that involves the listener by leaving so much unsaid. ◆

The Strange Saga of the Vulgar Boatmen, the Two-Headed Band

The Observer, 27 November 2015

The forest of rock family trees contains only one known instance of a band with twin trunks. If the existential notion of what a "band" is can stretch from an individual like Iron & Wine to a studio illusion (the Archies) or a parade of players (like those under the Fall flag), that *still* doesn't include the Vulgar Boatmen, who — in their early '90s heyday — defied a fundament of the form by maintaining fully functioning lineups in two different cities.

The subtitle of *Drive Somewhere*, an amateurish but worthwhile 2006 DVD documentary, is "The Saga of the Vulgar Boatmen." It begins in 1977 at Indiana University, where aspiring punk-rocker Dale Lawrence of the Gizmos met graduate student Robert Ray, who had grown up in Memphis.

"Robert taught the second half of a course about lyrics as literature, which became a history of American music. When he mentioned in class that he'd seen Elvis perform live while he was still on Sun, I immediately scheduled office hours with him, and we've been great friends ever since." Despite a thirteen-year age difference, the two had matching taste in books, movies and music — specifically Buddy Holly, Rogers & Hart, the Sex Pistols and Sam Cooke. After Ray moved to Gainesville to teach English at the University of Florida, they began co-writing songs by mailing cassettes back and forth. "We had no set collaboration method," says Dale. "The songs took shape about every way they could. Sometimes, he would add lyrics to a melody of mine, or additional verses; sometimes, a mostly finished song needed a bridge."

"Dale had the melody for 'Mary Jane'," Ray recalls, "but only a few lyrics and no guitar riff, both of which I provided. The best 50/50 collaboration on the first CD [1989's *You and Your Sister*] is 'Margaret Says.' It began with Dale's melody and a similar title; I renamed it for my older daughter."

The challenge of a long-distance collaboration gained bonus geographic complexity when they decided to record an album. Ray, who was disinclined to tour, had joined (or taken over, depending on who you ask) the Vulgar Boatmen, a Florida art-school combo founded by future Silos leader Walter Salas-Humara. After Lawrence converted his post-Gizmos Indianapolis band, Right to Left, to match, two completely separate lineups based 867 miles apart could fairly lay equal claim to the name, repertoire and releases of the Vulgar Boatmen. The Floridians were a recording unit that played out occasionally; with the same style and songs, the Hoosiers played out more but had — other than Lawrence — less of a recording role.

You and Your Sister was mostly recorded at Ray's home studio, with Lawrence commuting in as co-leader. A couple of tracks were done in Indiana with members of his group; good luck trying to guess which.

Lawrence recalls obsessing over the snare drum sound. "One of the best ones we got was on 'Mary Jane.' Trouble was, a lot of that sound was on the scratch-vocal track. When we tried to record a real lead vocal, we lost the great snare sound. So, what you hear is actually the scratch vocal, which luckily Robert sang all the way through."

Magically pulling a consistently economical and exacting sound (which elicited comparison to the Feelies) from more than a dozen musicians in myriad permutations, the two-pronged collective produced three albums of extra-ordinarily evocative, unornamented guitar pop music, using plain-spoken melodies to tell resonant American short stories that begin in the middle and end nowhere near a conclusion. Ray admits, "I do like elliptical, elusive things, often movies or poems or stories that seem allegorical, but for which the key has not been exactly provided."

The best songs on *You and Your Sister*, which is being reissued by Time Change Records this month in a 25th anniversary edition with three bonus tracks, use restraint and release to shape the music, which can be intensely intimate or wide open. The record summons enormous dynamic range from simplicity and understatement.

The pulsing, obsessive "Change the World All Around" describes the romantic angst of a man "standing in the driveway" at night and "calling your name." But rather than seeking the solace of one woman, the singer ventures a much grander plea: "Sometimes I just want to change the world all around."

The six-minute "Drive Somewhere" uses alternating picked chords and a metronomic snare to convey the obsessive-going-on-hypnotic expanse of a highway then turns on a splash cymbal into a joyful declaration of endless possibility. As Lawrence acknowledges, "It was always feel that we were after, rhythm. We just wanted to make music that we would like and want to own."

After two independently released CDs, the Boatmen signed to a British label in 1995, a seeming commercial break that, with all-too-familiar irony, ring proved disastrous, ending a dream encouraged by substantial critical support (Greil Marcus did liner notes for the *Wide Awake* compilation in 2003) and heavy rotation for "Drive Somewhere" on WXRT in Chicago.

First there was drama over which of the many players who could claim membership in the Boatmen were asked to be on the album, then record company politics kept *Opposite Sex* from a planned U.S. release. (Lawrence expects that failure to be remedied with a reissue.) Ray let the Gainesville band fade away, but the Indiana group — recharged by new bassist Jake Smith (also the singer-guitarist in the similarly minded Mysteries of Life, with his wife, ex-Blake Babies drummer Freda Love Smith) — carried on performing and still does a handful of Midwest shows every year, including an annual January booking at Schuba's in Chicago. The music endures. ◆

Opposite Sex liner notes (2018)

In 1994, after two albums, the Vulgar Boatmen — the long-distance partnership of two musicians, each leading his own live lineup — faced an uncertain future. Robert Ray, originally from Memphis, was (and is) a professor of film studies at the University of Florida in Gainesville. Dale Lawrence, a former student of his, was living (as he still does) in Indianapolis, after graduating from Indiana University and becoming a hero in Bloomington's punk-rock scene. Singly and together, they had established the Boatmen's finely honed blend of rhythmic insistence and evocative depth. *You and Your Sister* (1989) and *Please Panic.* (1992) established the template: enigmatic lyrics from a non-existent short story anthology set to tunes that seemed instantly familiar without quite being so. They had attracted a cult following, some Midwest airplay (acknowledged here with a namecheck for Chicago's WXRT in "Wide Awake"), and a fair bit of critical fervor.

Undistorted guitars, economical drumming, moody viola and handsomely natural singing insulated the band from the burgeoning grunge era; even with its amorphous membership, the Vulgar Boatmen maintained their stylistic clarity and purpose. Despite the odd logistics, the band managed a surprisingly effective interchangeability.

By the modest standards of early-'90s indie rock, the Boatmen had achieved liftoff — including second-stage dates on *Lollapalooza* in the summer 1993 tour — but they didn't have the commercial momentum to leave their 9 to 5s for the lives of professional musicians. Or the backing of a record company. Dale Lawrence explains, "The Boatmen were at an impasse. We'd broken with our label, Safe House, but had no real interest anywhere else. Because Rough Trade had picked up *Please Panic.* for release in Europe, I gave Geoff Travis a call, to see if he had any ideas. He did."

Travis had parlayed a London record shop into a powerful distribution firm and independent UK record label on the surprising commercial strength of such unusual young bands as The Smiths, The Fall, Cabaret Voltaire, Television Personalities and Stiff Little Fingers. He also had Blanco y Negro, which pushed the same kind of music (like the Jesus and Mary Chain) into the mainstream in a partnership with the formidable WEA group, whose labels were under the same multi-national corporate umbrella as several of America's top record companies, including Warner Brothers.

Lawrence explains that Travis "approached people who he thought might like the band, and found someone who did, in a big way: Simon Toulson-Clarke, an A&R man at East West. He visited Robert and me, signed the band, and helped us produce *Opposite Sex*."

Rather than be pulled into a flash big city studio with a big-name producer, the group opted to self-produce its third album, as with the first two, on an eight-track machine set up in the guest room of Robert Ray's house. Lawrence traveled there when he could; he recalls the project taking about six months. Toulson-Clarke, who had enjoyed British chart success in the duo Red Box, was on hand to provide advice, support, and a spot of guitar. Ray recalls him as "a wonderful guy [who] became both a good friend and a sharp critical presence." Toulson-Clarke's most audible contribution came in the person of English organist and arranger Alastair Gavin who, Ray feels, "added so much to the record. Coming from Memphis, I had always wanted that fat Hammond sound associated with soul, and especially Booker T. We had used substitutes: tremoloed guitars and double-stop viola. The organ was what I was hearing in my head, and Alastair provided it. I especially admire what he did with 'Call Back Instead'."

Including the two English guests, *Opposite Sex* credits a total of 15 musicians, representing both chapters. The Floridians were a recording unit that played live occasionally; the Hoosiers did so much more, but other than

Lawrence, they had previously participated less in the recording sessions. That arrangement, Ray says, had nothing to do with their abilities, but rather with their geographical remove from Gainesville. On *Opposite Sex*, however, Matt Speake, a core member of the Indiana band, is the album's lead guitarist, while viola duties are split between Indiana's Kathy Kolata and Ray's wife, Helen Kirklin. Andy Richards from the Indiana group is the drummer on about half the tracks. According to Ray, "Two Gainesville drummers worked on the three records: Jon Isley and Michael Derry. Michael is the best drummer I've ever played with. Jon contributed idiosyncratic drumming that always worked. Andy Richards was superb.") J.D. Foster, who would go on to a high-profile career with Dwight Yoakam, Marc Ribot, and Lucinda Williams, is the album's bassist — except for "Wide Awake," on which Jake Smith makes his Boatmen recording debut. Lawrence explains. "It was toward the end of recording the third album that our bass player at that time, Erik Baade, announced he was leaving. Jake, who was in grad school and thought he'd retired permanently from music, said he would do it for a year. 'Wide Awake' was the only track we were unhappy with the bass, so he got the call. His bass part was recorded in Indianapolis." One Indiana regular not on the record is vocalist-percussionist Janas Hoyt.

Ray is the album's primary vocalist; Lawrence sings lead on "Call Back Instead" and "Shake." Their styles (Ray, firm with conviction; Lawrence, softer and more fluid) balance so well within the band's music that the alternation is barely noticeable. That, however, is not true of "Genie Says" and the title track, sung, respectively, by Walter Salas-Humara, the Silos leader who co-founded the original Vulgar Boatmen band that Ray adopted, and Gainesville member Carey Crane. Ray explains, "Carey wrote the verses to 'Opposite Sex,' so he sang on it. Several critics objected to the song. I actually like it, but 'Nobody's Business,' probably a better song, whose lyrics Carey also largely wrote, could have replaced it." (It finally appeared on the re-release of *You and Your Sister*.) 'Genie Says' was an older song that Walter had sung on, although he didn't write it." The actual recording of a quintessential Lawrence-Ray composition was reclaimed from an '80s cassette.

Except for the effective employment of organ (notably on "We Can Walk," "Travelling," and "Call Back Instead"), *Opposite Sex* is of a piece with the band's two previous albums: lots of women's names, catchy melodies, crystalline playing, dangling conversations. The meaning of these one-sided dialogues can be elusive even when desires are finely outlined; rather than narrate action, the words are an essential component of the record's faintly ominous solitude and tenderness. (Ray: "I do like elliptical, elusive things, often movies or poems or stories that seem allegorical, but for which the key has not been provided.") There are three outliers: the blues-rock crunch and slide guitar of Crane's confrontational contribution; the cottony country-rock stroll of "Call Back Instead," which leans in the opposite direction, its flowing organ lines measured enough for a church processional; and the brief but fully developed solo acoustic finale "Susan, Goodnight."

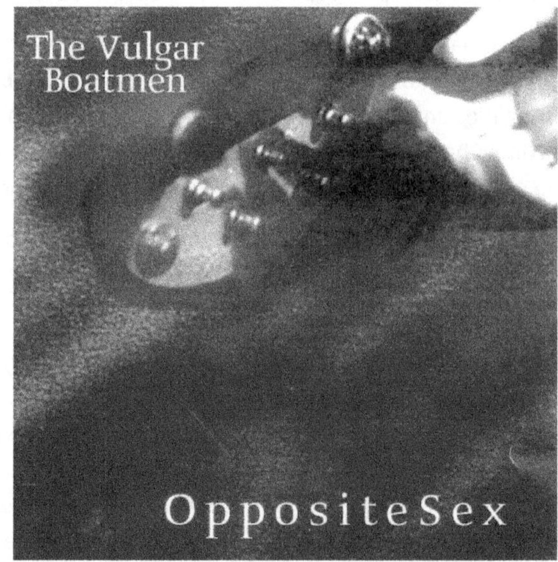

Lawrence, who came of age in Bloomington's goofy Gizmos, wrote "Heartbeat" for that band. What in 1979 was Ramonesy surf-punk is here alchemically sublimated into sweet three-chord pop so instantly familiar that it could be a lost Buddy Holly or Jonathan Richman classic. (That isn't the only artifact in the story. "Cry Real Tears" on *You and Your Sister* began as a Gizmos song; "Please Panic," became a Boatmen album title.) Ray sings "Heartbeat" here.

Lawrence explains what took them so long to put it on a Boatmen record. "We'd recorded versions of 'Heartbeat' earlier — there's one on the same cassette we lifted 'Genie' from. No deliberate reason it was held back until the third album other than that's the arrangement we were finally happiest with."

It is probably idle coincidence that *Opposite Sex* contains two pairs of similarly titled songs. "In a Station" ("let's make a hard decision, look it right in the face") is nothing like the funky (with harmonica) "In a Minute" ("I'm making a new investment"). "When We Walk" ("we don't talk about it") and "We Can Walk" ("there's not a dime's worth of difference between me and you") are closer in sound. As Ray notes, "We had been playing 'We Can Walk' for some time; I'm not sure the recording does it justice. It was always one of the Florida band's most successful live pieces."

"In some ways," he says, "'Shake' is a sequel to probably the band's most well-known song, 'Drive Somewhere' (which the *David Letterman* show used as a frequent outro to commercial breaks). Both songs began with the guitar riffs of Jeff Byers, a former student of mine who became a physicist. In fact, this way of writing a song around a guitar figure, a method that has become common (think of R.E.M. and U2), was very rare for us. Dale and I almost always started with a whole melody, to which we added lyrics. In general, I think that having only a riff puts an enormous burden on the singer, who has to come up with not only the lyrics, but also what has become oddly known as 'the vocal melody,' as if there were any other. The process with 'Drive Somewhere' and 'Shake,' however, resembled Duke Ellington's habit of constructing a song from an overheard phrase: he noticed saxophonist Johnny Hodges's warm-up figure and turned it into 'Don't Get Around Much Anymore.' I would never compare myself to Ellington, but with 'Drive Somewhere' and 'Shake,' the songwriting process was identical. I noticed what Jeff Byers was playing around with and asked him to regularize it; then Dale and I wrote words and melodies to those repeating riffs."

One benefit of being on a British label was access to London's television bookers. Around the time of the album's UK release, East West flew Ray and the Indianapolis lineup over for a live showcase and a high-profile TV appearance. On June 3rd, 1995, the Boatmen (with a session bassist standing in for Smith, who had been called home) played two songs on *Later...With Jools Holland*. One song from the show, "Heartbeat," can be found on YouTube and in the band's 2010 documentary film, *Drive Somewhere*. Ray, playing a Les Paul Special through a compressor pedal, concentrates on singing; to his left, with no microphone in sight, Lawrence rocks his Gretsch more demonstratively but with similarly intense focus. Only Kathy Kolata pierces the tautness of the moment with ascending drama in the lengthy solo that concludes the song.

Before *Opposite Sex* could be released in America, executive changes and label politics abruptly left the band high and dry, without an outlet in the U.S. For Ray, "Elektra's decision not to release the record in America was, if not traumatic, at least a decisive signal that I should invest my working energy in the academic career where I was more conventionally successful. The two books I had written had the international distribution *Opposite Sex* suddenly lacked. I didn't see a way forward." Events reinforced his view that the band had been a rewarding hobby. As he says in *Drive Somewhere*, commenting on an unwelcome label suggestion, "I would never have considered leaving my tenured teaching job for the lottery of a rock and roll career." He later told *Perfect Sound Forever* that the lack of an outlet made recording feel "more narcissistic than even I had intended."

For Lawrence, this reversal of fortunes forced him to accept that the band would not be his full-time career. But the Indiana group has carried on and still plays a handful of Midwest shows every year.

Which leaves this marvelous piece of art. For 43 minutes, *Opposite Sex* sets a mood, fills a gallery with pictures, and tells a dozen intriguing stories as only one amazing band ever could. Many of the characters here attempt to hold on to something precious, only to feel it slipping away. Ars longa, vita brevis. ◆

More Reviews

Before beginning his long and masterful career as the lead music critic of the *New York Times*, Jon Pareles was the reviews editor of *Crawdaddy*, the glossy descendent of the pioneering magazine founded by my idol, Paul Williams. Peter Knobler was the editor, while his dad was the magazine's wealthy publisher. (I used to be under the impression that Alf Knobler owned a printing plant, but a 1976 article in the *Times* described him as "a successful [ceramic] engineer, glass manufacturer and businessman.") The Knoblers were playing the same omni-cultural long game as Jann Wenner, then newly arrived in New York, was doing uptown: *Crawdaddy* covered actors, politics and social issues along with mainstream rock artists, so much so that the magazine eventually rebranded itself as *Feature*. Timothy White and Greg Mitchell were editors; so was Mitch Glazer, who befriended John Belushi and went on to become a bigtime screenwriter in Hollywood.

I enjoyed stopping by their well-appointed office at 72 Fifth Avenue, a world apart but only a ten-minute walk from the East 13th Street tenement where I once lived — and a few blocks down from the eventual home of *Trouser Press*. Other than *Circus* on Third Avenue, visiting *Crawdaddy* was my first exposure to the real world of professional publishing.

Jon once insisted to me that "Mystery Dance" was about wanking, I found that idea absurd. He was probably right.

Nick Lowe
Pure Pop for Now People
Crawdaddy, May 1978

Let me start with a heresy: As a summation of an era's musical styles, *Pure Pop for Now People* is 1978's answer to the Beatles' *White Album*. When the Beatles ended 1968 with their double magnum opus, legions marveled at the eclecticism in both songwriting and performance. Each song sounded different, as if the makeup of the group was changed for each track.

In Nick Lowe's case, there are 12 songs on his first solo album, but if a coin had a dozen sides, one song would fit neatly on each. Without giving any credit to other performers, and using only one non-original, Lowe manages to ape, satirize, insult, paraphrase and recreate such people/musics as Chuck Berry, David Bowie, MOR, the Bay City Rollers, reggae, Paul Simon, the Jackson Five, heavy metal and the Dixie Cups. In the process of all this musical thievery, Lowe tackles such diverse subject material as the record business, Castro, the record business, a silent film star who was eaten by her dachshund, the record business, the Bay City Rollers and, oh yeah, the record business. Not that Lowe is obsessed with one subject or anything, but what else can you expect from a man who could write and record the inimitable "I Love My Label" (a song which doesn't appear on this album)? The ones that do all come down strongly against everybody involved, from talent signers to writers to managers to the biz in general. Not quite the usual menu of "life at the top is hard why did I ever give up my teaching job" that self-important rock stars love to indulge in.

Until this debut, Nick Lowe has been known (to whatever extent) as a producer and sideman. If credentials count, Basher has produced 12-inch masters for Elvis Costello, Graham Parker, Dave Edmunds, the Damned and Dr. Feelgood, recorded with many of same, and held tenure with the premier pub band (remember the good old days?) of the early '70s, Brinsley Schwarz. His previous solo output includes a few singles ("Rollershow" was one), and an EP named *Bowi* in retaliation for the Thin White Duke's *Low* album. The tracks on *Pure Pop* come from recording sessions that began nearly two years ago, but there's no chronology obvious upon listening.

What is obvious from this album is that Lowe has an extraordinary pop sense. As he once told an interviewer, "I think of everything in terms of three-minute pictures. I'm a pop guy who grilled his brains on acid." Almost every track on PPFNP would make a tiptop single, yet Lowe ranges from intricate three-movement affairs like "Nutted by

Reality" to hyper-simple ditties of which "Heart of the City" is best. Every song is instantly memorable, wherein lies Lowe's main shortcoming: he makes it all sound so easy. The record is so well produced and performed that no rough edges show to prove that he's human. As a result, the album has some of the facile taint that has ultimately destroyed pop hit-making machines from Kasenetz/Katz to Chinn/Chapman. For Lowe, high standards present no challenge. I don't imagine Nick Lowe will ever run out of ideas, but I hope he forces himself to think through each recording, not churn it out simply because it's easy. When you're this good, your main problem becomes self-control.

Lowe, as the album title suggests, is young, fast and pop-conscious. If the world is ready for him, this is the album to bury in the time capsule. It's appealing, thought-provoking and representative of everything a bunch of pop singles should be, circa 1978. No one else is recording alternative Top 10 material of this caliber, so if it's not being played on your radio yet, make sure it's on your turntable. Now is the time for all now people to.... ◆

This long-winded whatsis was written for Michael Goldberg's pioneering online music magazine, a realm whose elastic word counts encouraged indulgent personal reminiscence and reflection that a print outlet would never condone. I'll give myself points for the provocative lede, but the easy-to-miss payoff ten paragraphs later is hardly satisfying enough to warrant the time it takes to get there. (For the record, the unnamed creative team behind the almost mythical *A. Ludden Sane* was led by Dave Schulps.)

David Bowie
Outside
Addicted to Noise, 1995

Had it not been for the stiff on line in front of me at the microphone in Avery Fisher Hall at September's CMJ convention in New York, I might have finally gotten to ask David Bowie the one question that has been hounding me ever since "Rebel Rebel" turned my 20-year-old world inside out.

Bowie had made a marginal impression on my glam-rock consciousness when WNEW-FM began playing "Changes" between tracks by Ars Nova and the Insect Trust. On that slender thread of evidence I took the Englishman to be some singer-songwriter type, better than James Taylor and Elton John but nothing to shake my faith in Slade or Roxy Music. Then a pal from high school gave me his spare ticket to see Bowie's *Ziggy Stardust* show at Carnegie Hall in '72, and, sitting a row behind Andy Warhol, I came face to face with an entirely different creature than the piano balladeer I imagined. I hated him. The strobe lights, the costumes, the posey overexertion, the space-alien role-playing, Bowie's fake fellatio of Ronno's Les Paul — it was all too much for this angry Alice Cooper (the music, not the gimmickry) fan who was already feeling out of step with the theatrical excesses of '70s arena rock.

But *Ziggy* — which I had not heard at the time of this now-legendary concert — turned out to be a truly great glam-rock record, a ludicrous fantasy dolled up in ferocious smears of attitude and axework. Bowie began making some sort of sense. *Space Oddity* didn't connect, but I had a good frolic in the humiliating back pages of *Images 1966-1967* (especially the drip-nosed "Please Mr. Gravedigger"). Then came *Aladdin Sane* to up the creative ante considerably (besides inspiring the parodic rock opera *A. Ludden Sane*, an extended ode to the late *Password* host, at George Washington University). A lot of it was easy to see through: the Jacques Brel delusions, the formulaic decadence and dissipation, the post-apocalyptic sci-fi-flick vision. But with "Drive-In Saturday," a fully realized portrait of an alternate universe that felt right but seemed all wrong, the ground began to shift. Like a superhero pulling some elemental brick out of the universal firmament, Bowie's dreams became my dreams, and the line separating my world and his started to bend and twist.

Although it didn't advance Bowie's place in the rock culture, *Pin Ups* was picture perfect, a masterful contemporary lesson in British Invasion music that affected my taste and listening for years. (My Pretty Things collection was paltry until Bowie provided the impetus for catching up with the group the Stones set out to be.)

So, it was with a clean palate and an eager mind that I encountered *Diamond Dogs* in the summer of '74. An even more irritating fantasy than *Ziggy*, the album had something more powerful than ambitious ideas: it had a sound, a profoundly desolate undertow of destruction and despair that came from well outside the familiar language of rock. Created by an artist who might as well have been speaking in tongues, the intense *Diamond Dogs* was impossible to deconstruct, suffused as it was in an atmosphere as poisonous as Agent Orange and as addictive as smack.

Diamond Dogs burned right through the theatrical wall behind which Bowie operated. Any pop icon worth her/his concert rider can make a memorable — even original — record, but Bowie had concocted an alien aura from rock's primordial soup of guitars and drums. It seemed somehow more real, more important, more frightening than what others were delivering. "This ain't rock and roll," Bowie announced portentously over riotous crowd noise at the start of "Diamond Dogs," "This is *genocide*!" And beyond the melodrama, he wasn't kidding.

The final battle in his mock war on youth took place in "Rebel Rebel." A nagging razor-riff, Tony Newman's crisp drum beat and a sneering melody made the song about a wanton glitter doll a taut chart package, but there was another, silent, aspect beyond the audible sounds — a microcosm of creation that redefined the time-space continuum for me. Like a mute ghost desperate to unburden itself, something about the track's recording process — of which I know no details whatever — hovered between its notes, the inescapable implication that the song's creation was more complicated (or inspired) than the usual Top 40 contrivance.

However "Rebel Rebel" came to be committed to tape, for two decades I've had an entirely fictional image of Bowie, in the wee hours of some bleak morning, riding an elevator up from a remote underground bunker studio, having just completed "Rebel Rebel." He is miles from anywhere; the only people with whom he's had any contact for weeks are the musicians with whom he is making the record. He is elated, knowing he's just dug a diamond out of solid rock, having no idea he knew where to find it.

I envision a control room full of people watching the song emerge full-blown with no warning: Bowie is supposed to be doing an overdub for, say, "We Are the Dead," when suddenly, he gives a little shudder, rolls his mismatched irises back and, in a four-and-a-half-minute trance, plays and sings something else entirely, something no one has ever heard, something [even he] has never imagined.

We identify with songs in many different ways — with people, places, events, emotions — but no other song has ever made me imagine its creation so vividly and absurdly. What I wanted to ask Bowie wasn't specifically about that, but it was related. Some questions in life you know you don't want answered. (Incidentally, the inquiry that preceded me, and turned out to be the final one in the time allotted to Q&A after Bowie's amusingly rambling keynote address, had to do with the college attended by his son. Jeez!) No, what I needed to know was this: How do you know how to be David Bowie?

Most people follow relatively straight paths, putting one foot in front of the other, facing the occasional forks in the road, making A/B choices, doing what they're told to. And then there's Bowie: a career of constant discontinuity, abrupt reinvention, geographical unpredictability, multi-media exploration, doing whatever total change of pace comes naturally. The guy is nearing 50 and he's still productively making it up as he goes along. Thinking of those whose toughest decisions every morning are one lump or two, drink or sobriety, wife or mistress, how does Bowie figure out what world — of all those he's already scoped out, and all those he has yet to envision — he'd care to inhabit this Tuesday?

It's not as if the vector of Bowie's life keeps him moving forward in one general direction. Coming in from the wilderness of *Black Tie, White Noise*, his 1993 trip-hopping style-sponge, *Outside* brings Bowie back into his old mutual orbit with Brian Eno (for the first time since completing their monumental sound collage trilogy of *Low, 'Heroes'* and *Lodger* in 1979), gathers together a bunch of familiar sidemen from various epochs (Reeves Gabrels, Carlos Alomar, Erdal Kizilçay, Mike Garson, plus drummer Sterling Campbell on loan from Soul Asylum) and sends the pair off on that most dicey of all middle-aged musical ventures: a narrative concept album. A *long*, narrative concept album. A long, narrative concept album created through the agency of that reliable tool of bankrupt fantasists: the William Burroughs cut-up gambit.

Even with Pete Townshend's *Psychoderelict* as recent and abundant proof of how bad an idea it is, Bowie role-plays his way through the diaries of one Nathan Adler, a detective investigating a series of "ritual art murders." Oh, I get it. Suffice to say, as surreal drama and social comment, this is not *Twin Peaks* set to music.

Outside, however, is by no means a bad album. Far from it. A bad idea, to be sure — an impenetrable colossus of oddly voiced characters and meta-plot that doesn't begin to reward the effort of trying to follow its logic — but, like Townshend's release, one that enshrouds some quality songs. It hardly matters that the bubbling techno calm of "We Prick You" is indicated as being sung by "members of the Court of Justice," that "Leon Blank" renders "The Motel," or that "Detective Nathan Adler" delivers "The Hearts Filthy Lesson" [*sic*], a modern dance track loaded up with random instrumental action. Bowie in whatever guise is still — as we have so often learned — Bowie.

True, he has joined Bob Dylan and Paul McCartney in that menopausal creative phase when songs as exceptional as "Rebel Rebel" and "'Heroes'" are no longer reliably within his reach, but his ability to line up the ducks of a melody and write words that convey some aspect of his authorly sensibility is unimpaired, and he has the skill and instincts to make music of compelling quality. "I'm Deranged," "Outside," the sedately sung "No Control," "We Prick You," "Voyeur of Utter Destruction (As Beauty)" and the alluring pop-plus-feedback closer "Strangers When We Meet" (which quotes the bass line from "Gimme Some Lovin'"), are all credible additions to the canon, but only as detached standalones. Taken as a cohesive package, they drag each other down into the conceptual mud. (As cool as the *Station to Station* stylings of "I Have Not Been to Oxford Town" are, however, it's hard not snicker at the narrative exigencies that lead to lines like "Baby Grace is the victim / She was 14 years of age.")

With Eno as his foil, Bowie's skill at creating fascinating sonic textures remains peerless, and that's where Outside's real strength resides. In an age where rock songwriting — other than the Green Day / Rancid / Smoking Popes axis — is headed back to square one ("I wanna fuck you like an animal" may be a catchy phrase, but the song in which it is contained hardly invites humming along on a wistful afternoon), Bowie's enormous talent for whipping up distinctive musical noise serves him well. Very much in keeping with the sound and vision of his first Eno era (also replicating some of Eno's other collaborative experiments with Talking Heads), *Outside* swarms with atmospheric instrumental layers, no two the same, and none overbearingly dense. Even songs that don't amount to much are easy to appreciate when these guys are finished messing about.

Having contributed significantly to the development of ambient techno, Bowie takes the flyover around the machinists' efforts into his own new version of sound for sound's sake. He sings "Wishful Beginnings" gently, against a growly "ha-ha-ha" loop, tapping percussion, a low-level buzz and noirish synthesizer accents; he recites the verses of "I Am With Name" against an amelodic background of harsh electronic beats and piano flourishes. *Outside*'s raucous highlights include "Hallo Spaceboy," a pulverizing industrial flip of the nine-inch tail, and "Voyeur of Utter Destruction (As Beauty)," a powerful, Crimson-like charge lanced by lines of feedback and colliding rhythms. But the album also contains passages of orchestral grace and quiet solace, like the febrile piano/drum jazz inventions at the heart of "A Small Plot of Land" or the nearly subliminal buildup of "The Motel."

Throughout the album, Bowie gets the framework and the details right, leaving the concept to flail for itself, doing little harm to those enjoying the rich scenery. The story of *Outside* is not one worth telling, but as a master of musical language, David Bowie still turns out brilliant sonic poetry. ◆

Public Enemy
Fear of a Black Planet
Request, April 1990

In the 1960s, youthful poets, inspired by radical politics and Woody Guthrie, took up acoustic guitars to deliver topical commentary in a folk music setting. The great protest singers — Bob Dylan, Phil Ochs, Tom Paxton — located a palatable sound and a lyrical language in which to castigate the government and other despicable institutions. Hit records of explicit radicalism were unthinkable, but a sizable universe of new-leftists — for whom songs attacking war, racism and imperialism were better than meaningless pop ditties — helped launch musical careers that outlasted the political movement.

As even *Newsweek*'s readers now know, discs of poetry with a beat are currently the hottest thing in popular music. Even if half the hip-hop world is busy doing the Humpty Dance, Public Enemy — Chuck D, the irrepressible Flavor Flav and DJ Terminator X — is about to become the biggest political pop group in American history. Through the auspices of CBS Records, *Fear of a Black Planet*, Public Enemy's stupendous third album, brings "War at 33 1/3" home to a potential audience of millions.

Being young no longer guarantees identification with rebel rockers: these are notes from the front in a struggle that is likely to exclude many potential fans. As Spike Lee demonstrated with *Do the Right Thing*, reality unbalances the aesthetic equation in pop culture. The subjective issue for record buyers is no longer just digging the sounds: the question of agreeing with (or at least tolerating) ideas must be faced. Where does this leave the ignorant and the impressionable? If the modern world is truly a terrordome, then kids who get their nutrition from fast food, culture from cartoons and education from TV might as well get their politics from a record.

Fear of a Black Planet is a masterpiece of art and articulation. Atop the hypnotic audio chaos — a roaring subway train of rhythmically looped sounds, a constant ebb and flow that precludes monotony — is an artfully poetic 100 mph harangue that reels off provocative views in verbal bursts of machine gun fire. Scraps of radio broadcasts and other found bits add vérité to this state-of-the-Black-nation report; instrumentals, cut-up edits and stylistically varied backing tracks provide depth and texture.

Escalating sharply from the half-baked generalizations of PE's first two albums, *Black Planet* unveils a powerfully focused and politicized consciousness. Standing on a beat-based soap box, Chuck D speaks his Afrocentric mind on assorted cultural and political issues with typical linguistic deftness. "Fight the Power" sets the album's tone, but *Black Planet*'s strength is the specificity of its attacks — on racism in buppie romance ("Pollywanacraka"), global genetics ("Fear of a Black Planet") and the movies ("Burn Hollywood Burn"); the mistreatment of African-American culture heroes ("Who Stole the Soul") and women ("Revolutionary Generation"); the unreliability of emergency services (Flav's "911 Is a Joke"); and, in a divisive dose of homophobia, AIDS ("Meet the G That Killed Me"). With so many shots being fired, everyone takes a hit. My advice? Just get off the bus when it reaches your stop.

One recurring topic is Public Enemy itself. As "Fight the Power" fades out to close Side Two, a question is posed about the future of Public Enemy. Chuck D begins to answer, but the record ends. Adding fuel to the flames with its "chosen"/"frozen" lyrical landmine, "Welcome to the Terrordome" recapitulates the fallout from Professor Griff's anti-Semitic ignorance without resolving it. (Although credited as a full member on the album, Griff has since left Public Enemy.) The most telling result of that disgraceful chapter, an orgy of hypocrisy and cowardice that shamed everyone involved, is that *Fear of a Black Planet* effectively replays Malcolm X's ideological split with the Nation of Islam, abandoning narrow-minded, anti-white Black nationalism to struggle for politically conscious Black power. Chuck D makes that crucial distinction in "Welcome to the Terrordome." ◆

[Footnote to the first paragraph: I must have forgotten "Eve of Destruction," which hit number-one in 1965.]

2Pac

Me Against the World

Newsday, 12 March 1995

Tupac Shakur is one gutsy brother. Or maybe two. The front-page Shakur is a punk, a convicted felon and a fool, a hard case on a collision course with authority, a hothead who checks himself out of the hospital hours after being shot five times and gives a stretcher-borne finger to the media. The 2Pac who inhabits the recording studio, however, is a sensitive, wise and loving commentator, a straight-up observer of life and death whose measured, melodic flow gives his pained lyrics searing universal power. Shot through the heart with grim reality and fatalistic courage, set atop smooth, gorgeous atmospheres of gently rolling funk and soul, *Me Against the World* is the hip-hop album to beat in 1995.

There's nothing unusual about reformed tough guys offering don't-be-like-me advice, but 2Pac cedes none of his gangsta hardness in telling young listeners not to join him in the thug life. "You could be an accountant, not a dope dealer... you could be a lawyer," he suggests, and he sounds serious. Such contradictions have always accompanied the tumult of 2Pac's combination of life and art, but never before has the dichotomy been drawn in such sharp relief.

The rapper-actor's fourth album (two prior solo discs and last year's unaccountably overlooked *Thug Life* group release) begins with news dispatches, but rather than devote the record to his harsh brushes with justice and violence, 2Pac makes only glancing references to his travails. His obsession is with death, not scores that might need settling. The fatalism that lurks through songs like "If I Die 2 Nite," "Me Against the World" and "Death Around the Corner" is matter-of-fact but ambivalent. "I'm having visions of leaving in a hearse," he rhymes in "So Many Tears."

"Temptation" does address the issues surrounding his sexual assault conviction, an attempt to put his love life in context. Before he gets to the winsome "Even thugs get lonely" line, 2Pac comes off patient and beleaguered, but careful not to impose himself on a woman in the way the jury believed he did. The album's other romantic number, "Get Away," is a sweetly posed, considerate come-on to a woman being mistreated by her man.

It would be facile to view "Dear Mama" as a conciliatory message from a dying man, but 2Pac's heartfelt expression of gratitude amid the album's prevailing gloom makes it hard to resist. This tragic and tender love song brings an uncommon and courageous dimension for roughnecks: forgiveness. Likewise, the ebullient tribute to the "Old School" comes to terms with the past in a way that makes the future seem like an afterthought.

If there's any way to separate the musician's reality from its creative translation, *Me Against the World* has to be seen as one of the saddest and most affecting expositions on young Black America ever offered for public display. Shakur makes the line between art and life nearly impossible to discern, but he's making the most of at least one. ◆

Sparks

My friend, colleague and onetime bandmate Michael Azerrad was for a time the editor of online content for eMusic, a subscription download service that initially offered only indie label music but later, in a futile bid to endure, mainstream recordings as well. It was always a pleasure to write for him.

Sparks
Angst in My Pants
eMusic, November 2007

Fraternal friction is a standard component among the many bands of brothers, but Sparks — in so many ways — take exception to the rules. The enormous oeuvre Ron (keyboards) and Russell Mael (voices) have created since launching themselves from LA in 1971 has many hallmarks, but internal antagonism is not one of its audible components. The absurdity and bizarre brilliance of which they are clearly capable arises from a shared mindset so in synch that it's scary. For outsiders, the challenge is figuring out where to begin introductions.

A decade after their dizzying spin through the teenybopper whirl of British glam-rock stardom, having worked through a pair of dud rock albums and a lucrative creative bask on the Eurodisco Riviera, the Maels returned to the sinfully witty realm of high-concept pop, finding the surest, smartest footing of a very entertaining stretch with this 1982 release. Produced in Munich by Mack ("for Giorgio Moroder Enterprises") with former members of LA new wavers Bates Motel as the band, *Angst in My Pants* is chockablock with the three essential components of Sparks: melody, ingenuity and highly cushioned but deeply sardonic irony. The cover of a demure Ron in a wedding dress, arm in arm with his brother, grinning in a silver suit, is a good indication of the absurdity at play here.

With deadpan charm, the Maels skip merrily through an eclectic menu that addresses such topics as cigarette smoking ("Nicotina"), Disney stars ("Mickey Mouse"), literary figures ("Sherlock Holmes," "Tarzan and Jane"), dieting ("Instant Weight Loss"). Oh, and sex: "Angst in My Pants," "Sextown U.S.A.," "Eaten by the Monster of Love." In a pinnacle of reflexive magic, like a film actor suddenly addressing the camera as himself, the tabloid-twitting "I Predict" fades out as Russell offers one final feat of prognostication: "And this song will fade out."

Holding a blinding Mael mirror up to the short-sighted, "Moustache" alludes to long-standing Hitlerian (as opposed to the intended Chaplinesque) comparisons to Ron's lip hair. (Such sensitivity was not a new topic for the Maels, who sang of bringing home a "Girl From Germany" on *A Woofer in Tweeter's Clothing*, their second album.)

If the music on *Angst* bears a residual trace of the time Sparks spent on the dancefloor with Moroder — namely, repetition — these songs have an unstoppable verbal momentum, with enough meaty verses to keep the choruses in their place. After inadvisably allowing collaborators to undercut their unique gifts as songwriters, the Maels here reassert the strength of their hermetic universe, a happy fraternal marriage made in rock and roll heaven. ◆

I wrote this for the booklet of a two-disc Rhino release compiled by Gary Stewart. I'd like to think of it as a preview of Edgar Wright's 2021 cinematic love letter, *The Sparks Brothers*. The Maels didn't have quite so many fans then.

Profile: The Ultimate Sparks Collection liner notes (1991)

Had Sparks never reached the pinnacle of teen pop sensationhood, or profoundly influenced the development of electronic dance music, the world would probably be content to view the voluminous body of songs meticulously crafted by Ron and Russell Mael over the past two decades as merely high-pitched self-indulgent non-commercial crypto-pop weirdness. (Or something like that.) Lofty intellectual standards and ambitious self-imposed stylistic challenges are hardly standard issue attributes for hit paraders, yet Sparks' career — even at its commercial Anglo-pop peak in the mid-'70s — has always held to just those credos. Providing encouragement to punny wiseasses the world over, thumbing a nose or two at stereotypes and constantly exploring unexpected artistic realms, Sparks have always charted their own course, regardless of the consequences. These twin beacons of creative independence have repeatedly proven that cleverness is no crime, that limbs are meant for climbing out on and that nothing (no, nothing) is sacred (anymore).

At the very beginning of the 1970s, when the world was young and things were fairly boring, the Maels met a third UCLA student, Earle Mankey, and started making music together at Earle's house. Ron played keyboards and wrote strange songs which Russell sang in a variety of uncommon voices, including a piercing falsetto; Earle played guitar and did the techie stuff. They sent a tape of their quirky songs to Todd Rundgren, who procured a record contract and graciously offered to produce their first album. Earle's brother Jim (now in Concrete Blonde) and drummer Harley Feinstein (now a California attorney) filled the ranks, and the quintet dubbed itself Halfnelson.

With true beginner's luck, their first Bearsville single ("Wonder Girl") was a minor chart hit, but that used up all their good fortune for a while. Following the album's release, the powers that were dictated a name change, so the group and its reissued debut became Sparks. For all the commercial good it did, they might as well have stayed Halfnelson.

A brilliant second album (*A Woofer in Tweeter's Clothing*) and a memorable appearance on *American Bandstand,* failed to advance Sparks much further down the road to stardom. As things grew bleak — the group was banished from its primary live venue (L.A.'s Whisky a Go-Go) and was living on food stamps — the Maels got an unexpected break. Island Records in England offered them a deal. Their parents had already moved to London, so Ron and Russell sold their worldly possessions and fulfilled the ultimate Anglophile rock'n'roll fantasy. Arriving abroad in the summer of '73, they wrote songs, recruited a trio of local sidemen and began recording an album of uncompromisingly bizarre pop masterpieces — which England's energy crisis very nearly prevented from being released.

For the first time, the Maels found themselves in a cultural environment that actually welcomed their novel imagination. They responded by writing and recording some of the most eccentric, mind-tingling pop the English charts had ever heard. (Who else would sing about sneezing, or name a pop song "Tits"?) Clever, tongue-twisting tunes and a colorful image that fit right in with the anything-goes aftermath of glam rock brought Sparks a string of hit records, turning the exiles into poster idols. The romantic pun-fest of "This Town Ain't Big Enough for Both of Us" led things off, followed in short order by "Amateur Hour," "Never Turn Your Back on Mother Earth" and a batch more. *Kimono My House* and *Propaganda* (probably the apex of Sparks' lyrical madness) both reached the Top 10 in '74; *Indiscreet* went Top 20 in '75. No matter how surreal and involuted Sparks' songs were, their live shows were total teen pandemonium. But as pop fads are wont to do, Sparks' stardom began slipping; by 1976, Ron and Russell had tired of inclement weather and were back in the U.S.A., bandless and ready to start over.

Neither *Big Beat*, recorded with New York rock and rollers, nor *Introducing Sparks*, played by L.A. session hacks, made any significant commercial noise. The Maels began casting around for a new challenge. What they came up with was studio-oriented dance music using synthesizers. Reaching out for an expert, they enlisted Giorgio Moroder and made *No. 1 in Heaven*, a hugely successful (in Europe) and influential (on the incipient Depeche Mode crowd) album derided by critics as a disco sellout. After a second project (*Terminal Jive*; unreleased in America) under Moroder's tutelage, the Maels adopted a Los Angeles band called Bates Motel and Sparks became a self-contained musical organization again.

Abetted by their fifth, sixth and seventh American labels, the reconstituted and recharged Sparks returned to pop music — albeit their own particular variation on it — for five diverse and frequently delightful albums. *Whomp That Sucker* (1981), produced in Munich by Moroder associate Mack, is a whimsical collection with songs about fear, Martians, faces and the agony of being teen-aged. The even-better *Angst in My Pants* (1982) manages, in the course of one record, to addresses pop icons (Sherlock Holmes, Mickey Mouse, Tarzan), personal health and grooming issues ("Moustache," "Nicotina," "Instant Weight Loss"), prognostication ("I Predict") and lust ("Angst in My Pants," "Sextown U.S.A."). With typical aplomb, the cover pictures Ron (moustache intact) as Russell's blushing bride.

Ron and Russell took the production reins for *Sparks in Outer Space* (1983), inviting Jane Wiedlin of the Go-Go's to sing along on two songs, including the delightful "Cool Places." Meanwhile, "All You Ever Think About Is Sex" revealed that, while Sparks may have been in orbit, the Mael mind was busy cruising in a convertible. The typically self-amused fraternal psychology cover of 1984's *Pulling Rabbits Out of a Hat* portrays Ron as the master of puppet Russell; the album inside is fairly low-key. *Music That You Can Dance To* (a 1986 release recently reissued as, of all things, *The Best of Sparks*) was the brothers' first dance-oriented album since *Terminal Jive*

In 1988, working in Russell's home studio with only a second keyboard player and a guitarist helping out, Sparks recorded *Interior Design*, a blend of romance and dance rhythms.

As of late 1990, that's where things stand. Be warned: the two decades of totally unpredictable pop music condensed here are only the tip of a most remarkable iceberg. ◆

The Songs:

Wonder Girl (1972, from *Halfnelson* aka *Sparks*)
Russell: This was one of the original Earle, Ron and Russell songs. The final recording of it that Todd Rundgren produced stayed really true to our home demo.

Ron: Everybody was telling us — and to this day still tells us — that we're a bit eccentric and out of the mainstream. Lo and behold, the first song that we ever released got into the charts.

(No More) Mr. Nice Guys (1972, *Halfnelson* aka *Sparks*)
Russell: We used to do this when we started to perform live; it went over real well at the Whisky, where Alice Cooper came and saw us. We're resentful to this day that he stole our wonderful title without credit.

Ron: A lot of our other songs didn't go over so well live but we liked doing them anyway. Our live shows at that time were hyperactive. We would play songs that were fast on our album and they would turn out twice as fast.

Girl From Germany (1972, *A Woofer in Tweeter's Clothing*)
Ron: Our lyrics aren't usually based on any outside event. There's a little universe we've developed over the years, with mythical people and situations. It's just an imaginary thing. "Girl From Germany" began as just a title, and one thing led to another.

Russell: People in Germany were real happy about it.

This Town Ain't Big Enough for Both of Us (1974, *Kimono My House*)
Ron: Before we went to England I was playing a lot of Bach etudes to try and become a better keyboard player. A lot of the stuff on *Kimono* was influenced by that. The gunshot came from a BBC sound-effects record. We debated for hours whether it was too much of a gimmick or not.

There was a phone-in competition on Capital Radio between "This Town" and Harry Chapin's "Cat's in the Cradle." We phoned in for our own record a lot, and that's how it got to be played on Capital Radio.

Hasta Manana, Monsieur (1974, *Kimono My House*)
Ron: This song has to do with wordplay, and the sounds of things, the fun of making up sentences that aren't tied down to one language. We felt in certain ways that we were more sophisticated than a lot of other rock bands. One way we could prove it was by doing *chansons* instead of songs.

Talent Is an Asset (1974, *Kimono My House*)
Russell: That was a single in America, not in Europe. It was always well received live. People requested it.

Amateur Hour (1974, *Kimono My House*)
Russell: One thing that's really exciting about England is that the lifespan of a single is about six weeks. "This Town" was still doing really well when we came out with "Amateur Hour." It was neat to see two songs that were really different in nature become back-to-back hits.

Something for the Girl With Everything (1974, *Propaganda*)
Russell: Another English hit single, melodically in the style of "This Town" — one of those melodies that couldn't be anyone but Sparks. Ron wrote them on keyboards and then forced me to sing those acrobatic melodies.

Never Turn Your Back on Mother Earth (1974, *Propaganda*)
Ron: We were wrapped up in our own little world, and we didn't think our songs sounded as much alike as other people did. But we tried — within the limits of what we do — to find different ways of doing things.

Russell: The record company was real nervous because this was the first ballad-like song from us. They were worried what the public might think of it, but it did really well.

Achoo (1974, *Propaganda*)
Russell: The series of echoing "achoo"s at the end is all me, done without the aid of any outside nasal stimulation.

Propaganda/At Home, at Work, at Play (1974, *Propaganda*)
Ron: We were trying different ways of combining things and doing "Propaganda" a cappella was a challenge for us. We're not trained musicians or anything. Russell would sing something, and then sing something else that sounded good with it.

Russell: You'll notice the operatic feel of "Propaganda" in several Queen albums that followed.

Get in the Swing (1975, *Indiscreet*)
Ron: We wanted to make use of [producer] Tony Visconti's abilities as an arranger. This song got into the English Top 30, but not into the Top 10. We were so upset at people not accepting it in a huge way that we thought about doing a version of "Louie, Louie" and releasing that.

Looks, Looks, Looks (1975, *Indiscreet*)
Ron: The English sales of *Propaganda* weren't quite as good as *Kimono*, and we wanted to do something different. At that time, if you faced that situation, you would push off in a different direction. Now the reaction is to go middle of the road. We were naïve enough to do what a lot of people thought was a really self-indulgent album. But to us everything is self-indulgent — that was our whole reason for doing music.

Happy Hunting Ground (1975, *Indiscreet*)
Ron: *Indiscreet* was recorded at Tony Visconti's house. He had a studio downstairs the size of a phone booth. It was incredibly tight, but it gave you the feeling you could concentrate without anyone knowing what you were doing.

Lost and Found (1974, B-side of "Talent Is an Asset")
Ron: We would write 30 or 35 songs in order to have an album's worth of material. We would rehearse all the songs in the studio and decide which would be on the album. Others that weren't as strong would be slated for B-sides.

Russell: It was fun to be able to come up with things whose main purpose in life was being B-sides.

Big Boy (1976, *Big Beat*)
Ron: We always liked the early Who, and this is our interpretation of a Who song. To our chagrin, it was a part of the *Rollercoaster* movie. They tried to get KISS, but KISS turned it down, and they got us instead.

Nothing to Do (1976, *Big Beat*)
Russell: This was a big favorite of Joey Ramone's. He was always trying to convince the rest of the Ramones to do that song. I would have loved to hear their version of it.

I Like Girls (1976, *Big Beat*)
Russell: We had proposed doing "I Want to Hold Your Hand" with Marianne Faithfull, and had contacted Rupert Holmes to do a lush, orchestrated version of it. Marianne Faithfull backed out of the project, but Rupert had already scored it, so we recorded it ourselves. [Sparks' version appeared on a 1976 single.] He also did an orchestrated version of "I Like Girls," an old song from our early days.

We asked him to do our entire album. But Rupert's strength is in his orchestration and, as it turned out, we decided that the album should be a stripped-down version of Sparks: more guitars and less keyboards.

Ron: We had recorded "I Like Girls" three or four times but never released it. I really liked the song, and it seemed good for the album.

A Big Surprise (1977, *Introducing Sparks*)
Russell: We were bandless again and back in L.A. We decided to do an album with session musicians. I like the songs, but they came out blander-sounding than they should have been.

Over the Summer (1977, *Introducing Sparks*)
Russell: We had done a demo of this — just keyboard and voice — that has more character than the final one that made it to the album, before we stuck on all those high-priced musicians.

Ron: We used the session backup singers that had done all the commercials that are supposed to sound like the Beach Boys.

The No. 1 Song in Heaven (1979, *No. 1 in Heaven*)
Ron: We're always trying to put ourselves in different musical situations, and the combination of electronics and a dance beat was exciting. We were introduced to Giorgio Moroder through a German journalist. He didn't want to spend a whole lot of money on the project, so we recorded over a bunch of old Donna Summer master tapes.

Beat the Clock (1979, *No. 1 in Heaven*)
Russell: We had loved "I Feel Love" which Giorgio Moroder had done with Donna Summer. We heard that song and were really amazed — it was a breakthrough pop record. We were looking for a way to combine that sort of thing with our kind of outlook and melodies, but we didn't know anything about synthesizers.

When I'm With You (1980, *Terminal Jive*)
Ron: We were still working with Giorgio. I played him 25 new songs and he rejected every one except "When I'm With You," and he still thought it needed a new middle. This single was the biggest thing we ever had in France. We spent eight months in Paris, doing television shows. It's a really good song but it doesn't really appeal to me, except that it brings back fond memories of living in France.

Tryouts for the Human Race (1979, *No. 1 in Heaven*)
Ron: We went to England to do press for the album and were absolutely crucified for "going disco." We felt as if we'd committed some major crime.

Russell: We were violently attacked for the blasphemy of using synthesizers in a band and doing dance music. Critics lashed out against us, but from the public's standpoint it was really successful. A good portion of the English bands in the Depeche Mode ilk — we know a lot of them — say that their careers were founded on this album.

Funny Face (1981, *Whomp That Sucker*)
Russell: Ron and I did a boxing match in London to introduce *Whomp That Sucker*. We had a couple of weeks of training with an English boxer, and they set up a full-size ring in the London Hilton hotel. It was staged that Ron would be the winner, so after three rounds he knocked me out, and they carried me out of the ring.

Tips for Teens (1981, *Whomp That Sucker*)
Russell: This song always reminded me of an album like the Who's *A Quick One*; lyrically, there's a certain similarity of slant. We were back to songs that were powerful and melodic with a lot of harmony.

Upstairs (1981, *Whomp That Sucker*)
Russell: We'd met an L.A. band called Bates Motel and got along really well with them personally so we asked them to join us en masse [except for one guitar player]. We spent a lot of time rehearsing with the band before we went into the studio to make *Whomp That Sucker*.

Modesty Plays (1982, French single)
Russell: A screenwriter friend of ours enlisted us to do a theme song for a TV version of the comic strip [*Modesty Blaise*]. The show never materialized, but we really liked the song and gave it to our French record company, which released it as a single. It got massive airplay as an import in Los Angeles; we'd do it in concerts here. A different recording of the song came out on *Music That You Can Dance To*. For legal reasons, we called it "Modesty Plays."

Angst in My Pants (1982, *Angst in My Pants*)
Russell: We had another song called "Angst in My Pants" with a totally different melody. It was going to be on the album, but we didn't like it that much. We'd finished recording all the other songs and needed one more, so Ron came up with a melody and stuck the old title onto the new song. The rest of the band had already flown home, so Ron played everything on the track, except for a David Kendrick drum loop that we snipped from some other tune.

Ron: The song opened things up for me musically. It's more sing-y and less herky-jerky. Maybe it can't be heard in anything we did later on, but it was really important to me as a songwriter because it led to other things.

I Predict (1982, *Angst in My Pants*)
Russell: An ode to the *National Enquirer*, an ode to the checkout stand. Live, we just kind of end it rather than fade out, but what are you gonna do?

Sextown U.S.A. (1982, *Angst in My Pants*)
Ron: We're definitely not repelled by sex, but we're definitely repelled by the typical crotch-rock stances, so we went out of our way to avoid anything that even approached a come-over-here-baby-let's-hop-into-bed sort of thing. We found a way to channel those urges in a Sparks kind of way.

Moustache (1982, *Angst in My Pants*)
Ron: We were kicked off a French TV show because the guy said I looked like Hitler and he didn't want Hitler on his show. A lot of people are weird, but French people are weirder. If I'd been smarter commercially, I would have altered my facial hair a lot sooner than I did. To me, it was a cartoon thing and, if anything, it was Chaplin. It was like a logo on my face.

All You Ever Think About Is Sex and **Cool Places** (1983, *Sparks in Outer Space*)
Russell: Our fan club got a really nice letter from the head of the Go-Go's fan club, saying Jane Wiedlin was a big Sparks fan. She had even once run her own Sparks fan club. I thought it was really neat, so I contacted Jane and asked if she wanted to do something together.

Ron: This was going to be a straight Sparks song. We played Jane a few songs, and she chose "Cool Places." It introduced us to a lot of people; Rick Springfield asked us to tour with him.

With All My Might (1984, *Pulling Rabbits Out of a Hat*)
Ron: We wanted to do a song that had all the irony removed. I really like it, but people look for the motive behind it. They wait for the punchline, and there isn't any.

Russell: We thought this could have been really successful. It sounds like the type of thing that could get played on the radio. For once in our career, Ron tried to make a song palatable for an American mass audience. But it didn't get played a lot. Even the stations that usually support us thought it was too soft.

Change (1985, *Music That You Can Dance To*)
Ron: We wanted to try something that was really involved, really challenging. We went to Telex's studio in Brussels and spent a month each on "Change" and "The Scene." "Change" is one of my favorite songs of anything we've done, partially because it was so much fun to work on. We set out to do something that was epic, and we thought we had succeeded.

Russell: "Change" is one of my favorite Sparks songs of all time, the kind of song you hope would be a worldwide number-one. It was a real disappointment when it didn't click commercially.

Music That You Can Dance To (1986, *Music That You Can Dance To*)
Russell: I really like the album because it's pure and focused. The production is rich, and it's stylized in a certain way that I like. After we finished the album it was eventually sold to Curb Records. Curb was producing a film called *Rad* and they thought this song would be great for the movie. So, they stuck it in. That was one of the worst movies of all time.

So Important (1988, *Interior Design*)
Ron: We were trying to write good songs in the way that maybe other people might write good songs.

Russell: This is as close as Sparks will ever get to being compatible with American radio. ◆

Sparks, 1976. Photo by Linda Danna Robbins

A few years ago, my wife Kristina and I attended an in-store the Maels did at the Rough Trade store in Brooklyn. After purchasing their latest CD, *Hippopotamus*, and waiting patiently in the receiving line to say hello, I received a tepid reception when I introduced myself, showed them this photo and mentioned *Trouser Press* and those liner notes. "Oh, yeah. Hi." Sure, it had been a long time, but it was hard not to feel slighted.

Oh, and *The Sparks Brothers*? Loads of great footage and, yes, it was fascinating to hear the Maels' talk about themselves and their work in ways I've never heard before, but the parade of random celebrities marveling at the stylistically diversity of Sparks' catalogue and what big fans they are made me want to kick the screen in.

Even before *Pitchfork*, the rise of online publications provided a welcome opportunity for long, thoughtful record reviews, a form which had been increasingly constrained by the cost of printing and the short-attention-span acceptance of efficiently encapsulated *USA Today* journalism. In a macro sense, record reviewing was being pushed away from its initial impetus — to give weisenheimers with a rock jones a place to show off by spilling their drug-addled brains all over the page — and toward the mercantile utility of helping music fans determine how best to apportion their discretionary cultural funds.

Album reviewing, for someone who does a lot of it, can be an exercise in swish-and-spit, where you taste, consider and then discharge the experience. For a couple of days, perhaps, you listen over and over to a single hour of music, digging yourself deep into it — the sound, the music, the words — analyzing the evidence, seeking reference points, formulating theories, confirming suspicions. Then you give it your best shot, balancing the paradox of growing familiarity with the need to judge it strictly on enduring merit, not momentary overload.

While you're writing, it's hard to think of anything else. You are buried, sonically speaking, in your work. But then you finished and move on to the next thing. An album that was your constant companion for a time is shelved, perhaps never to be played again. Years later, while you have evidence on paper of your time living with it, none of what you've written rings any bells. The song titles are utterly unfamiliar; reading what I said about them summons up zilch in the memory banks. I stand by my historical analysis of U2's progress and still have my copy of *Pop*, but until I fetch it up from the cellar, I can't even picture the cover. (And did I *really* use the word "reimagined"?)

Another issue this review summons up for me is the negative effect groupthink has on my critical thinking. Prior to the release of *Pop*, the U2 publicity machine did a brilliant job of feeding a group of prominent journalists a plate of spin that they all consumed and regurgitated to their readers. While it is entirely possible that a group of critics can hold similar views on a record, there were credulous hype-prints all over this one and that triggered my stubborn independent streak. Warily, I wasn't going to fall for it. I focused my attention on listening for those attributes the band had claimed and conveyed. When I didn't hear what I'd read about on the album, that became a mark against it. Now, I admit that's a wrongheaded way to think about music, but it definitely figured into this review.

U2

Pop

SonicNet, February 1997

Discounting the dimestore poetry of Bono's smug lyrical meanderings, density is a relatively new development in U2's music. The essential sonic aspect of the young rock group heralded on *Boy*, *October* and *War* was its exotic spaciousness. Shunning the strum and twang ethos of the punk era, the Edge had another idea than faster and louder. In an unprecedented embrace of electric pointillism, the guitarist picked out just the right notes, one heavily echoed string at a time, to fill the void with discrete sparkles rather than thick smears of aggression. For all the passion and the majesty, the stadium-filling power and haunting emotionalism, it was the Edge's reimagined guitar role that distinguished U2 in the '80s.

Though the group also indulged defiant whims, sending stylistic vectors off in random directions from that airy center, its next two albums — *The Unforgettable Fire* (1984) and *The Joshua Tree* (1987) — basically honored the economy of that original formulation. The hits from those albums are all, in one way or another, cut from the same stylistic template: the rhythm section's organic flow underpinning the Edge's tautly focused guitar detailing, held in check by, and in turn intensifying the relief of, Bono's unbridled vocal freedom.

With the evocative complications that resulted from that dialectic, U2 was able to paint the big picture in broad strokes and fill in the tiniest details in the same minutes of music; few quartets with standard instrumentation have ever made more original use of its assets. And in a world where compassion is too rare among those in a position to use it for something, the band's stirring contrast of surgical precision and raw feeling rang true to life.

Which is why the next giant step for U2 — evidently at the behest of the Edge, whose retiring public role appears at odds with his creative station in the band — was *Achtung Baby*, a thickly laid carpet of sounds surpassing songs. Inaugurating a new era of mature experimentation and tape-filling complexity, the group brought its once-skeletal sonic values to a modern factory where it was hammered by post-industrial blips and distortion, clattering synthetic rhythms and cyclonic dislocation, bending the purity of the band's compositional designs into unfamiliar and not entirely inviting shapes. As fingerpainting exercises, songs like "The Fly" and "Zoo Station" proved that it could be done and probably satisfied the group's craving for challenge and reinvigoration, but those weren't the songs that stuck. For all their productive and progressive window-dressing, "Mysterious Ways," "One" and "Who's Gonna Ride Your Wild Horses," which all hail from familiar U2 terrain, had the enduring virtues.

Then came *Zooropa*, 1993's untethered leap into the unknown, a sample sale of offbeat obsessions: the Edge's weird lead vocal on "Numb," mainstream-scorning atmospherics and other adventures in hi-fi. Seen as a courageous reinvention rather than a nervy attempt to escape preconceptions, *Zooropa* was a compelling success, a harbinger of further escapades in the Bowie-built arcade of cash-and-carry fads.

Time out. Throughout its career, U2 has been plagued by a variation on that pesky perception/reality dichotomy: the gap between the group's intentions and how those desires are ultimately perceived. Hoping to cast a p.c. vote against African-American oppression and wryly embrace the glitz and gilded dung of Americana on *Rattle and Hum*, U2 instead came off as patronizing and intrusive missionaries, lecturing the hapless colonial natives on how to improve their shallow and unfulfilled lives.

The *Zoo TV* tour was an even grander miscalculation, a triple sec shot of cynical detachment in which the pop star, in order to ridicule the trope of pop stardom without the inconvenience of abandoning its spotlighted trappings, pretended to be a pop star. Preening into a TV camera broadcasting his image to the masses, throwing his media weight around in contrived stunts like phoning the White House, Bono didn't lampoon his position, he exaggerated it in ways that were far too familiar to rock audiences to correctly register as satire or even critical commentary.

The spin cycle of well-orchestrated journalistic hype that preceded the release of *Pop* — typical of U2's of virtual reality, in which the group imagines how it would like to be perceived and then sets about achieving some approximation of that goal through any means necessary — would have you believe that techno has taken over, the guitars are gone, it's Village People time in Dublin and U2 is courageously blazing a trail to the new millennium.

Despite a few thrilling excursions into the ultraworld (most notably the boisterous tunnel travel of "MOFO"; the envelope-generator stutter of "Miami" is one of the album's few obvious flubs), *Pop* serves notice that U2 is firmly rooted to its own traditions. For all the fables of the reconstruction, the album returns U2, for the most part, to a solid safety zone of guitar-based ballads and songs in which trendy but accessible audio embellishments are worn as accessories, not armor.

In short, the Edge's guitars rock, the mild infusion of electronica here makes Bowie sound like the man who fell *from* earth, and the group's progress is more of the rearward sort, back towards cleaner, simpler sounds and appealing tunes that don't hide their better qualities under a mixing board. If this is a great leap forward, whoever is still in Depeche Mode had better get busy or find a new line of work.

It's no surprise that a rock group late in its second decade isn't as inclined (or able) to take creative risks, but U2's desire to move off the dime (or at least to be seen as having done) remains at odds with the album's effect, which dances colorfully in place. Signifying progress (as in the squiggly sequenced guitar trellis that snakes in and out of "Do You Feel Loved," a lovely and familiar-sounding melody presented in what sounds like a preemptive remix, and the My Bloody Valentine-thickened treble calamity that drifts in and out of "Gone") is altogether different from actually achieving it. Still, there's nothing intrinsically wrong in stationary exertion for a group of such estimable caliber. Unless the lyrics — big on Jesus, God and motherhood — are an insurmountable obstacle, *Pop* is easy to enjoy if you don't contemplate the absurd claims made for it.

When not playing it soft and supple in ballads like "If God Will Send His Angels" and the closing "Wake Up Dead Man," rocking to a slow Stones boil in "Last Night on Earth" or affixing a compelling club beat to rockist routine in "Discothèque," the group does nothing of greater shock than summoning up sour memories of *Rattle and Hum*'s cultural commentary in "The Playboy Mansion." Offered up as a lazy and laid-back '70s wah-wah soul allusion with a bridge borrowed from "The Mighty Quinn," the number finds the band's newspaper reader musing about OJ, Big Macs, perfume, obsession and talk shows. OK?

On the other hand, "Please" is typical of how U2 is able to smartly subsume its stylistic affinities into its own structures. Working between a snappy Larry Mullen snare and one of Bono's patented daydreamer vocals, co-producers Flood and Howie B softly squeeze in puffy layers of the latest textural frosting: an Adam Clayton bassline that pulses in and out like a cotton-covered mallet, keyboards that sputter rhythmically and shimmer calmly, a six-note Edge guitar lick. None of it seriously distracts from the vocal, which remains the song's focal point; the rest is just atmosphere.

More important than what "Please" says about U2's passing relationship with electronic dance music is what the track says about the techno genre. If Prodigy or the Chemical Brothers or Orbital could, or would, bring the noise via songs with this much structural integrity, they could easily bridge the generation gap being widened by the popularity of dance tracks that favor sensation over substance. Lyrics and melodies may not currently mean much in certain circles, but for U2, overweening ambitions and pretensions notwithstanding, those elements continue to provide a reliable beacon through the noise. *Pop* it is. ◆

R.E.M.
New Adventures in Hi-Fi
SonicNet, 7 October 1996

Well, it's a more appealing title than *Tuneless Noise From Weary Road Veterans*, but splitting the hairs of descriptive accuracy for R.E.M.'s tenth album would leave both choices equally wanting. Upholding the quartet's perplexing tradition of alternating good and bad releases, *New Adventures in Hi-Fi* is an improvement on 1994's horrifying *Monster*, but while it at least swings the pendulum in the proper direction, this ponderous exercise in offhand simplicity is too joyless and forced to even approach the heights of 1992's spectacular *Automatic for the People*, which is looking more and more likely to remain the band's '90s high-water mark.

Recorded in and around R.E.M's last tour, *New Adventures* betters the flat, shapeless songwriting that was poorly disguised on *Monster* by Pete Buck's radioactive guitar exertions. A little. Although some tracks again compound the failings of weak material with layers of blustery overstatement, the band wisely grants itself some sonic breathing room here, maneuvering a broader stylistic berth and paving its way with refreshing splashes of melody and instrumental variety. But the songs are still short on inspiration and elegance. And the performances, no matter how casually produced and uncomplicated, sag with creative weight in a way the seemingly effortless marvels on an album like *Green* don't. Having gone its own way for so long, R.E.M. appears to have found the way back home all uphill.

Once rich with bright splashes of fan-powered imagination, R.E.M. planted a glorious rebel flag in the Byrdsy '60s, turning innocuous nostalgia into a modern culture counter as a generation lay gasping for heroes. In the quartet's principled hands, jangle-pop somehow became a radical idea, a means to wax artistic, explore daring emotions and uplift the spirit all in the strength of (12-)strings and Michael Stipe's gauzy musings. As millions added *Lifes Rich Pageant*, *Document* and *Green* to their college curricula, that artistic victory became a heady commercial breakthrough; thanks to a recently signed deal, R.E.M. is now contractually the best-compensated entity in popular music.

On the way from the 40 Watt Club to the $60 million club, R.E.M. enhanced its stature by refusing to sell out to sponsors or advertisers, by supporting the independent music scene and good social causes. Sustained success helped the band lay down roots and then dig a deep and strong foundation. Now, a major art institution stands where a little old band from Athens once played. By taking the long, high road — maintaining commendable musical values and at least the *desire* to keep moving ahead well beyond the band world's nearly unpassable decade point — R.E.M. has achieved a mixed state of grace, free to succeed at whatever it chooses but equally unchallenged by things to prove or goals to imagine.

Of all the assets now at the band's disposal, youth and innocence are well out of its reach. While the brilliant fingerpainting that made records like *Murmur* and *Reckoning* comfortably real (and, paradoxically, accessible even in their elusiveness) still hangs in the band's gallery, context and stature make even the most colorful new canvases seem overly solemn and self-importantly significant. It's as if Stipe were doomed to view the world through a two-way mirror, observing his own response to every vision. Without any audible signs of it being the group's intent, *New Adventures in Hi-Fi* has a discouraging good-for-you tinge, that uneasy feeling that something is supposed to be gleaned from the experience even if visceral pleasures are not on the menu.

The album's whatever/wherever/whenever recording process — tracks were cut at soundchecks, in a dressing room, onstage and in quick studio sessions in Seattle — was presumably intended to bring immediacy and resonance back to the band's work. But rough edges and a few charmingly preserved botches are inadequate substitutes for enduring intrinsic qualities.

Despite a few musically rewarding numbers — the gripping "Departure" echoes the verbal cadences of "Pop Song 89" and "Exhuming McCarthy" as well as the rousing chorus of "Radio Free Europe"; the opening "How the West Was Won and Where It Got Us" slithers down a relaxed noirish path from the Crescent City; "Zither" finds fetching use for autoharp in a Southwestern setting; and the closing ballad, "Electrolite," handsomely inscribes Stipe's singing with violin and piano — it falls to such whims as Scott McCaughey's old ARP synthesizer to stir things up in R.E.M.'s museum. Splattering staticy wheeps, blurks and snargles all over the alluring "Leave" and the loud "Undertow" (one of the album's rare instances where feedback and volume actually serve a song's purpose rather than obscure it), he upstages the band, lighting a sonic fire that is elsewhere stifled by the slashing guitar power. (Patti Smith's background vocal, low in the mix of the somber and nearly spoken "E-Bow the Letter," however, achieves the opposite effect.) Generally, R.E.M.'s loud rock blasts still sound less like a deliberate creative decision than the absence of stylistic consideration, or at the very least a thoughtless concession to Buck, who is becoming less like the man with a plan than a big kid fooling with a fuzzbox.

If the album's balance of dynamic textures favors boisterous energy, consigning the acoustic or otherwise restrained digressions to serve as oases, not stylistic oceans, the emotional pitch of the lyrics — complicated by Stipe's myriad of unfamiliar singing styles — presents a more intriguing dilemma. Going along with the music like hitchhikers looking for a ride, the words propose marriage ("Be Mine"), reject religion ("Undertow"), reflect harshly on fame ("E-Bow the Letter") and remark on the banality of television talk shows ("New Test Leper"). Stipe, who once upended clichés (or at least carefully hid them in a forest of obscurity), here attempts to co-opt them, relying on his audience to know he couldn't possibly intend such banalities as "See ya/don't wanna be ya" ("The Wake-Up Bomb"), the Biblical "judge not lest ye be judged" ("New Test Leper") or "I'm outta here" ("Electrolite") to be taken at face value. It's a high-wire act, but Stipe knows whereof he leaps.

And, truly, he gets away with it here. His singing is as accomplished and involving as any in the band's catalogue, and his lyrics offer the usual quizzical considerations of moving targets that at least resemble a profound artist at work. But that element alone can't lift this over-burdened album off the ground. The music never soars, never transcends utilitarian intentions with the haunting beauty of the band's best. Adventures are educational, but they also have to be fun. ◆

When Bill Wyman (the incisive American journalist born with that name, not the erstwhile Rolling Stones bassist who borrowed it) became arts editor at *Salon*, he passed my name on to a cool editor in Brooklyn and I got a lot of room to blather on about music that mattered to me. (And some that didn't.)

50,000,000 Backstreet Boys fans *can* be wrong

Salon, June 1999

Until punk's neurotic attempt to abolish sex in the name of nihilism in the late '70s, the battle for rock and roll's soul had been a straightforward tug of war between god and the devil over the eternal fate of teenagers. Those sweat-drenched primal screamers of the '50s knew all about good and evil. They wiggled their whatsits to a thrusting beat and leered out of hi-fi radios in easily decipherable forni-code. The world wasn't quite ready for an all-out generation landslide, but what was boiling up in the backseats of those four-wheeled shrines of post-war prosperity must have seemed — reproductive evidence quite to the contrary — like something mom and dad would never have done. And they certainly wouldn't have written or whistled songs about it.

But those satanic verses sure did exist, and the proof comes tumbling out of Rhino Records' new *Loud, Fast, & Out of Control* box (subtitled "The Wild Sounds of '50s Rock") like silver dollars out of a perfectly prodded slot machine. These four CDs are packed with chewy passion candies, bite-sized treats pungent with the urges of youth. This sentimental education holds proof of a dozen different truths (like the joys of sax and the fact that the devil does have the best tunes, many of which — thanks to cover versions — may be familiar even to those ignorant of these particular recordings). The 104 tracks achieve a nearly unanimous standard of vigor and intensity, prodded by unhinged abandon or unmistakably bad intentions and nuanced into profundity by the artists' inscrutable mix of raw talent and dumb luck.

Again and again, slangy dreams are declared in fervent voices submerged in echo, driven by beats and slap bass, cajoled by virile horns, all documented in no time flat in recording facilities that were rudimentary beyond comprehension of modern technologists. Whether it's Eddie Cochran connecting his need for a flash car to his chances with a hot chick in "Somethin' Else," Frankie Ford's quizzical offer of a "Sea Cruise," Buddy Holly's surprisingly credible delivery of Chuck Berry's nervy Black-pride anthem, "Brown Eyed Handsome Man" or the male-bonding described without so much as an embarrassed shrug by an audibly straight-faced Elvis Presley in "Jailhouse Rock," the blissful optimism of can-do American spirit — and bug-eyed rockin' heebeegeebies — prevails.

Sexually, these tracks get as blatant as prevailing social mores could possibly abide. After all, making records has always been a business, and as such was subject to various forms of oversight. (The set omits three well-known emission-standards: Billy Ward and the Dominoes' "60-Minute Man," Hank Ballard's "Work With Me Annie" and Etta James' "Roll With Me, Henry.") While some Black musicians of the day prospered in the white world by singing about moon-June romance in smooth harmony, others diverted their church-learned spirit into songs about fucking. Little Richard somehow slurred "you sure like to ball" past potential censors of "Good Golly, Miss Molly." Wynonie Harris brags about his "Lovin' Machine." And Big Joe Turner carries off the wickedly euphemistic "I'm like a one-eyed cat peeping in the seafood store" and marvels salaciously that "I can't believe my eyes — all of this belongs to you" in the otherwise innocuous kitchen commands of "Shake, Rattle and Roll." Even Fats Domino, the genial Crescent City piano man in a rare state of ardor, declares "I'm Ready" (...and willing and able) "to rock and roll all night" — and you know he's not aiming to confine his nocturnal business to the dance floor.

White rockers, responsible for more than half the tracks here, get their licks in as well. The incomparable Wanda Jackson, who later traded in her libido for Christianity (a temporary victory for the lord: she's gone back to singing her hits, albeit with little of the same earthy euphoria), unleashes her multi-orgasmic volcano in "Fujiyama Mama" and promises more wanton immorality in "Let's Have a Party." (Writing about Jackson in his delirious paean to *Unsung Heroes of Rock'n'Roll*, the peerless Nick Tosches ventures "...she sounded like she could fry eggs on her

G-spot.") In the Collins Kids' "Mercy," 16-year-old Lorrie C. can barely contain her excitement: she sings "he makes my pulse go-go-go" with enough fuel to have you believe he's waiting outside the studio with the motor revved and a room booked right around the bend. Tune out the lyrics of "Great Balls of Fire," and listen to Jerry Lee Lewis share the sinful ways he learned growing up around Black juke joints in the deep South. He keeps his proverbial pants on in the peppy piano rag "Breathless," but there's no mistaking what's on his mind when he whimper-sighs the song's title.

Not all these iconoclasts were as lubriciously liberated. Bill Haley, the humble fuse curling into rock and roll's powder keg, sings "Rock Around the Clock" like a Sunday school teacher trying to prove he can let down his hair down and have fun with the kids. Buddy Holly, who I'm told once tried to force himself on a young Texas ticket-taker a decade before she begat a buddy of mine, never revealed himself so urgently in song. Chuck Berry, who, it later turned out, got his jollies taking sleazy snapshots of adults, kept his wily songs for teenagers good clean fun. (At least until 1972's painfully coy novelty "My Ding-a-Ling.") Nice guy Carl Perkins kept it clean, too, and all it got him was a chart loss on "Blue Suede Shoes" to his pal Elvis, a man who always sold sex, even if he had to park his pelvis when he came offstage to make records.

Sublimated sex, if that's what is, surfaces in the sounds of some seriously unhinged ravers here. Alabaman Jerry Lott, recording as The Phantom, gasps for breath from the bottom of a churning well in the fully crazed one-off "Love Me." Still, he's no match for Screamin' Jay Hawkins, R&B's great theatrical crypt-kicker, who spits up a double shot of dementia with the gurgling insanity of "Little Demon" and "Frenzy." (But, alas, no "Constipation Blues.") And for further walks on the wild side, Chan Romero's rabid delivery of his "Hippy Hippy Shake" makes it good, freakish company for LaVern Baker's weird "Voodoo Voodoo," Johnny Burnette's shrieking hiccough classic "Rock Billy Boogie," the obscure, harmonica-driven "Rockin' This Joint To-Nite" by one Kid Thomas and Gene Vincent's ominously mumbled "Race With the Devil."

Even instrumentals like Duane Eddy's "Rebel Rouser" and Link Wray's "Rumble," nonsense songs (Roy Orbison's "Ooby Dooby," Gene Vincent's "B-I-Bickey-Bi, Bo-Bo-Go," the Rock-a-Teens' "Woo-Hoo") and novelties (the Coasters' vivid "Charlie Brown," Billy Riley's inspired "Flying Saucer Rock and Roll") have the spunk to stick. No prissy posturing or nonchalant ambivalence undercuts the zest for life and love that makes this music move.

The '50s eventually settled down. Students did bomb shelter drills but were safe from sex, as cold war anxieties were balmed by mild-mannered vocal groups filling the tanks while Motown and the Beach Boys got themselves ready to roll. However, the moral scrimmage became much harder to follow when the explosive genesis of fundamental rock and roll was swept away by the megatonnage of mid-'60s youth culture. In the eye of the cultural storm, the Beatles took the high road, decontaminating hip-shaking R&B with the purity of romance. There was plenty of sexuality in their music (and lives), but they followed the literary mode and dressed it up, resetting the lust lurking in the pants of Clearasil kids into socially acceptable drama. But between the lines of their lyrics, in *A Hard Day's Night* and in their every bowl-haired head flip, the subversive message was loud and clear: freedom equals sex.

And they weren't the only game going. Taking a dirt road to hell, the Rolling Stones didn't waste their time on teenage tenderness: they looked down and pledged their troth to Jack Flash, serving up steamy platters of what, as they say, the little girls understand.

Come punk, the sneering disdain of the ironically named Sex Pistols' "Bodies" says more about the safety-pinned notion of intimacy than the *Hustler*-minded Dead Boys' song "Caught With the Meat in Your Mouth." The Buzzcocks ventured "Orgasm Addict," and the Stranglers sang "Bring on the Nubiles," but most punks liked to think of themselves as too cool to fuck. It finally took Duran Duran and other Chic-conscious new wavers to unlock the conceptual chastity belts. By inducing white groovers to dance for the first time since disco froze them like deer caught in mirror ball lights, funky style hounds got the temperature of pop to rise again, an effort only accelerated by Prince and the mischief of the 2 Live Crew party boys on the fringes of rap.

As hardcore hip-hop's credibility-confirming sex machine continued to vibrate mightily, it caught R&B ballad singers in its gears. These days, even songs with lulling melodies depict sexuality blunt enough to arrest the hearts of historic hellraisers. Macking down the red satin road to the bedroom, a glass of Cristal in one hand and a StarTAC phone in the other, young playboys and playgirls like R. Kelly, Total, Next, Silk and Shai serve it up raw and witless, less erotic lust than numb Skinemax thrust.

The Stones can still put fannies in high-priced seats, but what the men know, the little girls no longer understand. Today's teenyboppers — and, judging by the numbers going up on the sales board of late, some of their moms as well — are no longer entranced by the erogenous zones of grandpa old goat and his craggy-faced cronies. After their species' successive encounters with Michael Jackson, New Kids on the Block, Madonna, Mariah Carey, Color Me Badd and the Spice Girls, what they want, what they really, really want, is the Backstreet Boys.

The new Pat Boones on the block are five Florida preeners currently reigning in the vapid-chart-pop kingdom by selling the mechanics of recent best-selling R&B balladry minus the bump and grind (and the faux-spiritual uncertainty principle concerning the fixed position of notes in melodies.) Selling danceable soul that's safe as milk, the Backstreet Boys have picked up the soft-soap sensitivity of post-Barry White new age R&B lovermen and made it even less threatening to little ones. Slathering the overproduced vocal cream of melodramatic R&B balladry with the peppy techno beat-froth of crass Europop, *Millennium* is a gooey Hallmark-card confection that's hard to spit out. The album's mush-hearted romanticism defines itself — and the group, who couldn't possibly be as sappy as they sing — out of serious adult consideration. As catchy as the sing-song melodies of "Larger Than Life," "I Want It That Way" and "It's Gotta Be You" are, this formula fluff is strictly for consumption by love-idealizing adolescents. (For proof of just how young the group aims, Backstreeter Brian Littrell follows the lead of Boyz II Men and R. ("I Like the Crotch on You") Kelly here, flipping the parent-scorning script so basic to the teenage psyche by paying cloying homage to his mom in "The Perfect Fan." Sure, Elvis was big on mother love, but at least he put it away once his career got under way.)

Commercially calibrated songs and sharp trend-sweating production may help explain the Backstreet Boys' rising popularity in the Black community, but the group's appeal to adolescent white females — a demographic that can happily set commercial trends without regard to artistic merit — is intriguing. As a dynastic genre emanates from Florida (collectively, Britney Spears, 'N Sync and the Backstreet Boys have sold more than 20 million albums in the U.S. alone), never before has the primary pop audience found itself so thoroughly devoted to pop music that aspires to be R&B and owes next to nothing to rock. The conspicuous guitar solo in "Larger Than Life" is the same sort of outsider acknowledgment that prompted Michael Jackson to hire Eddie Van Halen to add six-string crossover potential to "Beat It."

It may be new, but it's hardly surprising. White masses are swarming to the Backstreet Boys because the tight connection to their parents' pop has been severed. Exposure to MTV, hip-hop, power producers and hit records by rappers, dance acts and style-crossing female singers has evolved a new consumer that, if not quite color-blind, is free of racial brand loyalty to the sound and symbols of electric guitar rock. Songwriting is no longer the dividing line between pop and serious artist. Timeless melodies are no longer the holy ghost of music. Blueprints that have been used to define music of quality and distinction since the '50s — originality, imagination, insight, individuality, creative ambition — have been erased. What's left is insipid pop in its purest form: meaningless, disposable, conformist, reactionary.

Such rockist doctrine seemed to mean a lot in those politically charged times when youth culture first opened traditional values up for debate. Mirroring the us-against-them polarity of left-wing activism, independently driven artists wiped the floor with the willing products of corporate design. It was a righteous notion, but it's time for a rethink. The Monkees' best records, as contrived and meaningless as pop of 1967 could be, stand up as fine examples of the form. Elvis Presley sure wasn't a songwriter, but neither were many of the Motown greats.

Bubblegum came from a song factory, but what was the Brill Building, where labored the likes of Carole King? When it all gets toted up, was *Tapestry* any greater a contribution to culture than "Will You Love You Me Tomorrow"?

Short-attention-spanners raised on samples and one-hit wonders no longer have any reason to value rock tradition. Let the hardliners cling to their reverence of self-containment, whether it's ABBA, R.E.M., Pink Floyd, the Replacements or Prince, autonomy ain't what it used to be. Today's flyweight rock titans (Matchbox 20 etc.) are no match for their debt to history, which only magnifies their failings. All they can do is fill millennial mall stores with full-priced product. They're followers, not leaders, with no courage beyond the obviously viable. For their hollow creations and paltry artistic ambition, they might as well be the Backstreet Boys.

For corporate rock in the late '90s, risks are dead-end detours off the yellow brick road. The creative motion that has driven pop music — and driven it to achieve great things from time to time — has all but ceased in rock. Through innovation, cycles, revivals, technology and detours, the music that matters avoided long-term entropy and continued to develop, even if progress wasn't always forward. Whatever motivated the barnstormers of Eddie Cochran's day lives as little in 1999's *Woodstock* stars — where you'd hope to find it — as in the callow grooves of the Backstreet Boys, where you wouldn't. In order to give squealing pleasure to white 10-year-olds, the Backstreet Boys have turned their back on the bullshit-busting values that long-ago typified rock and roll and tapped the commercial honey of Black pop. But their real debt to modern Black artists — turning the clock back two generations in the process — is for making the charts safe for sentimentality. ◆

Various Artists
The Best of Broadside 1962 -1988
Salon, September 2000

It's August 1965. The Beatles are set to perform at Shea Stadium, but I'm stuck at commie summer camp in upstate New York, a few miles from the farm that would later host *Woodstock*. I'm sitting under a big oak tree with an equally outsized acoustic guitar, learning to stretch my 11-year-old fingers into the awkward shape of a G chord from the camp's music counselor, a college student orphaned a decade earlier when the government executed his parents, Julius and Ethel Rosenberg, for leaking atomic secrets to the Russians. In the lyrics of Phil Ochs, we were building another link on the chain.

"Links on the Chain," which I learned to sing (if not quite play) that summer, is not the greatest protest song ever written. In fact, it's not a typical protest song at all. Amid tunes attacking oppressive governments, laws that need changing and assorted social inequities, this historically astute and stirring indictment of the labor movement for abandoning its progressive principles falls somewhere on the fringe. Ochs himself was not able to stay on course either, but his early work stands as a monument to those op-ed columnists of song, people who knew and believed things and made it their duty as soldiers of conscience to convince others. "Now it's only fair to ask you boys, which side are you on?" sang Ochs. He might as well have been challenging the whole artistic community around him.

As silly as that question might sound to a 21st century pop performer, for whom choosing up sides is more likely to mean endorsing Coke or Pepsi, self-styled folksingers of Ochs's day were all, to one degree or another, on the left. (Ochs later detailed those degrees in the scathing "Love Me I'm a Liberal.") Starting in 1963, as thousands of young people repeatedly gathered in Washington, DC and other cities to speak out for civil rights and an end to the war in Vietnam, singers like Ochs, Tom Paxton, Pete Seeger, Odetta, Pat Sky, Eric Andersen, Judy Collins and Joan Baez took the podium and spread the news their way. They weren't consciously "positioning" themselves as a marketing strategy, buying credibility with a little pro bono service to the cause, they were following through on the impulse that had drawn them to make music in the first place, building links on the chain fed to them by Woody Guthrie, Paul Robeson and others.

"Links on the Chain" opens *The Best of Broadside 1962 – 1988*, five CDs of music from the recorded archives of *Broadside*, a magazine which began publishing the words and music of topical folk songs just as they were needed to fuel one of the great grassroots political movements of the 20th century. Like many small publishing ventures, *Broadside* was a labor of love that barely stayed in business. But like many idealists willing to sacrifice their lives for a worthy idea, founders Sis Cunningham and Gordon Friesen never lost sight of their mission "to distribute...songs in which the 'commercial music world' had little or no interest." They published the mimeographed magazine from a series of Manhattan apartments, where they hosted monthly visits by young songwriters eager to see their work in print. Supplicants, who included some of the greatest poets of a generation, would sing into the couple's tape recorder, and Cunningham would transcribe the best of them for the next month's issue. Soon, *Broadside* began releasing records, some made in real studios, others using the lo-fi apartment office archives. If the 89 songs that make up this collection come from diverse sources (and sound it), the simplicity of the music — anything involving more than a guitar and an untrained voice sticks out — keeps the audio inconsistency from being a distraction. You won't have any problem hearing the voices here. You want to test your speakers? Get a Sting album.

Broadside disseminated songs the way it had been done until records became the lingua franca. For the 50 cents an issue cost, anyone could learn an evening's worth of new tunes, with words from last week's newspaper headlines and melodies that probably came from some old English ballad as duly annotated in the box's book-length liner notes, which also contain complete lyrics to every song and even the newspaper clippings that inspired them. (I'll leave the obvious preludes to hip-hop sampling and MP3 file sharing to any musicology or media student in need of a thesis topic. Help yourself. But be careful. In one of the set's most affecting songs, Sis Cunningham takes up the cause of Aunt Molly Jackson, an Appalachian woman whose songs were sung far and wide yet did nothing to alleviate her poverty. "No one thought to wonder whose [song] / Here it was for them to use," sings Cunningham. "The song became no longer mine." Maybe Metallica should learn that one for the next Napster court hearing.)

Collectively, these songs provide an unsentimental education about inconceivable catastrophes ("My Oklahoma Home (It Blowed Away)," "The Ballad of Martin Luther King"), monumental wrongs (racism, the nuclear threat, capitalist exploitation, the draft, the war, sexism) and courageous efforts to right them (like Paxton's "Ain't That News"). In our time, when knowledge of the past evaporates faster than instant messages on AOL, many of the subjects and events are so far off in the wasteland of times past that they might as well have never happened.

Like the social crisis of inter-racial dating. The 15-year-old Janis Ian's previously unreleased first recording (credited, in a *Broadside* in-joke, to Blind Girl Grunt) of "Society's Child" is here, in a 1966 version titled "Baby, I've Been Thinking." Of course, a climactic capitulation to prejudice makes it the only protest song in memory to give up and do the wrong thing ("One of these days I'm gonna stop my listening, gonna raise my head up high...but for now this is way [things] must remain"). Maybe its true cultural value is for the endorsement of pass-the-buck irresponsibility.

At best, these songs bring the forgotten past to enduring life. In "Ballad of William Worthy," Ochs sings of a 1961 incident in which an American journalist was jailed upon his return from Castro's Cuba, a place U.S. citizens were — and technically still are — barred from visiting. Writing before the birth of Elian Gonzales' parents, Ochs nails the entire absurdity of the government's position in two lines: "It is strange to hear the State Department say / You are living in the free world, in the free world you must stay." Peter La Farge's tragic "Ballad of Ira Hayes" notes how selective America can be about its heroes; the resonant profile of a Native American later became a hit for Johnny Cash. Pete Seeger, who to this day remains an unreconstructed protest singer, details an obscure and highly entertaining bit of history in Malvina Reynolds' deliciously witty "Do as the Doukhobors Do": five 19th century women, Russian immigrants to Canada, who expressed their objections to the nation's educational policies by attending a speech by the Prime Minister in the buff.

The Best of Broadside is such a motherlode that beyond fine recordings of the era's topical standards — Reynolds' "What Have They Done to the Rain," Seeger's "Waist Deep in the Big Muddy," Paxton's "What Did You Learn in

School Today," Matthew Jones' "Hell No, I Ain't Gonna Go" — many of the tracks that *could* have been omitted are still museum-quality, like "Song for Patty," a sympathetic 1974 number about the kidnapping of Patty Hearst which sounds a lot like Dylan but is credited to one Sammy Walker. (Another Walker contribution, "Catcher in the Rye," is even more Dylanesque than that. He also gets points for singing the version of Ochs' loving Woody Guthrie tribute, "Bound for Glory.") Ochs' heart-wrenching "Changes," a non-topical emotional outpouring that doesn't really belong here, is included in a tender live version that could well serve as the era's epilogue.

Even the post-dated songs warrant their place in such glorious company. Deborah Silverstein and the New Harmony Sisterhood Band's "Draglines" defies its 1984 vintage with the finely woven harmonies of Celtic folk singing to lodge a strong, not strident, protest against strip-mining. Although a dubious bow to star power would seem the only explanation why Lucinda Williams' "Lafayette," a good-times travelogue which was indeed published in *Broadside* in 1979, is here, the liner notes make its inclusion out to be a courtesy to Sis Cunningham.

Such forces are not to be underestimated here. Blind Boy Grunt — better known as Bob Dylan — was an ardent *Broadside* supporter (and beneficiary). His literal presence in this set consists of two performances ("John Brown" and "Ballad of Donald White") and four compositions sung by others. But, in a sense, *The Best of Broadside* is all about him. His arrival, influence and departure from the topical song scene each made a crucial difference in the lives of all these artists.

The earliest recording of a Dylan composition, a 1962 rendition of "Blowin' in the Wind" by the New World Singers, is sung the old way — handsomely, evenly, with idealism buoying what in the author's own voice would bite and sneer with the dawning anger of a new generation. Seeger himself walks the line on a 1963 version of "Hard Rain's a-Gonna Fall," singing out with conviction but little emotion, letting Dylan's lyrics speak for themselves in a way their clenched-jaw author never would.

Dylan, and all those influenced by him, quickly abandoned the traditional troubadour's twinned faces of smiling good humor and dolorous tragedy to indict injustice and hypocrisy with cutting sarcasm, indignant anger and the obliterating belief that the world was about to change if they had anything to say about it. Then Dylan released "Like a Rolling Stone" and pulled off his end-of-the-innocence electrification at Newport in the summer of '65. (Seeger, in the most myopic moment of an otherwise clear-eyed career, literally wanted to pull out the electric plug.) He was seen as a traitor, abandoning the cause for something as trivial as artistic vision or, worse, commercial ambition. Whose back pages were those? Like hardcore punk rock years later, commercial marginalization wasn't a hazard, it was a trademark of quality. If a lot of people liked you, how good could you be? (For more on the subject of how folk music became big business, read the section on Albert Grossman, the manager of both Peter Paul & Mary and Dylan, in Fred Goodman's excellent book *Mansion on the Hill*.)

Dylan may have left his compatriots behind, but he wasn't a traitor to the chain — his cutting wit was sharper, but the knife had always hung handy. Humor, from bitter mockery to lighthearted amusement, was the secret ingredient of topical singers, and this collection offers plenty of smiles amid the seriousness. Malvina Reynolds, who wrote and here sings the classic "Little Boxes," a wry commentary on conformity and suburbia, also has a comment on urban decay. "The Faucets Are Dripping," an anti-landlord screed, has witty couplets like "The reservoir's drying, because it's supplying / The faucets that drip in New York." Ernie Marrs raised a stink at the time with the jocular irreverence of "Plastic Jesus," but the Fugs ("Kill for Peace") and others really pushed the limits of ironic detachment (check "The Willing Conscript," Tom Paxton's deadpan depiction of a soldier asking to learn to kill and maim, sung here by Seeger). Paxton also demonstrates the danger of humorlessness, of hammering home a story with no leavening sense of context. He sings "Train for Auschwitz" as if the Holocaust was [still] news in 1963. Likewise, the piercing Canadian soprano Bonnie Dobson's "Take Me for a Walk," an anti-nuclear song also known as "Morning Dew," sinks into glum ponderousness with no firing pin to prick the mood. And Ochs' previously unreleased "Freedom Riders," while as commendable in sentiment as any tune here, is blunt and amateurish. Leave it to Reverend Frederick

Douglass Kirkpatrick, a singing civil rights activist, to let anger ring in the pseudo-spiritual "Nothing but His Blood," an agit-prop singalong that couldn't have failed to get fists pumping back in the day.

It's August 1964. A late summer haze of how the Yankees are doing, cute beatnik girls I'll never see again, a planned overnight trip to a nearby ski lodge and thoughts of the coming school year blows away as news filters into camp about the brutal murders of three young freedom riders in Mississippi. Two of the victims were from New York, and a couple of the counselors knew one of them, Andy Goodman. We had sung the songs and knew the battle was outside raging, but what we did not truly understand was how ordinary people, people we knew, were willing to die so that others they would never meet might move one step closer to freedom. The songs became personal and very, very real.

It's April 1965. I'm in Washington, D.C., protesting the war with thousands of other new lefties (and my mom). We chant "Hey, hey L.B.J., how many kids did you kill today?" Judy Collins, Phil Ochs and Joan Baez sing. I run into kids I know from camp. We know that our fight is different than, say, the freedom riders, or the Wobblies, the early trade unionists or the victims of the HUAC blacklist, but we know it is also the same. We know all the words to their songs, they are our songs, and we sing them, proud and strong, guided by the belief that we are part of a chain, and each song is a link on it. ◆

Newspaper writers are often called upon to do "think pieces," expounding on some vague topic using one timely item as a peg. In this case, it was two: an ABBA boxed set and repeated viewings of a music video that really pissed me off. (For the record, I liked ABBA's early records, especially the poignant "Suzy-Hang-Around.") Anyone needing a giddily positive spin on this topic can watch the *Stockholm Syndrome* episode of the Netflix docu-series *This Is Pop*.

Shlock Europop, From ABBA to ZZZZZ

Newsday, 14 May 1995

At a recently convened tribunal of one, the prosecution failed to produce the smoking gun that would prove ABBA's unwitting responsibility for two decades of appalling European dance music, but several hours of recorded evidence did move the jury to hand down a damning indictment. Americans didn't fight World War II so we could be overrun by hits from time-zoned hacks with disco phrase books and overactive synthesizers.

The immediate impetus for this enquiry was the current Top 40 success of "Cotton-Eye Joe," a traditional Tennessee fiddle tune retooled with dunderheaded techno-beats by Rednex, a Swedish studio creation whose obnoxious hillbilly caricature (complete with missing teeth and lyrics of stunning offensiveness to anyone born south of the Toronto-Montreal line) seems derived from incidental exposure to *Li'l Abner* comic strips and episodes of *Hee-Haw*. In a press handout accompanying the group's *Sex & Violins* album, Pat Reiniz — the Stockholm producer who masterminded Rednex's creation with evidently willful ignorance of the region and culture he set out to parody — attributes the band's music to *Bonanza* and its fashion sense to *Deliverance*. "The concept," he says with merry crassness, "is to make the band's members look filthy and uncouth."

Rednex's crude travesty, for all its momentary power, can't erase the memory of *The Gift*, 1993's eight-million-selling album by the vapid Ace of Base, another bunch of Swedes. And this year already has seen invasions by two new bands streaming across the borders to storm our charts: Dutch duo 2 Unlimited (whose hit "Get Ready for This" got a boost when ABC television used it as a promotional jingle) and the German trio Real McCoy. Add to this assault the still-echoing joker's laugh of Milli Vanilli and the return of the Belgium-based Technotronic –whose brand-new album, *Recall*, brings rapper Ya Kid K back to color the kinetic jams with her catchily insipid pronouncements — and it's hard to resist the obvious question: What hath ABBA wrought?

Speaking eloquently in the four Scandinavians' defense is *Thank You for the Music*, a four-CD retrospective of ABBA's work: 66 examples of the brilliantly contrived and irresistible '70s pop that sold an astounding 250 million records for Agnetha, Björn, Benny and Frida (a nickname for the Norwegian-born Anni-Frid). ABBA was delivered to the world via the *Eurovision Song Contest*, an annual competition in which participating countries select a song by an indigenous group to be performed as its entry. In 1974, Sweden sent ABBA to England with "Waterloo." Victory launched the group on its world domination enterprise.

Despite clumsy English lyrics and ludicrous costumes, ABBA produced hit after zippy hit in a masterfully designed global pop style that used richly massed vocals and extravagant productions to dart easily from American disco to Latin-inflected balladry with polyglot stylistic accents that were least of all Scandinavian. Nearly 20 years on, "Waterloo," "S.O.S.," "Knowing Me, Knowing You" and "Fernando" still carry that weight with more than nostalgia; having internalized and distilled decades of the world's pop, ABBA created songs of lasting power, as trivial and undeniable now as then. Strong enough to propel movies like *Muriel's Wedding* and *Priscilla, Queen of the Desert*, universal enough to support an internationally successful full-time tribute band (Australia's Bjorn Again), ABBA lives.

ABBA walked a fine line between magic and absurdity, non-English Europeans successfully participating in a realm pioneered and long dominated by Americans and Britons. And they weren't the first. The continent's campaign to competitively export its youth-pop dates back at least to the early '60s, when the Spotnicks — Sweden's answer to England's guitar-instrumental stars, the Shadows — began having international hits. Subsequent years brought Spain's Los Bravos ("Black Is Black"), Holland's Golden Earring ("Radar Love"), Shocking Blue ("Venus"), and Tee Set ("Ma Belle Amie") and Belgium's Singing Nun ("Dominique").

It wasn't until the mid-'70s, when the rise of synthesizers helped disco producers like Giorgio Moroder (the Italian resident of Germany behind Donna Summer and many others) and German native Frank Farian establish a power base and stamp "Made in Europe" on the international dance floor. Farian made his first killing in the late '70s by assembling Boney M, a quartet of Caribbeans who sang his giddy dance nonsense, songs like "Rasputin" (an ambitious history lesson in three sketchy verses) and "Rivers of Babylon." Segueing neatly onto the tail end of England's mad glam-rock era, Boney M became huge in the UK and was able to slingshot some of that momentum across the ocean for one solid hit.

A decade later, Farian regained the global spotlight with another cobbled-together group, a duo he dubbed Milli Vanilli. One degree more inorganic than Boney M — Rob Pilatus and Fabrice Morvan were ultimately discovered to have had no audible role on the records that bore their faces — the duo nonetheless scored three 1989 chart-toppers in America and won a subsequently rescinded Grammy before being found out. (The rich comedy of this boondoggle was only improved when a judge ordered Arista Records to offer refunds to anyone who had purchased Milli Vanilli albums, as if it mattered one whit whose voices or pictures were on them.)

Another decade, another band, same label. This year's crummy German outfit selling old-hat American techno-disco by the planeload is Real McCoy, an interracial trio whose *Another Night* album trots out hackneyed synthesizer bumps on a set of boppy house originals and covers like Redbone's "Come and Get Your Love," a 1974 hit they update to at least 1981. But if the energetic beats and appealing female voices are overly familiar, Real McCoy's original sin is mastermind Olaf Jeglitza's grunting raps, a melodramatic discharge of comic stupidity. Blame inadequate language skills, total witlessness, a fondness for stringing together non sequitur clichés or a hack's willful disregard for the meaning of words, but the lyrics crafted by Jeglitza and his creative cohorts for the group's first two U. S. Top 5 singles, "Run Away" and "Another Night," tackle English with the grace of a linebacker, rhyming "all that it takes" with "lovers and fakes."

Lovers and fakes. In current Europop, the difference is hard to discern. And with charmers like Rednex and Real McCoy, it hardly matters. But no one, it's safe to say, is innocent. ◆

Shoes

I was so excited to "discover" Shoes in 1977 that I rushed to stake my claim with a bug-eyed review of their first full-scale indie release, *Black Vinyl Shoes*, in *Trouser Press*. But someone else was hasty as well: the last line (and my byline) was lost in a layout error, so my "discovery" was inadvertently rendered anonymous. (I'll take all the blame for misusing the word "penultimate," however.)

I got to see Shoes several times after this remote introduction. Really nice guys, great musicians. I gather this review in a national magazine was of some encouragement to them; I'm proud to have played a bit part in their career. But Shoes fandom carries a price: the obligation of correcting people who attempt to add an article before the name.

Black Vinyl Shoes

Trouser Press, December 1977

"*Black Vinyl Shoes* is Shoes' debut album and is a completely independent effort by the band. It was recorded in my living room on a four-channel machine so it's admittedly inferior in quality to studio albums. Everything involved with the manufacturing of this disc, including the graphics, album design, arrangements, production, writing, and performing were done solely by the band. I hope that you can enjoy at least part of this effort and can appreciate the time involved in putting it together." —Jeff Murphy (guitar/vocals)

That (and more) came on a handwritten note attached to the cover of this album, hailing from Zion, Illinois. Inside, besides a 12-inch vinyl disc, were a sticker, iron-on transfer, technical sheet and much more, all done low-budget but well. It all looked fairly interesting, so it went on the turntable promptly, sidestepping the pile of ought-to-get-to-soon platters accumulating on the floor. To quote Phil Rizzuto, "HOLY COW!!" These guys have put together a twinky pop album that obliterates the competition on every level, including sound quality.

Shoes mix the best moments of Milk 'n' Cookies, Gary Glitter, Boston, Pilot, Cheap Trick, Artful Dodger, Tommy James and the Shondells, *Sell Out*-era Who, Creedence Clearwater, Raspberries, BTO, *Help!* Beatles, Spector, etc. etc. etc. They're not the penultimate band or anything, but when a group can sound like a Yardley commercial and still rock like this, they've got a little extra on the ball. The production techniques are so debonair and witty that the lack of real studio facilities seems not to have slowed them down appreciably. Having done it myself, I know what a pain it is to record anything more sophisticated than guitar, bass and drums on a four-track, but the inventiveness and resource shown here beats hell out of lots of discs that cost $40-50 thou to tape. If any band ever deserved a year of free studio time, Shoes do. What they might be able to produce under ideal conditions might be astonishing.

The sound of Shoes, for a good chunk of *Black Vinyl*, is a blend of multi-tracked fuzz guitar, handclaps or maracas, and wispy, high-pitched vocals with lots of reverb. Just when it begins to grate a bit in its uniformity (about 3/4 of the way through Side One), the tone shifts abruptly with a song called "Capital Gain," which rocks without the benefit of artificial attachments-straight aggro.

The three front-Shoes (Gary Klebe, John and Jeff Murphy) all write and sing lead, presenting the kind of multifariousness necessary to prevent singleness of direction. When Shoes start releasing records via a major label (shouldn't be too far off), they won't have any trouble coming up with a string of singles that will sound similar but different enough to stay creative. When a group combines an individual sound with a broad ability to write interesting songs, they're in business. Look out America; here [*the end of this sentence got cut off in the layout but probably said something limp like "comes Shoes."*] ◆

Shoes Hub

eMusic, 2007

Aficionados of power pop have, by acclamation, elected a small handful of bands to the genre's virtual hall of fame, a repository of the world's most winsome, affecting and sweetly rocked up tunefulness. Running the scale from twee to hard, the form's icons all share a willingness to put their backs into romance, singing timeless melodies with layers of harmony, a kickass backbeat, the occasional handclaps and enough electric wool to skirt the perils of commercial obviousness.

Shoes, one of American's quintessential power pop legends, hails from tiny Zion, Illinois. The quartet — bassist-singer John Murphy, guitarist-singers Jeff Murphy and Gary Klebe and drummer Skip Meyer — began in 1973, ignoring the implausibility of securing a major-label recording career with self-willed determination by putting their original songs on tape at home using a trusty four-track machine, eventually releasing the carefully produced results on the band's own Black Vinyl label in 1977, bridging the gap between power pop predecessors like Dwight Twilley and the punk do-it-yourselfers springing up all over the Amerindie landscape.

Made long before software drastically eased the virtual studio process, the intricately layered guitars and vocals of *Black Vinyl Shoes* make it hard to believe that it was recorded in a living room. The songs, telling tender tales of failed romance, are catchy and instantly likable. The band also put the record in an impressive package and distributed it as a vinyl demo; in fact, it's one of the finest home-brewed releases ever, a much more valid piece of music than many productions by well-known bands with far greater technical resources. After the small initial pressing sold out, the album was licensed to PVC and reissued with wholly different artwork.

After signing to Elektra, Shoes made *Present Tense* (1979) in a full-scale English 24-track studio with a professional producer but ended up sounding pretty much the same as before, only with much greater audio fidelity. Given the chance to experiment and open up their sound, Shoes opted to hold fast to what they knew — lots of vocals, lots of melody, lots of fuzzed-out guitars. Another triumphant LP that probably could have been made at home without losing any appreciable amount of charm or appeal, it's Shoes' talent, not studio technology, that matters here.

Tongue Twister (1981) successfully maintains the quality level of *Present Tense*, but Shoes were at a creative standstill. Having honed their style as far as it could go, they're stuck with it. *Boomerang* (1982), recorded near the band's home base without a strong outside producer, suffers from inconsistent song quality and an overanxious feeling, no doubt brought on by the band's failure to catch on commercially. (Early pressings of *Boomerang* included a 12-inch EP, *Shoes on Ice*, recorded live at the Zion Ice Arena in 1981, offering six of the band's best tunes as proof of their ability to play them in public.)

Parting company with Elektra and saying farewell to Meyer, the remaining Shoes set up shop in a studio they had built in Illinois (nominally re-creating the notion of home-made music, only in a fully equipped facility which became a focal point of Midwest poppitry) and continued writing and recording. Murphy, Murphy and Klebe made *Silhouette* (1984), which was released only in Europe. The sound (incorporating more keyboards and subtler dabs of guitar) is typically exquisite, and the songs — four by each man — are fine examples of the band's seemingly effortless pop suss. A fine, relaxed return that reasserts Shoes' considerable talent.

Acquiring the rights to their three Elektra albums, the group issued *Shoes Best* (1987), a 22-song non-chronological retrospective of album tracks that includes one live cut from *On Ice* and one new tune. (I wrote the liner notes.)

Stolen Wishes (1989), Shoes' first new album in five years (and the inspiration for an unprecedented bi-coastal tour in mid-'90), has all the band's hallmarks plus keyboards, including synthesizer dressing on several of the enormously catchy tunes. Ric Menck of Velvet Crush is the album's drummer, although the rigid, strident clatter on "Feel the Way That I Do" is surely electronic. (Ironically, mock horns add a handsome texture to the glorious guitar pop of "Let It Go," and imitation strings quietly shade in "Love Does.") The introduction of new elements into the group's sound

— whose intrinsically retro styling makes it anachronistic to begin with — is overdue, but Shoes' warm songs are better served by real instruments than by obviously fake simulations.

Another half-decade passed before another Shoes album, but as consistency is both the band's blessing and curse, precious few marks of stylistic change disturb the winsome Britpop familiarity of 1994's *Propeller* (at least not after the stuttering ZZ Top chug of Klebe's memorable "Animal Attraction," which gets the record off on a novel foot). With far less of the keyboard technology that characterized *Stolen Wishes* (but a weaker set of tunes), *Propeller* turns more easily, spinning out the usual romantic ups and downs with the typical mix of comely melodicism and muted aggression. Menck drums on half the songs; highlights include John Murphy's gauzy "Don't Do This to Me" and grabby "Tore a Hole," Jeff Murphy's riff-driven "Silence Is Deadly" and Klebe's "Never Ending." An equivocal placeholder.

The subsequent EP bridges *Propeller* and the live *Fret Buzz* (1995) with both studio and concert versions of "Tore a Hole" and two otherwise unreleased tracks from the same December 1994 Chicago club gig that produced *Fret Buzz*. With drummer John Richardson laying down the beat, the rocking set draws mainly from *Propeller* and *Stolen Wishes* but digs all the way back to 1979 for *Present Tense*'s "I Don't Wanna Hear It" and includes the previously unalbumized "In Harm's Way," recorded at a soundcheck. Energetically played and for the most part well-sung (without benefit of studio reverb or overdubs), *Fret Buzz* doesn't do much more than prove what these concert-shy studio hounds can do live — but that's enough.

Murphy's solo album, *Cantilever* (2007), ranges a little further afield than Shoes' music, cutting the old twee breathlessness with a tougher bottom, modest sonic experimentation and what can only be called maturity. Beyond the autonomy of writing, playing and recording eleven songs unassisted, Murphy brings a vague but tangible sense of purpose to the endeavor. If "It Happens All the Time," the dynamic "Won't Take Yes for an Answer" and the *Rubber Soul*-y "Never Let You Go" hearken back happily to aspects of Shoes' past sound, other tracks go off in different directions: "She Don't Drive" cranks up a vintage sound with banjo and "Some Day Soon" is a stately waltz with more acoustic strings than electric guitar.

If power pop dedication is a quixotic ideal, a dream that holding fast to the simple musical elements that made the Beatles a durable sonic blueprint should yield success — that "pop" and "popular" should have more in common than three letters — then Shoes are the true believers, the unwavering artists who can't help but make songs that stick. Dip in anywhere for a master class in the delicate balance that makes pop powerful and power pop. ◆

Green

The band Green arrived in my life in July 1987 when they played Maxwell's at a benefit for *Away From the Pulsebeat*, the cool fanzine run by photographer Monica Dee and writer Art Black. It was love at first sight. Regina Joskow and I befriended them and had them over for lasagna in Queens the next time they were in town. (We were shocked and not a little horrified when they announced, late in the evening, that they were fixing to drive home to Chicago.)

Jeff Lescher has made a lot of great music since then. Ken Kurson, who was a giddy 18-year-old when we first met, grew up to become a well-known journalist, publishing the financial magazine *Green* (geddit?), writing a personal finance column for *Esquire*, editing the *New York Observer* and ghostwriting the ghoulish Rudy Giuliani's best-selling memoir. We disagree vehemently about politics and politicians, but we've remained friends, even playing together in a cover band called The Editors NYC, which also included the founder of *Brownstoner* and a mainman at *Gawker*.

Looking at this manic review, I'm amazed at how divergent my style and tone could become when I thought the venue would welcome it. Usually, it was an assignment from the Lester-haunted *Creem* that would release me from the bonds of solemn, dignified journalism; in this case, it was *Spin*.

Green

Elaine MacKenzie

Spin, October 1988

Unless you come from Chicago, happen to be, like, unbelievably cool, or were sharp enough to read C. Eddy's brief but enthusiastic spiel on 'em in this here rag a year ago, you probably don't know from Green. That's OK. BUT IT'S HIGH TIME YOU GOT IN THE GAME, PAL!!! With the release of this enigmatically-titled LP, the trio from Bears & Cubs land has jump-cut its way from obscure localness to potential nationality in the post-Replacements/Hüsker Dü world of ruggedly incandescent pop rock. Pairing the most worthwhile Kinks influence since Big Star with enough hoarse R&B soul for a Small Faces LP on Paisley Park, if you get my drift, *Elaine MacKenzie* is an album of great accomplishment and even greater promise.

Guitarist Jeff Lescher wrote and vocalizes most of the 14 tracks; bassist Ken Kurson composed and sings two, also contributing album-wide backing vox-straight harmonies, Troggs-like "ba-pa-pa-paaa"-ing, and even Little Richardized "woos!" Echoing, among others, the Clash, Smokey Robinson, the Who and the pre-pot Beatles, this richly varied menu offers achingly sensitive but courageous fucked-up romance ballads — "Don't Ever Fall in Love With Someone When You're Already in Love With Someone Else," "I Know, I Know" and "She Was My Girl" — alongside the wonderfully wild Prince-inflected "My Love's on Fire" and Kurson's bile-shedding, punky ravers, "Beaten into Submission" and "Fingerprints." There's also "Saturday Afternoon," a charming piece of Kinksian nostalgia complete with subtly applied French horn; "I Can't Seem to Get It Through My Head," a dual-speed schizo soul / rock number that (hob)nails the Association to the Miracles; and "Radio Caroline," an endearingly silly salute to British broadcasting.

Lescher's voice is astonishing — a rough but melodic roar that seems to be straining for release. Leaping easily and often into a knee-jellying falsetto, he keeps a sexy whisper in reserve for appropriate mood shifts, but even on restrained songs reveals inescapable emotional turmoil; attractive settings never totally obscure the lyrical anguish. He also plays economical rockin' guitar (and painted a swell album cover to boot).

Amazingly, the album's cheap studio-on-a-tight-budget production and bluntly simple arrangements don't compromise the material. Full-throttle playing, redolent with desperate rock'n'roll conviction, gives the lapel-yanking melodies and wise-into-wiseass lyrics all the drive they need. The Greening of America starts here. ◆

Bigger Lovers

How I Learned to Stop Worrying

eMusic, February 2011

If words actually had meaning any more, the "pop" half of power pop would be short for populist, not popular. Any bedroom doodler able to write and deliver a breathtaking melody can be a listening class hero, but the full blast of stardom is generally reserved for the crass, the lucky and the fulsomely obvious. No devotee of tuneful auteurs really wants to know how minuscule a ratio will result from dividing the number of earthly pop hits by the vast fields of records that have been created in the Beatles' wake, if not their precise image. Yet, all praise the spirit of Shoes, Heavenly and Big Star, the music keeps getting made. Given the near certitude that most power pop will be heard by next to nobody, it's a bloody miracle how many faithful followers still apply themselves, occasionally with magnificent results, to the effort.

Pop has never thrived on obscurity, but neither has it been hobbled by the lack of commercial support. It is largely tunes for tunes' sake. Perhaps it's the possibility of being placed shoulder to shoulder with an idol (in even just one personal pantheon) that drives so many on. The occasional spectacular achievement — a little-known song that means as much to some listeners as a genuine genre standard — makes the lack of widespread endorsement merely a bagatelle (albeit the kind of buys houses and flash cars).

The Bigger Lovers came out of Philadelphia, gave it a good shot for three albums and then called it quits in 2005, all of which would probably matter to no one beyond the quartet's families and friends were it not for the brilliance and originality of their songs. In guitarist Bret Tobias and bassist Scott Jefferson, the group had two sterling singer-songwriters whose work meshed together rather than jockeyed for prominence. Credit as well production that pours on vocals like maple syrup and dresses up smart ensemble playing with oddball studio effects, making for a chewy confection that, on record, is both addictive and nourishing.

To mark a 2011 reunion, the group has reissued its wonderful 2001 debut with a couple of more recently recorded bonus tracks. The ironically titled *How I Learned to Stop Worrying* is a confident collection of anxieties, catastrophes and regrets, all set to richly realized guitar pop with occasional pedal steel that reasonably summons comparisons to Velvet Crush (rock and country periods). The songs benefit enormously from a lack of obvious chord patterns and melodic clichés, using textural dynamics and rhythmic diversity to further bolster their impact. The lyrics, which ruminate comfortably amid the joyous music, are just as thoughtful and uncommon. Jefferson's "Out of Sight" offers "Five years back / I had all different clothes / Maybe that's the reason he would never sleep with me." The second verse of "Forever Is Not So Long" is a brief concert review: "What did you think of those guys last night? / Were they OK? Do you think they're all right? / They sounded like something that I heard before / But the singer was a drag." The Bigger Lovers take small chances like that throughout yet always convey a positive spirit. They're a friend who wryly shares bad news without needing you to suffer along.

"Catch and Release" runs into "I'm Here" and concludes with a smattering of studio applause. With a stuttering guitar track upsetting the song's easy feel, "Change Your Mind" is not a complex creation, but still has a lot going on, all of which is a benefit. The band pushes and pulls back on the power before rising to a complete release on the gorgeous refrain; near the end, a lull in the action sets up a stirring instrumental coda that evaporates into a static loop. Other highlights include the rousingly resentful "Threadbare" and the sunny "Summer (of Our First Hello)." The odd track out is the gauzy, languorous "Casual Friday," which ends with a spoken interlude (credited to Tobias as "the Phil Everly part") about an airplane disaster.

Bigger Lovers developed nicely on their two subsequent albums (2002's *Honey in the Hive* and 2004's *This Affair Never Happened...*), upholding songwriting quality while growing more accomplished in presentation. It's safe to say that none of the group's music has reached even a fraction of the audience that would likely love it, but *How I Learned to Stop Worrying* was the starting point of something wonderful. And you never forget your first. ◆

Through the Past Lightly: The 1980s

In 1997, *Rolling Stone* endeavored to codify "the definitive library of the [200] best albums ever made" — not for the last time, as online listicle clickbait began to overtake music journalism. I don't remember writing this, but my name's on an entire section of it. I was paid well; you'd think that at least that would have left an impression, but no. Was a time when a music fan could make a decent living freestyling ideas in print.

The '80s was never my favorite decade, but the others were already taken. I didn't select the albums, either. (Compilations are a dodge. And somehow a *1979* Gang of Four record and a *1991* U2 platter slipped in.) Many of the LPs I reviewed here don't rate such acclaim in my book, so I had to dance, duck and dive a bit to make this work: it would hardly do for me to shit on some of "the best albums ever made." Or unconvincingly feign enthusiasm for them. If I couldn't write what I actually felt and still wanted to be honest, I had to beat around the bush. So, I did. If some of my entries in this sampling read like promotional squibs, I dare you to find any actual praise ("defiant"?) in these blurbs about the loathsome Don Henley, Guns n' Roses or Jane's Addiction.

Rolling Stone, 15 May 1997

GUNS N' ROSES

Appetite for Destruction (Uzi Suicide/Geffen) 1987
Except for the second coming of Aerosmith, wild-boy hard rock of the nut-busting, parent-shocking variety was as good as dead when the Gunners roared out of Hollywood in 1987, determined to be the hell-raising Rolling Stones of their generation. Although a sincere romantic ballad, "Sweet Child o' Mine," became the band's first and biggest hit, the mega-platinum *Appetite for Destruction* — a titillating hot shot of Slash's bluesy guitarsnake licks and Axl Rose's venomous vibrato — otherwise stuck to a decadent agenda of sex, drugs and animosity. If the album's ugly travel brochure, "Welcome to the Jungle," described an L.A. the Chamber of Commerce wouldn't recognize, the little girls (and boys) understood.

DON HENLEY

The End of the Innocence (Geffen) 1989
The crossroads of encroaching age and undiminished creativity stymied many performers in the '80s, but once and future Eagle Don Henley worked through that impasse, nursing his third (and best-selling) solo album over a zeitgeist hangover of hypocrisy, materialism and disillusion. With vocal assists from Melissa Etheridge, Sheryl Crow, Edie Brickell and W. Axl Rose, Henley takes a critical look back at a difficult decade — "The End of the Innocence," "The Last Worthless Evening," "How Bad Do You Want It?" — but doesn't wallow in spilt tears. In the defiant "I Will Not Go Quietly," Henley announces, "It's time to make some changes 'round here."

JANE'S ADDICTION

Nothing's Shocking (Warner Bros.) 1988
The title, of course, was meant as pure irony. With his naked-Siamese-babes-on-fire cover sculpture, dramatic adenoidal keen and ambivalent odes to sex, violence and drugs, Perry Farrell made it Jane's' mission to raise eyebrows and provoke outrage. And for those attracted to decadence delivered as blasting rhythm rock decorated by Dave Navarro's whiplash guitar, the Los Angeles quartet's first major-label album was a tantalizing ride on the wild side, complete with junkies ("Jane Says"), Freudian neuroses ("Had a Dad"), television culture ("Ted, Just Admit It..."), wanton bohemianism ("Summertime Rolls"), scatology ("Standing in the Shower...Thinking") and four-letter words ("Idiots Rule").

JOAN JETT AND THE BLACKHEARTS

I Love Rock-n-Roll (Boardwalk) 1981
No matter that Jett was an iffy vocalist and an average rhythm guitarist who never wrote enough of her own material — the ex-Runaway had what it took to become a full-blown rock star. A heartfelt mainstreamer able to capitalize on the American failure of '70s punk, Jett came equipped with diehard enthusiasm, a tough leather look

and popwise guidance by bubblegum veteran Kenny Laguna. All she needed was a few good songs. With hit versions of the Arrows' obscure "I Love Rock 'n' Roll" and Tommy James' classic "Crimson and Clover" leading her effectively direct second album to platinum success, Jett became a heroine to future riot grrrls everywhere.

JOY DIVISION

Closer (Factory) 1980 (Qwest) 1989

The withering chill of personal isolation found a warm body to inhabit, albeit briefly, in Joy Division leader Ian Curtis. Dead by his own hand at 23 soon after recording *Closer*, Curtis sang in the numb voice of chronic despair, thus resonating with countless bedroom hermits in need of guidance down alienation's barren path. On the Manchester quartet's desolately enveloping second album, Curtis' bandmates — who carried on as New Order — match his chronic dispassion with nearly mechanical post-punk and post-disco in such disconsolate enigmas as "Atrocity Exhibition" and "A Means to an End."

L.L. COOL J

Radio (Def Jam/Columbia) 1985

Nothing could be simpler than the hip-hop essentials — vocals, a drum machine and sparing samples, "reduced by Rick Rubin" — of *Radio*. But those ingredients were all it took to launch a handsome New York teenager into the longest-running star career in rap. Evincing confidence way beyond his years, L.L. Cool J (James Todd Smith) drops rhymes that are, by turns, rude ("You Can't Dance"), romantic ("I Can Give You More") and dubious ("That's a Lie"). For all that diversity, however, it was the basic maxims of "I Can't Live Without My Radio" and "I Need a Beat" that first made listeners love Cool James.

MINUTEMEN

Double Nickels on the Dime (SST) 1984

During the singular post-punk adventure that ended in a 1985 van crash, the Minutemen proved capable of inscribing endlessly fascinating ideas within the deceptively simple frame of wiry electric music. On this highway-bound (hence the title reference to a speed limit and an interstate) extravaganza, the sardonic Californians serve up forty-five diverse haikus of febrile ingenuity which sound like bare-bones rock essayed by funky free jazzers and read like entries in a political poet's journal. Plucking ingredients from disparate spheres of music, history and culture, the trio filled a treasure chest with cagey delights.

N.W.A

Straight Outta Compton (Ruthless/Priority) 1988

Hip-hop never seemed dangerous until N****z With Attitude — the posse that included Ice Cube, Eazy-E and MC Ren, plus Dr. Dre and DJ Yella — blew away the metaphoric line separating comfortably observed entertainment from perilous urban reality. If not quite rap's original gangstas, the callous Californians took the genre to another level on their uneven second album, raging in rugged street language over hard beats and sporadic bursts of gunfire. While harmlessly threatening violence all over the title track, N.W.A attracted FBI attention for its death-sentence prosecution of LAPD harassment in "— tha Police," thereby ensuring gangsta rap's rich and controversial future.

SINEAD O'CONNOR

I Do Not Want What I Haven't Got (Ensign/Chrysalis) 1990

Sporting the most famous buzzcut since Elvis joined the Army, Sinead O'Connor vaulted from a brashly impressive 1987 debut, *The Lion and the Cobra*, to the breathtaking achievement of *I Do Not Want What I Haven't Got* in one prodigious leap. Equally fluent in Gaelic folk heritage, American hip-hop, rock and theatrical orchestration, she rivets it all together on searingly personal — or fiercely political — songs. In "I Am Stretched on Your Grave," "The Last Day of Our Acquaintance," "Black Boys on Mopeds" and a cover of Prince's "Nothing Compares 2 U," O'Connor's conviction incites some of the most beautiful singing ever on record.

PRINCE

Dirty Mind (Warner Bros.) 1980

Purple Rain (Warner Bros.) 1984

Sign 'o' the Times (Paisley Park) 1987

The lesson that modern music was born rocking and a-rolling wasn't lost on Prince, who has made the joy of sex the central theme of his purple reign. On *Dirty Mind*, the third rump-moving missive from Minneapolis' one-man studio army, he promises to "Do It All Night," rhapsodizes about "Head" and empties the lustful contents of his "Dirty Mind," all with the zeal of an erotic missionary. While most of the album is state-of-the-art soul-funk, "When You Were Mine" — hummable guitar pop later covered to good effect by Cyndi Lauper — demonstrated how little Prince heeded pigeonhole perceptions of him as a genre artist.

Purple Rain, a mediocre film vehicle but an amazing soundtrack, brought millions who had never bought a Rick James or P-Funk record around to Prince's way of seeing himself. Sublimating his erotic frenzy into sanitized romance (save for "Darling Nikki," depicted "masturbating with a magazine" in a hotel lobby), Prince — joined, for the first time, by the five-strong Revolution — decreed himself a master of pop in its many forms. The spartan outlines of "When Doves Cry" virtually defy style, while the opulent orchestration of "Purple Rain," the contemporary rush of "Let's Go Crazy" and the vintage Spector-era dramatics of "Take Me With U" spread him all over the aesthetic map.

Prince relaxed a bit on *Sign 'o' the Times*. Facing a shortage of taboos worth violating, he stopped trying to astonish with his talent. Instead, he refined and consolidated past stylistic adventures into a relatively subdued double helping of obsessions, some — "If I Was Your Girlfriend," "The Ballad of Dorothy Parker" — more eccentric than others. Social consciousness (the sublimely skeletal title track) and religion ("The Cross") augment the familiar rut of sex drives like "Slow Love" and "Hot Thing"; late in the date, a manic live breakdown jolts the party back to full force. Even when he's not racing ahead, Prince makes wherever he is sound like the place to be.

PUBLIC ENEMY

It Takes a Nation of Millions to Hold Us Back (Def Jam/Columbia) 1988

Other rappers were content to keep their minds on their money, but the brilliant Chuck D stuck to his militant guns, making Public Enemy a potent and high-minded spokesgroup for Black America. On their strongest album, the self-declared "Prophets of Rage" preach the articulate polemics of "Black Steel in the Hour of Chaos," "Don't Believe the Hype" and "Bring the Noise" against mesmerizing beats footnoted with speeches by Malcolm X and Minister Farrakhan. Public Enemy's choice of public heroes didn't please everyone, but the impact of this incendiary record far outweighed any particular political issues it raised.

REPLACEMENTS

Let It Be (Twin/Tone) 1984

If punk was, by design, the province of thugs and morons, no one bothered to tell Replacements singer, guitarist and songwriter Paul Westerberg. His vulnerable intelligence marked *Let It Be*, an unmarked roadmap for a mixed-up generation, with deep-cutting emotional wounds in "Unsatisfied" and "Answering Machine." The intemperate Minneapolis quartet's third album rocks like crazy while giving the finger to expectations, paving a sincere indie path to KISS and daring to undercut such sophomoric jokes as "Gary's Got a Boner" with the fragile romance of "Favorite Thing" and "Androgynous."

RUN-DMC

Raising Hell (Profile) 1986

Run-DMC took rap's first giant step across genre lines with the screaming guitar riffage of 1985's *King of Rock*. On *Raising Hell*, however, the New York trio turned their crossover dreams to platinum, sampling the Knack's "My Sharona" for "It's Tricky" and marshalling a pivotal summit with Aerosmith, dropping an old-school beat, scratches and tightly interlaced MC-two style into a riveting remake of "Walk This Way." But while racing forward, the group kept it real for hip-hop purists with the straight-up rhymes of "My Adidas" and "You Be Illin'."

Got Live (If You Want It or Not)

People often ask us rock geezers about our first concert, seeking a vicarious experience they can only imagine (or view on YouTube). As best as I can reconstruct it, based on the available evidence and what remains of memories that are now more than a half-century old, my cherry-popper was Murray the K's Easter revue at the Brooklyn Fox Theater, at the corner of Flatbush Avenue and Nevins Street, on 11 April 1966.

Murray was the city's top rock jock, the self-declared Fifth Beatle, billed on the radio as "the boss of the swingin' soiree." He was a bubbling fount of weirdly accented patter, inventor of a slanguage (either called Meazurray or Bop Talk) that he used to rally the faithful.

I went with my cousin Frank, who was then 14, two years older than me. He must have come from Jackson Heights, Queens on the subway; I have no idea how I got there. (I lived two miles away, but those were rough times in Kings County, and I doubt I would have had the bottle to walk by myself, even for a daytime show. I was already a daily subway commuter to school, so maybe I took the train. Or maybe a parental unit was involved.)

Following the showing of some military themed adventure film that we fidgeted through (it was, after all, a movie theater), we thrilled to a parade of two or three-song sets by living proof of the color-blind power of AM radio in the '60s: Joe Tex, the Young Rascals, Mitch Ryder & the Detroit Wheels, Jay & the Americans, Little Anthony & the Imperials, Deon Jackson, the Shangri-Las, Patti LaBelle & the Bluebells, the Gentrys and the Royalettes. I do have a few clear memories of the event (which was probably done and dusted in two hours — the same show was staged four or five times a day): Joe Tex's riveting mic stand choreography, Mitch Ryder's dramatic splits, Felix Cavaliere's arm-waving organ playing, the cool UV light illumination of the white shirt plackets and gloves the Imperials paired with their tuxedos. I also recall a hysterical teenager a few rows ahead of us who somehow lost the ring off her finger in the excitement and had to clamber around on the floor to retrieve it before her boyfriend (who I guess wasn't there) learned of her carelessness.

Murray was a striver. The efficient New York native released a handful of albums documenting his concerts. Some, I later learned, were given away as premiums to ticket buyers. I have two, found in bargain bins in the '70s. One is on his own Brook-Lyn label, and I suspect the other, on KFM (Kaufman?) Records, was also his own doing. Neither is from the show I attended. I listened to one the other day and was struck by a few things: the coy smarm of Murray's "submarine races" spiel (he even gets an innocent laugh by suggesting that two guys in the audience might be necking), how difficult it must have been for the older vocal groups to be sandwiched between high-energy rockers and (perhaps due to a lack of stage monitors) the pitchy singing that afflicts nearly all the performers.

Some of the most bizarre, memorable and unique concerts I've seen since then:

◆ The New York Dolls at the Little Hippodrome in 1975. The show was arranged by Malcolm McLaren, who dressed the band in red patent leather and hung a Chinese flag behind them.

◆ The Who at the Fillmore East in 1969, when a political group called the Up Against the Wall Motherfuckers set a fire next door, inadvertently filling the concert venue with smoke. I recall standing on my seat considering my options: suffocate or miss part of the most thrilling concert I'd ever seen. I opted to stay and watched in amazement as a plain-clothes cop came onstage and grabbed the mic out of Roger Daltrey's hand, only to be crumpled by Pete Townshend's swift kick to the yarbles. To his credit, Bill Graham calmly stopped the show and directed us to file out onto East 6th Street.

◆ The Dictators at the Palladium in 1977, with the Michael Stanley Band and AC/DC as support acts. Angus Young (in full schoolboy clobber) had a guitar cable that must have been a couple of hundred feet long, because he rocked up one aisle of the 3,000-seat theater, out onto East 14th Street and then back down the other aisle to rejoin his mates on stage. I missed AC/DC at CBGB, although I *did* see the Dictators there.

◆ I stood a few feet from Kurt Cobain and Courtney Love (who amiably tossed jellybeans at the band) in July 1993 as the Melvins played a full-bore electric sludge gig in the Sheraton New York Presidential Suite.

◆ Chuck Berry and Albert King opening for the Who at the Fillmore East.

◆ The Who and the Doors at Singer Bowl in 1968 with Kangaroo as support. There's a lot about this show lost to the mists of my mind, including the chair-throwing riot that ended the Doors' headlining set.

◆ The Jam at CBGB in 1977: a show so frighteningly overcrowded that someone I know went outside and called the fire department, which got the show raided. I described the show in a *TP* article about the Jam that year, but all I remember of it now was being pressed against the back of someone wedged in front of me.

◆ The 1988 spoken-word "concert" by Hunter S. Thompson at which he brandished a hunting rifle. I left — that was a bit too gonzo for me. A *Post* subeditor helpfully slugged my writeup "comedy," but I didn't find it funny.

More loathing than fear

Hunter Thompson's election night "commentary" is a fiasco

By IRA ROBBINS

What sounded like an intriguing prospect — watching the election results with legendary political journalist Hunter S. Thompson — brought 1100 paying customers to a sold-out Ritz on Tuesday evening. Unfortunately, "Fear and Loathing on Election Night 1988" was as big a disappointment to the partisan crowd as Bush's victory.

Following an interminable program of rock videos interrupted by snippets of CBS-TV election reports, the best-selling author and Doonesbury character showed up late, foggy and totally unprepared. Introduced and joined by polling pundit Pat Caddell, Thompson mumbled halting, largely incomprehensible comments, wandered aimlessly around the stage, and engaged people near the front in brief exchanges concerning drugs, leather jackets and Nixon masks.

After 10 minutes, by which time a full-fledged fiasco was well under way, Caddell tried to take questions from the floor, but Thompson's insistence that questioners

COMEDY review

hold up a small flashlight added significantly to the chaos. The beer-drinking college crowd then baited their falling idol with absurd inquiries about John Denver, Elvis Presley, masturbation and football. A few wanted to talk serious politics, but that proved futile.

As disillusionment turned to outright hostility, Thompson continued to prowl around the stage, replying haphazardly, and rarely cogently, to shouted remarks. However, when he pulled a hunting rifle from a large case, shortly after 11, I hastily followed the stream of dejected kids out the door.

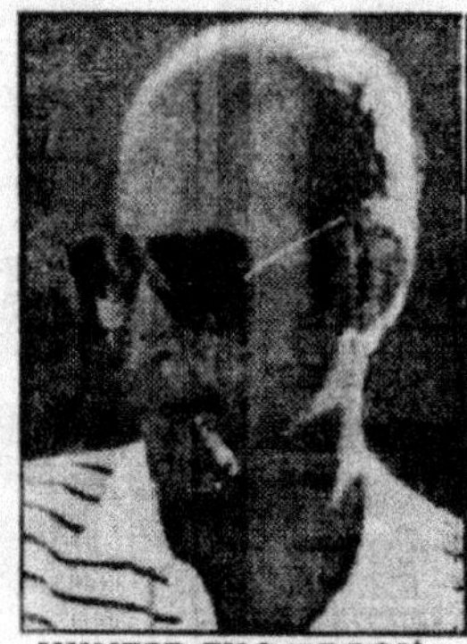

HUNTER THOMPSON
Enough is enough.

Enough is enough. Come the next presidential election, New Yorkers would be well advised to avoid any similar high-priced events and watch television at home.

YORK POST ON THE TOWN THURSDAY, NOVEMBER 10, 1988

◆ Sparks at the Rainbow in London in 1974, at the height of their British glam-rock fame. A girl ran onstage and grabbed Russell Mael around his white-suited knees and had to be pulled off him by a bouncer.

◆ The Ramones at Performance Studios with Tuff Darts and Suicide sometime in 1975: the audience, all three or four dozen of us, sat on the ratty carpet. There was no real stage in the rehearsal place. In my recollection, Johnny cut his hand and bled all over his Mosrite's scratch plate. If anyone else was at this show, please let me know!

◆ The original lineup of Television at Max's Kansas City when Richard Hell, rocking back and forth on his heels, fell backwards on his ass. Patti Smith reaching down from the stage and stealing a drink off my table at the same show.

◆ The Dead Boys at CBGB when Johnny Blitz threw a floor tom at Stiv Bators' back and knocked him out cold. The band left the stage with him still on the floor.

◆ The Eagles in Moscow (2001). Not something I'd do at home, but we happened to be in Russia visiting my sister-in-law, and they happened to have a show there. I wasn't even working. The Russian audience reacted to what they were seeing in ways I'd never witnessed. Joe Walsh stole the show.

◆ The fan at a 1974 Budgie concert at London's Lyceum who was probably tripping when he stuck his head inside a speaker cabinet while the band was playing at top volume.

◆ The K Fest in Olympia, Washington, August '91. The Smugglers blew the roof off the North-shore Surf Club, while the Melvins' outdoor gig by a lake pulled a powerful gloom over a bright blue sky. I got to see the Spinanes, Some Velvet Sidewalk, Beat Happening, Fugazi, L7, Billy Childish, Pastels, Stinky Puffs, Mecca Normal, Bratmobile, Lois, Sleepyhead, Fastbacks, Girl Trouble, Unwound and the Mummies. And the Pet Parade!

◆ Backed by Velvet Crush, Roger McGuinn performed a set of Byrds classics at my friends Melani and Edward's anniversary party at Fez.

◆ A Replacement show at CBGB where they played nothing but off-the-cuff covers. A similar show, only acoustic, by Dave Pirner and Dan Murphy of Soul Asylum at Siberia, an underground bar inside a Manhattan subway station.

◆ A bright afternoon concert by the Italian prog band Premiata Forneria Marconi in Central Park where I began a slow clap that ultimately ended a really boring violin solo. I believe you can hear it on their live album.

◆ Roger Ruskin Spear's Kinetic Wardrobe at the 100 Club in London, summer of 1974. Afterwards, I asked Roger to explain what a trouser press was (he wrote the song the magazine was named for), and he kindly drew one for me.

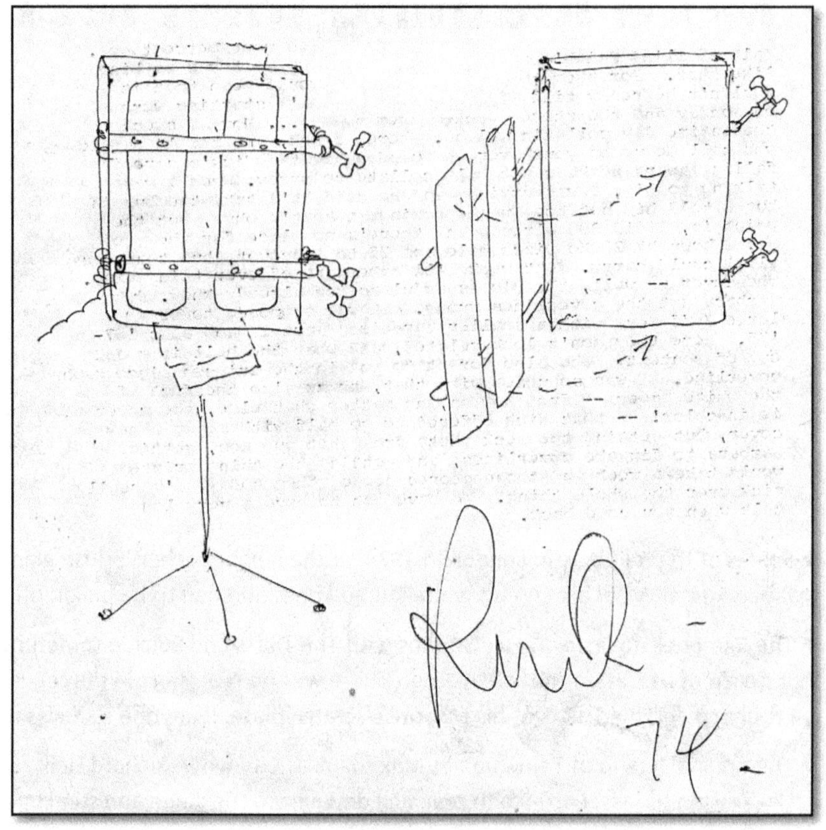

◆ Hawkwind at the Academy, the show at which audience howls of "Hawkwind" joined the rising tide of random "Whipping Post" cries. During "The Black Corridor," some brilliant balcony-dweller answered Robert Calvert's ponderous intonation of "Space is cold" with "*Take a blanket!*" "Space is dark" got "*Take a flashlight!*" and "Space does not comfort" elicited "*Take a friend!*"

◆ Status Quo at Irving Plaza in New York in 1997 playing to an audience that was largely Latin American.

◆ Green Day being pelted with buckets of mud at *Woodstock '94*. (Hey, they asked for it.) Nine Inch Nails showing up onstage the next day covered head to toe in it. (Unfortunately for my historical credibility, I didn't attend the original *Woodstock*. My friend Dan Slotkoff and I contemplated going but then decided there would be too many hippies there for our overly serious New Left sensibilities. I probably would have hated being there, but I am sorry to have missed seeing Pete Townshend treat Abbie Hoffman to a solid helping of British rock inhospitality.)

◆ My sister liked folk music but was not much interested in pop or rock. Still, she made several crucial contributions to my emerging taste in such things. It was on the table radio in her bedroom that I first heard the Beatles in early 1964. She later ceded me a small pile of 45s she owned, which introduced me to the Everly Brothers ("Bird Dog") and (the original) Johnny Thunder. And she and her first husband — a colorful mustachioed character who owned a beautiful Gibson Kalamazoo, smoked unfiltered Picayune cigarettes, worked as a substitute teacher and was friends with Dave Van Ronk — brought me to the *Philadelphia Folk Festival* a couple of times, starting in 1969.

The deal was we had to do some volunteer work in exchange for admission and a camping spot, so I ended up parked in the food tent, dodging the yellowjackets that swarmed around the soda machine, filling paper cups with boiling hot coffee from a huge urn well into the wee hours.

My serving post still allowed me to see the stage, so it wasn't so bad. The weekend's lineup presented an incredible cavalcade of folk, old-timey, bluegrass and blues stars (broaden the definition of country singers and it could have been the acronymic model for CBGB!), including Doc Watson, Reverend Gary Davis, Tom Rush, Bill Monroe, Tom Paxton, Pat Sky, Odetta, John Hartford and the Incredible String Band.

My fun was interrupted one night when I was distracted by something that made me turn my head — followed, thoughtlessly, by my cup-holding hand — and douse my sneaker-clad foot in steaming java. I escaped serious injury, but I was put off coffee for years.

◆ *A Musical Tribute to Woody Guthrie* at Carnegie Hall (h/t to my big sister Sara for taking 13-year-old me to such a historic event) in January 1968. All I recall of it is is Bob Dylan leaning toward Joan Baez for prompts while he sang "This Train" in an all-star sequence of vocalists.

CARNEGIE HALL/76th Season
Saturday, January 20, 1968, at 3:00 and 8:00

THE GUTHRIE CHILDREN'S TRUST FUND

presents

A MUSICAL TRIBUTE TO
WOODY GUTHRIE

JUDY COLLINS/BOB DYLAN/ARLO GUTHRIE
RICHIE HAVENS/BROWNIE MC GHEE
& SONNY TERRY
ODETTA/TOM PAXTON/PETE SEEGER
CHILDREN FROM
MARJORIE MAZIA SCHOOL OF DANCE

Narration by ROBERT RYAN/WILL GEER
Words & Music by WOODY GUTHRIE
Adapted and staged by MILLARD LAMPELL
Audio-Visuals by JERRY OBERWAGER

Produced by HAROLD LEVENTHAL
Assistants to Producer: TERRY SULLIVAN, IRENE ZACHS

Program subject to change

◆ The New York Dolls opening for Mott the Hoople at the Felt Forum, 1973.

◆ Mott the Hoople's midnight show at Radio City Music Hall, also in 1973, when the P.A. cut out, leaving only the kick drum and Ian Hunter's vocals audible.

◆ Queen opening for Mott the Hoople at the Uris Theater in 1974.

◆ Slade's excruciatingly loud sound system deployed to ear-splitting effect at Central Park, followed by a swank press party I got to attend.

◆ Tony Bennett at Radio City doing his wonderful ploy of putting down the mic and singing, unamplified but completely audibly, to the whole house. Absolutely magical.

◆ The Cars opening for Cheap Trick as the Boston band's success was exploding.

◆ Celine Dion opening for Michael Bolton.

◆ Three Dog Night opening for Canned Heat at the Fillmore East.

◆ R. Kelly opening for Salt-n-Pepa, mixing lurid vulgarity with religious reverence and mother-worship.

◆ Chicago opening for Johnny Winter (I recall Chicago guitarist Terry Kath body slamming his Ampeg stack).

◆ Rush opening for Rory Gallagher (I thought they were trying out to be the Canadian Budgie).

◆ Steely Dan (I loathed them that night and haven't changed my view since) opening for Electric Light Orchestra.

After publishing my first professional concert review (of PFM) in *Zoo World* in 1974, I didn't regularly practice the form until 1987, when I started freelancing for the *New York Post*. Even though I'd "been in publishing" for more than a decade at that point, the ways of a big newspaper were completely unfamiliar to me, and so leaving a show before the end, racing to a pub I knew near Madison Square Garden, scribbling a review out longhand and then dictating it over a pay phone (*stop....new graf....cap "L".... B as in boy, E as in Edward, D as Dog...comma, close quotes*) to a rewrite editor against a fast-approaching midnight deadline was a nerve-wracking shock to my system. (And, as evidenced below, no boon to my critical thinking or the quality of my prose.) And then I had to call back a little while later to see if any questions needed to be answered before I could head home.

But the angst of that nocturnal experience was washed away in the morning when I picked up the paper at a newsstand on Fordham Road. As accustomed as I was to the glacial pace of monthly magazine publishing, seeing my byline in print barely 12 hours after the event was a thrill.

I did reviews for the paper for a couple of years after that. It got old after a while, especially with the blunt exigencies of copyfitting ("We were three inches over, so we cut your piece up from the bottom..."), but I got to see lots of shows. Deadlines didn't allow for reflection or fence-sitting, and I should admit that some of my critiques now seem rash and/or a bit harsh.

The Cure keeps its promise

By IRA ROBBINS

ROCK review

THE political controversy surrounding The Cure's 1979 single, "Killing An Arab," was forgotten at the British band's sell-out performance last night at Madison Square Garden.

Thousands of enthusiastic young fans heard the sextet play an engaging two-hour set, drawn mostly from the current chart album, "Kiss Me, Kiss Me, Kiss Me," which has just hit gold sales status.

Over the past few years, the eccentric and unpredictable art-dance band has blossomed from obscure cultdom to major stardom. One of the pioneers of British new wave, The Cure onstage still embraces that era's spareness and modesty, so they avoid instrumental solos and any hint of rock idol pomposity.

Robert Smith, The Cure's charmingly waiflike singer and main creative force, ran the show with easy confidence, directing the tight ensemble through two dozen songs, including such popular repetoire numbers as "Let's Go To Bed," "Close To Me," "In Between Days," and "The Walk."

But many hits were passed over in favor of 14 songs from the new album. In fact, the set began with that record's lead-off track, "The Kiss." Throughout, Smith's unaffected vocals provided the band's most striking and attractive feature.

Although The Cure has gained most of its fans by playing melodic, quirky dance-rock, the band made a point of featuring many of its less accessible tunes, including such dirgey pieces as "The Snake Pit." The audience responded best to the songs they knew from MTV, but didn't object to the more esoteric selections.

Unlike other video-generation pop bands, The Cure's stage presence isn't especially colorful or cartoonish. The Britons dressed conservatively, moved very little, and dispensed with theatrics of any sort. The powerful personality that galvanized the arena was entirely due to the music. Without compromise or pandering, The Cure proved that it's possible to expand its following without losing the love of the faithful.

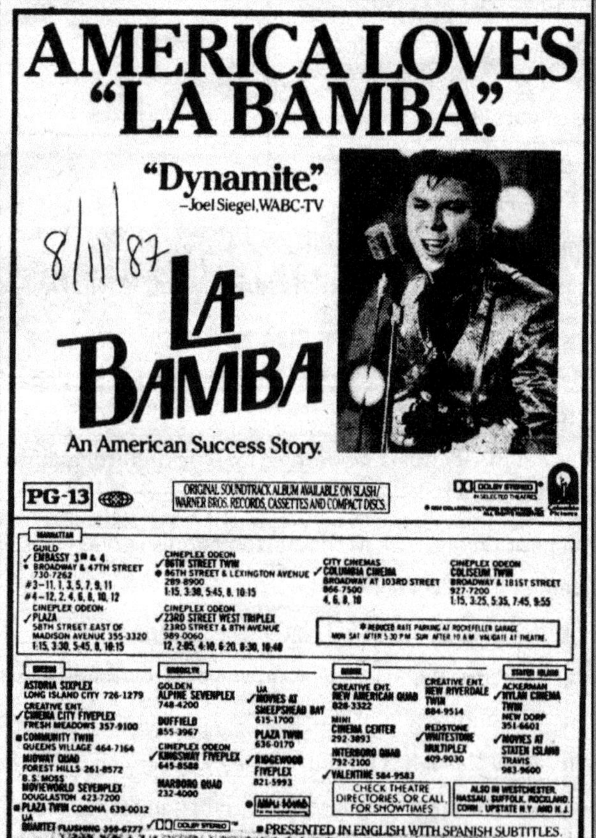

This review ran in the *New York Post* on 21 March 1989. At one of the shows of the engagement later that week, Reed bitched out "the guy from the *Post*" for my criticism of bassist Rob Wasserman, or so I was told by someone who was there. I guess Reed deserves credit for showing loyalty to musical colleagues.

It's nice to be read and noticed, but this minor scrape is nothing compared to the outrageous sneers and slanders against John Rockwell and Robert Christgau caught for posterity on Reed's *Live: Take No Prisoners* album, which — at least until the unbridled attacks of the Trump presidency — stood as a highwater mark in celebrity anti-press vituperation.

Lou Reed takes on urban decay

By IRA ROBBINS

ROCK *review*

NEVER mind the obvious irony of a comfortable rock star decrying the misery, squalor and corruption of New York from the stage of a posh Broadway theatre at $28.50 a seat while the homeless sleep outside in the cold. Appreciating Lou Reed has always meant granting him a unique moral position. So if he cares to perform his celebrated "New York" album in toto in the eminently civilized St. James Theatre, what's wrong with that?

The sold-out, six-show engagement began Sunday. Following an excitingly edgy, half-hour set by the Feelies, Reed and his guitar-bass-drums trio appeared on a stage containing just enough scenery to convey urban decay. Dressed in a dark suit and wearing glasses, Reed stood behind an intrusive music stand that hid his guitar and introduced the 14 songs of "New York" in order.

There were a few minor variations from the record. Reed corrected Richard Secord's name in "Sick of You," added an unexpected vocal twist to finish "Halloween Parade" and expanded the instrumental improvisation elsewhere. At first, Reed seemed a bit tense and reserved, but he and the band soon gained confidence and momentum, making the final third surge with power. Guitarist Mike Rathke provided excellent, sympathetic accompaniment, but Rob Wasserman, playing stand-up electric six-string bass, was a frequent source of irritation due to tonal imprecision, a distorted low end, and overambitious jazzy soloing.

Having rendered the album in 70 minutes, Reed took a short intermission and returned to play a half-dozen other songs, including "I Love You, Suzanne," "Rock and Roll" and "The Original Wrapper." The cheering crowd then brought him back

Steve Sands

LOU REED
Tense start.

three times, and heard fine versions of "Sweet Jane," "Walk on the Wild Side," "Vicious" and "Satellite of Love."

Lou Reed and the Feelies will be appearing at the St. James Theatre, 246 W. 44 St., today and Thursday through Saturday.

I posted this comment on Facebook on 28 October 2013:

What made Lou Reed great wasn't his musical talent — in traditional terms like melody, singing or guitar-playing he didn't actually have any — but his unselfconsciousness and his courage. He was an open-eyed observer — of people, his city, the (for want of a less hoity word) demi-monde — and his songs reported on those things without artifice or fear. That's what made them profound — he was first to make them into songs, and set them to the kind of propriety-destroying music no else had the courage or the dedication to attempt. The reason so many of the reminiscences that have been shared about Lou are of the "there was this one time he wasn't a dick to me" is because he never pretended to be anything he wasn't, and he didn't place too much value on consideration or civility. That's a very hard road to walk, but you can hear in his work that the ultimate object of his impossible expectations for people was himself. That's why he was a great artist, because he was unafraid to sacrifice himself for art. ◆

In March 1990, *Rolling Stone* Music Editor Jim Henke sent me on a quick northern jaunt to review a David Bowie show in Montreal. A low-key Midwesterner who managed to get along with Jann Wenner for many years, Jim later moved back to Cleveland to curate the Rock and Roll Hall of Fame Museum and died in 2019. He was great to work with ... when I could get him on the phone. He was one of those super-busy types who would leave a message for me to call him back urgently and then never be available when I did. Back in the days before mobile phones, that meant pumping quarters into payphones while going about my writerly rounds.

Bowie: *Sound + Vision* Tour Opener

Rolling Stone, 19 April 1990

"B*onsoir, Montreal! Merci beaucoup*!" David Bowie's greeting to a packed Montreal Forum may have been nothing more than a simple cultural courtesy, but it typifies the eager-to-please attitude that has led to a surprising move in a career built on the unexpected.

In an unprecedented conceptual gambit, Bowie has shelved his musical present in order to revisit his prodigious past. Beginning with a handful of Canadian dates in early March, he embarked on the hits-oriented *Sound + Vision World Tour 1990*, a world trek that will keep him and a four-piece band on the road for at least six months. By using simple musical backing and restrained staging, Bowie is finally the man who came down to earth.

The motivation for this massive give-the-people-what-they-want undertaking is neither generosity nor merely the desire for an enriching ride on the fortysomething nostalgia wave. Chastened by the critical rejection of 1987's outlandish *Glass Spider Tour* and the uncertain acceptance of Tin Machine, Bowie has struck a Faustian bargain with his audience, agreeing to relive his past in exchange for the right to escape it. He says this will be the last hurrah for his old songs.

Bowie and his touring band — guitarist Adrian Belew, drummer Michael Hodges and keyboardist Rick Fox (both members of Belew's own group) and bassist Erdal Kizilçay, a veteran Bowie sideman — reached Montreal on March 6th, two nights after a warm-up gig in Quebec City. In good voice and spirits, relaxed to the point of occasional giddiness, Bowie delivered more than two dozen of his best-loved tunes in a pair of 65-minute segments. Films of Bowie, Belew and dancer Louise Lecavalier were projected on a 60 x 40-foot gauze scrim backdrop; live video filled two round screens at the sides of the stage.

The retrospective began with "Space Oddity" and ended with "Rock 'n' Roll Suicide," drawing most heavily on records from 1971–'77, done in a faithful fashion.

This band has a more cerebral, less intense style than previous stadium-scaled Bowie touring ensembles. That reduced some of the drama but did nothing untoward to such staples as "Changes," "Life on Mars," "'Heroes'," "Let's Dance," "The Jean Genie," "Ashes to Ashes" and "TVC15." While Bowie proved able to reclaim virtually his entire diverse oeuvre — even those songs that now seem furthest from him — through sheer vocal power and charisma, the band wasn't always equal to the challenge, demonstrating too much respect for the songs' recorded arrangements.

"Suffragette City," "Panic in Detroit" and "Ziggy Stardust" could have used more glam-rock guitar sneer, while the funky kick of a soulful rhythm was notably absent from "Golden Years," "Fame" and "Fashion." What fared best was late-Seventies rock: "Stay," "Station to Station," "Sound + Vision" and "'Heroes,'" plus "Ashes to Ashes," from 1980. After a slow start, Belew — who contributed more as a backing vocalist than Bowie did as a rhythm guitarist — emerged from an indistinct mix to rip off rubbery, fluid solos.

The otherwise future-oriented Bowie first indicated his willingness to embrace the past by making a pact with Rykodisc, a young, independent record label, to reissue all of his pre-*Let's Dance* albums. But rather than just signing a contract and cashing a check, he took a great interest in the creation of *Sound + Vision*, an extraordinary box set of hits and rarities that was released last year. *Sound + Vision*'s success encouraged him to tour, which in turn led to the recent release of *Changesbowie*, a new hits compilation that includes a "Fame '90" remix.

For this tour, Bowie has ceded his artistic will to the masses, inviting the public — polled since January through 900 phone lines — to pick songs for this living jukebox. (Although the set played in each country will, to some degree, reflect the votes section tallied there, no phone polling was done in Canada before the March shows.) Bowie also delegated much of the artistic responsibility. As *Sound + Vision*'s bandleader, Belew, a veteran of the album *Lodger* and Bowie's 1978 tour, helped put together the band and work up the songs. Bowie gave Edouard Lock, the artistic director of the Montreal-based modern dance company La La La Human Steps, carte blanche to design the staging, Lock directed the films that let Bowie sing in rough sync with enormous images of himself and brought in artists to create the fiberglass gargoyles and friezes that framed the otherwise undecorated stage. Lock also choreographed the energetic onstage movements of Lecavalier and another Human Steps dancer who appeared (to an enormous ovation in their home town) for "Suffragette City" and will be on hand for a few other shows.

Bowie began the European leg of the tour in mid-March and is slated to bring the show to America in April. The tour will swing back through England in early August, with visits to Japan to be added later. ◆

I'm pretty sure this is the only concert review I have ever written that incorporated offstage quotes from the artist. *Blender*, one of several magazines that rejected my entreaties to become its reviews editor (J.D. Considine ended up in the position, followed by Rob Tannenbaum), had a format that required shows to be covered this way. So, when I went to see the White Stripes, I first spoke with Jack and Meg in the bar. Honestly, that part was more entertaining than the show that followed.

The White Stripes
Bowery Ballroom
June 16, 2001
Blender, Issue 2

"The shows I like the most are when we're trying to win somebody over," says Jack White, "When they're yelling at us, that really gets me going." Right now, the White Stripes are definitely going. The Detroit duo is indie rock's great white hope, and audiences are falling for them like a punch-drunk boxer throwing a fight. The guy standing with his wife behind the sound board heard one song on a college radio station, bought the White Stripes' current album, *White Blood Cells*, and drove in from Connecticut for the first of their three sold-out New York shows. He's not disappointed.

Jack White sings, whacks guitar and occasionally plays piano. He's an impressive and improving songwriter with great taste in covers. He loves Delta blues, Detroit bands and Bob Dylan. He hates live albums, Stevie Ray Vaughan, being pigeonholed, big venues and bands that don't change.

Meg White plays drums. Simply. No fills, no turns. She loves Mo Tucker of the Velvet Underground, Emmylou Harris and Keith Moon.

Meg and Jack are the most color-coordinated act since Prince. They wear cherry red and white clothes and play red and white instruments. Their albums are red and white. At least one of them lives in a red and white house.

Meg is not — as they have steadfastly claimed — Jack's big sister.

In the course of three albums, the White Stripes have done roaring blues that reeks of late nights in dangerous places, catchy pop froth, country stomp and (relatively) ambitious rock. With arrangements so elementary they wouldn't cut it as major-label demos, they still manage to summon the ghosts of the Rolling Stones, Yardbirds and Led Zeppelin.

Jack says, "The studio should always be different from the live show. The album is what lasts forever, the live show comes and goes." Thankfully, he's right.

This night, the White Stripes — who roadie for themselves and don't prepare set lists — burn their blueswailing first-album killer "Jimmy the Explorer," Dolly Parton's "Jolene" and the catchy "Pretty Good Looking" ("...for a girl") right off the bat and lose their reverb-caked charm not long after, as Jack's frantic yelp and fretwork and Meg's metronomic simplicity blur into a monochromatic rec-room blare. Only the timely arrival of four strong, diverse tunes ("Hotel Yorba," "We're Going to Be Friends," "Truth Doesn't Make a Noise" and "Astro") remedies the sonic two-dimensionality. What seems to be their draw — two members, no bassist — is in fact a footnote, a limitation, to the material. At an hour, the show — two dozen songs, including the old folk standard "Boll Weevil," served up virtually without pause — is plenty, exciting at times but in no need of further elaboration.

One time, Jack "forgot" his shoes and borrowed a friend's. "They were too big on me, and I had to stuff another pair of socks inside 'em to make 'em fit. When we were playing, [the extra] socks flew. I rocked my socks off!" ◆

Jack and Meg White, 16 June 2001

What's the weirdest thing that's ever happened to you onstage?
Jack: Not too long ago I forgot my shoes and I used a friend's shoes, and they were too big on me, and I had to stuff another pair of socks inside 'em to make 'em fit. When we were playing, they were falling out, and the socks flew off onstage. I rocked my socks off!

We don't have a set list. There's a couple of songs we love to start off with and love to end with. "Let's Shake Hands" was our very first single, it's like a greeting song.

Meg: He'll start playing songs I've never heard before.

Jack: We only have a couple of songs that Meg starts. The first song on our first album starts off with Meg. The last sound on the album is by Johnny Walker, who plays slide guitar with us on the last song.

We've been to New York a few times. The first time we came here we played the Mercury Lounge, and it was sold out. We were amazed because we thought no-one had heard of us in New York. We were on tour with Sleater-Kinney, and we booked our own show just to see what happened and it was really nice reaction. We always figured that New York and LA wouldn't like us. And here we are doing three sold-out nights.

Whenever we're onstage I never comprehend that there's more than five people in front of us. A couple of weeks ago we played in New Orleans and Ray Davies came to the show. Nothing was miked in the club, and my tuner didn't work. After the first song, I looked out and caught where he was standing. I couldn't stop looking over there — I don't know why, I've never done that before.

What if A&R men are watching?
I don't care. If God wills something to happen to us that's good, if not, we still have our house in Detroit and we can afford to live there. All we've ever heard is bad stories anyway, and I'm sure that if we do [sign to a major label] it's going to be a bad story, too.

My favorite bands to watch are Detroit bands. Whirlwind Heat. We're huge Bob Dylan fans.

Meg: Emmylou Harris, that was a phenomenal show.

"Jolene" was on a picture disc single. We do "I'm Bored" by Iggy Pop. We were going to do a Ziggy and Iggy single, but we never did it.

The best show we ever did was about a year ago in Asheville, North Carolina. The crowd was waiting for us, man. That was amazing. They knew all the lyrics to every song and would not let us go away. That was a really happy experience. We got the chance to open for Weezer in a small club in LA. I like Weezer. They have good songs. Then someone had tickets to see them in Detroit, and it really depressed me. It was sponsored by some computer company. I hate when those big lug security guards... We've had the opportunity to play bigger places and we won't do it. I hate being a spectator and getting frisked three times, getting yelled at for your ticket...

[If we get really successful], we'll just play small clubs for seven nights in a row. Wouldn't it be amazing if the Rolling Stones did a tour of small clubs?

The blues is my number-one love. I love it to death, yet I'm white. I wasn't born in 1910. When we're playing it I feel bad at the same time as loving it. It's difficult for me to think about. It makes me uncomfortable. That's why the new album is called *White Blood Cells*, and there's no blues on the album. Everything to me is derivative of the blues, that's why it's important to me, but I don't want people to think Stevie Ray Vaughan. It's not about guitar solos. Blues is a simple thing to play guitar solos — every guitar shop you go to in the country there's some idiot playing something like that. I don't ever want to be associated with... "Oh, check this out!"

We never want to make the same record twice. We don't want to get pigeonholed. I've never heard [an entire] Jon Spencer Blues Explosion album. People were saying that about us. It gets uncomfortable to just be "this is our thing, look at what we're doing." I get bored so fast.

I love blues to death, but I don't want to do the same thing over and over again. It disappoints me when I see other bands doing that.

Meg's influences
Mo Tucker, Keith Moon, the girl from the Gories.

Jack: I don't think artists should be at the service of the audience 99 percent. It should be 50-50. I appreciate Dylan that he doesn't kowtow to the hits or doing them exactly as they were on the album. Every time Dylan goes out he does a different version of his songs. He's not just phoning it in.

Critical praise?
There's so much more journalism than there was 30 years ago, and so much more knowledge. With mass communication everybody now knows everything that's ever been done, it just makes people so ready to knock things down.

If you were a completely original band, with a whole new idea, would it go over well?
I don't think it would. People would [compare it] to Devo or something.

The studio should always be different from the live show. The album is what lasts forever, the live show comes and goes. If a band has a string section [on a record], I don't think they should bring an orchestra along [on tour] just for that song. If we have a song on an album where I'm overdubbing piano and playing guitar, and Meg playing tambourine and drums that we should do it live with just guitar, drums and vocals. Different is better.

I just started playing piano a little on stage. Clubs don't have pianos. If they did, I'd play a lot more.

Goal of a great show?
The shows I like the most are when we're trying to win somebody over. When they're yelling at us, that really gets me going. It makes me feel something, it's much more exciting.

Someone made a rude comment to Meg, and I singled him out and made the whole audience look at me.

Last time we were here, during a break between songs, while I was tuning up, someone in the crowd said, "It better be good." We had just played Hoboken [the night before] and it was a whole crowd of rock critics — everyone was like, Oh, impress us. I said, "Where are we, Hoboken?" Half the crowd went "ooh." The other half cheered.

Everybody's got a garage in Detroit. Actually, it's mostly basement rock... ◆

Brian Wilson, card-carrying genius

After a life custom-made for cable catharsis, the force behind the Beach Boys is now being honored even for things he didn't do. Does that card ever expire?

Salon, April 2001

At last month's Brian Wilson tribute concert in New York, as a parade of esteemed pop music scholars pronounced familiar pieties, one of the short films shown to explain the night's present (if not quite accounted for) icon mentioned that Wilson had lived his whole life in fear and mentioned his "untreated mental illness." Were Dean Martin roasts ever this brutal?

Inexplicable host Chazz Palminteri, who not only heard but *liked* (!) Beach Boys records as a kid growing up in the anti-California Bronx 'hood that gave Dion's Belmonts their name, was followed at the podium by '60s survivor Dennis Hopper, Rod Stewart survivor Rachel Hunter, '70s romantic Cameron Crowe and Sir George Martin.

As tributes go, this concert staged for television — TNT will broadcast some of it on that most Beach Boy-like (not to mention James Wattest) of days, the 4th of July — primarily succeeded in making Wilson seem less than the genius so many of the speakers enthusiastically proclaimed him to be. Focusing on him as a songwriter rather than a studio auteur made for a self-defeating exercise, as Paul Simon, Elton John, Vince Gill, Billy Joel and others grappled with tunes inextricable from their original presentation. That the back-in-action Go-Go's rocked up "Surf City" and "Little Honda" like enthusiastic new lovers only proved the degree to which California punk-poppers have internalized the Beach Boys. And, as anyone who doesn't look down on the Beach Boys as a '60s novelty will know, those aren't the songs Brian deserves to be remembered for.

His legacy properly rests on innovative landmarks like "Surf's Up" and "Good Vibrations," which was oddly handed over to Ann and Nancy Wilson of Heart and opera singer Jubilant Sykes. In his introduction, Sir George suggested that the song, with its discontinuous complexity and harmonic sophistication, was all but unperformable. Perhaps he was unaware that the Beach Boys (and lesser bands armed with no more than a few true singers and a theremin) long ago put paid to the belief that Wilson's 3:35 studio gem had permanently relocated his creativity outside the reach of rock and roll, a form so simple any halfwit could play it. Even the stars of "Barracuda" and "Magic Man" — aided immeasurably by Brian's non-pareil touring band, an augmented incarnation of L.A.'s Wondermints, which played all of the songs with finesse and respect and provided the requisite harmonies — were able to hang on, at least until Ann's ill-advised rock improv at the end.

Brian's greatest achievements came not at the keyboard, where he composed his achingly beautiful melodies, but in the studio, where a guileless young man in his 20s, driven by faith in what he could hear in his head, believed that his future, and maybe that of all pop music, lay beyond three-chord odes to cars or girls. Brian took received wisdom — catchy tunes, sweet harmonies, teen-dream lyrics — and set sail beyond the horizon of AM haikus for music of greater ambition and no less appeal. That's not an easy idea to convey at an all-star tribute, and certainly not one Ricky Martin could explain with his wind-up pelvis. Brian clearly envisioned his creations as *sounds* more than structures — which explains their occasional lapses in logic as well as his inability to keep pace with the master craftsmen who followed his lead. (The effortless-sounding re-creations of "Good Vibrations" and "Strawberry Fields Forever" on Todd Rundgren's *Faithful* album underscore the acceleration of studio facility in a single decade.)

The concert's centerpiece — 1966's wonderful *Pet Sounds* done by Wilson and a procession of stars, many of whom turned in sensitive, heartfelt performances — dismantled the artistically advanced and arguably cohesive album (god only knows how the resigned alienation of "I Just Wasn't Made for These Times" can be understood to cohere with the Caribbean sailing misadventure "Sloop John B" or the pimply sexual longing of "Wouldn't It Be Nice") into a carelessly assembled K-Tel concert anthology of awkwardly juxtaposed singles.

What's more, only Brian — controlled and functional but still unnervingly remote at 58, an unblinking survivor retracing familiar steps — himself had the presence of mind and humility to acknowledge the true provenance of the songs for which he was being compared to Mozart. He singled out *Pet Sounds* lyricist Tony Asher and Van Dyke Parks (co-author of "Heroes and Villains," the poetic-sounding nonsense words of "Surf's Up" and one of the five men behind "Sail on, Sailor") in the audience and thanked them.

But he also left many debts unpaid, not the least of them to conspicuously unrepresented former bandmates, including his late brothers Dennis and Carl, who got a dedication for dying but less credit for living. And just because right-wing T-M creep singer Mike Love had to go to court in 1992 to establish his contributions to the Beach Boys oeuvre doesn't mean he didn't make them. (Actually, there was never any disagreement that Love co-wrote "Little Honda," "Darlin'," "Fun, Fun, Fun," "Don't Worry Baby," "The Warmth of the Sun," "Wild Honey" and the words he and Carl Wilson sang in "Good Vibrations." The lawsuit he won against Brian established his rights in 29 others.)

It was no favor to anyone that a tribute to an artist with no shortage of estimable compositions should include songs the Beach Boys didn't write. David Crosby took two awkward stabs at "Sloop John B," a folk ballad the group recorded but laid no claim to authoring. "Barbara Ann," which served as one of the all-star encores, was a hit for the Regents before the Beach Boys ever heard themselves on the radio. Then there's "Surfin' U.S.A.," which might as well be a cover. (In *Heroes & Villains: The True Story of the Beach Boys*, Steven Gaines claims that Brian and Mike borrowed the lyrical idea of a Chubby Checker hit and the music of Chuck Berry's "Sweet Little 16"; the song's joint credits were only formalized after Berry's camp sued.)

But who really cares about such music-nerd trivia? With creative evaluation being increasingly elbowed out by thoughtless consensus in our post-critical celebrity era — box office stats, chart positions, magazine covers and awards shows mean far more to people than the individual musings of effete intellectuals — public interest in nit-picky career details is no match for juicy personal details. Blame is banished in victim culture, and the cost for fucking up a life, whether one's own or someone else's, is no more than a cursory mea culpa of a misbegotten past, no matter how recent it may have been. And with that, life becomes the all-purpose excuse for lapses in artistry. Like the media-ready high school students who fill our screens with pithy soundbites every time TV cameras arrive at the scene of a shooting, the glossed-over-simplification of *Behind the Music* is now a blueprint for popular redemption. Brian Wilson's story is custom-made for cable catharsis: the bloated, bed-ridden burnout who sacrificed his soul to create his teenage symphonies to God and became a serial victim of drug-fueled psychosis, charlatans and thieves, all of it traceable to the spiteful dad-manager who deafened his ear, undercut his confidence and then sold off his songs. But a sad story with a happy ending hardly mirrors the arc of Wilson's work.

Like many of his surviving contemporaries, Wilson's 40-year career yielded timeless work only in its first decade. Even at top form, crafting the songs that made the Beach Boys "America's Band," he wasn't infallible. Then came the maudlin, weird and frequently embarrassing results of mental, physical and emotional stress. (It should be acknowledged, however, that there actually *are* people who play *The Beach Boys Love You*, the 1977 album that contains Wilson's ridiculous ode to "Johnny Carson," for enjoyment.) His sporadic releases over the past 20 years were only imitations of what we knew he could do, and the concert reflected that, proffering only two songs written since the early '70s — the sincere but ungainly memorial "Lay Down Burden" and the concert's coda, a solo rendition of 1988's almost-great "Love and Mercy."

Not to drown in semantics, but genius can't be such a fleeting gift. Do we now need to edit and excuse to safely recognize the demeaned idols of our time? J.D. Salinger, Joseph Mitchell and Ralph Ellison also peaked early, but they just stopped cold and so fixed their legends in ice. No one ever does that in eternal world of pop music, not unless they lose their minds or their lives. With its hacks, has-beens and one-hit wonders, rock and roll happily consigns the no-longer-creative to recycle past glories on the oldies circuit and can only forgive the self-deluded efforts of the once-great so long as they don't stop playing their hits. Pete Townshend of the currently reunited Who — which recorded its superfluous final album in 1982 and has been making rumblings about doing another — wrote earlier this year that "I have not discovered a single 'perfect' Who song in any of my trawlings through my old stuff or recent stuff." Thank goodness for "My Generation."

In fact, it's probably better for most of the old-timers if they keep their creativity under a basket. (Not Bob Dylan and Neil Young, however — they can keep going forever as far as I'm concerned.) Increasingly distant achievements can't keep a reputation aloft in the face of mounting evidence to the contrary. The eminence of "God Only Knows," "In My Room" and "Caroline, No" buys a lot of good will, but turning a blind eye to subsequent entries in the failure column only diminishes popular music's claims to enduring significance. Right now, up in Palminteri's Bronx, Chuck Knoblauch — the Yankees' millionaire infielder who lost the ability to hit the side of a barn last year — is being cheered every time he doesn't boot a routine play in his safer reposting to left field. The diminished expectations that now coddle Wilson have led to an equally condescending miscalculation of his past.

Palminteri mentioned that it wasn't cool to like the Beach Boys back in the day, but he didn't explain why. Before Brian turned inward, their wimpy idealism overshadowed the joy of their sound. Rock was the voice of anger, angst and rebellion, while surf music was the quintessence of good times. (Even Wilson's adaptation of the full-throated Phil Spector production style took it from tense drama to ebullient release.) Wilson's artistic stature improved as his life fell apart; a surviving victim of rock and roll whose body somehow outlasted his mind. In a twisted way, Brian's troubles — which also led to darker, more revealing songs — made his achievements more profound and went a long way to counter the awfulness of what his "Kokomo"-singing Disneyized bandmates got up to in his absence.

In hindsight, it was easier to appreciate the group's records if they could be viewed as the work of a solitary demented genius battling untold forces arrayed against him. In the process, Brian came to singly embody all that was good about the Beach Boys, from start to finish. Their work became his work, which reduced the others to tagalongs, or, worse, hindrances out to stymie his muse. Brian indisputably had the vision, conviction and sonic imagination. He was primarily, by a large margin, responsible for both the group's existence and its importance. But he clearly didn't do it alone. ◆

Surface Noise #2

TrouserPress.com, February 1997

It's tempting to rag on Smashing Pumpkins for all the obvious reasons (nice tunes, 'tude dude; love that Freddy Krueger voice), but watching the current figureheads of American "alternative" wow a hockey arena full of Long Island eighth graders recently evoked another sort of observation.

In a week of idealism regained by Bruce Springsteen, that literary lion draped in cowskin whom the *New York Times Magazine* saw fit to portray as the paragon of pure-hearted populism in a world now crawling with craven idols, the Smashing Pumpkins provided more compelling evidence of rock's static eternity. Who but the exceedingly young or gullible could honestly believe the soul of determined self-expression wears a carefully shaved dome and a "ZERO" T (available in the lobby for a functioning piece of plastic)? Going by their posture and purpose rather than the shadings of their guitar thunder, today's rock god hipoisie is indistinguishable from those pitiful fuddyduddies a full generation older. If you don't think the Smashing Pumpkins are lazy, fat dinosaurs in training, you just don't recognize the signs.

The Nassau night began with a typically delightful opening set by Fountains of Wayne, complete with an unannounced cover of ELO's 21-year-old "Can't Get It Out of My Head," a song one hapless newspaper critic earlier on the tour had mistaken for the Beatles tune on which it is loosely based; given its clear age advantage, the song could not possibly have been known by more than a fraction of the audience. Still too fresh to be jaded but too smart to be gullible, the deservedly ascendant New York quartet is in the early stages of a ground-up effort to win the hearts and minds of tune-conscious America, a campaign admittedly facilitated by personal and professional connections to the non-Corgan half of the Pumpkins. (Bassist Adam Schlesinger, also of the group Ivy, co-owns the PolyGram-affiliated Scratchie label with D'Arcy, James Iha and others.)

Fountains were onstage to do a job, trying to affix something to enough early arrivals to advance from zero recognition towards a rich, glorious future in which *they* get to dock the opening act for mischievous behavior. But they didn't go about it like a job; tightness hasn't yet squeezed the life out of them. Between songs played with enthusiasm and aplomb, singer/guitarist Chris Collingwood's dry quip sounded like things he just thought of, as opposed to the traditional "ALLRIGHT [fill in the current geographical locale identified on the TelePrompTer near your left-center monitor]!!!!!!!!"

Nothing about the quartet's brief set seemed more impromptu than that, but they still conveyed a sense of casual, comfortable fun, like it actually might be a hoot to be up there on a huge stage, getting to play songs they'd written for a sizable number of listeners who actually didn't mind if they did. By sharpened-needles-in-the-eye standards, it's a pleasant enough job, right?

Then came Pumpkins. Arrayed before a towering semi-conical lighting structure that looked like an alien steel Xmas bush, these determined rock gladiators dressed in their nightly uniforms — Billy the C in silver slacks and black "ZERO" T, James Iha dandy with a slick shirt and necktie, D'Arcy packed into shiny black jeans — attended to their jobs like pros, following theatrical rules of crowd-pleasing rock behavior that date back to Murray the K's de-uh-zay. The mass marketing of solipsistic anomie is old news (shit, the Rolling Stones did that in the '60s), and the Pumpkins seem content in the ranks of its door-to-door salesmen. Which doesn't say much for progress of any sort.

It's easy to see the route by which the spirit of raw challenge — born of playing to 15 people in a club, fighting for recognition, struggling to make a great (or at least faintly original) record, confronting hostility, all of that — gets sucked out of a band. In the studio, whether cutting a song for a fanzine flexidisc or finishing an album that will receive a full-tilt marketing blitz, musicians work in a vacuum, making music that will only later be taken from their control and offered to an outside audience. By the time that happens, the record will be immutable, an artifact to be encountered and judged by an uncountable and basically unknown populace. No one making a record has a reliable notion of how it will be received and by whom. The master tape of a record about to be released is a fully thought-out ball perfectly pitched into the darkness with everything on it. Only when the audience gets to take its swing will the artist know where it's going and who sent it there. Anyone who has ever slaved over a love letter or a job application knows it's not done till you drop in the box.

Onstage, however, all hope of communicating clearly and accurately goes up in dry ice. Even at its most controlled, a rock concert is a mess of variables, beginning with the sea of shining faces facing the stage. Who are they? What has brought them there? What do they expect? What will they accept? Unlike the recording studio, live events happen in real time. Once those lights go out, there's no timeouts for a band's strategy sessions. Rethinks happen on the fly, and emotions can run close to the surface.

After bludgeoning away for a tiresome hour or so at Nassau Coliseum (was this what the Kiss tour sounded like?), the Pumpkins brought out Jimmy Flemion, the gangly brother and Frogs bandmate of tour keyboardist Dennis Flemion, in the slot vacated by the late Jonathan Melvoin. Resplendent in glittering green angel wings and white feather boa, Flemion sang along with "1979" while his scraggly locks were sheared off by a roadie, who tossed them into the crowd. The fans, needless to say, didn't go wild.

Corgan evidently considered this incongruous break in the monotony a unique and significant art event. (It was certainly proof of some residual life in this moribund machine.) When the audience took this self-indulgent non sequitur in stride — in other words, collectively shrugged and waited for the next song — the disgruntled icon reiterated his disappointment. The only bit of onstage business that actually seemed to matter to Corgan as a person rather than a Pumpkin had proved futile, and he wasn't liking it. Can we expect a song about this whole tragic experience on the next album? ◆

Velvet Crush

I've always liked the lede to this review, one of my very few contributions to the insular and exclusive *Village Voice* music section. (Dawn Eden is a real person, known at the time for her encyclopedic knowledge of artists like Harry Nilsson, Curt Boettcher and Emmit Rhodes. As I recall, she was surprised — but amused — to see her name.)

Midnight at Maxwell's

By Ira Robbins

Velvet Crush

Dawn Eden frugged. Velvet Crush rocked. Life went on. But for that midnight hour at Maxwell's, school was out for summer, do anything you wanna do, and shake some action. One of very few bands with the vision to cherish power pop as an art form of endless possibilities, Velvet Crush evinces faith in something bigger than Big Star. Too many groups mistake the disposable nature of concise, melodic singles for cultural insignificance; Velvet Crush embraces pop's transience as its essential value, charging through alluring songs with the desperate joy and urgency of lifetime rock fans. VC resets new wave's sense of mission for the '90s, stripping the attitude off and leaving the heart to gush. Roll over Material Issue and tell Paul Weller the news.

A two-guitar quartet led by its rhythm section, Velvet Crush is motored by drummer Ric Menck,

Continued on page 81

VOICE July 21, 1992

[*from p. whatever*] a gangly contraption of flying wrists and forearms whose confrontational wit could make him an understudy for Adam Arkin on *Northern Exposure*. Onstage, the determination that lines his face isn't about fastidious timekeeping or tricky tempos — with a backbeat that swings like crazy and fills that resound like hand claps, he's a limber titan of pop rhythm. But like a bluesman canvassing the Lord for deeper feelings, Menck plays pop as soul music (cf. the band's "White Soul") and thus answers to a higher authority. Audience reverence is obligatory. Every few songs, Menck bounds out from behind his small silver kit to make bogus announcements or expound on pop aesthetics. At Maxwell's, interrupted during a rumination on rock's grail of lost innocence, he strode offstage to ream [out] an especially inattentive loudmouth.

Menck and bassist Paul Chastain, whose clear, weightless voice balances the band's surging distorto drive, have been partners through a decade of charm 'n' harmony ensembles like the Big Maybe, Paint Set and Choo Choo Train. The two Illinois natives settled into the louder Velvet Crush several years ago, coincident with a move to Providence, Rhode Island, where they acquired guitarists Jeffrey Borchardt and Dave Gibbs (also, respectively, of Honeybunch and the Gigolo Aunts). Pop arriviste Matthew Sweet produced the band's exceedingly pretty/tough 1991 debut, *In the Presence of Greatness* (Ringers Lactate); early this year, Menck and Chastain spent two months on the road as their old chum's rhythm section.

Loud and tuneful, the Hoboken set peaked with "Atmosphere," an evanescent number from the recent *Post-Greatness E.P.* rended by a furious drum attack, and the apocalyptic "Drive Me Down," a galloping drawbridge of descending chords and soaring melody that ended with Gibbs whacking his axe on a cymbal. "You gotta understand," said Menck earnestly during a Liverpool tour anecdote. "It's just about the songs." ◆

Newsday (1993 – 1995)

I was the pop music editor and critic of *Newsday* and *New York Newsday* from June 1993 to September 1995.

The job came my way through one of those completely unexpected twists of fate that emerge from the ether to alter the course of one's life. I was at a show at the Knitting Factory when and where Rachel Felder, a writer I knew (the niece of Doc Pomus and the daughter of super-lawyer Raoul Felder), was asked by Dave Herndon, a features editor at the paper, if she had any suggestions of journalists to fill a vacant slot on the paper's entertainment section. Kismet. She spotted me and, to my eternal gratitude (which I don't believe I have ever properly expressed), introduced us. Short-circuiting a process I would have found insurmountable unaided, I went in for an interview, weirdly confident of my chances, and a few days later I had the well-paid and prestigious gig.

Derisively known as "a tabloid in a tutu" for the juxtaposition of its modest format and outsized ambitions, the paper, which had the fifth-largest circulation of any daily in America, was based on Long Island but had launched a New York City edition to compete with the *Daily News* and the *Post*. Its music department had a deservedly strong reputation: my *Trouser Press* colleague John Leland had worked there, so had Robert Christgau and Dave Marsh. I joined a paper that then employed Wayne (one "b," no relation) Robins, Stanley Mieses, Gene Seymour and Tony Scaduto, author of an early book about Dylan. Tim Page, formerly of the *Soho Weekly News* and the *New York Times*, was the paper's classical music critic.

Management was conservative; policy obligated me to trek out to the paper's offices and printing plant in far-off Melville, Long Island to pee in a cup before I could formally be offered the job. Given the world of popular music, I wondered to friends whether the goal was to confirm that I *didn't* or that I *did* indulge in recreational drugs. Conveniently, it had been more than 20 years since I had inhaled, so I felt pretty confident about acing that, which I did.

My cubicle in the capacious newsroom at 2 Park Avenue was situated between film critic John Anderson and culture reporter Esther Iverem; both became pals, but all three of us had occasionally difficult personal lives that had to be managed over the phone without benefit of walls or doors. Maintaining a veneer of inattention while one side of a heated conversation went on loudly a few feet away became a necessary skill. Calling for the results (negative) of a routine HIV test was especially uncomfortable.

My job was to write, assign and edit features, album and concert reviews, previews, news, weekend squibs and whatever else came along. While I had a freelance budget for outside writers, I was also expected to use fellow staff. I was told Wayne Robins would be my primary resource in that regard, but he had seniority and standing at the paper and made it clear in an unpleasant lunch right before I started that he had no intention whatever of taking direction from me unless it suited him. Shortly after my arrival, he sought and received a transfer to the paper's food section; despite assurances, I was never allowed to hire a replacement. So, I made do on my own. I was young and single; what quickly became a routine 60 to 80 hours a week of work was exhausting, but I managed.

I started at *Newsday* the first week of June '93. On the Saturday, I woke up calm for the first time in five days. The whiplash of joining a big city newspaper, with its hierarchy of editors and stars (Jimmy Breslin, Liz Smith, Jim Ryan, Murray Kempton, Gail Collins), left me feeling like I'd been dropped into a foreign country where I didn't quite speak the language. I genuinely liked my new boss, Sylviane Gold (coincidentally the big sister of my high school pal Henry Gold), but newsroom dynamics, the Atex copy system, perceived public responsibility, deadline stress, the endless phone calls and frequent meetings were a lot to take on all at once, and those first few days were brutal. I still hadn't written a word but welcomed the chance to unwind and enjoy a pressure-free weekend.

I was brushing my teeth when the phone rang. It was Sylviane, with the news that Conway Twitty — a country legend about whom I knew zilch — had died. She listed three options: ask the city desk to run wire service copy, find a freelancer to whip up an obit or get into the office and do it myself. The wise course was clear, so in I went.

I used some of the wire service stories, read what I could find on Twitty in the reference library and summoned up any stories in the morgue (the newspaper's own archive, which was probably on microfilm — do I need to note that the Internet was not a handy resource in 1993?). With those meager resources in hand, I banged out 550 serviceably uninspired words. (Take that, Wikipedia!) Then I had to contend with the unfamiliar process of submitting an article. I muddled through the primitive technology and the paper's arcane file-naming convention, endured a grilling from the copy desk and went home. The next morning, I had my first byline in the paper.

Death Claims Country Star

Newsday, 6 June 1993

Conway Twitty, the 1950s rock and roll pioneer who went on to become a superstar of country music, died early yesterday morning in a Springfield, Mo., hospital. He was 59.

Twitty, a sentimental balladeer who reached the top of the country music charts more than 40 times in his monumental five-decade career, was returning home to Hendersonville, Tenn., following a matinee performance Friday in Branson, Mo., when he collapsed on his tour bus at a truck stop near Springfield. Twitty was rushed to the Cox Medical Center-South, where he died of complications from surgery after a blood vessel ruptured in his stomach.

Born Harold Lloyd Jenkins in Friar's Point, Miss., and raised in Helena, Ark., the son of a Mississippi River ferry pilot, he began singing and playing guitar on an Arkansas radio station at the age of 10. After high school, he was offered a baseball contract with the Philadelphia Phillies but was drafted into the Army instead. When he returned from two years overseas, he formed a band and dedicated himself to becoming a professional musician.

As the leader of the Rockhousers, Jenkins cut several demo recordings in the mid-'50s for Sun Records, the Memphis label of Elvis Presley, but none were released. While still a struggling young rockabilly singer with a slicked-back pompadour, he adopted a new handle, cobbling together (legend has it) the names of two towns he had visited: Conway, Ark. and Twitty, Texas.

Twitty's efforts as a rocker didn't make any significant commercial impression until he and a bandmate co-wrote and recorded "It's Only Make Believe" in 1958. The song went to number-one and became a million-selling international pop hit. He kept the hits coming, with "Danny Boy" and "Lonely Blue Boy." Like many of his southern contemporaries, Twitty stretched his musical reach into rhythm and blues, recording Muddy Waters' "Got My Mojo Workin'."

In 1960, Twitty became the thinly veiled inspiration for Conrad Birdie, the titular rock and roll star character of the Broadway show *Bye Bye Birdie*. As an actor, he appeared in several teen films, including *College Confidential* (1960) with Steve Allen and Mamie Van Doren.

Although he achieved a stretch of eight Top 40 singles in less than three years, Twitty's success as a recording artist waned after 1961, and he grew away from rock and roll. In 1965 Twitty re-emerged as a straightforward country-western singer, a specialist in heartbreak and regret. Twitty once described his forte as "three-minute soap operas."

Porter Wagoner, another country great whose career began around the same time as Twitty's, told Reuters that Twitty had a genius for picking material. "He had a great ear for great country songs that were commercial."

Beginning with 1968's "Next in Line," Twitty became one of country music's biggest-selling and most reliable hitmakers, scoring with such songs as "I Love You More Today," "That's When She Started to Stop Loving Me" and "Hello Darlin'." In the early 1970s, Twitty teamed with Loretta Lynn to record a string of duets, including "After the Fire Is Gone" (which won a 1971 *Grammy* award) and "Louisiana Woman, Mississippi Man."

Although he remained active on the road — in September 1992 he performed with George Jones at the Westbury Music Fair — Twitty's most recent number one country hit was 1986's "Desperado Love." ◆

I attended and reviewed loads of concerts for the paper. This is what I saw that first *Newsday* summer of 1993. (It's not a memory trick: I have long kept lists of the concerts I attend.) Beyond work obligations, I went to some just for my own amusement. Whether out of duty, curiosity or habit, with free admission just a phone call away, I saw whatever struck my fancy. (The July pileup came during a New Music Seminar convention, but multiple-show nights were not uncommon.) Most of these venues are gone, and so are my specific memories of most of the shows. But I have boxes of pads filled with notes as well as published reviews from some, so all is not lost.

2 June: Suede at Irving Plaza
3 June: Mellow Freakin' Woodies / Foamola at No Bar
8 June: Yanni at the Gershwin Theater (This was the first concert I reviewed for *Newsday*. It was not much fun.)
11 June: Paul McCartney at Giants Stadium
14 June: Pat Benatar at the Grand
15 June: Sloan / Hammerbox at Limelight
16 June: Mellow Freakin' Woodies at No Bar
16 June: Julianna Raye at the Bitter End
17 June: Gutterball at the Grand
17 June: Luscious Jackson / Kramer at Knitting Factory
18 June: Walt Mink at CBGB
18 June: Evertrue at Brownies
20 June: Tish Hinojosa / Los Lobos at Summerstage
20 June: Flaming Lips / Porno for Pyros at Roseland
21 June: Tiger Trap at Under Acme
22 June: Trashcan Sinatras at Limelight
23 June: Reverend Horton Heat / Frank Black - Academy
24 June: God Street Wine at Irving Plaza
25 June: Frank Black / The The at the Paramount
26 June: Bruce Springsteen at Madison Square Garden
28 June: Matthew Sweet at Wetlands

1 July: *Lollapalooza*: Primus, Alice in Chains, Arrested Development, Babes in Toyland, Tool, Fishbone, Front 242, Dinosaur Jr., Rage Against the Machine, Unrest, Vulgar Boatmen, Coctails at St. Louis Riverport
7 July: X and Dillon Fence at the Academy
8 July: Patti Smith reading with TC Boyle in Central Park
9 July: Screaming Trees, Soul Asylum, Spin Doctors at Jones Beach
10 July: Papa's Culture / Ohio Players at Summerstage
11 July: Twanglers, Y'all, Humphreys at 42nd Street Cafe
12 + 13 July: Pete Townshend at the Beacon
14 July: Melissa Ferrick at Sin-e
15 July: The Verve at Angel Orensanz Foundation
16 July: R. Stevie Moore / Half Japanese at Maxwells
20 July: Whitney Houston / Kirk Whalum at Radio City
21 July: Morphine at Ye Olde Tripple Inn
21 July: G Love and Special Sauce, Shootyz Groove, Del tha Funky Homosapien at the Grand
21 July: Magnapop / Juliana Hatfield Three at Irving Plaza
21 July: Madder Rose / Television Personalities at Wetlands
22 July: Melvins at Sheraton New York Presidential Suite

23 July: Jesus Lizard / Nirvana at Roseland
23 July: Moonshake, Yo La Tengo, Pavement at Irving
24 July: Jean-Paul Sartre Experience / Bats at Irving Plaza
24 July: Gigolo Aunts at Brownies
24 July: Melvins at Manhattan Center
28 July: Z100 Radio Festival: Proclaimers, Terence Trent D'Arby, 10,000 Maniacs, Duran Duran, Bon Jovi at Madison Square Garden
30 July: Madder Rose / Barbara Manning / Television Personalities at Maxwells
31 July: Pere Ubu / NRBQ at Central Park Summerstage (missed headliner They Might Be Giants)

3 Aug: Flaming Lips / Stone Temple Pilots / Butthole Surfers at Roseland
5 Aug: Grant Lee Buffalo / Paul Westerberg at Irving Plaza
7 Aug: Kevin Salem / Walter Salas-Humara / Vulgar Boatmen at Maxwells
9 Aug: Walter Salas-Humara / Vulgar Boatmen at Brownies
10 Aug: B.B. King / Buddy Guy / Eric Johnson at the Paramount
11 Aug: Barenaked Ladies at the Bottom Line
14 Aug: Motörhead / Leeway at the Ritz
18 Aug: Matt Keating at Fez
19 Aug: Jennyanykind at CBGB
20 Aug: Neil Young, Blind Melon, Soundgarden at Jones Beach
22 Aug: The Wind at Sun Mountain Cafe
25 Aug: Bay City Rollers / For Love Not Lisa at Limelight
27 Aug: Mekons at the Grand (missed Straitjacket Fits)
29 Aug: Cheap Trick / 38 Special / Bad Company at Sun Tan Lake, NJ

Brooklyn had not yet become a live music hotbed, so most of my nights out were in Manhattan, and I had the expense-account luxury of taking late-night expense-account taxis home to Queens, which became my regular routine. Still, there were plenty of shows that involved schlepping out to Long Island or New Jersey, with time-consuming hauls there and back on trains and buses.

I was on the go a lot in those days. In those pre-Bloomberg days, when cigarette smoking was still allowed inside venues, my pillowcases often reeked from the second-hand smoke that I brought home in my hair and needed to be changed a couple of times a week. I was wise enough to wear earplugs at shows, but I'm sure my hearing did not benefit from so much exposure to loud music, and the tinnitus I've long had no doubt was exacerbated by the experience.

One observation from looking back over the reviews I wrote in those days: my careful (and, I suppose, implicitly accusatory) mention of the ages of veteran performers feels ridiculous now that I am substantially older than most of them. Unlike other forms of music, geriatric rock and roll used to be perceived as an impossibility, if not a source of derisive arrogance. Now that it's commonplace I'm not sure what to think about that.

A Dylan Surprise: It's Positively 47th Street

Bringing it all back home, ascloseasthis. Wednesday night, late show at the Supper Club.

Newsday, 19 November 1993

It began Friday with a radio announcement and hit the newspapers over the weekend. By midnight Sunday, hundreds were camped out on a line leading up to Tower Records at Fourth and Broadway. For the price of a balmy November night spent curled up al fresco in sleeping bags, these devoted Bob Dylan fans — at least the first thousand or so — were rewarded Monday morning with free tickets to Dylan's unexpected four-show engagement Tuesday and Wednesday at midtown's small Supper Club. (Others paid as much as $150 a ticket to scalpers.)

Although Dylan's purpose was to have himself filmed in concert — indeed, the club was fully loaded with cameras, cranes and dolly tracks — the event revived the aura of high excitement his frequent appearances no longer inspire. Excellent but modest-selling albums like the just-released *World Gone Wrong* and nonstop touring have softened the image of this living legend. In recent years, this mysterious recluse has become a wanderer who drops by often enough to seem comfortably, if enigmatically, familiar. But seeing him up close in a 500-capacity room — now *that's* potential rock history in the making.

Reportedly concerned that the performances — not intended as full-fledged concerts — would be overly encumbered by film equipment, the star's camp denied the press access to Tuesday's shows. But Dylan was said to be so pleased with the first two concerts that he relented on Wednesday. Ultimately, the gear wasn't all that intrusive, and it ran like a regular gig, free of interruptions or extraneous business.

The late show began at 11: With simple white lighting and little fanfare, out came Dylan, wearing a white cowboy hat and carrying an acoustic guitar. As his sidemen arranged themselves at their instruments, Dylan removed his hat, squinted at the lights and without a word launched into "Ragged & Dirty," one of the traditional folk songs on his current album. The mix, initially an artificial-sounding mess that exacerbated the constricted nasality of Dylan's singing, was straightened out in time for "Lay Lady Lay," which Dylan rephrased to chop up the recorded version's syrupy flow. His voice required one more number to open up, but after "Tight Connection to My Heart" (from *Empire Burlesque*), which was warmly romantic anyway, he sang an unreleased (at least by Dylan) country blues ("Weeping Willow") with clarity and composure. Sensitively supported by John Jackson (acoustic guitar), Tony Garnier (standup bass), Winston Watson (drums) and Bucky Baxter (slide guitar and pedal steel), an alert, engaged Dylan contributed frequent scrappy guitar solos and one wailing harmonica break.

Besides a full-throttle rendition of "Queen Jane Approximately," a throat-lumpening "Forever Young" and an encore of "I Shall Be Released," the 70-minute program steered wide of Dylan's familiar canon [in favor of such songs as] "Delia" and "Jack-a-Roe" (both from *World Gone Wrong*), "Jim Jones" (from last year's *Good as I Been to You*) and "Ring Them Bells" (from *Oh Mercy*).

While the concept of Dylan performing in this intimate, egalitarian setting upped the emotional ante considerably, seeing this incalculably larger-than-life icon singing just a few yards away gave him a degree of real-world humanity full-size events by artists this famous always prevent. And although he didn't explicitly acknowledge it in any way, Dylan seemed to be getting off on the proximity of the audience as well. But it is emblematic of this cryptic genius's mesmerizing power as an artist that he remains just as inscrutable up close as in our dreams. ◆

Paul McCartney

Ageless pop icon travels the time tunnel with remarkable agility. Friday at Giants Stadium.
Newsday, 14 June 1993

Paul McCartney is a man at peace with his past. *The New World Tour*, which filled Giants Stadium for two-and-a-half hours Friday night, followed the model of his 1989-'90 shows and featured a generous helping of reverently rendered Beatles songs amid selections from his current album and a smattering of everything in-between. The 33-song program included 18 originally done by the Fab Four.

Carrying the weight of the Beatles' legend to fans young enough to barely remember Wings, McCartney willingly answered their desire for some entree to his rock and roll past. He performed the oldies with enthusiasm, respect and remarkable fidelity to the originals.

Abetted by superb state-of-the-art sound, stage lights and projections, the beloved entertainer fielded a sublimely skilled band. Where needed, guitarist Robbie McIntosh replicated George Harrison's solos, while keyboardist Wix Wickens fleshed out arrangements with synthesized horns or strings. Hamish Stuart began on rhythm guitar but spent much of the set playing bass, while McCartney concentrated on guitar and piano. Drummer Blair Cunningham played with modern sophistication but kept it tasteful. It wasn't entirely clear, audibly, what Linda McCartney was doing on keyboards.

Other than a few off-notes — the absence of Ringo's shuffle on "Hey Jude," the addition of clichéd boulevardier accordion to "Michelle" — the oldies were spot-on re-creations. Bob Dylan may rewrite his history every night, but Paul McCartney gives the people what they want.

Rock and roll's most boyish Dorian Gray, who will be 51 this Friday, has always been a crowd-pleasing ham at heart. If the glib Mr. Showbiz patter became mildly irritating, McCartney's genial, relaxed manner was nonetheless infectious. Only the animal-rights imagery in the short film that preceded the band onstage struck a strident chord in an otherwise fine, sweet-natured evening.

The show's first half was a masterpiece of pacing and balance. It began with "Drive My Car," an oddly chosen Beatles artifact that sounded frighteningly like a recording. "Coming Up," a buoyant 1980 solo hit, led into the tuneless but mild anti-vivisection protest "Looking for Changes" from the current *Off the Ground* album.

McCartney's first solo single, 1971's "Another Day," segued into the Beatles' "All My Loving," followed by a slow, ominous version of Wings' "Let Me Roll It." That provided enough momentum to carry the new album's "Peace in the Neighbourhood," a wan vacuum of a song, into the far more engaging title track. "Can't Buy Me Love" rounded the section off in vintage style.

Ten songs in, the band unplugged for a few appropriately acoustic chestnuts, including a nostalgically spine-chilling "We Can Work It Out." But the set ran decidedly hot and cold after that. Playing piano on the sappy "My Love," McCartney drained all the energy away, reclaiming it moments later with a pumping "Lady Madonna." Then "Live and Let Die" exploded with fireworks, flash pots and frenzied lighting effects. When the excitement finally settled after this incongruous, misplaced show-stopper, the quiet solemnity of "Let It Be" was a jarring come-down. With brilliant vocals and that surging bass line, "Paperback Writer" was a memory ticket back to junior high; a text by Trollope projected on huge drop cloths added a handsome visual component.

The show could have ended there, as McCartney's endurance and voice both began fading. "Fixing a Hole," "Penny Lane" (with gruesome synthetic horns) and a plodding "Sgt. Pepper's Lonely Hearts Club Band" that incorporated an endless, pointless guitar jam made for an anti-climactic ending, although McCartney recharged his batteries for the encores. The audience helped him sing "Hey Jude" and everybody went home happy. ◆

Ringo Starr's All-Starr Band

The drummer's gang of greybeards make great use of their memories in a smile-worthy oldies show. Thursday at Radio City Music Hall. Jack Tempchin opened.

Newsday, 17 July 1995

Three decades after he first cocked his head behind a cymbal and flashed that lopsided grin at the world, Ringo Starr has all but legally incorporated the word "lovable" into his name. Few figures in rock have made so many people smile, and not through any great expense of effort: His clowning days are long over. No, the key to Ringo's charm has always been his amused who-me? acceptance of fame and fortune.

If there's an arrogant, imperious side to this man, it was nowhere evident on the stage of Radio City Thursday, as the 55-year-old singing drummer led his third company of oldtimers (average age: 49) through a casually entertaining show that made no pretense to anything but nostalgic entertainment. The summit conference brought together Canadian guitarist Randy Bachman (Guess Who, Bachman-Turner Overdrive), New York keyboardist Felix Cavaliere (Rascals), British bassist John Entwistle (Who), Texas keyboardist Billy Preston and Midwest guitarist Mark Farner (Grand Funk Railroad), who, at 46, is the baby of the bunch.

Joined by Zak Starkey, Ringo's 29-year-old son (who looked like a teenager and turned out to be a great, inventive drummer) and saxophonist-percussionist Mark Rivera, Ringo and the lads ran through their two-hour program with little concern for details. Riddled by some very sloppy singing and a sound mix that repeatedly missed the beginnings of instrumental solos, the set mingled his hits and theirs (three each) in a show that ignored historical incongruities (John Entwistle playing a Grand Funk song??? Ringo drumming on BTO hits???) for good-natured teamwork. The musicians downplayed their individual styles — even the inimitable Entwistle kept his nonchalant bass thunder simple — in favor of a consistent group sound. That made the Beatles' "I Wanna Be Your Man" sound a bit more like the Who's "Boris the Spider" than one might have wanted, especially given the rich backing vocals. (Everyone but Zak sang.)

For all his avuncular charm, Ringo was not the most effervescent ringleader, announcing his songs with a measure of resignation and then singing them with effortless adequacy. Strolling the stage for some, delivering others from behind the drum kit, he trotted out "It Don't Come Easy," "Boys," "Yellow Submarine," "Act Naturally," "Photograph," "With a Little Help From My Friends" and a few others.

Although he and Bachman seemed awfully out of place in this enterprise, the geezer who seemed to be enjoying himself most was Mark Farner. He shook his long hair and blazed away on guitar through "I'm Your Captain / Closer to Home" and "The Loco-motion." Bachman's BTO hits — "Takin' Care of Business" and "You Ain't Seen Nothing Yet" — set the house to rocking, as did Billy Preston's "Will It Go Round in Circles." But it was Felix Cavaliere who took best advantage of all the onstage talent, turning "Groovin'," "People Got to Be Free" and "Good Lovin'" into lengthy, soulful workouts with the musical ambition the set otherwise overlooked. ◆

James Brown: The Godfather of Soul Still Has the Spirit

The soul king visits the realm of the Rockettes. Friday at Radio City Music Hall.

Newsday, 18 April 1994

He may no longer be the hardest-working man in show business, but James Brown, who will be 61 in a matter of weeks, can still lay credible claim to being the Godfather of Soul. Splits or sweat-drenched performances were never the meaning of his music; Brown's uniquely explosive gifts as a live performer only added legend to the real power of his art. More than 40 years since he began pouring it all out, Brown still hasn't lost touch with the universal emotions — overt and subtle testaments to pain, hope and pride — in his songs. Whether chanting

"Make It Funky" or "I Got the Feelin'" or fastening trademark ecstatic shouts to "Hot Pants," Brown still has all the spirit he needs to get his message across.

Friday's long and opulent Radio City show was often dismaying in its pandering to gutless glitz, but also timeless and profound in its dedication to unreconstructed soul music values. The program began with a wretched wedding-band medley of hits by Barbra Streisand, Mariah Carey and Whitney Houston sung by three of the Bittersweets, Brown's female vocal contingent, and a soundless video projection of a TV documentary. In the aftermath of the relentless steamroller of "Get Up Offa That Thing," the incongruity of Dick Clark's smiling face beaming over a formal-dress purebred 16-piece soul show band was dizzying.

Likewise, the eloquent and sensuous performance of "It's a Man's Man's Man's World" included two female dancers, a bass solo, a B.B. King-tribute guitar solo, a Bittersweet rendition of "Stormy Monday" and name checks to a string of dead musicians. But when Brown jumped into "Hot Pants," none of the Vegas trappings mattered one whit. Even an extended zodiac sign digression couldn't diminish the anguished impact of 1958's doo-woppy "Try Me."

The strangely ordered set put the funk up front, followed by a segment of gooey balladry ("Prisoner of Love," "Georgia-Lina" and "If I Ruled the World," which at least gave the lie to popular caricatures of Brown as a tuneless grunter) and some unexciting instrumental showboating. Amidst a return to soul power, "Georgia on My Mind" was inserted between "I Got the Feelin'" and a majestic rendition of "I Got You (I Feel Good)" done up like a USO show, with a stage full of costumed go-go dancers younger than the song itself.

"Please Please Please" began the lengthy wind-down process, as Brown enacted his traditional kneeling, robe-draping "help me!" business and briefly dropped the curtain. Before finally calling it quits, he pumped out a sizzling version of "Get Up (I Feel Like Being a) Sex Machine" and, after a moment of silence for writer and producer Dan Hartman, ended the night with an all-singing, all-dancing blast of "Living in America." No question: James Brown is still Soul Brother Number One. ◆

I was standing a fair distance from the stage at this show, writing notes in my pad, when the tail of a suddenly expanding mosh pit caught me and knocked me to the floor. I wasn't hurt, but I retreated further back for the rest of the set. That was the closest I ever came to a battlefield injury in the line of duty.

Fugazi

Putting out fires with gasoline: sophisticated, principled punk rock at its finest faces a crowd that won't stand still. Saturday at Roseland.

Newsday, 27 September 1993

For most of the world, hardcore punk began, peaked and — finding itself stuck up a stylistic tree — vanished into the clutches of fascist youth and nostalgists more than a decade ago. Yet Fugazi rolls on, keeping the form alive as much by moral virtue as by its music.

Formed in Washington, D.C., in the late '80s, Fugazi has built a huge underground career on thoughtful progressive politics and commendably strict principles. Although popular enough to sell out two nights at Roseland and get its most recent album (*In on the Killtaker*) in the charts, this devoutly independent quartet refuses to cash in or sell out. The self-managed group avoids publicity, releases low-cost records on its own Dischord label and prices concert tickets at $5.

But Fugazi's high-mindedness, which can border on cloying political correctness, becomes futile and more than a little ironic in the realm of crowd control. The group's entirely reasonable opposition to violent moshing leads to the absurdity of trying to regulate the chaotic response its music — a transcendent, supercharged mixture of punk-related idioms unbound by any formal strictures — so effectively induces.

Saturday, before playing a single note, Ian MacKaye — the sterner of Fugazi's two singer-guitarists, who preaches personal responsibility and addresses ill-mannered audience members as "sir" — delivered an admonition against slamming and fighting, recommending the safer up-and-down of the new wave-era pogo instead.

A squall of guitar feedback and a funky beat led into "Exit Only" and, for a minute or so, the mindful crowd moved vertically. But the tendency to Brownian motion is irresistible, and Roseland quickly became a roiling riot of flying bodies. By the time MacKaye had stopped and restarted the second song — "And the Same," a breathtaking assault of jackhammer pop punctuated by Guy Picciotto's slashing guitar bombs — there was no stopping the surging horde.

Or Fugazi. For 90 minutes, reviewing its career in songs like the feminist "Suggestion," "Waiting Room" and "Cassavetes," the group was a wild but tightly bound monster of raging dynamic control: convulsive guitar power locked onto Joe Lally's snaky bass riffs and Brendan Canty's intricate, imaginative drumming. In tapping rock's energy source and focusing it to pinpoint accuracy, Fugazi played a flawless, faith-renewing set of electric music that left the air charged, the crowd spent.

Two fine opening acts made the $5 show an even better value. The Spinanes, a delightful duo from Portland, Ore., with a debut album forthcoming on Sub Pop, showed that a diverse, powerful rock group need not include a bassist. Scott Plouf's drumming and Rebecca Gates' airy pop singing and inventive guitar work fully served the catchy songs, whether delicate mood setters or punk-level rave-ups.

Washington, D.C.'s Unrest completed the bill, showcasing its new album, *Perfect Teeth*. (If Fugazi won't entertain major-label wooing, they evidently don't hold 4AD's Warner Bros. link against Unrest: Picciotto obligingly changed a broken string for singer-guitarist Mark Robinson.) After years of odd stylistic experiments, Unrest has settled into a British-influenced pop sound — composed of brisk, constant strumming, contrapuntal bass lines and angular melodies — that recalls the Smiths and old New Order. Live, Unrest has become engaging and accessible, but the resultant moshing caught the group off guard. "I didn't know we were so rock," remarked bassist Bridget Cross. ◆

Madonna: Small on Pop, Big on Shock

Another dose of lurid sensationalism and, oh yeah, music. Thursday at Madison Square Garden.

Newsday, October 15, 1993

For all the talk about Madonna's assertive sexuality being a beacon of feminist empowerment, her latest concert spectacle, *The Girlie Show*, looked an awful lot like the cheesy bump and grind exploitation of a Las Vegas strip revue.

At Madison Square Garden last night, kicking off a three-show stand, Madonna, her seven-piece band and ten-strong company of dancers and backup singers teasingly simulated sex acts during grandiosely staged songs from last year's Erotica album and other phases of her career.

Music was hardly the prime consideration here; Madonna directed most of her efforts towards attempting to shock (within reasonable, if tasteless, PG-13 limits) her presumably jaded audience. Besides the female dancers who occasionally appeared topless, Madonna and her troupe intimated masturbation, sodomy, fornication and sado-masochism in the same fraudulent manner as has served sex shows for decades. It's all crude, good-natured fun, but hardly a serious pop music concert — and far from family entertainment.

PM Dawn had been announced as the opening act, but the group was an unexplained no-show, and Madonna appeared a little after 9 pm. Typical of the ambitious production, a huge red curtain lifted to reveal a topless dancer sliding down a very tall pole. Madonna entered atop a circular revolving platform that rose up from beneath the stage. Wearing a black mask, hot pants and patent leather platform boots, and brandishing a riding crop, she launched into "Erotica" as if she were performing for a camera crew: Her isolation from the audience was palpable.

"Fever" and "Vogue" maintained the same dispassionate detachment of well-rehearsed production numbers that seemed anything but live.

But then she changed gears, shelved the glitzy staging and sat down with her backup vocalists, Niki Haris and Donna DeLory, to sing "Rain," a lovely, melodic tune. Afterwards, she vanished offstage for a costume change while the company performed an unimpressive umbrella dance. Wearing a platinum frizz wig and colorful bellbottoms, Madonna descended to the stage atop a huge glitter ball as the band played "Express Yourself," which she visualized as a tribute to the disco era.

That led directly into the moving house beats of "Deeper and Deeper." Another modest effort, "In This Life" — a quiet lament about two friends who died of AIDS — worked on a musical level despite obvious and mawkish lyrics. But nothing made sense about "Beast Within," a piece in which dancers acted out military homoeroticism and violence while Madonna's disembodied voice intoned some crypto-religious nonsense.

The two-hour show — which finally ended with a slow encore of "Justify My Love" and a Sly Stone-citing "Everybody" — turned seriously strange with Madonna's waltz-time deconstruction of "Like a Virgin," presented in Marlene Dietrich top-hat-and-tails drag, complete with German accent and a snippet of "Falling in Love Again." Then came the catchy "Bye Bye Baby" (not the Four Seasons song), with a brief bout of spanky-panky. "What excites you?" asked Madonna, "What turns you on?" Judging by the way she keeps upping the ante, one can only imagine what she'll dream up next time. ◆

After this review appeared in the paper, a God-fearing gentleman with a lovely Caribbean accent left a threatening anti-Semitic message on my voice mail.

Whitney Houston

Diva with attitude and intermission. Tuesday at Radio City Music Hall. Angie & Debbie and Kirk Whalum opened.
Newsday, 22 July 1993

Many stars doing battle with the press take the high road, refusing to reply to negative stories or gossip. Some, like Michael Bolton, go on the offensive. But Tuesday evening, opening her five-night stand at Radio City, Whitney Houston took a page from Ross Perot's campaign book and brought her story directly to the public.

Several times during the 90-minute show (two halves with an intermission), Houston conducted spacey, defensive interview sessions with the audience. Occasionally prompted by shouted questions, she announced that she isn't fat, has never taken diet pills (as the *New York Post*, now the subject of a Houston lawsuit, claimed) and had defied skeptics by staying married to Bobby Brown for a year. She vowed that no one would run across the stage or slide down from the balcony (references to bizarre events that took place on previous stops of the tour in Florida and Virginia). She even praised her baby for sleeping through the night.

In between, Houston also sang. As it happened, not very well, at least not as well as one might expect of a singer with a voice as magnificent as hers. Slightly hoarse around the edges, a bit breathless and exerting little effort, Houston sang her hits with only flashes of real artistry. Armed with characteristic octave jumps and melisma, 0-to-60 dynamics and arrangements that finely integrated her four backup singers, Houston ran on auto-pilot most of the time, investing songs with enormous skill but little conviction.

"Saving All My Love for You" and "I Wanna Dance With Somebody" started the set off in low gear; Houston strolled listlessly while she sang, letting the band and the lighting do most of the work. Segueing out of a distastefully glib rendition of Ira Gershwin's "I Loves You, Porgy," she suddenly switched to powerdrive. Houston tore into "And I'm Telling You I'm Not Going," ending the *Dream Girls* song with a showstopping note that was drowned out in cheers.

Clutching a handkerchief (was she thinking Satchmo or Pavarotti?), she finished the segment with "I Have Nothing," giving the song all the overheated energy that frequently passes for great singing in an unsubtle age.

Houston returned for the second portion wearing a garish tutti-frutti bell-bottom pantsuit in place of the first half's white dress and began with "Queen of the Night." After delivering a rousing, defiant version of "All the Man That I Need" personalized with a reference to Bobby, she delivered a windy ramble about the Lord, and then offered her slick pop arrangement of "Jesus Loves Me." "I Will Always Love You" came complete with a sax solo by Kirk Whalum (who also did a fine warm-up set of his own instrumentals) and a spectacular sparkler shower that upstaged the music and turned Houston's vocal coda into a wet anti-climax. To cap things off, Bobby Brown strolled out from the wings after an encore of "I'm Every Woman" and escorted Houston offstage to signify their undying love. Or something. ◆

Janet Jackson

Wholesome, sexy entertainment with a beat and a smile. Friday at Madison Square Garden. Tony Toni Tone opened.
Newsday, 20 December 1993

The litany of production credits ("travel arrangements by...") that rolled on the large video monitors at the end of Janet Jackson's concert Friday was merely the most obvious post-pop hallmark of a live music performance rooted in television values. It's hardly surprising: Jackson was a TV actress well before she was a pop singer, and the ascendance of her music career was first accomplished not via touring but through carefully imaged videos that allowed audiences to "get to know" this wholesome charmer as she grew from idealistic youth to full-blooded woman. Her three most recent albums — 1986's *Control*, 1989's *Rhythm Nation 1814* and the current *janet.* — form a thematic procession from the assertion of virginal selfhood through an idealistic social conscience (and transitional romanticism) to hot, self-assured sexuality, all of which she was careful to embrace in the concert.

Staged like a variety show, with sporting-event video action and a melodramatic sense worthy of the soaps (a crucial difference from Madonna's equally videofied but clinically passionless crotch-grabbing), the slick, ambitious and entertaining spectacular looked like a series of live MTV clips, a modern rearrangement of the musical theatricality that predated the rock era. At the same time, it was built on the same sort of Disneyland fantasy magic and fast-food reliability that have shaped Michael Jackson's presentations. But Janet Jackson is a down-to-earth character: She offers more warmth and personal credibility than her brother's bizarreness and precision invite. (Michael, although nowhere in sight, was a presence at the Garden Friday, and not just as inspiration for lead dancer Tina Landon's uninspired choreography.)

Of course, reality and conviction in this contextual arena are relative concepts. Jackson seemed deeply sincere when she asked the audience to "bow your heads and say a silent prayer for my brother Michael," but the tears she choked back, haltingly trying to finish singing "Again," a bittersweet ballad of irresistible attraction, were strictly for show. The evening reached its pinnacle of believability in the delirious look that swept the face of a young man (presumably not a plant) who had been pulled from the audience and parked onstage in a chair when Ms. Jackson coyly asked if she might sit down.

A substantial part of Jackson's appeal is her seeming goodness, a side somewhat undercut by the crude lasciviousness of songs like "Throb" ("Boom boom boom until noon, noon, noon"). But while innocence is not a state that can be reclaimed in life, any similarity between large-scale pop music and life is strictly coincidental. Onstage, she switched at will between chaste teenager ("Let's Wait Awhile"), lovesick romantic ("Come Back to Me," "Alright"), take-charge woman ("If," "Nasty," "This Time") and sexy babe ("Miss You Much," "That's the Way Love Goes"). At times, Jackson's use of a headset microphone and constant dancing around the stage made it impossible to think of her lyrics as being addressed to anyone; maybe that's the trick to maintaining such a fluid persona.

Jackson performed on a white stage dressed with granite-and-grillwork — a Toontown twist on *Architecture Digest* — accompanied by eight dancers, seven musicians and three backup singers, who handsomely padded out her unremarkable voice. Frequent costume changes occasionally interrupted the two-hour show; video monitors (which doubled as risers for her to sing from) mixed stage action with graphics and footage from her videos.

Performers like Jackson are redefining pop spectacle, taking it miles away from the basic attributes of concertizing. The old ideas of theatricality — sets, costumes, projections — are being replaced by high-concept, integrated audio-visual entertainments. In the process, however, the sense of personal effort, of an artist painting broad musical strokes on a blank canvas under the watchful gaze of fans is being eliminated. Finely tuned, spoon-fed shows like this — perfectly reasonable fun for the whole family — contain no elements of tension or excitement, no risk, no adventure. America's love affair with the empty calories of culture — the familiar, the predictable, the safe — continues. ◆

Chrissie Hynde Coulda Been a Contender

Back on the chain gang. Tuesday at Irving Plaza.

Newsday, 26 May 1994

When Ohio native Chrissie Hynde made the transition from sharp-penned rock critic to sharp-tongued rock star in the late-'70s, she managed to do so without drastically altering her ironic distance from rock's gods and clichés. An easy victor over the music world's gender prejudice, this distinctive, affecting singer and hugely original songwriter carried the unpretentious ethos of punk's do-it-yourself plan up the charts with an air of candid self-consciousness that detached her (if not two death-by-overdose bandmates) from the destructive mythologizing of taking pop fame too seriously. The Pretenders' audience undoubtedly saw Hynde as a rock idol, but she always played the role from the outside, upholding her integrity by retaining a fan's appreciation for the context of rock history.

But time and adversity can erode even the steeliest determination and erase the last glimmers of idealism. As much as today's generation of strong women in rock owe this gutsy trailblazer a debt, Hynde herself now seems out of the loop. This onetime icon and role model has become just another hard-working rock laborer on the road to nowhere, confusing the pose for the spirit. A less-than-convincing assertion of the band's credibility, the titular bravado of *Last of the Independents* (Sire) captures Hynde's unfortunate past-tense position.

Leading a reconstituted Pretenders at the sold-out Irving Plaza Tuesday, Hynde was a journeyman, pushing the new album and playing old hits with little enthusiasm and less conviction. Despite the return of original drummer Martin Chambers, her current sidemen (zipless guitarist Adam Seymour, bored-looking bassist Andy Hobson and keyboardist Zeb Jameson) were woefully out of whack, shortchanging her songs with sloppy, seemingly under-rehearsed playing and an energy level that would have been hard-pressed to power a flashlight.

For her part, Hynde was, at best, diffident: Her vocals and guitar playing were weak, and the lack of juice flowing between her and the band ensured the show's state of enervation. The aimless 90-minute set drew from an eccentric song list that mixed such duly forgotten tracks from past albums as "Downtown (Akron)" and "Bad Boys Get Spanked" with such essentials as "Message of Love" and "Talk of the Town" and a half-dozen selections from the disturbingly ambiguous *Last of the Independents*. It wasn't until the halfway point, when Hynde removed her jacket and responded to a shouted comment [with] "If I'm so hot, why can't I get [laid]?," that the ice broke and the fun began. When the band booted some chord changes in the next number, she quipped, "This is a rock show: Wouldn't you feel cheated if we didn't [fuck] up?"

The venerable "Kid," in which Seymour's careful replication of the recorded guitar parts actually helped, was appreciably stronger and more exciting than anything up to that point. That was followed by a racing, full-bore

"Middle of the Road," complete with a Hynde harmonica break, and "Mystery Achievement," in which Chambers' choppy beat provided tense underpinning for her fluid vocals. Leaving the stage for the first time, Hynde had regained her dignity, if not her currency.

The encores added little to that burst of excitement. The choice of two ballads killed the incipient momentum, though "Precious" and "Brass in Pocket" were credible enough to end the night on a far better note than it began. ◆

Nine Inch Nails

Carefully packaged angst, just the way we like it. Friday at Webster Hall. Marilyn Manson opened.
Newsday, 16 May 1994

For a band that roots its songs in the most helplessly chaotic emotions and fantasies — sado-masochism, anguish, self-loathing, alienation, violence — and presents them via the unremitting, punishing excess of industrial rock, Nine Inch Nails puts on an ironically well-packaged and controlled show. In singer-auteur Trent Reznor's rock and roll theme park, makeup, shredded black costumes from the *Mad Max* lingerie catalogue, an ambitious set, evocative lighting and bales of fog add up to a seamy but safe treat for the *Lollapalooza* generation. (At least Reznor doesn't bring his analyst into it, the way Barbra Streisand does on her current tour.) Thanks to an excellent sound system and Reznor's articulate delivery, debauchery and disgust never sounded so clear.

No one you'd care to know actually expects Reznor to take his horrific world view seriously and flay himself with it onstage night after night, but that is, in essence, the effect that his band attempts to conjure. And Friday at Webster Hall, in an intense but uneven 65-minute spectacle, the enormously popular and unnervingly influential Nine Inch Nails turned in an effective piece of nihilistic rock theater.

A long delay followed the warm-up set by Marilyn Manson, a wretched bunch of boys who looked (and, playing a garbage-disposal variation of Alice Cooper records, sounded) like a sitcom version of a dress-wearing rock nightmare. With the overstuffed club reaching critical population mass, Nine Inch Nails hit the stage, obscured behind a gauze screen, a cloud of fog and a blitz of strobe lights. The curtain soon lifted, but the fog and blinding backlights kept the quintet in ghostly silhouette, or invisible, for much of the show.

As roadies worked overtime to right falling microphone stands, the band ripped into the awesome brutality of "Terrible Lie" and "Sin" (from 1989's *Pretty Hate Machine*), songs whose sonic frenzy still doesn't unravel the catchy, repeated anthem-like choruses designed for easy consumption and retention. Otherwise, the program mainly focused on material from *The Downward Spiral*, vicious things like "Reptile" ("My disease, my infection / I am so impure") and "Closer" ("Let me violate you / Let me desecrate you"). Powered by drummer Chris Vrenna's deft, thundering precision, the diverse, pulsing beats and harsh guitar-keyboards charge sent the young crowd into violent spasms of moshing. If the sound live wasn't quite as claustrophobic as Nine Inch Nails can get on record, it was no less involving an experience.

Ministry and Jim "Foetus" Thirlwell have both made more deeply disturbing use of the soiled-side-of-life thing, but Reznor seems to have cornered the market on McMisery. As offensive as his lyrics (and videos) can be, the music retains a humanity that makes it appealing, even when the emotions and images are revolting. And with covers like "Funky Stuff" and "Get Down Make Love" in the set, one has to admire Reznor's courage and imagination to explore the connection between the chilly antagonism of industrial thrash and the familial spirit of '70s funk. But as the author of songs like "Happiness in Slavery" and "Help Me I Am in Hell," it's obvious on which side of that divide Reznor hangs his hat. ◆

Aerosmith Searches for Its Second Wind

In the prime of their second commercial life, the aging bad boys of rock no longer seem so bad. Saturday at Jones Beach. 4 Non Blondes opened.
Newsday, 7 September 1993

Time cuts two ways for Aerosmith. When the hard-rocking quintet first roared out of Boston in the early '70s, so much of its look, sound and stance was borrowed from the Rolling Stones that no serious consideration of Aerosmith as a truly world-class rock'n'roll band could be entertained.

Despite massive success, Aerosmith was defined by its class roots as a second-generation derivative. By the end of the decade, even that position was untenable: drug-addled and dissipated, the group splintered and collapsed. Aerosmith's youth and time had both run out.

Ironically, as groups like Led Zeppelin and the Rolling Stones also discovered, years of inactivity only fanned the flames of legend. While sitting on the sidelines, Aerosmith grew from has-been joke to top-rank myth. For a new generation of young fans raised on classic-rock radio, the chicken-or-egg aspect of Aerosmith's origins was as irrelevant as the five-year age difference between singer Steven Tyler and Mick Jagger.

Ultimately, an older and healthier Aerosmith decided to get back in the saddle. But while Zeppelin has never returned and the Stones have never really gone away, Aerosmith was able to regroup and relaunch, using its enduring reputation and popularity as the basis for a whole new better-than-ever career. Now geared for the long haul, this moribund legend has become a present-tense cash cow not entirely beholden to history.

But — *time* again — the members of Aerosmith are no longer young upstarts. Opening a two-night stand at Jones Beach on Saturday, the band and its sexy guitar-riff raunch seemed tired and, in rock-spectacle terms, weak. The superhuman stars of ambitious, acrobatic video clips looked very much life-size; worse, their music sounds more exciting on records.

While nothing about the two-hour set was overtly wrong (except the botched chords on "Amazing," a ballad from the current *Get a Grip* album that Tyler announced had never before been performed live), it was a lackluster effort that never rose above adequacy. The sound was muddy, the energy level low. Although Steven Tyler, at 45, remains a potent sex symbol and remarkably athletic performer, his lubricious bump-and-grind routine seemed half-hearted and silly.

Aerosmith is a superlative old-school rock band. Guitar slinger Joe Perry is a skilled sharpshooter whose abiding taste for blues sparked the show's best moments: a 12-bar tune that he sang and the encore medley of Fleetwood Mac's old "Oh Well" and the Yardbirds' "Train Kept a Rollin'."

The rhythm section — drummer Joey Kramer, whose precise enthusiasm almost excused the incursion of a drum solo, and bassist Tom Hamilton — is a subtly powerful unit. Rhythm guitarist Brad Whitford, the band's expendable fifth wheel, and hired hand Thom Gimbel, a keyboard player / backing vocalist who also played some sax, completed the onstage ensemble. But Aerosmith was just going through the motions, without the customary tightness or venom.

The set mixed the catchiest tunes from *Get a Grip* — "Cryin'," "Eat the Rich," "Livin' on the Edge" — with such [past] standards as "Dream On," "Sweet Emotion," "Walk This Way," "Dude (Looks Like a Lady)," "Love in an Elevator" and "Janie's Got a Gun." Embracing both eras of its remarkable comeback, Aerosmith was armed but not especially dangerous. ◆

Iggy Pop

Raw punk power from an indestructible, inimitable legend. Tuesday at the Academy. Cop Shoot Cop opened.
Newsday, 14 October 1993

In the elusive pursuit of true grit in rock and roll, Iggy Pop is one performer who puts his body where his mind is: way past the safety zone, in a fearless realm of rebellion, sex, violence, fun and anger.

Around the time the members of Nirvana were busy being born, Iggy Pop — then fronting the Stooges — was busy inventing the wild style which they, along with countless other bands with a taste for primal truth and searing energy, would later embrace. Images of the muscular singer, dazed and bleeding after some stage misadventure or being carried on the upraised hands of a crowd, are luridly ingrained in the consciousness of every reckless soul who grasped the proto-rock significance of James Dean and Marlon Brando.

Now a lean, muscular 46-year-old, Pop could easily be forgiven if he (like such contemporaries in decadence as Lou Reed and David Bowie) no longer chose to compete in the dirt with his younger, faster and more irresponsible heirs. Since settling down a bit in the late '70s, he has shown a tamer side on his solo records, giving his darker impulses more intellectual than visceral exercise. Even his current *American Caesar* (Virgin) album, while plenty hard-rocking and tough-spoken, doesn't trip any serious chaos detectors.

Tuesday night at the Academy, however, Iggy brought it all back home with an over-the-top punk explosion that not only shamed the competition, it successfully confronted his own legend. Backed by a power trio (guitarist Eric Schermerhorn, bassist Hal Cragin and drummer Larry Mullins) that is fiercer and more effective than any group he's fronted in two decades, Iggy threw himself — literally — into his work, stripping rock (and himself) down to its barest sex-plus-electricity essentials in an unbridled and riveting display.

Pop's hallowed contributions to the punk jukebox — "Raw Power," "Search and Destroy," "I Wanna Be Your Dog," "No Fun," "T.V. Eye." — have been covered to death by bands from the Dictators to the Sex Pistols to the Dead Boys, but Iggy and his sidemen reclaimed them with incendiary pride.

With less historical weight riding on them, later songs like "The Passenger," "China Girl" and "Real Wild Child" received credibly energetic current readings; "Lust for Life," however, was a sluggardly bore that underscored the show's premature peak. Several selections from *American Caesar* slowed the pace and lowered the tension but added diversity to the program; the band's acoustic encore of "Social Life" was an amusing surprise, and "Louie Louie" topped things off royally.

Fluid, fast, precise, original and blisteringly aggressive, Schermerhorn is the guitar player of Iggy's dreams; his solos drew on decades of tradition and sailed magically into the present. Given such solid support, Iggy went to town, diving headlong into the crowd, throwing microphones and guitars, trashing mic stands and pushing monitor cabinets off the stage. Prancing around with carefree abandon and frenzied energy, repeatedly dropping his jeans to perform in nothing but red underpants, the unstoppable Pop acted just like a maladjusted infant on a sugar jag. Now *that's* rock and roll! ◆

Ice Cube

The West Coast's best rapper comes to town and nails it down. Thursday night at the Palladium.
Newsday, 1 November 1993

Dr. Dre may be a more visible alumnus of the N.W.A posse these days, but Ice Cube remains the untouchable giant of South Central hardcore rap. With the release of his new album, *Lethal Injection*, still a few months away, Cube brought the noise to New York, giving old material new shapes in a blistering but brief throwdown.

The show began at midnight with Mad Flava, three enthusiastic rappers totally upstaged by DJ Baby G's virtuoso exhibition of turntable management. Ice Cube appeared well after 1 a.m., using *Jaws* music and a fake-out intro. The stage went dark as a disembodied, official-sounding voice intoned "Ice Cube is not performing tonight," but then the spotlights came up to reveal a bearded, flannel-shirted Cube, his worthy onstage rhyming partner, W.C., and their solid DJ, Crazy Toones.

The Palladium's sound system is geared for the indistinct thunder of house music, not the razor-sharp enunciation of rap, so the masterful delivery of Cube's rhymes didn't come across word for word. But even the crashingly loud bass-and-drums beats being spun couldn't obscure the verbal thrust in the pair's hard-hitting rhythmic dexterity.

Stepping around the stage and trading their lines with intense force, Cube and W.C. demonstrated the aggressive strength of West Coast style without resorting to posturing or clichés other than one incongruous throw-your-hands-in-the-you-know-what interlude.

Although Ice Cube has broken stylistic ranks on record with such peaceful, low-key variations as "It Was a Good Day," his live show was strictly hardcore — relentless and pressurized — but didn't concentrate on the tough-guy gangsta stance that shapes many of his lyrics. Possibly as a result, the event's atmosphere remained static-free fun, a case of hero worship that never threatened to convert violent imagery to real life.

Recorded versions of songs — from Cube's most recent album, *The Predator* (Priority), as well as the old N.W.A catalog — went out the window as he and his teammates improvised and took creative liberties, using a different (actually better: more melodic and horn-driven) track on the murderous "Now I Gotta Wet Cha" and chopping together the first verses of N.W.A's "Straight Outta Compton" and its vinyl neighbor, "— tha Police" without pause. He turned two separate songs out of lines from "The N***a Ya Love to Hate," including one that began with a Cube-led audience cheer cursing him out.

The 40-minute set rocked in high gear almost to the end, when the momentum dipped with a pointless speech and a flagging finale of "Check Yo Self." Bringing the otherwise unstinting show to an abrupt finish, it was a weak way to go out, letting a power vacuum fill the vast room. ◆

Neil Young

An inspiring display of musical grit by rock's last iconoclast, backed by Booker T. and the MG's. Friday at Jones Beach Theater. Blind Melon and Soundgarden opened.

Newsday, 23 August 1993

Year after year, while most of his contemporaries have succumbed to laziness, repetition, fear, artistic bankruptcy or crude pandering, Neil Young remains the only middle-aged rock and roller with faith in the magic of the music. Whereas Bob Dylan's erratic remoteness and self-revisionism can often make his performances seem like the work of an impatient impostor unaware of the songs and the history, Young's enigmatic achievement is to reinvigorate selections from his vast catalog, balancing obligations to the past and the present with ease. An expressive singer and guitarist who still has a lot to say, Young can lose himself inside the emotions of an old, familiar song while still finding new ways to shape and color it.

This tour, in the wake of last year's poorly received solo acoustic outing, isn't quite a return to 1991's wanton noisefest, in which Young taught tourmates Sonic Youth a few lessons about splitting the atom with electric guitars. Rather than Crazy Horse, whose raw enthusiasm aroused Young's loudest, wildest impulses, his current backing band is Booker T. and the MG's, the peerless Memphis institution whose singular forte is electric soul played with subtle precision.

Given Young's predilection for abrupt stylistic shifts, this pairing might have signaled a sudden turn toward the Stax Records sound (and, indeed, Otis Redding's "Dock of the Bay" appeared as a delightful encore). Instead, Young pulled the innately restrained veterans as far as they could go toward his folk-to-freakout continuum. On "Southern Man," Booker T. Jones balanced the song's ire with handsome organ fills; during "Like a Hurricane," Steve Cropper intertwined flaming guitar solos with Young while bassist Duck Dunn and, drumming in place of the late Al Jackson, Jim Keltner kept the song from spinning out of control with a rock-solid beat.

When Young sat down at the piano for a plaintive "Helpless" and "Only Love Can Break Your Heart," the MG's' delicate shadings became almost subliminal. The finely arranged acoustic versions of "Harvest Moon" and "Unknown Legend" would have been beyond the capacity of a less sublime band. But when Young uncorked his firepower on "Rockin' in the Free World" and "Love to Burn," delivering hair-raising solos that screamed with imagination and energy, the MG's couldn't quite keep up.

Near the end of a skin-tingling rendition of Bob Dylan's "All Along the Watchtower" that ended the set, Young locked into a groove and began chanting the song's penultimate line, "Two riders were approaching," over and over, like a Van Morrison mantra. It was an extraordinary rock moment, fraught with mounting excitement. Young would not yield to the song's inevitable coda — "and the wind began to howl" — until he had finished some howling of his own. Wrestling with his guitar as if it were a flailing fish strapped to his chest, he hacked out a squealing, moaning solo laden with anguish and emotion. For a 47-year-old punk whose commercial appeal rests largely on ancient acoustic ballads, finding an utterly original path that led somewhere in a well-trod field was a triumph of true musical grit.

Hopelessly mismatched but not lucky enough to have been rained out, amateurish frat band Blind Melon (who, inexplicably, have a Top 10 album) and all-but-forgotten Seattle grunge pioneers Soundgarden did their opening sets in a heavy downpour. For all its heavy metal thunder, Soundgarden was upstaged by a bolt of lightning. ◆

Bruce Springsteen

Populist endurance contest for charity. Saturday night at Madison Square Garden.
Newsday, 28 June 1993

A concert to raise money for cancer research in memory of a 21-year-old friend could potentially be a grim, maudlin affair, but with Bruce Springsteen in command, it was anything but.

Donating the tour-ending show to the Kristen Ann Carr Fund, a foundation established after the death in January of his co-manager's daughter, Springsteen spoke movingly of the loss yet held the audience aloft with his music. If the gig was far from perfect, technically, nothing that went wrong seemed to bother the star at all. He remained ebullient and positive throughout, even when his fans booed occasional guest vocalist Terence Trent D'Arby. Springsteen hugged the singer, and that was that.

Songs like "Souls of the Departed," "Atlantic City" and "If I Should Fall Behind" took on new spiritual dimensions in this context. Jimmy Cliff's "Many Rivers to Cross" added further emotional resonance, as did the gospelly numbers that opened and closed the show.

The automobile, Springsteen's essential lyrical conveyance, provided a fair metaphor for the concert's strengths and weaknesses. He no longer relies on the showy but nonfunctional fins and hubcaps that once passed for conviction in his rock'n'roll act. Rather than overstate every gesture and stage gimmick, Springsteen now gears his manner to the downscaled music.

Early on, strumming an acoustic guitar, his voice clenched and twangy, he made "Darkness at the Edge of Town," "Mansion on the Hill" and "This Hard Land" the night's most powerful and affecting songs. Ironically, Springsteen's years as a rock'n'roller have made him a riveting solo artist, capable of dominating a huge hall all by himself.

The '90s-model Springsteen is a fuel-efficient family car, built for real-world needs, not some small-town fantasy of glitz. The sweeping bombast of oldies like "Born to Run" and "Badlands" seemed almost out of place — too big, too flashy. Springsteen almost acknowledged as much when he botched his unaccompanied version of the equally dated "Blinded by the Light" and joked about it. "Hey, help me out here," he yelled to the crowd. When he shared a mic with his wife Patti Scialfa on "Brilliant Disguise" their intimacy was nearly erotic.

However, the punishing length of the performance (more than three hours of music) harks back to the boat-sized cruisers of America's bigger-is-better myth. Near the end of the second half, during an infectiously boppy duet of "Jole Blon" with D'Arby, Springsteen's voice gave out. He limped gamely through an interminable version of his trivial Joan Jett soundtrack song, "Light of Day," and then left the stage.

With more than a few obligatory standards still to go (he never did get to "Born in the USA," "Dancing in the Dark" or "Hungry Heart"), Springsteen came back and continued the downward spiral with the encores. After a tuneless rendition of "Jumpin' Jack Flash" exacerbated by D'Arby's shrill vocal theatrics, he totally lost the melody on an excruciating "If I Should Fall Behind."

On "Born to Run," Springsteen had to search for alternate notes to the ones he could no longer hit. But he started getting some juice back in "Glory Days," squandering it on the night's second John Fogerty composition, "Rockin' All Over the World." After several false finishes, he fell backwards in slow motion, holding on to the mic stand. But he still wasn't through. Maybe it was because a long tour was finally ending and he wasn't ready to go home.

Amazingly, Springsteen was in full command and reasonable voice for the unfamiliar finale, a slow, swaying exhortation to "follow that dream." It was a graceful coda to a heartfelt show. ◆

Soul Asylum

Monday night at Tramps. Cellophane opened.

Newsday, 8 March 1995

It's hard to think of many bands that wouldn't be sorely upstaged by Bruce Springsteen. Dave Pirner allowed as much after the Boss paid a return call to Tramps Monday to join Soul Asylum for an entertainingly sloppy swipe at "Tracks of My Tears": "It's all downhill from here, ladies and gentlemen," quipped the dreadlocked singer-guitarist with typical self-deprecation.

In fact, the show — a casual semi-publicized club date slotted in while the Minneapolis post-punks spend time in New York mixing the follow-up to their platinum *Grave Dancers Union* album — only got better from there. Springsteen's designated hitter appearance might have added a few extra runs in the game, but the team was already on its way to an easy rout.

It hasn't been that long since Soul Asylum's career ascended to a point where playing clubs became a luxury, not a necessity, and the small stage fit the quintet like an old plaid shirt. If anyone expected the 15-year core of Pirner, guitarist Dan Murphy and bassist Karl Mueller — joined by hard-hitting new drummer Sterling Campbell (making his public debut with the band) and keyboardist Joey Huffman — to have forgotten its hard-traveling past since hitting the bigtime, such fears were quickly put to rest. Sure, the idea of Bruce Springsteen even knowing of Soul Asylum would have been inconceivable when the band was making monumental indie-label records like *Made to Be Broken*, and Pirner's movie star girlfriend, Winona Ryder, might have been waiting in the wings. If the first steps were a bit tentative, the quintet accelerated through the 70-minute set toward the ragged glory of all-out feedback rave-ups.

Other than a few covers, and "New World" and "Homesick" from 1992's *Grave Dancers Union*, all of the songs were new, but the band rose to the challenge and so did the audience, which raised no vocal objection to the absence of old favorites. (Or to Pirner's trumpet solo!) If he sounded a bit rigid for this loose-limbed band, Campbell held his own in the hot seat.

It would be absurd to hazard a guess about the qualities of the forthcoming album based on this gig, but the collection of songs premiered included some doozies. With Murphy and Pirner doing the joint lead vocals that were an early trademark of the group, the Tom Petty-ish "Bittersweetheart" sent the Top 40 commercialism meter into the red. "Just Like Anyone," however, followed the old Soul Asylum rock-rave mold and ended in howls of Murphy feedback. "I Did My Best," a finely wrought heartland ballad, sounded a lot like the Band's "The Weight," while "Crawl" contrasted mild-mannered verses with a barbed-wire blues chorus. "Eyes of a Child" was a wrenching folk-rocker about an adolescent hooker; the Dylanesque "Misery" put a memorably plaintive melody to lyrics about suicide; "String of Pearls" brought all of Pirner's storytelling skills to bear on a hallucinatory narrative in which Siamese twins grow up to be the first President with two heads.

Stardom has trapped Soul Asylum for the moment between its long-exercised creative will and a new audience hungry for another "Runaway Train." Judging by the divergently aimed raw material presented Monday night, the group is not unlike that fictional head of state: solidly of two minds. ◆

Having seen SA many times and hung out with them a bit in their pre-"Train" days, I was absolutely delighted to reconnect with Dave and Danny in 2018 when old pal Peter Jesperson asked me to write liner notes for a reissue of the 1986 cassette-only *Time's Incinerator.* They couldn't have been nicer, and I really enjoyed the opportunity to catch up with two musicians I greatly admire who had gone their separate ways. I submitted the liners and did some requested rewriting. It was going great until Pirner put the kibosh on the entire project, and that was that.

Technically, this wasn't a concert review but a critic's-notebook-type musing thing. But if it walks like a duck...

Eric Clapton: Time for the Cream to Rise Again

Newsday, 12 October 1994

The T-shirts and posters being sold from Madison Square Garden's concession stands this weekend depicted the grizzled, wire-rimmed visage of Eric Clapton, who was holding forth inside, playing his first all-blues tour. No thanks. What should have been on offer was the image of the man's hands doing what nature intended: making magic on a guitar. Because that was what people came to see, what they expected, what they responded to. Like a stupendous schnoz, Clapton's lead playing is an inescapable fact, an attention-grabbing attribute that makes it all but impossible to see him as a complete artist.

For more than 20 years, Clapton has musically been wearing the proverbial baggy sweater, giving his singing and his songwriting a chance to be appreciated. His success in that effort has built up an insatiable desire among fans to see him get naked onstage and play solos — which is what made him a demi-god in the first place — until the milk cows come home. With an album, *From the Cradle*, and this tour, Clapton has reimmersed himself in the music that provides him with the perfect framework for those unique lyrical inventions on a guitar string.

Essentially, this is a return to where he was — playing American 12-bar blues the British way in John Mayall's Blues Breakers — nearly 30 years ago. But that wasn't good enough then, and it isn't good enough now. At the Garden Monday, between blistering evocations of Freddie King and other legends of the blues, he tucked in a stomping rendition of Albert King's dispirited "Born Under a Bad Sign" and a duff version of Robert Johnson's elemental "Crossroads" that bent over backwards not to resemble in any way the version Cream used to play.

That got me thinking. In the minds of many of us old enough to have seen the British power trio, Cream remains the creative pinnacle of Clapton's career. In the pre-*Woodstock* '60s, Clapton, bassist-singer Jack Bruce and drummer Ginger Baker adopted the blues as their source material and improvisatory jazz as their technique. Huge amps and incredible amounts of overplaying produced protracted workouts on songs like Willie Dixon's "Spoonful" that managed to be virile artistic statements, not time-wasting displays of flashy technique.

Bruce, who had a better voice and more stage personality than the saturnine guitarist, did most of the singing. (To this day, Clapton sings with the diffidence of an amateur who has just been pushed on stage after a lengthy pep talk.) The band's songwriting was all over the place, from the barre-chord pop contrivance of "Sunshine of Your Love" to the arty pretensions of "White Room" to the crazed psychedelia of "Tales of Brave Ulysses." It was only when Cream turned to the blues power of old masters that all three men concentrated on their individual instruments (Bruce's advance of bass guitar's role in rock was revolutionary), and Clapton's glory found its most conducive vessel.

Back in the here and now, Clapton's tour through his museum of the blues consists of carefully rehearsed numbers culled from his vast knowledge of the genre. But for all his sincerity and reverence, the old songs aren't the point. I have no quarrel with the favorable reviews, but it was obvious that the structured role of his sidemen — play the parts, don't get in the way — left Clapton his designated solo space (never more than two verses at a blow) and nothing more. What he needs more than anything is to be part of a team that could start from there and proceed into uncharted ground, to rewrite the rules rather than accede to them. What he needs is...Cream.

The idea of reforming Cream isn't so outlandish: All three members are alive, active and able, something no other defunct '60s legend can claim. Baker's excellent new trio album, *Going Back Home* (Atlantic), is effectively Cream reconfigured as a jazz group. Countless bands of far less merit or historic stature have reunited. And with Clapton finally acknowledging his desire to do what his fans have long begged him to do, it would seem the last barrier has been erased. "Lay Down Sally" or "Crossroads"? The choice is clear. ◆

Salt-n-Pepa Shake It Up

The triumph of vulgarity. Can you spell c-o-n-c-u-p-i-s-c-e-n-c-e? Friday early show at Radio City Music Hall.
Newsday, 30 May 1994

Salt-n-Pepa don't just talk about sex. They rap it, sing it, dance it and mime it, wading into feminist issues of sexual politics with all the unguarded honesty, subtlety and dignity of their skin-tight cut-offs.

Mixed signals have rarely been meted out to better beats. Pop stars may be good role models, but few make enough consistent sense for social advisers: Delivered over canned music tracks, with moderate vocal skills, endless behind-wagging and occasional crotch-grabbing, the multi-platinum trio's spirited message of female empowerment ran from desire ("Whatta Man," "Push It," "Groove Me") through defiance ("Independent") and straight on to disdain. Several songs on the group's current *Very Necessary* album have harsh words for women and men alike; at one point in Friday's early show, Pepa pretended to whip several kneeling male dancers for the multitudinous sins of their gender, including her labor pains. Confusing matters further, during the deliriously horny "Shoop" finale, the three single mothers showed off their babies.

Joined by nine singers and five dancers, Salt (Cheryl James), Pepa (Sandy Denton) and DJ-rapper Spinderella (Dee Dee Roper) presented a compact hour as slick and athletic as any Vegas routine. In that context, on some level, the inversion of sexual dominance made a valuable and valid point. But the group's inclusive sex appeal — contrary to any explicit derogation of men in the show — works both ways. Women may cheer their notion of assertive female sexuality, but men probably don't have much of a problem with that, either. This kind of empowerment isn't that far from a night at Chippendales.

As pop rappers, Salt-n-Pepa are merely adequate, but their records have always demonstrated creativity in using varied musical settings. The show's selection of hits (including "Tramp," the old-school "My Mic Sounds Nice," "I'll Take Your Man" and a short but hard-hitting, bass-pumping "Let's Talk About Sex") touched on reggae, various realms of rap and soul; a gospellish performance by one female backup singer highlighted the God-praising "Heaven or Hell." But it wasn't enough to make a serious musical impression.

If Salt-n-Pepa equivocated, R. Kelly — who, as support act, did a longer, more ambitiously produced show than the headliners — made no bones about his purpose. Swoony soul ballads (the monster hit "Bump n' Grind," "Sex Me") and bouncy new jack danceables ("I Like the Crotch on You") alike, song after obnoxious song was, in no uncertain terms, obsessively concerned with his manly needs and desires. The only exception, which singly made Kelly's unironic presentation a campy exercise in conceptual absurdity, was "Sadie," an endless mother-love song (complete with ample praise for Jesus) so overbearingly sentimental it would have made Al Jolson weep. Kelly is a fine singer with catchy melodies and an impressive sense of theatrics, but any artistic credibility he mounted was rendered utterly laughable when he exited with a valedictory drop of the trousers. Classy stuff. ◆

Capital Night Opens Barbra Streisand's U.S. Tour

Tuesday evening at USAir Arena, Landover, Md.

Newsday, 12 May 1994

The carpets were gray. The mood was electric. Outside the USAir Arena, stretch limos swept through the parking lot. Barbra Streisand had chosen to begin her long-awaited American tour in the nation's capital, and the president was wise not to attend this opening. The night belonged to her.

Partly formulated as a self-congratulatory "This Is My Life" theater piece, the show began at 8:30 pm, as Marvin Hamlisch led the orchestra — seated behind an aristocratic white set sumptuously appointed with curtains, furniture and tall windows — through a lush, concise overture. Then the great woman herself appeared, glamorous in a glittering floor-length gown. Streisand's first challenge was to bring the reality of a mortal, tangible concert in sync with the absurdly high expectations her decades-long absence from touring has engendered. Feigning surprise at the response, she said "Wait! I haven't done anything yet."

Singing with confidence and strength, she began with several show tunes, including "Don't Rain on My Parade" from *Funny Girl*. In one of several long, stiffly delivered asides to the audience, Streisand talked about the reasons for the tour, her 1963 and 1993 presidential performances in Washington and what she called 30 years of criticism by the press. All of that was by way of introducing "I'm Still Here." Using her big voice to fill the 18,000-seat hall, Streisand still looked vulnerable and alone on the vast stage. It made a big difference when the backdrop was lifted away and she belted out a show-stopping rendition of "People" with plenty of people in plain sight behind her.

Throughout the first half of the show, the songs — a blend of classic show and film tunes, her hits and some new material — had to compete with Streisand's scripted patter and such bizarre theatrical business as singing to a video projection of Marlon Brando in the film of *Guys and Dolls* and sharing her romantic bewilderment with the disembodied voice of a therapist. But those incidental distractions added to the event's heightened sense of theater. And when she commenced to singing, Streisand demonstrated the skill and creative mettle to plumb the emotional depth and meaning in songs written to convey their messages more literally.

The second half alternated between unabashed sentimentality ("Nothing's Going to Harm You," a song for her son; "Ordinary Miracles," a call for grassroots social action) and partisan politics. Wearing a white suit and performing on a stripped-down stage set with two large columns and a few chairs, Streisand made repeated reference to Washington, D.C., and its local obsessions. At one point she even took a Democrat/Republican voice vote from the audience and seemed a bit nonplussed at the response, which wasn't entirely lopsided. Her attempts at topical stand-up comedy-cum-D.C.-roast were awful, and a pro-Clinton video montage that accompanied a slow, jazzy version of "Happy Days Are Here Again" was forced and conspicuous.

Nonetheless, her performances of songs like "Evergreen," "My Man" and "Somewhere" were everything the faithful paid big bucks ($50 to $350) for. Although by no means an overpowering musical experience, the show more or less lived up to its billing. It was a classy, traditional and richly turned-out showcase by and for one of America's best-loved singers. ◆

Frank Sinatra

Yet one more for the road. Tuesday at Radio City Music Hall. Don Rickles and the Count Basie Orchestra opened.
Newsday, 21 April 1994

Whiskey tumbler in hand, Frank Sinatra offered a toast to a packed, star-studded Radio City Music Hall Tuesday. "I hope you live to be 765 years old, and that the last voice you hear is mine."

Given the erosion of that fabled instrument already evident at 78, Sinatra's stubborn determination to be the last saloon singer standing after his peers have all thrown in the towel is an unwise and quixotic mistake. It in no way diminishes the greatness of the first 50 years of his career to suggest that the man on that stage — the same one from which he was unceremoniously hooked at the *Grammy Awards* in March — was not Francis Albert Sinatra, Crooner of the Western World.

The silver-haired legend's charisma was certainly there, and Frank Sinatra Jr. (doing yeoman work in what must be a nerve-wracking and possibly heartbreaking job) led the orchestra in sumptuous, subtle arrangements of 16 pop standards, including "You Make Me Feel So Young" and "Come Rain or Come Shine." And the star did make a good, relatively lucid effort in the hour-long show, getting through most of the tunes without dropping or fudging many lyrics.

But his voice was stiff and increasingly raspy, with burrs on the quiet notes and holes in the big ones. His pitch was neither sure nor steady. At this stage of the game, it requires willful suspension of reality to consider a Sinatra concert as a musical experience; it's more like observing the fine upholstery in a car wreck or cheering the courage of an injured athlete being carried off the field.

Audiences have become ruthless in their determination to witness their fantasies in the flesh, hence the endless appetite for tours by aging veterans and reunited groups. But, as Pearl Jam singer Eddie Vedder mused the other night, his fans would probably be happy if he stood there and cursed rather than actually took the trouble to sing. It hardly flatters an artist to be revered regardless of performance content.

Even sneaking glances at TelePrompTers, Sinatra occasionally fell behind and had to rush into lines, giving his already distinctive phrasing an odd syncopation. Although he rose to the song's brassy melody, "The Lady Is a Tramp" was choppy going with some missed words; his inflexible delivery put an anxious tinge to an eloquently gentle arrangement of the Gershwins' "Embraceable You." When he really reached into a song's heart — as on "What Now My Love," Stevie Wonder's "For Once in My Life" and a tender ode that he sang to his wife, seated down front — such struggles worked to his advantage. But most of the material suffered from his uncertain delivery. It was painful and sad to see him stumble through the end of "One for My Baby" and totally lose his place in "My Way," "Mack the Knife" and "New York, New York."

Unlike musicians who compose songs, interpretive singers must make their artistic statements through the nuances of imagination and pinpoint control in delivery. In his prime, Sinatra expressed the jaunty joys of youth, the bittersweet lessons of adulthood and the prideful spirit of individualism. And while Sinatra obviously has a worshipful following that delights in seeing him, the man lighting up the Radio City stage this week can only deduct from that artistic legacy. ◆

This one earned me a personal thank you and a compliment from the artist when I was introduced to him a few weeks later at some press event. Cool, humble, friendly, generous — what a guy!

Tony Bennett

Tender is the night for Astoria's favorite son. Saturday at Radio City Music Hall.
Newsday, 3 October 1994

It doesn't get much better than this. No TelePrompTers. No orchestra. No props. No novelty numbers. No fancy lighting. No guest stars. At one point, no amplification. All it took to make musical magic Saturday was Tony Bennett, the Ralph Sharon Trio and two dozen enduring examples of American songcraft.

After more than four full decades in the business, the 68-year-old crooner is supposed to be having a renaissance among young people. But even with MTV's imprimatur — an *Unplugged* special in June, with guests shots by kd lang and Elvis Costello, that yielded Bennett's latest album — Radio City Musical Hall was devoid of adolescents. The only relevant mention was a thin joke about being the "Madonna of my day — and I didn't even have to take my clothes off."

Bennett gives real meaning to the words living legend. His taste in tunes, his economical delivery, his musical values (and probably his stage patter) have hardly changed since recording "I Left My Heart in San Francisco" in 1962. Radiating warmth and sincerity through the creations of Johnny Mercer, Irving Berlin, George and Ira Gershwin, Jerome Kern, Johnny Mandel and others, Bennett projected the ease of a seasoned pro and the enthusiasm of a newcomer. If his voice was noticeably rough around the edges, it didn't diminish the joy of hearing a truly distinctive artist in perfect alignment with his material. And the incomparable Sharon anticipated Bennett's every nuance on piano, playing with all the energy or delicacy required.

After heartfelt readings of such romantic standards as "Old Devil Moon," "It Had to Be You," "Just in Time" and Hank Williams' "Cold, Cold Heart," Bennett applied himself with no diminution of affection to his signature tune, then praised the concert hall and requested that all the microphones be turned off. Once the audience settled into silence, the pure sound of Bennett's unamplified voice singing "Stranger in Paradise" floated out like an echo of Caruso, a more profoundly nostalgic suggestion of pop's distant past than any old song could possibly convey.

Taking a cue from his 1993 *Steppin' Out* album, Bennett made the 95-minute program's centerpiece a collection of songs associated with Fred Astaire. The otherwise stationary star pirouetted and promenaded through "Steppin' Out With My Baby," encouraged an audience snap-along to begin "A Foggy Day," kept his dignity through the corny geography of "You're All the World to Me" and finished off with a lovely "Who Cares?"

Bennett also paid tribute to Duke Ellington. "I'm a Lucky So-and-So" sparked the show's only ad lib ("If you ask me the amount / In my bank account / I'm slipping / Just ask Clinton") and a solo by bassist Doug Richeson; that segued into "It Don't Mean a Thing If It Ain't Got That Swing" and a showcase for drummer Clayton Cameron, who moved from behind his kit to demonstrate his fancy brushwork on a separate snare. When he finally finished, Cameron flipped the brushes over his shoulder and accidentally hit the boss, watching from a few feet away.

In a perfect finale spoiled by the addition of one more number, Bennett tenderly caressed "I'll Be Seeing You." With luck, this peerless singer and his fans will be seeing each other for many years to come. ◆

While I certainly shared the consensus critical opinion about Michael Bolton, I did give him a full and fair hearing before laying into him. It was a nice night for an outdoor show, and even his grotesque bludgeonings of soul music were an improvement after Celine Dion. My notes from the show are severe ("totally over the top rock bombast... kills song with smothering oversinging ... right gospel, wrong church"); I put my initial reactions in more measured form before sharing them with readers.

After the show, Columbia Records PR executive (and onetime *Trouser Press* intern) Fran DeFeo introduced us, and I got to hear his resentment of my ilk in person. Basically, his complaint about the press — the same vilifying illogic later wielded by Donald Trump — was that he'd read inaccuracies about himself and amateurish pieces by incompetent hacks, and that invalidated all critical media of him for all time. That syllogism — dismissing a practice by singling out a handful of its inept practitioners — turns bad apple logic on its head and is both unsupportable and hard to disprove. I voiced my disagreement with his perception, but it was clear we weren't going to settle anything there and then.

Still, he seemed like a decent sort of fellow, and serious enough that he might be up for a civil debate on the subject. I suggested he discuss his grievances with a self-appointed representative of his tormentors, a sitdown for an article to run in *Newsday*. They were open to the idea, but it never happened. Maybe he didn't appreciate this review.

Michael Bolton

Pouring it all out — and then some. Saturday evening at Jones Beach Theater. Celine Dion opened.
Newsday, 6 August 1994

By comic book convention, the acquisition of a super power requires a period of calamitous misjudgments while the hero learns to control it. Michael Bolton's gift is, of course, his formidable, larger-than-life voice — a virile, leonine roar in its middle register and a soaring falsetto on top (with a shredded horror in between). He's had plenty of time to tame it. But while Saturday's concert gave encouraging indications that the singer is finally reining in some of his excesses, Bolton ultimately reverted to heavy-handed love thug, repeatedly sacrificing emotional subtlety to steaming bombast.

Too often like his delivery, Bolton's romantic material deals with ultimates and absolutes. You "ain't got nothing if you ain't got love," he vowed in the song of the same name. "I'd rather be alone than be in love just half the way," he sang in "Completely." And in "Said I Loved You...but I Lied," he went even further: "This is more than love I feel inside."

The 95-minute show, which paused halfway for a wretched 10-minute instrumental interlude, had smart arrangements, great sound and excellent lights, but strung a confusing artistic message between soapy ballads like "Completely" and flashy rockers like the Bon Jovi-esque "How Can We Be Lovers."

In a quick speech, Bolton asserted his right to cover classics, and he did all right by "(Sittin' On) The Dock of the Bay" and the Bee Gees' "To Love Somebody." But he mistook the yearning of the Four Tops' "Reach Out I'll Be There" for desperation, and during a cloddish rendition of Percy Sledge's "When a Man Loves a Woman," grabbed a guitar for a wrongheaded rock solo. On a singing romp to the rear of the orchestra, he poured flaming passion all over "Georgia on My Mind" and incinerated the song's gentle nostalgia. Bolton's attempts to conjure up the ecstasies of soul music's church roots, while evidently sincere, fell far short.

Sixteen unintroduced people of color appeared onstage to sway and clap to the appealing "Time, Love and Tenderness" and the rousing finale, Bill Withers' "Lean on Me"; with no visible microphones near them, it was impossible to tell if they were contributing to the choir sound being produced by Bolton and his three regular female backup singers.

In an odd coincidence, the Isley Brothers — who recently won a lawsuit claiming that a song Bolton co-wrote infringed on a copyright of theirs — played in Manhattan over the weekend. At Saturday's show, Bolton sang the contested "Love Is a Wonderful Thing" without comment but later offered an unfunny comic set piece in which he initially claimed authorship of the opera *Pagliacci*. If there was a point being made, it was not taken. ◆

There are few bands I've hated as long and hard as the Grateful Dead. When confronted with the professional duty to finally face them live — and write about it — I asked my good friend Richard Gehr, a brilliant writer versant in experimental, progressive and world music (as well as a serious Dead and Phish fan) to accompany me and present a better informed (and more positive) side to the review. He agreed.

The Dead were awful in ways I never imagined, but I finally had my retort to people who for years had insisted "you have to see them to understand." (I didn't partake of the other routine Rx for appreciation, at least not intentionally.)

The Grateful Dead

One venerable band, one worshipful audience, two opposing critics. Friday at Madison Square Garden.

By Ira Robbins and Richard Gehr

Newsday, 20 September 1993

As has been observed often of the vast and enduring cult that follows the Grateful Dead, loving San Francisco's 27-year-old institution is not so much a matter of musical taste as an issue of faith. Some embrace the tie-dyed lifestyle; others can't get with the program on any level whatsoever. Why? What is it that makes a Grateful Dead concert — a sacred rite to so many — such a vast yawn to others? In the hopes of presenting a balanced perspective on this emotionally loaded topic, two critics — one an unabashed Dead fan, the other a skeptical neophyte — brought their longstanding difference of opinion and a couple of notebooks to Friday night's show.

Richard: I had a good time, Ira. How about you? The first set dragged a bit, yet much of the second was positively transcendent. Overall, I'd have to give it an 8 1/2 and a dancing bear.

Ira: Grrrr . . . Except for the time my ninth-grade class had to sit through a showing of Brigadoon in lieu of a rained-out field trip, this Dead show was the most boring cultural experience of my life. Sure, they can play their instruments (if you call endless, aimless noodling playing), but where was the stuff that makes music rock — backbeat, passion, energy, tunes, drama, soul, sex, fun, youth? I'd have had a better time if I'd gone with the band's flow and dozed off.

Richard: Were we at the same show? Criticizing the Dead for "aimless noodling" is like bagging on Don Mattingly for making all those boring outs at first base. If you weren't hearing the delicious counterpoint between guitarist Jerry Garcia, keyboardist Vince Welnick and bassist Phil Lesh in "Sugaree," you probably were asleep. The Dead possess all the traditional rock attributes you missed; they just don't slap their audience in the face with them.

Ira: I'm not objecting to refinement and sophistication, but the Dead goes way beyond dismantling rock's wall of sound: their music is a transparent, weightless fabric drifting on a lazy breeze. Snore. It's inoffensive, but the shapeless songs' lack of momentum (credit the non-propulsive drumming) made time stand still. I felt like I was stuck in a waiting room listening to elevator music.

And those much-vaunted Garcia solos — except for a bit of "Rambling Rose" and the silvery runs that embroidered the tender "Standing on the Moon" — were squinky, disconnected fragments, delivered in a weird MIDI-generated nylon-string tone, that made no musical sense. And for a band with twin drummers, how come no two people in the crowd were dancing in time?

Richard: Their polyrhythms are perverse, but that's the point. "Standing on the Moon" was definitely a keeper; likewise the wild oceanic jam in "Foolish Heart." The band's increasing digitization may have lent a little shrillness to the sound, but what elevators have you been hanging out in? Soundman Dan Healy transformed the Garden into a cosmic drum machine during the electro-percussion "Rhythm Devils" section of the second set; the ensuing free-form improvisation, "Space," was a wild and woolly game of musical 52 card pickup.

Ira: That this narcoleptic trance factory should suddenly switch gears into noisy, anarchic playroom chaos was quite a surprise. A sonically repulsive one, but at least a sign of life. The show's only other indication of a rock and roll heartbeat was the almost-energetic version of Chuck Berry's "Promised Land." But the "I Fought the Law" encore was a limp travesty of a great song, and Phil Lesh should really leave Bob Dylan alone.

Richard: Yeah, maybe, but Garcia's laid-back take on Paul McCartney's "That Would Be Something" was a sly hoot, even if it was a learn-while-you-earn band project. Still, I can't wait to hear what they Gratefully deconstruct tonight. Care to join me?

Ira: No thanks. I'd rather see Meat Loaf. ◆

Woodstock '94

Now, *this* was a time. I spent several days of August 1994 ankle-deep in upstate New York mud (one of my shoes got sucked off my foot by the disconcertingly organic muck; I saved for years it as a fouled souvenir of the experience), leading a small *Newsday* team which included my mentor Dave Herndon, photographer Bill Davis and a young Scottish news reporter loaned to us as a dogsbody, someone who could drive and do whatever else we OWME (Older Wiser More Experienced) staffers couldn't be arsed to. Matthew McAllester, as the likably eager lad was called, survived the experience handily and, undaunted, grew up to become a Pulitzer Prize-winning war correspondent, an editor at *Time*, the global editor of *Newsweek*, the author of several very fine books, including one about his captivity in Saddam's Iraq, and the CEO of a media company based in London. (Plus, his dad took the photograph for the cover of *Let It Bleed*.) I'm glad we didn't leave him behind.

First, the sweeping and ponderous cultural overview to preview the event:

How *Woodstock* Made (and Unmade) Rock and Roll

Newsday, 7 August 1994

Woodstock will always be the quintessential '60s event, but, in musical terms, the '70s were already well under way by the time Richie Havens hit the stage. Beyond the Bethel mud on that fateful weekend a quarter-century ago, the nation's No. 1 single was Zager and Evans' "In the Year 2525" — just the sort of commercial contrivance that would brand the '70s as a decade of hollow drivel and dopey fads. Meanwhile, back on the farm, the three overpopulated days of peace and music completed the elevation of rock and roll from teenaged cult to mainstream institution (quite an ironic achievement for a supposedly counterculture event); in doing so, *Woodstock* rang down the final curtain on '60s rock. The nominal peak of an era paradoxically proved to be its last call, as whatever innocence had once existed in rock was stamped out in the post-*'stock* gold rush.

Although *Woodstock* had little immediate career impact on most of the bands that played there, its enormity and its timing had an enduring effect on the pop culture at large. Other than the 400,000 hippies who actually witnessed the festival, few knew the musical details of what had transpired until the film was released a half-year afterward, followed by the live albums. (Even *Billboard*, the music industry's leading trade publication, had not one article about the event the week it took place.)

But as soon as the upstate highways choked to a close with traffic and the television news began reporting on the vast horde of kids gathered to announce the birth of their dying nation, *Woodstock* became a pivotal event in American social history, one whose significance went far beyond music. The attention *Woodstock* focused on a nebulous generation, its values and music's central role in its existence made rock and roll an inescapable fact of life.

Until then, the media had largely viewed rock with a mixture of curiosity and condescension, covering it casually as a cult that rarely demanded serious consideration. Outside the corridors of pop, rock's superstars — Elvis, the Beatles, Rolling Stones, Bob Dylan (none of whom, it bears noting, took part in the concert) — had been viewed more as extraordinary individual phenomena than as high-profile flagships of a bigger entity.

In the 15 years since Elvis, pop music had worn through a variety of social guises, from the outrageous heathen erotica of primal rock and roll to the innocuous puppy love of turn-of-the-decade pop to the wholesome hysteria of the Beatles to the overtly subversive sex-drugs-politics lifestyle rebellion of punk, folk-rock and psychedelia.

Woodstock finally made rock itself the story. When a concert was transformed by circumstances into front-page news, journalism — and, by extension, television, the movies and eventually pop life at large — could never again ignore the youth culture's noise. In short order, "rock" became a nearly universal trope for longhaired youth.

By 1969, rock had divided itself into two overlapping hemispheres: the straight world of AM radio and concise 7-inch singles, and the groovy underground (a real alternative, as opposed to today's crossover co-option) of FM radio, LPs and side-long songs. For a while, the two realms — a convenient generational subdivision and a technological rite of passage — co-existed peacefully. Some bands — the Who, the Doors, Rolling Stones, Canned Heat, Jimi Hendrix and others — were able to function and flourish in both, simultaneously maintaining their credibility and commercialism with a mix of musical approaches and formats, but most were strongly identified with one camp or the other. And audiences could be mighty willful when it came to deciding who was hip and who was irredeemably Top 40.

Woodstock's talent roster cut both ways across that line and, ultimately, helped erase the distinction. The bands may have landed on different spots on the groovy meter (imagine if Iron "In-a-Gadda-Da-Vida" Butterfly had actually made it to the gig), but playing *Woodstock* was good for underground cachet and above-ground market share. (Actually, only Joe Cocker, Ten Years After and Santana saw direct, substantial career benefits.) In this brave new world — the culmination of '60s pop radio's pluralism — the folk traditions of the Incredible String Band and the Top 40 swamp choogle of Creedence Clearwater Revival, the explosive rock of the Who and the rambling whimsy of Arlo Guthrie, the genius of Hendrix and the jazz-rock fusion of Blood, Sweat and Tears could all co-exist on a single stage before a single, tolerant audience.

The giddy, stylistic free-for-all of music in the 1960s acknowledged few rules and incurred little genre friction. Ultimately, rock and roll was the only name that could possibly cover the mad incongruity of *Woodstock*'s lineup: Richie Havens' folk rootsiness, Canned Heat's electric blues, Country Joe and the Fish's radical rabble-rousing, Sha Na Na's freeze-dried nostalgia, Mountain's overpowering sludge, Ravi Shankar's hypnotic sitar. In this explosive era, rock fans took it all in stride, open to whatever sounds might blow their way.

As *Woodstock* galvanized public attention, it broadened the audience for rock. Putting a brand name on such heterogeneity, *Woodstock* made rock more accessible and encouraged and attracted many young people who had been intimidated by what its rebellion and lifestyle promised. (In much the same way, the Age of Aquarius turned the New Left's five-year-old anti-war movement into a depoliticized campus fad, which, admittedly, finally did the trick.)

In making rock safe for the world, *Woodstock* widened the mainstream. But that led to an era in which pop music splintered as it never had before. By the end of 1970, with the blight of the Stones' bigger and badder Altamont fiasco compounded by the sordid deaths of Jimi Hendrix and Janis Joplin, rock had acquired an unexpectedly nasty reputation — as well as a voracious hunger for the bigtime. No longer was success on the Beatles' scale considered an untouchable feat; crassness, inspired by the ascending potentials of scale that *Woodstock* illustrated, became an essential aspect of the music business.

As record labels abandoned their late-'60s pretense of benevolence for an enlightened capitalism, they launched a Darwinian era in which the bands that survived were the ones that wanted to be turned by the wheels of industry. Unselfconscious about their ambitions, uninvolved in politics and disinclined toward idealism even as an illusion, the era's stars had no sense of mission, no commitment to cultural solidarity, no taste for rebellion as anything other than a James Dean pose. The folkier singer-songwriters made a token display of '60s left-wing piety, but that soon sounded old and out of fashion; the rising newcomers (and those old-timers sharp enough to shift gears for a faster track) that reached the upper echelons of rock were hard, simple, vacuous and carefully customized for mass consumption in arena settings.

The charismatic stars of '69 learned their giant-gig lessons — utopian misgivings and all — at *Woodstock*; the bands in their wake could build on an experience they hadn't even had. While many of the *Woodstock* bands found themselves on the outs as icons of a bygone era, the selection process encouraged the louder, simpler bands: Grand Funk Railroad, Black Oak Arkansas, Mountain, KISS, Bad Company. Alice Cooper, the new breed's most shamelessly entertaining huckster, may have put it best in 1972's "School's Out": "We got no class / And we got no principles."

The grand scale to which concerts aspired and rose in the '70s went against the essence of rock performance, moving artists away — literally *and* figuratively — from their audiences. Facing pinpoints on a distant stage at the far end of a football field, a new generation learned to take what it was offered: a video screen, not a real person. Concerts became more and more like sporting events; the idea of flogging peanuts in the stands while a band was playing turned quickly from intrusion on art to a gastronomic convenience. Thanks in part to the formal formatting of music radio and the conversion of AM into a spoken-word medium, rock's audience fragmented, quickly settling into narrow, stylistic prejudices. Music became an us-vs.-them issue, only now the combatants were all young fans. Racial segregation, which had been reduced in the '60s, returned with added virulence.

Musical movements began starting up in response to each other. Disgust with the hippies' idealism and casual dress begat the extreme fashions and over-the-top theatricality of glam (KISS, Slade, David Bowie, Jethro Tull), lumpen rock stupidity (Grand Funk Railroad) and mindless boogie (Foghat, Black Oak Arkansas). The overuse of electricity summoned up acoustic singer-songwriters and the Eagles' Southern California sound; the hegemony of guitar-driven blues-rock encouraged the rise of keyboard-shaped classical hybrids and other kings of the cerebral cosmos: Yes, Genesis, ELP. To the extent that it had not happened in the '60s, music in the '70s became balkanized into a disharmonious continent of incompatible armies. Disco filled a vacuum created by the absence of dance beats and the maturation of soul music; its arrival engendered a degree of animosity unseen since the burning of Beatles records by religious fanatics in the '60s.

As the industry increasingly concentrated its resources on the creation and marketing of broadly accessible, long-playing blockbusters loaded with hit singles, big genres and big albums — *Tapestry*, *Songs in the Key of Life*, *Frampton Comes Alive!*, *Hotel California*, *Rumours*, *Saturday Night Fever* — came to monopolize the airwaves. With the days of free-form radio gone forever, the narrowing process continued. All but the most conformist tastes were disenfranchised.

Eventually, an angry young generation lost all connection with commercial rock and began making harsh, aggressive music of its own design, ignoring sales potential in favor of sincere expression. The punks identified mass appeal as the root of all musical evil and made sure to be as abrasively anti-mainstream as possible. What bands like the Sex Pistols didn't quite consider was the power of infamy; their exploits eventually made them — and their genre — big news, which led to big sales as the music toned itself down and the world harshed itself up.

Peace and love are no longer much with us, but huge concerts certainly are. So, it's scant surprise that the rock bands chosen to play *Woodstock '94* have next to nothing in common with any but the least representative attractions of the original festival.

One crucial move the punks made (and the *Woodstock* nation overlooked) in the '70s was to set up a music business of their own. Thanks to their high ideals and lack of commercial conviction, bands of the late '60s had few defenses against the highly motivated, better-organized acts that displaced them in the '70s. But the punks who rejected them all later that decade had little choice but to erect a scrappy infrastructure that survived to eventually deliver (or at least facilitate) the stars of alternative rock. And led, directly, to the rise of the do-it-yourself culture that spawned *Lollapalooza*.

Since its 1991 launch, the annual tour has been portrayed as the whatever-generation's own version of *Woodstock*, another mass concert that serves up a sense of community along with the music. Strangely, just the opposite is proving to be true: a quarter of the bands scheduled to appear next weekend are past or present Lollapaloozers.

Classic rock radio, that graveyard of fossil bands that never grow old, may be stuck forever in the '60s and '70s, but the sound of *Woodstock '94* — conceived as a tribute to yesterday's youth — will, after all, be the sound of their children. ◆

The Music of *Woodstock '94*: A Review (Day One)

Newsday, 15 August 1994

King's X played Jimi Hendrix's "Manic Depression" and smashed their instruments. Cypress Hill's Sen-Dog body-surfed into the pit. In a seeming attempt to rip a hole in the time-space continuum, Melissa Etheridge draped herself in the mantle of Janis Joplin and unleashed a shriek that cut through the air.

In a parade of artists making a much stronger impact with symbols, nostalgic talismans and grand gestures than musical content, Trent Reznor delivered the festival's conceptual masterstroke Saturday night. Following a long set by Crosby, Stills and Nash that was capped by a rocked-up rendition of [*Joni Mitchell's*] "Woodstock," Reznor and the rest of Nine Inch Nails appeared onstage daubed in mud. It had already become clear that the so-called Mud People were the genuine stars of *Woodstock '94*. For all the irony of a vulgar, nihilistic thrash band helping celebrate the peace-and-love spirit, Reznor's show of solidarity was the initial evident connection between the doings onstage and the fans' experiences on the field.

The weekend's first defining moment was visual, not musical. When action painter Denny Dent flipped over the picture he had just thrown together live on the main stage revealing a portrait of Hendrix, it was as if the guitarist's ghost had been conjured up. The prayers of a vast crowd desperate to claim its piece of the past had finally been answered.

Over the first two days, the bands approached the event either by ignoring the situation or by consciously rising to the occasion. Etheridge used the opportunity to indulge the hubris of her Janis Joplin fantasies with a four-song medley that included "Move Over" and "Piece of My Heart." Metallica, who followed Nine Inch Nails on the path to Aerosmith, delivered its standard set, complete with artillery noises and pyrotechnics to accompany the anti-war "One" and an audience cheering "Die! Die!" during "Creeping Death." Peace and love just ain't what they used to be.

Such big symbols may have been the glue that held the first two days of music together. Or maybe it was just the mud. Or the sense of being at the biggest party in history. It sure wasn't the talent lineup, which was solidly second-drawer. No Springsteen, no Pearl Jam, no Dead, no R.E.M., no U2, no Led Zeppelin reunion. The bands chosen to play represented nothing, filled no stylistic map and surely suggested no artistic vision beyond a vague youth demographic. Short of Bob Dylan's peerless icon value, nothing on the bill was extraordinary enough to make this concert as special as it was large. But in the synergy between artists and audience, something powerful was definitely taking hold.

Some huge portion of the crowd stood for endless hours watching music Friday and Saturday. And had no discernible trouble shifting gears between the old-fogey harmonies and clumsy rock pretensions of CSN and the fury of Nine Inch Nails. Or grooving to the pot-centric raps of Cypress Hill, Sheryl Crow's robust country rock and Salt-n-Pepa's glitzy feminist hip-hop revue. Still, it may be too soon to credit Generation Whatever with a new openness; after all, its members also cheered helicopters, TV cameras and breast-baring women in the crowd.

On Friday night, which was described by promoters correctly as "MTV bands" and far less convincingly as "cutting edge," Pennsylvania's Live came off like a rehash of, alternately, R.E.M. and Pearl Jam. England's James put on a fine set of anthem-like pop that connected the Doors, U2 and Celtic folk. Collective Soul made some sing-along headway with its hit "Shine," but otherwise played generic Southern rock that belongs in a bar. Crow, however, had the opposite problem: Except for a surplus of flailing guitar solos, her set was good, but her hit, "Leaving Las Vegas," was a dud.

Saturday got under way with nostalgic favorite (and *Woodstock* '69 star) Joe Cocker, who included such venerable items as "Feelin' Alright" and "With a Little Help From My Friends." Wearing a white dress, singer Shannon Hoon of the wretched Blind Melon also borrowed from a Beatle, offering John Lennon's "Working Class Hero." Over on the South Stage, what's left of The Band, joined by a horn section, Roger McGuinn and other guests, played some weak material but also reprised such oldies as "Rag Mama Rag" and their cover of "Baby Don't Do It" with pleasingly old-fashioned sound.

Crosby, Stills and Nash (who were introduced by John Sebastian) took Saturday's déjà vu honors, pulling out such radio staples as "Marrakesh Express," "Love the One You're With," "Helplessly Hoping," "For What It's Worth," the Stills political action song originally done by the Buffalo Springfield in the '60s, and the Beatles' "In My Life." But the trio's entire set seemed to be a buildup to its speeding but profound rendition of "Woodstock." A quarter-century after Joni Mitchell wrote it, the song was finally delivered, readymade, to the first crowd that could properly receive it as a national anthem. As they sang, the sense of community was palpable. But in the time warp of attempting to resuscitate the past, it was also clear that music was just the medium, not the purpose, of this séance. ◆

The Music of *Woodstock '94*: A Review (Day Two)

Sunday in Saugerties, Bob Dylan finally fulfilled the ancient prophecy: Build a huge musical city in upstate New York and he will play.

Newsday, 16 August 1994

Holding the second *Woodstock*'s place of pride as the missing person of the original, and the only genuine '60s legend to appear in the flesh at its repeat [*Joe Cocker might have argued that point*], Dylan had the historic clout to give the young horde here a bridge to realize its fantasies about a bygone time. And what did Dylan — spokesman of a generation, poet laureate of the counterculture that set the agenda of an era — sing that truly moved the huddled, the muddy, the tired, yearning for an identity? "Everybody must get stoned."

Other than "Rainy Day Women," Dylan's solid, uneventful set — a dozen mostly '60s-vintage classics ("Masters of War," "Highway 61 Revisited," "It Ain't Me Babe," "All Along the Watchtower") revamped into lengthy, jam-expanded electric and acoustic arrangements — was received patiently but with no discernible enthusiasm; moshing even slowed to a rare halt. For an event that could have been An Event, Dylan's performance, good as it was, ultimately didn't count for much. He consigned the audience to a bystander's role at its own party. And while that is a perfectly reasonable approach for an ordinary rock concert, it didn't work here. The self-professed idiots of Green Day and the lightbulb-wearing goofs in the Red Hot Chili Peppers were the only bands with the insight to turn the crowd's power on itself. During Sunday sets that were, musically, par for the bands' respective courses, both created peak *Woodstock* memories.

Green Day demonstrated maximum punk-pop moxie (or unbelievable stupidity) by taunting a wired mid-afternoon crowd into hurling a barrage of mud at the stage. The good-natured trio not only continued rocking amid the flying clods of wet earth, mud-soaked clothing and stage-storming fans, singer-guitarist Billie Joe responded in kind, flinging it back and taking wry stabs at nostalgia. "Hey, where's Abbie Hoffman?" he asked, "I have to hit him in the head with a guitar." He also exposed himself and prodded a fan to sing a line from the Beastie Boys' "(You Gotta) Fight for Your Right (To Party)." But no further effort was needed: This punk-rock party was already way out of control.

Compared to Billie Joe's token effort, the Chili Peppers made a grand statement with a garment-removal gambit. Cavorting in just a sexy black mini-skirt himself, singer Anthony Kiedis requested that everyone take off their shirts and wave them over their heads. Enough complied to turn the field into a whorl of spinning cotton and bare chests; with the quartet's blistering version of Stevie Wonder's "Higher Ground" as the soundtrack, it was a shocking, amazing feel-good riot of uninhibited crowd compliance.

Traffic, the Spin Doctors, Porno for Pyros, Arrested Development and the Allman Brothers also played Sunday, a disappointing reminder that big-league rock music has not moved from its guitar-solos essence in three decades. That point was underscored by Paul Rodgers, the veteran British blues and rock singer (Free, Bad Company) who delivered the day's only significant surprise by corralling Guns n' Roses guitarist Slash to join his semi-star lineup for its last four numbers, including, as one of the weekend's numerous tributes to Jimi Hendrix, a version of his "I Don't Live Today."

After all was sung and played, Hendrix emerged as the spiritual star of *Woodstock 2*: ubiquitous, omnipotent, unassailable, universally praised, a martyred savior for rock's lost tribe. In the two-hour wait for Dylan — the weekend's only serious non-traffic delay — performer-painter Denny Dent killed time by reprising his upside-down Hendrix finger-painting; Melissa Etheridge's guitarist quoted "The Wind Cries Mary" as a song ending. And in a second conceptual coup, the Chili Peppers encored in mock-Hendrix duds, with Afro wigs, headbands, fringe jackets and bell-bottoms. Whatever else the new *Woodstock* nation achieved in this grueling initiation, it did elect an icon and attempt his resurrection. ◆

Look! Up on the Screen, It's Live Rock!

Newsday, August 28, 1994

I confess: I watched *Woodstock '94* on television. Yes, it's true. I went to Saugerties to do on-the-scene reporting about the supposed event of a lifetime. But without joining the roiling mosh pit down front, it was nigh on impossible to get near enough to the main stage to see more than an ant-farm pantomime with a disembodied, electronically delayed sound track. So, like most people at the Aquarian afterbirth, I instead found myself staring at one of the two huge screens flanking the 640-foot-wide stage structure. Even that wasn't always adequate: Lost at one point in the far reaches of a 90-acre field strewn with tents, I could hear music without being able to make out who was playing on the distant screens.

While sensible civilians spent the same mid-August weekend comfortable at home, admiring the biggest waste of effort in rock-concert history on the pay-per-view broadcast, the *Woodstock* battalion lived to tell a greater tale by braving the elements and disorganization to personally witness history through the impotent achievement of watching the damn thing live on TV. Whatever it was — a defining moment in American life, a rite of passage for Generation Whatever, a successful sally into passive anarchy, the world's biggest mud bath — *Woodstock* was, least of all, a concert.

One could stand and stare in the right direction for hours on end, but, ultimately, it was the sardine-packed crowd, the slippery ground and the crummy weather that ruled the ordeal. Bands were incidental to the *Woodstock* experience. (The weekend's mediocre lineup didn't help. For many of the artists who played, *Woodstock* was merely a stop on the summer tour; nearly half had shows of more reasonable scale in the New York City area this summer. *Woodstock* could get it for you wholesale, but as a transcendent musical event, the festival never left the ground.)

We've been asking for this. Once exclusively reserved for the great (Beatles, Shea Stadium, 1965) and the temporarily popular (Grand Funk Railroad, Shea Stadium, 1971), outsized outdoor shows have become a standard classic-rock graveyard. This summer saw Pink Floyd, Billy Joel and Elton John, the Stones and the Eagles all touring America's football palaces. Add *Woodstock* and *Lollapalooza* (at the rarely used Downing Stadium on Randall's Island) to the mix, and big gigs have become as common as the dinosaurs that can fill them.

No one can reasonably expect stars not to take advantage of the obvious benefits of playing to the largest possible audiences willing to pay top dollar for the privilege. Except in the sense that more get to partake in each diminished experience, that's not good news for fans.

Still, many raised on football games, sixplex movies and MTV, rather than 2,000-seat concerts — where eye contact (or at least some sense of sharing a couple of hours with an artist working to a crowd he or she can actually see) isn't entirely out of the question — are content to be passive, undemanding spectators, expecting the easy satisfaction of volume, excitement, show business and star power rather than artistic ambition or achievement.

As a rock-crazed teenager in the late '60s, I split my concert-going between a few New York venues. There was the Fillmore East, a cozy, once-glitzy legitimate theater on Second Avenue that provided a mystery-laden inner sanctum for "underground bands" such as Johnny Winter, Canned Heat and (yep) Chicago Transit Authority. In the summertime, there were Central Park concerts in the larger but manageable Wollman Rink, where twilight brought an array of intriguing bills and an inkling of rock's picnic-party future. At the top of the capacity spectrum stood the imposing, unthinkably (so much for thinking) vast Madison Square Garden. The impersonal cavern on Eighth Avenue was where one was remanded to see such certified big stars as Cream, Hendrix and the Rolling Stones from thin-air seats that could have been in a different state.

The Who played all three and then moved on to stadiums. In the Fillmore, the band's power was breathtaking, overwhelming; the sound came from everywhere, while the visual spectacle remained in sharp focus, mere yards away. At the Garden, during a four-night stand in June 1974, the first 30 or 40 rows received a similar dose of the quartet's visceral intensity and direct contact. To those down front, it felt like a small, private show with thousands of spectators looking on from a distant gallery. Sitting in the nosebleed section, the concert that remained riveting to some became second-hand, a roar of loud energy, but far less of an engrossing experience. In the following decade, at Shea Stadium, Who concerts took a giant final step toward emotionless, meaningless abstraction. Yet the fans still turned out in droves, desperate to see the remains of a legend before burial. They got what they deserved.

The Rolling Stones are the one group that has been playing stadiums as a rule since the '70s, an aging leviathan that has adapted to the sea-sized realm of outdoor bowls. Already hardened into extravagant caricatures of rock stars, the Stones have tailored themselves for performing at great removes from enormous hordes. Opening the *Voodoo Lounge* tour at RFK Stadium in Washington, D. C., recently, the Stones pulled out all the theatrical stops to produce the fiery spectacle they no longer can generate solely with music.

As they move from theaters to arenas to stadiums to *Woodstock*, musicians recede farther into the physical distance. What fans can see on the stage is all but useless compared to the super-real images on the towering video displays. Up close and personal, shot by sight-blocking cranes and slinking cameramen from otherwise inaccessible vantage points, the cool, flat, well-lit representation becomes infinitely preferable to the original.

The second-hand concert experience kills the cultural impact of music as an art form. When Pink Floyd kicked off its Yankee Stadium show with "Astronomy Domine," the oldest and most provocative song in its set, it was impossible to tell for sure if the musicians onstage were actually producing the sound or standing around waiting for a tape to finish. Throughout the show the audio system, for all its undoubted sophistication, only hinted at the group's pristine and precise playing.

Attributes that once distinguished mass sporting events from mass musical events have melded into all-purpose mass entertainment. Rock records, even videos, play between innings at baseball games; concert crowds bounce beach balls around, do the Wave and reflexively hone in on roving TV cameras with the same fervor as champion bench-warmers. There actually was a time when "getch-yer red-hots heah" was not a standard concert refrain.

Meanwhile, the attention span of concertgoers has gone the way of channel surfing. Arenas and stadiums have depersonalized music with distance and distractions, killing the one-on-one illusion tangible even in larger theaters. (Stadiums are worse than arenas, but only in degree, not kind.) The production demands of tons of equipment and hundred-strong crews corner artists into eliminating any shred of spontaneity, of the risk at the very heart of great rock music. It's not surprising that stage action is no longer the only game for fans, whose attention wavers and wanes, from solo to shout, tackle to homer, soda to program.

These days, people make their own fun. Traffic to concession stands doesn't diminish while the band is playing, neither does full-volume conversation. For many people, live bands are no different from any music playing at a party. Surrounded by a similarly motivated crowd of peers, feeling the same need to have a really great time — and, unlike partygoers, having paid outrageous ticket prices for the privilege — consumers are left little room to seriously consider what they're actually consuming. It was spine-tingling to hear tens of thousands chant "Piano Man" along with Billy Joel and Elton John last month, but the crowd was essentially singing to itself.

In any setting, large or small, where a patch of floor space is available these days, people seeking a major energy release slam-dance and body-surf. What began as an aggressive tribal dance ritual has devolved into a mindless, often brutal, exercise that completely ignores the music, to the point where moshers go at it between songs, during set changes, even for absurdly inappropriate bands such as Crosby, Stills and Nash (!).

The less fans are inclined to pay attention, the harder bands have to work this buyers' market to put on a great show, not play a great set. Few stadium-ready musicians could still be accused of trying to express some tangible emotion beyond technique in their instrumental work, or anything more than physical effort in their singing. Stadiums are poison to the art of rock. Selling an act to 50,000 means pumping up the gestures, cranking up the P. A. and making sure there's plenty for the fans to look at besides tiny little heads. Fireworks are becoming de rigueur; after the Stones left the RFK Stadium stage, a late launch was used to snuff out the crowd's encore roar. It's the rare artist who has the personal charisma to make a real artistic impression at a thousand yards; everyone else has to load up on pyrotechnics and lights, inflate those snarling pigs and make sure the video screens are large and sharp.

Too often, if the wind blows the sound out to the parking lots, or the flying pigs stay hangared, concert memories are made not of music but of things that go boom. ◆

Concert reviewing for a daily paper means deadline challenges. *Newsday* had an uncommonly early press time, so I filed most of my live pieces the morning after to appear in the paper the day after that. So, a Tuesday night gig would be covered to run in the Thursday paper. Not ideal, but that made the job (which included being in the office for morning meetings after staying out late at shows and still finding the time to write the reviews) more manageable.

For some big-deal shows, however, the marching orders were to file on the night for the next morning's paper. So, when the Rolling Stones set the kickoff of their *Voodoo Lounge* tour at RFK Stadium in Washington DC on 1 August 1994, it was deemed significant enough for me to fly down and file a same-night review.

Stones Roll 'Em

Rock legends back on road, full of energy in sweaty capital

By Ira Robbins 8/2/94
STAFF CORRESPONDENT

Washington, D.C. — Thirty years to the day after they first entered the American Top 40 with "Tell Me (You're Coming Back)," the Rolling Stones came back — to kick off one more age-defying concert tour.

Last night, a grotesquely muggy RFK Stadium became the Stones' "Voodoo Lounge," as the band's first concert tour (and studio album) in five years is being called. Some 50,000 fans turned out to see the 50-something rockers — arguably rock and roll's greatest living, active legends — embark on an international itinerary that will keep the group on the road well into next year. Opening night had a few rough spots, but the Stones' traveling hot spot is everything fans would want it to be.

Other than the presence of new bassist Darryl Jones (taking over for the retired Bill Wyman), the 1994 Stones look much the same as they did on 1989's "Steel Wheels" tour. But Jones' presence makes a big difference in the band's sound, adding muscle and meat to Charlie Watts' precise drumming, giving the Stones a rhythmic power they have never before displayed onstage.

Following an opening set by Counting Crows (who will also be on the New York area dates later this month), the Stones hit the stage — and quite a stage it is, 170 tons of steel that, illuminated, looks like a hallucinatory metal castle of lights — at 9:15. Amid hails of red flares, white fireworks and video projections, singer Mick Jagger and guitarists Keith Richards and Ron Wood started the show up with a fast take on 1964's "Not Fade Away."

From there, the Stones rolled out "Undercover," "Tumbling Dice" and "Live With Me" before unveiling any "Voodoo Lounge " songs. The new album's "You Got Me Rocking" and "Sparks Will Fly" sandwiched another vintage tune, "Rocks Off."

A one-two punch of "Shattered" and "Satisfaction" — the latter played as fast and hard as this rock classic ever has been — followed, then "Beast of Burden" and "Memory Motel," for which Jagger sat down and played piano. By this point wearing only a white T-shirt and black slacks, Jagger picked up a guitar for the new album's haunting lament, "Out of Tears."

Changing gears, the Stones then hit a funky groove with their own "Hot Stuff" and Al Green's arrangement of "I Can't Get Next to You."

The four official Stones were joined by keyboardist Chuck Leavell, saxophonist Bobby Keys, plus a three-man horn section and two backup singers.

Other than a surprise warmup club date in Toronto last month, the Stones have not performed in North America since the end of 1989. The "Voodoo Lounge" tour will reach Giants Stadium for the first of four New York area shows on Aug. 12.

The plan was to do a partial report (largely pre-written) during the show that could run in the morning and then file a full review the next day to have it appear August 3rd.

It was a warm, humid night. I was assigned to a desk and a telephone in the unlit press box. I brought my own state-of-the-art equipment: the paper's standard-issue Radio Shack
TRS-80 Model 100 laptop (a device known colloquially as "Trash 80"), a 1200-baud phone coupler modem, a pad, a pen and a pocket flashlight that I had to hold in my teeth.

Unless you're old enough to have used one (or even remember Radio Shack), it's hard to explain how ungainly (but, at the same time, miraculous) this primitive doorstop was. The LCD display showed eight wrapped lines of 40 characters each — 60 words or so — but a lack of backlighting made it all impossible to read once the sun set, around 8:30. Out of consideration for paying customers, the press box was kept dark. Shining a flashlight on the display only made it harder to read the letters.

Writing, connecting and filing under those conditions was a stressful nightmare. (Hearing the high-pitched screech that came down the phone line to indicate a successful modem link would now be a trigger for me.)

The actual goals of the lame piece on the previous page were to show we were there and obscure the fact that the show was half-through at the time I wrote it.

This is the proper review, published a day later.

A Sonic Overhaul for the Stones

Aged in the rock. Monday night at RFK Stadium, Washington, D.C. Counting Crows opened.
Newsday, 3 August 1994

The Rolling Stones had to wait 30 years for bassist Bill Wyman to finally retire, but his replacement didn't happen a tour too soon. At RFK Stadium on Monday, with new bassist Darryl Jones, Mick Jagger and company kicked off the *Voodoo Lounge* world expedition playing harder, faster and with a better bottom than they've had in years. How many other grandfathers can say the same?

Where Charlie Watts' economical drumming is the understated key to the Stones' mature rock energy, Wyman was a plodding plunker. Jones, who is a more aggressive, inventive bassist than Wyman, adds meat and muscle to the artful snap of Watts' timekeeping.

With Monday night's sloppy but grand return, the Stones have managed an impressive sonic overhaul. Compared to the brake-riding torpor of 1989's *Steel Wheels* tour, the lamest crawl in a career of unhurried concerts, these were speed trials. In an uninterrupted two hours and twenty minutes, Jagger, Watts, guitar twins Keith Richards and Ron Wood — aided by Jones, keyboardist Chuck Leavell, saxophonist Bobby Keys, three other horn players and two backup singers — blew through more than two dozen songs with the terse, jacked-up energy of concise singles.

Playing on another massive stage, this one a bizarre composite of wavy gridwork, turrets and catwalks that resembles a looking-glass steel castle, the Stones mixed half the current *Voodoo Lounge* album with a chronological jumble of hits. Arriving to a thunderous drumbeat and a steady barrage of smoking red flares, the Stones launched into a pumped-up version of "Not Fade Away," the Buddy Holly song that became their first American Top 100 single in 1964. "Undercover of the Night" and "Tumbling Dice" followed, then "Live With Me," in which the murky depth of Jones' bass failed the song's febrile riff and melted it into a dull blur.

The rusty beginning to this not-quite-perfect show didn't matter. Neither did the special effects: a cast of ludicrous, ineffectual inflatables during "Love Is Strong," a pair of costumed stilt-walkers during "Monkey Man" and enough opening and closing fireworks to incinerate a small town. Three songs in, the Stones had already answered their own million-dollar challenge. Yes, these old men can still rock a football stadium.

If Jagger's athletic displays were a notch less athletic than five years ago, the 51-year-old is by no means ready for a wheelchair. More unsettling was the degree to which prominent-in-the-mix backup singers Bernard Fowler and Lisa Fischer filled out his singing. With the confusing delays between the occasional video projection and the typically crummy stadium sound, there were many spots in which he appeared to coast — starting a line but letting others finish it.

"You Got Me Rocking" was the same nothing it is on *Voodoo Lounge*, and "Rocks Off" had rough patches in which the beat collapsed, but "Sparks Will Fly" was sharp and tight. "(I Can't Get No) Satisfaction" was a revelation, a fierce, angry rip through the most familiar song in the band's vast repertoire. "Beast of Burden" slowed the show down enough to let Jagger (playing piano) slide into a pretty "Memory Motel" and the new album's haunting "Out of Tears," on which he played guitar.

"Hot Stuff" and "Brand New Car" were torpid drones, and a version of the Temptations' (by way of Al Green) "I Can't Get Next to You" was a better idea than reality, but "Honky Tonk Women," "Before They Make Me Run" (sung with typical croaky aplomb by Keith Richards) and "Start Me Up" were impressively propelled by the band's newfound vigor. Ending with a gratuitous pyrotechnic coda instead of a climactic musical moment, the show's final section (a demobilized "Street Fighting Man," "Brown Sugar" and "Jumpin' Jack Flash") didn't lead anywhere but to the exits. But between the heat, the humidity and the exhaustion, it was definitely time to go. ◆

Outside My Comfort Zone

Most of the concerts I reviewed for *Newsday* were well within my realms of familiarity and expertise, but those limits could not be allowed to keep my readers from being informed about music and artists outside them. We had a diverse readership, and I was determined to serve it as best I could. Fortunately, the paper had a top-notch classical critic in Tim Page and a jazz expert in Gene Seymour, but that left a wide range of music for me to bumble my way through. I had to stretch myself to give due consideration to music and artists about which and whom I was a total ignoramus. And it had to be done without condescension or prejudice. Open your mind and your pen will follow.

That impetus expanded the breadth of my cultural knowledge and appreciation. Still, it was a lot harder to write about performances for which I lacked context or language (that was especially true when the language was Spanish, although my date for those shows was fluent, which helped). My guiding principles when I didn't have a clue were to (a) prepare as much as possible with research and listening (b) approach with curiosity and respect (c) share enough reliable detail to suggest familiarity (d) be generous (e) don't gape or act surprised at the unfamiliar (f) find reference points to comment on knowledgably (g) be informative and (h) lean heavily on description rather than judgment.

In other words: fake it.

Africa Fête: An Idyll in the Park

Boukman Eksperyans, Oumou Sangaré and Tabu Ley Rochereau star in the second day of the annual international music festival. Sunday at Central Park SummerStage.
Newsday, 11 July 1995

It usually takes a subway calamity or a blizzard to summon tales of New Yorkers overcoming their differences to function in positive harmony. Sunday, a free concert managed the same feat of unification without anyone having to be stuck in a tunnel or slogging through snow. All it took was three out-of-town bands and a couple of craft booths on a gorgeous afternoon in Central Park. Roll over *Woodstock* and tell the motherland the news.

Other than a bit of genial crowding, the third-annual *Africa Fête* (now a two-day affair, with Baaba Maal, Femi Kuti and Osibisa having made up Saturday's bill) was a utopian idyll Sunday, the final date on the show's coast-to-coast tour. The audience — a demographer's dream of national, racial, chronological and stylistic diversity — ignored language and culture barriers to bask in the low-key warmth of Zaire's Tabu Ley Rochereau, the keening traditionalism of Mali's Oumou Sangaré and the fiery drive of Haiti's Boukman Eksperyans. If they arrived sharing nothing else, the faces that enjoyed the afternoon all wound up wearing the same smile.

Tabu Ley Rochereau, the reigning icon of Zaire pop and the co-inventor of *soukous*, a lion whose career began in the late '50s, got the day started with a gorgeous, spirited hour of gently rolling dance music. Singing in a handsome, piercing voice over the sweet weave of a bassist, drummer, two electric guitarists, a pair of saxmen and two male vocalists, Tabu Ley (who sings in Lingala, one of Zaire's four national languages) poured out his bright, bouncy songs — engrossing circles of melody and rhythm that built on stable repetition but had definite endings. The numbers that departed from the prevailing clocklike tempo to rev up a quick-stepping ska beat, complete with appropriate verbal interjections, added punctuation to the set's otherwise temperate tone. At one point, Tabu Ley asked if the crowd was happy and got a vocal assent, but it was the gyrations of his two female dancers that elicited stirring roars of approval.

Compared with Tabu Ley's relatively contemporary sound and instrumental density, young Wassoulou star Oumou Sangaré was far more exotic and rootsy. Backed by a hand drum, flute, electric guitar, bass (which served as the band's rhythmic anchor) and *kamele n'goni* (an acoustic stringed instrument whose unstable notes suggested the sound of a sitar), Sangaré and her two sidewomen tossed beaded-basket percussion tools and sang in explosive bursts of fast, twisting melody that rose and fell urgently, like sinuous threads of Arabic chanting.

Sangaré is a traditionalist whose art spans centuries and cultures; her music is more for the communication of sometimes provocative messages than the convenience of dancers. In fact, the erratic rhythms and sudden dynamic variations made consistent motion all but impossible, and the fascinating sound ultimately became a bit grating.

Amid cries of "Ayi Bobo!" (which leader Theodore "Lolo" Beaubrun Jr. translated as "All right!"), Haitian headliner Boukman Eksperyans livelied up the day with ecstatic songs of praise and revolution that turned at least one of the bleachers into a dancing, whistle-blowing celebration. The 11-piece group incorporates many international elements in its energized dance groove — *soukous*, *merengue*, ska, psychedelic rock, Zulu harmonies — but surging shake-it power was the unifying theme. As the set reached its feverish climax in a long jam led by stuttering bass guitar runs and a joyous percussion breakdown, everyone standing near the stage wound up on it, making a literal display of the easy, unselfconscious fraternity that defined the day. ◆

I wonder if anyone caught my Janis Joplin allusion in the subhed...

Cassandra Wilson

Five men and one great, great lady. Monday (early show) at the Bottom Line.
Newsday, 23 March 1994

Strong, supple, rich and smoky, Cassandra Wilson's voice is a marvelous instrument, and her use of it is truly virtuosic. In concert, however, it modestly becomes a component of a remarkable sextet whose economy, detail and improvisation elevate songcraft to an entirely new realm. What Cassandra Wilson and her group perform is jazz for those unmoved by blinding flashes of instrumental fancy, pop for those disappointed by note-for-note studio reproductions. Unlike the jazz-vocalist stereotype, her singing resembles a gracefully chorded piano rather than a scat-happy trumpet or a mellow saxophone; she embellishes melodies with subtle invention and superb control.

Her current band — Brandon Ross (guitar), Lonnie Plaxico (bass), Jeff Haynes (percussion, from bells and whistles to pots and pans), Lance Carter (drums) and Charles Burnham (violin, mandolin, harmonica, bottle) — is equally untraditional and sublime in its approach to the repertoire.

At the Bottom Line Monday, Wilson performed most of her current *Blue Light 'Til Dawn* (Blue Note) album in arrangements that took the recordings as rough sketches and remade them from scratch.

Pulling mildly or determinedly against the structural center of a song, the musicians expanded numbers into deeply evocative sound paintings. "Skylark" was intoxicatingly sensuous, a lazy, fluid heatwave enfolding the listener, first in a bluesy harmonica wail, then in the weepy teardrops of a vibrato guitar solo.

Ann Peebles' "I Can't Stand the Rain" became a ghostly skeleton of vocals, string bass and incidental percussion; Wilson displayed sure pitch, timbre and volume, shaping the song while Plaxico played everything but a recognizable pattern in a stable key. Switching to a strong, swaying beat, the group moved onto Wilson's own "Blue Light 'Til Dawn," a serious song given a playful reading. "Want It to Be," a lovely new original, worked a jazzy folk groove before smoothly fading away to silence.

But the showstopper was Joni Mitchell's "Black Crow." After an introductory mallet drum solo, the song gathered itself up and suddenly switched to overdrive. As Carter and Haynes launched into a breathtaking African rhythm breakdown, Ross attacked his electric guitar in a choppy frenzy of tension-packed energy bursts, coaxing unreal sounds and feedback whistles from it. With Ross exploring uncharted ground and Haynes simulating animal noises on various implements, the kinetic mass of sound somehow became, in an inexplicable feat of musical magic, an extraordinarily vivid wildlife kingdom. That this highlight didn't even involve vocals was emblematic of this remarkable ensemble's organic democracy. ◆

Luis Miguel

Age is just a numero for this Mexican sensation. Thursday at Radio City Music Hall.
Newsday, 17 October 1994

Respect for one's elders may be a social tradition in Mexico, but singer Luis Miguel has made it a career cornerstone. His current *Segundo Romance* (WEA Latina), the highest-charting Spanish-language album in American pop history, is a collection of *bolero* standards; most of the ballads are much older than the 24-year-old Miguel, who has been a pop star half his life.

At Radio City Music Hall Thursday, beginning a nearly sold-out four-night stand, Miguel crossed generation-bound styles without hesitation and demonstrated the broad basis of his appeal. Hyperactive lights (often blindingly aimed at the house) and smoke machines keyed the show to the young crowd that was in attendance, but the music came from all eras: disco, traditional boleros, modern rock glitz, a lot of old-style crooning, even a spot of old-school rap. A full-dress mariachi group appeared, first to add incidental touches to "La Media Vuelta" and then to take the instrumental lead on three crowd-pleasers, including the classic "El Rey." Miguel also introduced Armando Manzanero, the venerated Mexican composer who contributed several numbers to Segundo Romance, to accompany him on grand piano for gentle and pretty "Como Yo Te Ame" and the handsome, carefully shaped "Somos Novios."

Backed by a high-tech 10-piece orchestra with a horn section, plus three female singer-dancers and a 23-piece string section, Miguel performed pop in the international style, largely free of any distinctive ethnic flavoring. Dressed for the first half in a conservative dark suit and tie, tugging thoughtlessly at his sandy hair (no longer worn in the Caesar cut of recent pictures), he looked like a cocky young casino manager: grinning, dapper, wired, shamelessly ingratiating. His performance style, however, leaned more toward soccer forward; in constant motion, Miguel lunged at melodies in the uptempo numbers with explosive bursts of energy.

As an able interpreter of Mexican pop chestnuts like the stately "Historia de un Amor," "Pensar en Ti" (done as quiet storm soul) and Manzanero's "No Se Tu" (a highlight of 1991's *Romance* album), Miguel conveyed ample enthusiasm and heartfelt passion without indulging in gratuitous melodrama; if he never sacrificed himself fully to the material, he did sing with more than enough conviction and skill to convey the endlessly romantic assertions.

Although Miguel acquitted himself equally well in more contemporary settings, the music foundered in arrangements that were close, but not quite up to date. The dated synthesizer sounds, backing chorus and dance beat of "Dame Tu Amor" suggested the *Love Boat* theme; "Sera Que No Me Amas," a fast rocker, called to mind the piffle of *Footloose*. In general, Miguel's swipes at soul-funk and midtempo bounce-pop (like "Suave") suffered from their inability to shake off the '80s.

By the end of the two-hour show, Miguel's female fans could not be contained, and several launched themselves onstage in kamikaze kiss missions that kept the bouncers scurrying and tackling. With strobe lights flashing, horns testifying and Miguel athletically covering the stage in "Cuando Caliente el Sol," the show took its final leap to the level of adrenaline-pumping chaos that defines true pop stardom. ◆

Reba McEntire

Down home never looked or sounded like this. Thursday at Radio City Music Hall. Rhett Akins opened.
Newsday, 22 July 1995

The twin video screens used to introduce songs and provide visual diversion during the frequent costume changes were a clue. Then there was the ten-strong cast of dancers acting out the simple plots of songs. But, finally, it was the well-populated barroom set unveiled for "The Heart Is a Lonely Hunter" that nailed it: Reba McEntire and Queensrÿche are stealing each other's concert ideas!

Hard though it may be to imagine a lapsed country queen and a ridiculous gang of heavy metal conceptualists who played Jones Beach Tuesday having anything more in common than lighting rigs and mixing boards, their proximate shows took unnervingly similar paths to spectacle in garish presentations that render music the least significant item on the menu. Ironically, McEntire was the one with the pyrotechnics!

Pander to the perceived entertainment desires of a jaded, attention-deficit audience, it seems, and a lot of differences get ironed over. Once a standard Nashville traditionalist, McEntire has become an all-purpose pop singer. A pedal steel guitar and a pronounced Oklahoma accent are her sole tangible connections to country music.

Otherwise, she applies her mannered singing — an irritating, gimmick-laden exaggeration of quavery country emotionalism — to rocked-up pop with forays into deracinated R&B, overly sentimental balladry and lite-fingered jazz. Her seven-piece band included a soprano sax, for Hank's sake!

McEntire's garish, high-tech presentation at Radio City Thursday (the second of two nights) was a multi-media Broadway extravaganza on a two-level stage complete with stairs and an elevator. Following an introduction by Donna Hanover Giuliani and a video vignette, the star arrived onstage in a yellow cab, emerging in funereal black to sing "Fancy" all alone. Fifteen costume changes, 21 songs and 105 minutes later, she finished with a re-creation of her recorded duet, "Does He Love You," with backup singer Linda Davis. The credits rolled, and that was that.

Throughout, the emphasis was on carefully calibrated pleasure. At the most unearthly point of an altogether unnatural event, Vince Gill appeared on video to introduce "The Heart Won't Lie," which McEntire then sang along with his pre-recorded image.

Amid all the visual hoopla, McEntire sang most of her current *Read My Mind* (MCA) album and such past hits as "Is There Life Out There," "The Greatest Man I Never Knew," "Take It Back" and "Rumor Has It," leaving her real oldies for greatest hits albums. Otherwise, she duffed up the Everly Brothers' "Cathy's Clown" badly (inverting the lyrics and stretching the word "clown" into five awkward syllables) and used Buck Owens' "Act Naturally" as the thread for a lengthy look-ma-I'm-in-the-movies production number, which incorporated scenes from such cinematic mementos as "Tremors."

The music, performed with far more skill than conviction, was clearly subordinate to the wardrobe, which included the slinky red number she revealed at the end of "Fancy," a blue suit, a simple print dress, glittery cowgirl threads and an unbelievable Elizabethan ball gown, which she inexplicably wore for the ambiguous moralizing of her promiscuity-leads-to-AIDS piano ballad, "She Thinks His Name Was John." Ambitiously aiming no higher than the cheap glitz of '60s TV variety shows, Reba McEntire has succeeded in processing once-heartfelt music into a traveling cultural theme park. ◆

This was certainly one of the strangest concerts I ever reviewed. It was insanely late; I had no idea where I was or how to get home to Queens. And the music was loud AF.

Voyager

A monster rave inside the Brooklyn Bridge, with DJs and the German group Air Liquide. Late Saturday night at the Anchorage, Old Fulton Street in Brooklyn.

Newsday, 8 November 1994

If the Brooklyn Bridge was swaying more than usual late Saturday, it wasn't because of high winds, heavy traffic or unusual seismic activity. The vibrations pulsing through the venerable structure emanated from the ear-splitting techno music driving *Voyager*, an all-night rave party within the span's Brooklyn foot.

One of New York's countless architectural surprises, the city-owned but privately operated Anchorage — otherwise used for art installations and private parties — is a cavernous collection of narrow chambers with stone walls and dizzyingly high vaulted ceilings.

This sepulchral void is perfect for the set of a gothic horror film, but with blitzes of strobe lights and laser graphics projecting down long hallways through clouds of smoke, the appearance of Indiana Jones pursued by a fireball would not have been too surprising.

Dark, cool and dank, with the deafening acoustic properties of a sealed well, the Anchorage made an excellent rave site — a protected environment perfect for disorienting sensory overload. (Those unable to imagine the entertainment value of this scenario would not be wrong to envision it as a self-inflicted headache in a can.) While DJs in different rooms filled every last corner with the booming high-pressure dance pitches of their punishingly loud distilled electronic beats, thousands of young people milled, wandered, grooved and cruised in an underground approximation of a crowded, blacked-out shopping mall. Some hung back in the Chillout Room, others bought T-shirts at several stands; no alcohol was served, and unless the lollipop sticks seen poking out from many mouths indicate a new delivery vehicle for hallucinogens, drug use — while undoubtedly taking place — was discreet.

Around 2 a.m., with absolutely no fanfare, Air Liquide took over the main stage and shifted the source of the music from spinning discs back to the digital sampling equipment whence it came. Standing over nondescript gear set on a long table that otherwise held turntables, the German duo didn't offer much visual diversion, producing its synthetic sounds with no correlation between physical action and audible result other than the occasional crisply hit button that stopped or released a galloping charge of pulverizing rhythms.

The intense speeding beats downplayed the unpropelled ambient excursions that fill one CD of the new double-album, *The Increased Difficulty of Concentration*. Still, the sonic components Air Liquide summoned up and controlled were occasionally offbeat enough to cut the tedium, and the duo managed its mixes with split-second precision, adding and subtracting squiggly synth melodies, voices and percussion sounds to vary the angle, volume and texture of its trance-inducing creations.

As much as rave culture seems to have lost some of its gathering-of-the-tribes cachet and subterranean influence — other than the extraordinary location, *Voyager* could have been techno night at any number of New York's large dance clubs — the high-profile success of *Ravestock* in upstate Saugerties in August evidently recharged the scene's batteries, upping its activity level and attracting newcomers eager for an organized excuse to stay up all night. Handbills for at least four additional November events, all at unspecified sites, were distributed to Voyagers. Trendy or not, raves are going to keep pre-dawn New York shaking for some time to come. ◆

Fania 30th Anniversary All-Star Concert

Celia Cruz, Eddie Palmieri, Johnny Pacheco, Yomo Toro, Ray Barretto and many others deliver top-flight worldbeat, direct from New York. Saturday at Madison Square Garden.

Newsday, 21 June 1994

Imagine James Brown, Al Green, Aretha, Wilson Pickett and Ray Charles all singing together, backed by a band joining Booker T. and the MG's, Tower of Power and P-Funk. That's how heavy-duty — and about as old as — Saturday's Fania All-Stars lineup at the Garden was.

If one has to approach live salsa from a point of complete ignorance, the Fania All-Stars are unquestionably the people to see. What better introduction to a populist musical genre than a gala concert by most of its widely acknowledged masters?

If bandleader, flautist and Fania Records co-founder Johnny Pacheco couldn't always keep the full stage of salsa veterans united in synch, most of the four-hour show was an utter delight, a traditional display packed with surprises. Whether music is truly a universal language or not, the infectious energy, rolling and interweaving intricate strains of Afro-Latin jazz rendered comprehension of the lyrics (beyond repeated outbursts of Puerto Rican patriotism, often wrapped in the island's flag) irrelevant.

Following a seductive dose of romance and nationalism from Marc Anthony and his duet guest, India, the individual All-Stars were welcomed with increasing roars of adulation. Ultimately, the stage boasted six singers — Celia Cruz, the inimitable queen of salsa; Adalberto Santiago, an expressively energetic grandfatherly type; Cheo Feliciano, a husky-voiced master of razor-sharp phrasing; smooth operator Pete Rodriguez, Ismael Miranda and Ismael Quintana — and more than a dozen instrumentalists, including a stack of horn men, conga great Ray Barretto, pianist Eddie Palmieri, keyboardist Papo Lucca, violinist Pupi Legarreta, *cuatro* player Yomo Toro and percussionist Nicky Marrero. Trombonist Willie Colon even put in a guest appearance.

The show's star was clearly the brassy Cruz, a spectacular presence in gold lamé, her hair done up like a blonde fountain. Cruz sang one of her two numbers against a tame, swing-style arrangement and the other over a rising and falling cauldron of dynamic salsa.

But Palmieri was the evening's most riveting figure. The pianist hijacked several of the long numbers with wild, free-form jazz excursions, contradicting melodies and rhythms with ferocious enthusiasm and imagination. When Palmieri wasn't seizing control on the electric ivories, he stalked the stage, exhorting other musicians to shift gears; he even took a brief (and equally contrary) turn on timbales.

The avuncular Yomo Toro hung in the background until late in the show, when he sauntered out for a jaw-dropping display of quicksilver runs on the eight-string *cuatro*. But that was nothing compared to the shock of his brief bout of rocking boogie-woogie.

Projected footage of the stars in their youth and salsa fans dancing in the streets gave the show — part of a short 30th-anniversary-of-the-label tour billed as the final go-round for the All-Stars (although radio deejay Paco, one of the night's three announcers, left that door wide open) — a sense of historic context, and spoke to the maturity of salsa's aging lions as well as its audience. Meanwhile, repeated tributes paid to Hector LaVoe, the beloved singer who died last year, added a solemn air of unreclaimable loss. For all its current vitality, today's salsa, it seems, owes a lot to the past. ◆

Michael Jackson

From time to time, my job at the paper meant entertainment news reporting. I was not highly skilled in that discipline and probably no better than adequate at it, but for motivation I had the competition between papers. It was one of Billy Joel's divorces, or maybe a DUI arrest, spotted on the *New York Post* cover when I stopped by my local newsstand en route to work one morning. I was called on the carpet by my boss and chewed out for not having the story. Good times.

Music doings were not among the paper's top priorities, so it was thankfully rare that the news desk asked me to cover anything. More often than not, it was a star's death. But no fatality was involved in my one cover story ("the wood," in newsroom parlance) for the paper, a sensationalized bit about the release of a weird Michael Jackson single and the artwork that accompanied it. (Not for nothing was *Newsday* known as "a tabloid in a tutu.")

Gloves Are Off

Michael takes on image tormentors.
Newsday, 31 May 1995

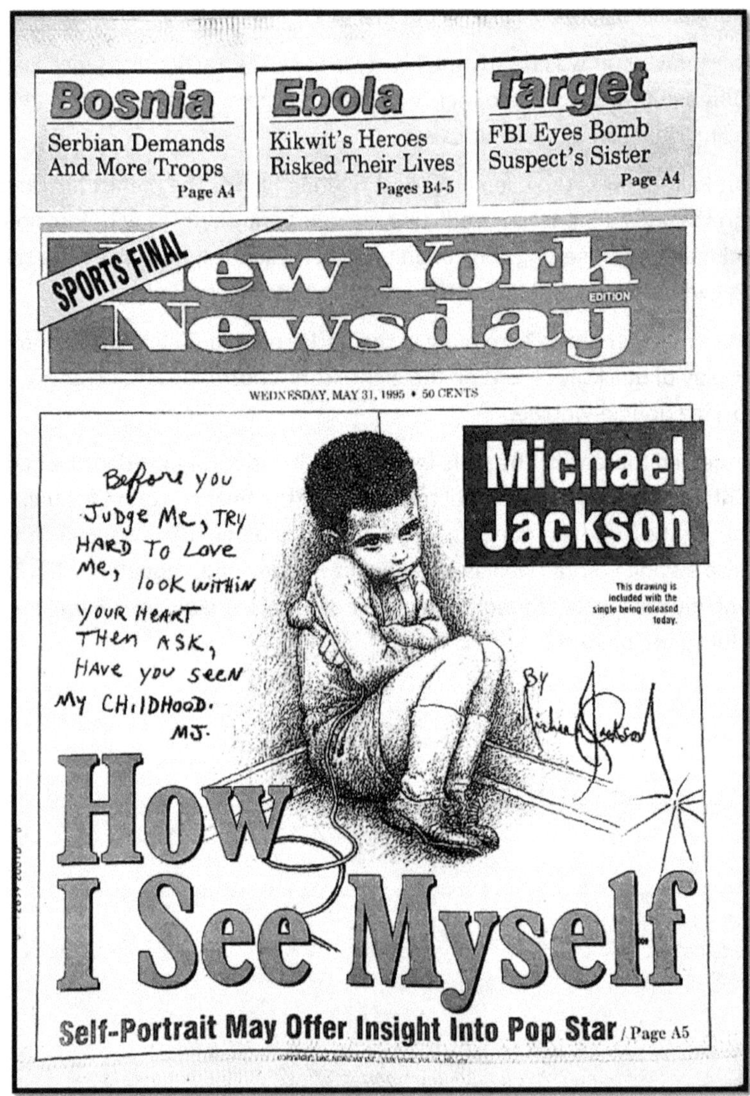

Bosnia
Serbian Demands And More Troops
Page A4

Ebola
Kikwit's Heroes Risked Their Lives
Pages B4-5

Target
FBI Eyes Bomb Suspect's Sister
Page A4

SPORTS FINAL

New York Newsday

EDITION

WEDNESDAY, MAY 31, 1995 • 50 CENTS

Michael Jackson

This drawing is included with the single being released today.

How I See Myself

Self-Portrait May Offer Insight Into Pop Star / Page A5

Judging by the beautifully rendered and poignant self-portrait Michael Jackson included in the two-song single of "Scream" and "Childhood" being released today, the superstar perceives himself — or wants to be seen — as a terrified toddler, huddled in a corner, clutching a mic.

It's a bizarre and shocking image for one of the world's wealthiest, most famous and powerful entertainers, and it stands in stark contrast to the enormous King of Pop statue unveiled in a multimillion-dollar promotional video for Jackson's forthcoming *HIStory: Past, Present and Future Book 1* album. A spokeswoman for Epic Records confirmed the drawing was a Jackson self-portrait.

Jackson, 36, who has been increasingly defensive in his public statements since being hit with allegations of sexually abusing a boy in 1993, is putting his pleas for sympathy into song. "Childhood," which Jackson wrote and recorded for the forthcoming movie *Free Willy 2*, is the most blatantly personal public appeal for tolerance and consideration in recorded memory, a virtual Checkers speech from the world of self-analysis. "Before you judge me, try hard to love me," Jackson sings in the sophisticated ballad's tearjerker chorus.

"Scream" is a duet with sister Janet that the pair co-wrote and co-produced with the hit-making team of Jimmy Jam and Terry Lewis. It offers a more aggressive response to those whom Jackson sees as his tormentors. While the verses challenge, the choruses howl and beg. In some versions included on the six formats being issued today on compact disc, vinyl and cassette, Jackson gets even more exercised, singing "Stop [expletive] with me."

Both songs, which were released to radio May 19, will be included on *HIStory: Past, Present and Future Book 1*, in stores June 20. In the wake of the scandal surrounding the abuse allegations (which were ultimately settled out of court), Jackson's first album in four years — a long-delayed double-length collection of new material plus solo hits — is a litmus test for the commercial future of the singer whose *Thriller* is the best-selling album of all time.

Epic Records would not provide exact numbers for how many copies of the single were shipped, although a spokeswoman did acknowledge that it had shipped platinum, meaning at least a million copies are in stores. At the Tower Records on Broadway in Greenwich Village, a spokesman said the store had ordered between 3,000 and 4,000 copies, a quantity he characterized as, "if not the store's biggest initial order ever, one of the top five or ten." ◆

Jackson had been the subject of intense media interest for some time, both for his successes and his bizarre-going-on-creepy behavior. Like many others, my mainstream paper made Michael — a household-name superstar *and* a salaciously suspicious freak — a regular subject of coverage. He eventually became the province of news reporters more than culture staff, but at this point it was all on me. So, when *this* dubious-sounding project was hastily assembled in early 1994, I went to Las Vegas to witness it. This preview, a mashup of verb tenses, had to be written in advance to run after the event — but before the broadcast.

It's a Tough Act to Get Together

Newsday, 20 February 1994

Big-budget television variety specials and musical fund raisers are both commonplace cultural events. But when America's foremost entertainment dynasty — the Jackson family — decides to throw its own all-in-one charity bash, personal tribute and TV special, things are likely to get complicated.

Late last week, some 30 members from three generations of the Jackson clan — parents Joseph and Katherine; sons Michael, Jermaine, Tito, Jackie, Randy and Marlon; daughters Janet and Rebbie; and assorted progeny — gathered in Las Vegas to rehearse *The Jackson Family Honors*, which was staged and taped last night. The two-hour extravaganza will air on NBC at 9 pm Tuesday.

It will be the first major family musical venture since Michael and his brothers undertook the 1984 *Victory* tour. *New York Newsday* will have full coverage of the show tomorrow.

As at the current Winter Olympic Games in Lillehammer, Norway, two colorful figures and a storm of will-they / won't-they controversy dominated the buildup to last night's show at the MGM Grand Garden, the same 15,000-seat arena that Barbra Streisand packed on New Year's Eve and Day.

First came the question of attendance by La Toya Jackson, who has been feuding with the family and broke ranks by not denouncing the accusations of sexual misconduct made in August against Michael. Would the prodigal daughter dare show up? Would she be allowed on stage if she did? The family says she was invited.

According to published reports, La Toya and her manager-husband, Jack Gordon, planned to attend the event in disguise but were discouraged by their belief that the family had hired 100 extra security people to bar them.

The other big issue was Michael's involvement in the event, which could have afforded him an opportunity to do an image-boosting show-stopper, as he did years ago on the *Motown 25* network television special. Michael recently settled out of court with a teenager who accused him of sex abuse, and a grand jury in California is reported to be hearing evidence related to the case.

But, no, it was acknowledged earlier in the week that the superstar's role would be limited to presenting achievement awards to his friend Elizabeth Taylor (attending despite her hip-replacement surgery scheduled for next month) and onetime mentor Berry Gordy, founder of Motown Records, who in 1969 signed the Jackson 5 from Gary, Ind. Michael also is joining the family for the musical finale, "If You Only Believe," a Jermaine Jackson composition with lyrics by the show's writer, Buz Cohan.

At a pre-show news conference held by the Jackson family yesterday morning, reporters asked mother Katherine Jackson if she felt as though she were living the American dream. In what may have been the best line of the conference, she said, "It was more like the American nightmare" over the past six months. And asked if rumors of a gag order on La Toya Jackson were true, she answered: "If we wanted La Toya to sign a gag order, we would have done that years ago."

Tickets for the gala also were a subject of some concern. Set high in keeping with the show's fund-raising purposes, ticket prices were slashed on Wednesday to counter slow sales. But with many thousands of visitors jamming Las Vegas for the three-day holiday weekend, producers were confident the show would be sold out by the 7 pm showtime. ◆

Big Gamble in Vegas Pays Off

Jackson concert a dud, but not for Michael.

Newsday, 21 February 1994

La Toya didn't turn up; Elizabeth Taylor and Minister Louis Farrakhan did, although only one of them appeared on stage.

It was late, it was long and it was far from an entertainment milestone. So much nebulous positivism prevailed it could have been a New Age teach-in. Tickets were still being sold at showtime, and a fishy "upgrading" system moved holders of $150 tickets into $500 seats. Amid all the hoopla, though, the *Jackson Family Honors* TV special was finally taped Saturday evening at the MGM Grand Garden. NBC will air the show tomorrow at 9 pm.

As a high-priced charity concert, the Jacksons' supposed extravaganza was a poorly conceived, cheesy dud. But as a live event, *The Jackson Family Honors* was a triumph — at least for one member of the clan.

The show was well past the two-hour mark when Michael finally appeared to present an award to Motown Records founder Berry Gordy. The diverse audience, having paid as much as $1,000 for the privilege, had already endured metal detectors, a 90-minute wait from the supposed starting time, camera-obstructed sightlines and a disconnected collection of routine, more-or-less live performances by Another Bad Creation, Janet Jackson, Celine Dion, Bruce Hornsby and Jermaine Jackson. The extended family (minus Michael and Janet) did a homey number; Smokey Robinson and Gladys Knight took part in a glib 13-fragment Motown medley; and Robinson sang a tuneless, fawning ode to Gordy. All the acts acquitted themselves adequately, but none of this haphazard hit parade quite fit the bill of a "special."

Then came Michael. Ever since his scandal broke, the $64 question has been whether his fans would abandon him. Judging by the unreserved enthusiasm that greeted him Saturday, those worries are over. Wearing black trousers, a black jacket with a leaf design and a red armband on his right sleeve, Michael basked in the adulation, grinning and blowing kisses, almost overtaken by emotion. Finally, in a strong, assured voice, he read a speech about the greatness of "Mr. Gordy." Like everything else said (or sung) during the cliché-and-platitude-riddled show, the effusiveness of this sentimental tribute would have shamed the most lovestruck schoolboy. When Gordy mounted the stage to accept the huge globe-and-doves statue, though, he turned the love light back on Michael. "I believed in you when you were nine," Gordy said. "I believe in you now. I will never stop believing in you."

The same thing happened a few minutes later, when Michael gave the evening's second Lifetime Achievement Award to Elizabeth Taylor, who limped a bit as she walked to the podium. Although she was the one being honored, Taylor praised Michael to the skies, calling him "glorious, loving and benevolent." (She also called for putting "tabloid media" out of business and, in a bit that just might not make it to TV, responded crossly to the crowd's loud demand that Michael sing.)

The unique phenomenon of Michael Jackson's appeal has never been made more obvious. His family goes to all this trouble to mount an ambitious special that hasn't got any impact at all, and then Michael brings the house down just by standing alone silently on stage. How this will play on the small screen won't be known until tomorrow, but, in person, it was a breathtaking display of true star power. ◆

As it all got sillier and sillier, I was obliged to produce this ridiculous postscript:

Hey Now, What's That Sound?

Newsday, 27 February 1994

Not surprisingly, the brief tiff between Elizabeth Taylor and the live audience attending last Saturday's *Jackson Family Honors* taping in Las Vegas was excised from the show's broadcast the following Tuesday. But in light of her pointed attack on "the tabloid media" (which *did* survive the editor's cut), it would have been deliciously ironic to leave the contretemps in, as it would have debunked the misleading, but now accepted, pack reportage of the event.

For the record: Michael Jackson was not booed. It was common knowledge to any reader that his role in the show was to consist of presenting awards to Liz and Berry Gordy and join in the family's musical finale. But in the wake of mounting "We want Michael!" cheers from the stands, Taylor made the mistake of lamely attempting to explain why he wouldn't be singing a solo as he stood mutely by.

Her explanation drew a collective groan and some mild boos, probably as much to express disappointment as for the whiny tone of her remark. Rather than let it pass, Taylor added to the confusion with a peevish comment ("booing is an ugly sound") and a hasty, frozen-smile exit.

Like the myth that the Rolling Stones played "Sympathy for the Devil" at Altamont while Meredith Hunter was stabbed to death in front of them (it was "Under My Thumb"), the myth of Michael Jackson — fallen icon — being booed has been ineradicably scratched into the framework of pop culture. Given his recent actions, he may not deserve unconditional adulation. But everyone is entitled to the dignity of truth. ◆

Linda Ronstadt

Working at a large newspaper gave me the juice to access big artists, but the downside of daily journalism is the relentless pressure of deadlines. In my time at monthly magazines, I could schedule and prepare for an in-person interview, record it, put off transcribing it for a few days, write a draft, come back to it a few days later and finally, after endless tinkering, turn it in. (Which meant getting on the subway to bring typed pages or a floppy disc to an editor in the city). At *Newsday*, where a lot of the stories I did were previews of weekend concerts, I might speak to a publicist on a Tuesday, do a phoner on Wednesday — in between meetings and other things — and file the piece electronically Thursday afternoon in time for Friday's paper. That made the delays inherent in taping and transcribing unthinkable, so I just popped on a headset and typed into the company's Atex system while we talked.

I very nearly flunked typing in junior high and still do basic hunt and peck, only at around 65 words per minute. When you're trying to have a productive conversation with a bored celebrity doing their job, listening and responding and thinking and probing can be a lot to juggle. It is nerve-wracking, imprecise, distracting and a whole lot of other bad things when your stenography skills are weak. If you miss something, there's no backup.

It was a real honor to speak with Linda Ronstadt, but I'm not proud of this critical and narrow-minded article that resulted. The focus is wrong; the easy route is rarely the best one.

Feels Like Linda Ronstadt

Newsday, 21 May 1995

"It all began with a pink skirt," says Linda Ronstadt. What pulled her into the TV tiff that turned into a radio assault by Howard Stern was an eye-catching garment Robin Quivers wore when she appeared on *The Tonight Show* to plug her book three weeks ago.

"I was in the green room, chatting," recalls Ronstadt, who was on Jay Leno's show that night to promote her latest album, *Feels Like Home*, one of the best in a three-decade career. "I looked over at the monitor and noticed this lovely African-American woman in a pink skirt. My interest was piqued. She was talking about penises and I felt sorry for her. Then she started talking about Howard and how she shouldn't be criticized for his racist remarks. I knew what he had said about Selena. He's also made a lot of Mexican remarks."

Once she joined the sidekick-turned-author on camera, Ronstadt took issue with Quivers' defense of Stern, saying that, as a woman and as a Mexican-American, she was offended. "[Quivers] went into overload and said I have no right to say I was offended," says the singer. The next day, Stern got into the act, lashing into Ronstadt on his radio program. Although she didn't hear the broadcast, Ronstadt says she heard about it. "A person who spends his life offending people was offended that I was offended. What an idiot."

One Ronstadt view Stern might endorse is the low esteem in which she holds some of her early work. In a 1993 article, she told the *Los Angeles Times*, "The album covers were [often] better than the records" and said of "You're No Good," her first chart-topping 45, "I didn't sing it very well." The subject has since become an interview staple.

"Peter Asher did very good production on those records," she now says, "but I didn't learn how to sing on a record until 1980. *Get Closer* [1982] was the first time I learned how to approach recording vocals. Most of my vocals before that were [recorded] live. Overdubbing gives me amazing freedom," she says of the process by which she assembles a final vocal track from numerous studio takes. "You can study those vocals in detail."

There's little to complain about on *Feels Like Home*, a superbly crafted and sung eclectic album that heralds her rebirth as a mainstream contemporary singer. Coming on the heels of 1993's encouraging but wan *Winter Light*, it continues her return from the cultural detours she took in the '80s. The album begins with a version of Tom Petty's "The Waiting," sung with rock gusto few others so familiar with the works of Gershwin and Berlin would be able to summon and ends with an exquisitely simple reading of the Carter Family's "Lover's Return," a homespun ode about the ravages of time.

Feels Like Home, which also has songs by Randy Newman, Neil Young and Matraca Berg, is the perfect calling card for a singer who has never limited her horizons beyond following a self-imposed edict that, stylistically, "It has to be something I heard in my living room before I was eight or ten." Using that compass, she has thrown herself into standards recorded with the Nelson Riddle Orchestra and, singing in Spanish, records of traditional canciones (from the Mexican side of her Southwest heritage) and Afro-Cuban salsa and balladry. "I didn't find enough good material to sing in contemporary pop in the '70s," explains Ronstadt. "It's rhythm music and it's suited for instrumental players. A Rodgers and Hart song is superb for a vocalist like me. It gives me a chance to exercise my instrument."

As a non-writing singer who embraces bluegrass, country, Motown, '50s and '60s rock and roll (from doo-wop to the Everly Brothers to Chuck Berry) and singer-songwriters as diverse as Jackson Browne, Bob Dylan, Warren Zevon and Jimmy Webb, Ronstadt brought a lot of guests to the Southern California country-rock-lite party in the '70s. Discerning and diverse though her taste in high-quality songs was (and is), not everything she put through the L.A. studio wash came out with the same bright colors they went in with. Her treatment of soul music, for instance, was never natural or convincing; careful singing wasn't what it took to get a toehold in songs eternalized by Smokey Robinson and Martha Reeves.

Even in more conducive genres, Ronstadt has never managed to fully commandeer any of the best-known songs that have become hits for her. But if she hasn't overshadowed the originals, Ronstadt has still done all right by many of them. Without much digging through the oeuvre, it's easy to point to Roy Orbison's "Blue Bayou," the Everly Brothers' "When Will I Be Loved," Zevon's "Poor Poor Pitiful Me" and even Buddy Holly's sacred "That'll Be the Day" and "It's So Easy" as fully positive beneficiaries of her efforts.

Throughout her career, the region in which Ronstadt has been strongest and most consistently engaging is country. (Not for nothing has she forged strong collaborative friendships with Dolly Parton and Emmylou Harris.) Ever since her chart debut in 1967 with Mike Nesmith's twangy "Different Drum," Ronstadt has used the tearful catch in her strong, clear voice to carve a unique place as a country outsider who can convincingly handle traditional Nashville music and the mainstream imitation pioneered by her pals in the Eagles. While becoming a model of crossover dilution, she also has stayed truer to the heritage of country music than the hat acts that have taken it over.

Feels Like Home has brought Ronstadt out on the road for her first English-language tour since 1990. The infrequency of her concert sorties is intentional. "I don't want to tour at all," she announces. "I've tried to quit for years, but I've put so much effort into the records, I don't want to throw them away. If you don't tour, they don't sell." If she doesn't remain on the treadmill, Ronstadt says, "I could live a comfortable — not lavish — lifestyle for the rest of my life." But, with a four-year-old adopted daughter to think of (they live in San Francisco; she also owns a home in Tucson, her birthplace), she's grown financially conservative.

"It's important to me to not make some move that means I don't have money for the future. I don't want to spend a lot of money on a record that doesn't recoup." (A record must earn back — "recoup" — the label's advance payment against its expected royalties before the artist receives any further revenue from it.) "I just want to recoup on each record so I can make the next one."

The next one she has in mind is a Christmas record. "I'm not religious, but I'm interested in the rhythm of the seasons and how people express their spiritual ideas in music," she says. Her plan is to sing carols from the 16th and 19th Centuries, and to feature the glass harmonica, a bizarre instrument invented by Ben Franklin that produces an ethereal whistle of piercing clarity. "It's a mechanical version of rubbed glasses. It was banned in the 19th Century: People were getting lead poisoning and going mad, so it was thought to be an instrument of the devil."

Meanwhile, she rationalizes the rigors of the road as "an excuse to rehearse. I love to rehearse, to refine music. Every song I sing is a work in progress. A record is [only] the starting point. I learn what makes a song tick every time I sing it; I explore it more, learn more about it, refine it."

Delving deep into the metaphysics of vocal music, this articulate, voluble woman says, "A really good song teaches you. [Singing] a Jimmy Webb song is like reading a classic book. Songs reveal things to you throughout your life.

"I resist singing stuff that is inappropriate for my age. I'm 48. I don't want to sing of an experience that was particular to me only when I was 16 or 28. There are some songs that address all those ages. Rosemary Clooney sings these beautiful songs about her girlhood, but they're about her hopes and dreams. You also get to hear how they turned out, so you get the cumulative experience of her lifetime. It's very powerful, more so than her just singing about being a young woman. Music is the sum total of your life experiences." ◆

These are the unedited notes I banged out while speaking to Ronstadt for that piece. Yes, I am a shit typist.

Linda Ronstadt, phoner May 1995

Intensity of singing in the waiting comes as a bit of a surprise
that was a song I had my eye for a long time. I'm a Tom petty fan. he's's a walking encyclopedia of rock vocal approaches. he's very derivative, but he's also so original. it's a sleight of hand. the whole approach to pop is cumulative, everything is derived from something else. you grow up admiring and emulating things. I'd wanted to do that song in a bluegrass setting, bit still approach it as rock and roll, put it into bluegrass instruments, but I told the tenors to sing like Roger mcguinn.

he's copying mcguinn who's copying bob Dylan who's copying woody guthrie. you get hooked up to a train that resonates through the generations, supercharged baggage that propels the train along. that's why I sang it that way.

the record started out to be a duet w/emmy lou then I asked dolly and the mcgarrigle sisters to join us here and there. we asked dolly to sing some trios and she said no, she was too busy. 6 months later she wanted to do a trio album, but the record company didn't want a trio record because country radio wouldn'y play it. I said we'd promote the record as a trio, because I feel very proud of the last one and country music wasn't paying much attention to traditional country music. dolly felt it was a commitment she couldn't honor and wanted us to wait until it was convenient for her to put out the record. if emmy and I had then gone back and made records of our own we would have had to wait 2 years to put the trio out. emmy got a few tracks out of the process, I got a few tracks. we took the record apart, and as the producer I had to steer this boat through the stormy seas. I had to take this material I was very close to and didn't want to lose it. I decided a mandolin was the continuous thread. the record had started out with this strong traditional bias. to make this a solo record in English, it had to have a contemporary. aspect to it. the trio wasn't interested in the waiting, but that had been a reject. so I was happy to see it get another airing.

I'm looking forward to getting another chance to sing with emmy. she's a singing sister to me. our sensibilities are more evenly matched than it was with the trio. our tastes are different than dolly's. on the trio albums we stuck to the traditional; material dolly is so good at. blue train and after the gold rush were both tracks we were using for the trio. they were charming with the trio, but they bloomed as a solo effort.

take me through your approach to album making
stuff is usually rolling around in my head. t has to be something I heard in my living room before I was 8 or 10. in my recording career I've gone back further and further in my childhood. I've done a lot of eclectic stuff, with my pop records, but the specialized stuff - Nelson, Mexican traditional - you can't mix it up, it does a terrible disservice, so it has to be in one clump as a concept. it's such a lot of prep. to make it sound like a professional.: research and practice and work. I get immersed in it and then I perform it so I'm several years in it before it's finished with me.

pleasure/pain in touring
I've never liked touring. it's an excuse to rehearse. I love to rehearse, to refine music. it's paid rehearsal. it's always work in progress. every song I sing is a work in progress. a record is the starting point. as I learn what makes a song tick every time I sing it I explore it more, learn more about, refine it. a really good song teaches you. 90% of

recording is listening. a producer listens to a song in microscopic detail and then makes tiny corrections. a song like a j. Webb song is like reading a CLASSIC book. reading Dostoevsky in h.s., reading it as a 40 year old you have no idea. songs reveal things to you through your life.

you were quoted by Robert hilburn in '93 as being less than proud of your early pop records. what's the cutoff point and what have you since improved?
I felt it at the time. peter asher did very good prod. on those records but I didn't learn how to sing on a record until 1980. get closer was the first time I learned how to approach recording vocals. most of my vocals before that were live. if you're singing a track and that's the version that's liable to stay there for years and years you get self-conscious. with overdubbing it gives me amazing freedom. you study those vocals in detail, the same way an opera singer does. I'm a recording artist, that's where I'm freest to sing, in the studio. my most intense emotional experiences and my best technical singing is in the studio.

having to travel every day is exhausting. eating crappy food is awful. for years I thought Cleveland was Dan Swingo's, this horrible rock and roll hotel where we used to stay.

folk/country music _ the erasing of some barriers and the creation of others
I'm too involved with my own stuff. I'm a singer and I've found not enough good material to sing in contemporary pop. it's rhythm music and it's suited for instrumental players. I didn't find enough to sing in the 70s. a Rogers and hart song is superb for a vocalist like me. it gives me a chance to exercise my instrument. I was so frustrated I climbed out of the box. I went to Joe papp and begged him for a job. I was working in places that were completely inappropriate for music. it was an artistic decision.

as I began to make records I used to look at Judy Collins as a role model. since then I've looked to other people for models. what was on my mind was making a living. I just want to recoup on each record so I can make the next one.

I've been working with this 18th century glass instrument called the armonica, invented by ben franklin, a mechanical version of rubbed glasses. it was banned in the 19th century because people were getting lead poisoning. people were going mad, and it was thought it was a devil's instrument. used on winter light record. its sound is so flattering to vocal tones, I put layers together. I want to use it for an xmas record. it's perfect for a xmas record. I've found 16th century, 19th and contemporary stuff I can do. as long as it's real music I'm really happy to do it.

I'm not religious but I'm interested in the rhythm of the seasons and how people express their spiritual ideas in music. music is prayer.

robin givens flap on leno: were you surprised at the vehemence of the reaction?
I didn't listen to his response. I only know second hand what he said. I was in the green room, chatting. I looked over at the monitor and noted this lovely African-American woman in a pink skirt and she was talking about penises and I felt sorry for her. my interest was piqued and she started talking about Howard and she shouldn't be criticized for his racist remarks. I knew what he had said about selena. he's also made a lot of Mexican remarks. no one complains about archie bunker she said. I said he's not speaking as a character, those are his own beliefs and I find it offensive. she went into overload and said I have no right to say I was offended. then he got on the radio and got after robin and said I'm not a character and that those are my feelings. a person who spends his life offending people was offended that I was offended. what an idiot.

how long do you look into the future as an artist?
I don't want to tour at all. I've tried to quit for years. but I've put so much effort into the records I don't want to throw them away. if you don't tour, they don't sell. I could live a comfortable, not lavish, lifestyle for the rest of my life. it's important to me to be responsible and not make some move that means I don't have money for the future. I don't want to spend a lot of money on a record that doesn't recoup because that would cut into my royalties. I also love to knit. I sing in Tucson with family and a choir. I resist singing stuff that is inappropriate for my age, I'm 48. I

don't want to sing of an experience that was particular to me only when I was 16 or 38. there are some songs that address all those ages. I watched these women flamenco singers sing of their entire lives, the whole works. rosemary clooney sings these beautiful songs of her girlhood, but they were her hopes and dreams. but I also get to hear the cumulative experience of her lifetime. her reflections. it's very powerful, more so than her singing about being a young women. music is the sum total of your life experiences.

neil young
he is the greatest rock star the world has ever known. I toured with him 4 months and I stayed for every single show. his music is that good. he's invited me many times to sing on his records. randy newman, who I don't think likes any vocal music, he listens to pop music. he's one of my biggest heroes. he once said to me that he listened to all these different singers and writers and he said Neil young is the best. this isn't a horse race, there are many bests, but pop music gets a lot of people through their lives and Neil does it a little better than most. ◆

A Disciplined and Distinctive Ronstadt

The life of the party. Saturday at Radio City Music Hall. The Williams Brothers opened.
Newsday, 15 May 1995

The pop singers of another era got their songs from Tin Pan Alley or the Brill Building, magical kingdoms that produced raw material rather than finished performances. An artist had to stake his or her claim to a prime picking by making the record that would become the one before someone else did.

That equation changed when songwriting became a point of pride for performers. Very few members of the '60s generation were able to sustain credible rock careers without a steady source of exclusive material; having to rely on other people's hits was an impediment to establishing a stylistic identity and creative independence.

As one of the very few rock-era giants who doesn't write music, Linda Ronstadt has made her way along a pre-rock path, building her exceptional career by choosing and covering songs, some of them extremely well-known, from a wide range of eras and genres. At Radio City Saturday, in what she called her first English-language tour in five years, applause greeted the familiar introductions to many of her oldies — like the smeary guitar leading into the Stones' "Tumbling Dice," the peppy beat setting off Martha and the Vandellas' "Heat Wave" — but it was impossible to be sure the recognition wasn't for the original songs as much as her renditions of them. The crowd's cool response to a downbeat set of Jimmy Webb tunes in the middle of the 105-minute show only increased that suspicion.

Ronstadt began by showcasing her excellent new album, *Feels Like Home*. Following the record's running order, she sang Tom Petty's "The Waiting," Matraca Berg's "Walk On," Harley Allen's "High Sierra," Neil Young's "After the Gold Rush," Jennifer Kimball and Tom Kimmel's "Blue Train" and Randy Newman's "Feels Like Home," easily navigating the transitions between rock, country and several stripes of singer-songwriterdom. Throughout, Ronstadt made good use of her powerful voice and finely tuned skills, carefully shaping sounds with precise control and subtle shadings.

Her accuracy came in most useful on "After the Gold Rush," for which she brought out four female backup singers and Dennis James, a player of the glass armonica, a contraption that produces haunting tone slivers like a high-pitched whistle. In a stunning display, this tender, not entirely graceful song reached to the heavens to become gorgeous music of the spheres.

While Ronstadt's discipline helped her tease distinctive qualities out of songs as diverse as Roy Orbison's "Blue Bayou," Doris Troy's "Just One Look" and Warren Zevon's "Poor Poor Pitiful Me," the band followed her careful lead right out the window of restraint. The eight musicians' clinical, soul-free exactitude, parceled into three-minute arrangements that did little more than re-create studio sounds, sucked life from some great songs. Perhaps by design, it fell to Ronstadt to carry all of the show's emotional weight, which she did, singing like she meant every word (even those she read off a foot-level TelePrompTer). ◆

Billy Joel

In addition to the many concert and album reviews I wrote for *Newsday*, I banged out a fair number of long features, all at a pace that made my previous life in monthly magazines feel like a leisurely stroll with plenty of time to reflect.

As the hometown superstar of Long Island, Billy Joel was a mandatory subject for the paper's pop staff, and so — upon the occasion of his *River of Dreams* album (the one with the childish painting by the then-Mrs. Joel on the cover) in July 1993 — I sat down with him. He had, as I recall, stubby fingers (kind of like Vienna sausages, if you will) for a piano player, and his brash, open honesty, an easy sense of self-deprecating humor to cut the satisfied confidence of stardom with a good measure of in-person charm, was enough to vanquish a few oddly pretentious attempts at intellectualism. He used the phrase *sturm und drang* in passing and quoted Flaubert, recalling the 19th century French novelist's "Be regular and orderly in your life, so that you may be violent and original in your work" as "An artist should live as normal and as dull and as regular a life so he can be completely insane for his art." Not bad for a rock icon.

As it turned out, finding nice things to say about Joel despite a lifetime of disdain for his music was no great hardship. I enjoyed talking to him and I liked the way the piece turned out. But when it ran, my mention of someone other than Joel in the lede for some reason ruffled the journalistic sensibilities of the paper's top editor, Tony Marro, and he conveyed his unhappiness to my boss, who shared it with me. That stung, and it made me wonder who I was working for.

He's Still Keeping the Faith

Newsday, 10 August 1993

John Sebastian of the Lovin' Spoonful was all of 22 when he sang, "I think I've come to see myself at last."

Billy Joel has taken twice as long to become sure of his own place in the creative world. In his third decade as a five-zillion-served pop composer and performer, the 44-year-old finally understands where he stands. Now confident rather than cocky, he seems remarkably comfortable and relaxed in the knowledge.

"I always found people who elevated themselves because they thought they were artists to be somewhat ridiculous and pretentious," he says during an interview Saturday. One is easily put in mind of Sting's haughty condescension, Paul Simon's world-beating appropriations or Bruce Springsteen's gold-plated populism.

America's real middle-class icon is a forthright suburbanite who has never striven to be placed above his audience or disclaim his beloved musical influences, a real-world nebbish whose stubby fingers put the Midas touch to instantly memorable songs. Without a trace of hubris, this superstar — who can attempt a Flaubert quote in one breath and compare musical sidemen to erstwhile Yankee utility infielder Fred Stanley in the next — says, "I've tried to stay away from the artsy-fartsy artiste aspect of it. Now I can see, at this age, I am an artist and very proud of it. I've come to understand that I don't need anybody else to tell me I'm good enough.

"You watch these award shows where all the artists are in one room hoping to win the *tchotchke*," he says, affecting an announcer's voice: "Here we are, ladies and gentlemen, the 25th annual *Tchotchke Awards*. And here you've got Eric Clapton, Sting, Nirvana, Natalie Cole, Whitney Houston, Billy Joel, blah, blah, blah. This is a pretty power-packed room, therefore you get some major advertising dollars spent on the time. The producers of the show make the money. The artist who wins the tchotchke gets a *tchotchke*, which is worth about $5.98. The plaque falls off, but there we all are, wanting that *tchotchke*. We think it is going to legitimize what we do. It never does."

Switching to the comic delivery of George Carlin, Joel continues. "'How many *tchotchkes* did you win?' '*He's* got three *tchotchkes*.' 'Well, he's a five-time *tchotchke* winner.' 'He's one of the living *tchotchke* legends.'"

On *River of Dreams*, his first album since 1989's triple-platinum *Storm Front*, Long Island's living *tchotchke* legend takes philosophical stock of middle age and what's truly important in life. "The essence of the album is a loss of faith, a search for and understanding of how to deal with that, and a renewal of faith in substantial things: faith in love, faith in one's self, faith in the things that have always been there." (For those keeping score, the word also appears in six of the ten songs.)

Although the album contains a compassionate, sweet lullaby to his seven-year-old daughter that, he says, answered her questions about what happens when you die, Joel rejects the suggestion that yesterday's angry young man has achieved serenity.

"I always assumed that when you got to this age, life would calm down, things would become boring and mundane. That I would start to vote...Republican. That when you got into your forties you were no longer in any way that crazy guy that you were when you were a teenager.

"I found that not to be the case. I am as crazy as I was when I was a teenager, and as wildly romantic, and as emotional. I just know more stuff. I have acquired some wisdom — not enough, I want more — and I don't get as angry about nickel and dime stuff. I get angry about bigger things now."

One of the bigger things Joel is angry about now provides a central theme of the album. Having spent much of the prior week giving depositions in his four-year-old lawsuit against ex-manager and ex-brother-in-law Frank Weber, Joel — who at one point in the conversation changes chairs, explaining that the one he's in feels like a witness stand — acknowledges that *River of Dreams* partly concerns "the foolishness of the search for justice. There is no justice. There is no justice," he says emphatically. His voice is steely and bitter.

The depth of Joel's disillusionment surfaces in a musical hate letter, "The Great Wall of China," clearly aimed at his former associate, whom he accuses of mismanaging and misappropriating his money. "Your role was protective, your soul was too defective," he sings. Asked about the song's use of the Great Wall as an anything-is-possible metaphor, Joel notes that he played Cuba in 1979 and the USSR in 1987. "China is still one of the last exotic unknown places to people who live where I live."

The stately and handsome "All About Soul" — which began as "The Motorcycle Song," a fast number about "middle-aged dentists and insurance salesmen getting themselves in biker gear and buying Harleys" — bears some of the same frustration at venality but mends the psychic wounds with love.

Through all the adversity, the love of a good woman — namely Joel's wife, Christie Brinkley, who painted the album's primitivist cover — comes to the rescue. The crucial line of the song (if not the entire album) provocatively announces, "Under the love is the stronger emotion."

What does Joel consider the underpinning of love? "The things that sustain love when you question love, when love alone isn't enough," he replies. "The basic inner something which I refer to as soul, the inner core: what you call on when the [shit] really comes down. Soul is what each person has within before there is love, or after there is love."

On this introspective, personal record, besides venting his spleen and opening his heart, Joel allows himself a long-denied indulgence: to sing the blues, on "A Minor Variation," a song he compares stylistically to the Memphis soul sound of Otis Redding and Wilson Pickett.

"Who the hell am I to complain? I'm supposed to have this phenomenal life. But I had the blues, and it felt good to actually say, 'Some days I have to give right into the blues.'

"I was suicidal when I was 21. I checked myself into an observation ward; it was a great experience for me because I saw people who had really incredible problems. When I got out of there I never looked back. I said I will never feel sorry for myself for another two seconds. This time, I happened to go, OK, I do have the blues, and I went on with it."

The year it took to write and record *River of Dreams* began last summer, in a Southampton church where Joel had installed a temporary studio to cut two Elvis Presley tunes for the Honeymoon in Vegas soundtrack. When he needed to relocate, "I looked around in my neck of the woods — out in the East End [of Long Island] — and I went over to Shelter Island. In a boatyard, I found a lobster shed, where they used to store lobster traps, which was big enough and secluded enough. That became the Shelter Island studio.

"I was producing; we recorded half a dozen or more songs. My idea of production is non-production. I don't do any more than three takes when we're recording, 'cause I still wanna like the thing."

Joel ultimately decided there was a "lot more that could be done" with the songs he had recorded. Enter producer-guitarist Danny Kortchmar, a New York-born veteran known for his Southern California work with James Taylor, Don Henley, Stevie Nicks and many others. Joel played Kortchmar the tapes from Shelter Island. "He listened to it and had some very, very strong ideas." The two decided to re-record the songs.

One of Kortchmar's ideas was to get Leslie West, the Mountain guitarist whose first band, Long Island's own Vagrants, had a big local influence on Billy Joel's late-'60s outfit, the Hassles. Ironically, "Shades of Grey," the track which actually invokes West's signature American Cream sound, features guitarist Tommy Byrnes firing up the fuzzbox. "Cream would write songs about so many fantastic colors, use these bizarre colorful images," notes Joel. "I was talking about exactly the opposite: shades of gray. I thought this was a terrific chance to use the Cream arrangement as irony."

River of Dreams was more or less created in the sequence it appears. "Each song got written in reaction to the song which came before it and recorded likewise. Once I've gotten to a certain point, [an album] becomes its own entity, and I work towards the resolution, which is why I don't write that many more songs than are on the album.

"Some artists write twenty, thirty songs and pick the best ones. What you hear is what I've written. [Although] there was a song, "You Picked a Real Bad Time," which didn't end up on the album but may end up on a B-side." And, he admits, there was one total reject. Joel describes the discarded number as "a dog. It was an art song called 'The Winter Crossing' which I took out back and shot. It was really pretentious and stupid." He played the doomed tune once for Danny Kortchmar and engineer Niko Bolas. "I'm watching Danny and Niko behind the console. I see their entire faces, and as the song goes along, I see less of their faces. Now I only see up to their noses. Then, as I'm further into the song, I just see eyes — very wide, open eyes. And I realize, as I'm singing it, that this really is a piece of [shit]. And I stopped and I said, OK. I'm sorry. And that was it."

With the album likely to follow its title track, already No. 28 in *Billboard*, up the charts, Joel is rehearsing for a tour to begin Sept. 10 in Portland, Maine. The New York dates, he says, will be in October at Madison Square Garden. (Word has it he will do six nights between Oct. 2 and 12.) But he firmly denies rumors of a Central Park show. In addition, Billy Joel's work may finally reach another part of Manhattan. "I talked with Pete Townshend in Cleveland; we went for the Rock and Roll Hall of Fame hodgepodge thing. I have a great deal of respect for Townshend. He said, 'Billy, you've got to write a Broadway musical.' He was insisting that I do this. He said, 'You're probably the guy best suited to do this in this day and age, to bring pop and the rock and roll sensibility into the musical theater.'"

"I had been approached by other people about doing a Broadway musical, but when Pete Townshend told me that, it was the first time I really seriously have considered that I am going to do that. I intend to do it."

For Billy the Man, at 44, the curtain also rises. ◆

Another surprising response to that feature came in a record review column faxed to me by a publicist pal, who scribbled a snide (but funny) note on it: "Wow! You can retire now! You made the Atlanta *Creative Loafing* — slagged by a podunk rock-crit who works at a book store!"

This is what said crit, David T. Lindsay, had to say:

> Normally it would be a waste of space to discuss someone like [Billy] Joel, space where I could be suggesting some new Sympathy or Hell Yeah release rather than discussing rock careerism, but recently I was thumbing through *New York Newsday* and ran across an Ira Robbins review that was glowing, gushing and hallowed-be-thy-name of Joel's newest. Now I respect Robbins both for his wit and his insights, so I grabbed a CD for a listen. To be blunt, *River of Dreams* sucks. By far the worst record of a ponderous career, Joel's cafeteria crooner searching has never been less focused; one song sounds like a Cars-ish ripoff to be followed by a pastiche of Sly & the Family Stone with a Fonziana accent. So, why would an established, respected rock critic bill and coo over an obvious shitcan of bile? Because of rock critic careerism — that obligation, not to one's integrity or craft, but to an industry that he's become parasitic to support. The joke here is that rock critics hold the power to correct the industry's indulgence but choose instead the path of least resistance so as to gain access to celebrity know-nothings like Joel. It's people like Robbins who come up with campaigns for Pepsi to give away Ray Charles "Uh-Huh!" sunglasses — think about it.
>
> So back to *River of Dreams*, it's a banged together collage of musical scrapage that leads nowhere, revealing just how arrogant this guy must be. Joel knows this isn't his best work. Ira Robbins knows it sucks. But then I'm not the least bit affected by the delusions of a dying industry too self-righteous to learn from its own mistakes.

I can only assume that commentary was prompted by the above article, since I don't recall (and can't find any evidence in my archive) having written a review of that album. And my description of it as an "introspective, personal record" and one of its songs as "stately and handsome" doesn't exactly read as "glowing, gushing and hallowed-be-thy-name" to me. And while I knew better than to shit on an album by the newspaper's hometown hero in the body of a friendly profile, I don't think that makes me the kind of person who would give away Ray Charles' Ray-Bans.

A few months later, Phil Collins turned out to be, oddly enough, pretty much the same sort of interview subject as Billy Joel — entertaining in person, convincingly humble, full of strong feelings barely held in check. Maybe not as self-aware. But open enough to consider (if not actually take) my lyrical suggestion. (I clearly missed a chance to note his cinematic confusion potential with Bob Hoskins.)

Phil Collins: "I am a very normal, straight-ahead person..."

Newsday, 31 October 1993

Some guys have all the fun; others do all the work. Phil Collins has it both ways.

After a teenage stint in London theater and one album with a band called Flaming Youth, Phil Collins entered music's big leagues well behind the spotlight, playing drums in Genesis — then an arty progressive-rock band of high critical standing and modest commercial appeal. That might have been enough for some percussion specialists. But not this one.

Collins' assumption of vocal duties from Peter Gabriel in 1975 coincided with Genesis's swing toward the middle, escaping its cult ghetto for the global pop arena. That same year, Collins began moonlighting in Brand X, a fusion jazz band. Even before that sideline wound down in the '80s, he revved up a hit-factory solo career that has co-existed with Genesis ever since. Next week, the spotlight turns back on Collins, with the release of *Both Sides*.

While he still finds time to guest on records by people like Eric Clapton, Robert Plant, Paul McCartney and Tears for Fears, the only musician to play *Live Aid* on both sides of the Atlantic has also ventured successfully into record production and film acting, appearing most recently in HBO's *...And the Band Played On* and an Australian feature, *Frauds*. What makes Phil run? "I only ever wanted a bit of respect from other musicians," he says, reflecting on his early days. "I wondered if other drummers liked me as much as I liked Keith Moon and Ginger Baker."

So, that's it. The Dangerfield factor. A likely clue to explain this restless, ambitious overachiever and his drive to collaborate with other highly rated musicians. Questioned about unfulfilled ambitions, Collins cites the greats he hoped to work with — Weather Report keyboardist Joe Zawinul, the late Miles Davis and big band drummer Buddy Rich — and explains the related appeal of acting.

"Maybe one of the reasons I'm taking [it] up is because I'm starting at the ground level," he offers. Here, too, his dreams are collaborative. "There's a lot of people out there that I'd love to work with: Tommy Lee Jones, Nicholson, Jimmy Stewart before he dies."

Whatever the motivation, Collins has reached a point of increasing returns in his professional life. "I just keep getting asked to do interesting things. The more I do, the more opportunities I get, and the more visibility I have to the people I want to work with."

In person, Collins exudes the common decency and awareness of a rock superstar still living in the material world. "I am a very normal, straight-ahead person. I save my money in case the bubble bursts; my mum and dad told me to do that," he says politely. Between such modest, workmanlike values and unbridled enthusiasm for his work, Collins seems like someone who has to pinch himself once in a while to be sure the incredible achievements of his 42 years aren't just dreams.

"From when I started playing the drums, before Genesis, I had my life mapped out. I thought I'd be in a pop group until that fizzled out, then a show band or a big band and then close my life in the orchestra pit." Back in the mid-'60s, while playing the Artful Dodger in a West End production of *Oliver!* he'd decided that was where serious musicians ended up. But other cultural forces were at work. Emblematic of his pop future, Collins was an extra in the theater scene at the end of *A Hard Day's Night*. Equally emblematic of his frustration at being overlooked and underappreciated, he doesn't actually appear in the film. "My non-image has worked against me getting on the covers of certain magazines, but [as an actor] it's a benefit; I don't have that strong rock-star personality to shake off, like Mick Jagger or David Bowie." He makes it sound like a fair trade.

Both Sides begins a new musical era for Collins. Three years ago, he culminated a decade of such smashes as "In the Air Tonight," "Against All Odds (Take a Look at Me Now)," "One More Night," "Sussudio" and "Groovy Kind of Love" by releasing *Serious Hits...Live!*, a concert album that includes them all. After a period of heavy Genesis activity (the 1991 *We Can't Dance* album and subsequent tour and live album), he began working on this somber, reflective album with newfound personal purpose — although he actually didn't realize what it was at the time. As he explains in the liner notes, "This batch of songs crept up behind me . . ."

Collins will discuss the album's subject matter in only the vaguest terms, but songs like "Can't Turn Back the Years," "I've Forgotten Everything" and "Survivors" all address a past love with melancholy, regret and a plea for forgiveness. "The lyrics on this album are very true, very real," he acknowledges. "Some songs are easier to talk about. But others, it's such a delicate situation, because life goes on."

Such discretion — always a bizarre conceit for an artist releasing cryptic million-sellers about personal business — is surprising in light of Collins's frank acknowledgment of the specific impulse that initially pushed him to write songs. (And, given the superficial evidence of his lyrics, may have done so again.)

Following the acrimonious end of Collins' first marriage in 1979, he says, "I was in a bad way, emotionally. I actually left the band. We had dinner one night and I said, 'Listen, I'm off to Vancouver tomorrow to chase the family. If you don't mind operating out of Vancouver, we've still got a band. Otherwise, I'm off.' The guys said, 'Wait. You go do your thing; we'll do our solo albums. You come back when you're ready.' Which was very wise of them. I came back two or three months later, and nothing had changed. They were midway through their solo albums, and I had nothing else to do. That's when I started to write."

Besides "In the Air Tonight" — the memorably atmospheric centerpiece of Collins' 1981 debut, *Face Value* — his first burst of solo composing yielded two tracks on Genesis's 1980 album, *Duke*: "Misunderstanding" and "Please Don't Ask," which Collins describes as "one of the most personal songs I've ever written, that lays out all the things I feel about my kids. I wrote all those songs around that time, just trying to get through the day. I was writing them really as messages. Not being very articulate, I thought, when [my ex-wife] hears this, she'll understand what I mean. Their real duty's for her. I must admit I was enjoying it. This was very creative for me, I was writing these songs and really enjoying it. But I was miserable as hell."

Now that he's happily remarried, raising young children and truly having it all, there's a perverse irony to his discovery of demons needing exorcism. Asked about *Both Sides*, Collins says, "I didn't write any of the songs specifically to fit in with anything. It's just a couple of things that happened to me, certain things in my past that I thought I'd worked out and dealt with. It became physically apparent to me that I hadn't. I would not necessarily choose to write songs about them, but when I sit down at a piano and these words, these feelings come out, I'm not going to fight it."

One thing Collins *will* fight is the critical brickbats aimed at the social concerns he expressed on 1989's *...But Seriously*. Though obviously well-meant, his sympathy for the homeless on "Another Day in Paradise" struck some as effete mush pitched from an ivory tower. Collins' remark to a writer from Canada's *Music Express* ("I see what is happening on the street from my car, the same as everybody else") didn't dispel that impression. Undaunted, he included another dose of urban reality on *Both Sides*. A verse of the album's first single, "Both Sides of the Story," was inspired by a scene in *Grand Canyon*, a film steeped in liberal insensitivity.

[The article quotes lyrics with a line about "ghetto kid."]

"*Ghetto* kid"? Why renew a dated word that Elvis Presley ran into the pop graveyard a generation ago?

"The reason it was 'ghetto' was to mean anybody," explains Collins. "I wanted to take the emphasis away from it being racist. What else could I have said?" Offered a few hasty suggestions, he fixes on one. "I guess if I had thought about it, I could have said city kid." The next afternoon, at the West Village loft where the video for "Everyday" is being shot, Collins is still ruminating on the choice of words. "I thought afterwards it's just like potayto or potahto, but if I'd thought of it, maybe I'd have used 'city kid.' When we play in New York, I may sing 'city kid'." [*P.S.: He didn't.*]

Such openness is clearly in Collins' favor. Where other superstars use their commercial clout as an excuse for indefensible arrogance and misbehavior, Collins — who has certainly done it all for long enough to be able to claim any haughty privilege he wants — remains a down-to-earth journeyman, vulnerable but optimistic, ready for any artistic challenge that comes along. In a business that generally rewards accomplishment with hubris and talent with laziness, Phil Collins's endless search for ways to prove himself has only made him more human. ◆

This sidebar ran with the piece:

Alone Again, Naturally

Where does *Both Sides* leave Genesis?

"There's no chance of any Genesis activity between now and, I'd say, the middle of 1995," says Phil Collins, explaining that guitarist Mike Rutherford is making a solo album and keyboardist Tony Banks wants to pursue film soundtrack work.

"I've just come off the most personal, exhilarating, fulfilling time making this record; I've touched the nerve on a lot of the songs. At the moment, there's no room for Genesis in my mind.

"Two weeks ago, Genesis did a charity show in England: Queen, Clapton, us and Pink Floyd. Suddenly I was onstage singing 'I Can't Dance,' 'Invisible Touch' and 'Turn It on Again' — it was culture shock. I was acting [the songs]; it wasn't what I feel. That worried me. Even though I was singing my lyrics, it was a different me. The more you hit that nail square on the head, the less you want to deal with anything else.

"I can see a time coming when we'll just make records, 'cause that's good fun. But to go on the road and play a potted history of the band, which involves lots of other moments I can't stand up and be counted for anymore — that might change." ◆

We did the interview for the piece in two sessions on consecutive days, which proved particularly helpful.

Phil Collins, 27 September 1993

How did you pick up all the instruments you now play?

They're all keyboard-based. I don't actually play bass or guitar, they're all sampled. The secret of the end result is that it should sound like someone *was* playing them. I was putting my hands on the keyboard to make the guitar sound.

One reason I did the album on my own is that I have such a load of talented friends, it was too easy to get them. Alongside that, the music that was coming out was very personal, and I started to think, did I really want someone's interpretation? It suddenly becomes a big production, a big album when you've got other people on it. Of course, people do it all the time. When you have something that you want to see through without other people's interpretation of your ideas, it seemed the right thing to do with this record, considering the kind of songs that I was writing.

I've always done my solo records at home. all my albums have been done like that. I've got my demos and taken them into the studio and overdubbed on top of my demos. What I do in a very casual way ends up being my masters. That is important in terms of the structure of the song and some of the performances you get. It's crystallized with this album — all the vocals except for one ("We Fly So Close," because I hadn't written the lyrics) were done at home. That was just me, no engineer, just me pressing play and record.

What kind of improvising are you referring to in the liner notes?

The kind of improvisation that leads to a song being a tangible thing, with a start and an end. Whenever you're writing you've got to start somewhere and that start is with just improvising. You literally just start playing and you're improvising: sometimes it sounds crap, sometimes it actually starts to sound good. Once I've got an idea I'll record it onto DAT, just to remember it. I may even speak the chords into the microphone so I won't forget it, and I'll write down the sounds that I have. Sometimes it'll all develop very quickly — a drum machine pattern, a keyboard sound, and suddenly you've got an atmosphere there that's giving you the whole picture. Then, in an ideal world, on a good day, the lion's share of the lyrical idea — or at least what it's about — will come at the same time. A lot of these lyrics did that.

Songwriting tinkering

I had something that I found that I wanted to use that felt like it would definitely work as an introduction to "Survivors," so I added it at the beginning. Lyrically, I wanted to sum up the whole song in that introduction, and it all happened in an hour. Also, the introduction to "Sons of our Fathers" was added because I had that thought, that little piece and it was the same sentiment. I don't often think that "oh the middle 8's not right, I'm going to take it out and start again" — obviously at the writing stage you do, but once I go into the studio...

When you work alone, the song's not really written until it's mastered. How can you stop yourself from tinkering?

If you *don't* stop yourself then you become Peter Gabriel. (I say that flippantly because he takes a long time...) You just have an instinctive feeling as to when it's right. Editing... [taking bits out] There was a tendency with me in the earlier years to go through things too quickly. now I try to double-guess myself, to let more space be used to allow for the eventuality of taking things out.

Your songs are long

I'm long-winded. I take a long time to get 'round the verse. Some of my verses and choruses are like a large clock.

The lyrics on this album are very true, very real. They're not written from a what-if circumstance. Consequently, as that started to materialize, I knew that what I wanted to do was make a record that you put on and it stayed in a mood. "Both Sides of the Story," in a way, grabs your lapels; the next song lets you down a bit. The next four, five, six songs — it's a mood. I wanted to make an album that you could put on if you felt in that mood. As opposed to my earlier records, which I stand by, but they take you up and down.

Is this a concept album?

I wouldn't want to tarnish it with that... I didn't write any of the songs specifically to fit in with anything. A concept infers that you get the bones of a concept and then pad it out. This is a succession of songs that I had written.

CDs vs. LPs

With CDs, that have only a start and a finish. There's no end of Side 1, start of Side 2 — you've got to keep convincing people to listen to the next song. I wanted to keep this mood going and try and pace the album in a way that was not jarring. 'Cause some of the sentiments you're dealing with, I think, are very dangerous in terms of what I get out of the lyrics. They're very intimate and so you don't want someone to slap you around the face at the end of it.

"We Wait, We Wonder"

To me, the album finishes with "We Wait, We Wonder," and there's a postscript, "Please Come Out Tonight," which is, 'Listen, after all the bullshit that's gone on, there's just you and me. Let's put everything behind us and just go out and be normal.' That was the sentiment.

The past: Is there something happening in your life that puts you in that frame of mind?

I'm not sure, really. I mean I *am* sure, of course, I'm sure. I'm just not sure if I want to tell you. There's never one answer. I'm 42, so I'm prepared to believe that some of this was, maybe, what I'm led to believe is what happens when you get to 40, 41. I never, ever thought I'd say that. I always felt that was someone else's problem — I'm far too well-balanced for this to happen to me. It's possible that's what it is. But there are certain things in my past that I thought I'd worked out and I thought I'd dealt with, and it became physically apparent to me that I hadn't, so that's why I'm looking back into the past.

Family matters?

People. I'm not talking about just thinking; I'm talking about something material. It's not just memories. Knowing that and looking at the lyrics you'd be able to see... You've got a song like "Can't Turn Back the Years" which is acknowledging the fact of whatever you want, whatever you *think* you want. The past is just that. "Survivors" is asking for forgiveness.

From whom?

You do something, you fuck up and you ask someone for forgiveness. To me, it's a minefield, it's a jungle out there.

You write the songs and put them out and five million people are going to buy them...

Yeah, but I've already done my stuff, I've already written the lyrics.

But we want to know...the context is always an elusive quantity

Some songs are easier to talk about. But others, it's such a delicate situation because life goes on.

But you've written a song about it, which means it wasn't delicate enough to keep hands off. The person it's about knows it's about them...

Yeah, I guess. It's just a couple of things that happened to me, that I'm glad happened to me, but nevertheless have been laid to rest. There are some lyrics that sum it up more than others — ghosts that come back to haunt you, and bridges that won't burn — and I would not necessarily choose to write songs about them, but when I sit down at a piano and these words, these feelings come out, I'm not going to fight it.

When did you start writing songs?

When we were with Peter, [the songwriting credit] was always "Genesis." Everybody figured it was Peter anyway. When he left, we decided to start crediting songs to the people that actually did write them. I'd written bits and pieces, I'd been responsible for this section here, that section there. On *The Lamb Lies Down on Broadway*, I'd written a piece. *And Then There Were 3*, during the period my marriage was starting to falter a little bit and we did a lot of touring. I still hadn't written a whole song. When the family broke up, I started trying to find something to do and operating this equipment I had just bought. Amongst the first batch of things that I was writing was "Misunderstanding," which is on the *Duke* album. The song would have been on *Face Value*, but the guys wanted to use it on duke. "Please Don't Ask," which is probably one of the most personal songs I've ever written, probably a lot of people have never heard it, buried somewhere in *Duke* — a song that lays out all the things I feel about my kids, and in the air tonight. I wrote all those songs around that time. Suddenly it was very productive, writing songs just trying to get through the day.

I was really in a bad way, emotionally. I'd been to school with my first wife — "Invisible Touch" was almost about her, she gets under your skin and fucks with you, it's like it's impossible to shake off — I was writing these songs really as messages. Not being very articulate, I thought, when she hears this she'll understand what I mean. Their real duty's for her. I must admit I was enjoying it: this was very creative for me, I was getting stuff out, writing these songs and really enjoying it. But I was miserable as hell.

I actually left the band. We had dinner one night and I said, listen I'm off to Vancouver tomorrow to chase the family. If you don't mind operating out of Vancouver, we've still got a band. Otherwise, I'm off. The guys said, wait, there's no rush. You go do your thing; we'll go and do our solo albums. You come back when you're ready. Which was very wise of them. I came back two or three months later, and nothing had changed. They were midway through their solo albums, and that's when I started to write all this stuff. I had nothing else to do because the guys were busy doing their albums. So, then we did *Duke*, and then *Face Value* followed. I found it very inspiring.

Melodies: "In the Air Tonight"

I had a drum machine, which I actually didn't want at first because, I thought, I'm a drummer, and then I thought, hang on, I can use this as a tool. it'll give my writing more space if I use this. So, I programmed a little thing on the drum machine, and I got a nice little mellow sound on my synthesizer, and I started playing. This chord sounded nice, and that chord sounded nice. I'd been so used to Genesis building and tracking and tracking, and then suddenly the vocals go on top and you're trying to be heard, so I thought I'd put the vocal on very soon. These were only demos, songs, ideas, mucking about — I didn't even know I was doing an album at this point — so I sang.

I thought I'd put the basic keyboard part down with the drum machine, then I'd just have the voice there, doing something so I could keep out of the way of it. I set the mic up and what I sang was what you hear on the record. I re-recorded it because the quality wasn't good enough, but I improvised all the words and the melody. I had no idea what that tune was going to be until I opened my mouth. That's the best scenario to happen. Sometimes you really have to work at a melody and hone it. I personally believe the first thing you sing, half the time, is the best.

Tony Banks will painstakingly work a tune out, and that makes it very hard to sing.

What incident sparked "In the Air Tonight"?

I have no idea. I literally opened my mouth...I didn't know what I was singing. I've been asked twice a week what it's about ever since. It's an abstract song about bitterness.

Why do Genesis and a solo career?

The group has become a vehicle for corporate writing rather than individual writing, and I think that's a healthy way to keep it because it saves any {internal quibbling}. The last three albums we've maintained that way of working. It's always worked. As we sit here, at this moment in time, I've just come off the most personal, exhilarating time making this record. Great fulfillment because I did it myself; I've touched the nerve on a lot of the songs; this is a great time for me. At the moment, there's no room for genesis in my mind. Once the intensity is burned off a little, and we've been on tour, and the novelty of taking this music on the road is wearing thin after 99 shows, maybe I'll say, Hey, fancy doing a record, guys? That's the way it works. There's no chance of Genesis activity between now and, I'd say, the middle of 1995.

And that's OK with them?

I guess. Mike's about to start an album. Tony would like to be doing soundtracks, but work's thin on the ground unless you're established. He's fed up doing solo albums because no one buys them. A lot of the time, he isn't a visible force. I often say, and I mean most sincerely, that if I was to leave Genesis, they could find a replacement. But if *he* was to leave Genesis, it would be harder to find a replacement and still keep the spirit of the band.

From a commercial standpoint, that's not true, but that aside, in terms of the music, he — and Mike a close second — are far more important musically to what Genesis fans conceive Genesis to be. If I had the guys playing on my record there'd be no point in doing it. I even went as far as signing to a different label to get away from Genesis; I wouldn't have them play on my records. In England, I wanted to be thought of as a separate entity.

Two weeks ago, Genesis did a charity show in England — Queen (with Roger Taylor singing), Clapton, us and Pink Floyd. Having just come out with this personal new album, suddenly I was on stage singing "I Can't Dance" and "Invisible Touch," "Turn It On Again" — it was culture shock. It was like I was acting, it wasn't what I feel. That worried me. Even though I wrote the lyrics to "I Can't Dance" and "Invisible Touch" and "Tonight Tonight" and "Hold on My Heart," and I was singing my lyrics, but it was a different me.

When I'm on stage with Genesis, it's me, but when I go out on that hoist, like we did on the last tour, and sing "Blood on the Windows," that's Tony Banks — I'm singing the thoughts of Tony. I have to act it. The farther I get down the road, the more you hit that nail square on the head, the less you want to deal with anything else. So, I can see a time coming when we'll just make the records and write the songs, 'cause that's good fun. But to go on the road and play a potted history of the band, which involves lots of other moments I can't stand up and be counted for any more, that might change.

Singing

I never envisaged singing. I used to sing in my school groups, but only from the drums. I only did the genesis job because we couldn't find anyone else. From when I started playing the drums before genesis, I had my life mapped out. I thought I'd be in a pop group until that fizzled out, and then a show band or a big band, and then closing my life in the orchestra pit; when I was in Oliver, watching these guys every night, I thought this is what you do, the logical conclusion. Even when I joined the band I only ever wanted a bit of respect from other musicians. I wondered if other drummers liked me as much as I liked Keith Moon and Ginger Baker...that was the way I was thinking.

"Both Sides of the Story" — social conscience this time after last LP's slagging?

I was right the first time. If there's two choices — not singing about it because you're worried that people might think you're a rich rock star and how will you possibly know what's on the street, which I take great offense at. I am a very normal, straight-ahead person — the man next door — I was brought up in that way, I still save my money in case the bubble bursts. My mum and dad told me to do that. I resent it when people think if you're rich you become an asshole and if you're poor you're a saint. There are some very poor assholes out there. It got me angry to read that.

The kind of criticism I get is from people who put me in a box. So, I didn't do it for any reason other than the fact that the lyric suggested itself. I could have said both sides of the story from an emotional relationship POV, 'cause that ties in with some of the other lyrics — about why you hurt someone and if they saw why you were doing it they would understand. But I thought I'd be broader than that and take four vignettes. the last verse is basically *Grand Canyon*.

"Ghetto boy"

If you say black .. .and if you say Hispanic... The reason it was "ghetto" was to mean anybody. What else could I have said?

Poor...street...city...see what's going on from your car...

That's just using the wrong words. I do walk down the street. I guess if I had thought about it I could have said city kid, that would have scanned as well. I wanted to take the emphasis away from it being racist. I'm aiming at a broad section here ... the guy's only got a gun because he's tired of being shat on. ◆

Phil Collins, 28 September 1993

I thought afterwards, it's just like "potayto" or "potahto," but if I'd have thought of it maybe I'd have used "city kid." when we play a show in New York and you come I may sing "city kid" just for you.

Live Aid

I did Wembley with Sting, we played each other's songs, then I got helicoptered to Heathrow, got on the Concorde, flew to New York, got a helicopter to Philadelphia, went on stage, checked the piano, checked the drums. The reason I did it was because I wanted to play drums. Nobody in Wembley needed me. Robert Plant asked me if I could get him on *Live Aid*: "How 'bout you, me and Jimmy Page doing something?" I said, "Yeah, ok, great." That became a Led Zeppelin reunion, and they wanted to rehearse because it was so much of a second coming. I couldn't do that because I was on tour. I finished a week before the gig, and I didn't want to rehearse. I said, "I can go on stage and play Led Zeppelin songs in my sleep." I grew up with them. Clapton was playing, and Harvey Goldsmith, who was helping Bill Graham organize the whole thing, said, if you can get there by 7 o'clock, we can do this, and it would link the two events. I said, OK, who else is doing it? They said Power Station and Duran Duran are doing it, one in each country, so a couple of them will be with you. I wasn't going to be the only person. But they didn't do it; in the end, I was the only person. Power Station played in America, and Duran Duran didn't play in England, so there was nobody else traveling with me apart from a posse of journalists and my wife.

I got on the plane and Cher was sitting there, and she rushed into the bathroom because she thought all this press were coming on for her. I went up to her and said hello, and she asked me what was going on. I told her it was *Live Aid*, and she said, can you get me on? I told her to just turn up. Later that night, she was onstage with a microphone. I just did it because my mates were in Philadelphia. It didn't really dawn on me that this was going to work until afterwards. People still ask me if I've recovered.

Remaining ambitions

There are certain people left that I'd love to collaborate with. I'd love to have made an album with Miles. I'd like to have produced an album for the Buddy Rich Big Band. we actually talked about that before he died. I'd like to play with Joe Zawinul, I'd like to have been a drummer in Weather Report. Professionally, I'd love to work with Blue Nile, I'd love to produce Eric again, but he's too together now, he does it himself. he doesn't need any one else.

As my music gets more and more insular, maybe one reason I'm taking up acting is because I'm starting at the ground level, I have all that to achieve. There's a lot of people out there that I'd love to work with. I saw *The Fugitive*, and Tommy Lee Jones is brilliant. Him, Nicholson, Jimmy Stewart before he dies. there's a lot of things I'd like to do.

I'm not bored with anything, I just keep getting asked to do interesting things. the more I do, the more opportunities I get, the more visibility I have to the people I want to work with.

Paul McCartney

He rang up once and said, will you come down and play drums? I was in *A Hard Day's Night*, although he wouldn't know it. I was an extra in the theater scene at the end, all the screaming kids. I see my friends, although I don't see me. I'm glad I put myself out there and had a chance to work with all these great people; it's made life interesting.

Tears for Fears: "Woman in Chains"

Roland said we want an "In the Air" type feel. I couldn't do that, but I gave them something that worked for them. I went in there and was finished within 3 or 4 hours. It was a simple song, and they used it pretty much as I did it.

Other projects

A film company came to me, gave me a book to read — *The Client* by John Grisham — and asked me if I'd write the music. I said, fantastic: I'd really love to do a legitimate soundtrack. I was writing pieces of music that didn't fit in a song format, didn't fit with a verse/chorus idea. So, I read the book and made all these notes and wrote all this music. I recorded it at home around the same time as this album and delivered it to them as an audition piece. Unbeknownst to them, the director had already hired another writer. Now I have all this music, which will surface.

The Genesis family

I see Peter quite a lot. more recently in the last six months. I don't think it's ever been anything but mutual respect. Tony Banks and Peter Gabriel were always the best of friends and they still see each other. I was always Peter's stooge, comically, on stage. it makes sense to stay in touch. I went out to dinner with him just before his last album came out. I went out to the show and came by the hotel the next day and signed a copy of the album. We've always got on. I don't know what he thinks about what I do: I think I have an easier time dealing with my emotions than he does; I think *Us* is more like *Face Value* in some respects because he was going through similar types of problems with his wife and his girlfriend: the eternal triangle. I know his way of dealing with it was through therapy, because he came from a public school background.

Even if Peter had been with the band [Genesis], which is inconceivable in a way, I think the kind of music we would be writing now is not the kind of music we were writing 25 years ago. He left 19 years ago. As we all change as people, our music has changed. Fans don't think of that aspect of it. I joined in '70; Peter left in '74, yet 19 years later I'm still the new boy, the singer that replaced Peter.

Flaming Youth

Our managers, Howard and Blakely, who wrote all the stuff for Dave Dee Dozy Beaky Mick & Tich and the Herd, had to spend a lot of money. Gered Mankowitz did the picture, with stained glass. They said there's a big display in this window down the Hampstead Road in a record shop, let's all go down and look at it. This was a big deal. They put the photograph in front of all these lights, and the lights had melted the picture. There was all this plastic melted.

We got together somehow; we'd arrived as a four-piece backing band for a four-piece 4 Tops-type group. We were the band, and they were the guys up front. We ended up being better than they were, so they got fired and we were suddenly the band. It was only a couple of gigs a week, nothing to write home about, and we worked up and down the country for a little while. And then Brian, the keyboard player, used to drink in this club in the West End and he met Howard and Blakely one night. They were looking for a band, and he said he'd got a band. We were playing at Eel Pie Island, rehearsing there day in and day out, and they came down to see us, and they offered us this record contract. It was a concept album called *Ark 2*, and we jumped at the chance because we were fed up with earning nothing — not that we went on to earn anything! We made the album, and it came out. It was *Melody Maker* album of the month — *Led Zeppelin II* came out the same week and we beat that — it was extraordinary press. We had a big launch at the London Planetarium.

We started doing gigs and nothing really happened. We used to go on stage and play this thing, which was ok, and then we'd play our own stuff. After a year of inactivity, I got fed up with it and started looking around for other jobs. That's when I answered the Genesis ad, although I auditioned for lots of other bands before I got the Genesis job.

Alumni: Brian Chatton was in the Warriors with Jon Anderson. Ronnie Carrol, the bass player, is still one of my oldest friends. he's not doing much. Gordon Smith is living in Holland and he's still recording.

I kept all the cuttings, the press was fantastic, and then nothing. We could have been something, but nothing.

It's always glorified that rock used to be rebellious and anti-establishment — the Pretty Things were and the Stones were, the Beatles. When I was a teenager, you were either a Beatles fan or a Stones fan. I did collect all the Beatles albums, and all the Stones albums, but if they warped or got scratched it didn't bother me quite as much. I was never on the rebellious side of things, I always wanted to play good songs and be a drummer. My son played me a Helmet album the other day, and I liked the guitar sound and the production, but the singer was terrible. He said, no, it's great. Sons of your fathers: There you are, sounding like your dad again.

I don't think all rock music was always rebellious; a lot of it was just about songs. There were Townshend and the other angry young men, but that was only one side of rock and roll; there was another side.

In England, the Doors never meant anything to me. I never understood Elvis Presley or Bill Haley.

My dad and mother used to belong to a motorboat club on Eel Pie Island, they built their own building next to the hotel. I was a cadet at the club: the young kids were cadets. Every Thursday we'd have meetings, and one night I was walking back with them towards the car and I heard this [imitates blues shouter]. I said what's that, and my mom and dad said it was beatniks, come on we're going home. The voice was something I'd never heard before. Someone who was coming out said it was Howling Wolf with the Rolling Stones. They were probably only 19 or 20 then.

Great drummers?

Keith Moon, Ginger Baker, Ringo and Charlie Watts - both underrated drummers who are unfairly ridiculed. People underestimated Keith Moon as well; people thought he was just a wild man, but he was fantastic, he was a one-off. Ginger revolutionized rock drumming. Robert Henrit, who used to be with the Roulettes and Argent. At one point I used to be a big fan of Bill Bruford, but that was a different period, a different area. Now I have very mixed feelings about that stuff, like I do with our early albums. The Motown guys, Al Jackson, Bernard Purdie, Earl Palmer — they were the kind of guys I listened to, as well as Ringo.

Carl Palmer?

I kind of like him — I've met him a few times and he's a nice guy. But he epitomizes the type of drummer I dislike. He was taught, and to me it has no natural swing, no natural groove.

John Bonham was one of the best rock drummers I ever saw: I saw him with Hard Meat, who were backing Tim Rose just when "Morning Dew" was a big hit in England. He did a drum solo that I stood up and applauded. He played with his hands, just did stuff I had never seen anyone do before. Then he joined Robert Plant in the Band of Joy and then the New Yardbirds. I saw the New Yardbirds at the Marquee; there were 30 of us in the audience, it was fantastic. They did all the first album stuff. He was a wonderful drummer, and he had a sound.

Drum solos?

In my tours, I do "The West Side," which is kind of a big band jazz piece. But I don't play a solo unaccompanied; nobody leaves the stage. The band just grooves for a minute, and I stretch out, and then we come back together and then we're finished. I've never felt comfortable as a soloist. I have never been a fan of drum solos. People are impressed by the visual elements. ◆

In the summer of '93, I wrote what now seems like a horrible cliché but then felt like a positive acknowledgment of progress — the inevitable "girls with guitars" article. The quotes came from interviews I did with Juliana Hatfield, Melissa Ferrick and Liz Phair. Having interviewed Phair for a *Rolling Stone* "New Faces" thing in May, I had plenty of unused material. I had no call to downgrade the Go-Go's' achievements to make my point, and I'm sorry I did.

Busting the Boys' Club

Newsday, 22 August 1993

Blame it on the Bangles. The do-it-yourself rock ethos that emerged in the mid-1970s brought countless boys out of the bedroom and onto the stages of rock clubs, but similarly motivated young women remained second-class citizens. Despite an open field supposedly cleared of rotten traditions, punk and new wave bands mindlessly accepted and maintained old sexist laws, leaving women to be singers or, strangely enough, bass players. The prized role of guitarist was out of the question: For all its radical reformism, punk kept men in control.

Appearances and impact aside, the Runaways — a hard-rocking teenage quintet that included future solo stars Joan Jett and Lita Ford — was a marketing experiment assembled by a male Svengali: bad girls with loud guitars, meant to titillate heterosexual male adolescents with anatomically correct rock stars to crave rather than worship.

The Go-Go's' 1981 breakthrough was significant in that they weren't exactly attempting to sound "male," but frothy songs and a sunny disposition undercut the band's long-term impact. The music, a pop outgrowth from southern California punk roots, was reasonably original, but the band was quickly elbowed out by other commercially acceptable new wavers who had more technical skill and showed more endurance.

Women would ultimately not be denied their place in pop music, but the Go-Go's weren't quite the missing link. Bananarama's entertaining nonsense was easy to ignore; radical guerrillas like Lydia Lunch and the Slits were hard not to; X, co-starring punk poet Exene Cervenka, fell somewhere in between. But with critical mass popularity provided by Chrissie Hynde's Pretenders and Annie Lennox in Eurythmics, the Bangles became the final ingredient needed for pop's sexual transformation.

Another melodic convocation of Los Angeles ex-punks, the Bangles took the power-pop template that had been richly explored by sensitive boys with pudding-bowl haircuts, shy smiles and thin, high-pitched voices, and used it to voice their own views of life. Forget the hits: It was songs like "Restless," "All About You" and "James" that stated mid-'80s don't-tread-on-me female independence with melodic precision.

The fact that they could play just about as well as their peers while writing and singing rings around them was a big asset. On one level, the Bangles sounded like every other '60s-inflected harmony group that could spew back the Big Star songbook; on another, this was the dawning of the *Sassy* generation's era in the musical sun.

Nearly a decade later, this summer's release of two debuts and a sophomore effort by three extraordinary young singer-songwriters is something of a watershed. Distinct from the aggressive gender warriors known as riot grrrls, these women are remaking pop music in their own image with wonderful results.

With the critically celebrated *Exile in Guyville* (Matador), Chicagoan Liz Phair vaults into the top echelons of independent-label cool. While professing a love for the radio pop she grew up on, Phair uses spare arrangements and captivating hooks to convey blunt, revealing commentaries on the battle of the sexes — '90s-style. Phair may be thinking "Feelings," but what comes out is "[Fuck] and Run," a searing, superbly constructed personal comment on sex without love. If not for its four-letter lyric, the song could be a hitbound teen anthem for enlightened refugees from the *90210* jungle.

Regarding her explicit choice of words, Phair says, "I think you can use any language you want. I love words, mixing large and small, obscure and direct. You exploit your strengths and weaknesses as they stand. That's what song-writing is about, how you explore your own art. That's the self-discovery that comes from the creative process."

Twenty-two-year-old Melissa Ferrick also has a personal tale to tell. A violin and trumpet prodigy who toured in China with a youth ensemble, she was a student at the Berklee School of Music when she acquired a guitar and embraced pop music. By 1991, she was at Madison Square Garden, opening for Morrissey. Now there's *Massive Blur*.

Armed with a powerfully dramatic voice and the prudent artistry not to overdo it, Ferrick writes about love and identity and family with piercing honesty and ingenuous uncertainty. "I started singing when I was 17," she says. "I screamed until I was in tune. Whatever hell happens to exist inside my soul definitely comes out that way. I'm wondering whether or not I'm ever going to write out all of whatever the hell it is that makes me so confused. Half the reason I'm doing this is because I want to figure everything out."

While her album's production sounds, in spots, overly commercial and adult, Ferrick's spunky zeal, gutsy reaching and spectacular voice give the record artistic credibility. And the harrowing "Hello Dad" — which Ferrick is quick to note does not describe her own father — conveys the same quiet cinematic terror as Suzanne Vega's "Luka."

Throwing curves all her own into the brave new world of pop women is Juliana Hatfield. The former leader of college radio's beloved Blake Babies made a big scene splash of her own with a memorable solo debut last year; the new *Become What You Are*, credited to the Juliana Hatfield Three, is tighter and stronger, a deft balance of airy tunes and brash guitar rock.

Hatfield, 26, a former bassist who now plays guitar, considers it a political act to lead an otherwise male rock trio. But she rejects any feminist tag, and once told Interview magazine that she considers women genetically incapable of rocking like men. Hatfield's wispy voice and obliquely reflective lyrics provide misleading signposts to her songs, however. The new record's "My Sister" might be taken as autobiographical if only Hatfield had a sister.

Then again . . . "Recently I was listening to it," Hatfield says, "and I think it's about me: I'm the sister. I thought of the concept of writing a song about a sister I never had, and the words just came out. The song isn't ambivalent; it's just like any relationship — it changes."

Given the current buzz of activity — bands like Tiger Trap and Bratmobile (female groups who have just issued nifty debuts), Heavenly, Small Factory, Madder Rose and many others — the relationship of the sexes in rock seems to have finally undergone a permanent change. ◆

Liz Phair, phoner 13 May 1993

Album being released as a double [vinyl]

I don't get a gatefold, but that's just as well. It's already a bit indulgent.

Stones song-by-song correspondence

Oh honey, I have a three-inch stack of notes, I'm not saying that anyone else would get this without my explanation, but I absolutely did that. If anyone wants to take the time and sit down with my notes, I would [explain it], I said it because it's true; and it mattered to me, but I think people would prefer to keep their own images. It makes for a richer structure, and people can tell there's thought in it, but I don't think anyone really cares.

Cloudy past in Matador bio

That's Johann [Kugelberg]; that's not me. He called me and started rambling off these lies, I edited a little. The worst I do is omit, but I'm revoltingly honest. You can ask the guys in the studio: I'd been listening to *Exile* [*on Main Street*] non-stop for a month and a half before we recorded it: I know that album so damn fucking I well. I know exactly how it corresponds to mine.

I categorized all the *Exile* songs by what type of songs they were using weird post-modern descriptions, exaggerating them. Lyric content was the main pivot point in terms of me feeling like my songs had to be dealing with the same issue. A discourse was arising out of what I thought was a focus point in each song. I tried to do the female version.

Lyrics
The truth is there's a huge difference between what clever Liz can tell you over the phone and what artist Liz does by herself. I just write them the way I write them because I have years and years of process training. I've been doing this forever, since well before I ever had any ability to articulate what I was doing. Sometimes I write songs that take a month, and I rewrite and I rewrite and I get very conscious about the words, and I play a lot of wordplay games; sometimes they come out entirely conceived in one fell swoop. I don't control it the way you might think.

Personnel on the album
I played guitar, Brad [Wood] played bass, drums and organ. [engineer] Casey Rice was the second most instrumental. He did some guitar leads on "Mesmerizing" and at the end of "Divorce Song," he did an amazing cymbal crash in the middle of "Shatter"... Tutti Jackson walked in and I threw her behind a mic for some background vocals; same with the harmonica [grabbed a friend) I have the credits instrument by instrument, just like *Exile* did.

I come from doing my own four-track stuff, and my main [goal] was that this would be a rock album, but I didn't want to be drowned out, I didn't want to be mixed in. I wanted to be a strong thread through that stood out: guitar and vocals. I wanted it to be like what everyone tries to do with a solo artist: accompany them yet have it meld with what the artist is doing and at the same time leave them prominent. We all agreed on that. Brad was extremely keen to do it that way; that's why my vocals are so high and clear.

I'm really into pop music. I love hits, I love catchy hooks. It's always a struggle because I write weird, dissonant chord structures sometimes; I'm always trying to counterbalance that with disgustingly catchy pop tunes, 'cause that's the kind of music I love. I'm basically trying to make the kind of stuff I want to hear on the radio. I grew up listening to the radio: I'm not much of a record buyer. Basically, I'm after radio-playable, but I just want it to come around to my way of thinking.

Would I sell out? That's a moot point. I don't think like that. All I think about is what sounds pop and awesome to me. I wouldn't do anything on my record that I thought sounded stupid: but I already have a fairly mainstream ear, I love radio stuff, I would never have to make that decision, because in my mind I'm making what I think sounds good. People who don't have a natural radio-type pop sensibility find themselves thinking along those terms, but I don't have to, because that's how my ear is tuned.

When you started out, were you a bedroom guitar player?
Totally. I still am. If I didn't have to play live ever again I wouldn't. I've played live ten times now, maybe eleven. Solo.

All in the Chicago area?
I went down to Champaign-Urbana once. I thought we were going to Bloomington, Indiana; but it turned out to be Bloomington, Illinois, and the gig was cancelled.

I'm going to do some shows solo in New York because I made a commitment to Matador, but then it's going to be with a band. Brad and I started practicing yesterday. I don't want to come out just another band onstage; I want it to be Liz Phair; and to do that I have to be an extremely strong vocalist on top of his drums, which I have in me but my embarrassment makes that difficult. ... It's horrifying to be in front of people singing your songs. It's really embarrassing. I'm one of those people that despise getting up...I would talk in front of the UN; but to actually sing songs in front of four people is nerve-wracking. I'm getting better. When I took piano lessons as a child and had to give recitals it was equally horrifying. [But] I'm not really a shy person, per se.

Do you have role models as a guitarist?
I don't know how to play anyone's songs but mine. When I had a piano I refused to learn to read music and wrote songs. When I had a guitar, I just started plunking on my own, I didn't model myself after anybody.

I started making Girly Sound tapes in the spring of '91. Before that I'd been screwing around in San Francisco, spending all of my savings for five months living in a loft and socializing like a motherfucker, stoned out of my mind all the time. It wasn't working out, I wasn't getting a job and I wasn't being responsible, so I came home, lived at home and found myself needing an outlet. A friend of mine in SF — Chris Brokaw from Codeine/Come — convinced me to make him a tape of some of my songs. So, I did and sent him a tape, I sent one to [my friend in] Kicking Giant and they just started dubbing and dubbing. It was like that Faberge Organic Shampoo commercial.

Favorite bands?
Urge Overkill. Antietam. Oddly enough, I'm informed in a lot of weird ways because I went out with a lot of guys who had extensive music collections and have a lot of friends who collect music and are very into it and know a great deal about Genesis and what has come from what band. I have, in very small segments, a great deal of knowledge, but on the whole I'm completely ignorant of [indie/mainstream]. It blurs in my mind. I behave very girlishly about it.

I consider myself a feminist.

Do you have qualms about using words like "cunt" in a song?
Not at all. You can use any language you want. I love words. I love mixing large and small, obscure and direct. What you do is what comes naturally to you. You exploit your strengths and weaknesses as they stand. That's what songwriting's about; how you explore your own art. That's the self-discovery that comes from participating in the creative process.

I was supposed to be a visual artist. I spent many, many hours in art classes critiquing art history, deconstructing. I find the direct approach — do what comes naturally and hone it well — is the way to go.

I got my first guitar in 7th grade, a Yamaha Classical. I still write a lot of songs on it.

Is the wooing by labels freaking you out?
It was, Badly. Over the winter I had a real crisis about it. I withdrew and freaked out and felt extremely threatened. Here are these things that everyone tells me I should be thrilled about and it feels like a gun pointed at my head. You want six years of my life doing what? It's frightening. You're stuck with the knowledge that you want to do something with yourself and they're offering you the chance to do that and you could take it and run but at the same time you realize that you're not there yet. You have to keep slugging it through, you're not just gonna wake up one morning the butterfly.

I have seasonal affective disorder, and I get real insecure and annoyed in the winter. It really pisses me off. I hate being here in the winter. Summer comes around and all of my confidence returns and I'm back in stride. I go crazy.

I'm doing another album and an EP with Matador, The EP will be Girly Sound: the album will be like a studio thing. It's a one-off, so we'll see who still wants me after that. After this whole out-of-nowhere wiz-kid label and you set back to being just a good pop artist, you see who wants you, see how they react to you then.

Personal relationships?
My real friends are mostly outside the music scene. They think it's a gas that I'm doing it at all. It was awkward with my family at first. My parents were a little shocked, but I prepared them for about a year and a half to listen to the album. They just heard it for the first time the other night. My mother said something like: "Well, that was intense." My lyrical content hasn't screwed up anything; I've always been outspoken.

"Divorce Song"?
They're all based on something in my life. That one is a mishmash of a couple of things. That is probably one of the less autobiographical ones. It's divvied up between three different situations and two different people. I haven't been divorced, no. I was using it metaphorically.

It's in my nature to be way too analytical [about my work). It's in my nature to do so, so I protect myself from thinking too much about it. I end what I can and stop when it freaks me out. ◆

So long as I filed my copy on time and filled out photo requests correctly, no one really told me what to cover at *Newsday.* I did this piece for my own fandom and curiosity, not because I expected it would register strongly among the paper's readers. Holly Beth Vincent's solo album had affected me deeply, and I was extremely curious to meet her. The long interview we did outdoors at Mekka, the then little-known chef Bobby Flay's Mexican restaurant in the East Village, turned surprisingly emotional and intense. Pulling an objective, level-headed article out of it was something a challenge.

Holly Beth Vincent: Rock's Pioneer Woman Keeps on Moving

Newsday, 30 July 1995

"Some people achieve greatness. Others have it thrust upon them. And then there are those who are... born Italian."

Replace the ethnic tag with "to devote their lives to writing and playing rock and roll, whatever the cost, regardless of the reward, for reasons too deep and probably too self-destructive to contemplate" and that invocation — which opens Holly and the Italians' 1981 album, *The Right to Be Italian* — thoroughly describes the woman who spoke it.

Long before Courtney Love or L7, PJ Harvey or Elastica, there was Holly Beth Vincent. If there's any value to such historical bragging rights, Vincent may well be the original riot grrrl, forming and fronting her own band while the younger Joan Jett was still stuck in the contrived Runaways. Emerging when womanhood was still a stigma in rock, this talented pioneer simply ignored stereotypes and did what came as naturally to her as it has to countless others.

"For me, music is personal," Vincent says. "I never really thought about gender. I come from a family of musicians. My brother Nick plays drums with Frank Black. My parents are big-band musicians. I grew up on Count Basie and Nancy Wilson. I had a drum teacher who worked with Billie Holiday. I come from a heavy musical background."

The fact that she didn't see much difference in the genders growing up also helped. "I've been a tomboy all my life, I've always been very competitive with guys and very athletic. And I always had this kind of androgynous look — tall, lanky, broad-shouldered. When I was in second grade," she recalls, "I got voted cutest boy in the class by my teacher's husband who didn't realize I was a girl. That was traumatic. Now, in retrospect, I take it as a compliment."

A sure-handed rhythm guitarist, hard-hitting drummer and possessor of the most alluring female rock voice since Chrissie Hynde, Vincent has made only four albums in a 15-year professional career; while failing to sell in numbers anywhere near records by those who have followed Vincent's lead, they form a distinctive and rewarding body of work. Despite commercial obscurity, influential admirers keep emerging from the firmament to move her career along. Joey Ramone cut a great 1982 cover of "I Got You Babe" with her and then asked her to join the Ramones. Indigo Girl Amy Ray released a '93 album by Vincent's band, the Oblivious, on her own label.

During Vincent's peripatetic saga in the rock wars, she nearly became the drummer in Dire Straits, briefly sang in the Waitresses and, most recently, joined forces with bassist-singer Johnette Napolitano of Concrete Blonde on a raucous project they [unfortunately] dubbed Vowel Movement. Typical of Vincent's bumpy and unpremeditated career, that collaboration began personally and casually.

"I saw a picture of Johnette on the cover of [California music magazine] *BAM*. Suddenly a light went on in my head: This was the girl I used to wait tables with a long time ago, and she's talking about how I influenced her." Contact was made and the Oblivious wound up touring as Concrete Blonde's opening act. Napolitano broke up her band in 1994, and the two women completed a casual studio experiment they had initiated as a way to spend a dateless New Year's Eve 1993, recording an intermittently exciting album in six days last July. By the time *Vowel Movement* (Mammoth) appeared this spring, Vincent and Napolitano had gone their separate ways on unfriendly terms. As she has been many times in her career, Vincent was back on her own, contemplating her next move.

A vivid storyteller with an infectious laugh and an amused sense of wonder at some of her own experiences, Vincent was born in Chicago. (Now in her late 30s, Vincent won't give her age.) Her father is Italian, her mother Swedish and French. Raised in Lake Tahoe and, later, Southern California, she ran away from home around 1972, and lived with the remnants of the Manson family in the Mojave Desert. "I read a lot of Edgar Allen Poe, practiced my drum lessons and ran around naked," she says with a chuckle. When that lost its charm, she moved back to Los Angeles and resumed her education, but "decided I wanted to play music" and quit.

At 18, she skipped off to London. "I ended up living with Chris Wood from Traffic and his wife. They kind of adopted me. I was around a lot of musicians: Mitch Mitchell, Jim Capaldi, Steve Winwood, Keith Richards, John Cale. Only months before I was listening to Traffic records, to Stones records and there I was hanging out with these people."

During her London stay, Vincent and a female bassist placed an ad for a guitar player in *Melody Maker*. "This guy, Mark Knopfler, showed up. He liked — y'know, *liked* — me. He was an English teacher at the time, like Sting, but he was a really good guitar player.

"Before he formed Dire Straits, Mark came to America on this big trip, hitchhiking across the country, and he came to Los Angeles and asked me if I wanted to play drums in his new band." She turned him down and stayed in California. After drumming in a punkabilly band called the Brothel Creepers, Vincent went to audition for the all-female Backstage Pass, who were actually looking for a guitarist, not a drummer. "Nobody knew how to play anyway, so..." Under cover of collective incompetence, Vincent switched instruments.

"The music was awful, but it was fun. That's where I learned to play guitar." She eventually quit and started a band of her own with drummer Steve Dalton (a high school classmate) and a series of bass players.

"One night in the Masque [a legendary L.A. punk club of the late '70s], I drank two giant cans of Schlitz malt liquor and came up with the name Holly and the Italians. I spray-painted 'Holly and the Italians' on the wall of the Masque. I think that must have been some subliminal Oedipal thing," she chuckles.

In Los Angeles with the now successful Dire Straits, Knopfler heard and liked her demo tape. "He played it for his manager, and they brought me and my drummer to England. Then me and Mark had a falling out." Dire Straits' *Making Movies* album, she says, "was written almost entirely about me, about when we separated."

Charlie Gillett, the London disc jockey who discovered Dire Straits, asked Vincent to make a single for his independent label, Oval. "Tell That Girl to Shut Up" came out at the end of 1980. "It got played and it was kind of a hit," says Vincent, who toured with the Clash to promote it. The song got a bigger chart ride eight years later, when Transvision Vamp cut an inferior carbon-copy.

Virgin Records signed the band and sent them to New York to record with legendary rock and roll producer Shadow Morton. The first day went okay, but, Vincent says, "When we showed up the next day, he had left a note at the reception desk that said, 'Gone out for blood transfusion, be back at 4 o'clock.' He never came back again." Richard Gottehrer was called in to supervise the album, and *The Right to Be Italian* — a canny new wave artifact of melodic originals like "Youth Coup," "Rock Against Romance" and "I Wanna Go Home" resonating with Vincent's snotty update of Ronnie Spector's robust wailing — was completed and released. But it didn't sell.

"With all these expectations I felt I couldn't meet, I was having a lot of trouble sleeping. When [Virgin Records] signed me, everyone was making such a big deal. My whole attitude was, 'Why are you making such a big deal over me?' I was trying to second-guess myself — what am I doing that they think is so great? Analyzing everything eventually drove me crazy. A doctor gave me sleeping pills and tranquilizers and I got strung out on them. I started doing a lot of LSD, too, which didn't help."

Despite (or perhaps because of) all the pharmaceutical interference, Vincent succeeded in making an extraordinary 1982 solo album which her record company perversely titled *Holly and the Italians*. As hauntingly atmospheric as the moments before a storm and as enigmatic as Freud, the album is a profoundly affecting ode to glamorous dissipation and bisexual romance, a document more than an invention. With violin and horns setting off the guitar and the whole thing drenched in echo, gorgeous songs like "Honalu," "Just Like Me" and "Samurai and Courtesan" pull the listener into the baroque salon of a private retreat. The only sign of life outside is a completely original rendition of Stephen Stills' "For What It's Worth." Vincent agrees that, "It was a very introspective record. Very personal. It's like a diary, truth mixed with fiction, as much as I could handle revealing at the time."

When that record flopped, Vincent was dropped by her label and deported from England. ("I think it had something to do with an interview I gave to *Melody Maker* in which I mentioned that I had worked as a dominatrix for a couple of months in California.") She moved to New York, played with local musicians (including Paul Shaffer, a session hand on her first album), did her stint in the Waitresses and stripped in a topless bar on Wall Street. "I stopped drinking, stopped taking drugs, met someone, had a baby and moved back to Los Angeles 'cause my family was there."

Vincent made a badly recorded but otherwise impressive Oblivious album, *America*, in '93, and returned to the racks this year with the stillborn Vowel Movement. She's currently cutting demos for a possible solo deal, keeping a hopeful eye on the future. "I would like to be more well-known to function as an artist," she says ruefully. "I've always had a lot of ambition to do this on a large scale and I haven't yet done that and I'm ready to do it. I've learned all my lessons." After all these years, she says, "I'm ready to actually go out on the stage and feel I belong there." ◆

HOLLY AND THE ITALIANS
***The Right to Be Italian* (Virgin-Epic) 1981**
HOLLY BETH VINCENT
***Holly & the Italians* (Virgin-Epic) 1982**
Trouser Press Record Guide, Fourth Edition (1991)

Chicago-born singer/guitarist Holly B. Vincent formed her band in Los Angeles, but it took a 1979 move to England to secure a recording deal. A single released there ("Tell That Girl to Shut Up") established her tough pop-rock style and briefly captured the full attention of the British press and public. The band's sole album was hindered by numerous problems (like firing the producer halfway through and starting from scratch with another, losing the drummer in midstream and having to find a replacement) and wasn't finished until over a year later, but it was well worth the wait. Richard Gottehrer's production on *The Right to Be Italian* fits the melodic rock songs perfectly, melding the hybrid LA/London sound — with glimpses of the Ramones, Blondie and Cheap Trick — into a powerful and original creation. The songs (mostly Vincent's) concern troubled romance, successful romance, teenage rebellion and kitsch culture; her convincing delivery gives them import, and the catchy phrases and solid rock foundation make it a masterful record by an important young talent.

The Right to Be Italian wasn't a commercial success, and Holly broke up the band, remaining in England for a time to soft-launch a solo career. The stunning result, produced by Mike Thorne, has a misleading title and bears little resemblance to its predecessor. *Holly and the Italians* plays up Vincent's voice and songs in a mesmerizing and mature swirl of baroque atmospheres, opaque introspection, sexual ambivalence and psychedelically distorted hallucinations. The striking music is based on violin (played by Bobby Valentino of the Fabulous Poodles) and keyboards (Thorne) as much as guitar. If Joni Mitchell and Ronnie Spector mated with Nick Cave and Leonard Cohen, the offspring of their offspring might have conceived something like this. Although Vincent took some flak for recording a totally overhauled version of the Buffalo Springfield's "For What It's Worth," she does manage to make something new and different out of the well-known tune. Elsewhere, sensitive, moody originals like "Samurai and Courtesan" and "Uptown" contrast with upbeat rockers like "We Danced" and "Honalu," all displaying a unique viewpoint in subtly evocative lyrics. Even more than its predecessor, this is an incredible album by an enormously gifted singer, writer and performer. (The American release has one different cut and far better sequencing.) ◆

When *Newsday*'s movie staff had its hands full with new releases, or someone was off covering a film festival, I got to do a little reviewing as well as the occasional movie star profile: Halle Berry was one of those, and we had a fascinating conversation that I enjoyed a lot. (There was nothing weird about it at the time, but I'd be awfully surprised to learn that male journalists are still doing one-on-one interviews alone with gorgeous young actresses in their hotel rooms.)

Still, I was a lot more excited to meet Ice Cube, who was in New York promoting the first of his *Friday* movies. I was a fan of his music but intimidated by his public image (and his permanently knitted brow); sitting across a table in a room at the Essex House, he was intense but pleasant. I was impressed and enjoyed the experience a lot. Here's the piece I wrote about it, followed by a transcript of our conversation, most of which I didn't have the chance to use.

Ice Cube Chills on Laughter

After the funny Friday, *he's got other film plans.*
Newsday, 4 May 1995

Ker-*plunk*!

The sound effects that surround rapper-actor Ice Cube on his million-selling records and in such films as *Boyz n the Hood* and *Trespass* usually come straight outta the ka-pow! section. The harsh depictions of urban violence that have made Cube a multi-media star demand the chilling report of guns, the ominous clang of jail doors, the whirr of police helicopters, the squealing tires of drive-by assassins. Ker-*plunk*?

In Cube's new film, *Friday*, a day-in-the-life comedy about two friends in South Central Los Angeles, the scene likely to linger longest in memory has Cube's character, Craig Jones, gasping for breath in his family's bathroom, while his otherwise occupied father, played by scenery-chewing comic John Witherspoon, harangues him about job-hunting.

Ker-*plunk*!

"I remember my father having conversations with me on the toilet," says Cube, who quickly acknowledges the reality behind the screenplay he wrote with old pal and occasional studio cohort DJ Pooh.

"You couldn't even frown," laughs Cube, who describes his dad, a UCLA groundskeeper, as "a very serious man." He swears that the unprintable explanation Witherspoon uses to justify the site and circumstances of the father-son tête-à-tête was an actual paternal sound bite.

Born O'Shea Jackson 25 years ago, budding filmmaker Ice Cube has used *Friday* as a breather from the hard-core intensity that has made him a powerful hero to a vast number of people and a sworn enemy of others — for instance, law enforcement, which didn't agree with the homicidal message of "[Fuck] tha Police," a song by Cube's old group, N.W.A.

A broad comedy made on the cheap, *Friday* borrows its showdown plot from *High Noon*, its look and feel from light-hearted '70s romps like *Car Wash* and '80s tributes like *Hollywood Shuffle* and its shameless humor from Cheech & Chong and *House Party*. The skits that make up the story, however, come directly from "events that happened in my life, friends' lives, things I've seen," Cube says. "The movie was actually written before I started writing. In my head."

Much as Cube's incendiary rhetoric and occasional descents to racism and misogyny can't erase the intelligence and conviction of his records' social and political outrage, the goofy hijinks of *Friday* don't sidetrack its moral message. (Guns are bad, fists are good.)

Portraying South Central not as a cesspool of criminals and drug addicts but as a loving, tight-knit community that contains solid two-parent families, Cube maintains that both Craig and Doughboy, the sensitive character he played in *Boyz*, "really represent most of the kids growing up in these areas. A lot of kids, they get caught up in it."

The film's real strength is its sunny-side-up sensibility, which Cube maintains is as much a reality as the violence and suffering intrinsic to hip-hop culture. "We've seen so many movies about the hardcore side, it's time to show how much fun we had growing up there. All the laughs."

The laughs in *Friday* open a warm, encouraging window into Cube's usually steel-hard persona. The role of a patient man who can balance his anger and principles without being ruled by either, one who doesn't throw bombs but is unafraid of catching them, is Cube to the core.

Sitting in a posh suite at the Essex House on Central Park South, Ice Cube looks comfortable but out of place, his film-star's right to luxury tempered by the likelihood that this particular flavor of affluence holds little allure for him. Even in these surroundings, it's bracing to find the self-declared "N***a Ya Love to Hate" polite, easygoing and articulate. "I'm a laid-back type dude. The records I do are all me, not a hundred percent of who I am, but a percentage that I decide to make public."

Reflecting on his decade-long career, a rarity in rap, Cube says, "I feel blessed for lasting this long. Five platinum records and I still don't see the ceiling yet. I'm like the Energizer Bunny . . . still going."

The secret to Cube's success may be his diversification into film. "A lot of doors are opening because of the rap records that I do, and I would be a fool not to step through them. The movies have taken my career to a whole new level. I'm going to take advantage of it."

Even if he's had to pave his own way down the yellow brick road. "After I did *Boyz n the Hood*, I thought every script was going to be that good. Unfortunately, they weren't. It looked like if I ever wanted to do another movie, I'd have to write one myself. So, I wrote one called *America Eats Its Young*." His second attempt, also unproduced, was a football story entitled *Defense*. Cube's motivation for adding all this extra work to his busy schedule is simple. "The only reason I started writing [screenplays] was because I like acting. I like seeing myself up there."

But busy he is. "I know what I'm doing months in advance. We sit down at the beginning at the year and figure out exactly what we want to accomplish by the end of the year. By the end of this year, I want to be directing [and starring in] a movie I wrote called *Fo Life*. We're gonna work hard to make that happen."

Cube says "I've been putting myself through a ghetto version of film school to get ready for this debut. I've done thirteen, fourteen videos. I've been hanging around John [Singleton, director of *Boyz* and *Higher Learning*]. He urges me on, to push it as far as I can. I was really on hand to see how *Friday* got directed, from a behind-the-scenes perspective. I've been studying films, movies that directors and cameramen look to for inspiration and guidance. I've been able to tell stories through my music. People get their own vision in their head, so I guess it was inevitable to evolve into actually starting to do them, write screenplays and think about directing."

Gary Gray, the neophyte director of *Friday*, is only one step ahead of its star, having learned his craft directing music videos for Cube and others. The movie was shot on the block — 126th and Normandie — where Gary grew up, and not that far from where Cube and Pooh were kids.

"I definitely wanted to do a movie for the neighborhood," says Cube, "'cause I've been gearing all my records for the neighborhood. Anything after that is icing on the cake."

White rap fans have always bought Ice Cube records; it's likely they'll also check out Cube's new movie. "Rap music is opening up that avenue of curiosity. Now that you got Black people making movies about Black life, if you ever wanted to get an insight to the community, here it is. This is it." ◆

Ice Cube, 21 April 1995

After I did Boyz n' the Hood, I thought every script was going to be that good. Unfortunately, they weren't. I got so many bad ones after that, it looked like if I ever want to do another movie, I'm gonna have to write one myself. So, I wrote one called *America Eats Its Young*. It was my first script, so it wasn't like the best one in the world.

I looked at all the scripts I was getting, looked at the format, and just did it from there. Then another opportunity came along for me to write a script called Defense that Universal kind of reneged on after we finished the whole script and stuff. Football. From there I just kept on doing it.

I figured if I wrote Friday that we was going to do it ourselves, we wasn't going to go through the studios. So, I felt like the movie was going to be made anyway, no matter what. That was my third attempt at writing a script and it actually came out pretty good. That's the only reason I started writing them, because I like acting, I like seeing myself up there. I'm not going to be corny with myself, so that was the move.

Luckily, all the movies I've done... John Singleton is never gonna write anything corny for me. So, I was cool with that. I worked on Trespass, and the director, Walter Hill, he was cool with me, changing the lines and making it myself and stuff.

Friday is the only script I wrote with Pooh. Pooh, he's always thinking in skits, he's always been a funny dude. Hooking up with him was the ultimate. He's been funny ever since I've known him. He's always been dying to really put something down and have it made into a film, so it was cool to hook up with him and write it.

We [DJ Pooh and I] came up in the hip-hop scene together. He was a little ahead of me, he's been around a little longer than I have. He worked on LL's *Bigger and Deffer* album.

What did you have in mind in writing Friday?
Cheech and Chong, Hollywood Shuffle, old Sidney Poitier/Bill Cosby movies, that type of thing. At first it was just going to be a movie with just us kicking on the porch and all these skits coming at you but then it started evolving into something different, an actual movie with a beginning, middle and end.

The first script took me a little under a month to write, and about two weeks of revisions.

You played a concert in St. Paul a couple of nights ago. How do you organize your life?
I know what I'm doing months in advance. I'm very tired right now, but after Monday, nothing's on my schedule, and I'm happy. What's going to end up happening is someone's gonna figure out that I have nothing to do, can we fit in here... It piles up. Whenever it's daylight, all these things pile up. I'd rather work now and play later.

We sit down at the beginning at the year and figure out exactly how the year is going to look, and what we want to accomplish by the end of the year. By the end of this year, I want to be directing a movie that I wrote called Fo Life. That's the goal. We're gonna work hard this whole year trying to make that happen. will be in the movie as well.

Last year, you said you weren't ready to direct.
I wasn't last year. But I've done 13, 14 videos, start really studying, hanging around John Singleton}, talking to John. I was really on hand to see how Friday got directed, from a behind the scenes perspective. I've been studying films, things like Visions of the Light and all these movies that directors and cameramen look to for inspiration and guidance. I think I've been putting myself through a ghetto version of film school to get ready for this debut.

[John Singleton] urges me on, to push it as far as I can. A lot of doors are opening because of the rap records that I do, and I would be a fool not to step through them, at least test the waters.

[As a kid] I thought movies was, like, it, the top. I've been able to tell stories through my music, people get their own vision in their head, so I guess it was inevitable to evolve into actually starting to do them, write screenplays and think about directing. I go to the movie theater now looking at the movies totally different, looking at it from a director's point of view. I love John Woo and these directors who are trendsetters.

America's more open because of rap music, Americans are more open to witnessing and sit and be patient and understand the things that are going on in a city like South Central Los Angeles, because it's the same story all through the country. The same things are happening.

Making a comedy doesn't worry me. They should see a different side. I don't want to get angled — this is Ice Cube, everything else is out of the norm — but people are going to enjoy the movie. They're going to go in there thinking one thing but after they see the movie they're going to enjoy it. And they're going to enjoy the fact that I haven't took the heavy and I wasn't the man. I wasn't no punk, but I wasn't the bully or these things people expect of me. I think it came out cool, no matter what.

I used all the talent around me, I wasn't trying to do too many jokes. I used people like Chris and let them get all the jokes and all the lines and all that, which still makes me look good. Up against me it just makes it even funnier, 'cause people say Cube has this hard image and to see me dealing with Chris Tucker, I think that's funnier than if two comedians were playing the roles and they cancel each other out.

Doughboy wasn't a punk by no means. Craig really represent most of the kids growing up in these areas. Punks by no means...ain't trying to start no shit, but if it's time to finish it, let's finish it. That's why a lot of kids, they get caught up in it. A person like Smokey is always starting shit, he's always in the mix, and Craig, who's down with Smokey to the fullest, to the end, both of them end up shot up or in jail. There are a lot of Craigs in jail 'cause they were down.

I don't think a lot of people want to really pull that trigger. They want to talk about it — I'm this, I'm that — but most people would rather fight it out, deal with it like that. Unfortunately, that's the world we live in, where the trigger is the thing. You're gonna have people walking out of the movie trying to be like Smokey and people walking out of the movie trying to be like Craig.

America promotes violence, America is in love with sex and violence. Until they get off that tip, you're always gonna have these problems.

Craig's pot avoidance, stable family, paucity of N-word usage — conscious?
I wouldn't say they was so strategic. The only thing we did that was strategic was comb the script for unnecessary profanity. When you're sitting in a movie, you always know when it's too much — I learned this from Reggie Hudlin — you never feel like, oh, there wasn't enough. If you comb the script for profanity, you can really get into the dialogue, into the characters more if you do that.

How much does this movie reflect your own upbringing?
A lot. Ideas for these movies was real-life events that happened in my life, friends' lives, or things I've seen. The movie was actually written before I started writing. In my head. I think that's why it comes off so funny, because it's so true.

No matter how much they promote the single parent, there's a lot of two-parent households out there. A lot.

Is Craig's father like your dad?
My father's not that loose, not that funny. He's a very serious man. I remember him having conversations with me on the toilet. You couldn't even frown. `What are you frowning at — what's the matter?' The line "I've been smelling your shit for 22 years, you could smell mine for 5 minutes" was his line. "Come in here, I have to talk to you." Those things I pulled from him. My father used to wear overalls to work, he's been a hard worker his whole life. He's a grounds keeper at UCLA.

Beyond the core audience, who's this for?

I don't know. I definitely wanted to do a movie for the neighborhood, 'cause I've been gearing all my records for the neighborhood. Anything after that is icing on the cake. Even if just the neighborhood goes to see it we're making a profit, 'cause the movie didn't cost nothing to make.

Rap music is opening up that avenue of curiosity. Now that you got Black people making movies about Black life, if you ever wanted to get an insight to the community, here it is. This is it. The news is not accurate.

Stereotypes hold a lot of reality — not enough, but they wouldn't grow to become stereotypes of people if they didn't. To me, nothing is ultra-wrong with them. If your culture is this way, or these things are happening in your community, why try to sweep them under the rug? Show the world. Maybe you can start dealing with it.

An alcoholic can never get rid of his problem until he admits he's an alcoholic. The Black community can never get rid of our problems until we admit that they're there, at least put 'em out in the open, and deal with 'em.

I don't think I could live in Africa, there's too many good things about living here in America. But I don't truly feel like...when I say America, I automatically think white. It's hard to include myself in that because it's a struggle for basic human rights. The thing with the juror on the OJ Simpson trial...they don't like the way people look so they're starting to pick people and throw them off the jury to get it to look like they want it to. That's bullshit. We should be way past that but it's not. Racism is in the core of America. America is a racist place.

White kids are starting to understand, because they're starting to hear it from our mouths. Their view: Our forefathers fucked up. They're still fucking up. We're gonna try and make this right. We're gonna listen to what y'all got to say. For me to have any white fans is incredible, it's progress period. I'm an artist who tells it like it is, say it how I feel, for the most part very brutal in the things that I say but I feel they need to be said, let's get it all out in the open. If you're willing to listen to me verbally say these things, then we can definitely talk. I think white kids is kind of like saying for things in the past I'm taking this abuse now, but I'm willing to take it so we can move on in these next generations and deal with each other on a different level.

I don't think they're taking abuse from my records, I think they're taking a whupping that they parents should be taking, or their grandfathers should be taking. They're saying we're just gonna take this. I think it's very necessary to say. The truth hurts. So what?

White fans turning off?
Radio's turning off, which they always do. They're gonna turn off for a couple of years, and then they're gonna turn back on and there's gonna be this surge. It don't matter, hip-hop still lives.

I remember when you couldn't say "ass" on the radio, anything about guns, or women or sex, nothing. Then radio jumped on the bandwagon, now it's convenient for them to jump off for a couple of years. It's music for the young. Youth created it, so it's always going to be popular. Out with the old and in with the new-type music. I feel blessed for lasting this long. I still don't see the ceiling yet. Five platinum records; hopefully, Bootlegs and B-sides if that go... My next record will probably be Helter Skelter.

Natural Born Killaz video?
That was beautiful. That was truly thought out. The media can do all these speculations about O.J., they can make all the money off that. Me and Dre was, hey if everybody is making money off it, let us make some money off it. I'm pretty sure nobody's taking that seriously. Once you go public, you have to absorb all that. I'm pretty sure nobody's investigating Ice Cube and Dr. Dre for the murders, but we hardcore rappers, we like stirring it up. It's in our nature, to stir up controversy. We love it. We got our first taste of it with Fuck Tha Police. That was like pure, innocent, like a baby putting a car in drive, like don't know what's going to happen...Damn. But after that, when you're writing a record, you say, this is going to start some shit.

"Natural Born Killaz" was supposed to go on the movie, part of the soundtrack. That movie is stirring it up for no reason, and we wanted to do a record that reflected the same feeling of the movie. Unfortunately, we was too late to get in the film, but we had this record. The track is the shit — me and Dre together — and if you can get past your hangups, it's a hardcore hip-hop record. We ain't heard a lot of hardcore hip-hop records out of the West Coast in a long time. Everything's been fluffy. We're getting past the fluffy stage and back to the rough stuff.

During the riots in LA, you had Asian store owners painting "Black Owned" on their stores so they wouldn't get 'em burnt down. That's like an LA joke. We didn't want to go too far. He's dressed him in the beanie with the big coat. Friday is strictly for laughs. We didn't want to do no after school special, we didn't want to be soft. Nothing to us was over the top. Most people at the studio level thought the fact that you hear the splashes was over the top, or seeing the stains in the guy's underwear was over the top. Naah. I think that's why Jim Carrey is blowing up, because nothing is over the top. *Naked Gun* and successful movies like that, nothing is over the top.

America is sick of this political correct shit. That shit is so fake, it's so watered down. America is sick of it and that's why we've been successful, because we're not politically correct. We're not watered down. We're who we are, and they ain't nothing wrong with that.

Fists vs. guns
You've got to figure Deebo's been around the neighborhood, it's not like he's from another neighborhood. We all grew up with him. You really wouldn't deal with it in no other way but fists. It would always come down to fists. If Deebo's from another neighborhood, you never know. But pulling that trigger would end the movie. All the messages that came out of the movie were spontaneous on-the-spot decisions. We decided to fight, that I was going to hand John Witherspoon the gun and fight, but all the other things was `let's do it this way. Let's flip on 'em right here. This movie's been funny all the way through, let's flip on 'em for a second. Then go back to the comedy. All of these things were spur of the moment, I think that's why they work and it doesn't seem preachy.

Do you envision kids coming up to you backstage and handing you scripts instead of tapes?
Maybe. I hope they hand me both. The movies have taken my career to a whole new level. I'm going to take advantage of it. I got people who know movies I've been in and don't know the records.

Image vs. reality
I'm a laid-back type dude. The records I do are all me, it's a percentage of who I am. It's not 100% of who I am, but it is a percentage, the percentage that I decide to make public. I can be as calm as I am now and tell you something deeper than I would on a record, but it's all me. I just decided to put my inner thoughts on a record. Most people think what I'm saying, but they're afraid to say it. I feel alive because I get a lot of people to hear what I got to say.

Some creative things that I have inside of me I put in other artists. I know I can't do certain records, I know these records wouldn't work coming from Ice Cube. I couldn't do a pop record, I wouldn't do it. No.

I could do a record, long as it has underground roots and it becomes a pop record — "It Was a Good Day" is underground as hell because what a good day to me looks like is underground: winning at craps and all that stuff. It becomes a pop record. That record is walking the fence for Ice Cube but it's a breath of fresh air that I think people like. It was done in a way that people can accept that from me. I couldn't go way out with it because I don't think it would be true enough to the people that supported me all this time.

Does being a member of the nation of Islam affect your work?
Not at all. I've had dinner with Farrakhan and he told me that to change what I'm doing now is the worst thing to do. Be yourself. You got fans out there who love you for doing hardcore, raw music. You can't talk to lions meowing like a cat. I have his support in whatever I do, and whatever I say. He definitely don't want me to flipflop at all.

I'm calm. I treat everyone with respect. In the Nation of Islam, the people who are true followers are taught to treat everyone with respect. You can do them around just by being a man, by treating them as well as they treat you.

I know Joe Blow down the street has nothing to do with my situation. I know that this lady right here, or you, have nothing to do with Black people being in the situation we're in. You have to understand that. Even if I met a person who was directly responsible — a person like Darryl Gates — I would treat him with as much respect as he treats me. I would know how to deal with him. I went on his radio show, and dealt with him on his radio show, but I was as cool with him as he was cool with me.

Hated the Palladium. When I did "The N***a You Love to Hate," "Fuck You, Ice Cube" was the chant on the chorus. makes sense, don't it? People around me was like, you're crazy, how ya gonna dis yourself on a record. It's done more out of love than hate. the crowd knows the record. they'll be some people who mean it, but that's cool, too. My show is different from my records. If you come out to see me, everybody have a good time. I don't get ultra-political with my show. It's more let's have a good time. Let's go over all the jams that you like over the years. I save all that stuff for the records, for interviews and all that.

Saying that chant — what else can you say? I'm so happy that I don't have a hangup about what the people, or the press, think of me. I'm not hung up like that. I think I have more freedom than other artists who are trying to live under the microscope. For the most part, Tupac could give a damn what the media is saying about him. Or Snoop. I saw Andrew Dice Clay break down, because he gave a damn what the media and what people said and it killed his career. Andrew Dice Clay is supposed to not give a fuck what anybody say.

In the last 6 years, I only think I've seen Eazy-E about seven times. We wasn't real close friends. We wasn't real close friends in the group. I was tight with Dre.

Over the last two, three years we really started talking every time we seen each other. We worked out all our differences, and we was trying to think of a way to do an N.W.A album. Last time I seen him was here in New York, and we talked for about two hours in a club.

A couple of weeks later I hear the rumors. I tried to get in contact, and then his assistant called me and said it was true, that there was going to be a press conference later that day and he wanted me to know. When I got down there he was unconscious. I didn't want to just go in there and look at him, so I said if he comes to, page me and I'll come down there, 'cause I want to talk to him. And he never came to. Then I heard he passed away. It still really hasn't hit me. As far as an entrepreneur, he's the one who set me off to be that way, always thinking about the biz.

No doubt I wrote the song "Boyz n the Hood."

Have not talked to DJ Yella since 1989. I've had two conversations with Ren since then. I don't know what they're doing. I never go out to clubs or functions or award shows. Still live in L.A. I can't live in South Central. I was standing there for a while, but after I did Boyz n the Hood, and released Death Certificate, I lived right up the street from a high school and it was murder. People coming by my house, ringing my doorbell, yelling and all this. I just had to move somewhere where I could get away from this Ice Cube shit.

We made Friday on the same block where [director] Gary grew up, 124th and Normand, something like that. That's what makes South Central so dangerous. It's unpredictable. You can be out there playing football in the street; next minute, some fool's gonna come by and spoil your whole day, spoil your whole life.

Little kid on the bicycle is a little dude named Chris. He was bad, man. Little youngster always riding his bike. Never went to school, just bad. We caught him and whupped him over the years. Now I go back, and he's straight gangbanging. He's maybe 20, 19.

My parents have seen the film. They like it. They see theyself in there a little bit now and then.

We've seen so many movies about the hardcore side, it's time to show how much fun we had growing up there. All the laughs. Unlike blaxploitation, today's Black movies are made by Black filmmakers. If we do it, it must be true. if we put it on the screen. ◆

The Ike Man Cometh — Again

Newsday, 30 May 1995

Singer, musician, composer, actor — not to mention outrageous fashion-monger, vitamin-gobbler and recent Scientology convert — Isaac Hayes makes it all sound so simple, as if writing a string of hits for the greatest soul duo of the '60s was easy. "Most of the time, Sam and Dave would be there when we wrote for them. If they were scheduled to be in the studio tomorrow, they would come in today and sit with [writing partner David Porter] and me tonight. We loved the pressure. The ideas just flowed."

Hayes' career as a professional keyboard player began as a fluke. The Covington, Tenn., native was a struggling saxophone player in Memphis when the sister of a musician friend who'd gone off to the Air Force passed along a call from a bandleader looking to hire a keyboard player. "I didn't know how to play. The only things I knew were 'Chopsticks' and 'Heart and Soul,' but I was hungry and had a wife and a new baby, so I had to do something," he recalls.

"It was New Year's Eve. I showed up at the gig, and it felt like I was going to an execution. I knew they were going to kill me when they found out I couldn't play." But neither, to Hayes' enormous relief, could the other musicians. "We got through the night because it was New Year's Eve and everybody was drunk. If we played 'Three Blind Mice' they still would try to groove on it." Against all odds, they were hired as the club's house band, and Hayes got on-the-job training that eventually gave him ivoried entree to the legendary Stax Records studio group.

Becoming a member of that elite group was an uncomplicated process. Hayes had begun working as a sideman to baritone saxophonist Floyd Newman, who also did sessions at Stax. When Newman got a shot at recording a single under his own name in 1963, Hayes co-wrote and played on it. While cutting the song, "Frog Stomp," at Stax, "[label co-owner] Jim Stewart saw my keyboard work and said, 'Isaac, Booker T. [Jones] is off in school, would you like to join the staff here?'" Drafted to fill in for the organ-playing leader of Booker T. and the M.G.'s, Hayes went on to become a Stax mainstay, writing (often as "Ed Lee"), producing and performing.

Even his trailblazing treatment of Glen Campbell's "By the Time I Get to Phoenix," which turned the country-pop ballad into a sprawling, monologue-extended soul epic in 1969, was, he says, just an improvisation. Enthusiastic about the song but undecided about recording it, he asked to sit in with the Bar-Kays at the Tiki Club in Memphis one night to try it out. "I showed up and the club was packed. I went up on stage. Everybody was talking, and I said, Damn, I got to get their attention, what am I going to do? I told the Bar-Kays to hang up on the first chord until I told them to stop. I started talking, off the top of my head, I had to do something that they could relate to in order to segue into 'Phoenix.' Halfway through my rapping, the conversations began to subside. When I hit the first notes, I had 'em." By the time he got to the finish, Hayes says, "The ladies were crying. They gave me a standing ovation." He reiterated the effort at a white club and knew he was on to something. The prolonged funk-pop jam was born.

Twenty-five years later, Hayes remains a multifaceted mountain in popular culture. His deep voice, shaved head and football player physique add up to an imposing image at odds with his avuncular personality; unlike the heavy he often plays, Hayes (who frequently refers to himself as Ike) listens closely and laughs easily while he recounts star-packed anecdotes with dramatic relish.

After a decade during which his work could most often be heard as samples in hip-hop records by Tupac, Ice Cube, Snoop Doggy Dogg, Dr. Dre and other rappers, the 52-year-old has resumed making albums. *Raw & Refined* collects undated instrumentals from Hayes' post-Stax stockpile, and opens with "Birth of Shaft," a vintage sketch for the themes he used on the 1971 film soundtrack. Released simultaneously with matching cover art, *Branded* is an all-new set of vocal songs that includes a cover of the Lovin' Spoonful's "Summer in the City" (done for, but not used in, the soundtrack of *Die Hard With a Vengeance*) and Hayes' first collaboration with Porter in more than two decades.

Shortly after he arrived at Stax, Hayes was teamed with Porter, and the pair began crafting material for various performers. They auditioned to work for the label's new arrivals, Sam and Dave, in 1965. The duo's "I Take What I

Want" and "You Don't Know Like I Know" got Sam and Dave started at Stax, while subsequent Hayes-Porter classics like "Hold On! I'm Comin'," "Soul Man" and "When Something Is Wrong With My Baby" made them stars.

It was around this period in the mid-'60s that Hayes happened on the first of his two career trademarks: shaving his head. (The other, the wah-wah pedal, came a few years later when he laid it all over "Shaft.") "Musicians of that time wore processes; to keep it in place you had to sleep with a doo rag. I hated it. It sweats in the summertime; if you don't put it on you wake up with your hair in spikes. I was sick of it. Around the corner from Stax was King's barber shop, and I went in and said, 'Mr. King, cut it all off.'" Hayes has been Mr. Clean ever since.

Hayes' tonsorial election "used to be the victim of a lot of jokes," he says. It proved especially troubling once in Harrisburg, Pennsylvania. "Booker T. somehow booked two gigs on the same day. One was in Oklahoma somewhere. Booker went to Oklahoma himself and used the house musicians there. I went along with the M.G.'s and David [Porter] to Harrisburg. I got up on the organ and we kicked off with 'Green Onions.' We were cooking. It was an all-Black crowd, and they'd been drinking. Someone said, 'That guy ain't no Booker T. — he ain't got no hair! We want our goddamn money back!' I jumped up behind the organ, me and David started dancing and singing and doing all kinds of [stuff] to entertain these people. We got away with it."

Another thing Hayes got away with was *Hot Buttered Soul*, the 1969 album that contained his 19-minute rendition of "By the Time I Get to Phoenix." The record had only three other tracks, one of them a dozen apocalyptic minutes of "Walk on By." *Hot Buttered Soul* was typical of a creative renegade who grew up listening to classical music and the Grand Ole Opry, gospel stars and B.B. King. He discovered jazz through players like Charlie Parker and pop through crooners like Perry Como and Nat King Cole. "They used to call me Nat in high school 'cause I tried to emulate him."

In an era when open-minded experimentation was on its way out of popular music, Hayes proved that he could do whatever he wanted with eclectic songs that might have gotten other funk giants laughed out of town. Now he takes credit for many of the adventurous efforts African-American artists made in his wake. And, to be sure, Barry White especially owes him for bringing symphonic lushness and the wah-wah pedal into funk and thereby setting the turntable for disco music, which made good use of both.

Hayes, who once billed himself "Black Moses," is unafraid to sing his own praises, but he is armed with enough evidence of his manifold achievements to be forgiven a certain degree of hyperbole. He can point to six platinum solo albums and a number-one single, "Theme from *Shaft*."

While Hayes' music remains a virtual sourcebook of funk and soul influence, he's maintained a parallel acting career in television (*The Rockford Files*, *Miami Vice*, *The A-Team*) and films (he's been in a dozen features, from *I'm Gonna Git You Sucka* to *Johnny Mnemonic*). John Singleton recently cooked him breakfast to discuss Hayes' participation, musical and dramatic, in an upcoming film project.

With his time split in so many directions, Hayes says that a full-fledged concert tour will have to wait until his next album. Although America hasn't seen him onstage this decade, Hayes says, "I want to stay out of the marketplace and let the interest and the demand build so I can put on the kind of production people are accustomed to seeing me do. I want horns and strings." So for now, the albums will have to suffice. No longer challenging any stylistic barriers, Hayes is sticking to trusty musical approaches and old-school romance. "I'm from an era when seduction was an art. Women don't want wham-bam-thank-you-ma'am; they want to be wooed. I use metaphors instead of describing anatomical parts."

Furthermore, he says, "Hip-hop is not live music, and people miss live music. That's why it's our time." ◆

An Operatic Turn From Marianne Faithfull

Newsday, 6 April 1995

The unexamined life may not be worth living, but that shouldn't trouble Marianne Faithfull. The singer has recently stockpiled enough introspection to convey her well into the next century. Thirty years after her brief bolt of mid-'60s fame as a convent girl who became a pop thrush and then doyenne of the British rock royalty's demi-monde, Faithfull published an oddly detached spew-all autobiography that erased decades of obscurity. Her lurid tale of sex, drugs and abominable behavior — spiced with celebrities, first among them '60s swain Mick Jagger — returned Faithfull, now 48, to the glare of sensationalism that had long since flamed out.

Following her stint on the pop charts, Faithfull starred in a film (1968's *Girl on a Motorcycle*) and acted in the theater, then vanished into the dissipated morass her book details. In 1979, she returned with *Broken English*, a parched, angry rock album that relaunched her career as a damaged adult. Three discs of whiskey-throated maturity followed, but her star stalled somewhere in the Tom Waits-Leonard Cohen galaxy. After 1990's *Blazing Away*, a live retrospective recorded at St. Anne's Cathedral in Brooklyn, Faithfull retreated to her estate in Ireland.

With an ambitious new album (ironically titled *A Secret Life*) and a career sampler (*A Collection of Her Best Recordings*) in stores, and a film (*When Pigs Fly*) on the way, the Englishwoman returns to Kings County — specifically the Brooklyn Academy of Music — for a weekend of Kurt Weill.

If the path from "As Tears Go By" (the 1964 hit written for Faithfull by her pals in the Rolling Stones) to a German composer of the '30s seems long, Faithfull considers it close to home. "I grew up with this music," she says. "My mum used to hum 'Alabama Song' while peeling the potatoes." Faithfull sang on *Lost in the Stars*, the 1985 Weill tribute album produced by Hal Willner, who later introduced her to *The Seven Deadly Sins*, the Brecht-Weill opera that Faithfull has performed around the world and is bringing to BAM tomorrow and Saturday evening. "It's a piece I identify with more than anything else in my whole life."

If it seems odd that an artist anxious to promote a new album of original songs should instead be singing a 60-year-old opera, the situation reflects the ambivalence that alternately drives Faithfull to bare her innards and then fret about overexposure. "I always get very anxious before the records come out. I feel like I'm laying my life on the line. I'm afraid of being unmasked. But by making these records and writing the book I'm unmasking myself. I want to keep the mystery, but I want to reveal myself, too. Artists that don't reveal anything are dull."

Faithfull's book put paid to that. "I now have permission to put my past, my burden, down," she says. By acknowledging her trespasses without the usual apologia of guilt and shame, however, Faithfull shouldered a new cross: public opprobrium. Stirring dormant embers renewed the thirst for dirt. "More than anywhere else, they judged me in England. They wanted to find some moral purpose in the thing. People were disappointed that I didn't make a demon of Mick Jagger." She has not heard from the demon himself. "He's much too grand, [and] we're not that close."

Since penning her memoirs, Faithfull has worked with an intriguing assortment of characters. Paddy Moloney got her to sing "Love Is Teasin'" on the Chieftains' best-selling *Long Black Veil* album, which also features Jagger. "I like the idea that we're on the record together," says Faithfull. Irish playwright Frank McGuiness (*Someone Who'll Watch Over Me*) wrote song lyrics with her. And Angelo Badalamenti, the composer-arranger who disturbed the musical atmosphere in *Twin Peaks*, co-wrote and produced *A Secret Life*. This marriage made in high-concept heaven has yielded a curious concept album of theatrical pop music about adult life, sprinkled with recitations of Dante and lyrics borrowed from Shakespeare.

"I could hear what I wanted before I met Angelo," says Faithfull. "I wanted a movie with no movie, it's part of my anti-MTV drive. I had just seen *Twin Peaks* and thought he was exactly the man I wanted. I think we did a new form."

That may be stretching it a bit, but Faithfull believes, "The whole point of being pop is continually pushing the boundaries." Pushing boundaries — moral, physical, artistic — is something she knows well. ◆

The Rock and Roll Hall of Fame

My employment at *Newsday*, which I can now look back on as a punishing but satisfying experience, ended in the summer of 1995. I covered the opening of the Rock and Roll Hall of Fame in Cleveland and then took a buyout after a corporate tool dubbed "The Cereal Killer" (for his downsizing of General Mills) took a tour of our offices, declared his full support for our mission and then shut down the New York edition. Before firing everyone unwilling to work in Melville, the company sought voluntary staff reductions. I agreed to a severance package and packed up my desk.

The timing was propitious. A modest chunk of change and a large amount of free time allowed me to organize, write and edit the fifth edition of the *Trouser Press Record Guide*, a book I had already contracted to deliver with precious little thought as to how I expected to do it while also working my ass off at the paper. As it happened, I spent from 14 to 18 hours a day, seven days a week, for roughly nine months to ready the manuscript by the deadline. There'd have been no prayer had I stayed on at the paper. (Coda: When I went to deliver it to my editor, having powered through the final printout process for two grueling days without sleep, he was away from the office. An assistant suggested I leave it — it being nearly a thousand pages of obsessive graft — on his chair. Bitterly disappointed at being greeted with a shrug at the finish line of my marathon, I did what she said, rode the elevator down to the street, shuffled out onto Third Avenue in a state of post-traumatic shock and burst into tears.)

I've visited the Rock and Roll Hall of Fame and Museum in Cleveland twice and have been moved, entertained and surprised both times. They've got great stuff on display, and the honorees room is quite moving. It's worth the trip. That said, I'm not here to debate the validity or choices of the Rock Hall. I've been a voter since the beginning, ticking boxes for artists I believe deserve recognition. My picks are not always the most popular ones, but some of them have been enshrined, many long after they first became eligible. I have repeatedly sought to get on the nominating committee, which wields the real power in the organization and which, despite the inclusion at times of many wise and honorable people, has made lots of inexplicable choices. So far, those efforts have come to naught.

It'll Go Down in History

Newsday, 27 August 1995

With the ribbon-cutting ceremony that officially opens the Rock and Roll Hall of Fame and Museum in Cleveland on Friday, the final thread holding up the illusion of rock and roll's rebel status will be severed; popular music's deliverance from heathen infamy complete. How, exactly, does glassed-in pedantry honor rule-smashing spontaneity?

A squalling runt born in back-street bars and grungy garages, rock and roll never was meant to be polite company. The lurid, licentious spawn of lust and a litany of bad habits, its very name — slang for sinfully recreational sex — was nearly unspeakable when first applied to upbeat electric R&B more than 40 years ago. And to this day, among the wide field of musicians answering its call are artists who strike terror into the hearts of decent folks, the very folks whose children are busy spending their allowances on those performers.

But even those who idealize its motives and imagine its purity of essence must admit that rock and roll — especially the safe, past-tense kind that fulfills the Hall of Fame's 25-year-career criterion — has been welcomed into the mainstream and exploited by it far too deeply to support its credibility as subversive.

With all of rock's successes and compromises, the opening of a museum dedicated to its history is really no big deal — symbolic or practical. As dubious as fetishistic exhibits of John Lennon's specs, Jim Morrison's report card or Sid Vicious's leather trousers might be, whatever potential there might have been for irony in such benediction of brattiness expired long before the Rock and Roll Hall of Fame was conceived in the mid-'80s. The faces of dead musical legends — including Elvis, Buddy and Otis — already grace the government's first-class stamps. Fleetwood Mac played the Clinton Inaugural. The Beach Boys (minus the loose-cannon genius of Brian Wilson) have come to be known as "America's Band." These aging sun gods provide just the cultural illusion the nation desires: freeze-dried, consecrated nostalgia, sex-free romance and innocuous fun, the kind that poses no present menace to society.

Rock and roll has never abandoned the three major chords and danceable backbeat of its guitar-grasping infancy, but the baby has picked up a lot of new tricks along the way. Within some vague border of sound and principle, rock now encompasses such opposites as Nine Inch Nail's infernal technology, Madonna's subterranean disco obsessions, Hootie and the Blowfish's unchallenging pop and Tupac Shakur's slow-rolling gangsta bravado — and just as little unanimity in its politics.

The graying of veterans and the endless infusion of teenagers feeds a wicked generation gap. Neil Young's creed to the contrary, most musicians neither burn out nor fade away — they hang around forever. So, while rockers at each age stratum may have common perspectives, the gap that once separated rock fans from their parents has been opened within the music community itself. Principles fly around like body surfers. For every belligerent hell-raiser throwing herself off the Lollapalooza stage, there are plenty of happy-face old-timers ready to bury their hearts at the local Hard Rock Cafe. Pearl Jam took on Ticketmaster, but R.E.M. opted not to buck the system. Youth-is-cool is no longer a reliable rule of thumb. For every Frank Zappa standing up to declare free speech the essence of rock and roll culture, there are plenty of got-mine youngsters glad to collect rock's riches and keep their traps shut.

If an anti-Hall of Fame case rests on any pretense of rockers' shared values, forget it. Every band that has ever opened a major tour has its tales of woe of being treated miserably by an arrogant headliner, but Sonic Youth, Nine Inch Nails, Soul Asylum and Nirvana all have used their clout to promote bands they like. Kurt Cobain took himself even more seriously, attempting to dictate fans' behavior and damn their prejudices.

Most successful acts simply take the money and run, resisting any role in the world beyond the exchange of money for product. The Hall of Fame provides them with a perfect career grail. Independent punk rockers Fugazi and singer-songwriter Ani DiFranco may see major record labels as the enemies of quality and freedom, but hip-hop rebels from Public Enemy to Snoop Doggy Dogg welcome their power and distribution.

Ultimately, in the complex calculus between artistic integrity and mass popularity, personal ambition and audience expectations, whimsical self-indulgence and big-bucks reality, every artist must balance his or her own equation. The Rock and Roll Hall of Fame may add an unexpected variable, but it's closer to a grandly resolved bar argument than the end of rock as we know it. Sure, it will be hard to accept the absurdity of mega-selling '70s no-talents like Grand Funk Railroad joining the Rolling Stones in the pantheon, or John Denver being spoken of in the same breath as Sam Cooke, but commercial radio makes such travesties audible on an hourly basis. Can Hall and Oates really be equated with Sam and Dave? Of course not, and their inevitable commemoration won't change that for most fans. And how will the Sex Pistols and the Clash, bands who swore opposition to all moribund cultural institutions (except, of course, those that aided and abetted them), talk their way out of rank hypocrisy when their peers call them to the podium early next century?

What the Rock and Roll Hall of Fame does is grant the world of three-minute marvels, initially dismissed as a passing fancy for fickle teenagers, full-fledged status as an institution, on a par with baseball and television. Once decried for its best values — rebellion, self-indulgence, violence, wanton sexuality, noise, mindless release, generational over-throw — rock and roll has become officially sanctioned Americana. Rock and roll now has a house of worship, a national monument as likely for summer vacation visits as Disneyland, the Grand Canyon, Cooperstown or Planet Hollywood. (Those seeking to limit freedom of expression in '90s music must be feeling a bit out of it this week.)

It's hard to pin down the point at which rock and roll was transformed from social pariah to American institution. Elvis was an irresistible, unmovable force in the 1950s, but he was the institution, not the culture that grew along with his global fame. As long as it could be viewed as something for the kids, and controlled by adults, rock culture remained a stratum for those who liked that sort of thing.

The bravado of Danny and the Juniors' brash declaration — "Rock and roll is here to stay" — could scarcely mask the anxiety that maybe rock and roll was just a '50s thing, an explosion of post-war giddiness that would fade away as soon as Elvis' popularity waned (as it inevitably would) and the decade's teens grew up to get the jobs the Silhouettes sarcastically sang about that same year. Little did anyone realize at the time that the rise of youth culture wasn't a phase, something to be tut-tutted about in polite circles, but a permanent state of grace, a social revolution that declared youth a private domain in which adult concerns were off limits.

America's youth didn't recognize its strength at first. Rock and roll, like everything else, was owned and operated by grownups, and artists functioned at their pleasure. Not every early icon was a rigged-up puppet like Fabian, but even Elvis Presley couldn't dictate the terms of his television appearances the way today's stars can. Prince was granted far more creative autonomy on his first record than the Beatles could swing for theirs; the amounts paid to top artists 30 years ago pale in comparison to the windfalls today's alternative buzz bands command.

The first waves of stars had no autonomy and little independence; Black artists were treated with all the dignity racist America accorded Black folks in general (that is, none). If managers like Col. Tom Parker and monolithic record companies couldn't always make artists toe the line, public morals and civil authorities were ready to keep high-spirited celebrities (such as Chuck Berry, convicted of statutory rape) in line. At concerts and movie showings, police made sure the fun never got too out of hand. Beyond the "race music" world of rhythm and blues — considered by racists as too far gone for mainstream redemption anyway — there were only a few '50s performers (Elvis Presley, Gene Vincent and Jerry Lee Lewis, to name some obvious ones) who could get away with the act of being themselves. And even they were made to pay for their most notorious transgressions.

But rock and roll's progress was inexorable. Reckless artists from Little Richard to the Rolling Stones and successors inspired by their examples pushed the boundaries of acceptable behavior (and dress, language, subject matter, volume, style, etc.) inch by inch, until there were no lines left to cross. At which point, a new generation of rebels arrived, identified barricades farther in the distance and set off to storm them.

It took the decade that witnessed Bob Dylan, the Beatles, hippies, Woodstock and the early inklings of celebrity drug deaths to catapult youth music, via the increasingly obsessed media, into the forefront of America's consciousness. As it became the soundtrack to everything from peace to war, rock — or the subject of rock and its outrageous characters — radiated out through a global culture in unprecedented flux, touching realms as clearly separated as church and state. Swept along in a wave of social unanimity, youth and rock and roll became virtually synonymous.

In short order, "relevant" college courses shaped around the obsessions of tuition-paying students became commonplace. (While last month's scholarly colloquium in Memphis on Elvis Presley was the first of its kind, the desire to treat rock with intellectual dignity is hardly new.) Books and serious magazines about rock and roll proliferated; television switched from taunting rock to accepting it. Although television's complete embrace of youth music as something more than dance-show fare would have to wait until the concert programs of the '70s and the creation of MTV in the '80s, the eight years that elapsed between Steve Allen humiliating Elvis Presley with a basset hound and the Beatles being given a clear path to overnight stardom on *The Ed Sullivan Show* marked a drastic change in the way we saw rock and roll.

Ultimately, the music demonstrated its greatest power in the apple-pie Americana of heavy financial traffic. Multibillion-dollar sales of records, concert tickets and related merchandise was just the birth of a many-striped cash cow. By the mid-'60s, beverage makers, auto manufacturers, the Army and other marketing monoliths had discovered the power of pop songs and their singers and began using them in commercials. If the alliance was shaky at first, the green light of dollar signs that bathed the high-stakes game of mutual back-scratching washed away any barriers. As baby-boom marketers moved up the ladder and targeted themselves as a prime audience, pop culture became as intrinsic to the world of sales as cash registers.

By the time the '60s ended, yesterday's bobbysoxers and greasers found themselves in charge. By the end of the following decade, the power to produce, distribute and publicize music was, to a large degree, theirs as well. Like the man who came to dinner, rock and roll was, for once and for all, here to stay.

But while sheer scale has turned it into as reliable and enduring an industry as the movies, rock and roll — through thick and thin, garbage and greatness, co-option and reinvention — has managed to keep its connection to the fringe, its escalator down to the underground. And that's why some like the Ohio punk-rock band called Thomas Jefferson Slave Apartments find the idea of its formal enshrinement in a $92-million multimedia palace designed by world-famous architect I.M. Pei so offensive.

They're not alone in clinging to music's outsider self-image. "If my dad were alive today," said Arlo Guthrie, accepting the Hall of Fame's induction of his late father, populist folksinger Woody Guthrie, in 1988, "this is the one place he wouldn't be." Like Groucho Marx, a lot of rock and rollers are rightly uneasy about being granted membership in a club that would actually have them. It would be encouraging if some aging rebel declined induction on conceptual grounds, but 25 years after the flush of novelty, who would have such unwavering principles?

It may be hard to watch the riotous music of youth settle down and politely gather dust, but that's what happens to the youth who created the music anyway. Rock and roll may never die, but the people who make it sure do. And since "My Generation" is probably not your generation, there's merit in offering today's 10-year-olds a vivid sense of what they missed. And I like the image of suburban parents packing kids into the station wagon to visit a museum to see the spangled wrestling jacket worn by Dictators singer Handsome Dick Manitoba. Rock and roll can certainly afford to fill one building with ephemera. We'll make more. ◆

In Huge New Shrine to Rock, It's the Details That Resonate

Newsday, 31 August 1995

Everything about rock and roll has always been big. Records that sell in the millions can still be deemed flops; stars go to extremes trying to outrage decent folks. Heck, just building a garage large enough to hold its junk cost $92 million. That garage — the Rock and Roll Hall of Fame and Museum, a glamorous I.M. Pei-designed building erected on the shores of Lake Erie — opens here tomorrow. The gleaming white structure with a huge glass pyramid houses four floors of historical exhibits and ephemera as well as the Hall of Fame.

It's big, all right. East German cars from U2's *Zoo TV* tour hang like a mobile in the lobby; a sizable chunk of Pink Floyd's wall holds down the fourth floor. Neil Young's oversized prop amplifiers look down on the entrance. But in a press preview held yesterday as workers hastily applied finishing touches, what resonated were details, little bits that said so much. (Not the jukebox-shaped cash machines or the cutely named Eat to the Beat Cafe.) Springsteen's popularity is easy to understand in light of the young up-and-comer's handwritten letter to a fan that ends with a humble "Sorry about the crummy paper." And the Doors need to be reconsidered in light of the poignant Jim Morrison display that contains his Cub Scout shirt, college degree (BA, major in theater arts) and death certificate.

One stock exhibit item is draft lyrics for hit songs. Paul Simon's are carefully printed on a ruled yellow pad; Dee Dee Ramone's "Gimme Gimme Shock Treatment" is scrawled on a bag. It's hard to imagine Billy Joel winning a *Grammy* for "Just the Way You Are" if he hadn't crossed out his original opening: "Don't go changing for some reason you've imagined I would need"? (And who knew that "We Didn't Start the Fire" was initially titled "Jolene"?) The museum is a veritable tribute to second thoughts: Jimi Hendrix' set list for Woodstock makes no mention of "Star Spangled Banner," the song for which the guitarist's 1969 performance will always be remembered.

A thorough, imaginative and well-organized multi-media effort that touches many musical bases with varying degrees of success, the museum was conceived, in the words of chief curator Jim Henke, as "a book on the history of rock and roll. It doesn't tell the entire story," he says, but there's still a lot to take in, from the revealing to the absurd.

The lower level, the main exhibit area, is the only place the noise and hubbub level threatens to be a problem. The upper floors are smaller, sparser and relatively serene, although the Alan Freed radio exhibit on the second floor seemed pretty loud. Features include a collection of stage costumes spanning Elvis Presley to KISS to Madonna, spotlights on seven time-and-place "scenes" (among them New York / London punk in the '70s and New York hip-hop in the '80s), and a bank of video terminals that offers visitors a chance to hear and read about "500 songs that shaped rock and roll."

The Beatles, Rolling Stones, Jim Morrison and Everly Brothers all merit individual exhibits that feature some of the museum's most prized acquisitions. Among them is John Lennon's chartreuse *Sgt. Pepper* uniform. There's a substantial and serious exhibit about rhythm and blues through the years as well as a wall of celebrity drumsticks assembled by Long Island collector Peter Lavinger.

Smaller showcases are devoted to a haphazard collection of artists, including the Who, Alice Cooper, Elvis Presley and Michael Jackson. (In two more revealing touches, the mannequins wearing Jackson's threads are white, and a plaque announces, "All objects collection of Michael Jackson, King of Pop.") In the Parliament-Funkadelic display, George Clinton's *Atomic Dog* shoes alone are worth the price of admission.

Carefully separated from the museum, the Hall of Fame is the building's top floor, in a small, darkened, high-ceilinged room at the head of a long, circular staircase. There are no brass plaques, no marble busts or gaping color portraits, no stereo blasting out the sounds of these musical greats. All it contains is four silent glass walls surrounding a large, round bench. The names and signatures of the inductees are etched in the glass, adjacent to small TV screens displaying a black-and-white photograph and elegiac quote from a relevant celebrity.

Running alphabetically from pioneering *Billboard* music editor Paul Ackerman to principled rock iconoclast Frank Zappa, the walls of fame celebrate some extremely rowdy heroes in a most dignified and reserved way. Rather than amplify or deify artists, the Hall of Fame honors them and their fans simply, by encouraging personal reflection. Presenting nothing more than names and faces, it allows visitors to carry in their own memories — that Temptations song that always made you smile, the Who's pulse-quickening power, the crush you had on Tina Turner — and indulge them. ◆

One highlight that goes unmentioned in my review of the marathon concert arranged for the Hall's opening weekend was meeting Jane Scott, a Cleveland icon who was then, at 76, the oldest living active rock critic in America. (As of this writing, the two coastal Roberts, Hilburn and Christgau, are older than that.) She was a delightful, enthusiastic character and made my time in the stadium press box where we were stationed so much more meaningful and memorable.

Ages of Rock

From Little Richard to Melissa Etheridge, the Concert for the Rock and Roll Hall of Fame spanned seven hours of tribute and travesty from musical lightweights and legends alike.

Newsday, 4 September 1995

Whoever said *ars longa, vita brevis* had a point, but it wasn't the one demonstrated by the *Concert for the Rock and Roll Hall of Fame* Saturday night. The show staged at Cleveland's crumbling Municipal Stadium proved that art is long — clearly, rock music remains an enduring and progressive stream of people and styles after 40-plus years. But it also underscored how fleeting human existence is. Hyperbolically billed by promoters as the concert of a lifetime, the nearly seven-hour ordeal sure seemed to take one.

Like other recent mega events in the world of rock, the efficiently mounted show was endless, pointless, geared for TV (HBO broadcast the whole thing live), weighed down by today's marquee names and only sporadically transcendent. On the other hand, the performances were almost all adequate, and the lineup *did* include Chuck Berry, Bruce Springsteen, Bob Dylan, Aretha Franklin, Jerry Lee Lewis, Johnny Cash, P-Funk All-Stars, Sam Moore and Little Richard.

Fittingly, in a program that granted too much stage time to current lightweights like Melissa Etheridge, John Mellencamp, Jon Bon Jovi and Sheryl Crow, it fell to real-deal Hall of Famers like Al Green, John Fogerty, Bob Dylan, James Brown and the Kinks to rip it up for the ages and show where the music's true spirit is kept. Fine performances from Springsteen, Lou Reed, Iggy Pop and the Allman Brothers kept the night moving along, but they weren't singing for the ages. And with 67 numbers performed by more than three dozen stars, gluttony, overkill and fatigue became major factors — enough so that HBO host Jon Stewart and Lou Reed could be seen and heard on the video screens at one point rhapsodizing about a duet Al Green and Aretha Franklin hadn't actually done.

The concert was organized both as a tribute to those artists enshrined in the Rock and Roll Hall of Fame and to raise money to fund its operation. While the reported 63,515 ticket holders — most of whom stayed to the bitter end, remaining on their feet for the entire marathon — saw to the latter, the former impulse was met in unusual, inscrutable and inexplicable ways. The discernible blueprint — the inductees on hand sang their own songs, those absent had their music interpreted by others — was not always followed, and the mixture of oldies night, tribute concert and stars-on-parade made for a confusing aesthetic. And to increase the confusion, the video screens occasionally filled stage change time with historic performances by Muddy Waters, Otis Redding, Jimi Hendrix and Janis Joplin that put all but a few of the live efforts to shame.

Backed by Booker T. and the M.G.'s, who served as the house band, the 50-year-old John Fogerty sang Creedence Clearwater Revival's "Born on the Bayou" and "Fortunate Son" as if he were a garage-rocking teenager revved up on rocket fuel. In a thrilling and surprisingly vehement performance, Fogerty was as unrepentant, unretiring and contemporary as Neil Young. (Young's absence was only one of many: there was also no trace of Beatles, Rolling Stones, Ray Charles, Bo Diddley, Fats Domino, Who or Led Zeppelin.)

Working the crowd as if it had assembled for him alone, Al Green was in top form, turning "Tired of Being Alone" and Sam Cooke's "A Change Is Gonna Come" into a showstopping display of inspired vocal prowess. The Kinks stormed through "All Day and All of the Night" and ambled around "Lola" with typical aplomb. Sam Moore, without mentioning his late partner Dave Prater, belted out "When Something Is Wrong With My Baby." And Dylan, an unannounced attraction, finished a truncated version of his typical '90s set by bringing Springsteen out for a beautiful duet on "Forever Young." Backed by Soul Asylum, Lou Reed, a bride still waiting at the Hall's altar, dedicated a ferocious and melodic performance of "Sweet Jane" to Sterling Morrison, the Velvet Underground guitarist who died last week.

Springsteen, the show's de facto star, served in a variety of capacities. He and the E Street Band (a reunion about which no fuss whatever was made) backed Chuck Berry and Jerry Lee Lewis, slowed "Shake, Rattle and Roll" to a dull snail's pace, wrapped two blasts of "Bo Diddley" around his similarly rhythmed "She's the One" and ended his 25-minute set with an epochal "Darkness on the Edge of Town."

James Brown, a grey-haired Johnny Cash, Aretha Franklin and Little Richard did their usual routines without incident, but some of the veterans weren't up to snuff. Eric Burdon, sharing the stage with Jon Bon Jovi, croaked a couple of Animals hits with no range; Martha Reeves couldn't find a mic she liked for "Dancing in the Streets." Chuck Berry, who, appropriately enough, kicked off the show by singing "Johnny B. Goode" also ended it with a disastrous rendition of "Rock and Roll Music" that defied Springsteen and Co.'s attempts to find a place or key in the song.

Some of the tributes were musically apt and richly rewarding. Dr. John did sweet justice to Fats Domino's "Blueberry Hill." The P-Funk All-Stars, joined by Family Stone bassist Larry Graham, poured funk power into the grooves of Sly's "Thank You Falettinme Be Mice Elf Agin" and "Higher." The Pretenders, a band that knows from drug tragedy, made poignant work of Neil Young's "The Needle and the Damage Done." The unplugged Gin Blossoms harmonized nicely on tunes by the Beatles and Byrds. And in a rare acknowledgment of an inductee in the early-influence category, Natalie Merchant presented her sexy side in a sultry version of Dinah Washington's "I Know How to Do It." The other possible pre-rock tribute was "Back Door Man," the Howlin' Wolf song Iggy Pop performed with Soul Asylum, but it could have been meant either for the benefit of the Doors, who covered it, or Willie Dixon, who wrote it.

Other conceptual conceits were an insult to musical history. The raunchless Sheryl Crow dishonored the Rolling Stones' "Let It Bleed" and "Get Off My Cloud" with her cloying sing-song delivery; the unworthy Bon Jovi stood up for the Beatles ("With a Little Help From My Friends") and John Lennon ("Imagine"). Slash and Boz Scaggs made a mockery of Jimi Hendrix's "Red House." John Mellencamp used Martha Reeves to re-create his hit version of Van Morrison's "Wild Night."

While Jackson Browne reduced Bob Marley's "Redemption Song" and Smokey Robinson's "The Tracks of My Tears" to bland singer-songwriter musings, Melissa Etheridge took show honors for singlehandedly botching the most great songs. Besides joining Browne for an oil-and-water duet on the Everly Brothers' "Wake Up Little Susie," Etheridge offered a crummy bar-band version of the Ronettes' "Be My Baby," stomped on the Supremes' "Love Child" and revved up a gender-switching "Leader of the Pack" which ran over the song's campy cool with melodramatic passion.

Ultimately, the sprawling show was an impressive display of marshalled talent and logistical precision. Griping about who wasn't represented (surely *someone* could have done a Beach Boys song) helped pass the time, but the show's intentions seemed good, and there were some memorable moments. The line between tribute and travesty was crossed too often for it to have been a clear artistic victory, but it was close enough for rock and roll. ◆

One last highlight of that weekend occurred during the press preview tour of the Museum. I wrote about it.

Newsday, 3 September 1995

The scheme several friends and I hatched to borrow instruments and perform on a remote stage at *Woodstock* last year didn't pan out, but now I have a consolation prize in the annals of modern music history. I'm in the Rock and Roll Hall of Fame and Museum!

Well, not exactly me, but close enough: Three issues of *Trouser Press*, the rock magazine I co-founded in 1974, are on display in "My Back Pages," an exhibit about the history of music journalism.

There I was the other day, doing my reporter's duty of checking out the insides of the long-promised institution that opened in Cleveland this weekend, when I happened upon the second-floor exhibit and discovered — to my total surprise — that *Trouser Press*, a 10-year labor of love, had been included alongside such pioneering periodicals as *Crawdaddy, Creem, Bomp, Punk, 16, Rock Scene* and *New York Rocker*. A friend from a Minneapolis newspaper [*Jim Walsh, thanks man!*], watching me exult in my unexpected moment of posterity, grabbed his pad and demanded a quote. "Uhhhhh," I said, "I had no idea. . . This is so cool. . ." The history of rock and roll marches on.

Surface Noise #8

TrouserPress.com, November 1997

The Rock and Roll Hall of Fame ballot arrived in yesterday's mail. Each year, a couple of thousand folks of some supposed standing in music receive a neat little package containing a card-stock folder with photos and thumbnail biographies (presumably provided for those too old to recall or too young to know) of a dozen-plus venerable nominees along with a cassette of their representative recordings to jog stodgy memories and bear audible witness to the long-ago musical achievements of those deemed worthy of honor and consideration.

This year's list runs pretty much along the lines of the dozen that preceded it, except that we're now up to 1972 (or '73 — I can never recollect whether it's based on balloting year [this one] or induction year [next one]) as the starting line for a contender's earliest record release.

There are, first and most evident, a handful of ancient R&B stars — unassailable strivers and stalwarts finally coming onto the Hall of Fame's radar screen long after their initial eligibility — whose fondly recalled names don't necessarily elicit accurate or extensive memories of their song catalogue. Solomon Burke, Joe Tex and the Moonglows certainly possess their full share of estimable hits, but none of these gentlemen clearly surpasses the sense of being simply a solid sender of some past era who rose to fame and left behind some fine records. With the glare of fame long extinguished, many beloved old-timers have receded into oldie status: proof of the past more than eternal figures aging against art's unstated wishes. Are these performers in the same league as indelible innovators like Al Green, Sam Cooke or Otis Redding? They don't seem that way to me, but others are surely more qualified than I am to speak to this topic.

The ballot also includes two pop acts (the Mamas and the Papas and, gulp, Billy Joel) whose enormous popularity, distinctive sound and basic goodness virtually define the very purpose of a Hall of Fame. But off to their side, the Eagles are this year's mainstream rock gods whose miserable plops left rotting on the cultural landscape have not noticeably improved with the passage of time. Santana is a group that was great in its day but doesn't seem to have grown in stature over the years. Spinning through so many different incarnations that they've become an inconsistent and unjudgeable institution rather than a proper band, Fleetwood Mac (in a severely belated nomination) raises the question of what band is actually being voting on: the tough and alienated British blues band Peter Green fronted or Stevie Nicks' bloated and affluent SoCal hit machine? How about the one after that, with Billy Burnette?

Beyond complicated characters like Gene Pitney and Lloyd Price, who — for those possessing historical knowledge beyond the ability to hum "Lawdy Miss Clawdy" and name "Town Without Pity" — deserve election but lack the bigger-than-life star stature to be shoe-ins, are the few artists on the list of nominees who actually mean something to me personally: the Stooges, Dusty Springfield, Gene Vincent and Del Shannon. Fuck what Billy Joel says, it's not all rock'n'roll to me. The Eagles are no more rock'n'roll music than [*Velveeta is cheese*]— they're the smugly synthetic post-industrial "improvement" on the real thing. Food that doesn't spoil. Tits installed by a surgeon. Natural wonders built by man. Demographic career designs to smoothly accompany yesterday's lifestyles.

No, my guys are the ones who did and do matter because they couldn't do anything else but spew their guts into the closest receptacle: a tape deck. They're life's losers, taking a last desperate stab at music's flimsy lifeline as they're being sucked under by the quicksand of personal circumstances. They're all outsiders, squirrely nutjobs thrown on the harsh mercy of those they'd never meet, weirdoes whose successful musical careers could never assuage their monumental discomfort with life.

Stardom failed to provide them with entry into a world they could only imagine, an oasis where pain and suffering would be replaced by acceptance and love. These sacrificial lambs could sell vinyl by the ton and have people lavish them with praise from airport lounge to radio studio to hotel bed, but they could never feel good enough about themselves to end the day with any less terror than they started out with. That's why the records they made still mean something: they came from someplace we've all been and truly don't want to revisit. That's art enough to me.

Even in the nonsense syllables of his eerie and imbecilic headstone "Be-Bop-a-Lula," there's something honest and true in Gene Vincent's incoherent hiccough, a laughably constipated attempt at romanticism. No matter how hard Gene tries to sound coolly self-confident, he keeps sliding into the humiliation of panting desperation. Dressed to kill in malevolent black leather, he's still a lonely stray dog with a game leg spraying an alley wall 'coz the scraggly spaniel around the corner won't let him do it to her. Life in the fast lane was no breezy cruise for a man whose dark rockabilly essays include such incandescent headlights of strangeness as the potently bewildering "Who Slapped John?" and "Race With the Devil."

Shannon was even more lost in this life. A heartbroken nebbish with the defiant bravado of a chilly wind looking for a warm fire to blow out, he radiates the pride and pain of each new emotional wound in every one of his great odes to romantic injury. No scars on him: every injury is dripping fresh blood. With a wrenching, nearly comical falsetto and the solitary flutings of a pitiful keyboard device called the musitron, he pours unappealing emotions into classics like "Hats Off to Larry" (a vindictive tribute to the guy who dumped the woman who dumped him), "So Long Baby" (getting even through infidelity), "Runaway" (obsessive misery on the whys and wheres of a real gone girl), "Little Town Flirt" (he can't have her, so he tells "every guy that goes by" that she's a cockteasing slut), "Cry Myself to Sleep," "Keep Searchin'" and so on down the line. Del's so lonesome he could cry, so he lashes out. Wearing each disappointment like a Boy Scout badge, Shannon does his stoic Midwest best to keep his lip from quivering and his real despair — an anguish far deeper than what any faithless lover could inflict — from showing. It didn't matter. No amount of public self-pity or adulation was enough to keep the minor-key maestro from topping himself in the end.

Springfield's strange ascent is harder to wrap a critical blanket around: in 1963 she's a high-stress British thrush doing delightfully disposable top-of-the-line factory pop like "I Only Want to Be With You." Five years later she's hanging with American heavies in Memphis, making like a lightweight Aretha on the subtly sexual soul-country dislocation of "Son of a Preacher Man." What message is being sent when an English girl starts "taking time to make time" and "looking to see how much we growin'"? [*If I may add some 21st century recognition: Dusty is one of the greatest singers ever. She was not Aretha, but then no one was.*]

As for the Stooges, it didn't matter whether it was 1969 or any other year with nothin' to do: Iggy and his fellow fuckups were always gonna be the rock barbarians banging their faces mindlessly against windows prudently barred against their passage. Their very existence defined rock as a loser's game, the playpen of misbegotten adolescents already over the hill, bored and jaded to the point of cynical disgust. "I say, oh my and boo-hoo." Any questions?

In this realm, rock's heroes-by-acclamation simply need to have their considerable achievements toted up like a bank statement at those pearly gates to be ushered into the hallowed halls. But the '60s was the last time when greatness in pop music was a universal slam dunk, and we're into trickier terrain. In my world, the Ramones, Clash, Sex Pistols, Elvis Costello, Johnny Thunders, Blondie, the Replacements, Hüsker Dü, Jesus and Mary Chain and T. Rex are shoe-ins, but this isn't my world. It took a couple of tries to get the Velvet Underground elected, ferchrissake. God save the Stooges and all who sail on their miserable seas. ◆

Each year's Hall of Fame inductees are memorialized in a lavish program book that is distributed free to attendees at the ceremony. Thanks to editor Holly George-Warren, I've gotten to author the profiles for some artists I really admire. (There was no live ceremony in 2020, but the program book that included my Depeche Mode essay was produced anyway.) I've done five so far. My essays on the Clash, Kinks and Cheap Trick are in those groups' respective chapters in Volume 2 of *Music in a Word*. Here are the others:

The Cure

Rock and Roll Hall of Fame Program Book, 2019

A review of *Three Imaginary Boys*, the Cure's debut album, ran in the *Melody Maker* of May 12th, 1979, under the headline "The Eighties Start Here." In England, the magnificent fury of '77 punk rock was already being consigned to cliché: The best bands were off to new stylistic adventures, and the ones they inspired into existence were moving even further afield. America gave most of it the cold shoulder, waiting for more colorful and diplomatic acts — the kind that MTV could embrace — to give the new decade a look and a sound, calling it everything from new wave to post-punk, new romantic, synth-pop, and college rock.

The Cure didn't need a calendar to see the future. While sharing many of punk's values — commercial nonchalance, willful self-direction, an aversion to showboating, solos and stage production — the Cure were emblematic of the next era, a singular sensation of atmosphere, intimacy, and occasional pop charm, brought to visual life in a stream of wildly inventive Tim Pope-directed videos. While some of their peers were crushed under grunge's wheels in the '90s, the Cure continued to grow and evolve, exploring joy and melancholy, whimsy and doom.

Early photos betray none of that. What they show is an anodyne group of clean-cut school friends (dubbed Easy Cure at the start of '77; slimmed down the next year as a more simply named trio) from Crawley, 30 miles south of London. Lol Tolhurst, the band's first drummer and a member through 1989, sees the Cure as a product of its environment: "suburban boredom and green forests and asylums for people who have problems. We wove all of that together."

Singer, lyricist, rhythm guitarist, and producer Robert Smith has been the life force animating the Cure for more than forty years now, joined at different times by a dozen other musicians. Nine are going into the Rock and Roll Hall of Fame. (Only three bands have had more members inducted: the Grateful Dead, Parliament-Funkadelic, and the Comets.) Michael Dempsey, bassist in the original trio, left in 1979. Guitarist Porl (now Pearl) Thompson was, for a time, in Easy Cure but didn't join the Cure until 1984, staying until 1993 and then returning for a third stint from 2005 to 2010. Boris Williams took over the drum throne in 1984, when Tolhurst switched to keyboards, and stayed until 1995. Perry Bamonte played keyboards and guitar in the band from 1990 to 2005.

The current lineup has been together since 2012: low-slung bassist Simon Gallup, who first joined in 1979, keyboardist Roger O'Donnell (three stints in the Cure, beginning in 1987), drummer Jason Cooper, a steady presence for more than two decades, and the new guy, Reeves Gabrels. The guitarist was in Tin Machine with David Bowie and joined Smith's crew seven years ago.

"The Cure has been several distinct groups over the years," Smith said in 1997. "There isn't any kind of linear logic to what we do. It all comes from a central core and it goes off in different directions from there. In the middle of it is me." Each iteration has ably shouldered the band's heritage while reinventing itself around Smith's current state of mind. It's no coincidence that one of the Cure's best albums is titled *Wild Mood Swings*. As he once noted, "The only common factor is me and my voice. And I'm a different person to the person that made the earlier albums." You might not know that to look at him: other than an unplanned home chop in 1986, he has maintained an unruly shock of black hair, smeared lipstick, heavy eye shadow, baggy black clothing, and sneakers. The look — gender disrupted, glamour gone bad — was adapted by Tim Burton for *Edward Scissorhands* (1990) and copied outright by Sean Penn in *This Must Be the Place* (2011).

While demonstrating a genius for pop singles that feel light, brisk and nearly translucent, the Cure have filled albums with extended expositions of opaque, downbeat layering and a measure of patience few stadium-scale artists can manage. On the diverse and satisfying *Disintegration* (and elsewhere), many of the long tracks start with a minute or two (even three) of an enveloping instrumental swirl before the vocals ever begin. Cure albums have been unutterably bleak (the first line of 1982's drum-driven *Pornography* is "It doesn't matter if we all die") and exotically romantic (*The Head on the Door*, from 1985), bare bones minimal (*Three Imaginary Boys*, revamped in the U.S. as *Boys Don't Cry*, adding the titular new wave pop classic) and loaded to the top with guitar, keyboards, horns, and more (*Kiss Me Kiss Me Kiss Me*).

The singles Smith has written and sung have provoked political outrage ("Killing an Arab"), titled an Oscar-winning film ("Boys Don't Cry"), and a Reese Witherspoon picture ("Just Like Heaven"), skewered conformity ("Jumping Someone Else's Train"), scored a number-two *Billboard* hit Adele later covered ("Lovesong"), and provided fodder for a million mixtapes ("Let's Go to Bed," the winsome sadness of "Pictures of You" and "Inbetween Days," the giddy joy of "Friday I'm in Love," "Why Can't I Be You?"). Yet outside of a few stray minutes in a huge library of music, the band's sonic signature remains immediately recognizable.

Artists from John Lennon to Morrissey have been lauded for their willingness to bare themselves in song; Smith has built his empire on vulnerability. The Cure is a compelling, if oblique, exhibition of his uncertainties, fears, anguish, anger, delight, and despair. At the same time, he's been married to his childhood sweetheart for three decades. He acknowledges the dichotomy. "I don't feel any conflict at all between how I am now in public when I'm with people and where the songs come from. The two are totally unrelated. I've got a house, I've got a back garden, I've got a telescope, and I live by the sea. I have all the ingredients of a wonderful life. The songs don't come from any of that." To some degree, they do come from Smith's avid literacy. His lyrics have been touched by everyone from Camus and Sartre to JD Salinger and Truman Capote. And those familiar with the symbolist poets will detect traces of *their* absinthe-infused anomie in the Cure's.

Currently without a manager, record label, or publicist, the Cure has never prioritized chart success over creative satisfaction. Smith once said the original idea of the band was "making music entirely to please myself" and characterized the selection process for singles as "the least obscure track on the album." All the same, five Cure albums and two long-form videos have gone platinum in the U.S. They've played football stadiums here and headlined many of the world's top festivals, doing shows as long as four hours.

If all but shunned by the *Grammys* (two *Alternative Music Album* nominations, no wins), the Cure has always connected powerfully with its fans. One of those is Trey Parker, who had Smith voice his animated self in a 1998 *South Park* episode, playing the superhero that destroys the Barbra Streisand monster. As he flies away, Kyle yells, "*Disintegration* is the best album ever!" In 1993, Smith told *Q* magazine, "Our audience gets caricatured as these tortured teenagers in their bedroom asking, 'Why am I here?' Well, what's so wrong with asking that? Kafka never stopped asking that. That sense of alienation doesn't go away. I'm not embarrassed to say that I still feel completely at a loss sometimes. If that's teenage angst, then I'm delighted I've got it." And, perhaps, he's been miscast along with them. "I hate people around me that wallow in despair. It really upsets me. I love people that do something. I don't even care if I hate what they do. I'm not a despairing person, but I'm not sure that I have a sense of true happiness, really. I get dead happy, but I always think it should be happier."

Early in the band's career, Smith was conscripted into Siouxsie and the Banshees as an emergency replacement for that band's departed guitarist. Exhausted by the rigors of leading the Cure, he later joined the Banshees formally for eighteen months. ("I'd got fed up with certain aspects of the Cure, which is essentially just me, so I'd got fed up with myself, singing and being the front man.") The sojourn broadened his musical outlook and gave the Cure a new lease on life but also saddled it with the "goth" designation, which explained less than it seemed to. As Smith reflected on it later, "We never were goth. A small section of our fans are goths, but that doesn't make us a goth band." The Cure has also been called mope rock, shoegaze, and even prog, but none of those labels do more than reflect one facet of a band whose vast catalogue, all of it powerfully mood-altering, defies generalization. As Smith once said, "I always wanted the Cure to exist outside of every fashion, every trend, so it would leave us free to do what we wanted."

The day after the Cure's election to the Rock and Roll Hall of Fame was revealed, Smith — who several decades ago said, "I'm going to hit 40 in 1999, and I think I'm going to embark on a different life" — announced that the band was at work on its first new album since *4:13 Dream* in 2008. So, in the year that he turns 60, Smith and the Cure have turned the fear of inadequacy he expressed in a song long ago into a proud vow of perseverance: "Whatever I do it's never enough." ◆

Depeche Mode

Rock and Roll Hall of Fame Program Book, 2020

However much we fancy that rock and roll is a thoroughly modern milieu of endless innovation, the vast majority of today's bands still employ the same basic ingredients — guitar, bass, drums, singer — taken up by the founders in the middle of the last century.

So it was of no small cultural import that, in the early days of 1981, an 18-year-old London DJ called Stevo hooked techno-pop into the grid with the release of *Some Bizzare Album*, a watershed compilation that introduced future stars Depeche Mode (or Depeché Mode, as the band initially mispronounced the name nicked from a French fashion magazine), Soft Cell, The The, B Movie and Blancmange, all of whom relied on, or at least used, synthesizers to carry their tuneful creations.

Timed perfectly for the rise of MTV, Depeche Mode was distilled in 1980 from assorted amateur guitar bands (No Romance in China, The French Look, The Plan, Composition of Sound and a duo called Norman and the Worms) in which Martin Gore, Vince Clarke and Andy "Fletch" Fletcher — school chums in Basildon, a town of 100,000, 26 miles east of London — and singer Dave Gahan first tried making music. Inspired by Kraftwerk, Human League and OMD, Clarke convinced his teenaged bandmates to forego the strength of strings for the clarity of keyboards. "To us, it was a punk instrument," says Gore.

While the designation scarcely covers the band's music over the past 40 years, Depeche Mode (on their third nomination) is the first "synthesizer band" elected to the Rock and Roll Hall of Fame. As they said during a 1990 press conference, "Electronics gives us more variety of sound, more possibilities. But we don't just use electronics. We use a lot of acoustic instruments. We have no restrictions." As Gahan puts it, "We've always tried to explore using technology, mashing it up with guitars and acoustic instruments, trying to find an interesting sound that will enhance a particular part of a song in an unusual way."

Depeche Mode speaks a language familiar to lonely, alienated and confused youth who find hope and comfort in the band's words and music: "a danceable solution to teenage revolution," as Roxy Music put it. With the force of Dave Gahan's deep voice and the firm pressure of upfront rhythms and dynamic, sometimes raucous, instrumentation, Depeche Mode balances beauty, sadness and power. Who would not take heart from lines that say you just need to achieve something that rings true?

Technology has another practical purpose. "Live concerts work really well with electronic music," Gore explains. "Things aren't a mishmash of sound. You can really hear everything precisely." Going further, he says, "How you make music is really unimportant. Songs are really important. Whether you record that song with guitar, bass, drums or you do it with electronics is really unimportant."

That same disregard for convention has been expressed in controversial lyrics, the gender-bending stage gear Gore wore in the '80s, unfettered musical digressions, enigmatic visuals and a refreshing lack of self-importance rarely encountered among stadium-level bands. (You don't title an album *Music for the Masses* without expecting some to take that the wrong way.) Their artistic choices balance a deep regard for their audiences and a firm commitment to their own impulses. The occasional critical bashing (including mine) has never fazed them. Gore says, "We make music for ourselves, music that we like, and then hopefully someone out there likes it." Fletch says, "You're influenced by music you don't like more than by music you like. We try and make original music, so there's no point emulating stuff we like. We know what not to do more than what to do."

Through 14 studio albums recorded all over the world and half as many live releases, nearly 60 (!) singles and two theatrical concert-plus-fans films (*101*, last year's *Spirits in the Forest*), what they've done is address greed, love, lust, religion, treachery, life and death in songs that are once both expansive and intimate. And done it with ambitious sonic experimentation and a refusal to stay stylistically still.

"People Are People" (once a gay anthem),"Personal Jesus" (inspired by Elvis Presley and covered by both Johnny Cash and Marilyn Manson), the kinky "Master and Servant," "Enjoy the Silence," the God-twitting "Blasphemous Rumours," "Never Let Me Down Again," "Stripped" and many other well-constructed songs range from transparent to enigmatic but are rarely opaque. Gore, a master at jamming round words into square holes, is reluctant to discuss his lyrics, but he does acknowledge their essential character — and impact on the band's identity. "There's always some dark quality to what we do because of the way I write. Most of my songs are about relationships, but there's always some kind of twisted element, a lot of suffering. And Dave's voice has an I've-been-to-hell-and-back quality to it, so there's always going to be that edge to anything we do." As Fletch notes, "Martin is fascinated by sex and religion. When he puts pen to paper, that's what comes out."

None of the genre names that have been hung on Depeche Mode — techno, dance, new wave, goth, pop, industrial, post-punk, electronica — adequately reflects the band's breadth. They've worked in all of those realms, aided by a diverse collection of producers (starting with Daniel Miller, the techno-pop pioneer who signed the group to his Mute label in 1981) and remixers, but they've never been bound by any. Strong melodies, upfront rhythms and a vast library of sampled sounds — as well as heavily processed guitars — predominate in a catalogue that has touched on blues, ballads, pop, gospel, grunge and rock, leading all the way back to "Route 66." Without ever sacrificing any essential character, Depeche Mode has redefined itself with each album.

"I just sit down and write songs," says Gore. "I write whatever I'm feeling at the time. Then [we] decide what direction we should be taking them in. There's no conscious move in a direction, it's just doing what you feel like doing and then taking the songs from there."

The fact that DM has, for long stretches, been more popular in concert than on record is down to the band's health-threatening amount of roadwork and to Gahan, a commanding singer who brings traditional rock star showmanship to the stage. In 1988, before they'd ever visited the Top 30 of the *Billboard* album chart, the group attracted more than 60,000 fans to the Rose Bowl in Pasadena, a show documented by filmmaker D.A. Pennebaker in *101*.

The band's commercial fortunes have only risen since then: eight Top 10 albums, five platinum albums (*Violator* is past three million), five gold albums, three gold singles and tours that play to a million or two fans each time they go out. And yet only one of their five Grammy nominations is for an album (2009's *Sounds of the Universe*).

Surprisingly, for a band detractors have thought of as chilly men-machines (that's Kraftwerk), Depeche Mode has survived more setbacks and calamities than Spinal Tap. Clarke, who wrote all but two songs on the band's carbonated new wave debut (including "Just Can't Get Enough," recently heard in a Discover TV spot), left afterwards to form Yazoo, then Erasure. The remaining three dusted themselves off and made *A Broken Frame* (1982), a darker, more serious LP written by Gore. Then came five increasingly accomplished albums as a quartet with Alan Wilder, a formally trained musician who became the band's primary sonic architect, bringing new technology, even live drums. In 1995, following an arduous five-month tour which Fletch left midway over mental issues, Wilder resigned. Fletch regained his health, and the trio soldiered on, although it took a while to, well, get the balance right. Gahan recalls, "After Alan departed, we had to have a rethink about how we were going to work in the studio. It took six months during the recording of *Ultra*" — which took more than a year to complete — "before we really settled in and became okay with each other [again]."

Depeche Mode has survived drug addiction, alcoholism, arrests, detoxes and rehabs, a suicide attempt, two heart attacks, seizures, a nervous breakdown, depression, broken ribs (a stage dive gone wrong), a tour that employed a drug dealer and a psychiatrist, cancer and kidney stones. Gahan flatlined from an OD in 1996 and later observed that "being in the same band for [a long time] is very much like a drug — it's hard to put down because it's all I know."

Throw in the usual stressors of marriage, divorce, parenthood, geography, ego and the divergence of maturing personalities that make long-term band membership an exercise in unnatural selection, and it's a small miracle that Depeche Mode has not just endured but flourished, passing through many chambers of purgatory to push, happy, healthy and sober, into its fifth decade. Credit the friendships forged out of common experiences (including broken homes) a half-century ago in Basildon, solid material, the safety valve of solo work and the lack of a clear leader. While Gahan is the onstage focus, a reliance on keyboards undermines traditional rock band hierarchy. As Fletch — one of the music world's few player-managers — explains, "Each member of the band has a function. Martin writes the songs, Alan is the main musician, Dave is the frontman and my major role is managerial. Luckily, I'm not creative one bit."

Like the very few other bands with similar creative arrangements (notably the Who), the fact that one bandmember supplies lyrics for another to sing has caused problems. Some of Gore's words are just too personal to be voiced by anyone else; Gahan's emergence as a confessional songwriter has been a salubrious development. "I don't write from Dave's perspective," Gore acknowledges. "You only know what you're experiencing. But we do have a lot in common." ◆

Features

I long doubted my ability to write long articles, the kind that land on magazine covers, accompanied by fat paychecks, maybe even contracts or a staff job. It didn't help that I was kind of bad at formulating sellable pitches.

Constitutionally incapable of mapping out pieces in my head (or even on paper) before writing them, I have always gone at the challenge willy nilly, thinking up a starting point — a first sentence at the very least — and then seeing where it would go from there. That approach undermines the potential for grandly mounted arguments or merry stylistic escapades; it also encourages structural dullness; rather than sailing around the skating rink, I tend to hug the wall and follow it to a logical conclusion. Add to that the fact that my mind is more fact-oriented more than fanciful, and that snappy endings (the journalistic equivalent of nailing a dismount in gymnastics) have always been hard for me. While a record review can come to an abrupt end if needed, a feature that doesn't have a strong "kicker" really doesn't cut it.

I was always inclined — probably not unconnected to my engineering training — to organize articles chronologically, using history as a framework and introducing other elements into that flow. That made me well-suited to liner notes projects and those Rock and Roll Hall of Fame program notes but was a drag in settings where a more adventurous, less predictable approach was called for. I always envied writers who could shape a long piece like a symphony, with movements, themes, returns and a satisfying final conclusion. I also didn't have a lot of experience as a reporter, and so I often went on research expeditions, integrating what I gathered into a semi-cohesive article.

It took me a long time to gain confidence in my ability to do long stories; I could have used more opportunities to practice Still, a few publications trusted me with pieces of 1,500 – 7,500 words. *Musician* was one of the first.

Bill Flanagan, a prodigiously gifted New Englander who wrote for *Trouser Press*, had become the editor of *Musician*. (He later added erstwhile *TP* editor Scott Isler to his staff.) En route to a top programming gig at VH1, Bill had befriended Elvis Costello, U2 (about whom he wrote a book) and a few other A-list rock stars. A few days after assigning me a piece on the Pogues, he called to say that Elvis — then married to Pogues bassist Cait O'Riordan — had enlisted him to help her quit the tour, the band, the whole fekkin' thing and get on a plane back to London. Bill asked if I could assist in the clandestine effort to get her to JFK Airport. In the end, I didn't do anything more than report the article, which was a fraught and challenging enough experience without any extra-journalistic drama. I suspect that I didn't write every last word of this piece (I have no idea how I would have known what happened in the hours after the World gig and I didn't follow after the band on the road), but I can't say for sure. I also can't take credit for the ungenerous, factually inaccurate and insensitive headline.

THE POGUES

BY IRA ROBBINS

NOT IRISH? NOT FOLKIES? ARE THEY AT LEAST DRUNKS?

The Pogues' brief legend has the well-worn air of an oft-repeated story, the kind old men tell each other in bars. Pogue Mahone (Gaelic for "kiss my ass") was formed in London a few years back by Shane MacGowan, a Dublin-born busker whose minor 70s punk career had been spent mostly in the Nipple Erectors (a.k.a. the Nips). On a rootsy lark, he rounded up English tin whistle player Spider Stacey and sang old Irish folk songs at a trendy rock club. Many months later, still enthused by the idea, MacGowan, Stacey, Jim Fearnley (another ex-Nip who dropped electric guitar for accordion) pulled together a six-piece band with a young female bassist, Cait O'Riordan, drummer Andrew Ranken and Jem Finer on banjo. Armed (mostly) with acoustic instruments, a collection of traditional tunes and MacGowan's original tales of misery, death and degradation, the Anglo-Gaelic sextet launched themselves, with drink in hand, onto the rock circuit. The British music press flocked to sing the Pogues' praises with the same red-nosed sentimentality previously reserved for Tom Waits to whom MacGowan's writing bears fair comparison. After

Shane MacGowan smiles for the dentists.

The Pogues: Not Irish? Not Folkies? Are They at Least Drunks?

Musician, May 1986

The Pogues' brief legend has the well-worn air of an oft-repeated story, the kind old men tell each other in bars. Pogue Mahone (Gaelic for "kiss my ass") was formed in London a few years back by Shane MacGowan, a Dublin-born busker, whose minor '70s punk career had been spent mostly in the Nipple Erectors (aka the Nips). On a rootsy lark, he rounded up English tin whistle player Spider Stacey and sang old Irish folk songs at a trendy rock club. Many months later, still enthused by the idea, MacGowan, Stacey, Jim Fearnley (another ex-Nip, who dropped electric guitar for accordion) pulled together a six-piece band with bassist Cait O'Riordan, drummer Andrew Ranken and Jem Finer on banjo. Armed (mostly) with acoustic instruments, a collection of traditional tunes and MacGowan's original tales of misery, death and degradation, the Anglo-Gaelic sextet launched themselves, with drink in hand, onto the rock circuit.

The British music press flocked to sing the Pogues' praises with the same red-nosed sentimentality previously reserved for Tom Waits, to whom MacGowan's writing bears fair comparison. After an indie 45, the Pogues released a 1984 debut album, *Red Roses for Me*, on Stiff and went on tour with Elvis Costello and the Attractions. Early last year, Dublin punk pioneer Philip Chevron, once the leader of the excellent Radiators From Space, joined as guitarist. Costello produced *Rum, Sodomy & The Lash* (titled after a Winston Churchill quote regarding life in the Royal Navy) and became engaged to O'Riordan. The newest Pogue is Irish folk veteran Terry Woods, who adds autoharp, cittern, concertina and dulcimer.

Every article about the Pogues mentions Ireland and drunkenness. Although both are partially relevant, mindless generalization [*leads to*] ethnic stereotypes. In this country, on the Pogues' first U.S. tour (nine East Coast dates), such questions can be partially forgotten amid the luxury of being a hot new band from abroad.

Friday, February 28

It's nearly 2:00 a.m. Several dozen people are milling around the door to the World, New York's latest late-night concert space, hoping to escape the bitter cold and see the band they've heard so much about. Fueled by the rumor that Elvis Costello will join his fiancée onstage, this chic crowd is very anxious to get inside. Suddenly, a body comes hurtling through the air and crashes against a bicycle chained to a lamp post. "When I say move back, I mean it asshole!" bellows the doorman. Upset but undaunted, the crumpled heap dusts his coat off, checks for serious injury and gets back in line, looking only slightly ashamed of himself.

Upstairs, beautiful people are busy being beautiful. Despite the hours, miles-from-nowhere location and difficulty in gaining admission, the audience — decked in designer clothes and hairdoed to the hilt — is poised for a Very Significant Event. Celebrities like Moon Zappa and Matt Dillon rub shoulders with the local rock biz establishment. A few actually look like paying customers.

After a lengthy wait, the Pogues amble onstage. Only O'Riordan uses an amp; the others play acoustic instruments into microphones. The sound is clean and not inappropriately loud; only MacGowan's hoarse vocals hint at rock'n'roll underpinnings. The rollicking collection of reels, ballads and boozers are rough and ragged, as emotionally raw as any punk shout. Through such items as "Dirty Old Town," "Jesse James" and MacGowan's "A Pair of Brown Eyes" and "The Old Main Drag," Stacey's puckish tin whistling and Ranken's insistent 2/4 thump on a two-piece drum kit provide an overriding Gaelic flavor.

It's an uplifting, rousing show. But out on the dancefloor the audience appears surprised and disappointed. Expecting hip cow-punks of some sort, they instead face a non-rock group with an altogether different take on decadence. Rather than Patti Smith quoting Rimbaud, this is Brendan Behan on a bender, caterwauling with some pals in an alley. Heads in the back half of the club start to look away from the stage; the Pogues sound remarkably like folkies, the kind rock fans in this country have shunned like an open sewer since Bob Dylan last played at Newport. The inappropriateness of this band appearing in this club is as wrenching as a funeral at Disneyland.

By the time the Pogues leave the stage, much of the audience is already gone. But a knot of open-minded fans in the front cheer enthusiastically, drawing them back for a pair of encores. A few of the less self-conscious attempt interpretative square dance and look like seasick yuppies. Costello, of course, has not appeared.

Saturday, March 1
As dawn breaks, the Pogues migrate uptown from the World to Limelight for some serious self-indulgence. By the time they stumble back to the Iroquois hotel it's mid-morning, and O'Riordan decides she has had enough. "I guess I'm just not tough enough to be a Pogue in America." Exhausted and distraught, she returns to London and Costello for a rest, phoning the band with the news from the airport. The Pogues, meanwhile, get on the bus and manage to play the tour's second date, in Washington, D.C., without her. Darryl Hunt, the band's roadie, fills in. An observer reports the show to be impossibly sloppy and the band utterly out of sorts.

Sunday, March 2
The Pogues appear in Baltimore, a town enthusiastic enough about Irish music to support a radio show devoted to it. Costello rumors apparently encouraged by people who know otherwise continue to spread. A writer at the show describes them as hopelessly drunk and barely capable of playing, much less playing together. The audience's reaction is mixed — traditionalists walk out; punks ignore the music and applaud the drunken demeanor. Later, a local interviewer's query about O'Riordan's whereabouts brings a quip from the band about menstruation.

Monday, March 3
My interview with the Pogues takes place in New York City. At the appointed hour, four members are present and accounted for. Stacey, Fearnley and Ranken are alert and friendly. Chevron is sleeping so soundly on the couch that someone actually checks to see if he's still breathing. Given the almost uniformly rowdy press reports, the three are surprisingly intelligent, sober, reasonable and witty. Allowances must be made, of course, for MacGowan's absence. Without the band's most notorious drinker and outrageous spokesman, a higher level of decorum is virtually assured. Stacey and Fearnley have the most to say (often simultaneously); after Chevron awakes, he volunteers a few cogent thoughts in a wan voice punctuated by coughs.

How's the tour going?

"Fine, but not without incident. The gigs have all been good, we've been getting good reactions."

What about Cait?

"That's one of the incidents."

Have you had any negative reaction from traditional musicians?

"Opinion is divided. The people who don't like us from the folk set are people who think we're trying to be a traditional folk group, which we're not. If we were, we'd have to learn how to play our instruments for a start. Some of it is sour grapes. From what we've heard, it's a minority that don't like us. We're not part of the folk scene at all."

To what do you attribute your image?

"Partly us, partly the way we've been marketed, partly down to the way we've been interpreted. Journalists are sometimes pretty dense, and they imagine they're writing for people who are as dense as they are. They come to our gigs and then start writing about brawling Paddies, which is nonsense. I read something in an American magazine about our tours in England being a succession of drunken fistfights. That's complete nonsense."

"*The Face* took me [Spider] and Shane out on a drinking spree to all these pubs along the Kilburn Highway because they'd got the idea that we spent our formative years drinking in these places. One of those I'd been in once in my life, and Shane only a few more times. They seem to have saddled us as being boozers because of the Irish connection. It's a bit insulting."

MacGowan, Finer and Woods arrive to join their bandmates for a hasty photo session. Shane looks terrible — bleary and disoriented, scarcely coherent. He shrugs off an invitation to talk and I leave him lurching towards a chair in the photographer's spotlight, wondering to myself just who the Pogues really are.

Outwardly, they appear to be a hard-drinking Irish folk band; not strictly traditional and certainly not unconnected to the rock world in spirit and heritage. But they do play folk songs using folk instruments and do sound like a folk group, regardless of costumes, lyrics or venue.

So why the vehement denial?

Poguetry in Motion, the wonderful new four-song EP produced by Costello, may answer that question. The Pogues are clearly testing their boundaries, and the two uncharacteristic MacGowan originals on the A-side offer proof. "London Girl" sounds like Los Lobos via New Orleans, with concertina leading a bouncy R&B romp; "A Rainy Night in Soho" is a wistful, bluesy ballad that uses piano, trombone and a 21-piece string section. There's a sense that the Pogues are no longer likely to be limited to the style with which they've become identified. "I would imagine the next album to be quite interesting in comparison to the first two," Spider Stacey declares. "The ideas that are being tossed around at the moment suggest that it will be a lot more diverse."

Postscript

That night, the Pogues attend a party in their honor at Limelight. They perform three tunes before a cinematic crowd that includes Matt Dillon, Molly Ringwald and David Keith. On Tuesday, the tour resumes with a gig in Hoboken, New Jersey (by which time O'Riordan has returned to the fold); three dates in and around Boston; a final faretheewell show at New York's Danceteria and then home to London, the city Shane's tipsy characters describe with such grungy lyricism.

"Shane's not seeing something that's not there," Fearnley says. "There's a line in a Sartre novel where he's walking down the quay, and everyone else is looking at how peaceful the water is, and all he can see is the shit beneath it. That's how Shane is." ◆

This is something Fearnley told me that didn't make its way into the piece:

"I've lived in London most of my life, and the places Shane writes about are familiar to me. Even if he's writing songs in the first person, they're not necessarily about him. He picks a lot of things up — he's the sort of person who talks to drunks and tramps in pubs and on the street. He's encyclopedic. It's not that he's created a persona. Tom Waits is a storyteller like Shane. I think there's a lot of similarity between the two. It's dangerous to narrow a songwriter down. Getting up on stage and singing is an act in the first place. The way Shane and all of us are onstage is more or less the way we are, anyway, it's just the kind of guys we are. Shane's got loads of different characters."

This was the first of three cover stories I did for my good buddy Jackson Griffith at *Tower Pulse!* The late record chain's monthly magazine, given away free in its stores, was a much better magazine than that might imply.

After some consideration, I've deleted two needlessly negative sentences from this piece, which is already a bit clunky. They served no purpose and made little sense. I don't know what led me to offer a handful of petty "demerits" in the third paragraph of a positive profile.

R.E.M.: Nice Guys Still Finish First

Pulse!, October 1992

A decade since obscurity and a cool guitar sound was all a young group paid to purchase surefire credibility at the hip rock counter, R.E.M. still seems too good to be true. Ten years is usually enough time for even the most superlative band to sink into the miserable cultural irrelevance of redundant million-sellers...or worse. Yet despite its longevity and colossal commercial success, the little ol' pop combo from Athens remains thoughtful, conscientious and genuinely responsible, musically and socially, making self-challenging records of real value.

Last year's quadruple-platinum *Out of Time* may have been only half a great album, but it was hardly the demographically blueprinted sellout some cynics claimed. The new one, an acoustic-geared / feedback-sharpened beauty titled *Automatic for the People*, is the band's most adult, accessible, reflective and gently proffered record yet, a rich, handsome disc that both ratifies and defies expectations. Is R.E.M. the Left Banke of the '90s? After all this time and momentum, the vision thing remains as much a function of whim as sales prospects. "We're all talking about the next album being kind of noisy," says guitarist Peter Buck.

It's been ages since anyone over the age of 12 expected perfection from a rock'n'roll band, but the members of R.E.M. have managed to become Genuine Rock Gods without making a public nuisance of themselves. (Except, perhaps, for Buck's bratty decision to wear pajamas at the *Grammy Awards* in February.)

"I think U2 tend to go for it more than we do," says Buck. "I had the feeling when I bought the first U2 record that they understood where they wanted to go a lot better than we did. They wanted to be the biggest band in the world. For us, fame and being on the world platform is a not really a necessary by-product of what we want to do — making records and playing when we want to play."

"We wanted to be successful," says bassist/keyboardist Mike Mills. "But, for me, we were successful the day in 1981 that I didn't have to have a day job." (He ran an inserting machine at the Athens newspaper.)

Success is a relative thing, and the members of R.E.M. now stand as low-key kings of an alternative rock colony they pioneered but no longer have much stake in. Nirvana and the rolling thunder of *Lollapalooza* don't appear to have much more impact than the fact that Mills calls *Nevermind* his favorite album of 1991 ("...except maybe for ours") and that Buck is interested in attending *Postpunkstock*. Too smart to crack up, apparently uncorruptable by the usual means, and determined to please themselves artistically, the band members continue to guide a grand-scale career with — God forgive me such gullibility — what appears to be sincere creative ambitions and human-being concerns other than just money, fame and power.

Are these guys nuts?

"Every time you make a record," says Buck, "You think, why am I doing this? When we get to the point where we don't have anything to say to each other musically, you couldn't pay me to do it. If we start making bad records, I'll quit. But I'm still learning things."

"There are songs on this record that I still don't believe we put out," allows Mills. "As long as we can keep surprising ourselves — I think that's the point — then we're doing all right. It's still fun for me to see what the three other guys do with music that I may initiate. Sometimes it's really annoying, but it's still cool."

Call Kurt Loder! R.E.M. has decided not to tour. For the second album in a row. The exhausting year-long *Green* excursion ended in November 1989; the current plan is to go out at the beginning of 1994, after the next album is released. "Touring can be great fun," says Mills, "but it's also very demanding. You have to be 100 percent into it to do it — to do it well." Doesn't the band worry that fans will take its staying home as a sign of arrogance? "I am concerned about that. But we don't want to go out and give somebody a half-assed show just because they want to see the band."

The last time R.E.M. performed was on January 31, 1992, at a benefit for a mental health organization in Athens. As Buck is quick to point out, "We played a lot last year, but we played for free: radio broadcasts, television shows [including *MTV Unplugged*], benefit things. For me, that's ideal: I can play for free every night of the week."

R.E.M.'s ambivalence about its business rings with disconcerting wholesomeness. *Out of Time*'s media-slaying "Radio Song" might not have gotten the airplay it theoretically deserved, but the group can accept its failure to become a hit single as a fair-market price for expressing those sentiments, and for giving a guest shout to Bronx rapper KRS-One. Likewise, if not touring costs the group a few million record sales worldwide, they evidently don't consider it a usurious penalty for peace of mind, or the time to do other things. Staying well outside the nouveau riche suicide class many big bands inhabit, R.E.M. evinces the sensible moderation of the working wealthy: its members know they've earned what they enjoy. "We do what we do," says Buck with the aplomb of someone who really believes that *que sera sera* stuff. "Eventually there'll be a time when we're not needed in the scheme of things. I'd like to think we'll figure it out before everyone else in the world does."

Nowadays, R.E.M. can take a relaxed front-porch attitude. A million miles from the gimme-it-now urgency of punk rock, its members can talk calmly about touring the year after next, of scheduling rehearsals for another album to begin on June 1, 1993, with a realistic sense of imminence and priority. These aren't pipe dreams relegated to some indefinite future, but realities on the horizon — just a long way off.

What's on the table right now is *Automatic for the People*, R.E.M.'s eighth album. Not counting compilations. Or reissues, a topic about which the group is currently steamed. I.R.S., R.E.M.'s former label, is rereleasing the band's back catalog (*Murmur, Reckoning, Fables of the Reconstruction, Lifes Rich Pageant, Dead Letter Office* and *Document*) in Europe. "They're tacking on three or four extra tracks to each record," Mills explains. "Most of the tracks were never released; they're not supposed to be released. The only reason they're doing it is to gouge people who collect records. One of the tracks is a version of 'Wind Out' that [R.E.M. managers] Jefferson [Holt] and Bertis [Downs] sing on." According to Buck, "I.R.S. doesn't have the master tapes. They're taking the shit off of bootlegs. There's some live stuff they took off a TV show." Sig Sigworth, the senior director of production for I.R.S. who assembled the European repackages, denies the allegation. "We have the master tapes in the vault that were delivered to us by the band."

Automatic for the People was recorded between April and July in Bearsville, N.Y., Miami and Atlanta, and mixed at Heart's Bad Animals studio in Seattle. "I would have loved to have been in Seattle two years ago," rues Buck. "You can tell it's like Athens was. Before you know you've got a scene it's a pretty great scene."

Following *Out of Time*'s arrival in March 1991, R.E.M. set about proving the old adage about work expanding to fill all available time. Even without touring, the foursome didn't exactly sit around Athens eating bonbons. They recorded "Fretless" for the soundtrack of Wim Wenders' *Until the End of the World*. Stipe attended the *Reebok Human Rights Awards* ceremony in Boston with Natalie Merchant of 10,000 Maniacs and met Jimmy Carter. (Recently, Stipe and Merchant did a duet vocal on an *Automatic* outtake that will be donated to the National Abortion Rights League for a benefit album.) Buck played guitar on Robyn Hitchcock's *Perspex Island*. Buck, Mills, drummer Bill Berry and former R.E.M. adjunct Peter Holsapple spent a week working on *Athens Andover*, a disappointingly bad album (save for "Nowhere Road," the one song they wrote) by the Troggs.

Buck iterates other ways R.E.M. passed the months. "We finished the promotional tour for *Out of Time* in May and started rehearsing for this record the first week of June. We did the fourth video, went to the *Grammys*, some of the guys went to the MTV thing, we went to England for the *BPI Awards*, went to Paraguay to look at some land for the Nature Conservancy. Then we started doing this record. We don't work in December. We demoed about 30 instrumental things."

Describing the songwriting process, Mills says, "Usually, one person will have done something at home on guitar. It could be just a little idea or most of a song. In the process of everyone learning the song they change it, write their own parts and it becomes a group thing. Sometimes it's literally noise from chaos. We all play without listening to the other and then all of a sudden some of it starts to go together. One of the first to come out of the chaos method was 'Orange Crush.' That was literally everybody just making noise in the studio and then it just fell into place.

"Our writing used to be all guitar-oriented; it was usually me and Peter, or me and Peter and Bill, sitting down with guitars and writing songs. You can only take that so far." Buck agrees. "On the last three or four records, there's been a few songs that we go, 'That's an R.E.M. song.' We never end up using them because we've done that. I could do 'Driver 8' three times a day. And I know a lot of other people can, too."

The lyrics — those elusive word paintings that have made Michael Stipe the messiah of university sensitivos everywhere — frequently go on last. But not always. "'Nightswimming' is something he wrote before *Out of Time*," explains Buck. "We were supposed to put music to it. We wrote three or four different things for it [that didn't work], so it didn't make the record."

While sharing some thoughts about the songs on the new album, Buck and Mills — forced, with no evident unease, into the odd position of having to speak for their bandmate, who opted to attend to video business rather than do interviews — gamely try to explain Stipe's lyrics (as much as their meaning can be deduced, a task for which membership in R.E.M. apparently isn't much help).

"Drive" is an atmospheric minor-key teen spirit song that sets the album's instrumental tone with acoustic guitar and moody strings (arranged by ex-Zepster John Paul Jones and played by some of the same Atlanta Symphony members who were on the last album) but refers, in the lyrics and the vocal delay, to David Essex's 1973 glam-rock classic "Rock On." The song, which will be the album's first single, "doesn't sound a whole lot like us, doesn't sound like anything on the radio," says Buck. "It's either going to totally stiff, or it's going to really stand out."

Mournful howls of guitar feedback (feedBuck?) unsettle "Try Not to Breathe," an affecting reflection on death and life. "When I was doing the demo," the guitarist recalls, "I had this little mic right in front of me and I was breathing really loud, and it was making too much noise. I said, 'I'll try not to breathe,' and Michael took that as the title."

If something about the title and Stipe's first four notes of "The Sidewinder Sleeps Tonite" sounds familiar, don't bother pointing it out to R.E.M. The group paid for the rights to tickle those memory banks, approaching the authors of "The Lion Sleeps Tonight," the Tokens' 1961 hit (itself a pop rewrite of the African folk song "Wimoweh"), to cut a deal. Why didn't R.E.M. just follow standard music-industry practice and pilfer whatever isn't legally nailed down? "If we did that," Mills explains, "some lawyer would call up [the songwriters] in a year and tell them they could sue us. We'd probably win, but who needs it? It's much better to just cut it off at the pass.

"Half of the song is about somebody trying to get in touch with someone who can sleep on his floor. The other half — you're on your own."

"Sometimes with Michael," notes Buck, "it helps to realize that there's an overall scheme to the song, but some verses don't refer to the body of the song." Hence the references to blackeyed peas, Nescafé on ice and The Cat in the Hat. But what's Stipe giggling about? "I kept trying to get Michael to say "Seuss, not Zeuss, and he couldn't do it," recalls Mills. "He tried, but he said 'Zeuss' anyway, and that made him laugh." And what is that catchy slurred refrain? "Call me when you try to wake her up." Oh.

The subject of "Everybody Hurts" is "exactly what it sounds like," says Mills. (What it sounds like is Simon and Garfunkel on a soul tip.) "I bought this awful $20 Univox drum machine," says Buck. "But it made sense because the song had a metronomish feel. Mike and I cut it live with this dumb drum machine which is just as wooden as you can get. We wanted to get this flow around that: human and non-human at the same time."

"New Orleans Instrumental No. 1" was done live, with Bill Berry on electric piano, Mills on stand-up bass and Pete on guitar. "It fit the mood of the record. It's not meant to signify anything. It's a mood piece," says Buck, who currently lives in the Big Easy. "It's the kind of thing we usually don't put on the record. This time we did. There's a 'No. 2' that will be a B-side; it sounds like an ad for some deranged piña colada mix."

"Sweetness Follows" addresses family estrangement with such evocative solemnity that, according to Buck, "Michael called his parents and said it wasn't about them when he wrote it." To Mills, "It sounds like he's getting back in touch with a sibling because their parents have died."

In an extremely pretty album's most incandescent thought, Stipe sings, "It's these little things that can pull you under/ Live your life filled with joy and wonder" (and then "thunder") in a voice heavy with sadness. "Michael likes to conflict what the lyrics are saying with the music or the way he's singing it sometimes," Buck explains.

"While we were doing the record, Michael met some guy who took photos of Montgomery Clift during *The Misfits*. I'm not sure what this guy told him," Buck admits, but it resulted in "Monty Got a Raw Deal." Regarding the other rock number on the same subject, he says, "The Clash song is real specific and ours isn't. It's more of a meditation on the movies and reality."

Offered a comparison of "Ignoreland" to the sound of early-'80s Who, Buck doesn't object, but doesn't agree, either. "More Neil Young-y; it's got that tuning he always uses." The track's harmonicat is co-producer Scott Litt, who also played clavinet on it. Mills considers it "a political song against the Reagan era, but it's basically a guitar fest." Ironically (or perversely), the album's most pointed topical message has its least discernible lyrics. "Michael really wanted to fuck his voice up. He's singing through an amp."

The actual title for the woozy "Star Me Kitten" is "Fuck Me Kitten" — but don't tell that to Walmart shoppers. The song was born, as Buck tells it, at practice one day, when "Mike started playing these oddball chords. I said, 'That sounds like it needs tremolo guitar, some lovely little *Twin Peaks* lead.' Me and Bill and Mike did it in like 10 minutes, put it on cassette and walked out. We said, 'Michael is never going to put words to that.' And that was the first one he got a melody and words to."

Besides Hammond organ, Mills is responsible for the song's ethereal background vocals. "I sang seven or eight different notes and put them on faders on the board. You play the board like an instrument, fading notes in and out."

R.E.M. may have come in second with Montgomery Clift, but "Man on the Moon" must be the first song about Andy Kaufman. As Buck plays '50s slide guitar over a warm samba beat, Stipe hangs such characters as Fred Blassie, Charles Darwin and Elvis Presley (a Kaufman specialty) onto a seductive melody. Buck claims there's no secret compartment here. "When Michael sings about Andy Kaufman and Elvis, he's singing about Andy Kaufman and Elvis. It's not about wheat prices in Russia."

Mills' increased role becomes most obvious with "Nightswimming," one of the finest pop songs in R.E.M.'s archive. His stately piano shapes the song, encouraging Stipe's heartfelt vocal to elevate a slice of small-town nostalgia into a song of aching beauty, an eroticized Norman Rockwell tableau with universal meaning. "We used to sneak on this guy's property in Athens and go swimming in this water hole," recalls Buck. "It'd be great: 30 of us all running around naked. It was before AIDS, and whatever happened happened."

Acknowledging the resemblance of "Find the River" to the music of 10,000 Maniacs, Mills agrees that Stipe's "approach for the melody is very similar" to that group's work. "I wanted the record to end with 'Man on the

Moon'," notes Buck, but he was overruled. "Now it ends with two slow songs, ending songs. 'Find the River' is kind of — dare I say it? — elegiac. It's a natural end to the record."

R.E.M. is in the driver's seat, a place all idealistic bands dream about in their youth. So, has it unraveled any of rock'n'roll's secrets? "No matter how archetypal we look, we're still making it up as we go along," says Buck. "It looks from the outside like there's some master plan, but we just do what makes sense on a given day. People look back over what can be described as a career and always assume that we knew what we were doing. All we knew was that we didn't want anyone else telling us what we should do." ◆

Mike Mills and Peter Buck, 17 August 1992

Is this an REM private record?
Peter: There's no one on the record aside from us except for the string players and the oboe player, although Scott [Litt], the producer, played harmonica and clavinet on "Ignoreland."

Isn't there harmonica on other tracks?
Mike: No. There's a real reedy-sounding accordion that actually sounds like a melodica on "Monty Got a Raw Deal."

Peter: It's a really cheesy accordion. I think it's made of plywood.

Mike: It's funny, it's a tiny little accordion. I've used the big ones and the good ones and the nice ones, and none of them sound as good — on our records, anyway, as the cheap one.

Peter: With a little reverb it's got that real Hang 'Em High / For a Few Dollars More feel.

That's not harmonica on "Find the River"?

Mike: No, the same little twinky accordion. I played all the accordion; all the keyboards. I usually do. Sometimes Bill or Michael will do little plinking noises.

Peter: Bill did piano on "Near Wild Heaven" last year, which was really cool. We were all out doing nothing and he just figured he'd play piano that day. It's kind of neat that all of us can do that, the drummer too can play a lot of stuff. Over the years, Bill's played drums, bass, guitar, keyboards and, of course, singing. Bill was the first guy that did a session outside the band. We were doing *Murmur*, and they were doing a Dodge commercial. It was that [demonstrates whistling thing] and someone came and in and said, 'Does anyone know how to do that?' And Bill did it, 'cause he's really good at it, and they gave him like twenty dollars. He called up his mom to tell her that it was him listening. So, before our record was out he was on this international...

What kind of keyboards do you play?

Mike: It's mostly [Hammond] B3, a couple of different pianos. I don't think we used any synths; maybe a little blended in somewhere.

Who are the songwriters?

Peter: All four of us.

Mike: The same as ever.

What's your songwriting technique?

Mike: The usual method is one person will have done something at home on guitar. It could be just a little idea or most of a song. You bring it in to practice and in the process of everyone else learning the song they write it, they change it, write their own parts and it becomes a group thing. Sometimes it's just literally noise from chaos. We just all play without listening to the other and then all of a sudden you find that some of it starts to go together.

Peter: We're still song-oriented. A lot of people, when they jam (I hate to use that word) they tend to do solos around E and A or whatever. With us, we tend to improvise song structures. We'll come up with a three-chord riff and then look at each other and go, ok here's where the chorus will go. It's amazing, 'cause I'll play a B minor and Mike'll play a C and go 'That's interesting...' It's really kind of chaotic until you force some order on it. Sometimes you never do. "Sweetness Follows" has an order, but it's kind of really unforced. When we were putting it down, we couldn't really tell what the order was, we just kind of did it.

The band's songwriting changed so strongly with Green. Was that a conscious effort? For a long time REM's songs were similarly structured, they came out of one place...
Mike: We realized that. Our writing used to be all guitar-oriented; it was usually me and Peter, or me and Peter and Bill, sitting down with guitars and writing songs. You can only take that so far. Now we have different methods. One of the first to come out of the chaos method was "Orange Crush." That was literally everybody just making noise in the studio and then it just fell into place.

Peter: Also, when we started out, we didn't sound like a whole lot of our peer groups, or whatever was on the radio. I think we were trying to carve a place for ourselves. For me, it was after Lifes Rich Pageant where we started...Like I had never played loud, distorted guitar because every other guitar player in the world had a Marshall and a Les Paul. So, consciously, I was trying to carve out my own little place as a guitar player, and as a band we were doing that [as well]. With Document, it felt like we were stretching the boundaries a little bit. And Green, now we felt we could do anything — without reason. We're never going to be a real get-down funk band...

Very little of the new record sounds like what R.E.M. is known for.
Peter: If you do it long enough, you feel like you can approach it as a tourist. We've touched a broad enough base of stuff that we feel like we don't really have to reflect some group vision or whatever.

Mike: It's no fun to be redundant. It is kind of limiting if you write songs the same way over and over again. You can really come up with the same after awhile.

Peter: Virtually every record we've made — the last three or four, anyway — there's two or three songs that we go, "That's an REM song." It's got the typical whatever... We always demo them and they're sitting around on tape so we never end up using them, because we've done that. I could do "Driver 8" three times a day. And I know a lot of other people can, too. There was a period about '86 when I'd turn on college radio, hear a record [and wonder] if it was me playing on it.

How does a band make a record that doesn't come from your basic well of creativity?
Mike: Well, it kind of is, though. It all comes from the same place; you just approach it differently. Rather than sitting down strumming an acoustic guitar, you'll pick it differently. Or you'll write the songs on keyboards. "Star Me Kitten" was this really bizarre set of chords on organ that turned into that song.

Peter: With my lovely little Twin Peaks lead guitar. My wife and Godfrey Cheshire were going to go see the Madonna movie, Truth or Dare. So, I went to practice and said I'd meet them after. I walked in, and Mike started playing these oddball chords. I said that sounds like it needs to have tremolo guitar. Me and Bill and Mike did it in like ten minutes, put it on cassette and walked out. We said, "That'll be a B-side; Michael is never going to put words to that." That was the first one he finished, the first one he got a melody and words to. Do we have to call it "Star Me Kitten"? It's called "Fuck Me Kitten."

The guitar on that song sounds like Santo and Johnny's "Sleepwalk." Did you ever cover it?
Peter: Great, I love that song. I've always wondered if they made an album.

Mike: I've played it on piano.

Peter: I think we played it in hotel rooms.

10 year time limit on rock band quality and originality and relevance...the Stones, Who, Beatles

Peter: It's something you've got to think about. Every time you make a record, every time you write a song you think why am I doing this? Am I doing it to pay the mortgage? This is what we do. To a certain degree, when I was younger, I'd look at these people and go why they don't just quit? What am I gonna do — stay home? Put it this way: If we start making bad records, I'll quit making records. As long as we're doing good work...

Mike: And get along...

Peter: Most of those bands were famous from the very first day. The Stones were like 19 and had done four months of gigs and were playing to 5,000 screaming 14-year-olds. We played in complete obscurity for six years. We had our first four records out and nobody, except for rock journalists and college kids — that's it. We didn't sell any records. For me, we're a new band to a certain degree. I think that's kept us fresh.

Mike: Everything has changed over the last five or six years, within and without the band. That keeps it different.

Peter: I can't imagine what it would have been like if *Murmur* had sold a million copies. We would have been dead; we would have made four records. It would have been the Go-Go's thing.

But what's the motivation? Is this an exploration?
Mike: There are songs on this record that I still don't believe we put out. As long as we can keep surprising ourselves — I think that's the point — as long as we surprise ourselves, then I think we're doing alright. And it is fun. When you write songs and demo them you think, this is a piece of fluff and the next thing you know it's a single off a record. That sort of thing is really intriguing. It's still fun for me to see what the three other guys do with music that I may initiate. It's really cool to see what it turns into. Sometimes it's really annoying, but it's still really cool.

Peter: We all bring in things separately and it's really weird how you view...this is going to be like this song, this'll mean this...and it turns totally around.

When we get to the point where we don't have anything to say to each other musically, then you couldn't pay me to do it. A lot of bands do it for the final payout, let's get our $10 million and go home. I'm not saying I'd be so above it not to do that, but we've avoided it so far. But I'm still learning things. I don't know what the next record's going to like except that we're all talking about it being kind of noisy. I have this picture in my head that we'll get to a point where we'll all know it immediately, probably in the middle of doing a record, we'll just go, you know we don't have it this time. Hopefully, we'll realize that before the record gets finished. It's over. There's no reason you can't keep playing. I see myself playing on a local level in Athens when I'm 50. I always wanted to have a five-piece — saxophone, organ, bass, guitar and drums — and do instrumentals.

Template for starting a band...You're an archetype...
Peter: No matter how archetypal we look, we're still making it up as we go along. In the South, in Georgia, there wasn't — there still isn't — a showbiz thing, there isn't a rock'n'roll road to success, so we just made it up. We toured, made a little independent record by ourselves, signed to a small label. I guess it looks from the outside like there's some overall master plan, but we just do what makes sense on a given day.

I'm pretty sure other [superstar rock'n'roll bands] make it up as they go along, too. If you look back over what can be described as a career (although I don't think of it like that), it looks like we knew what we were doing. People always [assume] we had firm control, we knew exactly what we were doing. All we knew was that we didn't want anyone else telling us what we should do. We never made sense as an organization that was trying to sustain itself.

How corporate is REM?
Mike: We have seven people that are fairly permanent...

Peter: ...but two of them — Jefferson [Holt] and Bertis [Downs] — are part of the band. Jefferson is actually a member of the band. [PiL comparison] In our contract we're a five-person corporation who provide music and videos and live shows. When we signed with Warner Bros. they wanted it in the contract that the four of us would actually appear on the records and that is not in the contract. If it comes down to it, we don't have to make the records. Jefferson could be the lead singer.

Mike: They're re-releasing the early catalogue, the IRS catalogue, and to each of those records they're tacking on three or four extra tracks. And they're bootlegs, and it should be illegal. Most of them were never released, they're not supposed to be released, and the only reason they're doing it is to gouge the people who collect records, who are now going to have to go out and repurchase the first five records. But one of the tracks is a version of "Wind Out" that Jefferson and Bertis sing on. [It was used on the *Bachelor Party* soundtrack.]

How did that get recorded?
Peter: We went out for lunch and they wanted to play a joke on us. IRS doesn't have the tapes. They're taking the shit off of bootlegs. There's some live stuff they took off a TV show. That's off a bootleg, because I know where the master tape is. We have it, we've never taped it. They're either taking it off a cassette or a bootleg CD. They're bootlegging our stuff — it's really infuriating.

Mike: [besides *Eponymous* and *Dead Letter Office*] IRS put out another compilation — which promptly sank like a stone — to coincide with *Out of Time*. They even copied the packaging. Now they're re-releasing the early catalogue.

Peter: I assume that every time we put out a record until the day I fucking die they'll find some way...

Mike: IRS will re-release another record. It's not so much IRS as it's EMI overseas.

Peter: We could let it go, as we're doing. I don't want to sue anybody.

Mike: They're within their rights. It's unethical, but I don't there's any point to making a big deal about it.

REM vs. U2
Mike: I think they're really good. I like the way they've gone about things as a rule.

Peter: I think they tend to go for it more than we do. I think they saw themselves as players on the world stage. We were reluctant to come to the understanding that, no matter how we look at this, we're famous, we're going to sell a lot of records and there are expectations. We can either live with it or not live with it, but we can't ignore it. I had the feeling when I bought the first U2 record that they understood the mechanics of it and where they wanted to go with it, a lot better than we did. They wanted it more. I'm not saying anything bad about that. They wanted to be the biggest band in the world. They wanted to be like the Clash, the last rock'n'roll band. For us, fame and being on the world platform is a not-really-necessary byproduct of doing what we want to do, which is making records and playing when we want to play.

Green quote
Peter: Well, I haven't been to any awards shows since the *Grammys* — my mom made me do that. We haven't done endorsements. We did a stadium tour, that was okay but I'm probably not going to do that again. That's why our faces aren't on the cover of the records; I'm hardly ever in the videos. I live a pretty anonymous life. Everyone in Athens knows me, but Christ, I've lived there 15 years, I'd hope so. I've never felt like I have to be in this position. I'm confident enough that I don't really care if people know what we do, or even what I contribute to the band.

Mike: We wanted to be successful, but for me we were successful the day that I didn't have to have a day job. '81. I was an inserter at the Athens newspaper, working the inserter machine and stacking papers. It was horrible, demeaning, menial, dull, dreary.

Peter: I lasted the longest, right up through the end of '82. I was a record store clerk: $3 an hour and a 50% discount.

Privilege vs. onerous responsibilities of rock success
Peter: We don't do much of that, and I don't use a whole lot of the privilege, either. I've got money, but I drive a four-year-old and I certainly don't dress all that well. You've got to remember that what we do that's important we

do pretty much behind locked doors and everything else is kind of silly. I feel pretty weird sitting here talking about myself all day. I'd much rather talk about records, or music industry gossip or how the Braves are doing. I'm one of those people who have no inner knowledge of myself: I don't think about why I do what I do, I don't think about why we make the records. It's just intuitive. At the end, when we finish a record, I realize that I've got to explain it. It's not something you can explain, it's something you kind of live. That sounds awful...a musician saying he doesn't know why he does it. You're afraid that if you explain it too much you'll figure out how you do it.

Touring...
Mike: We won't tour on this record. Touring can be great fun, but it's also very demanding and you have to be 100% into it to do it — to do it well. We don't want to go out if we're not going to do it as well as it can be done.

Peter: Nobody wanted to do it on the last record. This record, if everyone had voted and said, Peter we want to go out, I would have gone out. I'm not excited about it right now.

Mike: It's an inner feeling you get that tells you either it's time to go touring or it's not. For the first eight or nine years we toured because that's what we did for a living, and it was great fun. It's different now because you can't do little club shows that are great fun, you have to do something on a grander scale. You have to have an inner voice that tells you it's time to do that.

Are you concerned that fans will perceive this as arrogance?
Mike: I am concerned about that. I can see that people would think that. But we don't want to go out and give somebody a half-assed show just because they want to see the band. They'd be howling for their money back.

Peter: Our fans pay a lot more attention than a lot of bands'. But I don't think we demand the response Morrissey gets when he waves and they go nuts.

Mike: We got a little grief off the Green tour, and we worked our butts off on that. But it was a whole year of playing, and it just wore us out. That tour ended in November of '89.

When was the last time R.E.M. performed?
Peter: About three months ago. We did a benefit for this mental health organization in Athens. We did a couple of our songs, a Troggs song, a Robyn Hitchcock song and an Iggy song. We played a lot last year, but we played for free. For me, that's ideal: I can play for free every night of the week. We did radio broadcasts, television shows, a couple benefit things. I like that — you get up, do 40 minutes and leave.

Everybody talks about how long we haven't been on the road, but assuming we go on the road in '93, or the beginning of '94, which we're going to do — it'll be just as long between Green and that tour as it was between the last U2 tour and this tour. Nobody mentioned that about them.

Mike: There are a lot of internal things that go on as far as touring that people aren't aware of. There's nothing we can really do about that. For us to do a tour you have to start so far in advance — depending on what kind of places we want to play. We were pretty certain before the record we weren't going to tour, so we didn't get anything started. If we changed our minds, I'm sure they would have been more than happy to set the wheels in motion.

Peter: We could go out right now if we wanted to, but the days of hopping in a van are way over.

If the record gets really terrible reviews...
Mike: We'll make another. You can't polish a turd: if the record sucks, touring isn't going to make it any better.

Peter: I can't tell how this record rates. I think the songwriting is really good. My only concern when we were doing it was whether it was going to hold together as a group of songs. I'm happy with it, and it should get reviewed well, but if not, big deal, we're going to make another record in a year. People's careers go up and down, and ours so far has all gone up. Eventually, it's going to go down, and I've been expecting that for five years now.

Mike: We thought the backlash was going to come at *Reckoning*. We thought we were going to get the total grief thing for our second album. It never happened.

Peter: We were sure everyone was going to hate it. We've gone through phases where we were less popular than others. There was a period about three years where in Spin and all those magazines thought we were the anti-Christ. Then, all of a sudden, we're popular again.

When did you make this record?
Peter: April through July 1992. Three months and a week and a half. We did demos in Athens and New Orleans, and then Woodstock, Miami and Seattle. Then we did strings in Atlanta.

Why Seattle?
Peter: It seemed like a nice town and we just wanted to go there.

Mike: We were looking for certain technical things we needed that they had in the studio, and it's a town that we've always liked. Scott Litt co-produced with the band. We've always co-produced our records, but sometimes we demand credit. Might as well — it makes us look like we do something.

What's the Nirvana vibe like in Seattle?
Mike: Not a big deal. Chris [Novoselic] came by a couple of times, he's a nice guy. Eddie Vedder, the guys from Soundgarden came over. We met Tad — he was great. We had a real good time.

Peter: I would have loved to have been there two years ago. You can tell it's like Athens was. Before you know you've got a scene it's a pretty great scene. The minute that people start mentioning "scene," you get kids moving from other towns to be part of the scene, then everyone asking each other what the scene is like — where's the scene tonight?

Mike: It's the kiss of death.

Nirvana's success?
Mike: That's my favorite record of last year, except maybe for ours. I play it loud and often.

Peter: Bands like them and maybe the Black Crowes prove that there's kids who like hard rock that don't like the bands dressed up like their mothers. The Las Vegas aspect of heavy metal. Punk's not that threatening anymore.

Rock'n'roll's threat...
Peter: Kids are probably as excited by *Lollapalooza* as we were by the Stones in '72, or seeing the Dolls. What was considered really radical and wild when we were younger is now played for sedate older folks. Rolling Stones records get played to 50-year-olds on yachts in the Virgin Islands. I used to get beat up in Georgia for having long hair. Nowadays you can walk into any little diner in Georgia with a cock ring and a pink Mohawk and they go [drawls femininely] "How ya doin'? Want iced tea? Sweet or unsweetened?"

America's current disfavor towards incumbents?
Peter: If there's a process of sweeping things clean and we go, I guess that's probably justice in some way, although I think we made a good record. I don't think about stuff like that. We do what we do, and eventually there'll be a time when we're not needed in the scheme of things. You'd like to think that we'll figure it out before everyone else does.

Is there a theme to this record?
Peter: Quite the opposite, it's the first that doesn't hold together thematically to a certain for me.

Mike: Lyrically it's kind of introspective. It's surprisingly non-thematic.

Peter: Michael says what's there is there. You can look on the other records literally or metaphorically: this is more of a literal record. When he sings about Andy Kaufman and Elvis, he's singing about Andy Kaufman and Elvis. It's not about wheat prices in Russia or the drought. You don't have to look on four levels. Michael usually writes on a couple levels.

Mike: "Everybody Hurts" is about as surface as it gets. That is exactly what it is.

Songwriting
Peter: Michael usually writes the lyrics while we'll writing. We'll demo things without him hearing them and we'll give him cassettes. He travels a lot doing extracurricular things; he'll take our cassettes and listen on the plane.

"Nightswimming" is something he wrote before Out of Time. We saw the words written down, in order, exactly the way they were supposed to go and we were supposed to put music to it. We must have written three or four different things for it [that didn't work]. So, it didn't make the record until the last day of recording Mike came up with the keyboard thing and we demoed it.

What have you been doing for the last 18 months?
Mike: Making this record.

Peter: Mike and I were on the road four months doing promotion shit like this, the band did a month and a half in Europe doing interviews, playing TV shows. We did four videos. We finished the promotional tour in May last year and started rehearsing for this record the first week of June ['91]. While we were rehearsing we did the fourth video, went to the Grammys, some of the guys went to the MTV thing, went to England for the BPI Awards, went to Paraguay to look at some land; we're going to donate some money for something.

Mike: We're working with the Nature Conservancy, looking at some land

Peter: Then we started doing this record. We don't work in December. We demoed about 30 instrumental things. We work for two weeks, spend two days in the studio and put down five things and then take a week off. We decided that next time we're going to knock 'em all out and then go in and demo them. When the record came around, it was like doing cover versions.

Will you recycle any of the leftovers for the next record?
Mike: We usually don't. It's usually better to start fresh.

Peter: There might be one or two things we might think about reworking. There's one in particular — that noisy one in E — that I liked everything except the way we played the verse. We might mess around with that.

The Troggs record?
Peter: They just came over and we did it in five days.

Mike: Everybody knew that we did Troggs covers, we did "Love Is All Around" on MTV Unplugged. Larry Page saw a chance to do them some good; it's great to meet people who've been making music that you've been listening to.

Peter: A lot of the stuff was already demoed, we just overdubbed on it. We rearranged and re-recorded "That's the Way It Should Be," we wrote that song and put it down, Peter put a guide vocal down that's really good. There's a few things we didn't play on, there's a couple of songs I wasn't interested in. I enjoyed most of the stuff: it was easy, fun and simple. It's nice to work outside the group context.

Sequencing etc.
Peter: We had two extra songs in *Out of Time* at one point, but one of them was slower, so it misbalanced the record that way, and the other was a little instrumental thing that wasn't necessary and we thought distracted from things.

Mike: There's nothing wrong with being concise.

Peter: We try three or four different sequences. I lost this year. I wanted the record to end with "Man on the Moon." I thought that would have been a good ending. I did the first sequence and everyone liked it except they wanted to switch "Man on the Moon" from where it was.

Mike: It's a good ending, but with it that way there were a lot of slow songs right before it.

Peter: Now it ends with two slow songs, ending songs. "Find the River" is kind of — dare I say it? — elegiac. It's a natural end to the record.

Our album's coming out on vinyl. We sold four million records in America last year, and 25,000 on vinyl.

Stipe re interviews
Peter: He's just sick of it. He doesn't like the process and he did it all last year. We get asked technical questions and Michael gets all this soul-searching. They all want to go deep into his heart. Leave the guy alone, give him a break. He's home doing the videos now and finalizing the packaging of the record.

Stipe's film deal with Oliver Stone.
Peter: Michael has let it be known that he's got a script that his friends have written and he's executive producing this thing; Jim McCay, who's worked on some of video things, *Tourfilm*, is going to direct it.

Mike: I don't know if we can talk about it. It's an indie film with a small budget.

Peter: A few years ago he did *Arenabrains* with Richard Price and Eric Bogosian... He doesn't have a desire to be an actor. One of his strong points is his ability to soak up ideas.

Mike: We're in no hurry to put records out on a schedule. If Michael wants to take time and do a film, we've got other things that we do.

Peter: We're pretty good at scheduling. We've already scheduled when we're going to start working on the next record. June 1, 1993 we start rehearsing again.

Mike: I've got one song written...

Peter: We're going to make a record and then tour, so that gives us four months in the middle where we're not going to do anything. We've never had more than two weeks off in a row. The videos will be finished by Thanksgiving. I don't know what we're all going to do. Michael will probably be working on his film. I might do some weird adventure travel thing.

Mike: I might do some film scoring.

Peter: Bill's producing this country singer called Ralph Roddenberry. He likes to be around the house.

Mike: Bill's not a real crowd person. He's pretty private. He likes to keep out of the busy-ness.

"Radio Song"
Peter: Every DJ said "I know what you mean — about *some* DJs."

Mike: Some of them took it pretty personally and didn't play that song.

Peter: It had a nod in the rap direction, and rock stations that normally play the hell out of us wouldn't touch it. We had people suggesting we mix Chris [Parker, aka KRS-One] out of the record. I'd rather not have a hit single.

Peter Holsapple
Peter: There was a couple of misunderstandings. We're still friends, but it was best we not work together for a while. I love Peter. If he was in the band, it'd be his band in a week, because he writes so many songs.

Mike: He's got too much talent to be sitting around waiting on us. He's a dear person.

This is a very insular record.
Mike: We did the oboe in Atlanta with the rest of the Atlanta Symphony, the section of the Atlanta Symphony, most of whom are the same people we worked with on *Out of Time*.

Strings?
Mike: They're very emotive and evocative. If the arrangement is good they can really add a lot to the song. John Paul Jones and Mark Bingham came at it from different directions than we would have if we had done the strings ourselves.

Peter: I love strings. [But] it's so easy to be lachrymose and sentimental with strings. You've got to be really careful. When we're talking to the string arrangers we always emphasize that we want it pithy and angular.

Mike: And it's not like we just take whatever string arrangements are given us. There's a lot of work after we get that goes into chopping it up, putting it in the right place and not using what we don't need.

Isn't it strange?
Peter: Almost everything I do, I'll look around once and go, "This is really weird." If you're in the business and you aren't insane with ego, you've got to look around and think this is really odd. I do that every single day. You've got to have a well-developed sense of the absurd to do this.

The most absurd thing in R.E.M.'s existence?
Mike: Being at the Grammys. It was so not our scene, it was almost like slumming. Slumming up, although I don't look up to a lot of what was going on. It was like taking a trip to Mt. Everest or something.

Peter: I wore my pajamas. I met Bonnie Raitt.

Predominance of acoustic guitar
Peter: If I hadn't bought a Marshall amp halfway through the recording, it probably would have been all acoustic. I bought this Marshall and started sticking on all sorts of heavy guitar things. I love it, it's unlike any other amp. Most of the tracks are acoustic guitar, underneath there's feedback or distorted guitars, which is kind of backwards. Usually, it's the distorted one on top and the acoustic underneath. It just adds dramatics to the song.

Will Michael do a solo record?
Peter: Yeah, but it won't have songs on it. It'll have a cappella, drum beats, trombones...

Mike: That piano thing he's been playing for ten years.

Peter: I hope so. He's got this awful piano thing that he sits down and plays every time there's a piano around. Please record this so you can get it out of your system, and we'll never have to hear it again.

Does it have a name?
Peter: "That awful thing that makes us leave the room." Or "That which cannot be listened to." He does it on purpose, he knows it drives me insane.

"Drive"
Peter: The record is kind of odd for us anyway, and that's a nice choice for a single. It doesn't sound a whole lot like us, it doesn't sound like anything on the radio. It's either going to totally stiff, or it's going to really stand out.

David Essex reference and delay echo on voice:
Mike: "Rock On" is a great song.

Peter: It's a kind of political song (bushwhacked: take control of your life), and it seemed to fit in there. It blew my mind the first time I heard it. You don't have to see it as political.

Mike: It almost sounds like an anti-drug song to me, although there's no telling what Michael intended.

"Try Not to Breathe"
Mike: A song about choice as well.

Peter: It's funny. When I was doing the demo I had this little mic right in front of me and I was breathing really loud and it was making too much noise. I said I'll try not to breathe, and put the demo down, and Michael took that as the title. It's like an old man imagining himself dead. Michael said it's holding his breath till he dies.

Mike: It's reflective, looking back over his life.

Peter: I love feedback. It's so nontechnical, but it's so musical. You don't even play notes: you get a couple of notes going and you bend them and shake them. You can change what a chord is about. The feedback makes it discordant, a little threatening. I use a Vox with 2 12s and a little fuzzbox. I've got this hollow-body Rickenbacker, best feedback guitar in the world. I just hold it up, shake it, bend the neck. I usually do it one pass — that was the first pass.

"The Sidewinder Sleeps Tonight"
Mike: We had to work it out with the three guys that wrote "The Lion Sleeps Tonight." We paid them for the title and those notes. Let's put it this way. If we didn't, in a year, some lawyer would call them up and tell them they could sue us. We'd probably win, but who needs it? It's much better to just cut it off at the pass, say do you mind, we're going to use this, can we work something out with you so we can use this with no flak from you?

Peter: They were really cool about it. But there are nuisance lawsuits. We've never been sued, but you've got to protect yourself against that kind of stuff.

The chuckle re Dr. Seuss
Mike: I kept trying to get him to not say Zeuss, to say Seuss, and he couldn't do it. He tried, but said Zeuss anyway, and that made him laugh. Half of the song is about somebody trying to get in touch to set up a liaison with someone who can sleep on his floor. The other half you're on your own.

Peter: Sometimes with Michael it helps to realize that there's an overall scheme to the song but some verses don't refer to the body of the song. My picture of this song is a guy at a pay phone who's kind of pissed off. I don't need this shit — I want the good things.

"Everybody Hurts"
Peter: I think of it as white guys doing Stax.

Mike: It's got a '50s R&B feel; our first real shot with a Wurlitzer. Lyrically, it's exactly what it sounds like.

Peter: I bought this $20 drum machine, a Univox Rhythmer. It's got five little buttons — slow rock, fast rock, samba — and three things — hi-hat, woodblock, aguare. It's awful, but it makes sense, because the song had that metronomish feel anyway. Mike and I cut it live with this dumb drum machine which is just as wooden as you can get. We wanted to get this flow around that: human and non-human at the same time. Bill plays drums on the bridge.

"New Orleans Instrumental #1"
Peter: It fit the mood of the record. It's not meant to signify anything. It's a mood piece.

Mike: We ran through it once and we put it down. We didn't know what we were going to do with it. It sounds cool, let's keep this. I'm still not sold on that as being the right place in the sequence, but it works.

Peter: It's the kind of thing we usually don't put on the record. We always have these instrumentals and we never do. This time we did. There's a #2 that will be on a B-side. The next one sounds like an ad for some deranged pina colada mix. There's jolly piano; I'm playing stand-up bass. I was kind of drunk and as the song goes on I keep sliding higher and higher up the bass. By the last verse I'm up to F-plus-a-third.

"Sweetness Follows"
Peter: No e-bow: guitar feedback, cello, organ, no bass — we took the bass off because of the cello. I think Michael called his parents and said it wasn't about them. He's close to his family. Michael likes to conflict what the lyrics are saying with the music or the way he's singing it sometimes. It's unsettling to have the words undercut like that.

Mike: To me it's about family estrangement. It sounds like he's getting back in touch with a sibling because their parents have died.

"Monty Got a Raw Deal"
Peter: Michael met a guy while we were doing the record who took photos of Montgomery Clift during *The Misfits*. I'm not sure what this guy told him. The Clash song is real specific, and ours isn't. [There's nothing in the song that specifically alludes to Clift except for] the lyric "Monty, this is strange to me." It's more of a meditation on the movies and reality.

Mike: That song has a very definite place of its own because of the effects — delay and reverb — used on the vocals and the instruments. It's got a dry feel, I like that.

"Ignoreland" reminds me of the Who's "Eminence Front"...
Peter: Oh wow, that's pretty wild. I like "Eminence Front" but I would have thought more Neil Young-y; it's got that tuning he always uses where you tune the E's down to D's.

Mike: That's a guitar fest. It's a political song, but basically a guitar fest. It's against the Reagan era. When Michael found out, two or three years ago, what the budget was for defense spending it made a huge impression on him, and he's never gotten over it. He really wanted to fuck his voice up. He's singing through an amp. He didn't want his voice to sound normal. Like a lot of singers, he's not in love with his own voice, and keeps trying to trick it up.

Peter: He has such a great voice, but he's always asking for more reverb. That's fine, because I always try to bury my guitars as well.

"It's hard to walk in dignity with throw-up on your shoes."
Peter: I wanted to change it to "vomit," but "throw-up" makes sense.

Mike: Me too. I really like the honest disclaimer at the end. "I know that this is vitriol, spleen-venting, no solution, but I feel better having screamed — don't you?"

"Star [Fuck] Me Kitten" — Is that synthesizer?
Mike: No, that is a vocal technique. I sing seven or eight different notes and you put 'em on faders on the board and play the board like an instrument. You bring up whatever notes you want, you fade them in and out. "Star Me Kitten" was this bizarre set of chords on organ that turned into a song. I played the B3 in Athens, at John Keane's studio.

"Man on the Moon"
Peter: That just came out of nowhere. That's what I like about rock'n'roll. Sometimes you just can't figure it out.

Mike: You don't have to know. The only real touch point of that song is a little bit of the truckstop as St. Peters, a heaven allegory. But that's as close to pinning it down as you're going to get.

Peter: I never played slide guitar before. We went out to dinner and everyone goes, "Peter, you should play slide." I said OK. I used a bottleneck and a Telecaster, tuned down the E to a D and the A to a G. I just whacked it out.

"Nightswimming" — oboe, strings, cello, piano — reminds me of the opening chords of "#1 Record" by Raspberries...
Mike: Great song. I can see that. Who knows, I may have been thinking about that. It's about a real thing, historically based in fact.

Peter: We all used to go see rock'n'roll shows in Athens in '79, '80. Afterwards, we'd sneak on this guy's property and go swimming in this waterhole. It'd be great — 30 of us, all running around naked. It was pre-AIDS, we were all late teenagers, early 20s, and whatever happened happened. The results would be pretty obvious. ◆

Just as I was about to start at *Newsday* in 1993, I was asked to write a cover story for the tenth anniversary issue of *Pulse!* I can't imagine having the confidence or imagination to pull together an essay this paradoxically expansive and nebulous now.

The New Mainstream?

Pulse!, July 1993

Money changes everything. Way back in the summer of 1991, punk rock was just a recurring dream some of us had, a quixotic fantasy of music as the final chapter in a rebel culture that had already signed on to the anti-establishment establishment. The generation gap that opened four decades back by James Dean closed with the nobody-doesn't-like Sara Lee popularity of Michael Jackson, and any residual us-vs.-them fantasies were prudently jettisoned to ensure a smoother ride towards the American dream. Music for fucking and selling can never credibly feign any degree of innocence, but bands that at least smirked while they spit in the wind offered a reminder of how it used to be.

Whether borne on the malignant aftershocks of Alice Cooper / David Bowie glam-raunch, frenzied new wave nihilism or '80s art-roar, punk rock always defined a sound of music that could never — and for countless reasons, should never — be sold in convenience stores. Miserable teenagers may not know much, but the ability to offend normal sensibilities by making music tolerable only to other miserable teenagers is as basic a contemporary skill as rafting was to Huck Finn.

Into this pretty picture floated *Nevermind*, a dozen songs that introduced garageland to the wasteland and blasted whatever was left of punk rock straight out of the college radio ghetto and into the central social arena. Nirvana entered a stage set — by such up-from-the-underground victors as R.E.M., Living Colour and U2 — for a definitive sign from god (or at the very least David Geffen) as to what the Next Big Thing would be. With Nirvana lighting the financial fuse, in one mighty thrash explosion all bets were off.

One more posse of young white cowboys mounted on the creaky guitar-rock sawhorse, the Northwest's noisy auteurs headed for the commercial stratosphere, turning the mother of all pop cultures inside out. While the most pervasive influence on '80s style was unquestionably hip-hop, not since the Sex Pistols mouthed off to British TV geek Bill Grundy in 1976 had one group singlehandedly gouged such a deep dent in society's armor.

As *Nevermind* kept on selling, the ripples of Nirvana's splash flowed right out of the rock pond. The record industry did a flick-of-the-pick 180-degree shift and decreed that the couldn't-give-a-shit slacker ethos and undirected rocket power of Nirvana and their ilk (learned, of course, from the Replacements and their ilk) was no longer a free pass to hip oblivion but a ticket to the big time. Suddenly, the tested and the timid were out and the weird and wild were in; a new gimmick swept the land. As self-declared groundbreakers rushed to imitate the innovators, the elder statesmen from Aberdeen were joined by a generation of once-untouchable, now-exploitable, bands. Soon, stampeded by trendy clothing cannibals, the *Singles* Seattle-scene film and endless trees of drivel on the subject, even an institution as isolated as *The New York Times* saw fit to devote the front page of its Sunday Style section to a kiss-of-death declaration of GRUNGE as "a five-letter [*sic*] word...synonymous with a musical genre, a fashion statement, a pop phenomenon." Welcome to the topsy-turvy era of Nirvanaville.

The writer pauses to open a letter from a reader. "Punk will never die. Everybody thinks that it's just a bunch of wierdo's [*sic*] doing drugs that listen to that kind of music. Well, wake up and smell yourself, because it gets more popular everyday, and soon everybody will listen too [*sic*] it."

In less time than it has taken Nirvana to record a follow-up to *Nevermind*, punk rock — and its oblique dream-pop cousin (see My Bloody Valentine) — took its place as a highly salable commodity in the rock marketplace. By green wizardry, this noisy, antagonistic blight, once of interest only to young coffee-addicted losers with no future, no past and — most importantly, no money — became a Madison Avenue signifier for the Subaru Impreza, hyped to a heretofore unidentified American market share in a post-logic television commercial as "just like punk, 'cept it's cars!" Meanwhile, an upscale adult magazine ad for the same $16,000 metal box brags about its stability, smoothness, automatic tuning and Porsche-like engine technology. Now how punky is *that*, Mr. Businessman?

Moolah longa, rock brevis. Still, this temporary turn of the tables beats a poke in the eye with a busted guitar string. Looking at the beneficiaries of the record industry's newfound largesse towards anything that makes alternative-to-what noise, there are longstanding cultural wrongs being righted. Soul Asylum and Bob Mould have finally gotten their props after years of busting their balls for fanzine adulation and little more; Belly has effortlessly surmounted whatever barrier kept Tanya Donelly's alma mater, Throwing Muses, out of the MTV / *Billboard* loop. Love 'em or hate 'em, L7 — adult Runaways with no puppet strings — have empowered rock women as never before. Cool bands like the Goo Goo Dolls, Sloan, Television Personalities, Ween and Shonen Knife are on widespread release here for the first time. The Fall, Pere Ubu, Meat Puppets and the American Music Club — all of whose long, respectable careers have gone rudely unrewarded in this country — are still (or finally) being supported by record companies capable of remedying that frustration. Three cheers for our side.

Unfortunately, opening the floodgates allowed a lot of smelly bathwater to wash in. The Spin Doctors, those geezers-in-training disguised as groovy underground guys, slipped in the back door of pabulum nation. The Lemonheads, punk rock's very own Toto, owe their career to other peoples' songs, Hüsker Dü's sound and Evan Dando's lazy pothead grin. There's no shortage of young wanna-be-Dead goodtime ecologists to fill in when the real thing is off tripping somewhere else. Nine Inch Nails, a band whose songs pale next to Survival Research Labs', prove that, no matter how violently one goes at it, wanking is not a spectator sport. While Primus initially bubbled up out of the Bay Area, wearing we're-all-Peppers thrashfunk colors, *Pork Soda* pours its loopy lyrics over stretchy bits of instrumental jamming that threatens to evolve into Rush-ian prog rock. And if Soundgarden, Pearl Jam and Alice in Chains have, respectively, a sexgod hunk, an unassailable pedigree and a trip to hell as their calling cards, their successes only underscore how enormous the audience for a reformed Led Zeppelin — even beyond Jimmy Page's current David Coverdale trans-Plant — would be.

That still leaves (ha ha) the resurgence of interest in recreational drugs, and the bands riding that fuzzy bandwagon as an odd factor in this decade's musical trends. Back in 1982, a *Rolling Stone* headline noted the "End of an Era: Why the Sixties Generation Has Quit Smoking Pot." In 1993, there's a tribute album, *Marijuana's Greatest Hits Revisited*, to reefer music and a rising cloud of bands devoted to the stuff. Hey, don't bogart that lifestyle, man...

Despite Nirvana's numerical ascendance, the audience for this music remains a relatively small portion of the pop music universe. Of the best-selling 200 albums listed in a recent *Billboard*, roughly a sixth could sort-of maybe be filed in a store's "alternative" section. The same chart boasts as many country folk and a sizable posse of straight-up rappers. The rest of the slots go to the same fluffy-not-stuffy disposable diapers — crooners, dance bands and arena-sized rock gods — that have filled record store shelves since the dawn of time. The singles chart, where highly formatted radio still rules, has far less room for the stylistic fringe. Beyond the easy-lite romantic pap of Silk, Jade and Shai, whatever demand exists for diversity is met by random stylistic blips that pass in the night like Snow, the rapid-fire Canadian dance-haller.

While subculture pockets keep music's fringes (even those million-selling fringes) moving, the essence of mass taste has never really changed. Those who buy records now and then but consider music just another section alongside sports, fashion, alcohol, television and movies in the culture supermarket still take home mass quantities of undemanding romantic drool, Kenny G wallpaper and rump-shaking dance music.

One encouraging sound now in the air is the middle-class hip-hop of Arrested Development and Digable Planets. With the catchy, mild ambience of jazzy soul and the current-affairs snap of rap, this street-level version of college-rock intellectualism is forging a sweet center of extraordinarily broad appeal. AD's hippy-dippy idealism may be as precious as Lenny Kravitz's faux-naïveté,, and there's undoubtedly an element of balmed-out white guilt in the critical fawn-job the group has received, but *3 Years, 5 Months and 2 Days in the Life of...* set its own political and musical agenda and blew up strictly on merit. It's cool like that...

Early afternoon, April 5th. It's "Aerosmith Day" on MTV. The new Brady Bunch compilation is on the coffee table, alongside the latest issue of *Motorbooty*: the only 'zine with the courage to offer its own name to those "young Americans born too late to change the world and too soon to just throw it away." On the stereo, England's adroitly backwardized Denim sings its cultural manifesto, "The Osmonds." Meanwhile, Faith No More's Commodores cover, "Easy" is chasing Ugly Kid Joe's rendition of Harry Chapin's "Cat's in the Cradle" up the charts. Does anybody really know what time it is?

Once a harmless pursuit connecting a dismal present to the good bits of a distant past, nostalgia is now accelerating so uncontrollably that we will eventually reach existential meltdown. The Clash promised "No Elvis, Beatles or the Rolling Stones" in 1977, but 1978 came anyway. Despite Van Halen's contention that "Right Now" is everything, inveterate time wrinklers increasingly deem whatever preceded Right Now ready for reconsideration. Armed with an ironic sense of detachment, one can find redemptive qualities in anything — good, bad or, ideally, truly awful — that happened before Right Now. (I, for one, am about ready for the rehabilitation of good old Vanilla Ice. The Iceman's been and gone so long that it's high time for his return. I've already got my action figure — now $4.98 at Kitsch-R-Us — still in its original wrapper.) But time warps are no place for amateurs.

As Joe Levy observed in a recent *Village Voice* article on the Pooh Sticks, "It's Rob Schneider's Xerox Guy, making copies, the paradigmatic aesthetic strategy of the metacastic generation...metacasm elevates sarcastic in-jokes to a plateau where so much specialized information is necessary to separate the junk from 'junk,' where intentions are so thoroughly cloaked that meaning disappears, buried in a heap of references to '70s rock, punk, pop, TV, fanzines, Linda Blair movies and adolescence." I pity the poor ignorant. As much fun as in-joke bands are for the properly equipped cognoscenti, the notion of pop culture scholarship being a prerequisite for rock'n'roll appreciation runs deeply counter to its basic tenets.

The nostalgia clock used to tick slowly enough to let cultural corpses molder and ripen, for artifacts to go from dubious currency to bad memory to no memory at all and then bubble slowly back into consciousness, shorn of any associations other than fondness. But through the younging-down of the audience and the speeding-up of media overload, there's no longer any time to waste. Awash in the CD-driven reissue surge, which has made the most esoteric details of musical history more available than ever and might have sparked a serious revival of interest in music's great past, Rhino's *Have a Nice Day* crud-of-the-'70s series is considered a watershed. Beyond the duly appreciated Led Zeppelin boxes and Robert Johnson excavations, an enormous amount of insignificant trash is being enthusiastically scraped from pop's dumpster. And savored by those who, like young Bryan Adams concert-goers singing along to the "Summer of '69," feel the misty tug of a past they never actually inhabited.

Americans ignorant of political or social history demonstrate vast scholastic knowledge of Quisp and Quake, *Hogan's Heroes*, *The Jeffersons* (now being revived onstage with the original cast), Charlie Manson, Fluffernutter and big-eyed children paintings. Platform shoes are joining bell bottoms as the height of fashion. Lava lamps are everywhere. Hey man, this attic is getting mighty crowded. Sooner or later you gotta throw some stuff out.

Nostalgia helps explain the easy appeal of dance music and funk-rock to a white rock'n'roll audience whose forbears a generation back rebelled so adamantly against disco. Beyond those who danced to glitter-ball light in the '70s, it takes a nation of millions unstigmatized by life in that era of radio oppression to now consider disco charming kitsch nostalgia. Stretching that logic also rationalizes the popularity of the (George) Clintonian Chili Peppers and the living-wax-museum luck of the Black Crowes, the Spin Doctors and brain-dead cock-rock. Although blatantly derivative in origin, they can offer the photocopied semblance of novelty to Generation M(otorbooty) who, at the very least, can claim these bands, unembalmed by advanced age or history's baggage, for their own.

Twenty-five years ago, *Wild in the Streets* envisioned a youth-run future which deems turning 30 a crime; the film's ironic payoff is the inevitable uprising of pre-teens against the twenty-something establishment. Rock is currently suspended in a widening internal generation gap. Unlike the old in/out division of the hips vs. the straights, this modern gulf war is 'caused by the deeply divided values held by various music-loving factions and strata.

The cultural domination of greying baby boomers and the landfill of nostalgia has forced the hand of those born after the 1960s. How could a youth nation steeped in retro-everything be capable of forging an "alternative" to prevailing music? With pop's creative process revealed to be a Möbius band — a closed (and evidently shrinking) loop of repetition and reinvention bolted to a 40-year-old essential rock-band structure — participants armed with new guitar effects are doomed to dig in the same hard-scrabble ground, limited, by the audience's growing ignorance of reference points, to a dwindling array of usable roots.

So, the sorry choices facing Generation M include a recycled present and a poorly recalled past. Young bands daunted by the weight of history's challenge hanging over their amps, incapable of uncovering anything new in the minutely pillaged land of musical invention, have stopped worrying about it. Given the audience's tender age and short memory, hip new bands like Superchunk can dare to be ordinary, letting the needs of the moment vindicate their lack of innovation. Nothing is new, everything is permitted. After fronting a band firmly rooted in '70s metal, Perry Farrell — an obviously fine believer in such trappings of retro-rock stardom as appalling arrogance and cavernous self-indulgence — can become the saintly captain of the good ship Lollapalooza, that very model of p.c. multi-culturalism.

Beyond issues of taste and futile debates over sampling, sponsorship, free speech, drugs and the musicality of rap, it's obvious that any traditional belief in rock'n'roll as a vehicle for social and cultural progress are obsolete. Dylan warned about following leaders, but that dog still hunts. So, if Metallica's 29-year-old James Hetfield is hardly rock's first right-winger, his characterization, in David Fricke's *Rolling Stone* interview, as a "conservative anarchist" still inserts new variables in the old equation of musical youth and rebellion. (Truthfully, 'twas ever thus. Even in the '60s, hippie drag was a notoriously unreliable mindset guideline.)

Overwhelming economic synergy has rendered absurd the idea that rock still exists in opposition to anything. Above the lowest grassroots level of independence, everything is for sale. And with any serious political movement in America now twenty years gone, rebellion has become a marketing scam. MTV's promotional tagline aside, Gil Scott-Heron was right on in 1974: what's being televised is most assuredly *not* the revolution. Nowadays, when I hear the word rebellion, I reach for my credit card.

Even hip-hop, pop culture's greatest do-it-yourself success story, was largely motivated by traditional capitalist desires; with some notable exceptions, rappers who took old-school to the malls viewed freedom of expression as a sales tool, not a political goal. And why should they have been any different? In the 1990s, everybody plays the game. Youthful idealism may still produce outcroppings of responsible social action, but fewer and fewer rockers have been able (or willing) to resist the seductive tug of corporate tool-dom.

Thanks to Spike Lee's good intentions, Malcolm X has been reduced to a letter, a pop icon whose ideas remain in the shadow of his legend. Rising-up-angry politics take a timeout so Chuck D can batter up at MTV's charity Rock n' Jock ballgame (money by Pepsi; as Gil Scott-Heron said, "The revolution will not go better with Coke"). And how about that righteous voice of uncorruptable independence, Henry Rollins? Watching him coyly rationalize the hypocrisy of his off-camera attacks on MTV as the network's red light winked dollar signs at him on *Alternative Nation* made me squirm more than the flustered but indignant Kennedy.

The common bond of music as a defining lifestyle no longer applies. In becoming really big business — not just records sold, but as an indistinguishable ingredient in the blurry crossover media mix that makes up contemporary pop culture — music has left the private preserve of fans to become public property. As the background noise in every walk of commerce, popular music has sacrificed its unique cultural significance.

At the heart of this change is the reduction or absence of the cult of personality, either in or behind the grooves. Unreconstructed fans remain devoted to icons like Keef or the Boss or the King, but the truly modern consumer follows product rather than its creators. The hit single, always a medium in which the artist is subordinate to an artifact, has been conceptually broadened to cipher-like careers by anonymous sound factories — from C+C [Music Factory] to Billy Ray [Cyrus] — in which contextual items like inspiration and intention become insignificant to the sound of a record and the look of a video.

This new vacuity feeds into another stage in rock rebellion, inspired by no opposition more tangible than the relentless tug to have a riot of one's own. While some find their rock jones can be satisfied by whatever bands manage to hurl up from the underground — Living Colour or Sugar or the Pixies or L7 or Faith No More or They Might Be Giants — others remain desperate for icons who can, for the time being at least, escape the attention of MTV and the emotional dilution of a full-sized audience. Fed by a limited realm of media — college radio, its attendant trade journals and skeins of kneejerk new-music consumer magazines — Generation M has made indie-scene stars of numerous bands, including Sonic Youth, Fugazi, Superchunk, Pavement, Beat Happening, Unrest, Sebadoh, Velvet Crush, Mudhoney, Teenage Fanclub, Urge Overkill, Jesus Lizard, Yo La Tengo and Velocity Girl.

That many of today's hippest "underground" groups are on major labels — some through indie/major hookups, like the Matador/Atlantic and Slash/Warner Bros. alliances, others on crypto-indie labels used to obscure corporate parentage (Sony's Chaos, PolyGram's Stardog, Atlantic's Seed) — no longer packs much irony. If it ever did. In their day, the Velvet Underground, Stooges, MC5, Clash and the Sex Pistols all made records for the man.

In 1993, "indie" describes a state of mind, not a state of affairs. What's truly amazing is that there still are genuinely independent record companies. (And that so many of them, despite red-ink returns, are turning back to 7-inch singles. What better medium for young bands to identify and build their faintly Luddite underground cults?) Following their idiosyncratic — and by no means commercially reliable — visions, Touch and Go, Dischord, Shimmy Disc, K and Sub Pop have all weathered brutal economic times, all the while functioning in plain view of rich corporate monoliths quick to cherry pick any long shots that happen to pay off. In the past two years, major labels have demonstrated an unnerving willingness to sign just about anything with cachet or sales potential — no matter how weird, difficult or dubious — from the Butthole Surfers (now on Capitol) to Ween (on Elektra) to Babes in Toyland and the Poster Children (both on Sire) to Cop Shoot Cop (Interscope, via Atlantic) and the Melvins (Atlantic). And some of them (Helmet, for instance) have rewarded their financiers' faith.

The winning archetype for '90s rock success is the slacker, that sleight-of-life slumper who makes it in a harsh, competitive world by refusing to evince any desire or concern. Not caring, or at least managing a convincing semblance of not caring, is passive aggression at its best and grants the bearer an unmistakable eau de cool in the cynical eyes of hip youth. The old joke about Marc Bolan composing hit records during the elevator ride up to the studio has been elevated to a zen ideal. Who wants to be caught slaving over a lyric or spending months in a studio, racking up self-indulgent bills like an old fart? Even putting last names or faces on record jackets is now considered somewhat déclassé, (or at least overly careerist).

No wonder rock's grizzled veterans are looking around the hallowed halls of their corporate patrons and wondering what's up. Faced with the new kids in the halls — sloppy, uncooperative problem children who play too loud and don't give a shit what anyone thinks (in short, the living ghost of all the rock'n'roll attitude that was long ago auctioned off to breweries) — these never-say-diehards now have to face facts. Their aging constituency has either lost its interest in music or spawned a generation who can't see any reason to worship Eric Clapton or Pete Townshend or Grace Slick like mom and dad did.

Unless they can find more conducive settings, like acoustic restraint (rock's new rule of commercial thumb: electric music sounds different without amps) or theatrical maturity (witness the Who's deaf-dumb-and-blind boy, Tommy Walker, joining the felines, the French Revolution and Little Orphan Annie as ladies-who-lunch Broadway entertainment fare), rock's warhorses face life in the past, doomed to endless, timeless lock groove repetition of whatever they did in the war, or careers in the slow wane. And while no one need cry for an acclaimed superstar selling a scant two million copies of the follow-up to a ten-million monster, numerical deceleration rarely reverses itself.

The problems for fossils (and that designation may well come to include young arrivistes who align themselves too closely with traditional rock values) run deeper than the bottom line. Besides losing their grip on teenagers' pocket money, they're being relieved of their cultural influence as well. Artists older than your parents don't make good role models for those in the rapture of youth. Overexposure, creative inconsistency, dated irrelevance and endless degrees of compromise have left the spokespeople of a generation speechless. Why would anyone under 30 care what Jagger, Reed or even Bono or Strummer thinks about anything anymore? If they feel obliged to continue making records, that's fine, but that doesn't put them in touch with the sound of the suburbs anymore. Of course, old rockers don't have a lock on needless prattle. Soon after the release of *Incesticide*, Nirvana's odds-and-sods stopgap, a revised version of the record's idiotic liner notes ("if any of you in any way hate homosexuals, people of different color, or women, please... don't come to our shows and don't buy our records") — with a bonus paragraph gracelessly libeling *Vanity Fair* writer Lynn Hirschberg — were sent, by a source both anonymous and obvious, to the media as "An Open Letter from Kurt Cobain."

The true activists of the '90s rock world are women. In the '70s, while still swathed in its scabrous, vindictive anti-sex misogyny ("girl" was once British slang for a wimp of any gender), the punk/new wave's anarchic open-door policy readily admitted female musicians, who took whatever encouragement they could find and armed themselves instrumentally to rock out, with or without the boys. Sonic Youth's Kim Gordon, Bikini Kill's Kathleen Hanna, Babes in Toyland's Kat Bjelland (among those who have been lumped together, rightly or wrongly, under the riot grrrls moniker) and others, including Come's Thalia Zedek and Hole's Courtney Love — all of them essentially following in the Slits' giant footsteps — are establishing a sexually conscious aesthetic based neither on male fantasy or doctrinaire feminist canon. Their spectrum of values, styles and viewpoints runs from apolitical gender-pop fandom (as in the delightful and influential fanzine *Chickfactor*, where "cool guitar girls" like Amelia of Heavenly and Bridget of Unrest talk about their crushes and their music) to the angrily determined activism of L7. While still in a transitional state where simply being a woman in a band remains, on some level, an issue, the indie-rock scene (at least; how this will disseminate deeper into the music world is hard to see) is progressing towards an ideal situation in which women can assume any musical role and image they choose without being stigmatized, much less marginalized, as the sexual other.

One side effect of women's rise in rock is the demystification of sex and its liberation from, to borrow a New York Times subhead, the "virgin-vixen-bimbo stereotype." As three-dimensional people who won't play by the wrong old rules, female musicians are at a point where they don't have to satisfy anybody's lust. Then there's Madonna. Ms. C's overly strenuous devotion to equating and connecting her sexuality and her art is tired and offensive. That there's a sizable audience for her routine self-exploitation is sad but unsurprising; that otherwise rational critics have rushed to defend her as a courageous libertine is laughable. Madonna may have the good taste to buy Frida Kahlo paintings, but she's in danger of becoming a post-modern Charo, someone whose frantic need to provoke has long since passed the point of diminishing returns. It used to be only mid-life-crisising rock studs who needed to reassure themselves that old organs can be made to do new tricks; Madonna's breasts have become the most ineffectual cultural emblem since Mick Jagger's lips. Licky boom boom now...

For the final word on the state of music, circa 1993, one has only to clock the resurgence of early '80s dawn-of-MTV new wave. Even if Boy George's hit is a soundtrack-driven fluke, Duran Duran's seven-year commercial absence does justify the comeback tag; despite his 1990 success with electronic disco, Adam Ant's recent tour was built on good old Antmusic. But while the unwavering popularity of Depeche Mode, who haven't made a good record in years, can be written off to strong marketing and deep-seated pin-up inertia, the group's unexpected critical rehabilitation (ooh, look — they've got guitars!) indicates some greater pathology at work. In the U.K., two years after the Clash's ironic 1991 Levi's commercial surge, the delightful, long-gone Bluebells land a song on a TV ad and wind up bigger than ever. Add in the sudden surge of techno-pop (and related phenomena) reissues, assorted reunions of late-'70s/early-'80s punk bands and the appearance of new groups devoted to covering new wave standards and it's clear that we've begun digging up a lot of relatively fresh musical corpses. Find it, sell it, kill it and then revive it. Don't stop thinking about tomorrow. It'll soon be here. Again. ◆

The article elicited a marvelous reaction from Ben Kim in his *Raw Material* column for Chicago's *NewCity*. I may have felt a bit stung at the time, but now I relish the insightful and amusing praise. And being compared to Tom Carson is an added honor. (I've broken it into paragraphs, which were not in the original.) But who's Stu?

> This tastes like...yeowch, my tail! (Or, "Critcrit Corner.") Ira Robbins' "The New Mainstream," the cover story of July's PULSE magazine, is a sprawling, thrillingly overwritten rant on the rotten state of rock and the complete absorption of the "alternative." It's packed with breathtaking generalizations, death-defying syllogisms, received wisdom (a long quote from Joe Levy's *Village Voice* essay on the Pooh Sticks — feels like we're sticking corncob grips into a can of Niblets here), free-wheeling puns and sub-references, and plenty of keen insights. In other words, it's the kind of rock writing I love to read.
>
> Robbins nicely summarizes the fate of rock taste under the postmodern condition, particularly the hyper-acceleration of nostalgia: "The nostalgia clock used to tick slowly enough to let cultural corpses molder and ripen, for artifacts to go from dubious currency to bad memory to no memory at all and then bubble slowly back into consciousness, shorn of any association other than fondness. But through the younging-down of the audience and the speeding-up of media overload, there's no longer any time to waste."
>
> Some of this reminded me more than a little of another earth-tamping rock's-all-used-up tract, Tom Carson's "What We Do Is Secret: Your Guide to the Post-Whatever," from the fall 1988 *Village Voice Rock & Roll Quarterly*.
>
> Robbins: "Overwhelming economic synergy has rendered absurd the idea that rock still exists in opposition to anything."
>
> Carson: "Rock and roll's assimilation into the cultural norm was inevitable, but one side effect of the Reagan era has been that popular culture in general is also now establishment culture."
>
> I prefer Carson's piece because its dead-end thesis focuses specifically on post-punk guitar rock, the site of a huge chain-reaction pileup of bands and critics (myself included) searching for something new to say after Sonic Youth and Big Black (Carson depicted SY shoulder-riding past another pileup just up the road), and he's more or less able to chew this beyond-Rotten bite. "The current scene comes up with all sorts of moves, but all of them end up as just one more convolution of a radicalism that's become a genre, dealing in extremes that have become constants." Kind of makes you want to go back to bed (as if you needed a good excuse).
>
> So, rock's used up, and rock's-used-up articles are used up: that won't stop any of us from trying. Boot up that motherfucker, Stu, I'm gonna kick out the jams! ◆

The Queers

Rolling Stone, 14 November 1996

One of the golden rules in the punk handbook is to confuse and irritate people at every opportunity. So, naming a band of straights the Queers — thereby upsetting narrow thinkers of both orientations — deserves a merit badge. As do the resilient dispositions of grown men who can make a proud punk-pop career of shamelessly dumb but irresistibly catchy ditties like "I Can't Stop Farting," "Ursula Finally Has Tits" and (true scout story!) "Kicked Out of the Webelos."

Inspired by the cartoon delinquency and three-chord blare of the Ramones, Portsmouth, New Hampshire singer, guitarist and sometime surfer Joe King formed the Queers in the early '80s, taking crude and bratty shots at everything in sight, starting with the scruffy punk he saw in the mirror. The original Queers didn't last long, and King bounced around California and Hawaii for a time, playing sporadic gigs with assorted lineups when he was home. In 1990, he and drummer Hugh O'Neill met bassist B-Face (Chris Barnard) at a Social Distortion show and relaunched the band, making up for lost time with a vengeance.

The Queers have since released five delightfully quick-and-dirty studio albums (the superb new *Don't Back Down* owes its polished clarity to the unprecedented luxury of nine days' work), a rarities compilation, two pseudo-live discs and a cover of the Ramones' *Rocket to Russia*. While some of the band's early numbers were too raw or derivative to be much good, 1993's wonderful *Love Songs for the Retarded* brought the group into its stylistic own, staking out the genial animosity and melodic soft spot at the Queers' core. For this band, "fuck you" is used (frequently) as a nearly neutral interjection.

"We're laughing at ourselves. The Queers are about having fun," says King, who admits to being 35 but has the energy and gee-whiz enthusiasm of a horny high-schooler. (If no longer the drinking habits. *Don't Back Down*'s inclusion of "I Only Drink Bud" is a confusing hangover from the now-sober rocker's intemperate past.)

With the Ramones retiring this year, the Queers are poised to fill their Keds and carry the breakneck banner. But while *Don't Back Down* has its share of typically entertaining bashers, the album steers toward '60s pop, specifically the Beach Boys. Queers' records have always made room for tuneful candyfloss, but never to this degree.

"We wanted to get into more vocals, more background vocals and have lead guitar solos on this album," King says. "The kids are coming along with us. When we do the pop stuff, that's what they grasp onto — the simple three-chord 'Louie Louie'-type shit. A lot of them think the Beach Boys aren't cool, so we figured we'd throw that at 'em." The title track is a stirring Brian Wilson surf oldie; "Sidewalk Surfin' Girl" was a '64 Hondells B-side. "Born to Do Dishes" (not, King insists, an ode to his three years as co-owner of a New Hampshire cafe) is downright winsome in its depiction of a dead-end job — quite a contrast to the usual "Born to...Kill/Be Wild/Run/Die" choices. The Queers don't need menacing tough-guy poses to make their loud-fast rock rule.

After all, appearances can be illusions. "There's a lot of phonies," King says. "Lesley Gore's more of a punk than any of these kids in leather jackets and mohawks." It takes one to know one. ◆

Pavement

This was great, enlightening fun. When Jackson Griffith, whose roots in Stockton (he even wrote a song about the town!) made Pavement something of a hometown band for him, asked me to do a story for *Pulse!,* I had to caution him that I wasn't much of a fan, having found the band's appeal something of an indie rock snob mystery. I couldn't hear what it was that got people so worked up.

It felt like a generational divide, but I was curious enough to consider this assignment a good way to find out what I was missing. I went in with an open mind and came away with a deep appreciation for the band and its music. I found their intelligence and openness refreshing and stimulating, amplifying without explaining their records for me.

The band members all lived in different states (only one in New York: bassist Mark Ibold, who tended bar at the beloved Great Jones Café in NYC), so the logistics were tricky. Matador publicist Spencer Gates — a great, tough-talking lady who died a few years later — made all the arrangements. I could only speak with Malkmus by phone, but Spencer was able to fly me out to Berkeley to meet Spiral Stairs (Scott Kannberg) in person. It was a whirlwind trip (my first time there; I recall the late-night taxi from the airport driving over the breathtaking Golden Gate Bridge), but he was very cool, offering a great conversation and generously giving me a numbered copy of *Slay Tracks*, already a valuable Pavement rarity, which I have proudly kept. In addition to talking music, I was intrigued about the civil engineering graduate thesis he was incubating on the role of fences in urban development. Rockers come in all sorts; the smart ones are always worth meeting.

Alternarock is dead, right? So how come nobody told Pavement?

Pulse!, March 1997

It's deconstruction time again. Right now, there's a sophomore somewhere hunkered down on the floor of his dorm room, a cigarette in one hand and a pen in the other. Every so often, a look of recognition followed by a crooked smile crosses his face, and he stabs at a notebook, scrawling out his observations and analyses of what's on the stereo.

For our kid, *Brighten the Corners* — Pavement's abundantly tuneful follow-up to 1995's sorely undervalued *Wowee Zowee* — isn't just a carefully arranged collection of Daliesque pop contraptions. As a Pavement record, it's another enigmatic challenge of shaggy dog riddles and obscure signifiers, arcane allusions and wry ironies. The Beatlesque "We Are Underused" mentions wedding invitations, which makes sense to student boy since he's read that guitarist-singer Scott Kannberg and drummer Steve West both got married last year. He recognizes the sweeping 12-string Byrds guitar sound of Kannberg's "Date With IKEA" and the Roxy Music sounds coming from "Embassy Row." He knows from checking an Internet phone directory that someone with the same surname as singer/guitarist Stephen Malkmus lives on a "Shady Lane" Court in Kansas; that might explain the title of the airy album's most Kinks-like delicacy. The serious philosophical issues touched on in "Transport Is Arranged" and "Old to Begin" slow his progress, though he guesses the whimsical geography in "Starlings of the Slipstream," a sweet harmony breeze, is just a joke. Still, it's a couplet in the sing-songy "Stereo" that really pulls his beard.

What about the voice of Geddy Lee — how did it get so high?

Whoah nellie, eh? Is this Pavement's doubly dry way of ripping the Canadian trio? Maybe it's a pop culture quiz, a snarky e.p.t. for collegiate cool, dividing the true-blue disciples of all things alternative from those harboring revisionist tendencies towards the evil behemoth of corporate classic rock.

Try door number three. Reached by phone at his home in Portland, Oregon, Malkmus willingly professes his admiration for Rush. "*2112* was the album we were into when I was a kid. I still listen to *Caress of Steel.*" There's a brief pause. "Maybe we can tour with them or something." But then he shrugs off the notion: it wasn't meant in earnest.

Or was it? Besides defying most conventions of rock careerism (like having its five members live in one geographical area), Pavement has spent eight curious years thriving on the uncertainty principle, arranging common and disparate elements into distinctive, influential and occasionally popular art that never quite gives itself away. Solidly rooted in the individualist self-expression of indie-rock but willing to meet commercial acceptance on their own terms, Pavement have progressed from amateur flailings to enticingly poised accomplishment without sacrificing their dignity or integrity. Those who found the band's early records too lo-fi and in-jokey will be surprised by *Brighten the Corners*' easy allure.

Having laid a solid foundation of critical acclaim from its first 7-inch sputters, Pavement established a beachhead of commercial viability in 1994 with *Crooked Rain, Crooked Rain*, an album that has sold nearly 200,000 copies in the U.S. (*Wowee Zowee* did maybe half as well). The accessible pop of *Brighten the Corners* — the band's bow via the newly united forces of super-groovy independent label Matador and the thunderously establishment Capitol — puts Pavement on the threshold of a major breakthrough.

Still, the group — which duly gives its fans credit for more intelligence than the average KISS Army foot soldier — playfully continues to keep listeners in the dark, flashing eclectically borrowed riffs and far-flung cultural reference points to provide blurred and illusory illumination. So, whether it's the recognition of *Wowee Zowee*'s graphic tribute to German '70s prog-rock trio Guru Guru or the discovery of a Coleridge poem which rhymes the words "slanted" and "enchanted" (as in the title of Pavement's 1992 full-length debut, which Malkmus attributes to a book of drawings by college pal David Berman, leader of the Silver Jews), the band's work is rife with fodder for examination, imagination and auto-didacticism — honey to rocking academic bears.

"Our fans understand that we're into history," says West, 30, by phone from the vast old fixer-upper he recently purchased in Lexington, Virginia. "Stephen was a history major. I'm huge into history and the history of music." If the recycled clues scattered throughout the band's records encourage fans to seek out Pavement's own musical sources, that's fine by him.

Nursing a cup of joe in a coffee bar near his house in Berkeley, California, Scott Kannberg connects the tactic to his own experiences growing up. "The way I discovered a lot of music was by reading R.E.M. interviews and seeing them say 'We're really into the Velvet Underground' or 'We're really into Wire.' So, I'd go out and buy those records. We try and do the same thing."

For all the depth of meaning people are able to extract from Pavement's increasingly sheer fabric, the designs or accidents that put it there generally remain clouded. Even with inside information, songs are subject to multiple interpretations, less likely to enlighten curiosity-seekers than lead them down an intellectual cul-de-sac.

"Ninety percent of the songs are just words put together in that kind of way, so they're really not about anything," admits Kannberg. "They're phrases and stuff that sound good together." At its best, Malkmus's free-association imagery invokes the imprecision and acid-fueled imagination of vintage Bob Dylan, a notion reinforced by the *Blonde on Blonde* coloring of the new album's "Type Slowly." For a generation of channel-surfers, magazine-flippers and web-browsers, his scampering poetry has the tempo of the times.

But he won't make too much of it. "Lyrics are mostly automatic things. I don't know where it comes from, but it's not a big heart-on-my-sleeve, here's the sadcore truth-of-the-world-type thing. I use stuff that came out of nowhere and steal things that come out of somewhere. I don't try to overwork it. It's playful; it's done pretty quickly." Malkmus declines to be the singer he plays on television. "People should know it's an act. Some of it is really you, but a lot of it's just assuming a voice and fucking around. It's not a situationist prank or anything — there's emotion and soul and stuff in there, too — but I feel like it's distant from me. Like the rap guys, I just gotta say it's entertainment."

Discussing motives and tactics with Pavement — who, individually, are as forthright as their elusive records usually aren't — is an exercise in unresolvable contradictions. Through some organic combination of design and naïveté, the leaderless group functions like a motivated amoeba, resolutely moving along an eccentric path it appears to be concocting on a need-to-proceed basis. As a business, Pavement is a fascinating model of laissez-faire socialism, valuing individualism and the collective good, letting each determine his own ideal role in the enterprise. As a band, Pavement shuns gang-like insularity for a looser but no less cohesive association. Living in different states and convening only to record and tour, the five remain bound by their friendship, their work ethic and their admiration for the songs Malkmus (and, once or twice per album, Kannberg) writes and sings. "If we all lived in the same town, our records might be better," allows bassist Mark Ibold, "but nobody wants to." And there's nobody to make them do it.

The frugal and self-reliant band is managerless. Kannberg, aided by an outside accountant, handles business affairs in consultation with Malkmus; major decisions are put to a band vote. They drive themselves to gigs and hump their own gear; they had never worked with a real producer before engaging Mitch Easter and his North Carolina studio for *Brighten the Corners*. And his contribution was more encouragement than guidance.

"We've made some mistakes," says Ibold during a vegetarian lunch on Manhattan's Lower East Side right before Christmas. "We make 'em all the time, actually. Fortunately, they haven't been really huge." At 34, the onetime skate punk is Pavement's pragmatic elder, the one most likely to consider career and life in conventional terms. (He is also the only Pavement member still living in New York City. Though none are natives, West, Malkmus and percussionist/Moog player Bob Nastanovich — who now makes his home across the street from Churchill Downs racetrack in Louisville, Kentucky — all resided in New York for a time.)

Despite the near-unanimous sense that their live shows could be better, Pavement keeps rehearsals to a minimum; the first few weeks of each tour, they say, are spent shaking off the cobwebs. The group doesn't demo songs before recording final versions and attributes sonic shortcomings of their records to self-imposed time and money constraints. "We don't have much of a game plan when we enter the studio as far as what anything is going to sound like," Malkmus allows. And while he notes that "Our songs never reach their peak on record — they get so much better once we've played 'em forty times on the road," he is mildly nonplused by the suggestion they try reversing the process.

The band's benign mystique of casual informality and seeming indifference is free of rock's typical measures of greed and ego; there are no arrogant bozos on this bus. West, recalling Malkmus's invitation to join Pavement (both were then employed as security guards at New York's Whitney Museum), says, "If I was in his place, I don't know if I would have picked someone who isn't a complete drummer. My actual playing has improved a whole lot, but I am in no way now, and was not then, a super drummer. I'm no Neil Peart."

Malkmus thinks his voice sounds "stupid." The new album? "I don't like it much. There are some good songs, but the vocals are too loud and the kick drum's too loud." Defying decades of frontman arrogance, Malkmus brings resignation to the role. "I wouldn't sing in Pavement if there wasn't a need for it. In the end there was no one else to do it."

By all accounts, Malkmus takes a less passive view of his studio responsibilities. The boast in a Matador press release that, in a first for Pavement, the new album was "record[ed] with the entire five-person band in the same room at the same time (playing, not just watching)." Ibold concurs. "Most of the songs are all of us actually in the same room playing everything at the same time. About four are first takes."

The band's early records were made by Malkmus and Kannberg with drummer Gary Young; rumor has it that, in Pavement's name, the pair — who contractually *are* Pavement — have continued to record solo or together on occasion. Ibold praises Malkmus for sometimes doing bass parts he then copies to play live; Nastanovich describes his studio job as "a cheerleader" and says the sessions for 1992's *Watery, Domestic* EP were the first he attended.

"Stephen is pretty much the songwriter and song-structurer," says West. "We back him up with our stuff and he edits accordingly. When it comes down to the mixing, he'll put in and take out what he thinks is going to work." Malkmus's self-effacement notwithstanding, "He's got a good idea of what he wants."

And can't have. "There's lots of music I would like to play that we can't," says Malkmus after praising Canned Heat and Creedence, declaring his thwarted desire to sing like John Fogerty on "Harness Your Hopes," an outtake from *Brighten the Corners* which Ibold insists will be the next album's hit. "It's just too technical. We make the best of what we have."

Recording the new album together, says Kannberg, made some difference. "But it still felt like [Stephen and I] were calling the shots, telling people what to play. I think it'll always be that way."

Contrary to common belief, Pavement did not spring into existence on January 17, 1989, the day childhood chums Scott Kannberg and Stephen Joseph Malkmus strolled into Gary Young's Stockton, California, studio, Louder Than You Think, where they spent the day cutting a few scraggly, intermittently sharp songs as their prismatic fan response to the Fall, Can, Clean and Swell Maps.

Malkmus was born in Los Angeles and moved to Stockton when he was eight or nine. He and Kannberg lived in the same neighborhood and met in the third grade. "We were jocks," says Scott. "We were on the same soccer team. We played tennis together."

Malkmus was the bassist in a hardcore band called the Straw Dogs until he left town to attend a private school in Santa Barbara for two years. When he returned and rejoined Kannberg at Tokay High School, Malkmus brought with him important fun from the new world — cool early-'80s records by happening bands like X and Devo.

After graduation, Malkmus enrolled in the University of Virginia ("the only school people said was good that I got into"); Kannberg spent a year at Arizona State. Before dropping out, he says, "I thought up the name Pavement and had a band that played one show at a party in 1987." Pavement's first singer, he notes, is now in an Arizona band called Beats the Hell Out of Me. Back home, Kannberg spent a year working in a used record store and then resumed college in Sacramento, where he studied urban planning. When Malkmus visited, they tried to form a band, Bag o' Bones, that never got off the ground.

Malkmus had met Nastanovich at school, where they were members of a band called Ectoslavia and DJs on WTJU. "Stephen and I got along famously right off the bat," says Bob, a garrulous straight-shooter with a hearty laugh. "We had similar tastes in just about everything. We were both into pinball, sports and drinking beer."

One thing they didn't share was the need to perform music. Unlike Malkmus, who even had a second group, Lake Speed, Nastanovich was content to be a fan. Still, he wound up banging on stuff in Ectoslavia. "Nobody could really play except for Malkmus and Rob Chamberlain a little bit, it was just noise."

Broadcasting was another story. While Nastanovich devoted himself to WTJU enough to become its station manager in his last year, Malkmus was no Casey Kasem. "The station had an amazing library," recalls Bob. "Stephen was less interested in putting together a radio show than he was in listening to albums he'd never heard." Typically, Bob would do the late-night shift while his future bandmate devoted himself to getting a musical education.

Between semesters, Malkmus continued to jam with devout California boy Kannberg in Stockton. Finally, they decided to commit themselves to posterity. "He thought we should just make a record," says Kannberg. "He had these songs and I had a couple of songs; we wanted to put the single out just to have something in the history of rock."

"We weren't trying to get big or anything," says Malkmus. "We were listening to a lot of obscure music — Chrome, Swell Maps, the Television Personalities — and celebrating obscurity was fine with us." With such humble aspirations, the two found their way to Young's studio. Taking advantage of his musical abilities, they got the much older Young to drum on "Box Elder" and "Price Yeah!," doing the rest themselves. Kannberg pressed up a thousand 7-inches and released the little bugger as *Slay Tracks (1933 – 1969)*, an artifact that now fetches $100 or more from collectors. In the tradition of heroes like Epic Soundtracks and Nikki Sudden, they identified themselves on the record as SM and Spiral Stairs, the latter a meaningless pseudonym Kannberg clung to through *Wowee Zowee*.

"There was a lot of mystery to the bands we liked," explains Kannberg of the nomenclatural conceit. "They didn't want their picture plastered all over. We wanted to keep our band mysterious. I wish we still could be. We had these visions of trying to do things a little differently, try to fuck things up a little bit."

Slay Tracks led Pavement to Chicago indie label Drag City, which released the duo's next EP, *Demolition Plot J-7*, in 1990. By this point, Malkmus had finished school and returned to Stockton after an extended personal tour through Europe, Asia and the Middle East. Following his 1989 graduation, the vehicular-minded Nastanovich had fulfilled his dream of driving a bus "in the big leagues" — New York City — and moved north with Berman, who got a job guarding paintings at the Whitney. Together, they persuaded Malkmus to join them in Jersey City.

Despite the fact that its two principals were now living on opposite coasts, Pavement-the-intermittent-recording-project moved closer to making its public debut. Several months after aborting a 1990 itinerary and making a solitary performance in a Davis, California radio studio, Pavement — Kannberg, Malkmus, Young, Nastanovich and Ectoslavia guitarist Rob Chamberlain — emerged from its cocoon and hit the road. The road, not too surprisingly, hit back.

"We practiced for three or four days at Gary's parents' house in Mamaroneck, then went on tour in [Bob's] station wagon," recalls Kannberg. "At the first show, a club in New Brunswick, New Jersey, we saw how much of a drunk Gary was. Then we played the Middle East in Boston, and he was out of control. Gary was out there doing this weird hippie dance to the opening band and fell down and sliced his leg open on a bottle. We had to play five or six shows without him. Bob switched to drums and I played drums, too. Gary finally made it to the New York show we did at the Pyramid." Fatefully, that 1991 gig was witnessed by Mark Ibold — then of New York's Dust Devils — who had bought *Slay Tracks* "just because of the way it looked."

Kannberg recalls the band's calamitous first adventure as "so much fun. We were so innocent. If 50 people came to see us, we thought, this is great." Nastanovich has a different memory of the episode. Before the tour, "Stephen had told me that I was going to be the drummer. Then he decided he needed somebody that could play a kit, and so he got Gary. He said, we'll just figure out something for you to do." (The fact that Bob owned wheels and volunteered to drive the band didn't hurt, but he has never been a secondary member in the band's odd hierarchy. As Malkmus notes, "There was no plan that the sound of the band needed two drummers to really beef it up like the Dead or the Allman Brothers. We created a role for him because he's such a great friend and I wanted him to be in the band.")

When Nastanovich first joined the band, "I couldn't think of anything to do other than play a floor tom and a snare. But when I realized Gary was going to be inconsistent; it became necessary for me to keep the beat. After Gary cut himself, we went down south, to live situations where I could name over half the people in the room. I told Stephen I could play decent drums on only six or seven of the songs, and he'd better adjust the set list or else it's going to be a complete disaster. He wouldn't do that. On several songs I had no idea what to do — I only had two drums, anyway. It was harsh, but because I went through that, anything immensely humiliating that's happened subsequently has been not [so bad]."

Malkmus, Kannberg and Young had recorded *Slanted and Enchanted* at the beginning of that year. "We wanted to make a rock record, a record that should be easy to play, that we could tour to," is Kannberg's offhand explanation for the craggy, seductive album — recorded in a week — which sold something near 100,000 copies and topped many critics' year-end lists in 1992.

With Chamberlain out of the picture, Pavement decided a bassist would lively up the party mix. They considered Michael Duane, the Dust Devils' main man, but — fearing the English expatriate would compound the Young situation — instead selected his protégé, Mark Ibold. Without quitting the Dust Devils, Ibold joined Pavement a few months prior to the release of *Slanted and Enchanted* in '92. The following summer, to the relief of all concerned,

Young bowed out of the band and was replaced by Steve West. (Young still runs his studio and leads a band called Hospital, which released an album on Big Cat in 1995.)

Displaying the nonchalance that belies his bandmates' confidence in his creative vision, Malkmus invited West into Pavement drumming unheard. "I didn't even try him out. I figured it would work out fine 'cause he's such a great person. Bob [Nastanovich] went to high school with him and said he was pretty good on the drums. I knew him. I figured I could mold his drumming style." West seconds the emotion. "I feel like my audition with Stephen was working with him for nine months and getting to know him, realizing what our similarities are." Here's a third perspective: When a lead singer hates his audibly imperfect voice, how much expert technique should he want or expect from colleagues?

West's unveiling came at the *Drag City Invitational* in Chicago in 1993. "That was a really hard time for me," says Nastanovich. "I told Gary on several occasions that I would not go on in this band if he wasn't in it. I felt a certain amount of personal immorality that I had to overcome." Fans also had their reservations. "In the beginning," says West, "there were shouts of `Where's Gary?'," but no longer. "Most listeners don't even know what record I started to play on."

The revised lineup proved entirely salutary. "Steve West is a solid and stable individual that I knew would provide an element of consistency that had never been there," says Bob. "I really didn't know if it was necessary or worthwhile for me to be in the band anymore. I had to change my role. So, I got a Moog [synthesizer] and figured I'd make some noise on it and add some spice."

Thus bolstered, Pavement promptly took a great leap forward, making 1994's monumental *Crooked Rain, Crooked Rain*. The accessible and chewy consideration of the rock life contains the most coherent songs of Malkmus' canon, as well as Kannberg's urgent Fall clone, "Hit the Plane Down," and "5 - 4 = Unity," a witty interpretation of Stockton homeboy Dave Brubeck's "Take 5." The album became Pavement's biggest seller, lost out to Hole's *Live Through This* as top album on the *Village Voice*'s prestigious *Pazz & Jop* critics' poll and brought the band to the following summer's *Lollapalooza* tour, where they again took a back seat to Courtney's crew. With *Wowee Zowee* not wowing much of anybody, Pavement found its poorly attended afternoon slot a trying ordeal, but the band did enjoy the generous pay and comfortable traveling conditions.

Other than recording *Brighten the Corners*, doing a short tour that began on the West Coast in January and the Tibetan Freedom Concert in June, Pavement laid low in '96. Malkmus cut a version of X's "Unheard Music" with Elastica for the soundtrack of the upcoming *SubUrbia*; otherwise, the band mostly attended to such post-rock affairs as matrimony, moving, mortgages and, in one case, an "off-season" career. Nastanovich, who publishes a thoroughbred tipsheet called *Lucky Lavender*, owns shares in two race horses: Steinlen's Promise and Fast Irish Lass. "I never intend to be in any other band," he says. "I consider myself to be a member of Pavement more than a musician. At the end of a tour, I go home and forget that I'm in Pavement."

But for the first half of '97, Bob and the others are most definitely neck-deep in Pavement. The well-rested band is armed with its best musical shot yet at joining Oasis and Bush in the MTV-sponsored alternarock winners' circle. (The band's apathy toward making videos, however, remains its Achilles heel in that campaign.) A bit older and more settled, the five are perhaps less tolerant of some rigors they once welcomed. Though confident enough to accept that putting a roadie or two on the payroll isn't a complete sellout, Pavement still operates beneath the hard-headed career radar of those other bands. "I never have any idea what's going to happen with this band more than six months in advance," says Ibold. "We never have plans." ◆

Kirsty MacColl

Sometimes it's just work, collecting what you need during a professional obligation. But there have been times when an artist I've interviewed has made a real human impression. When I went to do a front-of-the-book *Rolling Stone* feature on Kirsty MacColl, she proved to be one of those vivid, delightful, frank and funny people I immediately wanted to become friends with. And wish I had. She struck me, paradoxically, as both vulnerable and gutsy, tough and fragile. That comes across in a lot of her music and may be what gives it so much power. She was a prodigious talent. I loved (and still do love) her voice and her songs; her accidental death in 2000 felt like a personal loss.

This article, which I wrote in May 1990, never ran.

Kirsty MacColl's name may not be familiar to many Americans, but she's probably at home in quite a few record collections. Besides writing and recording catchy pop songs for more than a decade, the London native has led a second life as backup singer to the stars. Her distinctive voice and skill at arranging multiple harmonies have been utilized by the Smiths, Pogues, Billy Bragg, Robert Plant, Simple Minds, Talking Heads, Rolling Stones and many others.

The pop-minded daughter of folk legend Ewan MacColl traces her vocal roots back to the Beach Boys' "Good Vibrations," which she discovered at age six. "I played it for weeks. That was enlightenment for me." She grew up listening to everything from Bach to glam-rock, developing eclectic musical tastes and the burning desire to write and sing.

Through a punk band called the Drug Addix, she came to the attention of Stiff Records, which released her debut solo single in 1979. "They Don't Know" didn't set the world on fire, although comedienne Tracey Ullman later had an international hit with a version of the song. MacColl's album debut came in 1981, with the Rockpile-styled *Desperate Character*. She scaled the British charts with the bent wit of "There's a Guy Works Down the Chip Shop Swears He's Elvis," did a "disastrous" tour of Irish ballrooms and cut several more winsome singles that went nowhere.

Hamstrung by her second label, MacColl stayed solvent and busy by doing backup sessions. Working for Simple Minds in 1983, she met producer Steve Lillywhite. They fell in love, married and produced "A New England," a single which climbed into the British Top 10 just as MacColl delivered their first son. While devoting the next four years to parenthood, she kept taking singing jobs that sounded interesting, widening her circle of musical acquaintances. "I like working with talented people. It's very inspiring."

By 1989, when MacColl was ready to make her own album, she had plenty of friends — including ex-Smiths guitarist Johnny Marr, with whom she co-wrote two songs, Robbie McIntosh and David Gilmour — happy to help. Lillywhite produced, using the couple's home studio to overdub layers of her unmistakable harmonies. Just out in America (a year after its British release), *Kite* is a contrast of sweet sounds and strong words, a mature and unpredictable collection that has some country swing, a film noir plot sung in French, a lovely rendition of the Kinks' "Days" that earned the Ray Davies seal of approval and pointed attacks on both Margaret Thatcher and shallow celebrity seekers. "I'm not from the Laura Ashley school of prose. If you've got something to say, just say it. There's no point trying to be obscure when you know exactly what you're talking about. Why say 'mounds of flesh' instead of 'tits'?"

Lacking any plans to tour, MacColl is busy with her next album. Although she's married to the man behind the mixing board, she's not married to the idea of keeping her recording career a family affair. "I'd rather Steve produce me, but if he was busy I'd use another producer."

Like most strong, independent women, MacColl is rankled by the sexist attitudes she encounters. "Steve is better known than I am in America, so people assume it's a teaching-your-wife-to-drive sort of thing. I get pissed off with that. You can't be talented just because you're talented; you have to be talented because your husband is showing you the way, or because your father was famous. Steve is very talented. I don't produce as well as he does. But then he doesn't write songs." ◆

Kirsty MacColl, 23 April 1990

I don't mind interviews. It's only English ones that I have difficulty with.

Deja vu of re-promoting a year-old album?
I spent so long wondering if and when and by who it was actually going to get released in the States that it's a relief. I'm glad if it reaches a new audience. I've never had anything released over here before, so it's exciting.

Why wasn't it released simultaneously?
Virgin were hemming and hawing about it. They wanted to put it out, but they didn't want to put it out then. When they were starting up Charisma, Phil [Quartararo] was really keen on it, so I'd rather go with people who haven't been buggering around for nine months.

Have you been working on new things?
Yeah, I was in the studio [two days last week] and I put down five backing tracks with a band. I've got a few more demos to put down. I kept recording after the record was released because we had so many formats out. For the English charts you have the CD single, the 12-inch, the 10-inch, the 7-inch. If you put the same things on every format it's just a con, I think. What I used to really enjoy about the Smiths was that you'd buy a 12-inch and get two tracks that are probably better than the single, which aren't on the album. I like that value for money aspect of it instead of just being a con to make you buy more versions, you actually get something else. So, I put a load of new songs in various different formats. I've probably written an album's worth of stuff since the album which I've already used and I'm still writing.

Synching up US/UK releases?
If I don't get [the new LP] done before the end of the summer, it won't be out in Britain this year anyway.

Have you heard of French and Saunders? I did their series. They asked me to do a guest spot every week. Doing the music, but some of it was songs for specific sketches, like a girl biker sketch, so I wrote that for them. They used a couple of songs off the album: "Cowboy" and "15 Minutes."

How well did the LP do in the UK?
It's done about 85,000.

Has it gone Top 20?
No, but it's done better than anything I've had out before, but then everything I've had out before has been a joke in terms of getting it to the shops. That seems to be a major problem.

Which singles were released?
"Free World" was the first. Then "Days," then "Innocence." "Free World" did pretty well, considering I haven't had anything out since "A New England" apart from the Pogues. "Days" was a big hit. I did it because I thought a lot of people my age and younger wouldn't know the original, 'cause it was 21 years old when I recorded it. I covered it because I thought I could do a good job on it. I'd heard if for years and a lot of people don't know that song well.

I met Ray once before. When I had "Days" out he sent a message of goodwill and invited to sing it with him at the Town and Country club when the Kinks played there last summer. I was very nervous, but it was good.

You haven't done much performing, have you?
No. I went out with the Pogues after "Fairy Tale" was a hit, and I did some very disastrous touring when I started out around the time of the first album. I did a tour of the Irish ballrooms, which is not really the place to start. The band on that tour was Lu Edmonds, who later joined Public Image, John Dillon on drums, Gavin Povey, and [a bassist].

With the Pogues I did the British tour, the French tour and half the German tour. I'd come on to do "Fairy Tale" and then stay on and do backing vocals for half a dozen numbers.

Pete Glenister?
He worked on "A New England" and we write well together, so it's an ongoing thing. He's going to be working on the new album as well. With him and with Johnny [Marr], or whoever I write with, if they come up with a guitar riff, they can put it down on cassette whether I'm there or not. Johnny usually does it in my house; Pete usually sends me a cassette he's done at home. All I need is an acoustic guitar. If I get off on the chord sequence, then I get a melody and lyrics straight away. If I don't get off on the chord sequence, then I don't use it. It's a catalyst. I write the melody to the chords. Often they've had an idea that "this is the chorus and that's the verse and this is the bridge" and by the time I give it back to them that's the chorus, that's the bridge and that's the verse.

How did you first hook up with Gavin Povey?
The Edge played on my version of "They Don't Know" and they were the backing band for Jane Aire. I did backing vocals on her record. I enjoyed working with Lu and Gavin; I wrote a lot with Lu.

Liam Sternberg [producer of her first single] used them. I didn't get a day off work when they were putting the backing track down, so I arrived, met the band, heard the track and sang it. Then I thought it's a bit short, it needs a bridge or something, so we wrote the bridge while we were down there.

What were you doing careerwise at that point [1979]?
I was selling advertising space for an industrial magazine. It wasn't anything I planned doing long-term.

Your career was a bit slow to get off the ground...
No it wasn't. I had my first record out when I was 19. It just got slower after that. Initially it was very quick. After "They Don't Know" came out, nine months later Stiff didn't want to put out the follow-up, so I said sod this and went to Polydor. That was a nightmare, something I'd prefer to forget altogether. (The Stiff follow-up was called "You Caught Me Out" but it was never officially released.)

What would you have done if Stiff hadn't signed you?
I'd have gone to another record company, I suppose. I really like recording and you've got to have an outlet, someone paying for it. My primary thing has always been writing and recording. I was in this band, the Drug Addix, that split up, and we did an EP on Chiswick. I can't even remember if I sang on it. They chucked me out. I was the backup vocalist, just the spare tart, really.

How did you fare during the punk era?
I was always into pop music, I wasn't into folk music. Most people don't automatically take on all the things that their parents like, most people do the opposite. I did. I wasn't in the slightest bit interested in anything that they had to offer. I was a teenager and I liked David Bowie and the Beach Boys. Folk music is something I grew to like later.

How old were you when the Sex Pistols started?
In 1975, I was in the sixth form, just before I left. It was a great time. All I'd been thinking for years is to wait till I get out of school and write songs. Be a better guitarist. I always liked choral music and Bach. I listen to a lot of classical music. I like the structure of building up harmonies, that's why I like the Beach Boys and Requiem, Messiah, things like that. The power of voices is so much stronger than any other sound. When the punk thing happened, it was like suddenly anybody can do it. You don't have to have a special in or be a fabulous instrumentalist. Anyone could start a band, and anyone could get a deal.

Were you a pogoing punk?
On weekends, yeah. A weekend pogoer.

But it wasn't very vocal-oriented.
Some great artists came out of that era that weren't ever punk bands. Because it spawned so much energy, a lot of people who had nothing to do with punk — like XTC, the Buzzcocks. I was really into the Ramones.

Billy Bragg wrote some extra lyrics for A New England for you...
I said it was too short to be a hit. He wrote two more verses and we cut out half of each one and put what was left together to make one. I did all that bit in the middle.

That was a big hit? How did he like it?
Yeah. He loved it, but he liked the B-side better. The B-side was one of my songs, called "Patrick," and Billy was mad for it.

You sang on an album of his, didn't you?
I sang on "Greetings to the New Brunette."

How do you approach being a backup singer now, getting the call from some childhood idol or another?
It's a good buzz. It's flattering to be asked, because it means that people you admire know what you're about. They don't get me if they want three gospel singers, 'cause obviously they can get three gospel singers. If they want something different and they don't know what they want usually, that's when [they get me]. If it sounds like an interesting project, then I'm quite into doing it. There's no pressure on me when it's someone else's record. You don't have to write it, you don't care if it's not a hit — the end of your job is when you've finished your last bit of vocal.

They usually give me a free range to suggest. It starts off that they might have a few ideas, but then I sort of suggest that they let me just get on with it, and when they hear how it works then they usually like it. You have to build up the parts; you have to sing them the other eighteen voices that go with it.

Do you get involved with the artists on such projects or are they off somewhere by the time you arrive?
They're usually there. Some are more fun than others. I've got a bit wary. I did this last Robert Plant album — he was the last person in the world I expected to ring up and say would you like to do some backing vocals. I do the low bits, do I, while he's going *waaagh*! It was good fun, it was totally different, a new experience and everything, but... I did about four songs and charged very little for them and then one of the songs I sang on was sold to Coca Cola as an ad for about two million quid ("Long Cool Hot Woman" or something...) I ran into them about six months ago and he said, "Hey we just used eight bars of you on the new record, we sampled it off the album." Well, thanks for telling me. I felt a bit pissed off — I would have gone down and done it if they had phoned me up. It doesn't seem that he needs to save money that badly.

It must be a strain working for people when you have top people working for you.
That's the way it works: extended families. I knew Mel Gaynor 'cause I worked with Simple Minds that's how I met Steve Lillywhite. I did a whole album for Polydor with Pino [Palladino] that was never released. [her unreleased second LP for Polydor] When "A New England" was a hit, Polydor put out half of it as a greatest hits album with "Chip Shop" on it and half the album that they wouldn't release in the first place. So, what was the point? Either they like it or they don't. Don't release it if you think it's a pile of shite.

I really enjoyed doing David Byrne's Latin thing, that was great 'cause you get to meet all these great musicians. You're working with the best, and you're learning all the time. I've never done anything like that before.

Do you envision a point at which you'll be too busy to do backup?
No. I used to do it because I needed the money; I do it now because I enjoy it. I think it's a challenge to go in and sing a song that you had nothing to do with writing. Some you like better than others, but it's a challenge to do your best on that particular thing and to make it applicable to that song.

Have you ever bailed out after hearing what you've been asked to sing on?
No. I've said no to things before I heard them — you can't do everything you're asked. If you say no after you've heard it, that's a bit worse than saying no before you've heard it. I'm lucky that my people that I've worked with that I know it's going to be good. Morrissey rings me up and says come down and sing and I know it's going to be fun.

Besides the Pogues, have you been asked to do duets?
I don't especially want to do duets with people. It's not something I think about. You get caught up in the thing of who's famous, then. 'Cause if you're not as famous as they are, then you're jumping on their bandwagon. Who needs the hassle?

The lyrics to "Chip Shop" don't sound like something you'd make up off the top of your head.
I did. I made it up off the top of my head. It's not about anyone who looks like Elvis. Most women understand the title immediately. Every guy thinks he's Elvis under the skin — he's an egotist, this guy, looking he's in the mirror all the time. Elvis is a state of mind, not a persona.

I don't want the songs to be totally ambiguous, but every time you hear a song you add your own interpretation to it. You don't have to ring up Paul McCartney and ask him what it meant to him to make it mean anything to you. Beauty is in the eye of the beholder, and meaning's in the ear of the listener.

I think I'm getting better as a writer, and what I'm trying to do is to have it working on two levels. There's the personal politics, relationships and all that, but it's also a reflection of what's going on on a more global scale.

"Lonely Teenager in Love" — autobiographical?
No, that was just a piss-take of a country song. For some reason that I don't understand at all, I seem to have an affinity for country music. I seem to find it really easy to write country music. I think it's because I don't play very well. If you don't play very well, it's much easier to play a waltz than an upbeat guitar thing. I work out chords and I don't know what they're called.

[answer to an unasked question about songs]
The good ones are those that everyone can relate to. There's a lot of singer/songwriters, especially from England, who get that elitist I've-been-to-college-listen-to-my-record. I don't want it to be like that, I want people to whistle it while they're working on their cars. You can enjoy it for different reasons: the lyrics could make you laugh, or they mean something to you, or you just like to dance to it, or you just like to hear the voice.

"Sonny Jim" could be a country hit in America.
That would be great. I'd love Dolly Parton to do it, someone like that. That would be ideal.

The original game plan was to have something out for the college market and then put that out for the country market. I don't know if they're still going to do that. I'd really like that, because I've always been such a diverse writer. I don't ever want to stick to one style. There's not any one kind of music that is my kind of music. I'd like to reach more people and get on different sorts of stations. Here, there's so many categories. People ask what's your music like, and I say I don't know, it's bloody pop music! Someone said it's post-modernist. What's that?

How influential (on you) is working as a backup singer?
It gives you ideas of who you want to get on your own album. Working with David, I want to use his string and brass arranger. I want to come to New York to do the strings and the brass. There's good players in England, but we didn't use a lot of the brass that we put down for the album because it was too much Radio 2 (MOR). Over here, the brass is hot.

You're doing a new form of networking.
A lot of my friends do it as well. Johnny Marr does it. Johnny played and I sang on "Nothing but Flowers" off [the Heads'] *Naked* album. Yves N'Djock was on that as well. He's Salif Keita's guitar player. They worked with him in Paris and we all met here doing a video and I used Johnny and Yves on my album. Johnny worked on the same stuff with Billy Bragg that I worked on as well. We tend to do a lot of the same things. We both really like records, and we turn each other on to different music. I like working with interesting, talented people. It's a very inspiring thing to do.

There was quite a long time when I wasn't writing and I was having kids and stuff, when I couldn't write, I couldn't get it together and it was an opportunity to keep working without having the pressure. You don't feel completely useless. When you're working you can keep working. It's just when you have a block it's hard to get back. I'd had hit records out before I became a backing vocalist, and I was only asked after I'd had a certain amount of attention as a recording artist and a writer.

What was your first backing vocal gig?
I did stuff before I had records out. The first big band was Simple Minds. I did all the backing vocals on Tracey Ullman's "They Don't Know."

You were her writer for a while?
She was on Stiff Records and Stiff know a good partnership when they see one. She's really good at selling them, she does great videos, she's really fun and she can handle all that attention. I don't like all that, but I like writing, so it was a good partnership.

Who did "Terry" first?
I recorded it first. They used my backing tracks. We shared all kinds of things at Stiff Records. That's why I'm down as a co-producer.

How did you hook up with the Pogues?
We used to have the same manager. Frank had worked with me for five years and then I got married and started having babies, so there wasn't much for him to do. He met the Pogues and started managing them. I used to go down to gigs and say to Steve, c'mon, listen to this lot.

[*"Fairytale of New York."*] It's a great song. I wish I had written it. It wasn't planned out that I was going to do the duet with them. They'd recorded all their half and they were looking around for a girl to sing the other bit. I ended up getting the gig. I said I'll have a go and if you don't like get somebody else. No skin off my nose.

You record at a home studio?
Not the band stuff, but all the overdubs. We went in with the band last week and put down five tracks in two days, of which we'll use all the bass and drums and some of the guitars. Then we'll take them home and we'll get people in to do overdubs. I'll do all the vocals first, and if there's any space left we'll get some overdubs. The group was Mel Gaynor, Pino Palladino, Pete Glenister and Mark Nevin [ex-Fairground Attraction].

Is that going to be a touring group?
No. I'm not in the same league as Pink Floyd. I'd have to be them to employ all those musicians to go on tour. Touring is such an expensive thing to set up that I'm a bit loath to do it until I'm prepared to commit myself to doing it for months and months. It's not really worth it.

I feel like more of a writer and a recording artist than anything else. If you write a book no one expects you to go on stage wriggling about in front of TV cameras. I find it vaguely embarrassing. If it was all set up and there was a band ready to go that knew all the songs I'd do it. I just think you've got to be really committed, you've got to want to tour indefinitely otherwise it's not worth setting up. I wasn't in a position to do that with my kids being so young. I don't particularly want to be 7,000 miles away in some crummy hotel room phoning them up.

Creative marriage tensions?
With "A New England" we just thought we'd try it. I wanted to do that song and no one else was sure. I was sure it was a smash, like a Beatles song that's never been done. Steve was into it, so we got a band together and did it and that was a success. I'm happy when I'm working, I'm a dragon when I'm not, so I think he'd rather I was working than not. I'd rather use Steve to produce me than someone else, but if he was busy then I'd use another producer. He knows what I'm about, and he works very well with instrumentalists as opposed to techno machines.

I'd had records released that I'd written and I'd had hits before I met Steve. In America, he's much better known than I am, so people assume it's a teaching-your-wife-to-drive sort of thing. I get pissed off with that attitude. It's like you can't be talented just because you're talented; you have to be talented because your husband is showing you the way or because your father was famous. What's it got to do with anything? They always assume the male figure in the background is the one that has the talent. Steve is very talented but he doesn't write songs. I don't produce as well as he does. I like to listen to the things he's working on, but I don't interfere. He asks my opinions sometimes and he gets it. I don't sugarcoat it first.

Your half-brother is in The Bible...
Neal MacColl. My real brother, Hamish, I've written a song with him for my next album. I've got another half-brother, Callum, who's been in various bands.

Your father died last year. Were you very close?
Yeah, I love my dad because he's my dad, but I didn't always agree with his politics or anything. I thought they were quite old-fashioned and had been proved wrong a long time before they brought down the Berlin wall. People automatically assume that if your parents are very dogmatic about what they believe in that you're going to inherit it, and that's not the case. My dad was a bit surprised that all his children wanted to be pop musicians. I think he'd rather we'd been terrorists or guerillas. He really liked the last album. I'm glad I'd done that before he died. I don't think he thought much of what I'd done before, 'cause it was teen ballads and he couldn't relate to teen culture. It had to have a political message otherwise it was worthless in his eyes. I overcame that for him with this album.

Had he retired?
No, he was still working up to fairly much the last minute.

When did your parents divorce?
He left my mum before I was born. I saw him once a week, but I didn't grow up with that family. I feel sorry for my mum when she reads that I'm the daughter of Ewan MacColl and Peggy Seeger, because she brought me up. She spent 18 years putting up with me, why should someone else get the credit?

Why is the album titled Kite?

I wanted to call it *Al Green Was My Valet*. Virgin weren't too keen on that. We had to think of something else. Nothing [presented] itself to me that wouldn't mislead people when they're looking at the album. We needed something different. When we got Gilmour down to play, after we'd finished, we said thanks Dave, that's really great. Can we pay you, do you want to invoice us or whatever? He said, no that's all right. He said, just send a kite to Armenia, meaning a check for the earthquake disaster. I thought that was such a nice image, a hopeful bit of optimism rising above a sea of crap.

The dynamic between the strength of your lyrics and the sweetness of your voice? "Free World" sounds like a conscious attempt to sound angry.
I don't think I was trying to sound angry. The lyrics are angry enough just written down. I don't think it works to hit people over the head with what you believe in. I try to put a bit of humor in, a bit of wit to bring a smile to your lips while you're listening to something that might be quite aggressive. I get rid of my aggression writing songs, but I don't have that Tina Turner styled voice. It wouldn't sound convincing. I sing how I sing. I think it's good to have a laid-back kind of voice that's melodic. A lot of people don't listen to the lyrics.

I'm not the talking kind of singer, like Bob Dylan. It's melodic and it's musical and it's choral, but it's also saying something. I love the Mamas and Papas. Some of the songs weren't great, but Mama Cass's voice made everything sound fantastic, so it didn't matter.

When I pick covers, there's an edge to them. "A New England" was like that. I like an angle on a song. I just tell it how I see it. I'm not from the Laura Ashley school of prose. If you've got something to say, just say it. You don't have to fuck around trying to put it into words that don't offend anybody. If it doesn't offend anybody it's fucking meaningless. Either people are going to listen or they're not. If they are going to listen, you want to tell them what you feel. Why say "heaving mounds of flesh" instead of "tits"? I don't think there's any point in dragging it out and trying to make it obscure when you actually know exactly what you're talking about.

When did you first realize you could sing?
I always assumed I could, so there was never a question. I thought everybody sang. I didn't realize that other people didn't automatically do it all the time. When I was little, my brother was nine years older than me, so he had records and I didn't. I think I was three and a half when I got into "Good Vibrations," 'cause it was there and I was allowed to use the record player. I played it for about six weeks and I knew every single note on the A-side and the B-side. I knew every part. I began to understand where the different instruments came in, and how did they get that sound and what's that [imitates theremin]. That was enlightenment for me. It started there.

Have you worked with Brian Wilson?
No. I'd love to. My hero. I really like the stuff he wrote with Van Dyke Parks, like "Surf's Up," the best. I know people who have worked with him, and I'm so jealous.

Have you made overtures?
No. I did do a Beach Boys song once, "You Still Believe in Me," off *Pet Sounds*. It came out on Polydor as a single in '82. It didn't get any airplay or do anything.

The fire song on Smile...
That is so weird. We were thinking of doing something with that, 'cause you could sample it but it just started freaking us out. I started playing it and it started getting really creepy. There's something about that track that I think you don't want to mess with it.

Did you like Brian's solo record?
Yeah, I liked it. I wasn't so hot for the lyrics. (If you need lyrics, Brian?)

Who else would you really like to work with?
Mark Moore, who's got a band called S'Express. He's very talented and he's in a league of his own. I like Neil Young, but I wouldn't expect him to come and play on my record. I wouldn't mind going to sing on his, though. There's lots of people around that I like working with. It just depends who's in town.

Traveling with small children?
I usually leave them home. When we've come [to NYC] to work, if Steve's here for three months, we come as a family. They're in school now, so you can't really take them out every time you feel like it.

How old are your sons?
Three-and-a-half and five. The oldest one's been to New York twice, and the youngest one's been to New York once. They get around. We go to France a lot. We're going to Australia at Christmas. We're going to try and tie in some things to support the holiday.

I've worked in Paris and I've worked here. I really enjoy the difference. I like working, full-stop. But I don't mind where I am to do it. I don't need to be on a tropical island to be creative.

You did something on the last Stones album?
I did some backup vocals, but I wasn't specifically asked. It was anybody that happened to be hanging around the studio that night. [That was in New York.]

You got to know Johnny Marr through singing on Smiths' records...

Morrissey wrote to me in the first place and said that he'd read that I liked them, and that he liked my stuff and would I working on something or consider recording one of their songs at some point. I said, yeah definitely. Then I ended up speaking to him on the phone and he said he'd be in London soon we're doing some recording, and I should come down to the studio.

Is it hard to sing along with him?
He's a really good singer. He gets a lot of stick for his voice. I really appreciate people who don't sound like everybody else. Holly Johnson and John Lydon have great voices and don't sound like anybody else. Put anything on and I can sing harmony to it.

I don't demo the harmonies. I just demo the lead vocal. I do it on the spot. I know what I'm going to do, but it's time consuming, and there's no point to do it twice.

Can you explain to another singer how to do a harmony?
I never have yet because I always do my own, but I'm going to use other singers on the next album just for the vibe. And there's so many good singers around that haven't got any work as well. It wouldn't be worth getting in a load of singers and making them sing one of my parts, because then I might as well do it. It's what comes out of your head that matters.

Sound of your voice.
If I was nervous about letting my lead vocal come to the fore, I would just do more and more harmonies so you'd never have to hear it. The more of me there is, the better it sounds. But I'm trying to work on it the other way now to clean it up a bit and simplify it. A strong lead vocal worked on "Fairytale" and I think I should try a bit harder at that because otherwise it's going to be impossible to ever do it live.

Why did you sing in French on the new record?
I played that Kate and Annie McGarrigle track to Johnny Marr. He said, oh, you should do that. I thought, why bother? They've done it great. I don't think my version is any better than theirs; it's just different. I just thought I'd do it to see if I could, as an exercise. I go to France a lot, and there's a sign on the motorway in the South of France that says La Foret de Mimosas. That's so romantic: you don't get signs like that in England. You get good signs over here, you could write songs about Oklahoma City and stuff, but you can't write songs about Croydon, Rochdale. They don't have the same kind of ring to them. It's a film noir kind of thing: she's having an affair with this guy and she goes to the car park in the Foret de Mimosas to meet him every day and he shoots her and buries her because he doesn't want her going back to her husband. I like a bit of blood and guts in my films. *Red River*, anything with Montgomery Clift, Peter Weir is my favorite director. I like John Waters. I like *Eating Raoul.*

Covers of your songs?
I've got the German language version of "They Don't Know" which I put on when I need a good laugh. It's by Heidi somebody. There's a Japanese version which I'd love to hear. A NY punk band did "Chip Shop." They must have gotten the lyrics off the record and misheard. All the lyrics were slightly different.

Country women are strong...
That's true across the board: women have always had to be strong to do anything. They have to have kids, look after things, still earn enough money and still run their lives. When a man has children, nobody expects it to change his life. It might change it in little ways. That thing of kids not knowing who their mother is if she works, what about kids who don't see much of their fathers and still know who they are. Contraception has changed the world.

Gavin Povey and the whole Lowe/Edmunds crew?
I'm friends with them all, but we've never got around to working together. [My first LP] was very influenced by Rockpile. One of the first records I bought was Edmunds' version of "I Hear You Knocking." I like his voice and I love the guitars. I've always been a guitar-oriented person. Edmunds was going to produce me at one point, and then I

met Steve and I thought I might as well use him. It would have been all right. But I don't want to fall into that rockabilly kind of... I did a lot of that sort of stuff, but they do that and they're going to do it for the next 20 years and I want to do something else.

It's alright to write teen ballads when you're 19, but you don't want to be doing it when you're 30. I've got children, I've got more concerns about things than I did then. When you're young you can be totally selfish, but when you get older and you get responsibilities and stuff, you can't forget about them.

Do your kids like your records?
Yeah, they sang one line on "Innocence." But they prefer Michael Jackson. All kids like Michael Jackson. It's a fact of life. There's something on those records that only kids can hear. I used to love him as well, but not so much now. Who they really like is They Might Be Giants. They had a big hit with "Birdhouse in Your Soul." We played it a lot at home. I really like the album.

Do you take reviews seriously?
You take them seriously if they're really good. If they're really crap, you just think, what a wanker! This guy doesn't know shit.

Do you ever get people approaching you or Steve through the other?
Everybody that's ever come around the house has got a cassette from someone that they want to give him. You get an electrician round and his sister's in a band, and will Steve listen to this?

He's also got people writing to him saying I'd really like Kirsty to sing this songs. People send me reams of poetry and say, do you like my songs? One guy sent me a whole load about trout and asked me if I'd write the music for it. I didn't know what to say. It's funny. They say, I really like your work and then they send you all their lyrics. If you like mine so much, why do you send me yours?

Being a singer.
What I do matters to me very much. I wouldn't want to release anything that I didn't think was good. It's my life. It's what I do. It's what I've always done and it's what I need to do. I don't do it because being a pop singer is a good job I do it because I need to write. If I don't write, I'll feel ill. I'll get unhealthy.

Do you have a lot of unused songs?
Yeah. Loads. But I don't want to start dragging out songs that I did years ago to redo them. I want to get on with new stuff. Although I wrote a song with Marshall Crenshaw about three or four years ago that I'd like to do for the next album. But I have to have Marshall playing on it.

Stiff round 2
I bought my way out of my contract shortly before "Fairy Tale" was a hit. That was lucky: I would have been more expensive otherwise. It was worth every penny. I had to give them money to let me go even though they weren't doing anything anyway. ◆

Strolling Down Punk-Rock Lane

New York Times, 7 July 1996

The Class of 1976 held a reunion in the lobby of the Gershwin Hotel late last month. While inspecting a photography exhibition documenting their youth, several hundred New Yorkers gawked, caught up and swapped war stories. Familiar faces eyed each other with collegial recognition, extrapolating the passage of two decades behind fashions no longer matched in style or station.

If the congestion, smoke and din smacked of a packed rock club, the ambiance was entirely apt for the event that gathered aging rockers, a publication party for *Please Kill Me* (Grove Press), an oral history of the punk bands that rattled the walls of Max's Kansas City, CBGB and other fabled New York dives in the 1970s. Eddie (Legs) McNeil and Gillian McCain, the authors, mingled with punk elders like Richard Hell, Jayne County, Dee Dee Ramone and various Dictators, Demons and Dead Boys, whose unabashed and sensational testimonies to drugs, sex and debauchery fill the book.

On the previous night, Mr. McNeil and Ms. McCain took a walking tour of the East Village, stopping by some of the places that figure prominently in their story. With one exception, the sites have long since been converted and forgotten. The Dom on St. Marks Place, once a stronghold for Andy Warhol and the Velvet Underground, is now a bustling community center. Mothers, a bar on West 23d Street where Blondie used to play, is now an empty storefront. The Mercer Art Center, home to the New York Dolls, collapsed in 1973 and has been replaced by a dormitory for New York University's Law School. Only CBGB perseveres as a concert venue.

It was in 1975 that Mr. McNeil, now 40, first walked into CBGB, at 315 Bowery. Prodded by the promise of free beer, Mr. McNeil, a teen-age refugee from small-town suburbia, had moved into a 10th Avenue storefront with two friends to found *Punk* magazine. Talking his way into the club that momentous night, he spied and interviewed Lou Reed, the former Velvet Underground leader, and caught a set by the Ramones.

"In Connecticut, rock was this big thing that came to a stadium," Mr. McNeil said. "The concept of people playing their own rock and roll in a hole in the Bowery, to maybe 30 people, was amazing. I really felt like I'd walked into the Cavern Club," he added, referring to the Liverpool spot made famous by the Beatles.

Serving as the magazine's "resident punk," the budding journalist played his delinquent role to the hilt. "I came to CBGB every night," he recalled, stepping into a telephone booth he said was ideal for sexual encounters. "CBGB was like a clubhouse. You could work your way down the bar talking to everybody: Debbie Harry, David Johansen, Joey Ramone, Richard Hell, Johnny Thunders."

Protective of their local fame, the punks could be highly selective in their awe of celebrities. "When David Bowie came with Bianca Jagger and a bunch of bodyguards, I stole the hubcaps off his limousine," Mr. McNeil confessed with punkish pride.

Around the corner, on East Second Street, Mr. McNeil pointed to a fenced-in community garden. Somewhere behind all the vegetation was a brick wall where the Ramones posed for the photographer Roberta Bayley. Her portrait became the cover of the band's first album and helped set punk's visual style.

Across Second Avenue, next to the Strada Caffe on East Fourth Street, is the door that led downstairs to the 82 Club. In the 70's, this lesbian bar featured shows by cross-dressing glam-punks and their friends. Mr. McNeil, who noted that the New York Dolls made their drag debut at the 82, added: "This is where we had the famous drinking match between me and Handsome Dick Manitoba. It was the prize in some stupid contest in *Punk* magazine."

In the doorway of St. Marks Church, at 131 East 10th Street — where the poet and rock musician Patti Smith began her career — Mr. McNeil said it was rumored that he set a fire there in 1978. "I probably didn't have a good alibi," he added with a laugh. The supposed motive, he said, was that "we hated art and literature and poetry." As Ms. McCain noted, Richard Hell was curator of a Monday night series there before she became the resident Poetry Project's program coordinator in 1991.

Just off Union Square, a delicatessen is the only street-level business at 213 Park Avenue South, where Max's Kansas City, ground zero of the cultural decade, operated. Beyond the tales of Iggy Pop's bleeding chest and Lou Reed's scatological pickup lines, *Please Kill Me* details Max's role as a subterranean social club, the pre-Studio 54 hangout where Warhol's art crowd, Bowie's rock-star contingent and impoverished punks could meet and cross-pollinate.

"I did a famous Richard Hell interview here," Mr. McNeil said. "I passed out, and Richard continued the interview with my tape recorder." Mr. McNeil said he had to return the next day with a hangover to retrieve his tape recorder.

Mr. McNeil acknowledged that his behavior did not endear him to everyone. "Lou Reed hated me," he said. "I would have hated me, too. I was so obnoxious. I got away with everything. We just did whatever we wanted, and no one ever said no," he added with a laugh. "We used to come out of clubs and just take people's limousines." The musical glory days ended in 1979. "Everybody was on tour by then," Mr. McNeil said. "The New York scene went on the road."

He said he stopped drinking in 1982. "It was a big blow for me, waking up," he said. "I didn't know how insane I was. It wasn't until I got sober that I discovered how boring life really is."

He joined *Spin* magazine in the mid-1980s, extending his career to travelogues and international affairs. In 1988, he went undercover to write an unpublished book entitled *Yuppie Like Me*. He also contributed to *Details* magazine and in 1993 edited a short-lived magazine called *Nerve*. It was the failure of that project that led to *Please Kill Me*. "I couldn't do magazines anymore, and I wanted to do something I really loved," he said.

"The book is my memory," he said. "We might not have captured every fact right, but emotionally the book brings it back for people. I loved living there in my head again. And this time, I was sober." ◆

Other than one Cheap Trick marathon, this interview — conducted over two days — was the longest one I've ever done. It's amazing how personal things got. I don't know how I had the bottle to ask a lot of it, but Mac was game and never seemed put out. A true Scouser, Mac was loquacious, arrogant, open, a bit full of beans, larger than life and utterly fascinating. Unlike many artists in my experience, he seemed to enjoy being interviewed. While I've remained a fan, I've never since crossed paths with him.

A lot of the references in here no longer mean anything to me, but I will note that Lorraine was his wife at the time. And *Candleland* remains one of my favorite albums, a hauntingly beautiful masterpiece of loss and longing.

The impetus for this extensive interrogation was a *Rolling Stone* article that was assigned at one length (probably a one-pager), cut down due to space considerations and then binned. (Thank goodness for kill fees.) Here is the piece I submitted, with a title I've just given it, followed by the (much longer) first half of our conversation.

Ian McCulloch: Po-Faced on the Pitch

Unpublished, 1990

An hour before Echo and the Bunnymen went onstage in Osaka, Japan for the final date of a world tour in April 1988, singer Ian McCulloch was told his father had suffered a heart attack. He flew home to Liverpool immediately after the show, only to learn that his dad had just died. For McCulloch, so had the group. "I was determined he didn't die on that day for nothing." It was a sign to begin the new career he'd been contemplating. Last fall saw the release of McCulloch's first solo album, *Candleland*.

For ten years, the passionate, poetic Bunnymen ran on artistic ideals and conceptual whimsy, designing tours, records, videos and assorted happenings more to amuse themselves than to advance their fortunes. But as the four inspired amateurs matured into a successful, highly regarded band, the classic symptoms of a teenage marriage on the rocks surfaced. The Bunnymen, once an insular and close-knit unit, began coming apart.

From a Bowie-mad teenager harboring pop-idol fantasies alone in his room, McCulloch had become a genuine pin-up star, an articulate and opinionated media darling dubbed "Mac the Mouth" Although quick to deflate his self-importance in public, McCulloch could no longer sacrifice his individuality to the group. He resented the others' refusal to grant him first-among-equals status.

"I was getting frustrated," he recalls. "It was still meant to be a democracy, but it obviously wasn't. It had stopped working on that level." For one thing, communal songwriting was no longer productive. "I wanted to be able to come in with a song I'd written at home and have it be an Ian McCulloch song. In the early days, [guitarist Will Sergeant] would come in with chords, I'd put a tune to it and we'd have a song. Maybe I'd put some chords in, or [bassist Les Pattinson] would do something. It got to where egos were so fragile we'd all sit around a room for weeks trying to come up with a riff."

Sergeant was nonplused when McCulloch requested individual credit for his lyrics. "Will tried to make me feel guilty and selfish for that. They wanted to remain this selfless group where we were all in it together." After the 1987 *Echo and the Bunnymen* album was recorded twice with different producers and still wound up an artistic disappointment, McCulloch decided enough was enough.

"I couldn't see making another record with them. My self-confidence would have totally vanished if we had done another album that wasn't great. I needed to do something different."

In March 1988, McCulloch informed Sergeant of his desire to end the Bunnymen. "I said, 'As much as I'd love for us to carry on if we thought we could do it, I'm not happy. And I don't think you are. We all know in our hearts that it's not what it was.'" He finished the tour and called it a day.

When not spending time with his wife and baby, rooting for Liverpool's soccer team or going to pubs (an activity he describes cheerfully as "one of the pivotal things" in his life), McCulloch made *Candleland*, a wistful, autobiographical album that is more refined and poppier, but not that far removed from the Bunnymen's later sound. Producer Ray Shulman handled bass and keyboards, while McCulloch rose to the challenge of songwriting and guitar playing by himself. (Sergeant, who claims not to have heard the record, wishes his former associate luck but adds, drily, "I'm not going to be a fan.")

McCulloch subsequently assembled a band, the Prodigal Sons. Perhaps mindful of *Candleland*'s critics, he describes their style as "heavier, harder, a lot more layers; more what I want for the next album," to be recorded this summer. The quartet, which will accompany him on an American tour in March and April, played on three new songs for the British "Faith & Healing" single.

Sergeant, Pattinson and drummer Pete De Freitas (who had left the fold for much of 1986) decided to carry on with two new members: longtime musical associate Jake Brockman and singer/lyricist Noel Burke. Over McCulloch's vocal objections, the quintet — presently at work on a new album — is calling itself Echo and the Bunnymen, even after the loss of De Freitas, who was killed in a motorcycle accident last June on his way to meet Burke at a rehearsal.

McCulloch accepts *Candleland*'s relatively modest success — a no-show in the American charts and Top 20 in the UK, where every Echo album reached the Top 10. "People who leave groups generally sell less records. I feel better and more worthwhile selling less than the last Bunnymen record. I feel more important." But he still harbors affectionate feelings for his former partners. "When all's said and done, I wish them well. I wasn't just the one that ranted a bit in interviews and thought he was great. I thought the group were great." ◆

Ian McCulloch, 24 January 1990

You were once quoted saying the Bunnymen were the greatest work of art since Michelangelo's David.

I think actually it was about *Porcupine*, but it was still — probably more — extravagant a claim. It got to the point in Britain...You lead this sheltered life when you're in a hip English band. Two albums down the line and you're still hip. People say... It's titles like "Promise of Rock Reborn." You think I'll take advantage of this. Just before the backlash, the third album will be the greatest work of art since Michelangelo's David, which I don't think is one of the greatest works of art anyway. It's a nice statue, but that chair [pointing] is much more of a work of art. I'd met quite a few of these journalists and I thought if they can say we're that good, then I can. I was trying to deflate the whole thing. It wasn't meant to be pompous.

Great rock music is art, I think, but so what? The art you go and see in a museum is kind of lifeless, really. It was just me trying to take the piss out of a few people, including meself.

You've never been afraid of sounding arrogant or pompous to the press.

I think I'm like that in life, but whether that's a product of doing so many interviews and becoming more like that I don't know. Lorraine says to me, 'That's not really you, it's not the you I know,' but it is the me she knows because she always moaning at me for being like that. I do think people are too boring in life. That's one of the fears [I have] about meself: bloody hell, am I boring? Then I look at most other people and I think I'm not.

Xmas Melody Maker

I'd refused to read it. Even Mick Houghton, my press person in England, he said to Lorraine [after] a bit of a rant. Then I heard from other people they said it was fantastic. Then Lorraine got sent a photocopy and gave it to me and I started reading it and I thought this is the best interview I've ever done. There was a point just after *Candleland* that I did an interview for the *NME* [Danny Kelly] and I loved that one, it made me feel really sad, and Chris McCaffrey's girlfriend phoned me up and said I've read that piece and I'm so proud of you, and then she started crying. It became a weight and a burden and that's why the next interview I got drunk and went for it. I'm always flip-flopping from one style of interview to another. I don't mind, 'cause it goes along with me schizophrenia anyway. It's only mild, but if you're not schizophrenic in this business you go mad.

Before I did *Candleland*, the idea I had in me head — I was writing a lot of songs — and it was all becoming kind of 3/4. I thought yeah, I'll get some kind of Hungarian nose flute in there and be Jacques Brel. And then I couldn't write any words for it, apart from "I Know You Well," which I'd written before I started. It was nearly on the last Bunnymen album but I kept it back. I thought, you're not Jacques Brel. Then I saw Marc Almond, and if anyone was going to be Jacques Brel, or the camp Jacques Brel, then it was him. I write rock-based stuff anyway, although I do like singing with strings and stuff, and doing cover versions of Kurt Weill songs or something. It just struck me that you have to write songs that mean something to you. All the things that had been happening kept filtering through in the lyrics and I found the lyrics really easy to write, whereas the more European Brel-y type thing I thought it would be I just got stuck on. That was a really important part of me life. I knew from then what direction it was going to go in, instead of poncing about trying to incorporate as many variations or directions as it/I could.

The band's self-importance
Especially in America initially, we never encouraged the audience to like us one way or another. We just demanded that they respected us. In England, there's a lot of self-important little 15-year-olds who don't want to have written on their school bag a group name that anyone else has got. And that was the kind of thing we attracted. I think when I was that age I was like that: Bowie, the Velvet Underground. Bowie was kind of known then, but the Velvets certainly weren't. We were doing that when we were 25, and maybe we should have left that kind of mentality 10 years ago when we were 15. I do see groups now doing it and it's oh god, go and have a sodding game of football. I've started playing football again, and you can't be po-faced on the football pitch.

British football vs. British foreign policy
I've never seen any mass violence, although it's obviously happened. Liverpool was always a safe ground to go to as a kid. This season I went to see the 'pool vs. Man City in Manchester and we were in the Manchester section in seats. We were beating them 3-nil and these kids were giving me a bit of stick and I was giving it back. There was no way it would blow into something else. I've seen 50-year-old men about to do battle — in the seated area. From what I can gather, the hooligan element abroad is yuppie-type people, people who are lower class in background, but they've got this yuppie lower-middle class attitude. It's the kind of people who don't understand it, probably don't even play it. The yuppie thing in Britain is frightening. They think they've bettered themselves and that's given them some strength, arrogance. That's more common in the South. The suburbs of London, that's where a lot of the `lager lout' violence happens. Violence has always happened in Liverpool, but it's very rare that you see something blow up. I don't think I've ever seen a really heavy situation in Liverpool. It's burglars who are trying to become yuppies.

Crime seems to have become less prevalent in Liverpool. I don't know if that's because ecstasy's around and people are liking each other. Liverpool has come up in the last four years. There's been development in the center of town, the dock areas.

Is there a shadow of the Beatles left in Liverpool?
In Liverpool, the Beatles were always looked on that they left Liverpool in '64, '65. They say, yeah they're a good group, but... People like the fact that I still live in Liverpool, as though I could afford to live anywhere else. People think I must be a millionaire but I'm still living in Liverpool, and I go to football, so he's... They like that. When I go down to the old part of Liverpool town, near the river, and walk around, the wind's blowing and I think gee, the lads walked down this road with their winklepickers on. I always imagine it in black & white. It's great around there. You do get a sense of the Beatles carrying the guitars around.

Based on Tony Fletcher's book about the Bunnymen, was the desire to become ambitious, to achieve big-league success, especially abroad, the reason for the split?
Yeah, when I read the book it struck me like that, and thought, I never sodding felt, I was never that bothered. We had to get some kind of proper management, because our affairs were all in a mess, but at the back of our minds was proper management, proper results. You need a manager who understands the music, and I don't think [Martin

Kirkup and Steve Jensen] did. I don't think they understood us as people. They came in at a time when I was getting more and more frustrated with the way it was still meant to be a democracy when it obviously wasn't. It had stopped working on that level. Things had to change structurally within the group. I said to them it's either got to change or I'm going to leave at some point. I wanted to be able to come in with a song that I'd written at home. I knew I could never do that and say I've written a song and have it be an Ian McCulloch song.

Songwriting was always a group effort?
We used to sit around for like three weeks trying to come up with a riff. In the early days, Will'd come in and say I've got these chords, which was fine. I'd put a tune to it and we'd have a song. Maybe I'd put some chords in for the chorus, or Les would do something. It got to the stage where, because egos were so fragile, we'd all have to sit in a room playing dirty little bits. Once we got the groove going after a couple of weeks. We'd sit around, and nobody would say, let's get this written and finish it and we've got a song. [It became more like] Does anybody like this, or am I the only one? It was too intense. I wanted to be able to come in and say I've got this song, let's do it. It was always a bit like that with the Bunnymen, even in the early days. We were all a bit wary. More me and Will, 'cause he was negative and I was positive. I tried to pull him more into the center and by doing so pull meself more in the center instead of allowing the positive side to come through.

In the end it just got so I couldn't handle the pressure anymore. I know they resent me for...I don't feel happy just being a quarter. I felt it's great being a quarter of something that's working and being proud to ?, but I'm not going to stay being a quarter of this thing that's falling apart. It just got to the point where it could no longer work, and I couldn't see meself making another record with them, going through possibly two months of compromise and being around that kind of atmosphere. I felt it was crumbling.

Mentally, I wasn't in a particularly good state, and I needed to get out to save meself. If we had done another album that wasn't a great record in our eyes and the real fans' eyes, then the likelihood of wanting to make another record, either a solo one or with a band would be remote. My self-confidence would have totally vanished, which was happening towards the end. I need to do something different to get me self-confidence back.

Were you very disappointed in the last album?
Yeah. Even at the time I remember coming over to America to do interviews and all I said was "it's a good album, it's fairly straightforward. Maybe we've got rid of a lot of the pretentious side." It was hard talking about an album when I couldn't say I think it's fantastic. Or even I think it's crap. Or too heavy. *Porcupine* did me head in when we did that, and all I could say was it was a nightmare to make, but at least it was something I could talk about.

Do you regret having Laurie Latham produce it?
In the end it was partly me who did it. We'd done "Bring on the Dancing Horses" which I thought was really good because it was kind of a change in direction, it adds something. It was fairly Bunnymen, but different. It had a kind of solemn majesty. Then it went wrong, 'cause what we started doing was we wanted to get back rocking out, and we'd forgotten how to do it. We came out with all these riffs that were half-baked. It was all kind of tailored for mass appeal. I think the reason the Bunnymen were getting more popular in America was because the essence of the Bunnymen was finally becoming more liked. Just at that point, when what we were all about was getting to do something, we made it sound all weird, and the essence had gone. I do like "The Game" and I think "Bedbugs and Ballyhoo" is great, but that was probably better on the B-side of "Dancing Horses." I liked "Bomber's Bay" at the time because I liked the feel of it, but if I listen to it now I think it's not about anything. "The Game" was all about I was going to leave. It was funny writing that — it was like a two-year premonition.

Did the band suss that from the song?
No. I don't think they did.

Were you surprised?
I was, 'cause I think it's so obviously about them. I wrote it as Pete had left — he'd gone off his head in New Orleans — and the three of us went in and did some demos. I kind of wrote the chords, it was my song. Pete had sodded off and there was this little period of "let's do it, this could maybe be the thing we need to go on and do something different" and the demos for that album are much better than the album. Fragile, more the way we were at that point. I wrote the lyrics in about 10 minutes and after we'd done the middle bit — the Earth is a world, the world is a ball, stuff — Will said to me, "Mac, that's poetry that, innit?" Will was not the most academic of schoolboys, but I thought "cheers, Will, after ten years you finally..." Not that you don't expect that in a group, but you expect certain phrases to be "oh, I like that..." It was nice, but I could see he didn't really know what it was about.

Did you write that as an effort to set things in motion?
It was exactly that. I knew that they weren't getting the clues, and it made it a bit more interesting for me knowing I was going to leave, but let's play it out a little bit. There were certain things I'd do onstage, maybe start destroying the myth by not being moody and intense, having a good laugh. Maybe isolating the band from me and the audience. Little things. I thought if anyone set up the myth of this band it was me, so don't stand in the shadows and hide there forever. It's going to end. It was the most important thing to us, but the Beatles broke up and the world went on. It was less hard for me for it to pack in because I wanted it to end and I was the singer so I can go and sing.

Did you expect them to go their separate ways when you told them you were leaving?
It wasn't a case of me telling them I was leaving. I told Will before the end of the tour in Japan. It was roughly a ten-month world tour with two weeks off here and there. We'd just come back from an American leg and we were coming back to America for the second part of the last tour. We went out for something to eat, and Lorraine came, and Will's wife. I said, look I don't know how to say this but I'm packing it in at the end of the tour. He was really shocked and stunned (as we used to say from the Rutles film). I explained why. I said whatever part of history we'll have in the rock annals, we've got to make it as big as we can by leaving now, by packing it in now. I said as much as I'd love for us to carry on if we thought we could do it, I'm not happy. That will show through. And to be honest, I don't think you are, and I don't think Les is, or Pete. I think we all know it in our hearts that it's not what it was. There were all these arguments: if we do another record it could do a million in America. Will is the one who purported to be against that kind of reason for writing music. I thought maybe I'd be the one to say sod it, it's only music, but in the end I was glad it was me who called it a day. It makes me feel better as a human being, I don't feel as mercenary. Not that I ever felt mercenary, but I could see that I might become that. He agreed. Finally the tour ended. April 26 was the last show in Japan, and that was it. I went home. It was the 27th [me dad] died. It was too many predestined things going on. I was determined me dad didn't die on that day for nothing. I felt that me dad was going to say it's the end of the third era [decade?] of your life and it's time for the fourth.

A couple of months went by and people were saying what's happening, what are we going to do? When are we going to start writing some songs? I was quite surprised that anyone was bothered.

They didn't take it seriously?
They didn't know. Only Will and me. I don't think he'd told anyone. I think he thought I might change me mind. Although it was obvious — I never went out for a meal with Will. It wasn't me phoning him up saying I think I might pack it in. It was a guaranteed certainty. A couple of months went by and I thought, Sod it, I'll tell 'em let's meet, have a drink and stuff in the pub. I think they knew kind of what was going on. We sat down in the pub and I was nervous about it. It was very difficult to say. Particularly to Les. I felt Will would maybe go on and do some Enoesque stuff, maybe get some film music. I always thought he resented me for tying him down to songs. Maybe his forte was going off on tangents. I'm not sure if it is, because Will wasn't an extended solo person, he was little melodies. I thought Pete was already getting interested in bongo music, and he liked making films and riding his bike, and just

getting by. Plus he was a great drummer and could always play for another group. But I felt Les was more the boat-builder. He kind of picked up the bass one day. I thought he was great, but not as natural maybe.

Where did you and Will discuss your leaving?
In a restaurant in Liverpool. Prior to the second leg of the American tour; sometime around February [1988].

Did you cancel the last date in Japan because of your father's heart attack?
No. We cancelled one Tokyo gig because I had a throat infection. The last gig was where it would have been anyway. It was just an hour before going on that I found out. Someone had rung up the road manager, and they were keeping it from until after the show. He died as I was about half an hour from Liverpool on the plane. I'd spoken to him a couple of days before on the phone. [evidently he had previous heart problems] He didn't sound great, but he sounded like he'd be alright. He was mad, me dad. He'd go in the telly room and watch football and get all excited and have a cigarette and stuff. He was like that, you couldn't stop him watching football.

The shows are on at half-past six in Japan so I'd been to a sake tent and had a few drinks. I walked into the dressing room and Les said, "How's your dad?" I said, "Oh, he's alright, I spoke to him the other day." And Les said, "Oh." What the sod does he know that I don't know? I went up to him and said what the sod is going on? I've just felt the weirdest feeling. Curly, the production manager, said, look, he's had another heart attack and he's not too great. He'd gone into a coma. I thought he'd died.

I got meself together after a bit and did the show and it was fantastic, for me anyway. There was something in the air that had been missing for all that last year of touring. Certain songs were just out there. Will later said to me, when I'd told all the band, I knew that was the last one. The way you were, he said, I've never seen you like that. It was a fantastic show where the audience went mad which is funny in Japan; 'cause they're normally held back. They went over the barriers. It was a strange night that followed. I cried for hours non-stop.

Was your wife with you?
No, which I was glad about. She was at the hospital and she was there for me. If she had been with me it would have felt too weird.

When you told the rest of the group it was over, you expected them to go off and find different things to do.
Yeah. They actually all agreed. But it was unfair of me to expect that. They put ten years of their lives into it. The idea was we'd all go off. I'd said to Will maybe we could write together, but that was me lying to myself and him. I knew exactly what I wanted to do. When Will phoned up a few months later, I said why don't you try writing some stuff? He'd bought a computer and was started getting into programming some stuff. I said to him that's maybe what you'll be good at, and I'll just write songs, 'cause I think that's probably what I'm good at. A few months later he panicked and phoned me up a few times and said are we going to do anything or what? I said, well, I've got all these songs I want to demo. I was just puttin' it off. That was the final thing that he [???]. Then he phoned up a few days later and said Mac I've got something to tell you. I don't know how you feel about but me and Les want to carry on together. I said to him, great. I just took it as being a different project.

It wasn't the idea of them working together, it was their decision to use the name that bothered you...
Yeah, it was that more than anything. I still think that's pretty strange. I don't see why they can't set it up with a different name if they've got belief in something. Other people have done it.

They've got a new singer?
Yeah, he was in St. Vitus Dance.

Have you heard what they're doing?
A few people have said it's alright but it lacks something. I've heard a couple of songs I wasn't meant to. It was very rough, but it lacked something even at that stage. Maybe it was the first lyrics the singer had written for a new song.

Does he sound like you?
No, which is good. I think they should have gone for a girl, though. I do think it'd have been better getting a charismatic voice, more particularly a girl. They would have written differently, taken it somewhere else. When I first heard this fellow's voice, I thought it sounded like a weasel. It's not a particularly strong voice, but the tune's not bad. The lyrics aren't quite there.

Contracts?
We were all contracted to Warners. We had three albums left. Even me leaving the group I was still under contract for three albums; it doesn't get split between. I heard they were auditioning again, whereas I didn't have to do that. It must have been very hard for them. It wasn't particularly hard for me. The record company just said, yeah. They tried to guide me away from sounding like the Dead Kennedys, but there's not much danger of that anyway.

When all's said and done, I wish them well, whether it's with the name or not. They finally were left in a position where they should have understood what I did in the group more than just being the one that ranted a bit in interviews and thought he was great. It was more I thought the group were great. If they had understood that maybe they wouldn't have been left in a situation where I know Will and Les went through real doubts about what to do. Even now, I think. I do wish them well and hopefully they learn something from it, more so Will as a person — that what you have to do with anything is be positive for anything to work.

Who's in your band, the Prodigal Sons?
Steve Humphreys is the drummer who played in La Magia, which is one of Marc Almond's names. I met Steve and seen Marc Almond live and really enjoyed the show, found it camp and funny. I thought the drumming was great. I used [Almond bassist] Billy McGee as a string arranger on *Candleland* ["Horse's Head"] and happened to mention to him that I was looking for, initially, a drummer. [Humphreys] came in and met up with me and he's such a nice lad. On the first meeting, within five minutes, he was talking about his grandmother and stuff. I thought this is too weird. This fellow's too nice. I can't handle him. He's so enthusiastic about everything. Nobody in this group's scared to say what they want to say and to look enthusiastic. If anything I'm the least enthusiastic because I'm older.

Mike Mooney played on the *Albert Hall Tour* in 1983. It was New York, Boston, Reykjavik, Roskilde, the Isle of Skye, Isle of Lewis, Blackburn and the Albert Hall. It was a great tour. He was the extra guitarist on that tour when he was about 19 or 20. Used to wear shorts on stage: he's a right poseur. He throws all these shapes; does everything that Will didn't do. Which is good. I do enjoy having a guitarist that takes some of that burden off me. He's the lead guitarist and the resident mad comedian. He comes out with these weird monologues with a Yorkshire accent. The rhythm guitarist is John McEvoy. Edgar Summertime is the bassist; he's 19. He's dead dozy; the kind that frustrates me. He's got lips like tires.

Have you recorded with them?
The "Faith and Healing" single has the first songs with them playing. They're great; it's got more of what I want to get for the [second] album. It's heavier, harder, a lot more layers. A thicker sound. More reverb for a start.

Songwriting and guitar playing.
Songwriting wasn't a bother at all. You miss certain things not writing with other people. I think the songs are really good. I've proved to meself I can write a proper song — well, I always knew I could; "The Killing Moon" was my chords, and "The Cutter" and stuff. That's why it's important now to have the group on the next thing so that other elements come out. I still want to be able to say I've got a great guitar line here and I want to put it down. It's really difficult with a group — you don't get the time.

How much guitar playing did you do on the Bunnymen records?
I always played the acoustic 'cause I could press the strings down better than Will. I did a lot of rhythm stuff, but it was always mixed kind of low. Not too low on certain things. I never did any lead parts.

The guitar playing on Candleland is amazingly similar sounding.

The first thing was "Proud to Fall." I wrote that around the Christmas of '87. Just before I left. Although I knew anyway, that was the moment when I thought I can do it. Even though it was just the one song. I think I came up with the chorus first, and that line, "from start to finish, I was proud to fall." I thought, yeah, it was the first thing I've said that I'd wanted to say for yonks. I came up with the [sings guitar hook]. I thought, bloody hell! I'd never really done things like that. I had a little four-track and I was playing; not complicated things but nice melodic guitar. Then "In Bloom," I did that and came out with all this mad stuff. It was all very hamfisted, but kind of good. Then, in "White Hotel," I came up with that Lou Reedy freakout bit on the end. I wouldn't call meself a great guitar player, but for some reason on those songs I came up with the right parts.

Is "In Bloom" a doff of the hat to Will?

I wrote it on an acoustic initially; it was just three or four chords and me humming the tune. We had this groove and got a drum beat for it. I kept thinking if the Bunnymen, if I'd have gone in with that riff it wouldn't have been In Bloom, it would have been maybe something else that was good but that was a really important track because it was one of the last tracks I wrote. Then I thought the next album's got to be more in that vein. It was a doff of the hat, but also me saying I can do it as well. Will was possibly my favorite guitarist of the '80s.

Was the five-month hiatus Echo took in '85 important to you in making your decision to leave the band?

We had five months off and then did a cover versions tour which wasn't exactly taking the Bunnymen anywhere, and then we had more time off. We eventually ended up doing a few demos around August which became Dancing Horses. It was a year that not a lot happened. We never got back from there. That was just before Pete went off his head. I'd planned to do a few singles; I did "September Song." That came out and [misquotes the book regarding the impact of the single's failure on him]

Was that December 1984? Was that before the Bunnymen's hiatus started?

Yeah. It came out around November. Bill Drummond phoned me up during a tour and asked me if I fancied doing the single. It was the same day he said how do you fancy being the lead role in this play at the Crucible Theatre in Sheffield, which is this prestigious provincial theatre. I said it sounds interesting, but he said the thing is you've only got a week to learn all the lines, rehearse and get onstage. I was flattered to be asked, but then I met the director at the theatre and got on the stage and it was...no chance. It was ludicrous to expect me to do that in a week. I thought I can't even act me way through a Bunnymen set never mind a show...

Was "Start Again" hard to write emotionally?

Yeah. I've never really written a song like that, that kind of self-explanatory. There was a night in Paris [during the recording sessions] when I got drunk and I went in and thought about me dad as I sang it. I was choked up and I thought it was the best vocal I've ever done. Then I listened to it and it was all over the place. It was emotional, but it was crap. The following day I came in and sang it and it was a lot better; just understated. I do think it's a great song, but it's not necessarily what people want of Ian McCulloch. They might like me being the blaggard and rocking out...

Was that for Pete as well?

We were nearly at the end of mixing the album when I found out about Pete. I came home for the weekend and got this phone call. It was Les's wife. They'd just found out and thought I should be phoned first. We hadn't seen each other, or talked much. I still see Les every now and then. I love Les. I always said at various stages throughout the 10 years you're my favorite Bunnyman. I think he was, really. He was very important in the longevity of it. He had the most niceness about him. More naive.

It wasn't even particularly about me dad. Bits of it were, but it was more about me. It was about the Bunnymen as well. About me always being pulled towards sadness and getting meself in situations where I'm sad as though I like it. Now I've got this new band and laughter's become the thing I push meself towards. It's much healthier. Everyone goes through lows and stuff.

On the last Bunnymen tour, I isolated myself to a certain extent from them. I was flying everywhere 'cause I hated doing overnighters in a coach. A group is already the most claustrophobic thing you can be in, never mind sleeping on top of them. I remember Will saying to me, You seem to do things to make yourself sad. I said, I know, yeah. He tried to talk to me a few times because he saw me becoming a bit strange on tour, very remote and down. I talked to him for a little while, but it had gone too far. I couldn't tell him the real reason I was sad.

Is "I Know You Well" written for them?
You're the first person who's spotted that bits of it might be. Yeah, it is, kind of. Yeah, it is.

Was "Faith and Healing" written for someone?
That was one of the last or the last lyric I wrote for the album. It starts on a guitar riff that's a bit Barney-ish [Bernard Sumner of New Order] it became even more New Order-y. I had all these different tunes and finally I got this one that I thought was the right one. I was about to do me vocals and I phoned Lorraine at home and we had a bad phone call. It wasn't that heavy, it was just frustrating and unnecessary, I thought — not that it was Lorraine's fault, it was probably me being remote again — and I came back in and wrote the lyric. That's what it hinged on, or what created it, but it's also about the past again. I like the opening thing — the twisted end to all the words that I'd hung onto — it was kind of about me. I'd steeped meself in all this mythology and self-importance and it kind of left me clutching for things that weren't there. It's about that, really.

Were you once considered to replace Barney in New Order?
When we did that tour [together] I used to hang out with them more than I did with the Bunnymen. Barney hates going on tour. I was always in their dressing room. It was either them or me said, you might as well come and sing for us. Do you want to join our band? On that tour Barney asked me if I fancied writing with him and I said yeah, I'd love to. At the end of the tour Hooky [Peter Hook] asked me and I said yeah, I'd love to. I never did either because I couldn't have done both. I wouldn't have wanted to make the choice. I didn't want to get into projects, it had to be something definite.

Are you planning to do something with Peter Hook?
He has a solo group. It's actually pretty good. We meant to be doing the tour together in March. Initially we had a plan that we'd co-headline again and flip-flop as well. But his record won't be out in America in time for our tour. The plan was to do multiple nights in each city — three in New York, three in Los Angeles and two in most of the other towns. It would have been weird: a traveling circus type thing. I love Hooky and I'd love to do something like that with him, but I think to do your first American tour like that is a bit dangerous. For him as well. If New Order split up by any chance and he's going to do that, I don't think it's good for him.

How's your singing changed over the years?
I think it's less posey. I still miss going for the big notes, but they're coming back again just by having a rock band behind me. I know how I'd like me voice to sound. Most of the singing on *Candleland* is how I'd always heard me voice. If you listen to "The Cutter" it's more operatic. There's something in the tone of it that I don't like.

Have you gotten better over the years?
I don't know if me lungs are as strong. They are after I've toured. They take a lot of inflating in the studio. I think it's gotten a lot more honest, a lot more personal. A lot of people maybe think I sounded better when I was younger. I like a lot of the early stuff — "The Killing Moon." I do think I'm more of a crooner than a rocker. I do like the rocker things, but there's always that tendency to bring out the stadium twang. You need to convince people that this isn't just a rock song, that it means something. You can get a bit over the top. I like Leonard Cohen's voice a lot and Lou Reed's. As long as you communicate. It's something I do think about a lot. What's better? Me opening me lungs up and doing massive notes or doing the "Start Again" thing where it's more spoken and maybe means more for it?

Have you met Bowie?
He's the one that I haven't. It's probably just as well. I wouldn't mind meeting him when I'm about 50 and he's 60-odd. I've met Leonard, Lou and Iggy, and that'll do. They were all really nice, particularly Leonard and Iggy. Lou was nice, but he's Lou. You don't expect him to get the champagne out. I liked him for that, but I wouldn't like to be his best friend. I've had Leonard Cohen's number for a couple years. I phoned him once but he wasn't in. We were playing Montreal and I phoned and Leonard was in Los Angeles. Iggy's just a lovely, friendly fellow. But Leonard's the biggest gentleman you could meet.

How much education have you had?
I used to play truant a bit. Me eyesight went... I got two A levels. You do O levels around 16, A levels take you to 18. I only stayed on 'cause the idea of getting a job — at 16, I was about 11 compared to most kids. All these people were writing off to banks. Even now I find it hard to believe that at 15 going on 16 these people were writing off for jobs. You start your life around 10, so I was 5 really. I stayed on to ward off the job hunt. I wanted to be in a group — or a singer more than being in a group — and the punk thing started when I was 16 or 17 and I was going to a club at 17.

I was always the best in my year at what we call art, which means drawing and painting and messing about getting your hands scummy with clay, which I always hated. Because I was the best me mum said you'll be going to art school and I said no, I'm going to be a singer. She still says I promised her I'd buy her a cottage by the time I was 20, but I forgot to tell her you have to recoup the advances.

Me dad was into [me being a singer] because he used to sing himself in pubs and stuff. It was what I always said I was going to do when I was 13. I know that they were really proud — more than being proud of me doing something with me life, being proud of knowing it when I was 13 is what they should be maybe.

How does it feel to be 30 and grown up?
I'd call it late 20s. I'm only months into 30. (May). Feeling more mature felt good for a month. Then I couldn't keep it up: I just wanted to go to the pub and get drunk, do *Melody Maker* interviews. It's like the *NME* represent one side of me and the *MM* the other. There was all that stuff about it being a mature album and at the time I took it as flattery, because people said it's mature, but in a good way. The songs for the next album, it's more me being...there are some me out-Louing Lou lines. The next batch of stuff isn't about me, it's... thoughts, little comments on things. I'm not even sure what the comments mean, but I'm glad about that. I thought when I did the songs for *Candleland* that that would be the way I'd write forever, that it would always have to move me somehow. But I don't think it has to be. That happens when you feel like that and I'm going through a phase now where I'm happy and more outward, just a bit lippier and cheeky. That's part of me character as well and I'd rather write like that.

How old is your daughter?
Three and a half. She's getting cheeky. She's so clever. I'm sure she's telepathic. Lorraine says she keeps saying things that are weird, that are kind of what you're thinking. Maybe that's rubbing off on me. I love it when she says "sod." She got that from me. I say "sodding" so much. As long as she doesn't use any heavy words.

When was the meeting with the rest of the band in which you told them the band was over?
July 8th. [1988]

Besides songwriting, what did you do in the 6 to 8 months between then and the beginning of work on Candleland?
Went to see Liverpool a lot. Played with me daughter. Went to the pub.

Was it like a vacation?
Yeah, in a way. Taking stock. Evaluating my position. It was a break that I needed. I don't think me brain was in too healthy a state. It did me a lot of good. I'm still making all the same mistakes, but at least I make them less often.

So, you spent the time getting your head back together...
And now I'm getting it untogether again. ◆

Julian Cope

Moving on to my time with another member of the Crucial Three.

I wrote for *Spin* a bit in the late '80s. I never felt much connection to the magazine, which I could not help but see as a well-funded, less principled and better-timed alternative to the one I'd recently put to bed. But people I knew kept getting jobs there (a lot of them cycled through) and that meant freelance work for me now and again. Also, I never liked the magazine's design, but that didn't prevent me taking a tiny bit of Bobby Guccione's money.

The strangest experience I had there was when James Truman, on his way to becoming the mysterious creative overlord of Condé Nast and (more recently) the proprietor of a wonderful (but now defunct) vegetarian restaurant, Nix, in New York, was *Spin*'s Executive Editor. He pulled a paragraph from near the end of an article I'd submitted and moved it up to the beginning and relocated a sentence to somewhere that made no sense. As it ran, with this lazy, lame hed, the story petered out as if I'd just stopped writing in mid-thought.

I found three different drafts in my file — admittedly, it got better as the editorial process proceeded, so there must have been some beneficial feedback — and used them to construct a version of the article that makes sense, at least to me. Apologies for his occasional use of offensive language.

Julian Copes

Spin, May 1987

The gospel according to Saint Julian:

- People who are not horny make half-assed records.
- Artists have an obligation to serve as cultural proxies, and if that means substantial pharmaceutical self-abuse, so be it.
- It's totally cool to have hang-ups and really important to be tense.
- Pere Ubu, the Stooges and the MC5 were brilliant.

In the beginning, there was Liverpool. Not the Merseyside cradle of '60s beat groups, but the artified 1977-79 mecca that begat such musical catalysts as Echo and the Bunnymen, The Teardrop Explodes, OMD and Dalek I Love You. (It would also produce Dead or Alive and Frankie Goes to Hollywood, but every cultural upheaval has its residual trade-off.) The renaissance began when Julian Cope, a transplanted Welshman, formed a band with his friends Ian McCulloch and Pete Wylie. As Cope remembers it, "Wylie said, 'Let's call ourselves the Crucial Three — we're going to be the most legendary group in the world!'"

The apocryphal trio, which lasted for a few rehearsals and numerous arguments, came to be viewed as a seminal development in the Liverpool new wave scene. Within a year, McCulloch had formed Echo and the Bunnymen; a couple of years later Wylie was at the head of Wah! Heat. Cope, meanwhile, founded The Teardrop Explodes, an often oblique but attractive pop band that, by his own account, "took ridiculous amounts of drugs."

"When the Teardrops and the Bunnymen started, Mac and I wanted to be absolute megastars. We wanted to be the biggest cult heroes in the world, to be millionaires, to look brilliant and to be total bastards."

But that was all a long time ago. The Teardrop Explodes put out two albums and split up in 1983. Having met his American wife-to-be, Cope decided he was unsatisfied with his professional situation. "Halfway through recording the third album I realized I was still in charge, and all I had to do was say no. I woke up one morning and Dorian and I went home. I rung up from Tamworth and said, 'I think we've split up.'"

Cope went solo. Working with the Teardrops' drummer and a new guitarist, he took a batch of songs he'd written for the band and recorded *World Shut Your Mouth* (which doesn't contain the song of the same name, as he hadn't written it at the time). World offers relatively upbeat, idiosyncratic neo-psychedelia. His second solo album, *Fried*, released in 1984, is a tougher chew. "*Fried* was written in about a month of total depression. The reason I'm like this" — meaning sane, coherent and healthy — "is because I wrote *Fried* and came out of it. If I'd tried to do an album that was really together, I'd still be in a semi-fucked-up situation." Cope's logic may be obscure, but he does make sense.

After *Fried*, Julian did no gigs or recording until the middle of last year: "I was Mr. Paranoid — I never opened the door." The present activity of this popstar phase of his career got under way when he recorded demos of several new songs, including "World Shut Your Mouth," which recycled not only the LP title but two out of three chords to "Louie, Louie" as well.

To Cope's chagrin, "My A&R man said, 'These songs are shit, go away and write some more.'" He declined and was soon free to sign with Island, who liked the tunes just fine. By the end of last year, "World Shut Your Mouth" hung in the British Top 20 (a 12-inch mini-album, issued in the States, included a neat pair of covers: "Levitation," the 1968 13th Floor Elevators song, and Pere Ubu's odd romantic ode, "Non Alignment Pact"). His next 45, "Trampolene," also did well, setting the groundwork for the album, *Saint Julian*, his most impressive and accessible record yet. (Double DeHarrison, credited with keyboards and some production, is actually Cope.)

And with the album, of course, a tour. In a late February show [*at the Ritz, 2/26/87*] being taped for MTV broadcast, the quintet is dressed ominously in black leather, enveloped by the occasional spew of smoke generators. Cope plays very little guitar, concentrating instead on singing and posing through a career retrospective in a variety of styles that suggests everyone from Donovan to Iggy to the Doors to Echo. Cope's psychedelic sensibility is obvious: songs stretch and writhe with abandon; sounds ebb and flow in the mix in disordered, unsettling fashion. He sings without restraint, seeming only semi-cognizant of the audience. He wraps himself around a custom-built, industrial-strength mic stand contraption with steps built on it. ("We wanted the most low-tech, Luddite thing. We didn't want something that was kind of faggy or too rock'n'roll. What I like about it is you can throw any shape you want on it and whether it looks ugly or beautiful, it's a good shape, a good ugly shape, a good, beautiful shape. I've always thought of the mic stand as the altar, and the lectern, and a phallic symbol. It's almost like sucking your own cock onstage.")

With his steel pipe whatchamacallit for assistance, Cope is a slithering serpent, alternately lurching out at the audience and resting back, sated. He's a right poseur, to be sure, but with enough unselfconsciousness to make it more play than pomp. His true dramatic value comes to the fore when the band finally gets around to playing what the audience of MTV kids came to see: "World Shut Your Mouth." Cope begins it as an easygoing lounge lilt, sticking to just the verses, teasing the crowd by withholding the anthemic chorus, and threatening to finish it without ever making it sound like the record. After what seems like an eternity, the band accelerates into total rev and runs through the entire number the way it's s'posed to be. The result is orgasmic, dizzying. The audience gets just what it wants, delivered in a fashion that makes it seem far more than the obligatory performance of a hit single.

Asked a few days later about the revision, Cope offers a fascinatingly convoluted explanation. "So much of *Saint Julian* is the idea of newness. I love the idea of the first person to have sex. It's like the Mona Lisa — there was a time when Leonardo sat back and said, 'I think it's finished.' The idea of the long version of 'World Shut Your Mouth' was going into this garden and the idea of everything being so cool that you let certain things go past that are really not good. But when you've got a relationship, you think, I won't question that bit for a while 'cause this scene's really good.' The long version has got a real shape to it. It's very erotic, isn't it? It keeps building — it's like a massive orgasm!"

With some justification, people often reckon Cope to be postpunk's answer to Brian Wilson or Syd Barrett — a harmless, drug-addled lunatic with a penchant for inactivity and isolation. With some justification, he vehemently disputes the comparison. "However depressed or untogether I've been, I've always been aware of it, and I've written songs that explained those things." Although his ability to function like a normal individual in the world is obvious onstage and off, the acid-casualty rep has proven hard to shake. "I really don't want people saying, 'There's Julian Cope — he's really off his box.' I've spent the last few years being really together.

"When people expect you to be off your tree all the time, you really straighten out. People are so pleased I'm lucid." In fact, he's not only lucid but extremely intelligent, analytical and rather charming, if a little spacey at times. He fights for the right to be mundane. "Sometimes you just feel bland — everybody does. Sometimes Vincent Van Gogh must have thought, 'I think I want some coffee.' You've got to live day to day."

Cope is admittedly no stranger to controlled substances. "I never advocate drug-taking, but for myself it's all right. Artists have to feel more brittle and tense; they have to be more fucked-up. A lot of people enjoy things by proxy — it's a necessity of the world. If everybody goes around out of their minds, nothing gets done. I get paid to be Julian Cope. It's like when you listen to Nick Drake: not everybody wants to be Nick Drake — it's the most tortuous thing you could be — but thank god for his existence."

Despite the hippy-tinged vocabulary, Cope is no stuffed paisley shirt with flower-power pop tunes and a cabinet of Kaleidoscope records. "I've taken acid over 150 times. You get so much into your system that you get to a point where you question everything. There's absolutely no way your everyday life is not seething with that questioning and bewilderment."

Through the agency of Owsley, Julian Cope has made a veritable religion of questioning and bewilderment. He's located a unique path of intelligence and sanity that is bordered on the edges by idiocy and madness. His whole-hearted commitment to love and humanity is primary and true. Through his music, this mundane saint fancies himself a selfless tool of society, somehow serving the greater good by pounding stages like a clown. If that exalts the chosen one and thus dignifies the lot of man on Earth, then Julian Cope is a pretty good musician. ◆

Cope was a strange and challenging interview subject; among other things, his leather clothes gave an aroma that smelled like semen to me and — not coincidentally, I thought at the time — his ideas kept circling back around to sex. And drugs. At lunch, he drank six cups of black coffee. At the time, he was preparing to marry Dorian Beslity, an American Who fan I'd met through mutual friends from New York University. Almost 40 years later, they're still together, living in England.

Julian Cope, 28 February 1987

When the Teardrops split up, I had to smash what had become a really big business. Dorian and I went to live in Tamworth. I met her March '81; Teardrop split up May '82. Dorian and I got the house in April '82. We had a year that was quite hellish 'cause we were miles apart. We started to get that domestic scene together, and that's what really crippled the Teardrops. I met Dorian and thought, I can do this much better. We spent all that time in Tamworth.

I'd written the entire third Teardrops album, and Dave Balfe said to me, "Why should you write all the songs?" He said, "You get all the money." I didn't get all the money. He said, "I want to write some songs." So, he went away and I think listened to every Teardrops song ever and came back with facsimiles. Very accurate. He stuck me in the studio with his backing tracks and I sang away.

When I finally got these songs, it seemed preposterous. They were horrible. Halfway through recording the album I realized I was still in charge and all I had to do was say "no." I woke up one morning and Dorian and I went home. I rung up from Tamworth and said, "I think we've split up." *World Shut Your Mouth* was really the third Teardrops album played by me. The LP was positive in a lonely way. *Fried* was the album where I suddenly thought, wow. The strange part about that is that my most untogether period was when I was recording *World Shut Your Mouth*. Luckily, I had all those songs, so I went in and did them. I was together enough to know how they should sound. *Fried* was written in about a month of total depression — feeling hellish. Then people started to appear on the scene who were really helpful — Callie, Donald. All my albums have been like an apologia.

The Teardrops did take ridiculous amounts of drugs.

Mac's not part of a very horny relationship. It's completely different from Dorian and me. Dorian and I still go out and fuck on trains, we still get completely out of it and trip out in the country." "I don't think the Bunnymen are such tense human beings as me. It's really important to me to be tense."

The Crucial Three was Wylie saying, "Hey, let's call ourselves the Crucial Three — we're going to be the most legendary group in the worlds. At the time, Mac and I were such spazzes. If you'd seen me and Mac and Wylie — we were complete dorks. I've got photos from this period, and Wylie's the only one who looks cool — Mac and I were such young punks. Wylie was into Springsteen and the Blue Öyster Cult. We were into the Stooges. We were the cool ones. I don't mean to slag Wylie off, but he was always trying to convince us the Boss was a really a punk.

We were very aware of creating history. I don't know whether that spoils it or not. We were all basing ourselves on Detroit and the 1974-75 New York scene. Gary had been playing drums eight weeks when we did our first single. When the Bunnymen did their first single, Will had got the worst guitar in the world and the only things he could play were the two songs they did on the single.

"Books" is from 2/78. We wrote a lot of songs together. In Los Angeles in 1981, a girl played me a tape of me and Mac doing "Louie Louie" together in a Liverpool coffee shop in 1977. It was the only time we'd appeared onstage together before the Teardrops and the Bunnymen. We did a version of this song of Mac's called "Robert Mitchum." She wouldn't give me the tape.

The title of "World Shut Your Mouth" came from a guy who said to me in 1978 that "the reason I like this music is because it sounds like you're telling the world to shut its mouth." We record everything because I always have this stream of consciousness thing. We recorded the whole Italian tour last year where we were doing this long version where I would garble. I went through five different takes; as it came along it started to take shape what the song was about. So much of the St. Julian idea is the idea of newness. I love the idea of the first person to have sex when Adam and Eve were here. They landed here and thought, everything is brand new.

It's like Mona Lisa — there was a time when Leonardo sat back and said, I think it's finished. I love that kind of brand newness. Everybody's got this love of nostalgia. They forget how wonderful it is when something is brand new. With "World Shut Your Mouth" the idea that came out of the long version was that it was going into this garden and the idea of everything being so cool that you let certain things go past that are really not good. But you know when you've got a relationship you think, "I won't question that bit for a while because this thing's really good," this scene that we're going down here. I used to have a great hatred of taking things apart and then working them out. With the long version of "World Shut Your Mouth" it's got a real shape to it now and it's really beautiful. It's very erotic, isn't it? It keeps building — it's like this massive orgasm. It's a wank!"

I find the Bunnymen just a little bit half-assed. So, my rock'n'roll life is not separated from my domestic. The whole thing is one big course. I'd like the Bunnymen to sound less... it's very nice, but I wouldn't have gone the orchestrated way.

My songs are completely based around the way I feel, the way that I'm living at the time. By writing songs that way, you write them out of your system and you go into another phase. The reason I'm like this is because I wrote Fried and came out of it. If I'd tried to do an album that was really together, I'd still be in a semi-fucked up situation.

I think it's totally cool to have hangups — I'm really hung up about a lot of things. Everybody tries to throw their hangups off as quickly as possible; I think mine are my most appealing side.

When I first started writing songs, everything had to be the most unusual thing in the world, to be brand new and not have roots in anything. Now my songs are much simpler. When you get older, you stop worrying about everything having to be brand new.

I've never been like Syd Barrett or Roky Erickson, because however depressed I've been or untogether I was, I've always been aware of it, and I've written songs that explained those things. Robyn Hitchcock's always been far more whimsical than me — his songs seem far more in a Monty Python area, which is not what I'm interested in.

I get people saying, 'Hey, you're really normal' and so pleased I'm lucid. Sometimes you just feel bland. Sometimes, Van Gogh must have thought, "I think I want some coffee." You've got to live from day to day.

When I went to Tamworth, Donald [Skinner] was a 17-year-old Teardrops fan. I was Mr. Paranoid — never opened the door. Dorian opened the door for me for about the first year. He would knock on the door, but we would only answer for people who'd rung [called] first. Then one day my father was due to come 'round, and there's this knock on the door and I opened the door and, "Hello, I'm Donald." Donald came in and he was the most fresh person I'd ever met. He was into Lee Underwood — Tim Buckley's [lead] guitarist — and I thought, a 17-year-old guitarist in Tamworth being even aware of Lee Underwood, that's amazing. I heard his demo — he was in this group that were really crap, but the guitar was fluent and beautiful, like Robby Krieger. I asked if he'd like to do a Janice Long session on Radio 1. His A-levels were trashed. He actually made me see things really better. He's been around for ages. He was on *Fried*.

Who are the musicians on Saint Julian?
Chris [Whitten], who's playing drums, played on *Fried.* He was in the Waterboys, and he'd had such a burning experience where Mike Scott would be horrible to him. James [Eller] played bass on the second Teardrops album. I was always a real paranoiac as far as bass was concerned because I'd been a bass player and to meet someone who's technically capable of everything but doesn't need to do it is great. I'll play him the bass line and he just makes it his own. And he plays it so sexually. The fourth member is Double De Harrison, who's me. The extra guy on stage is Keith-Richard Frost [Richard Frost]. He's going to be playing on the next album: He's someone Callie knew and he's played with a lot of people.

I took the demos for "World Shut Your Mouth," "Shot Down," "St. Julian" and "Eve's Volcano" to Polygram and David Bates, my A&R man, said these songs are shit, go away and write some more. I said, no. This is the fifth album that I've done. So, he said, I'm not really interested then, we might as well forget the whole thing. As soon as Bates found out Island was interested, he changed his tune. I love the fact that he dropped me on those songs.

I've always been completely anti-heroin. I've always had tremendous morality in my drugtaking. I think coke is a real bad drug, speed is a really bad drug. But they're really bad for other people. Caffeine is a real bad drug, but I have as much as I possibly can. This isn't meant to sound elitist, but I think artists have to feel more brittle, and they have to feel more tense and they have to be more fucked up. A lot of people enjoy things by proxy — it's a necessity of the world. It's like the way Morrison used to go on about the shaman. If everybody is going around out of their minds, nothing gets done. In a way, I get paid to be Julian Cope, to be a celebration of yourself. If taxi drivers and everybody are going around tripping out, then nothing gets done, but if they come and see me, or they listen to the music, there's a certain release. It's like when you listen to Nick Drake. Not everybody wants to be Nick Drake — it's the most tortuous thing you could be. But thank god for his existence. That's why I never advocate drug-taking, but for myself it's right. It's not meant to be elitist, it's that we can't all be exactly the same.

I've always been anti dressing in a stylistically psychedelic way, because psychedelia to a lot of people is paisley shirts and all that. I've taken acid over 150 times, and I'd never do one trip, I'd do like five trips — the most I ever took was 15 trips at once — you get so much into your system that you get to the point where you question everything. There's absolutely no way your everyday life is not seething with that questioning and bewilderment. I've never called it psychedelia which has become a retrospective term.

I've spent the last few years being really together. When you go so far over one way, and people expect you to be off your tree all the time, you really straighten out. I'm being really together, and I enjoy being really together. I meet loads of people and they meet me, and they act really flaky. I met Zodiac Mindwarp, and the guy walked up to me and said, "Haiiiiihhhhh." I said hello, how are you and immediately I went into this super straight trip, 'cause I really don't want people saying, "There's Julian Cope, he's really off his box." If you stick me in a suit I'll act like a guy in a suit, 'cause I can do it.

I did an interview in San Francisco. The guy was really pissed off. He said, "I didn't enjoy the show — you're really together." I said, "What are you saying?" He said, "I've always thought of you as one of rock's great eccentrics." I said, "So, therefore, I have to be untogether?" I felt the most eccentric thing I could do was to make an album that was really together, without a sleeve of me hanging upside down with my dick hanging out. I'm not going to apologize.

When Zoo [Records] started, and the Teardrops and the Bunnymen started, Mac and I wanted to be absolute megastars. We didn't want to be small cult heroes — we wanted to be the biggest cult heroes in the world and we also wanted to be millionaires, and we also wanted to look brilliant and be total bastards. We wanted everything! When we recorded [Treason] on Zoo, Dave Balfe immediately went out and booked a holiday, thinking it was going to be Top 20 immediately. I loved that optimism! It was understood in Liverpool that you had to make it, and that you weren't going to sell your ass to do it — you wouldn't even consider that. You really had to try and sell!

I only slag people off who are the best at what they do.

I always used to break up mic stands. When we did the Hammersmith Palais gig about three years ago, I cut myself up pretty badly — loads of people fainted and all that bullshit. So, when we did the Italian tour last year, I was doing the same stuff again, breaking all these mic stands, and it was becoming financially not viable, so my manager said we're going to have to make something more brutal that you physically cannot destroy. We looked into what would be the most low-tech, Luddite thing you could have, 'cause we didn't want something that was kind of faggy or too rock'n'roll, so we just started to work on something that was very, very heavy that I could actually get into. I've always thought of the mic stand as the altar, and the lectern, and a phallic symbol. It's almost like sucking your own cock on stage. You get really into the microphone. We started to formulate what it was, and we asked this old guy, Tommy the Welder, if he could build us something really brutal. We didn't want something that was going to be chromed and perfect. What I like about it is that you can throw any shape you want on it, and whether it looks ugly or beautiful, it's a good shape, a good ugly shape, a good, beautiful shape. ◆

Tears for Fears

The cassette of my 90-minute hotel room interview with Roland Orzabal went to the *Rolling Stone* research department to confirm his quotes and never came back. (Ditto for the even longer Curt Smith interview I did the next day.) Fortunately, I had transcripts of both in my files. I *do* have tapes of my phoners with Nikki Holland and Oleta Adams, neither of whose comments are in the published piece.

Orzabal was a full-on British snob: self-assured to the point of smugness, a bit condescending and chilly. Some of his answers were unhelpfully brief. But in expansive mode, he was extremely thoughtful, smart and articulate. I couldn't agree with a lot of his ideas and was struck by the insane pointillist approach he'd used to create *The Seeds of Love*, basically editing it together note by note, using sampled instruments triggered by recorded performances. The album came out fine, but it's hard to hear how it benefited from being created that way. If top-notch musicians are incapable of playing songs adequately to be released to the public, maybe they're not the problem.

I listened to the album for the first time in a while recently, and found it sterile, unaffecting, soulless and dull. The audio quality is amazing, but all that musicianship went in service of what? To be sure, the single is brilliant, and "Woman in Chains" has a certain glossy power, but otherwise the LP is no better than a baritone-voiced Steely Dan.

Fear of Finishing

Songs From the Big Delay: How Tears for Fears Took Four Years to Sprout The Seeds of Love.
Rolling Stone, 16 November 1989

Rome wasn't built in a day, but any group that can while away four years perfecting eight songs might consider hiring an efficiency expert. The Beatles, after all, knocked off *Sgt. Pepper's* in four months. Still, singer, songwriter and guitarist Roland Orzabal and singer and bass player Curt Smith — the two members of Tears for Fears — are quite content with their investment of time, energy and money in their new album, *The Seeds of Love*. Orzabal calls the period "the best years of my life — I learned so much and had a really good time." Smith says, "This album was time-consuming but easy to make."

Tears for Fears' second record, *Songs From the Big Chair*, and their ensuing 1985 world tour elevated the uncommonly literate musicians from Bath, England to superstardom but left them exhausted and uninspired. Rather than exploit their commercial ascendancy with similar-sounding product, Orzabal and Smith, now both 28, clung to the freedom such success grants. They took a year off and then, like other shell-shocked artists from Brian Wilson to Tom Scholz, sought refuge in the recording studio.

Two false starts, roughly a million dollars and 17 productive months later, Tears for Fears emerged from their co-coon with a challenging, ambitious album that Orzabal likens in its density to a Tolstoy novel. Detailed and intricate without sounding belabored, the record is both a striking departure and a sizable achievement for the band. Forays into jazz pop, blues and soul — plus a delicious Beatles parody, "Sowing the Seeds of Love" — reflect the pair's creative progress, as well as the profound influence of two piano-playing women: Nicky Holland and Oleta Adams.

Holland, who was Fun Boy Three's musical director, sang and played keyboards on Tears for Fears' 1985 tour. She began composing onstage with Orzabal during soundchecks, complementing his guitar-oriented style with her classical influence. She receives co-writing credits on five songs on *The Seeds of Love*.

Holland and Orzabal's first collaboration, "Badman's Song," struck him as the perfect vehicle for a duet with Adams, whom he had seen performing in a Kansas City supper club. Although Orzabal hadn't realized it then, Adams would eventually answer many of his concerns about the band's musical future.

Determined to expand their stylistic and emotional range, Orzabal and Smith had begun working with producers Clive Langer and Alan Winstanley at the end of 1986. They quickly deemed the experiment a mistake and returned to longtime collaborator Chris Hughes. Ten months later, however, finding the results sterile and convinced that

Hughes wanted to remake their old records, the two musicians scrapped the unfinished tracks and decided to produce the record themselves. "To be artist and producer is a lot of work," says Orzabal. "You have to get into very boring, mundane things — what producers should do. You either look for someone who is at least one step further than you in their vision or somebody who can help articulate yours." They chose David Bascombe, engineer on *Songs From the Big Chair*, to be their co-producer.

After fashioning two albums mostly on Fairlight synthesizers, the duo aimed to add spontaneity to the process by involving more live musicians. A band, they reckoned, even a temporary one, would provide the extra dimension they were lacking. To that end, Oleta Adams, drummer Manu Katché, guitarist Neil Taylor, bassist Pino Palladino, percussionist Carole Steele and keyboardist Simon Clark assembled in a London studio in February 1988. Smith and Orzabal taught them several songs and then retired to the control room.

For several weeks, the band played dozens of takes, exploring the songs. Then Orzabal and Smith began the painstaking process of editing miles of digital recording tape, note by note, into what Orzabal calls the ultimate performance. "Musicians have their own style, which is wonderful," he says. "You take what they've done and insert your own personality, doctor it, structure it. The trick is to create something greater than yourself. A lot of spontaneous things have been collected and assembled on this album." Ironically, the sextet's efforts appear on only three songs. The five remaining tracks were, like the band's previous albums, performed by Orzabal and Smith, using overdubbing.

Orzabal and Smith both soft-pedal reports that Phonogram put pressure on them to hurry their project along. Their label was "a bit concerned, but pretty much left us to our own devices," says Smith. Then he adds wryly, "Not that they had tons of choice in the matter. They couldn't physically make us make a record." Nonetheless, to mollify the label executives at the end of 1988, producer Bob Clearmountain came in to mix "Woman in Chains" and "Year of the Knife." (Ever the perfectionists, Orzabal and Smith ultimately edited together two different mixes of the latter song — one Clearmountain's and one Bascombe's.) *The Seeds of Love* was finally declared complete this June.

On the eve of another massive world tour, which should begin in Ireland in the first week of January, the two musicians defend their painstaking efforts to meet their artistic standards. "Complex characters create complex visions and complex music," declares Orzabal with the ingenuous arrogance of the truly self-righteous. Smith is more modest, saying, "Maybe if we were smarter and better at what we do, it wouldn't take us as long." ◆

I doubt that my questions, as rendered here, are the actual words I spoke; my feelings about the tenor of our interview led to a bit of passive-aggressive self-amusement when I transcribed it.

Roland Orzabal, 25 September 1989

What's the story, Roland?

For a long time on *Q*'s Mutterings page they kept talking about TFF still doing their difficult third album, so in a sense the story was already written. It was totally, ridiculously biased, almost verging on the gutter press.

Are there ways in which the story is factually incorrect?

My perception of what happened is simply this: not a great desire to get back into the pop circus. Quite definite, not so much time-wasting, as an investment in time in the sense of taking our time over things, getting them right and not believing there was a hurry. Just trying to live outside of the evil eye of the television or the media, just to live a normal life.

I'm very, very critical. I know what I'm happy with [about the album], I know what I'm not happy with. I know it backwards, I know every thread, every single line. Ultimately, other people are going to hear it slightly differently. To some degree it's like looking in a mirror.

What was the net result of your ten months work with Chris Hughes?

It's quite amazing, but there was nothing I could have actually sat down and played you. It's almost like we were looking for the essential missing piece of the jigsaw with Chris, but funnily enough we didn't actually find it 'til we stopped working. There was a problem with the structure, i.e., the arrangement of the persons involved in the creative process. Because we'd made the first two albums with Chris we naturally thought that it'd be OK to make this one with him, because he's a good friend. But all the time there were musical differences, so that when we stopped working with Chris and we reassessed the situation and realized the only people who could produce this record was ourselves, working closely with Dave Bascombe, who engineered the last album. Chris is a very active producer, and he has a certain vision of things. If you don't follow it, all hell breaks loose. Dave Bascombe is a passive producer, he lets you get on with it. He's an engineer/producer.

Did you consider working with any other producers?

No, because we knew Dave Bascombe. That was it. I couldn't stomach a new relationship. It felt comfortable.

If Chris Hughes is such a good friend, why couldn't you work with him?

Even with people you get on with you step into an element of role-playing. I wasn't pushing myself. I wasn't using all of my talents. I was falling into the role of the artist as opposed to the artist/producer, which is a different thing.

Can the audience tell the difference?

People are incredibly sensitive to sound, more so than you give them credit. What you're in a sense hinting at is that musicians or artists are working at a completely different level to the way people perceive music, and I don't think that's correct. When one understands how these things work, there is a chance of getting lost because there are so many things you can do, it's virtually limitless. I don't know how people paint, I don't understand the technique behind it, but I know when a painting's good or not.

Are musicians no longer competent to play by themselves?

Musicians have a specific style, their own personality, which is fine and wonderful. But if it's not what you completely require, you then take what they've done and insert your own critique, your own personality and doctor it, structure it to what you require. We don't work in a band situation all the time. If we had a drummer and a keyboard player, that kind of stuff, a common personality grows out of the group situation. We are a duo and therefore there is a risk of getting anonymous performances. There is that risk that there isn't enough relating between session musicians. That's the process of editing, to get it back to a more personalized sound.

The old way of working with studio players: delineating what you want.

That way, you end up with something which is the same size as your vision. The trick is to create something which is greater than your vision, greater than yourself. Had we spent years playing with these people, some common identity would have occurred. But we didn't. Session musicians have an awful lot to offer, only it doesn't come quickly.

The editing process

It's the difference between a live performance and a record. The edited version was the ultimate performance. We didn't do it that good in one take. We simply couldn't have done it. There may have been a few mistakes, or there may have been a good ending, but not a good beginning, or vice versa. Somebody did an ad lib on one take, which wasn't a good track. That way you can stick it all together and get the perfect.

It's more than [fixing tracks] because these people are capable of phenomenal bits, little pieces of expression. Normally, you get a session musician in and you sit him down to a track that's already been worked out, and he plays. But it's a very sterile way of doing it. Because everybody was playing together over a period of a couple of weeks, people would do things they wouldn't do...risk taking. The people who played are amazed. The differences aren't drastic, but they're not subtle. For me the initial isn't acceptable, and the final thing is.

Weeks of drum edits?

It does take lots of time. You can have 30 takes of a track, done to a click track. They're all the same tempo, but the feels vary. It's quite amazing. It's simply a lengthy process.

Your own instrumental involvement?

The way Curt works is far more rational in terms of his bass playing: he gets a part and that's it.

Are you hands-off?

No, not necessarily. Some of his bass parts were taken a stage further by me.

Do you feel compelled to play on every track?

Certainly not. I play the guitar, but there are certain things which I know someone else could do better. The same with Curt. Ultimately what matters is what comes out of the speakers. That for me is the statement.

So much of me goes into it that I couldn't really care less if I played guitar or I didn't. So much of the Fairlight program, the drum programming, so much of the vision... It doesn't satisfy my ego any more to have my guitar playing on it.

If we had done this album on analog we wouldn't have been able to edit like we edited. It's only through digital offsets and all this kind of stuff, 'cause you never really lose what you've done. Having said that, another reason it took so long, aside from just the editing, is that if there was a direct-to-disc system which was up and working we could have done it like that. The way we're working is very much a stage, a way of doing things which I think will become the norm. I was aware that you could do it. I don't think anyone else has done it to the degree that we've done it, so far.

This wasn't an arduous process?

No. If somebody's away for four years, you can fantasize all kinds of things that are going on. People love to paint a black picture, especially because we don't go out of our way to paint a bright one. We don't. It's been the best time of my life, the best years of my life. I had a really good time, I learned so much.

I'm not bothered in the least by the quantity [of creative output). The information on that record is so dense, anyway. You could have watered the whole thing down and spread it over three albums. But there's a lot of information, a lot of stuff to wade through...it's like a Tolstoy novel.

How arduous a process is songwriting?

Not very, when I let myself go, things come to me. I get inspired. I wrote "Sowing the Seeds of Love" one week and I wrote "Woman in Chains" the next. I do spend a fuck of a lot of time on lyrics 'cause I get very fussy about that.

Kick out the style/bring back the jam

That came from "Kick out the Jams." I thought it was neat. Nothing personal. I don't have strong feelings about it.

Nicky Holland

She played piano on tour with us in 1985. We were jamming at soundcheck. She would come up with a piano motif and I would sing a tune on top. It was that simple and that instant.

Oleta Adams

[On that tour] we only had two albums worth of material and it was very programmed. Although it worked in the studio, there was something lacking in it in a live situation, especially a stadium situation. We came across Oleta in a bar in Kansas City, just piano, bass and drums. I could hear so much in that piano, especially with Oleta playing 10-finger chords, Nicky's a bit like that as well — hammer it out on piano, rather than arrange it. All on the piano, no room for anything else. I thought, yeah, that's where I have to go. The way I used to do it was really much more bits of information, threads which would go through the music and meet up, whereas it's all there on the piano.

Nicky Holland's input as a songwriter?

She would come up with bits on the piano. I could write with a lot of people. Nicky is a songwriter.

Oleta's input?

She played on the live sessions, and she came in to do the vocal tracks. [Working with her live] was fantastic.

What did you get from her as a musician?

It's very much a religious feeling, the sense that music was sacred in terms of the communication from one soul to another. Yeah. That you can express yourself in music in a very emotional way, yet it be very, very musical, not angst.

What was her music like?

Some of her own stuff, some standards. Very simple piano stuff. It's just the delivery — it's quite frightening, the accuracy of her expression. It's absolutely structured, but absolutely loose.

What was your first instinct?

The first thing we did was tell David Bates, our A&R man, you've got to see this woman: she's just incredible. So, he flew from England to Kansas to see her, thought she was great but didn't know how to market her. Which I think says a lot about the music industry: that you could see somebody so obviously talented and not know how to market her, as if that wasn't enough. That's the first thing we did, then it was forgotten. It was just one of those fantastic evenings that makes a great impression. I was kind of realizing that soul music was a good vehicle — that I could do with getting a bit of soul, that it would make what I did more fluid. In '87, when I came up with "Woman in Chains," which was a natural duet — singing high and singing low — I thought Aha! I know the woman that can do that. We had "Badman's Song" lying around from the tour but it had never really come together. I thought, if I played it with her she can really take it. So, I rewrote the song into another duet, and I rewrote the verse specifically for her to do all the lows and highs gospel style.

A lot of this record is geared toward the live setting. I made quite a few mental notes.

Was there thought of having more live performances on the record?

Yeah, we tried quite a few songs, but it didn't really work. We tried "Woman in Chains."

Frustration onstage?

What frustrates me is that sometimes you aren't in the mood. Then you are professional.

Your American record company?

They were absolutely patient.

Is it a big problem if the record doesn't sell 10 million copies?

No, not a problem. I like making music...I'm driven. I like to hear things coming out of the speakers which are somewhat representative of the way I feel. That's what I do, and enough people allow me to do it. I'm in a duo the name of which people recognize. That's the way it works.

There's a dichotomy between the freedom selling millions of records gives you vs. the straitjacket that it puts you in.

Very true. It's that dichotomy which can you force you to take a long time on a record, because you might as well. In a sense you do have two ambitions to fulfill: your own, and other people's. I had specific things which I wanted to do, specific things which I wanted to achieve for my own sake, for my own sanity. The rest is really understanding what is expected. I did want to prove that what happened in '85 wasn't a fluke, that we can do it again. When we want to. In our own time. When we're ready.

"Sowing the Seeds of Love" seems the most obvious thing on the record.

To you. Not everyone says that. I'm very pleased with it. It was good fun to do because there's a lot of humor in it.

Any response from the Beatles?

No, not yet...

The music, I understand, is meant to set the tone for the political commentary of the lyrics. That seems esoteric.

Oh yeah. What I meant was the familiarity of the sound cuts through, gets straight in to people. There's no resistance because of the optimism of the chorus: anything's possible when you're sowing the seeds of love, and then, by the way, blah blah blah blah — this is wrong, this is wrong...but anything is possible. I suppose in a sense that's what was one of Lennon's strengths — his absolute faith in life and love — the archetype of love — yet his absolute Cynicism towards the establishment. This fantastic combination of energies. That's kind of what the song does: it's all couched. It could have been overt, it could have been direct, it could have been straightforward, but people wouldn't have heard it as much, it wouldn't have got in.

How customized is the music to the thoughts in the lyrics?

I can't answer that question. I don't know.

You're of the new wave generation, yet you've become the Pink Floyd of the era in terms of being extremely studio oriented and perfectionist. Where you started versus where you've gotten to.

I think it was inevitable, because there was always an element of complexity, right from the beginning [in TFF). And maybe that's right, maybe it needs that setting to be justified.

Like Sting, are you buying into indigenous American sounds by working with Oleta?

I can't see it like that at all. That's an objective, outsider's view but it's nowt to do with that. That's very cynical, I think, and very detached way of seeing it. No, the fact is that both Oleta and I have our moon in Capricorn, that's why I like her, that's why I used her. It didn't bother me if she was American or Pygmy or Scandinavian. We have more in common than we have not in common — on a very soul level, on a musical level. There was definite empathy — it's nothing to do with her color, her background, her tradition, or what — other than that her background has allowed her and trained her to express herself in that way. I would say my background has done the reverse.

How subsidiary is Curt's role?

In one sense he's very, very equal. He doesn't write as such, although he did come up with possibly the biggest hook on the album. So, you've got to hand it to them. There is more to being in a pop group than just making music. In a sense we both get out of it what we both require. I'm not fully at ease with the promotion bit, which is fair enough, not everybody is. Curt's understanding of the actual business is remarkably developed. He's not stupid.

Groups of this era are not simply guys with guitars.

It used to be like that, but it isn't any longer. To develop, we've had to develop different talents.

Have you ever considered making TFF into a full-fledged group?

No, because no one drummer would satisfy us. Chris Hughes played "Sowing the Seeds of Love" the fantastic way he did it, it's beautiful, but there are certain things he couldn't have done. The same with Manu Cache. He's got a highly stylized way of playing. And Phil Collins. It's very difficult to throw a group together that can trace all those styles.

Are there are any instruments you're less capable of judging?

No. It's music and you feel it. If it sounds good, then that's it. It doesn't matter what it is: an accordion, or a harmonica or Jon Hassell. I knew when Jon Hassell was playing well and when he wasn't — and so did he. That's the way it works. You just sit there and listen to it.

How long did you work with Clive Langer and Alan Winstanley?

We just did one track with them: "Badman's Song," pre-Oleta. It's a shame because I'd really liked Clive's production:

"Shipbuilding" by Robert Wyatt, all the Madness records and Wilder by Teardrop Explodes which, for the time, I thought was a beautiful record. I was hoping it was going to work out and, funnily enough, if I had been a bit more relaxed, and a bit more liberal, it may have done, but I was still buggering about with machines at the time.

It was the two of us and Nicky was there. I had programmed the whole bass and drums part on the Fairlight. And the piano. That's how we started. Then we replaced bits of piano, added some guitar...

How much input does a producer have in that process?

Not a lot. Type a record. Everyone's sitting around criticizing programming. It's not really an area for discourse or debate. I can't really comment on the role of the producer.

Does a producer have a fair chance to influence?

Probably not, no. It's almost like when you're sitting by a Fairlight you have a monopoly.

It wasn't so much that you couldn't work with Langer/Winstanley — you just couldn't work with anybody like that.

Clive and Alan were into it. They thought it was good — we didn't.

Were they pushing you into things you didn't want to do?

No.

You were unsatisfied working with them, they were satisfied working with you, and you had the upper hand creatively. So, what's the problem?

If you have the ability to produce yourself, if you have a vision of how it should be and an ability to know what is a good and bad sound and when something works, not just subjectively, but objectively — i.e., you're hearing what everybody else is hearing. If you have that ability, but you work with somebody who is supposed to be in that role you have to give that part of yourself up to some degree or else there'll just be fights of vision, or production techniques or that kind of very subjective [disagreements] like I like that snare drum, you like this snare drum.

To be the artist and the producer is a lot of work, and you have to get into things which aren't even necessarily artistic — very boring, mundane things. That's what producers should be doing. If by giving up that part of yourself and handing it over you're not getting what you want, then there's something wrong. You either look for somebody who is at least one step further than you in their vision, or somebody who can help you articulate it, and you end up with an engineer/producer. That's the way it works.

The point is this: all the time I wasn't using that part of myself, we weren't getting the results. The moment I took it upon myself to really manifest to realize it. to make it materialize, that's when things started to happen.

You had to come to grips with the fact that you had to produce yourself. It took a long time to get to that point.

Yes it did because that's not something the record company had prepared us for. Or were prepared for. They like hierarchical situations — they like record company, producer, artist. They like that. Because then the whole pyramid of power, the chain of command gets set into operation and they can hopefully get what they want. When the artist is in control, it becomes more difficult. It becomes more of an equal relationship. It's not uncommon, but when you sign to a company when you're 19 there are a few relationship changes you have to go through. Business puberty.

The record company found the notion of you producing yourself unsettling?

Absolutely.

That seems short-sighted.

Yes, it is.

Was this lack of faith on the part of the record company difficult for you to deal with emotionally?

Yes.

Is the company satisfied with the record?

They're very happy indeed, especially the American company. I don't know why. Record companies are money-making machines. I don't know how much they concern themselves with an artist's long-term development. At the end of the day they've got a budget, a balance sheet they have to meet. And shareholders they have to keep happy.

Why are there audience noises on "Year of the Knife"?

The initial idea was to start the album with that because we were gonna start the set with it live. We were gonna play audience noise to the audience. That was the why. We set it up to start up where we'd left off in the live situation and take it from there. We [ultimately] didn't feel it was the right track to open the album with and we were left with many versions; Some had the audience, some didn't. In terms of a segue which we wanted to do from "Swords and knives" it didn't work without the audience. So, we put the audience in. The audience is [from our show in] Toronto. Massey Hall.

Did your work with Langer/Winstanley create an emotional problem with Chris Hughes? Was he peeved at not being asked to produce the record?

Maybe...I don't know. Probably.

Was there any big problem when you went back to work with him?

He's a friend, so it's alright. Chris is very affable. He has an amazing ability to rise above emotional situations and understand the reality involved. He would have made a better band member than producer because he has some wonderful ideas.

[response to quote about working to achieve spontaneity]

You can learn to structure spontaneity. There are times when you'll be spontaneous, and times where you need to sit back and analyze and criticize and edit that which has been spontaneously produced. It takes a long time to learn how that fits in, to respond to your impulses, things that are going on inside of you. Something can be spontaneous and then edited. It was spontaneous. I think you can develop spontaneity. I think one of the outstanding features of this album is that you have a lot of spontaneous things, things which came about by magic, but they have been collected and assembled, and put together, they have been structured.

How much has been lost in the development of music-making?

It really depends what you want. [Bashing it out] doesn't satisfy me. It doesn't satisfy me because there are elements of the human condition which that doesn't involve, doesn't even get anywhere near. It doesn't touch melancholy, it doesn't touch violence, anger, depression. I think it's a lot easier to do that nowadays. You can paint a far bigger than ever before. There are more colors to play with.

Have you ever thought of being an acoustic solo performer with one guitar?

No. Complex characters create complex visions and complex music. It's as simple as that. When rock'n'roll came about it was straightforward because people's vision was straightforward. Life was simple, in a sense, a lot more simple — on the surface. There were so many post-war restrictions, like get a job, do this, try and carve a future — and that's the way music mirrored that. I don't think it's like that nowadays, I don't think it's like that at all. Things are so complicated.

Gary Zukav [reference to heavy-looking book lying open on desk] is talking about developing from a five-sensory animal into a multi-sensory animal, and that's the way we have to develop. Yeah, it's going to get bloody complicated. That doesn't mean it has to be pompous and bombastic and brash and too deep you can't get anywhere near it. One should develop one's art so that it is both complex and simple at the same time. That's when it's right. Honestly, the way things are going, our understanding of ourselves psychologically is far greater than when rock'n'roll started. We are only learning the words to use now. That's why this is complicated. ◆

After we worked together at *Newsday*, Lois Draegin, a top-shelf entertainment editor, moved on to *TV Guide* and, in 1997, asked me to do a piece for a 20-years-gone Elvis issue (hyped with four "collectors' covers.") The gig paid well and was in a magazine I'd grown up reading and really — at one time, at least — admired. (I still have a box of old *Fall Preview* issues in the cellar — I loved seeing what ridiculous fare the networks had in store for America.)

My job was a short oral history of the TV hosts who'd presented Elvis early in his career. Which, amazingly enough, meant getting on the phone to speak with Steve Allen, Wink Martindale, Jimmy Dean and the nearly 89-year-old Milton Berle, who signed off a bizarre but entertaining conversation by saying, "Alright baby, let me hear from you."

Here's Elvis!

TV Guide, 16 August 1997

Television in the mid-'50s was nothing like the MTV world we now know. The entertainment establishment considered rock and roll a teen fad. Elvis was initially treated as a minor attraction, a hillbilly singer unworthy of national exposure. Then, in 1956, his spiraling popularity made him the most wanted man on television.

In his early days, Elvis was a musical barnstormer, playing concerts wherever and whenever, often at the drop of a hat, all over the South. In early 1955, he was booked to perform on a boat that cruised the Potomac River. The promoter, Connie B. Gay, also owned a local variety show, *Town and Country Time*, hosted on WMAL-TV in Washington, D.C. by country singer Jimmy Dean. With tickets still to be sold, Elvis stopped by the station for a last-minute plug.

Jimmy Dean: "In all probability, it was the worst interview I ever did. I would say something like 'I understand you're going to appear on the SS Mount Vernon tonight, Elvis.'

'Yep.'

'Have you ever appeared on a boat before?'

'Nope.'

'Are you looking forward to a good evening?'

'Yep.'

"It was like pulling teeth. I was glad to get rid of him. But he turned out to be a good friend. Later, when we worked together in Vegas, he apologized. He said, 'I know I was terrible, but I was scared to death.' He had just started, and I don't think he felt comfortable with anybody, including himself."

In 1956, Elvis headlined a Fourth of July concert in Memphis to raise money for a local children's charity. On June 23, in order to promote the event, he visited the *Top Ten Dance Party*, a local *Bandstand*-type show hosted live Saturday afternoons on WHBQ-TV by disc jockey (and future game show host) Wink Martindale. Martindale had first met Elvis at the radio station that fateful night in July 1954 when Dewey Phillips began spinning "That's All Right."

Wink Martindale: "With Dewey's help, I had been trying to get Elvis on my show for a year and a half. At that point in his career and in my young life, it was quite a coup to get him to come on.

"I did the morning show on WHBQ radio, and I had plugged the fact that he was going to be on the [TV] show for a couple of weeks. So, we had a tremendous traffic jam in East Memphis that day, everybody waiting for Elvis to arrive. He wasn't going to perform, just talk about the Cynthia Milk Fund and his career.

"At the time, I didn't know a lot about his background. I was just asking biographical-type stuff I felt people would want to know. I wasn't leaving anything to chance, everything I wanted to ask him was on cue cards."

"We were really surprised he would have pictures made with kids that were there from the high school, and also get out on the dance floor and run around and make a fool of himself.

"When I came out to California in 1959 and started my *Teenage Dance Party* on KHJ, I replayed the kinescope of the Elvis interview. I also called him in Germany, and he gave me a real nice ten-minute chat on the telephone about how the Army was going."

Following six musical appearances on *Jackie Gleason's Stage Show*, hosted by the Dorsey Brothers in early '56, Elvis was booked by Milton Berle for one of his pioneering color variety specials, broadcast April 3, 1956 from the deck of the U.S.S. Hancock in San Diego.

Milton Berle: "My agent asked if I would consider putting this young fellow on. I asked to see him, so they gave me an audition. They brought him to me. I put him on a special with Harry James' Orchestra (Joe Williams was singing) and Esther Williams.

"I told my assistant George Schlatter to round up three or four buses and go over to the high schools and get girl students and bring 'em over to the boat. We gave them five dollars apiece. We said, 'Scream, 'cause the cameras may be on you.'

"I picked Elvis and Col. Parker up in the limo from the airport. Elvis was very charming, he was cute, adorable, shy, good-looking and soft-spoken. I introduced them, and Harry James said where's your orchestration? Elvis picked out one sheet of music, a lead sheet, not an orchestra arrangement, and said, 'Here it is.' They laughed at him. He started to strum on the guitar, and I caught a glance of James and [drummer] Buddy Rich looking at each other. Rich made a square sign with his fingers and pointed at Elvis. I walked over and had a little beef with them. I said, 'That's very rude of you. Wait till you see him, you're going to be surprised.'"

After the rehearsal, the buses arrived and Elvis took over, singing "Heartbreak Hotel" and "Blue Suede Shoes" to the girls on the boat as well as the national television audience.

"They were screaming because of his looks. Then he started to wiggle with his butt and all that stuff and they're standing up screaming naturally. I didn't even have to tell 'em. "When the show was over you couldn't keep the dancers in our cast away from him. They were all after him. He was a sensation that night.

"I received about 300,000 letters from parents. They were not fan letters, they were pan letters. They thought it was out of line with the gyrations and everything. 'We'll never let our children watch your show if you're going to put a performer like that on. The way he wiggles is really rude and distasteful and all that.'

"I booked him back right away. I was concerned that maybe I would lose my audience, too, but I didn't. I was concerned for myself, but more happy for him."

Presley's return appearance to the Berle show was on June 5, 1956. In addition to a frisky performance of "Hound Dog" that enraged and disgusted conservative critics, Elvis did shtick with the star, whose clever asides and mugging to the music left Elvis in stitches. (Replying to a comment about finding a nice girl "to relax me," Berle quips, "You don't want a girl, you want a Miltown.")

Berle: "I used to work with the performer, whoever it was, in an after piece, or I was weaved into their act. So, when he got through, I did some stand-up talk with him. Berle-isms. He was very shy. This was new to him, and I broke him up. He couldn't keep a straight face. I put my arm around and said 'This is make-believe. Laugh it up.' I said, 'Come on, I laugh when you sing.' He was one of the nicest young gentlemen I ever met. I really loved him."

Steve Allen, no friend to rock and roll, wasn't so enthusiastic. He had booked Elvis after spotting "this goofy, gangly kid" on the Dorsey show, and so had him under contract when the ruckus erupted. On July 1, 1956, Elvis made what Allen wryly referred to on air as "his first comeback," dressed in a tuxedo and reluctantly singing "Hound Dog" to an actual basset hound. Later in the show, he did a western comedy sketch with Allen, Imogene Coca and Andy Griffith.

Steve Allen: "Because ours was a comedy show and not a variety show, I intended to have Elvis sing his little heart out but also get laughs, and he did. When he sang to the dog all dressed up that way, everybody loved him.

"I had written [the sketch] years earlier, it was a satire of cowboy shows that were on the air in the late '30s and early '40s. By 1956, there weren't very many of those corny shows on anymore, so it was no longer a very legitimate target. I just remembered it was funny. We changed a few little lines, and basically went out with the same old script. Elvis was very cute in it."

Even before the live broadcast had finished, Allen's Sunday night competitor, Ed Sullivan, reached Col. Parker backstage with a deal for five appearances at the exorbitant fee of $10,000 per show. Parker extended Allen the courtesy of matching the offer. He passed.

Allen: "I thought it over for about three seconds. I was being largely magnanimous, but not solely so. We were doing a comedy show, and I didn't want to have to think of five other clever ways of making Elvis seem funny." ◆

Steve Allen phoner 19 May 1997

I gather in the '50s you weren't much of a fan of rock and roll.
Well, it depends on what you mean. Either I still am not, or I still love it, depends on how you interpret the evidence. If you put the thousand most popular rock songs in a blender and got something you could analyze in a laboratory, it is simply not as good as what we got from George Gershwin, Hoagy Carmichael, Duke Ellington, Jerome Kern, Richard Rogers, all those people — the great composers of the truly golden age of American melody. That's an important distinction. As regards the other side of the ledger, I write rock music, I have recorded rock music and some of my big band jazz arrangements are constructed with rock rhythms. All I am interested in is quality. It just happens to be the case that the percentage of really high-quality music with coherent lyrics and gorgeous and original and harmonically innovative melodies, was considerably higher than that same percentage in the rock field.

In my comedy concerts, which always include some music, one of the things I do is play rock music and I explain to the audience that what I am playing is the first form of rock. A lot of young people have no idea where rock came from. They don't even know who the founding fathers were. If you ask them, they give you such irrelevant names as Elvis Presley or Buddy Holly, whereas rock, of course, originated in the late 1920s in the Black musical culture. In its first form, which still is used, it's called boogie-woogie. A classic instance would be Jerry Lewis' recording of "Great Balls of Fire." You still hear it in some of the better rock forms now.

You had Elvis on in the wake of his appearance on the Berle show, which got a critical outcry that he was a savage who would corrupt the youth of America. You booked him a month later, and announced it as his first comeback.
I announced that on the show? I haven't seen it recently. Oh, I see. It must be interpreted surely as a joke.

Believe it or not, it was only about ten years ago that I found out he'd been on Berle's show. I knew he didn't appear first on my show, because I found him on television. I'm often praised for having brought Elvis into television, which is nice of people to say but it's not true. I found him on television. As I say I never heard that he'd been on Milton's show; where I found him was on a summer replacement show on CBS hosted by the great bandleaders Jimmy Dorsey and Tommy Dorsey. I had no idea who he was. It was in the middle of the show somewhere, and I saw this goofy, gangly kid. I guess because my mother and father were entertainers, and I grew up in the business and spent my early years in and around vaudeville theaters, I have always been very good at telling who has it and who should get out of show business.

They never listen to me as to who should get out, but that's ok. I recognized that this kid, whose name I didn't even catch, had something, to use that old phrase. He certainly did not have a glorious sound in the sense the young Sinatra did or Perry Como does, or Andy Williams, or a lot of the women singers who enchant you with the beauty of the noise their mouth makes when they sing. He was not in their category of singers, but the same is true of some of the very best singers of all time: Louis Armstrong had a pretty dumb sound but he was a great singer, and one of my favorites, Johnny Mercer. There's not only a beautiful sound that makes a great singer. Personality and image are also important.

Elvis also had a cute face. I could see that face being appealing to high school, and it was. One thing that struck me as odd is that about 20 years ago, I began to notice that teenagers of that day didn't give a damn about Elvis.

Your show was opposite The Ed Sullivan Show on Sunday nights. Did competition induce you to book Elvis?
No. He certainly wasn't a name the night I saw him, so that had nothing to do with my deciding to book him. We just had a stroke of good luck. I'd never heard that he'd been on television before that night, and if there was any controversy about his wiggling or whatever, it had escaped my attention. The controversy did not come to my attention until after he was booked for our show. I think it was about a five-week lapse between my memo to book him and the time he appeared, and it finally did come to my attention that, of all people, Ed Sullivan had made some dreadfully insulting comments about Elvis, that he was a danger to the youth of America, that he would never put that sort of fare on his fine family show. [He changed his mind] As soon as he saw what ratings we got — and he knew before the show what ratings we would get, because by then all that complaining plus his own talent had made Elvis the biggest.

The fee of $7,500?
That was the top price, no matter whose show you were on. If you were a major star, you got $7,500. Sullivan, who was a journalist of the old front-page school, he did a gutsy thing. He called Colonel Parker backstage at our theater. I was busy finishing the show, but I've been told by our people that he called during our show. How the hell he got offstage to call I have no idea. He also talked to the Colonel after the show was over. He was so desperate to do something, he suddenly felt threatened, I was not interested in the ratings part of it all. I knew we would do a better show, but that does not give you the higher ratings in television.

Was having Elvis sing to the hound dog your idea?
It was my idea. The other night I was doing a show at a comedy club in Boston, and a good part of my show consists of answering questions sent up by the audience. Somebody asked the other night, "What do you think of Elvis Presley?" My answer was "I think he's dead" The other question was "Whose idea was it to have Elvis sing to the hound dog?" I said it was the dog's idea.

Those shows are rehearsed. Nobody walks onstage and surprises you. There was no way for me not to know what he was going to sing or what he was going to say.

The very first day he showed up, we were told that he would like to sing a song called "Hound Dog." I said, "terrific." Because ours was a comedy show and not a variety show, I naturally intended to have Elvis sing his little heart out but also get laughs, and he did. America loved him doing that. We also dressed him in Fred Astaire attire, white tie and tails, in which he looked very handsome, by the way. When he sang to the dog all dressed up that way, everybody loved him. It was only 25 or 30 years later that I began to hear nonsensical reports that Elvis took that as a personal insult and we'd demeaned his dignity. Nothing of the sort ever happened. He was just a kid at the time, a lovely kid. We were always friends for the rest of his life. Whenever I would run into him we would hang out for a little bit if I saw him in Vegas or wherever he was. His success never seemed to go to his head as it has done unfortunately to some other performers. He was still just good ol' country boy Elvis.

Any recollection where the dog came from?
No idea. On television, if you want a dog or a goat or a horse or a chicken, there are people that do that for a living. In the New York area, which is where we were, there was a place in New Jersey that had a little compound, and we used to get a llama from them.

History is a matter of revising reality long after the fact. The historical significance is often totally unrecognized until quite some time has passed. At that time, Elvis had yet to be deified.

I liked his work. I didn't give a damn whether we had rock people on or not. Over the years I've had a lot of them on. Jerry Lee Lewis named one of his sons after me; he interpreted his appearance on that same show, the old NBC Sunday night show, as saving his career, which I never understood until I saw the movie *Great Balls of Fire* in which I played myself. Just by booking him, because I didn't give a damn about that gossip stuff, he was back on top again.

Elvis's comedy sketch, the Range Roundup. Did he have acting talent at that point?
Not really, but he was able to do something that many professional actors cannot do, so it's a talent of a sort. And that is: Be yourself. It's amazing how many actors, some of them who've been in the business for 40 or 50 years, who when chatting on the phone or at the golf course talk just the way you and I are, just plain old talk. But you write down those same lines in a script, and they can't seem to be themselves. They become stiff, artificial or square sounding. Elvis never had that problem. Later in his films he had to do some acting, obviously, but even in those roles he was being himself.

We had the dog sitting on a Greek pillar. It was somebody else's idea to put a little top hat on the dog with a chin strap; it was just one more cute little look. Somebody told me they had been in Graceland a year or so ago and noticed one of the souvenir shops had a ceramic dog, that actual dog, 'cause it had the same little black hat on.

Was the sketch written for him?
No, I had written it years earlier. Like a lot of comics of my generation, I came out of radio comedy. I had written it on a radio comedy show a long time before. At the time that I did, it was satire.

In the late '30s and early '40s, there were actual country and western shows, cowboy shows, on the air that were kind of shlocky. The MC or the star or the host would do a lot of what would now be considered corny talk about mom's apple pie and America — kind of a mixture of religion and patriotism and selling albums. My original version that had appeared on the radio had been a satire on that kind of show. By 1956, when Elvis appeared with us, it was no longer a very legitimate target for satire. There weren't very many of those corny shows on anymore. I just remembered it was funny, and we had Imogene Coca and Andy Griffith, who were very funny people, so it just came to my mind. We changed a few little lines, and basically went out with the same old script I'd written years before. Elvis was very cute in it.

Did you try to book him back?
I was quite willing to. The same night, Bill Harbach, our producer, came up to me and said did you hear about Sullivan calling Col. Parker and offering Elvis five bookings at $10,000 apiece? I said, no. Bill said what do you want to do because the way Colonel put it, we could stop that. According to Harbach, the Colonel had said "Sullivan wouldn't book us when you guys would, so we owe you something. All Sullivan had been doing to that point is criticize us, and we didn't like that. So, check with Mr. Allen. If he wants to have us back..." What he was implying was that I'd have to meet the offer, but he would do it with us rather than them. I thought it over for about three seconds and I said, Billy, tell the Colonel that I really appreciate his approach, it was a lovely gesture, but tell him to go right ahead and take the $50,000 with my blessings. I was being largely magnanimous, but not solely so. We were doing a comedy show, and I didn't want to have to think of five other clever ways of making Elvis seem funny.

Milton Berle's cameo.
I think Milton was on another part of the show. As I say, it was years later that I found out that he'd had Elvis on. That had nothing to do with booking Milton; he and I are lifelong friends. He was my babysitter when I was about three years old. He worked on the same bill with my mother when he was a teenage entertainer in vaudeville, and she hired him a couple of times to keep an eye on me.

Some critic in Newsweek *criticized you for Elvis' appearance.*
No, I didn't hear any of that kind of nonsense until 25 or 30 years after the appearance. The only words I heard were joy from all the teenaged fans who loved him and the grownup folks loved the way we made him seem so funny and so entertaining. There were no complaints that I heard.

People were afraid of rock and roll...
There was always a gentlemanly side to Elvis. He would address my wife as Ma'am, that kind of approach which was very sweet.

A couple of years ago, there was an awards ceremony, I think they're called the Angel awards. Jayne [Meadows] and I were the co-emcees of the ceremonies several months ago here in town [LA]. I realized that every single play-on [the music accompanying entrances] that I was hearing was in the rock style. I said it wasn't very many years ago when a lot of folks right here in this room were very forthright in calling rock music the music of the devil and now here in these dignified proceedings that's what we're hearing all night long is rock music. They all laughed.

Of course, there is still rock music for which people should be arrested — and I mean that in an almost literal sense. It's been very well publicized in the Congressional attack and other widespread media criticisms of some of the lyrics of the hip-hop and street language some of it is so vulgar I don't even know you well enough to use it, but you probably are hip to what it is. Killing policemen, justifying rape — it's really disgraceful. There's still that element in rock and pop-rock music. But there's nothing wrong with the rhythm.

Did watching Elvis up close change your opinion of his music?
I enjoyed his performing when I first saw him on the Dorsey Brothers show.

If I saw him for nine minutes [on my show] it was six more minutes, but it was the same thing. He was no better. I enjoyed his work originally and I did then and I still do when I see him on an old special.

I liked him from the very first. Charisma is in the eye of the beholder. What Elvis had done for a living before he had any success as a singer was drive a truck. I can assure you, knowing what I do about human nature and Elvis and trucks, that absolutely nobody who ever saw him drive past in his truck ever stood and stared and said, My god, look at the charisma on that young truck driver. They might have noticed if one of his tires was flat, but they never noticed him.

Another relevant factor is that the American people do not now and have never had any particular interest in talent. Trust me. What they are morbidly fascinated by is celebrity and success. They don't even care how you achieved your celebrity. You can achieve it by sleeping with Frank Sinatra or trying to shoot Ronald Reagan. Whatever gets your picture in the papers, then you've got fans. You can even have murdered people to become a celebrity. Every time there's some real monster who gets arrested for serial killing or whatever, these idiots, too, get their proposals of marriage. Look at all the people who scream when John Gotti walks out of a courtroom. They're screaming adulation at him because he's a celebrity. ◆

This was a deeply strange experience. Berle was a legend, a figure so engrained in American culture and yet so far outside my cultural world that talking to him on the phone didn't quite feel real. When I called, a manservant answered, which already put me in mind of a Nick and Nora picture. I can only imagine the mansion.

Berle was old and hard of hearing, but completely capable of reeling off ancient anecdotes with élan. And that voice was unmistakable. I suppose he might have been the most famous person I have ever interviewed.

Milton Berle phoner 21 May 1997

I was on the air since '48 when I started the Texaco show. I've been with the William Morris Agency 65 years. Lastfogel, who was the president of the company, was approached by Colonel Tom Parker. Lastfogel spoke to me. He said that Tom Parker has this young fellow, Elvis Presley. Lastfogel, who was my agent, asked would I consider putting this young fellow on? It was Parker who got in touch with the Morris office. He was the backbone of the kid, of Elvis. I said, can I see him, can I hear him? So, they gave me an audition.

They brought him to me. I saw him, and I heard him, and I said fine. I had been on television a long time, from '48 on, but this happened in '56. At that time, I had specials, and I put him on a special, and I remember who was on the special that I had booked. I had Harry James' Orchestra (Joe Williams was singing), Esther Williams and this young fellow that was referred to me by Lastfogel. Parker was his manager.

We did it from the deck of the Hancock in San Diego. When he showed up, I had him picked up in the car from the airport. I did four big specials in addition to my show, and he was on one of them.

At the drums of Harry James' Orchestra — and he's gone, may he rest in peace — that's Buddy Rich playing the drums.

He came in, we picked him up, and he was with Parker. I picked him up in the car, personally, in the limo. Now we're driving back, and he was very charming, he was cute, he was very adorable, very shy, and very good looking and very soft-spoken. He was very nice. Col. Parker, who I knew before he had Elvis, I did medicine shows for him in the '40s. He was very sharp and worked very hard, and very bright.

Anyway, coming back in the car over to the boat, Elvis said, "Very pleased to meet you Mr. Berle, I watch you on the television," like a young fan. I was very nice to him, I think. I must have been. The three of us are riding in the back seat of the limo toward the ship and I had the contract for his appearance in my pocket, we're talking, and I opened the contract with the three of us sitting back there and Parker grabbed it away from me. He said, "Don't show that contract to the boy!" I said, "I'm sorry, I didn't know that, Tom." I don't think he wanted Elvis to see the contract that Elvis was supposed to sign. He kept everything away from the boy. He was taking care of Elvis. He wasn't cheating him, but he didn't want him to know... "I'm the boy's manager, just let me see it." It was Parker that really worked on him, public relation wise, put him on the right track and all that. Parker deserves so much credit.

The first time there on the boat, we did the rehearsal. We had the band and everything and we had put little folding chairs on the boat for an audience. I remember I did this with Sinatra back in '43, when he opened at the Paramount. We loaded the audience with young people so when we got to San Diego, I told my assistant — who was George Schlatter by the way, he's a big producer — I want you to round up three or four buses and go over to the high schools and get me a lot of girl students and bring 'em over to the boat. The show at that time was completely live. You saw what you got and you got what you saw. I remembered when Sinatra — I was close to Sinatra — and what happened with loading the audience, not with plants.

Schlatter went and got three busloads of young students, girls, so we could have an audience. It was like a studio audience, but it was on the boat and we planted all the girls in the audience. We had cameras doing reverse shots over his shoulders from the back with the girls screaming and everything. We gave them, I think, five dollars apiece to do it, just for a little present. We said, "Scream, the cameras may be on you." That was set up.

When we started to rehearse, he come in unassuming, cute. He come in with his guitar. I introduced them and Harry James said where's your orchestration? He said I don't use an orchestration and he picked out one sheet of music, like a lead sheet, no other parts. No saxes, no trumpets — not an orchestra arrangement. He said here it is, and it was one sheet of music for rhythm. I watched and they started to laugh at him. Look what we've got here, a hick, the new kid on the block. He started to strum on the guitar and said all I want is rhythm.

The band kind of faked whatever song he was doing, and I caught a glance of Buddy Rich and Harry James looking at each other. Buddy Rich made a square sign with his fingers and pointed at Elvis. They looked at each other like, what have we got here? Where the hell did he come from?

I caught their eye and I walked over and said why did you do that? I had a little beef with James and Buddy Rich. I said I saw you make those signs to one another, that's very rude of you. I caught you. Wait till you see him. I saw him, and you're going to be surprised. You're mocking him. Don't put him down until you see him. He hadn't performed yet.

Then he started to rehearse and he started to wiggle and all that stuff and sing. The audience was not in, this is at the rehearsal. They looked at him — it was something new, they never saw a kid like this before. He was an original.

Then the buses showed up and we did the performance. They were naturally, of their own will, screaming because of his looks and he was so adorable. And then he started to wiggle with his butt and all that stuff, you know, his style, and they're standing up screaming. We had cameras all around. Regardless of being set up, they did it naturally. I didn't even have to tell 'em. We caught everything on camera and it was live.

The show went over tremendously. It was one of the first color specials. When the show was over you couldn't keep the dancers in our cast away from him. They were all after him. He was a sensation that night. He was terrific.

It was the second show I did with him "Hound Dog." I was the MC of the Texaco Star Theater Starring Milton Berle. It was strictly a variety show.

When he got through, I used to work with the performer, whoever it was, we worked together like an after piece, or I was weaved into their act. So, when he got through, I did some stand-up talk with him. And he was very shy. This was new to him, and I broke him up. He couldn't keep a straight face. This was a new business, a new alley, for him. I liked him and we got along very well, but when we got to do the live performance, he broke up while I was doing shtick with him. I put my arm around and said, "This is make-believe. Laugh it up." I said, "Come on, I laugh when you sing." Berle-isms. But by laughing it up naturally at me, he was more relating to the audience — like a new kid on the block, he was enjoying me. It set a pace for our audience.

I booked him back right away because he was a big hit. He was fresh and he had a new thing to show an audience. He jived and wiggled and all that stuff, with his foot and everything.

When he appeared with me, he was in the first of four specials. After my audience, and I played to a lot of young people, kids, with my style, I was obvious with visual hokey bits, pie in the face, falls, flops, etc. Today it's Jim Carrey doing this. I had been doing that for years, I did this ever since I started doing a standup, we used to call it a monolog, that format turned out to be Texaco.

After the first appearance of Elvis, I was still number-one in the ratings. A week later, instead of me receiving thousands of fan letters about me, written to me, I received about 300,000 letters from parents that said — they were not fan letters, they were *pan* letters, which was the first time I got them in my career on the air — Uncle Miltie or Mr. Berle, how dare you allow that young boy whose name was Elvis something...

I got the blame for booking him on the show, because they thought it was just out of line with the gyrations and everything and they never saw anything like that. We'll never let our children watch your show if you're going to put a performer like that on gyrating and doing those things. The way he wiggles is really rude and distasteful and all that. They thought that was terrible.

After having all these letters opened, they were practically all pan letters from my fans who loved me all those years. We're going around in circles because all that shit is happening again with cable. Censorship in those times was terrible. But this came from my audience.

I immediately called Parker. Before I told him I received these letters against Elvis and blaming me, I said, Colonel, you've got a star on your hands. If they were all of the same taste — how dare you? — when you receive that many don'ts against the yeses, it means they watched him. Elvis never knew anything about this; it was just between Tom and myself and Abe Lastfogel 'cause I'm kind of show-wise, because when you receive those kind of letters and they're all the same and they come that heavy, they're watching him. He must be hot. And he's going to be hotter. He was an original, not a copy. He was who he was and he created a new style.

That's one of the reasons he was such a sensation. That's one of the reasons I booked him back. We're talking about ratings and numbers.

I was very broad, a wise guy, very flippant, very brash in my style, but that was my style. Critics said I was too wild, too visual, too slapstick. This is before the Three Stooges. I was broad. I did all the broad visual things to please the public. In the '30s, Walter Winchell wrote something in his column I never forgot: Nobody likes Milton Berle except his mother and the public. [It was the same with Elvis.]

He was one of the nicest young gentlemen I ever met. He listened because he was new to this side of show biz. He had respect. I never knew him to say anything bad about anybody. I really loved him. As I look back, I don't feel I'm responsible for his success, I contributed to his success. I felt very close to him. He was always a nice guy and he did his duty with the war.

I had four specials and I had done two. I had him for the first one and the third one, then the season ended. I was ready to use him again. He wasn't available for the fourth special. I should have signed him for the four specials. We did the fourth special and that was the end of the season. I was ready to book him on, but we only had this one show and we couldn't do it.

Were you afraid to book him again after 300,000 letters of complaint?
Of course I was. I was concerned that maybe I would lose my audience, too, but I didn't. I didn't. I just stayed where I was. I was concerned about for myself, but more happy for him. They had never seen him. It was like a discovery. When you receive that many fan letters or pan letters, you know you've got something. So, I was happy. It did affect me a little, but I got over it. I was too busy working and doing the show and other things and producing and writing and performing. Fortunately, audiences who have favorites forget the scandalous things said about them. If the audience likes you, and they're with you and your fans are with you, and you're on top...so many stars overcame adversity of bad notices.

Did I feel a hurt? Was I afraid it would do something to me? Yes, but just for a few weeks until it got around that I had something to do with discovering him, and the plaudits went the other way. It didn't worry me. I stayed on. This is my 50th year in television and my 85th year in show business. And I got a birthday coming up in July, I'm going to be 89.

I wouldn't tell you all this shit if I didn't want to be quoted. I want to be truthful with you. I want them something on Presley that's different, that they don't know about it, don't read about. Something that you got a scoop on.

Alright, baby, let me hear from you. Take good care of yourself. ◆

In the early '90s, I was contacted by an editor at *Condé Nast Traveler*. He knew my writing and asked if I had any story ideas. I didn't fancy myself as any sort of budding Jan Morris, but the magazine had a huge editorial budget and a willingness to consider anything that involved, well, travel. And for a freelancer, an offer of possible work is never to be taken lightly.

In a flash of inspiration, I suggested what turned out to be a dream assignment: a four-day blues pilgrimage to the Mississippi Delta, seeking out the graves and other notable shrines to great musicians I had long admired. I'd never really been to the South, so I enlisted my intrepid high school friend Fred Wasser to go along, which proved wise for a number of reasons. For one thing I'd only recently learned to drive, and there was no way I was taking a road trip to the South by my lonesome.

In February 1992, we flew to Memphis and rented a car — an ostentatiously sporty silver job — that we drove down through Mississippi to New Orleans, where a great aunt of Fred's lived in the Garden District. After trying a stretch of Highway 61 to honor Bob Dylan we switched to Highway 1, which better served our geographical needs and turned out to be more scenic. At times there was so little traffic on the ruler-straight road that we gunned it to 100 mph.

En route from one hard-to-find grave marker to the next, every time we spotted a plume of smoke off the road we stopped and ate some of the most amazing barbeque imaginable. The trip was eventful. Our conspicuous ride drew the brief attention of cops in one town; we heard threatening mutters from crack addicts in darkened doorways; we were turned away at the door of a boisterous and melodic juke joint with the bouncer's firm insistence that there was no music going on inside, at least not for two white boys from up North. It was a little scary, but we had a blast.

The magazine never ran the piece, so it turned out to be an all-expenses-paid adventure that was educational, enlightening and enormously tasty. Fair enough.

Birth of the Blues

Condé Nast Traveler, 1992, unpublished

"You may bury my body down by the highway side...so my old evil spirit can catch a Greyhound bus and ride." When blues legend Robert Johnson sang those lyrics in the 1930s, Highway 61 was just a gravel road running up the west edge of Mississippi parallel to the Big Muddy. But to the children of slavery who had been raised on cotton and rice plantations in the Mississippi Delta — the triangle of fertile farmland between Memphis and Vicksburg fanning out east from the Mississippi River — this lonely strip of dirt was a lifeline to the big cities of the north. Among 61's frequent travelers were musicians, the working men and women now revered as the pioneers of the blues. Electric blues ultimately exploded out of Chicago, but this profoundly American music was born and raised in the Delta.

Highway 61 has become a modern thoroughfare, but traditional blues lives on, with a worldwide audience that feels right about music made for the soul, not the checkbook. Fortunately, people in the Delta are justifiably proud of their musical heritage and some have dedicated themselves to preserving and promoting it. So, if your taste runs more to Muddy Waters than Mariah Carey, a few days spent on the Delta blues trail can be a tonic well taken.

Before setting off, a little homework is in order. For a concise and illuminating history, read Robert Palmer's *Deep Blues* (Penguin); order your geography lesson, the *Delta Blues Map Kit*, from Stackhouse Records, 232 Sunflower Avenue, Clarksdale MS 38614. This hip pamphlet identifies enough blues shrines to plan your next trip as well.

The starting line for this expedition is Memphis, a city that has made music history a leading local industry. There's Graceland, of course, Sun Studios and Beale Street, a well-kept (but not entirely sterile) tourist district brimming with live music venues. BB King's Blues Club, as smoothly commercialized as its namesake, is at 143 Beale; across the street, the Center for Southern Folklore (152 Beale) mounts fascinating historical exhibits of the region's music and culture. Culinary tip for visitors to Sun Studios (706 Union Avenue): drive over to the bustling Cupboard (1495 Union) for an inexpensively memorable down-home lunch.

Memphis's newest blues stop also happens to be its best. Located within a record/guitar store facing the Peabody Hotel, the Memphis Music & Blues Museum (97 South Second Street) is packed with an afternoon's worth of vintage memorabilia. The well-organized exhibition cases devoted to legendary bluesmen like Furry Lewis, Robert Johnson, Robert Jr. Lockwood and Albert King, as well as Elvis, rockabilly and gospel are filled with photos, bios, records, guitars, harmonicas and more; many have earphones offering relevant musical accompaniment.

Get an early start the day you leave Memphis. Find the beginning of Highway 61, which is what Third Street becomes at Crump Boulevard, and head south for an hour. Turn west on Highway 49, which traverses the Hernando DeSoto Bridge into Helena, Arkansas. Every October, Helena's 8,000 residents are joined by 50,000 fans for the King Biscuit Blues Festival. (This year's dates are October 9-10. Contact PO Box 247, Helena AR 72342.) The rest of the year, Blues Corner is the town's main magnet for blues fans. Situated within This Little Pig Antiques at 105 Cherry Street, Bubba Sullivan's more-than-a-record-store mingles music with Delta artifacts and friendly conversation and serves as the headquarters of a group raising money to restore the decrepit Helena building (427 1/2 Elm Street) in which Sonny Boy Williamson lived and died. Although born in Mississippi, the wizard of the blues harp became a Helena celebrity as the star of the *King Biscuit Time* radio program. Fifty years later, KFFA (1360 AM) still blasts a half-hour of blues every weekday at 12:15, but the music now comes from records rather than live performance.

From Helena, it's a half-hour drive to Stovall, the cotton plantation where Muddy Waters lived and worked before he moved up to Chicago. Take 49 east until it meets Highway 1, then turn south for about fifteen miles. After the Clarksdale turn-off and several more intersections, turn left onto Stovall Road for two miles. The forlorn remnants of Waters' house, in which he ran a juke joint on weekends, are on the right. Originally built as slave quarters, the cabin was battered in a 1987 tornado; what's left is a roofless, fifteen-foot square of weathered cypress. Around back is an amusing injunction against removing souvenirs, signed by Howard Stovall, chairman of the Sunflower River Blues Association: "We will lay a BIG NASTY MOJO on you if you take anything."

Eight miles southeast of Stovall lies the unofficial capital of Delta blues, Clarksdale. The birthplace of John Lee Hooker (who'll celebrate his 75th birthday August 22nd) and Ike Turner now also boasts the Delta Blues Museum at the Carnegie Public Library (114 Delta Ave.). The recently expanded institution houses videos, records, literature and instruments (including the Muddywood guitar commissioned by ZZ Top, using a plank blown from Waters' shack) for entertaining perusal or serious research. One of the most interesting collections is blues art: paintings, sculptures, photographs and an extraordinary life-size figure of Muddy Waters that dominates a corner of the front room.

Clarksdale's other blues mine is Stackhouse Records (232 Sunflower Avenue), lodged in a former ice cream parlor built to resemble a steamboat. The shop not only sells a fine selection of old and new records, publications and related paraphernalia (need a John the Conqueror root?) it also houses the Rooster Blues label and has a hand in the annual *Sunflower River Blues Festival*, held the second Friday and Saturday of August. It's also one of the many stops on the blues circuit where friendly conversation and advice to visitors flows freely.

Finding graves can be a real challenge, but those with a sense of direction and history should make the effort to visit the final resting places of the men who made the music.

Sonny Boy Williamson's grave is not that far from Clarksdale. Take 49 south for 15 miles. (Incidentally, the junction of 49 and 61 — a disappointing Clarksdale corner with a couple of gas stations — is identified by Stackhouse's Jim O'Neal as the fabled crossroads where Robert Johnson is supposed to have met the Devil.) Right after you blink through Tutwiler there's a fork; take 49W and make a hard right immediately after the "ROME 4" sign. Go half a mile through the field, then make a left at the fenced-in gas pump. The abandoned Whitfield church, an unmarked white building with a green roof, is a mile-and-a-half down the road, on the right. Ninety feet to the left of the church is the handsome headstone — inscribed with Sonny Boy's given name, Aleck Miller, and strewn with harmonicas, guitar picks and other items of tribute. If you're done for the day, you can drive through Indianola (birthplace of BB King, who has a park named for him) and stay in Greenville, a good-sized town 60 miles from Tutwiler. If you do, try Mr. Jay's Q at 1003 Highway 82W for a spectacular plate of smoky ribs.

Otherwise, follow 49 to 82 and head east to Holly Ridge, a hamlet just off the highway about nine miles from Leland. Shortly after the turnoff you'll see a cotton gin. The New Jerusalem church is on the near side of the mill; the cemetery is a bit further along. At the far left corner is the grave of Charley Patton, twenty years Robert Johnson's senior and generally credited as his primary influence.

As befits the object of endless mythologizing, Johnson's own whereabouts are a matter of debate: two separate cemeteries in Leflore County contain markers and claim his remains. One is outside Quito. Take 82E for 25 miles; turn south down Highway 7 and go through Itta Bena. (Be careful to stay on 7, which makes a funny little jog west before exiting the town.) About three miles later turn right onto a dirt road (512W) and look for Payne Chapel, where, in 1991, an Atlanta rock band placed a modest stone with the epitaph "Resting in the Blues."

That same year, Columbia Records celebrated the astonishing success of its Grammy-winning *Robert Johnson: The Complete Recordings* boxed set by erecting an impressive memorial in a peaceful spot at the Mount Zion church, the cemetery noted on Johnson's death certificate. It's northeast of Morgan City: Leaving the Quito site, take Highway 7 south for three-and-a-half miles, turn left on 511 and it's right there.

You can improvise the rest. Vicksburg isn't a blues center, but it has other attractions, such as the Old Southern Tea Room (801 Clay Street). Mississippi's cosmopolitan capital, Jackson, has clubs and juke joints — try the Queen of Hearts at 2243 Martin Luther King Jr. Drive. The region has plenty of other blues sites which local aficionados will gladly recommend.

So, pack some tapes, bring a hearty appetite for barbecue and adventure, and let the music set your course. ◆

What remains of Muddy Waters' shack on the Stovall plantation:

😈😈😈 My Greatest Hits 😈😈😈

I've written some harsh appraisals in my time. What does that make me? Funny, demanding, intolerant, gutsy, curmudgeonly, peevish, rigorous or just another angry asshole fixing some private hurt by breaking butterflies on a wheel? Perhaps all of those things. The mean stuff is often what people remember, and I'm alright with that. Although I do regret the venom I spewed in an obnoxious early *Trouser Press* article titled "Is Patti a Patsy?" I am proud of these broadsides and stand by the opinions they convey.

Some particularly sanguinary selections from my critical abattoir:

Sting

Alighting in Switzerland, Sting produced the effete intellectual masturbation of *Nothing Like the Sun*, one of the most self-important records on record. Aided by a new batch of virtuosos and famous guests (Andy Summers, Gil Evans, Eric Clapton, Mark Knopfler and Rubén Blades, credited on one track with "Spanish"), Sting stretches a dozen delicate songs over two short discs, coming down off his high horse long enough to show Jimi Hendrix aficionados a numbingly dull way to perform "Little Wing." It's a tedious, bankrupt and vacuous cavern of a record. Even as the nouveau sophisticate sings "History Will Teach Us Nothing," his pedantic instincts and bulging ego inform the lyrics at every turn with political dilettantism, literary name-dropping and prolix pseudo-profundities.

There's an epistolary footnote to that one:

> Michael Roberts, *Syracuse New Times* / 17 Jan 92
>
> Dear Michael: A friend at Chrysalis Records brought your *Hero Worship* piece from October to my attention. While I am flattered to be referred to as the "great Ira Robbins," I must point out that I did not actually write the Police quote you cited from the *Trouser Press Record Guide*. While I did, in a separate entry, refer to Sting as "smug and pretentious," called *Nothing Like the Sun* "effete intellectual masturbation" and wrote that "his pedantic instincts and bulging ego inform the lyrics of 'History Will Teach Us Nothing' at every turn with political dilettantism, literary name-dropping and prolix pseudo-profundities," the Police entry was actually written by the great Jim Green.

The Fixx

A xeroxed quote from this review was tacked up on a bulletin board at WLIR-FM; I spotted it during a visit to the studio for an interview with Ben Manilla. The pacesetting alternative rock station on Long Island was a big supporter of the band, and my contrary review was evidently a source of amusement and derision.

Although they sound like a dozen other pretentious synth-heavy atmospheric English dance bands of the early '80s, London's Fixx, aided immeasurably for a time by producer Rupert Hine's ability to sculpt their mundane songs and uncover marginal tense appeal, have managed to become enormously successful, regularly drawing a couple of irritating hits from each album. *Shuttered Room* offers "Red Skies" and "Stand or Fall"; *Reach the Beach* contains "One Thing Leads to Another" and "Saved by Zero"; *Phantoms* has "Are We Ourselves?" Showing remarkable consistency, they are all equally unpleasant and trivial.

Barenaked Ladies

As cute as a baby and as appealing as a loaded diaper, Toronto's Barenaked Ladies — in truth, a bunch of guys whose only discernible fashion statement is their heinous haircuts — rope together the hyperactive lyrical imagination of They Might Be Giants, the overbearing sentimentality of Harry Chapin, the folk-rocky musical conviction of Jimmy Buffett (the group most often sounds like it's hitting the Squeeze sample button on its stylistic synthesizer) and the hip rock sensibilities of a high-school principal to produce a gut course for impressionable liberal arts majors. (You haven't fully loathed a concert crowd until you've seen boxloads of dry Kraft macaroni and cheese gaily thrown onstage in ritual response to a line from *Gordon*'s "If I Had $1000000.")

Jane's Addiction

Pulling himself further into a private world of self-congratulatory decadence (the inclusion of a methadone bottle on the back cover's botanica shelf is bad news, whatever the intention), Farrell fills the absurd *Ritual de lo Habitual* with ravings that, when they manage to coagulate into coherence, describe the joys of shoplifting ("Been Caught Stealing," the pathetic bleat of a spoiled rich asshole that inexplicably begins with barking dogs), masochism ("Ain't No Right"), supposed solidarity with Black people ("No One's Leaving") and a nebulous 11-minute opus about a *ménage à trois* ("Three Days"). The band's swirling demi-metal — still limited by Navarro's slow progress toward the guitar heroism he would ultimately achieve — is loudly functional, but Farrell's expanding ego and detachment make the album unbearable.

Alanis Morissette

Either an astute bandwagon jumper with exquisite timing, the sharp-tongued mouthpiece for calculating commercial interests or a maturing young artist clumsily finding her creative purpose after two premature hack jobs (or all three), Ottawa-born singer Alanis Morissette helped define the mid-'90s by downloading all the ethernet enthusiasm music-buyers had developed for stand-up women like Chrissie Hynde, Madonna, Sophie B. Hawkins, Liz Phair and Courtney Love and, with *Jagged Little Pill*, galvanizing it. At just the right cultural moment, putting a slickly commercialized spin on the trendiness of youthful angst, Morissette made herself the lightning rod for polar sympathies, offering a potent but misleading combination of cheap fantasy thrills and the illusion of female empowerment. Basically, Morissette — who sings in a piercing yet throaty warble that some find unendurable — owes her stardom to the supposed shock/titillation value of "You Oughta Know," a petulant post-breakup song that crudely asks, "Would she go down on you in a theater?" and "Are you thinking of me when you fuck her?" It's amazing how little it takes to get people off these days.

Falco

The late Falco (Johann Hoelcel) was something of a hero in his native Austria; although he sang (in a random pastiche of accented English and German) like an arch, continental smoothie, his shtick was slick, thematically simpleminded chart fare, syncopated and fashionably automated (lots of synth, computerized drums with roto-tom and cymbal overdubs). The best parts of *Einzelhaft*...are tedious rock; the tracks that brought him international viability ("Der Kommissar," a U.S. hit when badly covered in English by After the Fire; "Maschine Brennt") are repulsive pseudo-funk with obnoxiously patronizing attempts at African-American lingo, accents and music, sung in a constipated gurgle as appealing as hearing someone vomit outside your window.

Greil Marcus

There's so much stupidity in rock journalism that I hate to come out on the side of anti-intellectualism, but *Invisible Republic, Mystery Train* author Greil Marcus' latest Ivy-league tome, is — in the words of Eric Burdon quoting Bo Diddley appraising the Animals in their tributary song about him — "the biggest load of rubbish I ever heard in my life!"

The unbearably pretentious *Invisible Republic*...turn[s] each passing reference into a protracted soliloquy that leaves the book's supposed subject stranded by the side of this winding highway. Under Marcus's microscopic analysis, the chorus of "Lo and Behold!" (which consists of the title three times, the words "looking for my" and a coda of "Get me out of here my dear man") reveals a 1931 book about American national character, 18th-century Puritan preacher Jonathan Edwards, Martin Luther King Jr., William S. Burroughs, blues singer Frank Hutchison and West Virginia's mine war. If that seems like a lot of baggage to hang on such a wee bit of music, you're in for a bumpy ride.

Grand Funk Railroad

Of all the rock acts I have loathed, Grand Funk was barely a bad memory when all my old objections to the band crystallized one morning in the spring of 2000. I banged this out with little greater purpose than to shed some long-stewing bile and air a long-harbored cultural theory. Years later, the ridiculously talented and courageous bomb-thrower Tim Sommer would relaunch his writing career with high-octane broadsides of this sort, only wielding a sharper and wider wit than I could manage at the time.

There stands before you a murderer — the band that killed rock'n'roll.

Salon, 10 April 2000

Among cultural historians, it has long been an article of faith that the '60s dream died in an ugly bar fight at Altamont Speedway in December 1969. Given the evidence, it's not a bad guess. After all, the Rolling Stones' well-intentioned fiasco proved that rock and roll wasn't about good vibes and peace (man) and made it clear that the Woodstock nation was far better equipped to destroy itself than take on any nebulous "establishment." Within a year, superstars would start ODing like flies, the Beatles would sue each other and Don McLean would write "American Pie." How much more habeas corpus do you need?

As Freddy Krueger later observed, you can't kill something that's already dead. By the winter of '69, rock was already flat-lining. If the bad news had yet to reach the front lines — and some might argue that it never has — the monument to virile youth the Stones helped erect only a few years earlier was an edifice about to be wrecked.

And, ironically enough, not by its sworn enemies or its craftiest exploiters. Not by MTV, hip-hop, the Internet or even Celine Dion. No, rock and roll was done in by three well-intentioned nobodies who, to their credit, worked hard and believed in themselves. That their values ran counter to the counter-culture might have left them on the outside looking in a year earlier, but the '60s were ready for last call. That party had gone out of bounds with hard drugs and the discovery of death as a lifestyle and was facing a grim and uncertain morning-after. The new left politics [that] rock had inadvertently fueled had diverged into feel-good Moratorium marches and self-obsessed bombers. Stardom corrupted musical idealists and left them easy prey for commercial interests. With Newtonian certainty, the great leap forward was ready for its about-face.

The world didn't need any more fixing, at least not of the sort that had turned to mud at *Woodstock*. There was nothing to be nostalgic about, since youth culture needed to see its reflection, and the Elvis '50s didn't look familiar at all. The future was too hard to comprehend, and far harder still to imagine shaping. No, what the world needed, in the eyes of those unaware of its possibilities, was the kind of fun that didn't mean anything. As the social pendulum began its great swing back, Grand Funk Railroad rolled up to embody that know-nothing reactionary spirit and make it the soundtrack of the '70s.

The Railroad arose from Michigan's working class industrial fug around the same time as the Stooges, but their garage-bred ineptitude was a completely different American breed. The Stooges were bad seeds, pollution-fueled aliens who had abandoned life's assembly line to make music of enormously negative appeal as they accelerated blindly towards a personal hell. Ugly, depraved, unsophisticated but knowledgeably honoring some worthy predecessors, these vicious bohemians fit into the cultural fabric like cigarette holes in a couch. Their clothes and demeanor, if at all conscious, were not meant to help them fit in but to stand out, to inflict whatever offense was still possible in a time of great moral decay.

Grand Funk were Nixon's silent majority, living proof that long hair and loud music signified nothing more than the Prez muttering "Sock it to me" on *Laugh-In*. Arriving on the scene too late to grasp rock's pivotal role in shaping the '60s, they observed a landscape of no-account hippies, foreign influence and dissipating idealism — and didn't like what they saw. (The bra-less chicks, drugs and ready cash were another story.) Unlike the sissies and bookworms who had found rock and roll their court of last resort, Mark, Don and Mel were hard, simple and strong — macho moral descendants of John Wayne and Billy Jack — and they knew their country needed them. Owing nothing to history, unashamed of their shortcomings and undaunted by their obstacles, they suited up and got to work. Though hardly in the same league, they shrewdly fashioned themselves a power trio after Cream, who conveniently dissolved just around the same time.

Others could lock themselves away, spending unconscionable amounts of time in the studio making grandiose art-rock of increasing intricacy and technical reach; Grand Funk displayed the rugged efficiency of line workers. These get-it-done types released two albums in each of their first four years, paving the way for cynics like the equally unselfconscious KISS, who also knew to keep striking while the iron was on fire.

In addition to a career-launching appearance at the *Atlanta Pop Festival* a month before *Woodstock*, Grand Funk released a pair of LPs in 1969 and began their inexorable plod to superstardom. Appearing only weeks after Altamont, their second longplayer, *Grand Funk Railroad*, is a textbook classic of sweat-rock, a lumbering collection of clichés played with the conviction of Charlton Heston parting the Red Sea and the mindless determination of Rocky Balboa leaking blood on the canvas. Whereas the Stooges presumably noticed the vast chasm between their work and the sound of young America — and thought themselves the better for it — Grand Funk comically gave it their best shot with quavering vocals, grunting bass and high-school guitar licks. And they were richly rewarded.

With three additional decades of rock history to consider, their ineptitude can actually be forgiven. After all, punk couldn't have happened if instrumental ability were a prerequisite. But lack of skill has to be mortgaged against some brilliant idea, or at least a clever novelty. Grand Funk, God love 'em, didn't have an original bone in their body. They went from being puppets of an autocratic manager to willing servants of strong producers like Todd Rundgren without ever demonstrating a shred of individual creativity. Their best work, save for the dumb-luck power of "We're an American Band," came via covers of classics like "The Loco-Motion" or "Some Kind of Wonderful." And uncredited borrowings, like the Ten Years After chorus ("Love Like a Man") in Grand Funk's subsequent "Walk Like a Man." The significance of their merciless decimation of "Gimme Shelter," the Stones song for which the Maysles named their documentary film of the dismal doings at Altamont, however, is too dense to contemplate. No, GFR were bad singers and players, but success calls its own tune, and their unmitigated shittiness became an acceptable '70s benchmark.

With the green-eyed gods of commerce on their side, Grand Funk sold an unheard-of ten-million albums within two years. And that was that. Critics could carp all they wanted, but it was a new decade and a new generation had spoken. The '60s suddenly felt like a pitifully naïve oasis, pre-school for the big boys. In the wake of Grand Funk's jolly thuggery, the era they had wiped away felt like it might have been a mass hallucination, and rock was revealed to be just another cynical American industry, free of social consequence and solidly status quo. Flag-burners be damned — the irony-impaired Grand Funk posed nude in a barnyard full of flags and made it look respectful.

The success of Grand Funk dragged rock back to Earth from its wildest imaginings, as if the space program had been taken over by McDonalds and NASA's rocketry breakthroughs [repurposed] to broiling burgers. In their clumsiness, Grand Funk inadvertently knocked down the wall that had divided rock self-expression from market-driven factory pop. Shorn of its pretensions and dreams, its politics and its effeminacy, rock entered *Have a Nice Day* hell, the vapid wasteland of the early '70s in which musical styles became random buttons on the Top 40 jukebox. While Britain's teens embraced the future in platform heels and eye shadow, Americans would go years before rediscovering music's artistic and cultural ambitions.

But, in their own minds, Grand Funk were ready to save America. Weighing in late on the Vietnam saga (14 months before the signing of the Paris peace accords, as it happens), they declared, "People, Let's Stop the War" on 1971's *E Pluribus Funk*, reducing years of protest against the military-industrial complex to three incoherent lines. On the same album, which is the most outspoken for singer-guitarist-songwriter Mark Farner, he takes a bold stand to "Save the Land." More typical of the group's spiritual concerns is the unbridled passion of "Heartbreaker," a minor hit released in early 1970.

Critics raked them over the coals, but Grand Funk had the last laugh. Victory was theirs, no matter how many pussies with pens proclaimed that they sucked. Their sales as much as their sensibilities cleared a path to football stadiums, where rock, sports and other testosterone-fueled mass gatherings could finally meld into one universal crud culture. That would lead to even worse things. (Maybe you don't care that rock songs have become "jock classics" or that hot dogs are hawked in the stands at Pink Floyd shows, but I do.) Farner went on to become a survivalist and born-again Christian. In the liner notes to the band's *Thirty Years of Funk* box set, he writes, "Just for the record, I despise the men and women who under the influence of darkness have compromised the sovereignty of the People of the United States." Can you spell W-A-C-O?

There have been far worse bands than Grand Funk Railroad, but try and imagine what might have happened if it had been, say, Melanie who had been able to outsell the Beatles at Shea Stadium. That would have fixed rock's male paradigm, wouldn't it? What Grand Funk did was establish banality as a mass-market ideal, inverting the idealism that had once driven artists to strive for creative progress, testing and shedding styles like babies learning to walk. For a brief, exciting time, rock could not bear to stand still, and its greats were those who constantly sought new challenges. Between 1966 and 1969, it was swept by waves of psychedelia, sitar, folk, blues, country and more. The arrival of Grand Funk stopped progress dead in its tracks. Ill-suited to do more than sweat, stomp and sell, they were neither capable of, nor inclined to, advance. By the time they got out of the way, ushered into the past tense by two albums that tanked, the latter having been produced by Frank Zappa (bless his bearded little head), the '70s were more than half over. As if on cue, the Ramones were counting it down on the Bowery, and it was time to begin again. ◆

Joan Jett

Far from my finest hour, this juvenile display of my inability to pick hits (in this case, with a regrettable dollop of gratuitous sexism) elicited separate replies from the future Rock and Roll Hall of Famer and her manager/producer.

Joan Jett

Trouser Press, September 1980

In one swift kick, this record disproves four conventional rock tenets: First, that anyone, given time and a chance to practice, can learn how to sing and play guitar. Second, that women are making real strides in establishing themselves on an equal footing with men in rock'n'roll. Third, that record labels don't throw their money away on artists with absolutely no talent. Fourth, that recording techniques can make any singer sound at least OK.

Joan Jett has a few things going against her. She can't sing outside a range of about five notes; anything higher forces her to screech flatly. Her dynamic scale goes from very soft (where she sounds fairly good) to shrieking in one neat step, without an inch of middle ground. Her delivery is also totally expressionless. She evidently doesn't play guitar very well; record credits indicate that other guitarists handled lead. And she apparently doesn't write too many usable songs: of the eleven here, she composed only one herself and co-wrote two more with producers Kenny Laguna and Ritchie Cordell.

So, what does Joan do? Why has she made this album? Who at Ariola made the mistake of paying for this and the gumption to release it? Why is Joan still as futile as when the Runaways first began shaking their underage tailfeathers?

What's interesting about this record is Laguna and Cordell, both of whom have long and involved histories. The latter produced and wrote hits for Tommy James and the Shondells. *Joan Jett* contains a version of James's first hit ("Hanky Panky"), a number he covered (the Isley Brothers' "Shout") and a tune co-written by Cordell and his partner in Shondellia, Bo Gentry. *Joan Jett* is the direct descendant of *I Think We're Alone Now* without any of the good stuff. ◆

In response to that churlish (but not unwarranted) review, I received indignant letters from Jett (a handwritten defense of herself as a rhythm guitarist "in the company of Brian Jones, John Lennon, Greg Kihn and Bruce Springsteen") and Laguna (dictated and typed: "I cannot believe how extreme your review was... Perhaps if you'd listened to the record with more of an open mind, you might have enjoyed a fun album by a great rock and roll person who knows that rock and roll is supposed to be fun.")

I can agree ... to a degree. The album is not good, but I surely could have written a less vengeful pan. I evidently felt some contrition, since my review of her follow-up 18 months later was a *lot* more generous. (The eponymous debut was retitled *Bad Reputation* for its major-label reissue.) And I seem to have echoed Laguna in the first graf.

Joan Jett and the Blackhearts

I Love Rock-n-Roll

Trouser Press, March 1982

Joan Jett's first solo album, *Bad Reputation*, suffered from a number of flaws I pointed out in my review of the time; listening to it now, I must admit I might have been somewhat curmudgeonly about it. Joan's skills are unquestionably rudimentary, but her straight-ahead goodtime sound and good taste in picking non-originals make for unchallenging rock'n'roll fun — something lacking in many of today's more cerebral bands.

While her last record was a production hodgepodge — a collection of recording sessions at various studios over twelve months, using three different bands and songs of inconsistent quality — Jett's new one is well-conceived and cleanly executed. She's also writing more, and a competent new set of Blackhearts make for a stronger presentation all around. There's a fair amount of hackneyed and failed material, but as long as this album is accepted in the uncomplicated and unpretentious spirit in which it was evidently intended, everyone goes home happy.

Jett's readings of "Crimson and Clover" and "Bits and Pieces" are plain and simple, and okay if you relish familiarity. Doing "Little Drummer Boy" in time for the holidays is a nice touch; it's always fun to hear a delicate song bludgeoned with a rock treatment. The title track, originally done by the Arrows, sounds appropriately raunch-and-rabble.

The originals are solid rockers not far removed from what Suzi Quatro built her career on — not as catchy but certainly more liberated. The best of the lot, "Nag," works the refrain "Nag nag naggity nag" into a rocky little bopper. Joan Jett may not be the greatest, but there's certainly room for her on my turntable and yours, too. ◆

The Trouser Press Guide to '90s Rock, 1997 (excerpt)

Always a contradiction of commercial accommodation and left-of-the-dial aspiration, Jett sounds unfazed by the incongruity of songwriting collaborations with both Paul Westerberg and Desmond Child on the slickly run-of-the-mill *Notorious*. Likewise, Jett's covers album, *The Hit List*, includes her renditions of "Pretty Vacant" and "Roadrunner" alongside AC/DC's "Dirty Deeds Done Dirt Cheap" and the Kinks' "Celluloid Heroes." Like the good [Baltimore] Orioles fan she is, Jett keeps her eye on the ball.

Even on *Pure and Simple*, the most ambitiously uncommon album of her career, Jett can't simplify her life. While moved to unprecedented levels of boisterous energy by her obstreperous disciples — Kathleen Hanna (Bikini Kill), Kat Bjelland (Babes in Toyland), Donita Sparks and Jennifer Finch (L7) all stop by to write and play with her — she still employs the same old song-factory pros. (In one of rock's oddest culture clashes, Hanna, Child and Jett all share songwriting credit for the tunelessly hostile "You Got a Problem.") Still, a renewed sense of purpose and Hanna's random antagonism helps Jett survive a daunting stack of big-league producers, and *Pure and Simple* is a punchy, no-frills collection of chunky electric guitar chords, 4/4 beats and melodically shouted choruses as catchy and cool as any in her past. Searching for a sense of place, Jett spends the album trying to deny her self-consciousness: "As I Am," "Wonderin'," "Spinster" and "Insecure" all acknowledge uncertainty and plead for acceptance — if not understanding. Her tributes to new pals ("Activity Grrrl") and murdered Gits singer Mia Zapata ("Go Home") are too oblique and awkward to convey much, but the point of her concern is well-taken. Whether she is a riot grrrl or just plays one in the studio, Jett has never been better. Even her handlers might have learned something from this one. The album, CD and cassette contain different sets of songs that suggest a careful bit of demographic calculation. Bjelland's "Here to Stay" and Sparks' "Hostility" appear on vinyl but not CD; the reverse is true for Child's schmaltz-slathered "Brighter Day" and onetime Bryan Adams songwriter Jim Vallance's wonderful "Wonderin'."

Jett subsequently deepened her involvement in the indie-rock world and her commitment to the memory of Mia Zapata by performing three early-'95 benefit shows fronting a band with the former Gits, who had already regrouped as Dancing French Liberals of '48. *Evil Stig*, the pro temp quartet's semi-live album (the proceeds of which were marked for a fund to find Zapata's killer) consists largely of Gits songs — half of them from the 1994 *Enter: The Conquering Chicken* album — but also contains *Pure and Simple*'s "You Got a Problem" and "Activity Grrrl" (not "Go Home" — that went to the *Home Alive* compilation), a needless remake of Tommy James' "Crimson & Clover" (the song was a hit for Jett in 1982) and a poppy *Evil Stig* original, "Last to Know." It's weird the way the album doesn't differentiate between the freewheeling stage work and overproduced studio efforts, but that's always been typical of Jett's not-quite-in-tune career. No matter. This gutsy, hoarse and rousing record that strikes a workable balance between the veteran's arena experience and the younguns' raucous punk animation is an important and impressive step in Joan Jett's creative rehabilitation. ◆

Second Thoughts

I have written very little about Bruce Springsteen over the years. Not that I don't have strong opinions about him and his work — anyone who knows me has heard them vociferously expressed. I am, as one says when one prefers not to provoke an argument, not a fan. Although I am obviously no subscriber to the "if you can't something nice" school of thought, I do try to sheathe vindictive criticism when it would serve no purpose.

But I am not a fan. So much so that when the *Trouser Press* brain trust decided to run a story about him (by my longtime friend Wayne King, a proud New Jersey native with whom I vehemently disagree on very few things other than his Springsteen fandom) on the cover in 1980, I still found a way to do so without having him appear on it. (The vintage Fender Esquire, standing-in for Springsteen's venerated axe, was a ringer. It belonged to *TP* editor Scott Isler. We brought it to the Record Plant and stood it there, Zelig-like, to be photographed by Mitch Kearney.)

Bruce Springsteen

Greatest Hits

Newsday, February 1985

One needn't have much regard for his music to agree that Bruce Springsteen is a genuine American rock god and has been for two full decades. Too distinctive to be imitated and as profoundly popular as any musician alive, this proletarian troubadour of white suburbia became the rear-view mirror for a vast, culturally disaffected audience that worshiped him for being their kind, their flesh-and-blood saint.

Transplanting a hybrid of Spectorized R&B and Bob Dylan verbosity into bombastic arena rock, this principled believer in the honor of being a musician refused to play the game. He wouldn't ransom his songs or tours to advertisers; he was reluctant to make promo videos or pimp himself with TV appearances. In concert, he gave to the limits of his physical endurance, converting passion to sweat in a dubious alchemy of musical greatness.

While the esteem in which Springsteen is publicly held remains a high and mighty stone monument (individual album sales notwithstanding), the arc of his career seems headed toward the living statue of a venerated but inactive great like Joe DiMaggio. Whether due to adult satisfactions, a conscious retreat or just a fallow creative patch, Springsteen no longer swings the musical bat like a boy of summer. He has made exactly two credible studio albums (*Born in the USA* and *Tunnel of Love*) in the past 13 years; *Human Touch* and *Lucky Town* did nothing to improve his '90s profile. If not for the one-off "Streets of Philadelphia," he wouldn't have no luck at all.

So, the arrival of a one-CD *Greatest Hits* album — the most standard concession and place-keeper for an artist treading water, if not drowning — feels less like the pause that recharges than a dire turning point, a stock-taking that promises nothing. If nothing else, it's an ineffectual echo of his retrospective 1986 live box. Even the new material — a momentary reunion with the old E Street Band, tucked in here to up the ante rather than to solidify a major new effort — increases the backdated sensation.

Paying oddly selective attention to Springsteen's past, *Greatest Hits* neglects *Greetings From Asbury Park, New Jersey* and *The Wild, the Innocent and the E Street Shuffle* to join the saga in chronological progress with the title track and "Thunder Road" from his third album, *Born to Run*. That decision — which omits several concert and radio staples more essential to the oeuvre than 1992's tuneless *Human Touch* — and an unsteady focus (the synthesized pop of "Dancing in the Dark" but not the same album's nearly as big-charting "I'm on Fire"; "Brilliant Disguise" rather than "Tunnel of Love") provides a revisionist view of Springsteen's work. *Greatest Hits* downplays the brawny youth that made him a star in favor of durable Big Statements and somber maturity, like "The River" and "Atlantic City."

The four previously unreleased tracks salting the 18-song selection include an '82 outtake, "Murder Incorporated," that sounds too much like Bryan Adams and not enough like Neil Young. The newly recorded "Secret Garden" follows the moody keyboard template of "Streets of Philadelphia" to mushier effect; "This Hard Land" finds Springsteen reclaiming his Woody Guthrie epic mode for a sweeping drifter's tale.

The Dylanesque "Blood Brothers" is a pretty but pat rumination on adulthood that includes such typical profundities as "Now the hardness of this world slowly grinds your dreams away." Judging by the tenor of this collection, Springsteen knows what he's singing about. ◆

Although I can now see that I was way more patronizingly scornful than I should have been in that review, I can't say my overall enthusiasm for Springsteen's work has grown much in the years since.

I praised a 1993 benefit show he played: "Springsteen's years as a rock'n'roller have made him a riveting solo artist, capable of dominating a huge hall all by himself." (My full review of the 33-song marathon is included in a previous chapter.) The notes I took at the gig include the phrase "rock's greatest plebian." I'm not sure quite what I meant by that, but you get the drift. Also from my notes (written in darkness at the heart of town, as it were): "By now, his moves and poses are so familiar that he barely has to suggest them to elicit a response — proof of how little they meant in the first place." Not sure that bears scrutiny, and that's probably why it didn't end up in the piece.

But the one time I was persuaded to attend a full E Street Band show in December 1980 I was bored off my ass by the bombast, the monotony, the overbearing endlessness of it all. When the musicians finally left the stage after what seemed like an eternity (all concerts have always begun losing their luster for me after an hour), I turned to Wayne and said something along the lines of "thank Christ that's finally finished" only to be informed, with some amusement, that we were in for a whole second set of equal (if not greater) duration.

That same year, I assigned myself to review *The River* for *Trouser Press*. Other than that greatest hits collection, it's the only album of his I have ever commented on in print. Reading this now, it's apparent I had not yet grasped the fact that few words add less to a piece of criticism than "interesting." I let Wayne King, whose enthusiasm for Springsteen matched his love of the Who (a dichotomy I have never understood), read my review before it went to print and his letter to the editor castigating me for it ran in the same issue. Why postpone the inevitable?

Bruce Springsteen
The River
Trouser Press, January 1981

A *Saturday Night Live* sketch of a few seasons back poked fun at Roy Orbison by reducing him to a caricature: motionless stance and ever-present shades. With this overdue collection — given added weight by being a double album — Bruce Springsteen has proven himself to be equally typecast. Unable or unwilling to cast off the clichés of his past records, *The River*'s attempt to Make a Statement is buried in an avalanche of repetition and evident lack of inspiration.

Like a painter with a monochromatic palette, Springsteen is limited to working with his too-familiar "street" character. As a result, we get a batch of undynamic tracks lacking both the urgency and clarity of past successes. Instead of impact or emotional urgency, Springsteen substitutes a ridiculous "party atmosphere." *The River* adds up to a water-treading exercise that neither upholds his standards of excellence nor explores any new avenues.

Springsteen deservedly commands a lot of respect; despite all the drumbeating done on his behalf, nothing he's ever said or written would suggest he believes any of the messiah hype. His ethics, overall accessibility and commitment to maintain self-imposed standards are both rare and commendable. Now, if only the results were more interesting. Throughout his recording career, he's repeatedly done things that repel my sense of rock aesthetics and reduce his music to laughable bombast. Springsteen has two major stumbling blocks: stunningly bad vocals and perennially flawed lyrics. His wounded buffalo noises should be reserved for football grandstands. He also repeats lines mercilessly and meanders into a high register that is not his domain; the sound of his voice cracking and straining destroys any mood he might have built up (e.g., "Drive All Night" on Side Four). Lyrically, Springsteen is capable of powerful tableaus and stories, but he insists on tossing in his crutch words — "night," "street," "darkness," "drive" — as if he were totally unable to imagine a sunlit world not moving along a thoroughfare. That sort of monomania might be okay for an entire album, but not a career.

The River paints a bleak picture of the American dream gone sour: kids forced into marriage and adulthood; people disgusted with their lives and jobs; lovers and families who know they're doomed to grow apart. Everything is wrapped in automotive settings and metaphors that are tenuous at best. All Springsteen's songs are about those same dismal lives in one way or another, just as the highway metaphor runs through his work. Almost all *The River*'s themes, in fact, could have been consolidated into one song.

With a few exceptions, the album's music offers little excitement and less novelty, relying on fairly routine Springsteen moves. The songs can be classified as lightweight, uptempo party tunes with familiar phrases and Jukes-like joviality; slow, somber workouts that sound (at worst) like Jackson Browne; and medium-tempo numbers in the vein of "Tenth Avenue Freezeout" which work about half the time. Numbers that seem likely to survive include "Two Hearts," "Independence Day," "You Can Look (But You Better Not Touch)," "Cadillac Ranch," "Fade Away" and "I'm a Rocker." The remainder adds up to precious little, and all of Side Four is simply awful.

The ultimate failure of *The River* lies with its language. When he started out, Springsteen's songs were embarrassing fairy tales populated with foolishly named characters and crammed full of juvenile cleverness. By the time of *Born to Run,* he had developed a knack for scene-setting and story-telling, replete with poetic descriptions and insights. With each successive album it appears less likely that Springsteen will ever match those tales of urban lives and individual fortitude. For this outing, he's reduced to writing trivial nonsense in the guise of good-time rock'n'roll on one hand and ponderous pomp on the other.

Springsteen's reliance on a limited vocabulary points up his artistic limitations. Out of 20 tracks, 13 use "night"; nine use "street" and there are four with "highway" and two with "avenue"; "drive" turns up in 10 songs, as does "heart." And these few words appear constantly throughout many of his previous songs as well. Repetitive language might be forgivable if the songs dealt with different subjects, but Springsteen just goes back over the same ground, neither refining nor elucidating — merely restating.

All that said, I'm sincerely glad Springsteen exists. He's had a tremendous (and I think positive) effect on the rock community; fans, musicians and industry people have all been inspired by his work. His dedication, principles and heart have reawakened a lot of dormant enthusiasm among ex-rockers who thought themselves beyond the music's magic grip — no mean feat. Disregarding overzealous fans and generally boring records, I respect Springsteen for proving you don't need to trade your soul for stardom (even if people try to do it for you). But that doesn't make *The River* a better record. It's a stagnant talent who can't or won't dig himself out of the mud. That's a shame. ◆

In the four decades since I wrote that, I've heard some of those songs played countless times, and my critical harshness in general has softened with age. So, what do I make of *The River* in 2020? (And, yes, I still have my copy.)

The songwriting is clearly in thrall to the music of the '60s; most of the material is rebuilt on the chassis of various styles of AM radio hits. That's not a criticism, but it does give a musty aroma to a 1980 album. And the fact that Springsteen's subject matter is rooted in the same era adds to the sense of *déjà entendu*. If the goal was generational signifying, 35-year-olds of the time would certainly have felt comfortably at home in this home-cooked mush. The production is all over the place; with so many instruments vying to be heard, the album sounds like it was mixed to replicate the sound of a worn 45. Overly generous echo exaggerates the blurry roughness of Springsteen's voice, while the backup singing is pushed so far behind it that it barely registers.

Right off, I will take one thing back: Side Four is not "simply awful." I was probably exhausted and disgusted by the time I flipped the vinyl over for the last time and may not have given it a fair hearing. Or maybe I lost hope amid the hackneyed sexist garage-rock rubbish of the first track on the side, "Ramrod," which Springsteen sings with smarmy swagger: "I wanna ramrod with you honey till half-past dawn." (Also, the drumming by Max Weinberg is absolutely dreadful in its rank heartlessness.) The rest of the side — which in essence is a recapitulation of the previous three, adding nothing but more of the same — has more merit. "The Price You Pay" has the handsomest and best-sung melody of the whole album; the production and playing all serve the song well. However, the abstract immigrant drama lyrics don't make a whole lot of sense — stringing together pungent phrases that don't go together in any meaningful way (the two elements of "you've gotta stand and fight for the price you pay" would make more sense inverted) is not a hallmark of strong writing. (Dylan has been guilty of that, but he created entire worlds in his songs, which is not the same as throwing words together without care.)

"Drive All Night" is a bookend for the title track, an endless (8:26) slow, magnum ballad, this one celebrating love in vague terms rather than recalling it ruefully with detailed storytelling. Starting off understated and nearly eloquent, it never gains the dramatic momentum of "The River" and ultimately dissolves into unbearable self-defeating wounded-animal roars of the phrase "heart and soul" over and over. Merciless. And then, of all the weird ways to conclude a 20-song opus, "Wreck on the Highway" takes a mild detour toward country music to limn accidental death on one hand and the affirmation of life on the other; it's nice enough until Springsteen's shoehorn effort to sing the ungainly, unmusical title at the end of three verses.

What about the rest? "The Ties That Bind" (*bi-yi-yi-yi-yi*), "Sherry Darling" (Hey, hey, hey, what you say"..."She can take a subway back to the ghetto tonight"), "Jackson Cage," "Out in the Street," "Crush on You" (nowhere near as good as the Clash's "1-2 Crush on You," issued two years earlier), "You Can Look (But You Better Not Touch)" and "I'm a Rocker" are all tossed-off retreads of '60s rock genres that bring no discernable imagination or innovation to the effort. "Point Blank" is six minutes of Tom Waits butchering a rejected Elvis Costello ballad: some of it is atmospherically pleasant, the rest harshly gruesome melodrama. "Fade Away" comes over like a totally oversung stab at rewriting "Alison." The keyboards add a lot, but the awkward bridge does nothing for the song. "Hungry Heart," the breakthrough hit, reduces a thoughtful romantic sentiment to a Hallmark card cliché, hammered home with extremely bad drumming. But props to Flo and Eddie (wtf????) for the background vocals.

In the plus column, "Two Hearts" has a really catchy chorus and the song's speeding velocity makes it exciting. Springsteen's vocals are beneficially buried in the mix and layered. "Independence Day" has repetitive lyrics, a powerfully somber mood and an unneeded sax solo. (Clemons' horn serves a much better purpose firing up the piffle of "Cadillac Ranch.") Oddly juxtaposed with "I Wanna Marry You," which precedes it, the romantic misery of "The River" offers solid storytelling and handsome imagery, all sung with restraint and sensitivity. That concludes Side Two. ("Stolen Car," another tale of marital failure, ends Side Three. Again, a spare arrangement and vocal restraint hit the mark, but the lyrics sink [it].

Springsteen later claimed that it was his purposeful intention to include *both* good-time rock and roll nonsense and solemn contemplation of deep life issues (i.e., the "I meant to do it" defense). Apparently, he had finished a single-disc LP when Landau told him to go big, and the result was a half-year spent recording a second disc's worth of material. The final result pinballs emotionally in a most disconcerting fashion, each extreme undercutting the other. According to Wikipedia, this interview remark he made to Robert Hilburn explains his motivation, "Rock and roll has always been this joy, this certain happiness that is in its way the most beautiful thing in life. But rock is also about hardness and coldness and being alone ... I finally got to the place where I realized life had paradoxes, a lot of them, and you've got to live with them." (Really? Dude was 30 at the time he made *The River*.) I can think of other reasons for creating and releasing a 20-track mash-up monument, but that would require impugning Springsteen's veracity and integrity, and I have no basis for doing that. And, truth be told, it was not uncommon (or inadvisable) for double studio albums of that era to jump all over the place, stylistically speaking: *The White Album, London Calling, Todd, Layla, Songs in the Key of Life*. But *The River* doesn't just try on different sounds, it is basically two distinct albums — one Seriously Artistic, the other proffering Mindless Fun — shuffled together like two decks of cards. Or, less charitably, an album of real effort and an album of tossed-off filler that was probably fun to play live but hardly merited inclusion on what was clearly intended as a Major Artistic Statement.

While Springsteen surely came to this undertaking with a vision, which is half the creative battle for artists right there, his depiction of it, lyrically, is often simple-minded and, well, dumb in a *Rocky* sort of way. LCD appeal is an expressway to the charts, but it does not flatter him or his audience. And isn't that, in a way, how Trump got elected, by scorning complexity and sophistication, wit and subtlety, in favor of a bullhorn appeal to people's worst instincts?

My opinion of Springsteen, which began as simple college-days dislike of the bellowing all-American voice, of the verbosely depicted cartoon characters, of the car-highway-darkness-town clichés of his early albums, hardened, without conscious intent but no doubt spurred on by the hype of his elevation to universally acclaimed rock god, into implacable cultural opposition. At the height of his celebration as the new Dylan — and just two months before his mug landed on the covers of *Time* and *Newsweek* the same week — I heard the August 1975 Bottom Line show that was broadcast live on WNEW-FM. I recall finding Springsteen's extended "Big Man" spiel as corny and lame as anything I'd ever heard. I craved immediacy and improvisation, risk, surprise and danger in rock and roll and this felt like a shaggy dog story on endless replay, a mock-sermon comic book bid for boardwalk myth-making. If one was supposed to buy into the transformational legend and join the faith, I was sent running for the proverbial exit.

Following on from the lyric concordance I wrote about in my *River* review, I've done a little more research. Here are the number of times certain words appear in the lyrics of *Darkness on the Edge of Town*, *The Wild, the Innocent & the E Street Shuffle* and *Born to Run*:

	Darkness	*Wild*	*Born to Run*
(to)night	35	33	41
down	9	25	13
street	10	17	21
work(ing)	16	0	3
dark(ness)	10	1	6
dream	8	3	5

Admittedly, that's no match for the 100+ times the word "no" (or "nobody") is sung in the Human Beinz' "Nobody but Me," but I still take it as a sign of limited imagination, paltry vocabulary and a hick-town bar band worldview. (Incidentally, Springsteen's most-sung word on these three albums is "all," but I don't know what to make of that.)

We can't blame artists for their audiences, but — as I felt daily during the Trump presidency — undeserved exaltation is a potent irritant to unbelievers, underscoring inadequacies by exaggerating them. Springsteen has always come on the humble servant, making no hyuuuge claims of biglyness, but his fans (including critics who worship him) have shouldered that burden, and done a helluva job all these years.

That's another thorny issue — in the face of overwhelming odds, clinging to a minority opinion can feel like David facing Goliath. (I hasten to note, perhaps unnecessarily, that I have never been dissuaded from a critical position simply because few others share it. Artistic quality is not decided by democracy. Furthermore, popularity is not a valid measure of creative achievement, hence my rejection of the sillier elements of poptimism.) But it can be hard to be heard in that arena, and that can lead to throwing rocks harder than need be. For me, that situation has occasionally led to resentment and dogmatism in my writing. I'd be lying if I said I have always been able to remain emotionally stable when something worthless in my view is widely praised. I had that feeling the first time I heard "Sweet Child o' Mine" by this L.A. band everyone was raving about. I was lying on the couch at home, resting with a miserable head cold. When Axl started singing I laughed so hard that I rolled onto the floor.

While any rock star with sky-high populist everyman cred is inevitably in the grip of an obvious contradiction, that isn't really my issue here. I am happy to acknowledge that he is a devoted performer whose public conduct has always seemed responsible and respectable. He has always evinced the highest regard for his audience, his family, the heritage of rock and roll and his musical peers and forbears. He's demonstrated social responsibility about public issues on occasion. There are plenty of artists I admire who fall far short of all that, so good for him.

First off, I can't stand his voice. There's no subtlety to his singing. Like his horribly stiff cardboard box drummer, he hits too hard, mistaking brute force for the conveyance of emotion. His lyrics generally leave me cold. And I just don't buy his whole schtick. Ever since he came under the guidance of Jon Landau, I have never been able to shake the suspicion that he is playing a part crafted for him as a deep-thinking and soberly serious auteur. (Fred Goodman's *Mansion on the Hill* provides some support for that view, but I will admit it's not far from a conspiracy theory, evidence-wise.) It's easy to fake sincerity, and pseudo-intellectualism has increasingly become a refuge of aging rock dudes. True, he's never come close to the arch self-important twathood of Sting, but I found it suspicious that his media persona, which began as good-time knockaround Jersey romantic, a sensitive Fonzie with a Fender bound to sing because it's the only way he knows, was overnight recast to be a profound poet of the American condition. I don't imagine Bruce is a Lonesome Rhodes character, shucking and jiving while looking down his nose on the yokels who admire him, I just don't believe that he is quite what he appears to be, and that he didn't come to it all by his lonesome. I can almost believe that he's grown into it, that he learned enough along the way to become a wise elder statesman, but I will never believe that he came up with the strategic positioning concept to channel Woody Guthrie and John Steinbeck in *The Ghost of Tom Joad* on his own. (And don't get me started on *The Seeger Sessions*...)

In 2002, when Jon Pareles visited Bruce at home for a *New York Times* profile, this bit reeked to me of contrived pretension:

> "You're mining, soul mining," Mr. Springsteen added. "And sometimes you're just not around the rich veins, and a long time can go by. And then all of a sudden, boom! You hit one."
>
> On a table sat a blue spiral-bound Mead notebook, with a handwritten label reading "Work Book" and a sticker with a picture of an eagle from Exile Cycles, a custom motorcycle builder in Sun Valley, Calif. It held, in its handwritten pages, the making of *The Rising*, starting with a page of potential song titles, including keepers like "Into the Fire" and nonstarters like "Hard Drive." Then came draft after draft of lyrics, a few dead-ended songs and, eventually, finished lyrics with notes on arranging and mixing. The last pages are sequences of songs for the finished album. Mr. Springsteen has stacks of these books; after all, he has been making albums for Columbia for 30 years.

I'm enough of a cynic to easily imagine a publicist or manager urging Springsteen to, y'know, consider casually leaving a notebook or two out for the visiting journalist to spot and ask about, thus allowing the Artist to make a generous show of allowing a rare peek into the mysteries of his creative process.

I recently did an inventory of my record collection, using Discogs.com. Which means checking run-out grooves for pressing plant codes, inspecting label variations and other picayune shit. So, when I pulled out my copy of *Darkness* I was forced to see if it might be a rare mispressing ("center labels display Side 1 & 2 tracks as normal, while actual tracks on both sides are Side 2 tracks"). I put it on the turntable (of course, my copy turned out to be bog-standard) and went back to what I was doing. A line from "Badlands" got stuck in my head: "Poor man wanna be rich, rich man wanna be king." A precise, economical populist observation sung, with a bit of swing, as a matter-of-fact announcement. Thinking I might have unexpectedly found a portal into the world of mild Springsteen appreciation, I got to wondering about its provenance. So, I checked online to see if there was anything to know about it. And, whaddaya know, it's a direct lift from the Elvis Presley soundtrack song "King of the Whole Wide World," featured in the 1962 boxing flick *Kid Galahad*.

As you were. ◆

Where Were They Then?

In 1984, the year *Trouser Press* closed up shop, I was contacted by Jonathan Wells and Tim McGinnis (R.I.P.), who were running Rolling Stone Press, the magazine's book division. Borrowing a concept from Virgin Books in the UK, they were keen to launch an annual series of *RS*-branded music yearbooks.

At *Trouser Press*, we had taken notice of the Britons' inaugural edition, *The Rock Year Book 1981*, because a section called "Quotes of the Year" drew liberally from our pages. That was a bit of a surprise — we'd had no advance notice of it — but fair use and all, and they did credit the source. The following year, with St. Martin's on board to distribute *The Rock Yearbook 1982* in America, Al Clark — a Virgin Books editor who would go on to become the press officer for Virgin Records and then a bigtime movie producer — saw fit to add a lengthy section of album reviews, using brief extracts from the British music weeklies, *Rolling Stone*...and *Trouser Press.*

This was different. Quoting pungent remarks from published artist interviews was one thing, lifting bits from numerous original record reviews without permission seemed well out of order to me. Since we could hardly afford a lawyer, I fired off an indignant letter (a species known in the office as an "Ira-gram") of complaint. I have in my files a very nice note I got back from London, apologizing for taking liberties and offering, as a pre-emptive sort of recompense, an editorial role on the next edition: Associate Editor (US) of *The Rock Yearbook 1983.*

That experience/credit might have had something to do with the offer I got from Rolling Stone Press a year later, but it also could have come at the behest of Michael Pietsch, the editor at Scribner's who was going to publish the book. Michael had signed me up to do *The Trouser Press Guide to New Wave Records* a few years earlier, following a lunch meeting at which we nervous greenhorns must have consumed a gallon of coffee and ended up jabbering away like pilled-up speed freaks. Like many people I have befriended along the way, Michael has risen way beyond the humble station from which we first met and now occupies the CEO chair at the Hachette Book Group.

In addition to a fair fee, I got a small office adjacent to *Rolling Stone*'s art department (populated at the time by scum-rock legends Jerry Teel and Lisa Wells of the Honeymoon Killers, Kurt Hoffman of the Ordinaires and other colorful multi-media talents), a phone and an eager young intern, Seth Schachner, who grew up to be a successful digital media and music consultant. (It's too bad the rock kids didn't get to design the book: I had a tough time dealing with the high-price firm they engaged.)

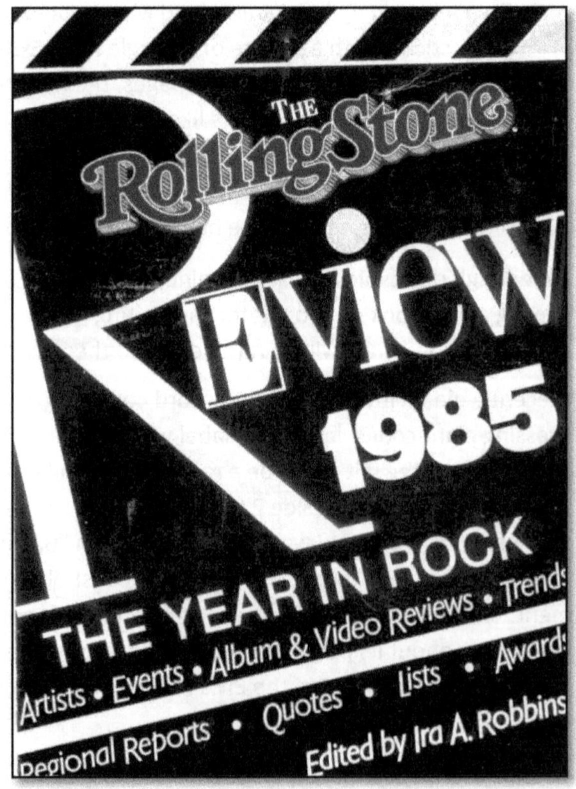

And so, *The Rolling Stone Review 1985: The Year in Rock* came about — never to be repeated, as it happened. We worked hard, I gave good-paying freelance work to fine writers who'd never been in *Rolling Stone*, recycled local scene reports from *TP* and offered, as "Picks for 1985," the Bangles, Red Hot Chili Peppers, Hüsker Dü, Replacements, Scritti Politti and Bronski Beat. One Band of the Year, sandwiched between R.E.M. and the Smiths, was Run-DMC, who we somehow booked to rock the launch party. I was quite drunk when I introduced them at what, I suspect, was the Queens trio's first show for a downtown (read: white) crowd. They were in fine form, I was thrilled and I am grateful no tape (so far as I know) exists of my ravings.

And that is how I got to become a semi-regular contributor to *Rolling Stone* and found myself, on the 10th of January 1985, in Jann Wenner's office, accepting an assignment to satisfy his aging cultural curiosity by researching and writing an ambitious "Where Are They Now?" feature. He had assembled a target list of musicians, actors, artists, producers, promoters and broadcasters he remembered from his California youth and was curious to hear about. I suggested some British musicians I thought would be fun to speak with.

The money on offer was quite good, but I was going to earn it by tracking down a whole pile of off-the-radar folks using nothing more than Ma Bell (I had to add call waiting to my home phone so that I wouldn't miss the inevitable callbacks), the U.S. Post and the powerful cachet of the *Rolling Stone* name.

Nowadays, with social media, celebrities have become a lot easier to find and contact. Back then, however, it was full-on detective work. (The CD reissue boom, which brought a lot of forgotten musical figures back into currency, was still a few years in the future.) It took three months and hundreds of cold calls — to past managers, song publishers, former record companies, onetime sidemen and other sorts — to clumsily network my way from person to person until I finally got a useful phone number. And that still didn't guarantee a result. There were numerous unreturned messages, but it was thrilling when the phone rang and it was someone from a band I'd idolized — the Lovin' Spoonful, the Blues Project, the Fugs, the Bonzos, Raiders, Zombies, Rascals — happy to be back in the spotlight.

I found, reached and spoke to all of these folks on the phone, one on each side of a cassette. (The magazine paid to have them professionally transcribed, a time-saving expense and luxury I'd never before enjoyed.) Steve Alaimo, Paul Atkinson, Long John Baldry, Hank Ballard, Steve Boone, Don Brewer, Gary Brooker, Arthur Brown, Joe Butler, Luria Castell, Felix Cavaliere, Lester Chambers, Gene Chandler, Michael Cole, Jayne County, R Crumb, Lonnie Donegan, Georgie Fame, Mark Farner, Matthew Fisher, John Fred, Craig Frost, Daria Halprin, Ersel Hickey, Neil Innes, Wanda Jackson, Chris Jagger, Jerry Kasenetz, Steve Katz, Kelly, Al Kooper, Wayne Kramer, Andy Kulberg, Tuli Kupferberg, Michael Lang, Mark Lindsay, John Mayall, Curtis Mayfield, Buddy Miles, Chip Monck, Mouse, Earl Palmer, Michael J Pollard, Keith Reid, Paul Revere, Russ the Moose, Ed Sanders, Mel Schacher, John Sebastian, John Sinclair, Roger Ruskin Spear, Peter Stampfel, Mark Stein, Barrett Strong, Screaming Lord Sutch, Dallas Taylor, Lloyd Thaxton, Maureen Tucker, Barry White, Chris White, Wes Wilson and Zal Yanovsky. If I tell you it was a formidably educational experience, I'd still be understating how much I learned from speaking to all these greats.

Barry White's velvety bass voice was a sensual pleasure; Mark Stein of the Vanilla Fudge demanded to know how I'd gotten his number. Alex Chilton wouldn't talk to me. Try as I might, I could not find or reach Syd Barrett, Ginger Baker, Alvin Lee or Mel Lyman. I had to call Gene Chandler every day for two weeks before I finally got him on the phone. I tried Noel Redding at his home in Ireland at random times for eight days with no success.

Lee Michaels, the organist-singer who had a hit with "Do You Know What I Mean," had a duo with a drummer known as Frosty. Unable to find Lee, I called him, hoping he could hook us up. Did he know where Lee was living? He said a few years back he'd been on Venice Beach. I'm thinking some swank pad overlooking the ocean. Do you have his number? "No, dude, he's *living* on the beach. No house, no car, no phone." Yikes.

Some members of the Lovin' Spoonful had longstanding grudges to revive; rockabilly hottie Wanda Jackson talked to me about God. Lester Chambers was out mowing his lawn when I called; he was nice enough to stop and come inside to talk to me. Michael J. Pollard, the character actor famous for his role in *Bonnie and Clyde*, had the disconcerting habit of saying my name each time he answered a question. Paul Revere wouldn't stop talking (not that I had any problem with that). Fearsome "Fire" singer Arthur Brown turned out to be a lovely bloke now resident in Austin. Hank Ballard, the originator of "The Twist," sent me a tape of a country album he'd made. Through it all, most of the stars I spoke to were upbeat, either settled happily in a post-fame life or excited about the record that was just about to come out or plans for an upcoming tour. It was amazing, but also kind of sad sometimes. No one likes being asked questions so loaded with the inference of has-beendom, but I preferred to think of what I was doing as offering them well-deserved publicity at a time when the chances of that were otherwise remote.

I wish I'd been able to spend more time with each of them, especially such now-gone giants as Curtis Mayfield, Earl Palmer, Barry White and Lonnie Donegan. But I had a job to do, and all I needed was some basic information and a couple of good quotes. Finding and reaching people took a lot of time and effort, and I was under serious deadline pressure, so I did the calls quickly, rarely spending more than 15 minutes with an artist. Gathering historical facts meant wasting a golden opportunity to really learn something from these unique and important figures. I've had that thought several times recently — too often in my career, I didn't take enough advantage of the incredible opportunities I've had to meet and speak with cultural icons.

When all the calls were done, when I'd given up hope on the lost causes, I did the writing and handed in 42 compact articles. And how many of those pieces appeared in *RS* 456 (12 September 1985), a special issue with Prince on the cover? 17 of them. Unbeknownst to me, staffers had been brought into the project, and their contributions made up the bulk of the section.

This is my first opportunity to share the manuscript, more than half of it previously unpublished.

Long John Baldry

British singer John Baldry led some historically significant blues and R&B bands in the '60s, among them the Hoochie Coochie Men (one of whom was Rod Stewart) and Bluesology, which included a 19-year-old Reg Dwight (better known as Elton John). Popular at home but never a star in America, Baldry, at 44, remains an important — and, at 6' 7", very tall — figure in British blues.

Baldry spent several months of 1976 in an institution for a neurological malady that "was affecting my coherence and coordination." At the end of '70s, he emigrated ("I was getting pretty bored with England and always wanted to live in North America"). He lived in L.A. and New York before settling in Toronto, although, he says, "I've seen so many savage winters up here, I'm thinking of moving on sometime in the next year." Baldry, who has never married ("I came dangerously close on a few occasions"), became a Canadian citizen in 1980.

He continues to record for a Canadian label and tours extensively with five backing musicians and longtime cohort American singer Kathi McDonald. "In addition, I've been doing occasional solo performances [accompanying himself on guitar] at blues festivals and folk concerts." On a commercial front, his baritone voice has helped him build a successful career in radio and television advertising, singing jingles and doing announcements for companies like Kawasaki, Levi Strauss and Chrysler.

"Getting up and singing on stage with people I've loved since I was a kid is always a big treat, because I feel very much in awe of people like that. I've always been nervous referring to myself as a blues singer. I tend to think of myself as a bluesy singer."

Hank Ballard

In the mid-'50s, Detroit's Hank Ballard and the Midnighters built a career on raunchy R&B songs like "Work With Me, Annie" and "Sexy Ways," whose substantial erotic content generated moral indignation (and airplay bans) but were million-sellers all the same. Posterity, however, may remember Ballard best for writing "The Twist." He doesn't mind that Chubby Checker is the person most associated with the song. "We have never been enemies. He used to date my sister-in-law before he even recorded it. I don't hold any resentment at all because otherwise I wouldn't have made a dime from `The Twist.' I knew the song was going to be a hit, it just didn't work out for me. My company didn't believe in the record and Dick Clark did."

Now 48, Ballard — married for the second time, with six grown children — lives in Long Beach, California and continues to record and perform, "practically every weekend. I'm getting a big response; everybody wants to hear the old stuff again. I guess it's the baby boom. For a long time I didn't want to do those old songs — I got tired of them — but now I'm doing rock & roll, blues and love songs. I get a lot of requests for blues. A lot of people are back into the blues; I guess because of the economy."

Ballard's own economy has had recessions as well. In the mid-'70s, he ran afoul of the IRS and had to borrow against future royalties to pay off a $90,000 tax bill and lost his rights to "The Twist." "If I'd had the publishing, I could have retired. I only had the writer's share. It's still earning a lot of money." But not for the song's author, who receives no income from it — a situation he is attempting to rectify through legal efforts.

The Blues Project

More rewarded critically than commercially, the Blues Project disbanded (for the second time) in 1972 but has reunited sporadically for concerts and tours ever since. The group's original members have spread out into several areas of the music world and number many accomplishments among them, yet still find time and inclination to get back together once in a while.

Brooklyn-born keyboard player Al Kooper formed Blood, Sweat and Tears, "which turned out to be the monster that strangled Dr. Frankenstein, so I left before I got strangled." He became a staff producer for CBS Records ("I was the first rock musician hired by a major record company on a corporate level") owned a label and has continued a career as a solo artist and producer "with a proclivity for acts [Lynyrd Skynyrd, Tubes, etc.] doing their first album" ever since. Now the Director of West Coast A&R for PolyGram, Kooper, 41, lives in Los Angeles but still finds time to "play about three times a year in New York; every two or three years I do tours, primarily East Coast. I have a de facto band, but the last two times I've played solo."

Kooper has made over a dozen albums under his own name but is not currently active in that area. "The hardest thing to do when you're a recording artist is to get out with dignity. I've watched so many people not able to do it. When you're a solo artist, it's hard to [restrain] yourself from making a solo album, because it's the ultimate masturbatory exercise." But he's not swearing off the habit just yet. "I think the trick is to put a lot of time between records and have something else to fall back on."

Andy Kulberg, the Blues Project's flute-playing bassist, is now 40, married with three kids and living in San Francisco. After the Blues Project ended, he and drummer Roy Blumenfeld formed Seatrain, but Kulberg doesn't play much anymore. "I'm mainly a composer, conductor and arranger." His projects cover a wide range. "This year I did a serious classical score for a PBS documentary, *In Search of Excellence*; I've done work for the Disney cable channel. In the past I've done [soundtracks] for *Starsky and Hutch*, *Sesame Street*, B-movies — one was called *Cardiac Arrest*." Kulberg also writes orchestral music, produces records and does music for advertising. Additionally, he collaborated on a musical, *Dead End Kid*, which had a successful run in San Francisco. "Basically, I like people to pay me to compose music and I'm not real touchy about which way I get there."

Guitarist Steve Katz, 40, was in Blood, Sweat and Tears for four years, became a producer (working most notably with Lou Reed) and spent three years on the A&R staff of Mercury Records. He subsequently formed a production company with a partner who "didn't like Patty Smyth's voice and didn't like Dexys Midnight Runners." They also had a shot at signing Cyndi Lauper but didn't. Katz's partner "put all his eggs in one basket" and made an album with the Drongos. "It was not a satisfactory experience." Katz, whose first musical group was the folky Even Dozen Jug Band, is now getting back to those roots. "Two summers ago, I was invited to play the *Waterloo Folk Festival*. I had never performed alone on stage before but figured I might as well try it. For a month, I practiced and practiced and got up in front of 5,000 people and played acoustic guitar and sang and I got an encore." It was an encouraging experience. "I produce in order to make a living, but I really want to try being an artist and put out an album." Katz feels he's entitled. "My line is that if Al Kooper can do 15 albums in the last 20 years, I can do one. And his were expensive. Mine will be real cheap."

As for other ex-members of the Blues Project, Roy Blumenfeld is a drummer in the Bay Area — playing mostly country music — and does some production work, although Kulberg produced an album by Roy's group. Danny Kalb recently sold his apartment in New York City and moved to San Francisco, where he teaches guitar and plays live.

The Bonzo Dog Doo-Dah Band

The Bonzo Dog Band's dadaist humour and British blend of rock and trad jazz may not have won the band pop-star immortality but has had lasting influence on the worlds of music and comedy. As Neil Innes notes, "Eric Idle acknowledges that working with the Bonzos in the early days gave him ideas about the anarchic approach which the Pythons then controlled, very successfully, on television." Since disbanding in 1970, Innes and the other alumni have worked extensively in television, films, books and, of course, music.

Innes became an "affiliate" member of Monty Python, writing and performing music for the troupe's television show, live appearances and many of their movies. "Every film I've been in with the Pythons ends with something being slung at me. I don't know whether they're trying to tell me something." He had a musical show, *The Innes Book of Records*, on British television and has released a number of solo albums. In 1977, Innes co-starred (as the John Lennon-like Ron Nasty) in the Rutles' Beatles TV mockumentary *All You Need Is Cash*, for which he also wrote, produced and performed the music. Unfortunately, the project led to an embittering legal tussle with the owners of the Beatles' music, who claimed Innes's parodies were copies of Beatles songs. He eventually relinquished half the royalties. "At least I'm not being roasted for the 90% they wanted. But I did lose a lot of money."

He and his wife live in East Anglia with their three sons. "I spend a lot of time writing and developing things, until I get sick of the sound of my own voice and thoughts. Then I go out and do a one-man show," which he brought to the U.S. for the first time early this year. Innes, 40, is currently collaborating with ex-Python Terry Jones creating a new series of fairy tales for British television.

Vivian Stanshall, once notorious for his outrageous exploits in the company of Keith Moon, has made musical and spoken-word solo albums, hosted a radio show, written a book and film (*Sir Henry at Rawlinson End*) and been involved in many other cultural endeavors. For a long time, Stanshall and his wife lived on a houseboat in the Thames until, as Innes tells it, "on his birthday last year, a huge log came down on the high tide and holed his boat. It sank in five minutes flat, all his possessions went to the bottom." Stanshall, 42, now runs a floating theatre and restaurant-bar called the Old Profanity Showboat on a converted tanker docked in Bristol.

Roger Ruskin Spear made two albums in the '70s and has continued performing, solo accompanied by home-made robots, and with more-populated outfits, while also earning teaching three-dimensional design at London's Chelsea School of Art. Recently, Spear, now 42, hosted a ten-episode music and comedy television series. "It was billed as the worst television show ever made. In fact, it was."

Spear describes his current duo, the Slightly Dangerous Brothers, as "sort of the Bonzos with computers, really, the same old rubbish." The pair have performed in Stanshall's club. The longtime Surrey resident is married and has two sons, one of whom is following dad's footsteps and leads Departure, an avant-rock band.

When he first moved to California in 1967, Crumb lived in Haight-Ashbury. "I tried to get involved in the whole concert poster scene but that was before I was famous and [the people in charge] wouldn't use me — they already had enough poster artists." Times were tough for a struggling cartoonist. "I was on welfare for a couple of years in the '60s. In the hippie culture you weren't supposed to be so gauche as to ask anybody about money. But after a couple of years the comics really caught on and I started being able to make a living off my work.

"I've never done advertising art — I draw the line at that. I can still somewhat pick and choose what I do. If I like the politics, I'll do something. I'm still basically a communist at heart."

Arthur Brown

The Crazy World of Arthur Brown shocked music fans in 1968 with a hit single called "Fire" and a stage show that climaxed with singer Brown igniting the specially rigged helmet he wore. After the Crazy World ended, Brown pursued other musical avenues in a group called Kingdom Come and had a small role in the movie of *Tommy*. In 1980, "I was wanting to move to America, and Robert Fripp — from whom I'd been taking guitar lessons — suggested Austin, Texas. He said I would earn money quickly in California or New York, but life would expand in Austin." A good call? Brown chuckles. "It's expanded in a different direction from the one I thought." He doesn't elaborate.

Brown left London for Austin, planning to continue his musical career. "When I first came to Austin, there was supposed to be a nice big record deal, but as often happens, that fell apart." Instead, he has released albums of synthesizer music on two independent labels, including his own Fig Productions. He also took up carpentry, and currently runs a house-painting business with original Mothers of Invention drummer Jimmy Carl Black. Brown notes a helpful relationship between his two careers. "We've gotten a lot of jobs because of the music," but adds, "I charge extra for lighting my head on fire." Now 41 and the father of a young son by his Texas-born wife, Brown performs occasionally in the area with a couple of synthesizer players. "I just did a track on the Austin Christmas album on Felicity Records that also features Willie Nelson." He's working on an album and has hopes of touring the US and Europe this year.

Lester Chambers

Following such hits as "Time Has Come Today" and "I Can't Turn You Loose," the Chambers Brothers — Lester, Joe, George and Willie — stopped performing together in the early '70s. "We just got tired and decided to go on a little vacation, and it lasted for a while. We got into management that wasn't correct, which is why we went on vacation. We were doing seven nights a week and we decided we had to think about us, our health and stuff like that."

The group existed sporadically during the '70s, performing at no-nuke and peace benefits, guesting on a Maria Muldaur album and doing Levi Strauss commercials. (The four are also members of the Chambers Family Singers, an all-kin gospel choir that has sung on the West Coast for the last four years.) Otherwise, Joe and Willie remained in California, doing session work, George sang gospel and Lester moved to New York in 1980, forming a band with Harvey Brooks and doing "some stupid things just trying to keep my name alive" that he declines to identify. He moved back to the San Fernando Valley in California at the end of 1984 to reunite and reincarnate the Chambers Brothers.

Now 45 and married with a young son, Lester is very enthusiastic about the newly revived Chambers Brothers. "We're planning a fantastic career now. A totally new concept." The group will continue its tradition of mixing inspirational and secular songs. "I say we always have a debt to pay to the Master. So, we do it by giving him a song." He recalls that the group "got a lot of flak from both Black producers and promoters as well as whites" about their original drummer, Brian Keenan. (Keenan is white; the Chambers are Black.) "I think he was the greatest drummer around in those times, at least for us. The music didn't have any colors, so we [decided] not to let people that don't think like us stop us. We liked it, so we kept it going." Lester stays in touch with Keenan, who he says owns a small recording studio in Connecticut.

Gene Chandler

Chicago soul star Gene Chandler found success early in his singing career, reaching number-one in 1962 with "Duke of Earl." He recorded with Curtis Mayfield and Jerry Butler, scored another gold single in 1970 and performed on and off while also owning record companies, managing bands and producing records. At his busiest, Chandler had "25 acts [on his label], was managing about 15 of them, and producing them all myself. I was [always] in the studio recording, mixing or something, but I was so energetic and hyped that I didn't realize I was doing as much work as I was. I just backed out of it — it was like burn-out."

He served a brief jail sentence for drugs in 1976. After acrimoniously leaving the now-defunct Chi-Sound Records —

"I was disgusted with that particular situation" — Chandler didn't do much for a few years. "I thought I'd sit back and get my head together rather than just rush out and try to record again."

Chandler, 45, recently signed to Fastfire, a new label in New York, and recorded an album. "As soon as we put a record out and it starts moving, we look forward to beginning to perform again. "I've seen the greatest of them come and go. But people like Tina Turner and myself, we just keep rolling along." According to Chandler, it's not that easy. "You have to really concentrate and keep on top of things; you have to work at your craft, stay away from heavy drugs and be an adult. You cannot assume because you were good that anything you do is going to be great."

R. Crumb

Cartoonist Robert Crumb was one of the '60s most influential counterculture image-makers, mainly via "underground" comics and other magazine work. But Crumb was not as interested in rock music as his audience may have imagined. A devotee and player of old blues and jazz, he "actively disliked psychedelic music. I thought it was real boring. I never liked the Grateful Dead or any of that stuff. We all got lumped together as part of the hippie culture, maybe because we all took LSD."

Crumb stopped taking drugs in 1975. "I got tired of being stoned — I got what I was gonna get out of it." Now 41 and living in California's Sacramento Valley with his wife and small daughter, he draws comics (including *Weirdo* and *Zap*) and illustrates books. Crumb also creates trading cards of early blues, jazz and country musicians. As a guitarist, he plays locally ("weddings and private affairs — no clubs or anything") in the Rural Sophisticates.

Lonnie Donegan

Best known in the U.S. for "Rock Island Line" (1956) and "Does Your Chewing Gum Lose Its Flavor (on the Bedpost Overnight)" (1961), Lonnie Donegan was, for six years, hugely successful on the British charts. As leader of the anyone-can-do-it skiffle (jug-band) craze, Donegan paved the way for the Beatles and others who began their careers emulating him.

Now 54 and married with five children (one an infant), Donegan has lived in Lake Tahoe, California since 1976. Accompanied by a four-man band, he tours six months of the year — mainly in England, but also Australia and Canada — playing "folk-country-rock, about 75% American folk material." Last year, he did a stage musical, *Mr. Cinders*, in London's West End. "I might be doing another one in the fall. It breaks up the monotony of singing the same songs over and over."

Donegan feels he has been shut out by the record industry in recent years. "There are very few performers over the age of 30 that have much of a recording career anymore, probably owing to the preponderance of young people in recording companies. The middle-age audience is virtually uncatered to.

"People will ask, 'What have you been doing since 1961?' What they mean is the last time we had a hit record from you was in 1961. And if they're not hearing you all day on the radio or seeing you on television, mentally you've died. As far as they're concerned, you haven't done anything even though you may be working your buns off. I'm earning pretty good bread and I know many people of my age and musical attitude that have done just that."

Georgie Fame

As a singer and keyboard player, Georgie Fame has had a remarkable, varied career, from accompanying Eddie Cochran and Gene Vincent to a partnership with Alan Price to singing at the Royal Albert Hall with Count Basie. He is even the subject of a song written and performed by Blossom Dearie. Nowadays, "I'm sort of condensing everything I've done in the past. I'm singing jazz with big bands, ballads with orchestras, and playing rhythm and blues with my own band, the Blue Flames. And I've just written a musical called *Singer* with a friend of mine. I've written all the lyrics and a couple of the tunes and I'm performing in it with Madeline Bell."

Fame's found time to record as well. "Since '78, I've made seven LPs, including a reggae album with some Jamaican cats and a tribute to Hoagy Carmichael called *In Hoagland*. I wrote to him while we were making the album and asked if he'd write sleeve notes. He liked it so much that he went into a little studio in Palm Springs, California and sang 'Rocking Chair' and asked us to include it on the album. I think that was his last recording — he died in 1981."

Originally a pianist, Fame (who was born Clive Powell) switched to organ in 1962. "I used to play piano down at the Flamingo Club — John McLaughlin was the guitar player in the band. A G.I. walked in one night and asked me if I'd ever heard of Booker T. and the MG's, which I hadn't. He gave me a 45 of 'Green Onions.' The next day I went out and bought a Hammond organ." Now 42, Fame lives in Somerset, England with his wife and two sons. "I'm not a millionaire, but I've got a nice house and am blessed with a good family. I just keep on working."

John Fred

After a decade together, John Fred and His Playboy Band topped the charts in 1968 with "Judy in Disguise (with Glasses)." The Louisiana band continued a few more years without similar success and then broke up in the mid-'70s. "I worked for a studio and then ran a record company called R.C.S. for four years. We did a few good things, but it wasn't financed enough." Nowadays, alongside a Clio-winning career singing jingles, Fred leads a revived Playboy Band. "I make most of my money playing gigs — between $1,500 and $2,000 a night." He's writing songs and working on a new album.

"The last time Paul McCartney was in New Orleans I asked him how much money the Beatles got screwed out of. You just figure from the Beatles on down, no matter who you were in the '60s, they just didn't pay you. I didn't get screwed as bad as a lot of people because I'd been in it so long." Still, Fred has a gripe. "'Judy in Disguise' sold about four million records; I saw maybe 50 grand." (That works out to 1.25 cents per copy.)

"We were the band the parents didn't want their kids to see 'cause we played Negro music, as they called it back then." At the height of the civil rights movement, "We played in Little Rock, Arkansas and they shut us down, because the Black people were dancing with the whites. They told us, 'Don't play any more Negro songs.' That was stupid — it had nothing to do with that. If we'd'a played 'Ave Maria,' they'd'a danced anyway." Now 44 and divorced, Fred lives in Baton Rouge and has a 20-year-old son.

The Fugs

Vulgar, irreverent, anti-establishment drug-exalting hippies, the infamous Fugs camouflaged several of New York's best left wing-beatnik-poetry minds for the latter half of the '60s. Over the course of a shambling recording career that led to such notorious albums as *It Crawled Into My Hand, Honest*, the loosely configured (around Ed Sanders and Tuli Kupferberg) group did their level best to outrage and offend; by and large, they succeeded gloriously. Dormant for over a decade, the Fugs have recently undergone a renaissance: last year, Sanders and Kupferberg resurrected the band with sidemen and toured.

Ed Sanders emerged from the group's 1969 wind-up with a solo recording deal but spent more (and more profitable) time writing a bestselling book (*The Family*) about the Charles Manson trial. He also taught, co-authored a book with Abbie Hoffman, published books of his poetry and wrote for numerous magazines. In the late '70s, Sanders traveled with the Eagles and wrote an as-yet unpublished "gigantic analysis of the group that runs — with appendices — 1,200 pages." Sanders also "began inventing a whole bunch of new electronic musical instruments that I used when we had the Fugs reunion."

"There had been pressure over the years to get the Fugs back together; I always turned it down or just asked for such an outlandish price that made it impossible." It took a number of different forces to finally change his mind. "It was 1984, which is a symbolic year, fraught with Reagan and Orwell, and I had been writing a lot of topical songs and poems. Plus, a lot of people that had been in the Fugs were dying at a rate faster than biology would want it to be. So, Tuli and I got together and made some decisions." The Fugs did two engagements at New York's Bottom Line and then toured eight European countries. A live album recorded along the route was recently released. "The next Fugs thing is going to be a full-length left-wing opera." Sanders, 45, lives with his wife in Woodstock, New York.

Tuli Kupferberg has published songbooks of political satire and cartoons on his own Vanity imprint and founded a radical vaudeville theatre group, The Revolting Theatre. He writes a column on journalism for a New York arts paper and remains part of the New York beat literati. About the Fugs' reunion, Kupferberg notes, "I always thought of us as musical theatre. The poetry and the music and the writing — even the theater I did — is sort of the same thing. What we were doing was a continuation without the band." Kupferberg is 61 and lives, as ever, in New York City.

Peter Stampfel was half of the Holy Modal Rounders, who doubled as the Fugs' backing musicians. He left both groups after the Fugs' first album and has led several bands (currently the Bottlecaps) since but earns a living writing for magazines and working for a science-fiction book publisher. Now 46, Stampfel and his wife live in New York.

Grand Funk Railroad

Following a career filled with gold records and world tours, macho Michigan rockers Grand Funk Railroad disbanded in 1976. Three of the four stayed together and formed a new band, Flint; guitarist/singer Mark Farner, however, struck out on his own. "I've got 40 acres in Northern Michigan. I bought a saw mill and cut down a whole bunch of trees, sawed them into lumber, and constructed a 4,000-square-foot log cabin," where he lives with his wife and two young sons. Now 36, Farner owns a recording studio as well as an alternative energy store and warehouse, which his wife looks after. Except for a Grand Funk reunion in 1981, Farner's worked under his own name, producing two solo albums in the '70s and currently leading a trio, touring "ballrooms and small concert halls," playing "rock & roll, but more soulful." He's been writing new songs and plans to record for a new album shortly.

Bassist Mel Schacher has been "retired from music for a number of years," and declined to join the '81 reunion, but remains involved with rock & roll: he owns Platinum Cat, a record store in Flint, Michigan that incorporates Grand Funk's old lights in its high-tech motif. "We have a computer sequencer that can run them just like stage lighting," he says proudly. Schacher also putters around in a makeshift home studio and has produced a couple of local bands, something he'd like to do more of. Once a mechanic in his father's body shop, Schacher now restores and collects cars. "I had thirty at one point, but now I have about fifteen, seven of them Jaguars." Schacher turned 34 in April and resides outside Flint with his wife and two sons, one of whom they adopted earlier this year. As for future musical projects, Schacher says, "I'm game for anything — I just don't like traveling."

After the group Flint folded, keyboardist Craig Frost joined fellow Michigander Bob Seger's band, with whom he has happily toured and recorded ever since. "I really enjoy it. Seger's a really good guy, a rich person that doesn't think he's rich." Frost sees other benefits in the situation: "In Grand Funk, we were all bosses; that can be real weird sometimes. Seger's the star and it works better this way. Everything goes a certain way and there's no fighting." He doesn't mind playing a supporting role. "I don't consider myself a star and I don't want to be — I like the fact that I can walk into a K-Mart and nobody runs up to me." Frost, 37, lives in Temperance, Michigan with his second wife. He has a daughter by his first marriage.

Don Brewer was in Seger's band as well, briefly, for a 1983 tour. The 36-year-old drummer lives with his wife and young daughter in Boca Raton, Florida and is launching a new trio called Top Secret with two former Ted Nugent sidemen. "It's real commercial — a lot of melody, good vocal harmonies, good music. We're looking for hit singles." Recalling Grand Funk, Brewer says, "When I listen to the records now it sounds so innocent."

Ersel Hickey

Even if his name isn't familiar, odds are a photo of Ersel Hickey as the quintessential '50s rockabilly cat is recognizable: his enduring silhouette has appeared numerous times in books and magazines and on album covers. Hickey, now 51, acknowledges, "That picture has done so much good" for his career, whose high point, the self-penned "Bluebirds Over the Mountain," was a moderate 1958 hit, earning him a spot on *American Bandstand* and comparisons to Elvis Presley. (Hickey's comment at the time was "I gyrate from the waist up.") Covered a decade later by the Beach Boys, "Bluebirds" has proven to be Hickey's annuity. "The song is on seven albums [including repackages] by the Beach Boys." Hickey estimates the tune has sold "all told, two-million records. It's been a fair source of income." He's written other songs and done production; a new compilation of Hickey's early recordings has just been released.

A farmboy from upstate New York, Hickey now lives in Hoboken, New Jersey, stockpiling songs and releasing sporadic singles. He hasn't played live in a long while, except "several years ago I performed with the Beach Boys in Atlantic City. They invited me down and I did a whole weekend with them, all the shows and everything. It was exciting."

Wanda Jackson

In the late '50s, Wanda Jackson made red-hot rockabilly records like "Fujiyama Mama," "Hot Dog! That Made Him Mad" and "Let's Have a Party," as well as "Silver Threads and Golden Needles" and other country songs. "On June the 6th, 1971, my husband and I received Christ personally." She became a gospel singer.

Wanda Jackson is 47; her husband is her manager. The couple live in Oklahoma City and have a son and daughter in their early twenties. Wanda's career combines "one-night revivals, singing and giving testimony" — in churches all over the U.S. — with secular concerts, although she won't work in nightclubs. "I'm a Christian first and foremost; I go wherever I feel that the Lord would have me go. The appeal is to a different type of audience than in my church work, but I get to give my testimony to the Lord in these places, so it works out fine."

She doesn't do a lot of extended tours, but does make occasional trips to Europe, where her rockabilly records are well known. (During a Swedish tour last year, she recorded her first non-gospel album in many years with local Scandinavian pickers. In keeping with her beliefs, she insisted on including at least a religious number amidst tunes like "Rave On," "Stupid Cupid" and "Breathless.") Given the suggestiveness of the songs she once sang, Jackson has to be "selective. There are some lyrics that I couldn't sing because of my convictions." But she has no problem with her dual career. "I can sing [rockabilly] in order to tell people about my relationship with Christ and how it's changed my life — that's the purpose of my singing these days."

Jerry Kasenetz and Jeff Katz

In the late '60s, Jerry Kasenetz and his partner Jeff Katz spearheaded and dominated the bubblegum sound, finding songs and producing records by the Ohio Express, Music Explosion, 1910 Fruitgum Company, Rare Breed and others. They also did their own radio promotion, pulling off many outrageous stunts to help push their records into the charts. Between 1967 and '70, the two young New Yorkers masterminded more than 40 hits, earning millions each.

Kasenetz picks up the story. "From '71 to '74 we retired. In '74 we built our own studio in Great Neck [Long Island]. We had a label. We had a big hit with Ram Jam — 'Black Betty' — that covered us for the '70s." Coincident with Kasenetz's 1981 divorce, they closed and sold the studio (as well as the land around it — the two are active in real estate) and retired again at the end of '81. But not permanently. "We've signed a few new artists and we're gonna come back. I think we still know what a hit is today; we're looking to have a hit in 1987 to make it three decades ['67, '77, '87]. That would be unusual.

"We're not into the artistic part of this anymore. We're into having hits. We've had an incredible career; we had hits with seven different artists on the first shot. As far as I'm concerned, if it ended tomorrow it was almost too good to be true. My son should only appreciate it — he thinks the only good thing I ever did was Ram Jam."

Kasenetz and Katz, both 42, still live on Long Island; Jerry with one of his two sons; Jeff with his wife and son. Kasenetz sums it up: "We keep a low profile. [We] do rather well and are continuing along quietly. We'll be making records in heaven."

Michael Lang and Chip Monck

Michael Lang was 23 with only some skimpy experience promoting concerts in Florida when he made rock'n'roll history by instigating and executive producing the *Woodstock Music & Art Festival* in August 1969. A bona fide Legendary Event, *Woodstock* was a financial disaster, replete with attendant legal problems that were resolved only after "a couple of years. We had six months of pretty intense work. It wasn't anything catastrophic, but they were myriad." While remaining in concert promotion for a while, Lang pursued other aspects of the music business, forming Just Sunshine Records (whose roster included the Fabulous Rhinestones and the Voices of East Harlem) in 1970. When the label's distributor left the record business, he converted it to a production company. He worked with Billy Joel and Stuff and developed film and television projects ("nothing spectacular, just some small music shows and scripts — some we're still working on").

In 1977, Joe Cocker "came to a jazz-rock festival we did in Europe. He had been on tour with Stuff. It was a rough point in his life, and he I asked if I would get involved. Management was something I never really wanted to do, but he's a really delightful guy — I'd known him from *Woodstock* — and he needed help." Lang successfully repaired and has managed Joe Cocker's career ever since. His company, Better Music, has taken on other artists as well. Lang and his wife have three children and divide their time between a house near Woodstock and a place in New York City.

Although hired to handle the festival's lighting and technical design, E.H. Beresford "Chip" Monck — who staged the *Monterey Pop Festival* in 1967 and was then technical coordinator at both Fillmore Auditoriums — gained more notoriety at *Woodstock* for introducing the acts and making other stage announcements. ("The brown acid that is circulating is not specifically so good." "Wheatgerm: Holly has your bag with your medicine...") "Michael [Lang] turned to me at seven o'clock in the morning and said, 'Oh, by the way, Monck, we forgot [to get] an MC, so since you haven't got all your lamps hung, why don't you start now?'"

After *Woodstock*, Monck continued as a highly-regarded lighting designer and production manager and has added industrial illumination consulting to his main work in music. He briefly hosted a TV music talk show, *Speakeasy*, in the mid-'70s. For the past three years, Chipmonck Enterprises has produced MOR concerts to immediately follow sporting events; his newest venture is the design and manufacture of architectural lighting fixtures.

Monck, 46, and his wife live in Hollywood. "This age is one of the most rewarding of my life." As for the Woodstock era, "We had a wonderful time, but it's past. I'm not as occupied being a music person as I was. I'm delighted to have had the experiences, and I've made a good living from it, but there are other, perhaps more exciting things. [Music] isn't all the fun it's cracked up to be, and certainly isn't the fun it was in the '60s and early '70s."

Lovin' Spoonful

Following such hits as "Do You Believe in Magic" "You Didn't Have to Be So Nice" and "Summer in the City," the Lovin' Spoonful broke up in 1968 when John Sebastian went solo; he is now the only original member still doing music full-time. The others — guitarist Zal Yanovsky, who left the band in 1966, bassist Steve Boone and drummer Joe Butler — have pursued quite different paths, although the four did reunite briefly to appear in Paul Simon's 1980 movie *One Trick Pony*.

Zal Yanovsky, 40, owns and operates Chez Piggy, a restaurant in Kingston, Ontario. As credentials for opening a restaurant, chef Yanovsky says he "ate in them" and describes the cuisine as "sort of continental Jewish, mix and match." Musically, "I have about six or seven guitars and I'm a paid-up member of Local 149 of the American Federation of Musicians, but I hardly ever touch it." Asked whether the Spoonful will ever reform, Zal's distaste for the music business he left behind surfaces. "At one point some of the guys were really anxious that we should get together but I'm not anxious to do it. Who needs it? It's finito." Yanovsky is married and "living quite comfortably in a nice place out in the country."

In 1970, Steve Boone says, "I threw up my hands in total disgust because the IRS had attached all of my publishing and royalty income, so I bought a sailboat and moved to the Virgin Islands. I sailed around the Caribbean for the next three years." His tax problems were the result of "the way the Spoonful got paid — large sums all at once and then long periods with no money. I was more impulsive than the rest and didn't really listen to the little advice we got. It was easy get a large sum and spend it all with very little thought to paying the taxes."

Boone's earnings finally paid off the liens — "in excess of $50,000 after the penalties were added" — several years ago. In the meantime, he bought a recording studio in Baltimore and relocated it onto a houseboat floating in the city's inner harbor. "On Christmas Day 1977, the studio sunk. There was speculation that we had sunk it for the insurance, but the police did an investigation and never found why it sunk. We didn't have insurance anyway. The studio was just at the point where we were getting national clients — we could have turned the corner in six months — but it was not to be."

Boone, 42, occasionally tours and writes with Sebastian and is "trying to maintain a career as a songwriter. I started my own publishing company and I send out whatever songs I think I can match up to artists." Also, "a friend of mine here in Baltimore has a double life as a car dealer and a blues singer, so whenever we both get the feeling that we need to play we throw a pickup band together and do some jobs in the area." He is married with no children.

Joe Butler, also now 42, remained in New York, where he studied method acting and has appeared in Broadway shows and films. He also builds and renovates houses, although "it's not a major business at this point." He has mixed feelings about the Spoonful. "When I hear the music, it's double-edged. Sometimes I enjoy the memory, sometimes it gets me bitter, realizing that none of us are making a penny on it. We're still owed a lot of money and have no way of tracking it. We got together and hired a lawyer, but he gave up after six months. We were given an advance against future royalties, but we've never been paid on any of the hits. Most of the money we got was from concert tours and television."

On the other hand, Butler cites as his fondest memory a trip the band made to Ireland around 1966 to play at the 21st birthday party of an heir to the Guinness fortune. "We stayed at this castle for about a week, it was like living in another time. My family is from Ireland; it was a very romantic, beautiful time."

Butler recalls Yanovsky's reaction to the idea of a Spoonful reunion. "He basically said show business is cancer, it eats people. He thought [our motivation] was middle-age menopause. He said that was then and this is now and was totally disinterested." Butler doesn't strongly dissent. "I'm not really aiming to get back into music. The music stands up, but in terms of getting four old men together and dragging them around on the road..."

John Mayall

A seminal figure in British blues lore and the early employer of many very well-known musicians — Eric Clapton, Mick Taylor and Jack Bruce included — John Mayall has released "between 35 and 40 albums" in a wide variety of traditional and progressive blues styles. He's been a resident of Laurel Canyon, California for the last 16 years and, now 51, recently became a grandfather for the first time.

"In 1982, [Mayall band veterans] John McVie and Mick Fleetwood suggested that sufficient time had passed for a new generation not to have heard the original Bluesbreakers; that started the idea of having a revival." And so Mayall reassembled the Bluesbreakers to play "strictly hard-core blues." Originally featuring McVie and Taylor, the lineup has been in a state of flux ever since — the current cast boasts no English luminaries. Still, Mayall has been "very busy" and cites a full tour schedule of America and Europe, including a June date at New York's Carnegie Hall as part of the Kool Jazz Festival.

His recording career, however, is "non-existent." Since his last album came out in 1980, "I've made [three] albums that didn't appeal to record companies — one with Mick Taylor, another with a band I put together in Memphis and one with my current lineup. So, I've put the best of all three together on one album; now it's a case of getting someone interested in releasing it. It's an uphill battle these days because the record companies are not willing to take the chance on anything they can't get a video out of and on MTV."

Curtis Mayfield

Singer, songwriter, film scorer, producer, musician and label owner Curtis Mayfield has had a profound impact on soul and pop music for almost three decades. Mayfield's career ran into a snag several years back when Boardwalk, the label he was signed to, went bankrupt. "I got caught up in the terminating of that company, trying to get my contract cleared away and all." That situation has been resolved, but he hasn't released any records since, a victim of "the economy, I guess, and just kind of slow times for Mayfield."

However, "I went on to record and produce a new album myself which I hope to release on [my own label]. The name of the album is *We Come in Peace*. Hopefully we can release it within the next month." Now 43, the Chicago native moved his family (he has six children) — and his Curtom Studio — to Atlanta, Georgia six years ago. "Music was sort of drying up in Chicago. All the musicians moved to either LA, New York or Philly." Also, the Windy City's "cold weather moves you out. I always adored Atlanta. I always had a place here that I'd come down to and do a lot of writing."

A 1983 reunion tour with the Impressions has Mayfield contemplating the possibility of recording the group again. "I've been talking back and forth with them. I've been talking with Sam [Gooden] and Fred [Cash] — they live right over the next state in Chattanooga, Tennessee — and seeing that I have the studio here, we've been thinking about putting things together and doing some recording."

The MC5

A decade before the Sex Pistols, Detroit's MC5 put the revolution in rock, extolling angry anti-establishment views with equally uncivil music. Although their ideological commitment kept the group well out of the commercial mainstream, it did attract a large, like-minded cult following and remains a punk icon. The 5 split up in 1971, with most of its members — Dennis Thompson, Michael Davis, Fred Smith, Wayne Kramer, Rob Tyner — remaining in music via various outfits.

In 1980, guitarist Fred Smith married Patti Smith and has since lived quietly in the Midwest. After being sentenced to jail for a minor marijuana charge, manager John Sinclair was the subject of a John Lennon song; the Clash likewise honored guitarist Wayne Kramer in "Jail Guitar Doors" when he went up for dealing cocaine. Sinclair still lives in Detroit and runs a management company that handles the up-and-coming Urbations. "I was out of artist management and out of rock & roll professionally for several years. I worked for jazz artists and as a journalist."

No longer the firebrand activist of his White Panther days, Sinclair nonetheless remains politically aware and locally active. But, as he says, "You really have to concentrate on making a living. The interesting thing in the '60s and early '70s was that people were disgusted in a way, so there was room for interesting ideas to circulate and things to happen, But now they wish they were in Nicaragua already — you can't even talk politics with them, they want to beat your ass."

After jail ("You'd be amazed to find out how much you can really adjust and adapt"), Kramer returned to music and has led several bands, including Gang Wars with Johnny Thunders. Now living in New York, he does production, plays in several bands (including the Delancey Street Hawaiians Social and Drinking Club) and has a theatrical work in progress called *The Last Words of Dutch Schultz*. He returns periodically to Detroit, but only to record with Was (Not Was).

"After the MC5 ended I had to keep busy, so I moved into the Motown stream of things — even though Motown itself had left, a lot of good people were around — and I got a fair amount of session work and club dates working with R&B cats. When Was (Not Was) got together, it was perfect." The white funk duo's next album will in fact contain a cover version of the MC5's "Kick Out the Jams" on which Kramer overdubbed nine tracks of guitar.

Kramer has no interest in an MC5 reunion. "It's a great old legend; let's just leave it. We were just crazy like street hoodlums — all our relationships with the record companies were impossible. We were into it for the rock & roll of it, for the spirit of the music and the politics and the parties. We didn't really think about money. Had we thought about money, we probably would have been smarter and not broke up and we'd all be millionaires today."

Buddy Miles

Since his glory days with Jimi Hendrix in the Band of Gypsys, Buddy Miles — who has played with everyone from Wilson Pickett to John McLaughlin [to Carlos Santana] — has had what he describes as a "haphazard" career. He served time in California's penal system on two separate occasions and released records only irregularly.

But, at age 37, Miles is making a comeback with two separate trios. Besides a new Buddy Miles Express, the singing drummer has joined forces with guitarist Randy Hansen and Tony Saunders to form Band of Gypsys: A Tribute to Jimi Hendrix. (Original bassist Billy Cox, who lives in Nashville, declined to participate, Buddy reckons, "because of his domestic responsibilities and life style: He's an insurance salesman.") "It is really an extension of what Jimi and Billy and myself were trying to achieve in the Band of Gypsys when we first started it." The tour, scheduled to start in late February, hit an unexpected legal snag regarding Miles' travel restrictions and had to be postponed.

"I've been acclaimed as a drug addict, as a foul person by the [music] industry. I've been more or less told that I've been 86ed. If the world feels that way, let me prove different. I have the energy to do that. I think that I am the most sound and sane of body and spirit that I have ever been. I have taken a lot of time to know what it is to be responsible. I'm paying my own dues; I put it on myself. I'm just trying to get myself together, prove to myself that I still have it."

Earl Palmer

Earl Palmer's been drumming on records since the early '50s, when he became one of the top session men in New Orleans, working on "90% of Fats Domino's recordings [and] most of Little Richard's," as well as platters by Sam Cooke, Lloyd Price and many more. Palmer moved to California in 1957, where his credits broadened with names like Willie Nelson, the Beach Boys, Frank Sinatra, Jan and Dean and the Ventures, plus film work with Quincy Jones.

At age 60, Palmer is now back playing after a two-year stint as Secretary/Treasurer of the 15,000-member LA County local of the American Federation of Musicians. "There isn't too much work out there now. Three years ago, work was beginning to get slow, and I was beginning to wonder if I wanted to continue playing. I wanted to do something in music and the opportunity came along. I was elected and learned that aspect of the business. It worked out alright, although it was somewhat nerve-wracking."

During his tenure as an administrator, Palmer had to put his sticks down, professionally. "As an officer, it would be a conflict of interest to perform for pay, competing with the guys who pay your salary. Not that the salary was that big, but it's something you have to live with. It was a job."

Michael J. Pollard

Imp-faced actor Michael J. Pollard earned an Oscar nomination for his 1967 portrayal of C. W. Moss in *Bonnie and Clyde*; his career, while never receiving the same level of acclaim, continued in such films as *Hannibal Brooks* (1968), *Little Fauss and Big Halsy* (1970) and many others. He even made a memorable appearance in an episode of *Star Trek*. In the '70s, Pollard "moved to Woodstock and didn't work for a couple of years. I hung out with the Band — they were my neighbors — and just had fun and relaxed."

Pollard's latest projects are manifold. "I just did a movie called Jungle in the Philippines. I've got two movies that I'm going to do: one in England called *Kerash* and then one called *The Price of Gold* when I come back." Then there's

Rider in the Dark, "a western about this blind guy, but he's like a karate champ or something." A twelve-minute pilot starring Pollard was shot in upstate New York; "I think they're going to do the rest of it now." Pollard also has a film in the can that he did "about three summers ago with [director] Bob Downey, called *Moonbeam*. They kept editing it and editing it. I spoke to him a couple of weeks ago; he said it's going to come out, but he doesn't know when."

Married and divorced twice, Pollard, 46 this year and a California resident once again, has a son in Boston and a daughter who lives with her mother, *Alice* actress Beth Howland, in Santa Monica.

"I thought the '60s were pretty exciting. Everybody now says that it wasn't so good, but I didn't think it was that grim." The current music he likes includes Talking Heads, Trio, Los Lobos, T-Bone Burnett, Cyndi Lauper and Madonna. "She's sexy."

Procol Harum

When Procol Harum broke up in 1977, the group left not only an impressive catalogue of recorded achievements but also a legacy of musicians who've gone on to careers in varied segments of the music industry.

Singer and keyboard player Gary Brooker remained with the group he co-founded until the very end, took a year off and then began a solo career, finding time to join Eric Clapton's band and do some outside production work. He and Procol lyricist Keith Reid have remained occasional songwriting partners; for his latest album Brooker contacted another ex-bandmate, Matthew Fisher, whom he hadn't seen "since about 1970" and the two renewed their collaboration — writing, producing and playing the record together.

A pioneer in melding rock with classical music, Brooker has continued to perform with symphonies. "I've done concerts in Poland with orchestras and played quite a lot in Germany, including an annual televised night of rock and classics with the Bavarian Radio Orchestra." Reflecting on the band, he says "Procol always seems to have been well thought of. Everyone's heard 'A Whiter Shade of Pale,' so there's something in common with everyone I meet. It's a mutual focal point." Brooker, 40, and his wife live in southwest Surrey on a "smallish" farm and own a local pub.

Organist Fisher, who played the signature riff in "A Whiter Shade of Pale," became a record producer and engineer after leaving Procol in 1970 and now owns a 24-track studio, the Old Barn, near his home in London. He's made four solo albums. Despite his musical notoriety, Fisher has "always been very incognito. I don't think I've been recognized once in my whole life," which seems to suit him. Not getting credit for playing keyboards on Captain Sensible's *Power of Love* album (recorded in his studio), however, is a different matter. ("I was rather pissed off about that.") Fisher plans to resume his recording career and is experimenting with a synth-adapted Apple computer.

What about touring? "I don't mind the idea of actually playing on stage, what I dislike is when the whole thing is a big show. It always involves hours and hours of waiting around doing nothing. I don't like the ceremonial aspect of it. It's not like playing in a pub. If I was to do any gigs, I'd much rather play at little clubs."

Now 39, Fisher is married and has two sons. He stays abreast of modern music and is "quite keen on a lot of the stuff they're making now," citing Howard Jones as a favorable example. "But I really hated the music of the '70s."

Keith Reid, who occupied an uncommon rock-group role as Procol's full-member lyricist, now manages ex-bandmate Robin Trower, Frankie Miller and Mickey Jupp. He got into that side of the business by becoming "involved in some of the managerial aspects of Procol Harum. We were on the same label as Frankie Miller. I got friendly with him and he asked me to manage him." Reid has also remained active as a songwriter. "I'm interested in writing for other areas — I've gotten interested in writing for the theater. That's something that I will do."

Reid and Brooker own Bluebeard Music, which publishes their material as well as other peoples', but they don't control the rights to the mega-hit they co-wrote. "'A Whiter Shade of Pale' must have sold more than ten million copies as a song" and, Reid notes, "has certainly made a fortune for other people." He has no complaints about that. "I can't say we did badly."

Reid is 38 and lives in London. Ending Procol Harum "wasn't difficult. It was the only sensible thing to do. The band did a lot of good things, but I don't miss it. I think the worst thing is when you read people moaning about the good old days. I can't stand that."

Paul Revere and Mark Lindsay

Although their colonial costumes and ever-changing lineup made Paul Revere and the Raiders seem more like a theatrical troupe than a rock & roll band in the '60s, the group did sell lots of records and attract millions of devoted fans. As house band on the TV show *Where the Action Is*, they had a huge daily audience for their antics; after it ended, they hosted a Saturday morning children's show called *Happening*.

Organist Paul Revere formed the band in 1958, and with the exception of a brief retirement, has kept it going ever since; like the Beach Boys, the Raiders are now an American institution. "We had an incredibly good year in 1976 because everybody was looking for a red, white and blue band in three-cornered hats. We made a lot of money and had great crowds and I thought it would be good to go out in a blaze of glory. I had no idea that I would go crazy — it got very boring, and I started feeling old and useless. The one thing I know how to do is run a rock & roll band, make people laugh and have a good time, so I went back to work. Since then we've been on the road 300 days a year, working places like Harrah's Reno and Harrah's Tahoe an awful lot."

The Raiders do a '60s show, playing the era's hits at casinos, clubs, state fairs and amusement parks. Revere is the consummate showman, playing keyboards built into vintage car fronts. Former lead singer Mark Lindsay calls it "funny, zany: a combination of the circus, Marx Brothers, Three Stooges and Paul Revere."

Revere is now 47. He and his wife, who travels with him, have a son and a daughter. The couple owns homes in Idaho that they "don't have a chance to use." This April, Revere became involved in the drive to make "Louie, Louie" (which the Raiders recorded before the Kingsmen's better-known version) the official song of Washington and performed it on the steps of the state Capitol with an orchestra.

Mark Lindsay, the Raiders' pony-tailed heartthrob (also major songwriter and producer), began recording solo in 1969 and quit the band a few years later. "I stopped recording pretty much the same time I left the group. Without getting into details, there was a contractual thing I didn't agree with, and I just stopped." He began doing voice-overs and singing on commercials, built a recording studio and wound up, for several years, as an A&R man for United Artists Records. "It was invaluable experience now that I'm actively writing and recording again."

Lindsay's become very successful in advertising — doing spots for Yamaha, Datsun, Kodak, Pontiac and Levis. "There was a record I did called 'Silverbird.' Yamaha Motorcycles decided they liked the tune and used it for a campaign. It became 'Yamaha, won't you fly me away?' I made more money on the commercial than I did off the single, which was not quite gold." Lindsay has collaborated on film scores, including *Shogun Assassins* and *The Killing of America*.

When did he cut off those trademark tresses? "Columbia Records had a big convention in '72; that was the first time I appeared *sans* pony-tail. It was a big shock." Now in his early 40s and divorced with no children, Lindsay lives in Beverly Hills and is "planning some major moves in the music business," but declines to provide details. "It will be a surprise, that's all I can say."

Mark Stein

After the Vanilla Fudge called it a day in 1970, organist/singer Mark Stein toured and recorded with Alice Cooper, Dave Mason and guitarist Tommy Bolin. He made a solo album for CBS that was never issued and relocated from the East Coast to California.

In 1982, "Carmine [Appice] was doing a benefit for UNICEF at the Savoy in New York and had a lot of people jamming. All the Fudge guys were in town, and we did a couple of the old tunes. The band was really happening — there was a lot of energy and a buzz when we started to do the old stuff. People started talking about the Vanilla Fudge...it could be exciting to reform and do records and see what happens. Ahmet Ertegun was real excited about the project."

The reunited Vanilla Fudge re-signed with Atlantic and issued an album, *Mystery*, in 1983. "That was a mentally exhausting experience. It took a chunk — about two years — out of everybody's lives." The band never toured. "A lot of political nonsense went on, a lot of ego problems, management problems, legal problems stopped it from really being born." Also, guitarist Vinnie Martell, who hadn't remained as active in music as the others, "didn't know how to get a sound. His playing was really old-fashioned. Spencer Proffer, who produced the record, decided to get other guitar players that could cut the mustard."

Now 38, Stein, who is married and has one child, is assembling a new band to play "symphonic heavy metal — in between a Dio and Led Zeppelin/Purple thing. I feel real good about this new situation. I feel like I'm reaching where I should be. Talking about the old Fudge leaves a real lousy taste; it's real negative." But there is still pride in his voice. "We were one of the pioneers of big business rock & roll as it is today; we broke in bands like Led Zeppelin and Deep Purple that came on tour with us. As far as the business end of it, things could have ended up in a healthier state, but that's just life. But I'm here and I'm talking to you and I'm doing it again. I survived it."

Barrett Strong

One of the first signings to the fledgling Motown Records in 1959, Barrett Strong, a young songwriter-singer from Mississippi, became a star the next year with "Money," the first million-seller of Berry Gordy's empire. Contrary to popular belief, Strong didn't pen the song; in partnership with Norman Whitfield, however, he subsequently did write a number of classic soul hits ("I Heard It Through the Grapevine," "Papa Was a Rolling Stone," "Just My Imagination," "War," etc.) for the Temptations and other Motown artists. Strong also continued as a recording artist, although his last album was released in 1976.

Married, with four daughters and two sons, Strong, 44, still lives in Detroit, producing "a lot of people, some young artists" and writing songs. While his partnership with Whitfield ended and he left Motown in the early '70s, Strong has never abandoned the music business. "It's like anything else — there's a dry period and you go through soul-searching and figure which way you're gonna go. I just kept on going independently, producing and writing.

"The whole thing is a learning process. [The past] bettered me for this period. I'm pretty happy with my past; I have no regrets. There might be a few things I might do differently, but I don't find anything that happened so bad."

Screaming Lord Sutch

David Sutch, who claims to be the fifth Earl of Harrow, is better known for the musicians who began their careers in his employ — Ritchie Blackmore, Nicky Hopkins, Matthew Fisher to name just three — than the records he's made during a career that began in 1960. England's answer to Screamin' Jay Hawkins, Sutch dresses in Jack the Ripper garb and has been known to use coffins, cages, knives and other macabre theatrical devices onstage.

Although he's never had any big hit records, Sutch is a living legend in England, and his outrageous publicity stunts, including perennial candidacy for Parliament, have not changed over the years. His current organization, the Official Monster Raving Looney Party, ran eleven candidates in England's last general election; Sutch himself tried to unseat Prime Minister Thatcher by running in her constituency, receiving "about 360 votes."

"I'm still at it, recording and doing one-night stands. I do mainly colleges. I've just played Oxford University, and I've got Cambridge University coming up." His latest album, *Alive and Well*, features Cheap Trick guitarist Rick Nielsen on some tracks. Sutch, 40, lives in London and Harrow, but regularly visits his 10-year-old son, who lives with his remarried mother in Texas.

"I was a name act long before the Stones. Mick Jagger and Brian Jones used to come to my gigs. When they were a support act in clubs, some of it went okay, but sometimes they literally died on their asses." Drummer Carlo Little, a member of Sutch's band who played a few gigs in a nascent Stones lineup, "told me he didn't think they were going to make it" and recommended a replacement. "He can still vividly see himself writing Charlie Watts' number down."

Dallas Taylor

Dallas Taylor spent the '60s and the early part of the '70s as a top session drummer, recording and touring with Crosby, Stills, Nash and Young, Manassas, Bill Wyman, John Sebastian and many others, playing on seven gold and two platinum albums. Although Taylor did perform and record a bit, mostly in Europe, little more was heard of him until January, when an *LA Times* story about "middle-class junkies" described his successful efforts to kick a long-standing heroin addiction. Having admittedly been unemployable for ten years, Taylor is enthusiastically returning to music, writing songs and recording with a new band. Now in his mid-30s, Taylor lives with his wife, Trudy, in L.A.

Maureen Tucker

Mo Tucker of Levittown, Long Island was "playing drums on a $50 set just for fun" when a childhood friend, Sterling Morrison, asked her to join his band, the Velvet Underground. "Lou [Reed] came up to my room to see me. I was a nervous wreck." Having passed muster, she understood it to be merely a temporary position, but wound up a full-fledged member, staying until the band was finally laid to rest in 1973. Afterwards, she married, had children and lived quietly in California and Arizona. Now divorced, the 40-year-old mother of five returned to New York this year to support her family by resuming a career in computer programming. But she also plans to make music and wants to try producing records.

Although otherwise musically inactive, Tucker did record and release a home-made album, *Playin' Possum*, in 1981. A label in Boston had convinced her to record a single. "The reaction to it was so nice, plus making it was a lot of fun. People started asking, only half-jokingly, when the album was coming out, so I figured what the hell." She recorded it in her living room. "It took a long time because I was doing it alone with four kids running around."

Tucker is very happy about the "new" Velvet Underground album, VU, and "proud of every inch we recorded. I don't regret any of it. The whole time I was in the group I really enjoyed the people and loved the music." Her fondest hope, given the resurgence of interest in the Velvets, is "to do a concert again. I really think it would be tremendous, let alone fun. I wish the guys would cut the crap and let's get together."

Barry White

One of disco music's creative pioneers and biggest stars, Barry White had been a successful songwriter and producer for over a decade when he also began recording sexy love songs under his own name in the early '70s.

Collecting dozens of gold and platinum records worldwide, White racked up a phenomenal string of hits, but he hasn't done as well in the '80s. As an artist, that doesn't bother him. "I'm not hung up over number one. If a creative person is depending on the charts for motivation, they're in big trouble. I make music, I don't get into what was the last chart position and all of that." Until the end of 1983, the label he owns, Unlimited Gold, was a CBS affiliate; now independently distributed, "We're getting ready to come out with our new product. We've been recording a Barry White album, a Love Unlimited Orchestra album, a female group called Holiday and two male groups, New World and Tara." Off the road now for several years, White plans to embark on a world tour this summer.

Although he is only 40 years old, 1985 marks White's twenty-fifth year in the music business. He lives in Los Angeles; he and his wife have seven children. "I listen to everything. I like a lot of the new music that's out there — Bruce Springsteen, Michael Jackson, Prince, Tina Turner. Music is endless. There's always going to be new fads, new sounds, but it's still fundamental, still basic."

The Zombies

Although well-remembered from the '60s for "Tell Her No" and "She's Not There," the Zombies made only two albums and had already disbanded by the time of their second gold single. Vocalist Colin Blunstone worked for an insurance company then launched a solo career, initially under the pseudonym Neil MacArthur. He is presently a member of the group Keats and has sung on the Alan Parsons Project's records.

Keyboardist Rod Argent formed his own eponymous group and made a number of successful albums but has since expanded his scope to include classical music and theater. A musical he wrote based on the book *Masquerade* was produced in England. Drummer Hugh Grundy has left the music business.

Chris White decided to retire from performing because "there were better bass players around." He did continue to write songs and produce records, both on his own and with Rod Argent. In 1979, he moved his family to Spain. "I got fed up with things falling through and decided to have a rest; there were also tax reasons. I was only going to go for 18 months and ended up there for five years." He moved back to London last year and is now involved in a record production company and embryonic film projects.

White, 42, admits that there has been some consideration of a Zombies reunion, but they "decided to leave it as it was. I'd love to do it — we might play for fun at a party — but it could really fall flat on its face commercially." He's pleased about Rhino Records' newly-released live Zombies LP. "It's not bad at all. I had forgotten half the stuff on there, forgotten what a jazzy feel it had."

Paul Atkinson, the Zombies' guitarist, is now Vice President of West Coast A&R for RCA Records; he previously held an A&R directorship for Columbia. Following the Zombies' 1968 breakup, he worked in the computer field, but decided music was his life and re-entered the business. "I actually prefer what I'm doing now to traveling around England in the back of a truck, which is what I did for five years," he remarks wryly. His background has proven helpful as a record executive: "[Bands] usually find out what I used to do, and it enables me to be more effective because they can accept advice from someone who has been in their position, taken the hard knocks and survived. I regard it as a great advantage."

As Atkinson notes, "Most 18-year-old guitar players in the '60s weren't thinking about business." Nonetheless, "We did manage to stop for a few minutes to think about it and formed a limited company. We were each a director, had a secretary and a chairman and annual general meetings. The company received all our income — which was derived mostly from sales of singles — and we voted each other an annual salary. If there was anything left over at the end of the year, we would give ourselves a bonus. We actually just dissolved the company last year."

Atkinson, 39, lives in Santa Monica with his second wife and has two sons. "My 13-year-old in London gives me advice on which bands to sign. I listen to him intently. The four-year-old watches MTV and tells me what he likes as well." ◆

J. Geils Band

As long as I'm back on the subject of *Rolling Stone*, I was bowled over in 2017 when I read — in *Sticky Fingers*, Joe Hagan's ambitious biography of Jann Wenner — that the publishing mogul had once toyed with the idea of buying *Trouser Press* in order to eliminate a small but evidently irksome competitor. On page 436, Peter Wolf, the J. Geils Band singer who is a close friend of Wenner's, recalls the publisher's wife telling her husband about meeting a kid who said, "*Rolling Stone* sucks, *Trouser Press* is really fucking great." As Wolf recalls, "[Jann] threatens, in a half-joking way, 'I'm gonna buy *Trouser Press* just to put it outta fucking business.'"

Holy fuck! Who knew? It's like finding out years later that the hot girl in high school, the one that was galaxies out of your league, was planning to seduce you in order to make her college-age boyfriend jealous. I would probably have turned down the offer, but I sure would have relished the moment of being asked. Anyway, that really set my mind reeling, wondering how close I came to a life-changing experience without ever knowing about it. (And before I forget, let me express my great and fond appreciation to Susan Ollinick, a circulation executive at Straight Arrow, who provided crucial advice and assistance. She was incredibly friendly, kind and helpful to a young publisher.)

Maybe Ian Fleming was right when he named a 1964 James Bond novel *You Only Live Twice*. In the summer of 1992, Yves Beauvais of Atlantic Records engaged me to compile and annotate a two-disc J. Geils Band compilation. I went to town in the company's vaults at 1841 Broadway, listening to outtakes from various studio sessions as well as the original multi-track recordings of the four Detroit shows that were culled for the *Full House* album. I hoped the project might turn an audience that only knew their overplayed '80s MTV hits on to what had made me fall in love with the band a decade earlier — the wild, loose-limbed, jive-spattered R&B frenzy of "First I Look at the Purse," "Looking for a Love," "Homework," "Whammer Jammer" and "Hard Drivin' Man."

I found a hysterical band introduction by cornball comic George Jessel. I rediscovered their covers of "Peanut Butter" and "Dead Presidents" and was smitten with an amazing scrap — an offhand studio jam that really swung and ended with a funny talkback interjection from producer Bill Szymczyk. There were unreleased live tracks that made the band's smoking power clear. (Sure, there were a few small goofs here and there, but what's wrong with that?) I put it all together on cassettes in a sequence that flowed like a funky stream. (Tom Silverman, a colleague I hadn't been in touch with in years, mentioned recently that I gave him a copy that he played to death back then.)

Excited by what I had in hand, I wrote Wolf about a couple of things I'd found, seeking permission to include them:

1) "Hold Me Just a Little Longer": cool song, great dirty lyrics, and never released. I found this removed from the *Nightmares* master, so it's a finished take. I don't want this just 'cause it's rare, but because it fits in so well with the band's work of this era.

2) "Harp Tune": I know this is just a minor studio jam (it sounds a lot like the roots of "Orange Driver"), but to me it captures the feel of the band perfectly: a bunch of friends finding a groove and enjoying it. The fact that it's just a fragment will prevent listeners from seeing it as a "real" track, and it's short enough that it doesn't displace anything else in the collection. And the unexpected talkback line at the end — "You're fired, Geils" — to me crystallizes the spirit and good humor of the J. Geils Band. I've played this cut for a few friends and it always gets a great response: I think it would make a perfect end to one of the discs. I understand why you wouldn't want to release something this minor, but I think it humanizes the band and cozies up to the listener in a really special way.

I tinkered with the song selection and the sequencing for weeks. The friends who I played it for were knocked out. I still think it tells their story fully and faithfully.

The band *hated* it. Far from the blues-loving reputation savior I imagined myself to be, the band — at least some of the band — must have seen me as some corporate hack trying to mess up an easy paycheck and ruin their newly groomed self-image in the process.

They rejected what I'd done out of hand. It turned out they wanted it to be another hits collection with an emphasis on their recent successes. (Mind, there had already been a 1985 single disc of that stuff and two compilations of their earlier work.) They wouldn't hear of including anything that had not been previously released (I'm paraphrasing — "Why do you think that stuff didn't come out in the first place?"). Seth Justman, the keyboard player who was a less-than-magic dick to me, was incensed that I had the audacity to supervise mixes of four-track live tapes (not the most difficult thing in the world to do) without the band's permission or involvement.

They threw out all the stuff I'd unearthed and let me reassemble the two-disc collection just the way they wanted. And someone else wrote the liner notes. *Tant pis*, as the French say.

Compilation lesson learned: bands don't care what you think. If they have a say in things, they will follow the money. Don't try and tell a group that their old stuff was better or that outtakes are worth releasing.

Still, I got paid, received a producer credit and even got a gracious personal note from Wolf.

Blink and it's 2021. Going through my diary from that year for this project, I found this:

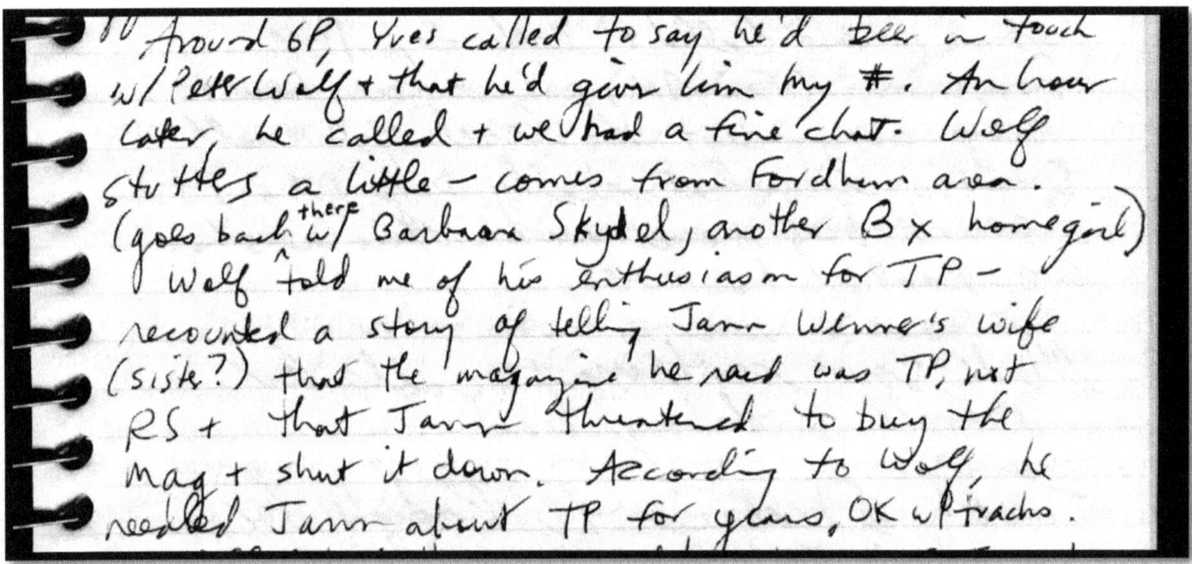

10 Around 6P, Yves called to say he'd be in touch
w/ Peter Wolf + that he'd give him my #. An hour
later, he called + we had a fine chat. Wolf
stutters a little – comes from Fordham area.
(goes back there w/ Barbara Skydel, another Bx homegirl)
Wolf told me of his enthusiasm for TP –
recounted a story of telling Jann Wenner's wife
(sister?) that the magazine he read was TP, not
RS + that Jann threatened to buy the
mag + shut it down. According to Wolf, he
needled Jann about TP for years, OK w/ tracks.

So, in 23 years, I had completely forgotten a mind-boggling story told to me directly by a major rock star. The kind of amazing tale a onetime rock magazine publisher could have dined out on for years. And not just, "Oh yeah, that sounds vaguely familiar" but the details are hazy. No, in this case, any and all knowledge of this exchange it had been thoroughly scrubbed from my memory.

I wonder what else must've got lost along the way...

Other Books by Ira Robbins

***Music in a Word Volume 2*: Fandom and Fascinations (2022)**
Collected works from a 50-year career about the Who, the Clash, Cheap Trick, Ramones, Nirvana, Kinks, Keith Richards, Elvis Costello and the Replacements, plus previously unpublished interviews and much more. Paperback and E-book.

***Music in a Word Volume 3*: Whipping and Apologies (2022)**
Liner notes, critics polls, obituaries, correspondence, essays and reporting. Paperback and E-book.

***Marc Bolan Killed in Crash* (2020)**
London, 1972: An ordinary schoolgirl is pulled into the world of a fading rock star and becomes the secret weapon in a plan to revive his career in the time of glam. The mysteries of sex and songwriting, connivance, fame, family and the music business collide to bring her to a life she has never imagined. Paperback and E-book.

***Kick It Till It Breaks* (2009)**
This novel about underground activism in the 1960s is long, complicated, profane and at times dishearteningly bleak. *Kick It Till It Breaks* is rich with offbeat characters vividly drawn against a tableau of antiwar violence and unsparing in its depiction of dedicated idealists failing to uphold their ideals. Paperback and E-book.

***The Trouser Press Guide to '90s Rock* (1997)**
Picking up where the four previous editions of the *Trouser Press* record guide left off, this all-new undertaking is an indispensable addition to the bookshelf of every fan of alternative music. As someone described it, "Avoiding the callow 'more alternative than thou' attitude that sinks so much criticism of new music, the entries have an edge, but when they're smart-ass, which they often are, they are also intelligent." Out of print paperback, but all of the content is online at TrouserPress.com.

www.ingramcontent.com/pod-product-compliance
Lightning Source LLC
LaVergne TN
LVHW081313110826
845149LV00006B/1497

* 9 7 8 0 9 8 4 2 5 3 9 7 5 *